The Jewish Political Tradition

EDITORS   Michael Walzer
           Menachem Lorberbaum
           Noam J. Zohar

The Jewish
Political
Tradition

VOLUME III *Community*

EDITORS

Michael Walzer

Menachem Lorberbaum

Noam J. Zohar

COEDITOR

Madeline Kochen

Yale UNIVERSITY PRESS

New Haven and London

Published with assistance from the Castle Fund, endowed by John K. Castle to honor his ancestor the Reverend James Pierpont, one of Yale's original founders, and administered by the Program in Ethics, Politics, and Economics at Yale University.

Yale University Press books may be purchased in quantity for educational, business, or promotional use. For information, please e-mail sales.press@yale.edu (U.S. office) or sales@yaleup.co.uk (U.K. office).

Designed by Sonia L. Shannon. Set in Bembo type by Tseng Information Systems, Inc. Printed in the United States of America.

Library of Congress Control Number: 2017946596
ISBN 978-0-300-22834-2 (hardcover : alk. paper)

A catalogue record for this book is available from the British Library.

This paper meets the requirements of ANSI/NISO Z39.48-1992 (Permanence of Paper).

10 9 8 7 6 5 4 3 2 1

In memory of our teacher David Hartman,
a man of vision

Contents

Contents for Volumes I–IV

Preface and Acknowledgments

The Jewish Political Tradition has its origins in a conference on Jewish philosophy, religion, and politics, sponsored by the Shalom Hartman Institute in Jerusalem, that has convened every year since 1983. Its participants are political theorists, philosophers, law professors, and historians, brought together with scholars of the Talmud and of Jewish literature generally. The discussions have ranged widely but have come back again and again to political questions of the sort that we have tried to engage in these volumes. The idea of a "reader with commentaries" arose out of the conference discussions, for the discussions have exactly the form that we have reproduced here: we read texts together and argue about what the texts mean and what value their arguments have. From the beginning, the project has had strong support—intellectual, financial, and logistical—from the faculty and staff of the Hartman Institute. David Hartman, to whose memory we dedicate this volume, provided critical guidance and encouragement.

The first, rough proposal for a book on Jewish political thought was circulated by Michael Walzer in 1987. Menachem Lorberbaum joined in launching the project in 1989 and played a major role in fleshing out the proposal and producing the first long list of readings; he is responsible for translations of medieval and modern texts. Noam Zohar has worked on the project since 1991, helping to revise, supplement, and reorganize the list and undertaking the translation of all our talmudic and midrashic texts. Madeline Kochen spent three years, 2002–5, working on the successive revisions and reorganizations of this volume and helping with the translation of medieval and modern texts. The introductory essays for all the chapters were drafted by Michael Walzer and then rewritten with the benefit of comments and criticism from the other editors. Headnotes and footnotes are the primary responsibility of Menachem Lorberbaum and Noam Zohar. The glossaries for this volume were drafted by Yuval Jobani, who also read through an early version of the entire volume and contributed many valuable comments. The choice of commentators was a joint responsibility.

For reasons of space, we have been forced to omit from this volume, as we did from Volume II, some of the front matter that appeared in Volume I: the Foreword by David Hartman, the general introduction to the series by Michael Walzer, and an essay on reading Rabbinic texts by Michael Fishbane. Readers may consult the first volume for this material, which helps to explain the project as a whole.

A host of friends and colleagues have provided moral and intellectual support, counsel, and criticism, telling us about their favorite texts and advising us on editorial matters of all sorts. A significant part of the materials for this volume was discussed in a special weekend seminar on Jewish Ethics organized by the Ethikon Institute in Los Angeles. We thank Ethikon's director, Phil Valera, for making this possible, and also acknowledge the valuable input offered by the participants in that seminar, some of which eventually evolved into commentaries in the present volume. For help and advice in many forms we thank again the individuals mentioned in the prefaces to the first two volumes; in addition, we would like to note particularly the help we have received from Julie Cooper.

The project has required and received a great deal of financial support. The Institute for Advanced Study in Princeton, where Michael Walzer is a professor (now emeritus), provided funds to bring each of the coeditors, and several other contributors to these volumes, to Princeton for two or three years of residence and research. A grant from the Delmas Foundation sustained our work for a critical year. The National Endowment for the Humanities supported the project for several years. The Castle Fund at Yale University has provided a subsidy for the publication of the three volumes produced thus far—and the fourth still to come. The commitment of the Hartman Institute, already mentioned, has been critically important. We are deeply indebted to the men and women who manage these institutions and funds, a number of whom have taken a sympathetic interest in our work; without them we could not have seen it through to completion. We can single out only a few of them here: Patricia Labalme of the Delmas Foundation, Ian Shapiro of the Castle Fund committee at Yale, and Donniel Hartman in Jerusalem.

We are honored by the scholarship of the commentators whose

critical essays appear in these volumes. Their contributions express a strong commitment to our larger enterprise: to make this tradition of political thought vivid and accessible, a subject for engagement as well as study.

We are also the appreciative beneficiaries of the Yale Judaica Series, whose fine translations we have used whenever they were available. Ivan Marcus, the general editor of the series, has even permitted us to publish translations in progress, with the agreement of the translators. Further acknowledgments to translators and their publishers are listed below.

Grateful acknowledgment is made for permission to reprint selections from the following books and journals.

Adler, Rachel. *Engendering Judaism: An Inclusive Theology and Ethics* (Philadelphia: Jewish Publication Society, 1998); reprinted by permission of the University of Nebraska Press; copyright 1998 by Rachel Adler; published by the Jewish Publication Society, Philadelphia.

Agus, Irving A. *Urban Civilization in Pre-Crusade Europe: A Study of Organized Town-Life in Northwestern Europe during the Tenth and Eleventh Centuries Based on the Responsa Literature* (New York: Yeshiva University Press, 1965); reprinted with permission from the publisher.

Capsali, Elijah. *Me'ah Shearim* (Jerusalem: Ofeq Institute, 2000; Hebrew); many thanks to Ofeq Institute USA and its director, Rabbi Avraham Shoshana, for allowing us to reprint pp. 273–75 in an English translation.

Cygielman, Shmuel A. Arthur. *Jewish Autonomy in Poland and Lithuania until 1648 (5408)* (Jerusalem: n.p., 1997); reprinted with the permission of Raamah Cygielman.

Dubnow, Simon. "Autonomism, the Basis of the National Program," in *Nationalism and History: Essays on Old and New Judaism,* ed. Koppel S. Pinson (New York: Atheneum, 1970); reproduced by permission of the University of Nebraska Press; copyright 1958 by the Jewish Publication Society of America.

Elon, Menachem. *Jewish Law: History, Sources, Principles,* trans. Bernard Auerbach and Melvin J. Sykes (Philadelphia: Jewish Publication Society, 1994); reprinted by permission of the University of Nebraska Press; copyright 1994 by Menachem Elon.

Feldblum, Meir Simcha Hakohen. "The Problem of Chained Women and Mamzerim—A Proposal for a Comprehensive Solution" [in Hebrew], *Dine Yisrael* 19 (1997–98): 203–16; used by permission of Ayalah Levy Feldblum.

Hanover, Nathan. *Abyss of Despair (Yeven Metzulah),* trans. Abraham J. Mesch (1950; reprint ed., New Brunswick, N.J.: Transaction Books, 1983); re-published with the permission of Barry Mesch.

Loeb, Morris. "Federation or Consolidation of Jewish Charities," in *Trends and Issues in Jewish Social Welfare in the United States, 1899-1952,* ed. Robert Morris and Michael Freund (Philadelphia: Jewish Publication Society, 1966); reprinted by permission of the University of Nebraska Press; copyright 1966 by the Jewish Publication Society of America.

Maimonides. *The Guide of the Perplexed,* trans. Shlomo Pines (Chicago: University of Chicago Press, 1963); reprinted with the permission of the publisher; copyright 1963 by the University of Chicago Press.

Marcus, Jacob R. *Communal Sick-Care in the German Ghetto* (Cincinnati: Hebrew Union College Press, 1947); reprinted by permission of the publisher.

Rubinow, I. M. "What Do We Owe to Peter Stuyvesant?" in *Trends and Issues in Jewish Social Welfare in the United States, 1899-1958,* ed. Robert Morris and Michael Freund (Philadelphia: Jewish Publication Society, 1966); reprinted by permission of the University of Nebraska Press; copyright 1966 by the Jewish Publication Society of America.

Zevin, Shelomo Yosef. "On the Drafting of Yeshiva Students," trans. David Wachsman, *Tradition: A Journal of Orthodox Jewish Thought* 21, no. 4 (Fall 1985): 52–55; reprinted with the permission of the Rabbinical Council of America.

Selections from the following texts are reprinted with the permission of the Yale Judaica Series and Yale University Press:

Halevi, Judah. *The Kuzari: The Book of Refutation and Proof on Behalf of the Despised Religion,* trans. Lawrence Berman and Barry Kogan, forthcoming; used with the permission of Barry S. Kogan.

Maimonides. *The Code of Maimonides, Book Three: The Book of Seasons,* trans. Solomon Gandz and Hyman Klein, 1961.

Maimonides. *The Code of Maimonides, Book Four: The Book of Women,* trans. Isaac Klein, 1972.

Maimonides. *The Code of Maimonides, Book Seven: The Book of Agriculture,* trans. Isaac Klein, 1979.

Maimonides. *The Code of Maimonides, Book Eleven: The Book of Torts,* trans. Isaac Klein, 1954.

Maimonides. *The Code of Maimonides, Book Twelve: The Book of Acquisition,* trans. Isaac Klein, 1951.

Sifre on Deuteronomy, trans. Reuven Hammer, 1986.

The staff of Yale University Press have been helpful and supportive ever since we first approached them. John Covell and Larissa Heimert provided valuable assistance and advice at the beginning of the project; William Frucht has been a strong supporter and helpful guide at the Press in more recent years.

The editors are grateful, again, to all their family members—spouses, parents, children, and grandchildren—who have provided abiding love and steadfast support for the past many years. We have a strong sense of the familial character that Jewish politics sometimes takes and an even stronger sense that there is a world beyond politics, a world of infinite human value, which good political arrangements ought to protect. We intend this book to serve all our generations.

The Translation and Presentation of the Texts

The textual world of the Jewish tradition is complex and, for the unaccustomed reader, often more than a little bewildering. A comprehensive orientation is provided in Michael Fishbane's introductory essay in Volume I. We offer here a brief overview of the main texts and their interrelations.

All Jewish traditional discourse relates to the Hebrew Bible as its canon. Initially, Rabbinic teachings were expounded and transmitted in connection with the biblical books. Thus the *Mekhilta* follows many parts of Exodus line by line, just as the *Sifre* follows Numbers and Deuteronomy. Since the same legal topic is often addressed in more than one biblical location, there was a need to organize the material according to subject, independently of Scripture. The Mishnah—a concise collection of Rabbinic legal teachings (and arguments) redacted by Rabbi Judah "the Prince" early in the third century C.E. is organized into six "orders," which are further divided into tractates, chapters, and individual sections (each of which is also called a *mishnah*—not capitalized).

The Mishnah became the core document of Rabbinic Judaism, and its redaction (c. 200 C.E.) marks the end of the era of the *tanna'im*. A supplementary collection of the teachings of the *tanna'im*, the Tosefta, as well as both the Jerusalem and the Babylonian Talmuds, follows the order of the Mishnah. The talmudic discussions (*sugyot*, sing. *sugya*) take the mishnaic clauses as their point of departure but often also revolve around independent statements and traditions of the *amora'im*. Unlike the Mishnah, which focuses almost exclusively on *halakhah,* the Talmud also incorporates much aggadic material. In talmudic times aggadic collections were also compiled for many books of the Bible—primarily the *Midrash Rabbah* series for the Pentateuch.

Subsequent generations continued to study the Bible directly and to produce commentaries thereon, although they often consulted and quoted talmudic interpretations. The halakhic tradition focused, however, on the Babylonian Talmud (BT), which was considered authoritative—yet whose *sugyot* rarely conclude with decisions in the myriad controversies recorded and elaborated. Initially the intricate Hebrew-Aramaic talmudic discussions were barely decipherable even by the learned, and rulings based on the Talmud were rendered centrally by the Babylonian Geonim, the heads of academies. By the eleventh century, however, the Jewish world had become strongly decentralized. Rashi's classic line-by-line commentary finally made the talmudic text widely accessible. Much of medieval talmudic scholarship was written in the form of commentaries or novellae—that is, new interpretive insights and discussions—relating to the talmudic text. Rashi's contemporary Isaac Alfasi produced the first major code of talmudic law. Alfasi's abridgment of the Talmud still closely followed the order of the tractates. It was Maimonides' *Mishneh Torah* (MT) that first provided, in fourteen "books," an independent reordering and restatement of Rabbinic *halakhah,* with all the arguments resolved. Another such scheme, including only the sections of *halakhah* that apply "in these times" (i.e., in exile), was designed by Jacob b. Asher in his *Four Columns* (*Tur,* pl. *Turim*); this scheme was also adopted by Joseph Karo in his influential *Shulhan Arukh.*

These various codes themselves became the focus of study and comment. Karo's code, for example, is based on his own extensive commentaries on both Maimonides' *Mishneh Torah* (*Kesef Mishneh*) and the *Tur* (*Bet Yosef*). Even halakhic works not directly addressing the clauses of the codes, such as the numerous collections of responsa, are normally loosely organized according to the four "columns" of the *Tur.*

The works mentioned in this overview, as well as many others, constitute the rabbinic (with a small *r*) tradition. We have reserved the capitalized adjective "Rabbinic" for the classical period of the *tanna'im* and *amora'im,* collectively "the Rabbis." The generic (lowercase) "rabbis" refers, accordingly, to the agents of the tradition over many generations—until they were joined in modern times by writers, scholars, and public intellectuals of a new kind.

Many of the selections are from works not yet translated into English (or, as a rule, into any other language). This is true especially of the responsa literature, which is the main repository for legal and "constitutional" Jewish writing, both medieval and modern, and for the bulk of the medieval codes. Of the five classical codes (Alfasi, Maimonides, Rosh, *Tur,* and *Shulhan Arukh*), only Maimonides' *Mishneh Torah* and the *Shulhan Arukh* have been partially rendered into English, and this without their accompanying commentaries. The independent commentaries and the collections of novellae on the Talmud have not been translated at all.

With regard to medieval philosophical tracts, the situation is generally better: many of the basic texts have already appeared in English. We have used reliable English versions whenever they are available. Indeed, we are fortunate to have been able to select passages from the excellent translations of the Yale Judaica Series, including (with the agreement of the translators and the assistance of Ivan Marcus, the editor of the series) some translations not yet published. In all these cases, we have omitted the translators' footnotes and added our own so that the annotation of texts is consistent throughout the book.

Although many translations exist of Rabbinic works, they are often not readily usable for our work, and we have generally provided our own. Of course, new translations come at a price: they differ from the editions currently available to the larger public. We have therefore made use of existing English versions and standard editions whenever possible: most importantly, the Yale Judaica Series editions of the *Sifre* and the *Mishneh Torah* and the new Jewish Publication Society (NJPS) translation of the Hebrew Bible (1985), but also many other texts, medieval and modern. The cost of this is an occasional sacrifice of consistency. A partial remedy is provided by the glossary of terms, which indicates the range of meanings carried by some protean Hebrew words. A complementary tool is the general index, especially its subheadings, through which the reader will be able to trace appearances of some important Hebrew concepts (e.g., Torah).

Our biblical translations sometimes deviate slightly from the NJPS version to fit the context in which the text is used or the commentaries that follow. In rare cases, we have altered the rendering of a particular word or phrase in a published translation. In all such instances, the change is explicitly noted.

Rabbinic texts are both condensed in substance and elliptical in style. In our translations we have striven to reflect this character of the originals. At the same time, we have provided some minimal expansion, always in brackets within the translated text. In doing this we follow the traditional mode of studying the Talmud: one finger on the text and one finger on Rashi's commentary, which, since the first printing of the Talmud (Venice, 1520–23), has been published alongside the text. It has guided our own expansions and annotations. Occasionally we have inserted a line or two from Rashi directly into the text, in brackets, as follows: [*Rashi:* . . .]. Where we use existing translations, brackets indicate additions by the translators; any additions we have made are marked as editors' notes [—Eds.].

Individual selections are preceded by headnotes. These serve to provide background information (historical, legal, and conceptual) and to suggest connections among the texts. Biographical information on particular authors and on the more important persons or groups mentioned in the selections may be found in the glossary of names. Where particular points in the text or the translation require explanation, this is offered in accompanying footnotes. As a rule, the notes serve simply to clarify the texts. Citations in the introductions and commentaries are given in parentheses.

In some cases, we preserve the original Hebrew (and sometimes the Aramaic) term in transliteration, either beside or instead of an English equivalent. Non-English words are italicized (unless they are proper names), and recurring words and phrases are explained in the glossary of terms. We have resorted to transliteration in cases where the Hebrew term is in common use and where it carries multiple meanings. In these latter cases an English translation would require different words in different places, and the thread of the tradition would be lost. In addition, using the Hebrew sometimes draws the reader's attention to significant semantic links between key terms; these are elaborated in the glossary. In transliteration we generally follow the ("nonscientific") form adopted in the *Encyclopedia Judaica*. Hebrew names are reproduced as precisely as possible. For both terms and names, however, we depart from this practice if another form is in common English use. We refer to certain figures by their Hebrew acronyms (for example: *Rashi* for Rabbi Shlomo b. Isaac). We transliterate the Hebrew acronym and treat it as a proper name, capitalizing only the first letter.

All omissions are indicated by three ellipsis points. Brackets indicate all manner of additions to the original. Parentheses are used for references (e.g., to biblical texts) and sometimes for a phrase that is part of the original when this is the best way to convey the author's meaning. This latter use of parentheses is in line with our more general practice of adding punctuation, mostly absent in ancient and medieval texts.

For classical Rabbinic texts, manuscript versions have become increasingly accessible, through websites such as that at the Israeli National Library (http://web.nli.org.il/sites/NLI/Hebrew/collections/jewish-collec tion/Talmud/Pages/default.aspx) or at Bar Ilan University (http://www.biu .ac.il/js/tannaim/); hence our not uncommon departures from the text of printed editions.

Citations are given to specific editions when appropriate. Many traditional works, however, from the Mishnah to Rabbinic responsa and novellae, are available in numerous editions (including electronic versions), and we saw no reason to refer the reader to one edition and its pagination rather than to another. Instead, we follow the practice that is common for biblical citations, providing references by section (and subsection, when appropriate) in accordance with the original or traditional division of a work. As a rule, the original subdivisions of a text are reproduced in the body of the selections. We depart from this rule only for the biblical selections, where including the verse numbers would detract too much from the natural flow of the text. But here, too, we remain true to the Hebrew, for in the original scrolls there is no division into chapters or verses.

The work of translation in this volume—as for the project as a whole—is a collective effort. The contributions of those who translated texts from various languages and of experts who helped verify specific translations are acknowledged in notes to the relevant texts. Final editing of all translations was done jointly by Menachem Lorberbaum and Noam J. Zohar.

Ancient Rabbinic texts were translated mostly by Noam Zohar. On many matters of Rabbinic usage, we had the privilege of consulting with Shlomo Naeh. Modern texts, medieval responsa, and Rabbinic commentaries were translated mostly by Menachem Lorberbaum and Madeline Kochen. Nahmanides' *Mishpat ha-Herem* was translated by Yehudah Mirsky.

Menachem Lorberbaum and Noam J. Zohar

Abbreviations

¢	chapter; used to refer to chapters in *The Jewish Political Tradition*
§	selection; used to refer to selections in *The Jewish Political Tradition*
b.	ben/bar (= son of)
BT	Babylonian Talmud
1 Chron.	1 Chronicles
2 Chron.	2 Chronicles
Dan.	Daniel
Deut.	Deuteronomy
EH	Even ha-Ezer
Eccles.	Ecclesiastes
Exod.	Exodus
Ezek.	Ezekiel
Gen.	Genesis
Hab.	Habakkuk
Hag.	Haggai
HM	Hoshen Mishpat
Hos.	Hosea
Isa.	Isaiah
Jer.	Jeremiah
Jon.	Jonah
Josh.	Joshua
JPS	Jewish Publication Society
JT	Jerusalem Talmud
Judg.	Judges
KJV	King James Version
Lev.	Leviticus
1 Macc.	1 Maccabees
Mal.	Malachi

Mic.	Micah
MT	*Mishneh Torah* (The Code of Maimonides)
Neh.	Nehemiah
NJPS	Hebrew Bible (New Jewish Publication Society 1985 translation)
Num.	Numbers
OH	Orah Hayyim
Prov.	Proverbs
Ps.	Psalms
R.	Rabbi/Rav
1 Sam.	1 Samuel
2 Sam.	2 Samuel
Song of Sol.	Song of Solomon
YD	Yoreh De'ah
YJS	Yale Judaica Series
Zech.	Zechariah

The Jewish Political Tradition
VOLUME III   Community

Introduction

Years ago, Yitzhak Baer suggested that we think of the *kahal* as the Jewish polis. The idea has an obvious attraction, and we have taken it seriously. But it requires two large qualifications. First of all, because of the circumstances of the exile, there never was a sovereign *kahal.* No community of Jews in the diaspora was ever in control of its fate in the way that the citizens of Athens were. No Jewish assembly ever debated issues like those that were standard in Athens: whether to destroy Mytilene or form an alliance with Thebes or invade Sicily. Foreign policy for the *kahal* meant nothing more than its dealings with its gentile overlords—we will take this up in Volume IV, when we address the external politics of exile and consider the court Jew and the *shtadlan.*

Hannah Arendt famously argued that the loss of sovereignty was also the end of Jewish politics and the explanation for the "lack of political ability and judgment" that in her account marked European Jewry. The government of the *kahal,* she wrote dismissively, was mere "housekeeping." Our texts tell a different story. The internal politics of exilic life was limited, indeed, and undervalued by the Jews themselves, but it was vital nonetheless, raising many of the central political questions—about authority and legitimacy (as we saw in Volume I), about the policing of the community's borders (as we saw in Volume II), about the distribution of the benefits and burdens of the common life, and about the interpretation and enforcement of the law. The absence of sovereignty made this politics precarious and difficult, but it also required and evoked in the scattered Jewish communities both "ability and judgment."

The second qualification of the idea that the *kahal* was the Jewish polis follows from the fact that, even in exile, the Jews were a more cohesive nation than the Greeks, with a singular and coherent religious culture. Monotheism ruled out anything like the city-gods of the polis, and exile ruled out anything like the wars of the Greek cities. The Jews had what paganism could not provide: a divinely sanctioned and universally accepted law. Though local customs had a certain legal status, the members of the *kahal* recognized expert interpreters of God's law from around the Jewish world — scholars who often had something like diaspora-wide authority. No local assembly could determine the standing of a sage. The *kahal* might choose its rabbis and establish its own *bet din,* but it commonly regarded itself as bound by the rulings of men it had not chosen, whose renown and prestige were produced by informal and nonpolitical means. So the role of the "good men of the town" was doubly limited: by gentile rulers and by Jewish sages. We have already seen the working out of these limits in Chapters 6–9.

Still, there was a lot of room left for the internal determination of the everyday life of the *kahal*. Its members possessed, if not sovereignty, then a kind of autonomy, whose boundaries were fixed from the outside but, in good times, subject also to negotiation. That regime of autonomy is our subject in this volume. We deal first with the bond that held the *kahal* together and then with the men and women who made up the Jewish community. The "members" were actually families (and male heads of families) rather than individuals in the modern sense, and so we need to take up the role of the family in the *kahal* and the interventions of the *kahal* in the family. We then deal with the public activities and institutions of the various diaspora communities: first, with the provision of welfare through charitable gifts and through taxation (and with the ambiguous distinction between these two: *tzedakah* and tax); second, with decision-making in the assembly (when there was an assembly); and finally, with the communal courts. The texts that we have gathered come, as in the first two volumes, almost entirely from the sages and rabbis, who had to be consulted about every aspect of communal life. The "good men" are largely silent. Whereas the Greeks preserved the speeches of their political leaders, the Jews preserved the legal decisions (responsa) of their intellectual and religious leaders. We have no *kahal* orations and very few reports of public debates. We have to draw out the Jewish understanding of the autonomist regime from the questions posed to legal scholars and from their legalistic but also, often, politically shrewd responses.

Autonomy allowed the members of the *kahal* to address issues of distributive justice, law and order, and crime and punishment. But it also required them to address what we might think of as the central political question: How and by whom were decisions about these issues to be made? Who ruled? Given the authority of the law and the sages, that question was especially problematic, and it was only gradually that the *kahal* developed some collective self-awareness about its own decision-making powers. But with regard to the practical necessities and the frequent crises of the common life, the sages were fairly permissive from early on, recognizing the necessity of prudential decision-making and of ordinances adapted to local circumstance.

The actual history of each *kahal* took shape as a compromise between a universally binding law and a set of particularist arrangements and decisions. We can hardly capture the particularism in any adequate way in our selections, though we are able to provide some striking examples of local conflicts and creative rulings. But our aim is to suggest the more general features of the *kahal* regime and the characteristic arguments that went on among its members. We also mean to celebrate a remarkable political achievement that has hardly been recognized in the past: the members and leaders of the diaspora *kehillot* managed to sustain a common life without sovereignty, without territory, without the authority and agency provided by a state. Our texts reveal the thinking that went along with and made possible that achievement.

Our focus in most of this volume is on the *kahal,* but as with the discussion of membership in Volume II, we can't avoid considering how this communal-political history has moved on in our time from universal exile to emancipation in the democratic West and sovereign statehood in the Middle East. Many of the same issues are now addressed in dramatically new settings: the relation of civil and religious laws and courts, the forms of distributive justice, the "needs of the hour," the permissibility of capital punishment— and even the question of gender equality, just barely raised in our texts but not entirely a modern question. Our selections from contemporary writers are necessarily tentative; we don't know which ones will endure. But we have chosen texts that resonate with, and also suggest the end of, the experience of exile as previously known.

As in Volumes I and II, the texts are arranged topically by chapter and then chronologically within the chapters. Interspersed among the texts are commentaries written by contemporary philosophers, political theorists, and lawyers. The commentaries are not intended to provide historical information; we try to do that, though only in a minimalist way, in the headnotes and the glossary of names. We have asked the commentators, instead, to join the arguments of the texts, to interpret and evaluate, to revise or reject, the claims made by their authors. As with authority and membership in the earlier volumes, so with the internal life of the Jewish communities here, the issues debated in the past remain central to contemporary political debates, and so it seems especially important to avoid treating the tradition as if it were merely ancient and venerable. It is contested and vital, and the point of the commentaries is to bear living witness to that fact.

Introduction

What is it that holds the Jewish people together? That may seem too big a question; our focus in this chapter is more specific: What is it that holds the members of the *kahal* together? But the two questions are closely linked, for the *kahal* is understood simultaneously as a microcosm of the larger congregation of Israel and as a particular association of Israelites. Its members are bound to one another both as Jews and as men and women living together *here,* in this time and place. Our texts move back and forth between the particular and the general union.

So, what bonds of sentiment or duty account for the survival of the *kahal,* this complex and vulnerable communal structure, over so many centuries? We need to ask this question before turning to the families out of which the community is constituted and then to the activities and institutional arrangements of the community itself. For the families would never have come together and the common enterprise would never have succeeded without some underlying and widely shared sense of what a *kahal* was, and why it was, and what claims it had on its members. Issues of this kind are almost never raised directly or dealt with systematically in Jewish literature. But directness and system are not all that common among non-Jews either—not when it comes to the deepest political understandings.

The immediate problem is that no one has ever seen a state or a polis or a *kahal.* These are invisible entities, and so they invite indirect, allusive, and metaphorical descriptions: the body politic, the ship of state, the social contract, the political system (with its checks and balances), and so on. One of our purposes in this chapter is to expose the basic metaphors with which Jewish writers expressed their legal-political views. But we also want to provide an introductory sense of what those views were in the age of the *kehillot* (and, more briefly, before and after that).

In two different ways, the *kahal* rested on consent. First of all, its members were Jews, all of them, and therefore subject to the same set of divine commandments—which had been delivered at Sinai and accepted by the people (see ¢1, where some doubts are expressed about the precise nature of this "acceptance"). And second, the members were partners in an enterprise: they had come together, joined one by one or family by family, to *make* a community. The history of the various *kehillot* was too well known to allow for any widespread use of organic imagery. The *kahal* was a constructed, not a natural body; the imagery of partnership is pervasive. But this was not an entirely voluntary partnership. The second consent followed necessarily from the first. Diaspora Jews recognized that they were bound to form communities of this sort, for otherwise they could not give concrete expression to their religious and legal obligations. Judaism is not a religion that emphasizes the relation of the individual Jew to his or her God. The pronouns are always in the plural: "our God and God of our fathers." And the laws themselves presuppose a community, whose members worship together and are bound to certain patterns of mutual help.

This mutuality is not only legal and consensual; it is also familial. The "children" of Israel are descended from a set of natural and spiritual "fathers" and "mothers," the biblical patriarchs and matriarchs, and they acknowledge at the same time the common parenthood of God—hence they are doubly "siblings." The most common expressions of solidarity make use of this familial imagery, drawn from crucial passages in Leviticus and Deuteronomy, where what is asserted is an absolute obligation to help "your brother." Sometimes in both the Bible and later rabbinic writings, other terms are also used, variously translated as "your fellow," "your neighbor," or "your colleague." But "brother" is dominant.

The imagery is consistently patriarchal and fraternal, though there is one Hebrew root for brother and sister, and in some contexts a gender-free translation might be plausible. In any case, so far as the helping activities go, women are not excluded. As subjects of charity or welfare, they are clearly "brethren," members of the family. They are active helpers, too, whenever, like Queen Esther, they are in a position to help. Converts, too, according to Maimonides (see ¢14), are members of this family, having adopted Abraham as their father and Sarah as their mother and joined the "brotherhood" of Israel. As Mordecai tells Esther, the fate of one is the fate of all.

Two near-contemporary writers demonstrate the continuing power of Jewish familism. Joseph B. Soloveitchik quotes Mordecai's line and invokes the biblical idea of brotherhood, though he also provides a more mod-

ern account of shared experience, of a historically constructed consciousness, to explain the long-standing obligations of Jews to one another. Again,
however, this isn't an entirely voluntary construction; it is, in his view,
"fated"—determined by the often painful circumstances of Jewish history.
Emma Lazarus worries that this "tribal" consciousness, to which she remains
deeply committed, is not strong enough to produce the solidarity necessary
for mutual aid. Jews living freely and comfortably in the United States need
to be reminded of their obligations to persecuted brethren. (We print these
two texts in reverse chronological order, because Soloveitchik seems to write
from a pre-emancipation standpoint, whereas Lazarus reflects the specific
anxieties of emancipated Jews.)

In the days of the *kahal,* the obligations of Jews to one another were
clear enough, though they were always subject to debate at the margins.
Their full extent, and the arguments they engendered, will be revealed only
in the course of the next five chapters. Here we provide some exemplary
texts, designed to suggest the character of the *kahal* as a moral union. The
members cannot abandon the union: "Do not separate yourself . . ." is its first
commandment. They can move, of course, and join another *kahal,* and there
are intricate discussions in the responsa literature about precisely when their
obligations shift from the old to the new community. But they are never
without obligations. It follows, then, that no one can ever be definitively
expelled: excommunication, as Meir of Rothenburg makes clear, is always a
partial sanction (see ¢23 for a full discussion).

The partners-brothers are bound to share the burdens of the community, not only paying taxes but also contributing their time and energy.
They must support one another in adversity, redeeming (ransoming) captives, helping the poor, lending money without interest. And they must admonish one another in matters of personal conduct—for their partnership is
of such a kind that they are all liable for the moral and religious failures of
their fellows. They live, very much like Rousseauean citizens, in each other's
watchful eye.

Caring, sharing, helping, scolding: the model is closer to familial
love or concern—though the obligations of the brethren are subject to legal
determination—than to Aristotelian "friendship" or to anything that we

might recognize as modern civility. Political relations imply for us a certain distance, a distinction of public and private, that is largely absent here. It is worth stressing, however, that the only familial connection invoked in the literature of the *kahal* is brotherhood. No political analogies are drawn from the marriage tie or the bond of parents and children (leaders of the *kahal* are not called "fathers"). The nuclear family is not a model for the political community, and the family generally is shielded from communal interference and regulation—though the authority of the *kahal,* as we will see in the next chapters, can sometimes be brought to bear to protect women against their husbands or children against their parents. When this happens, women and children are, again, treated like "brothers."

Brotherhood is inclusive of Israel as a whole, not merely of this or that *kahal.* Were we to map the obligations to help brethren in trouble incumbent upon every Jew, we would need a complex grid in which need as well as proximity would have a place. The redemption of captives, for example, takes precedence over all merely local charities (because of the religious as well as physical dangers of captivity), but one redeems a captive from one's own *kahal* before someone from far away. Similarly, one's "own" poor take precedence over all others, though one has at least residual obligations to all the others. In these discussions, Israel is rarely described in organic imagery, as a holy body of which each individual Jew is a "limb" and each *kahal* a miniature "embodiment." But it is always understood that both individuals and communities are set within something larger, more inclusive, and far more ancient.

The obligations of the brethren to help one another had, however, certain limits, which cannot be understood from within the family analogy. In a sense, the obligations of kinship never cease; they are unlimited; hence the idea of limits was usually expressed by combining kinship and consent. The crucial formula here is that Jews are "brothers with respect to the commandments." Their brotherhood is constituted not by descent, or not only by descent, but also by agreement. When they break the agreement, transgress the law, they leave or they are excluded from the community of brethren. More accurately, they leave or are excluded *in some sense,* for some purposes, with reference to some of the entitlements of membership. Depending on the degree or kind of their transgression, disobedient brethren are not entitled to redemption if captured, to loans without interest, or to ordinary charity. But there was much debate about these matters (and the arguments, as the selection from Eli'ezer b. Samuel of Metz suggests, were complicated). For the transgressors— so Rashi had written early on in the history of the *kahal*—"though they were sinners" were still Jews. They can never move entirely outside the community or be definitively expelled from it. So, again, the debate about eligibility for communal help was really a debate about sanctions, and the sanctions were always incomplete and temporary. Whenever they were successful, brotherhood was vindicated and all entitlements were restored. Still, at the very end of life, a boundary was drawn. Maimonides says that the rituals of mourning should not be observed for heretics, apostates, and informers; and Solomon b. Abraham Adret denies burial rites to a similar list: apostates, informers, and anyone convicted of a capital offense in a Jewish court.

We may, perhaps, best understand these ideas about responsibility and obligation if we consider how they were tested in the recurrent crises of Jewish history. It is a standard claim of virtually every political theory that individuals must be prepared to risk their lives for the safety of the community. The point is most often made with reference to soldiers in time of war. Among the Jews, who for two thousand years had no army, it commonly arose in the context of persecution, where what was at issue was not military heroism but religious martyrdom. Here the individual's duty was to sacrifice his life for "the sanctification of the Name," that is, for God's sake. But it was never forgotten that the martyr was also defending the integrity and honor and therefore the spiritual survival of the community (see ¢11).

Martyrdom is hard enough, and there were, as we have seen, significant efforts to set limits on the requirement of self-sacrifice. An even harder problem, and one that is unhappily more specific to Jewish political experience, arises when it is the community that is required to sacrifice itself or put itself at risk for the sake of one or more of its members. The cases are ancient as well as modern; the earliest accounts, reported in the Terumot selections, describe heathen gangsters or tyrannical rulers demanding the surrender of a member of a Jewish city or town and threatening the whole community with destruction if the demand is refused.

Here we encounter in dramatic and frightening circumstances the question so hotly debated by utilitarian and anti-utilitarian philosophers: Do the numbers count? The dominant view of the rabbis was that, in certain circumstances, the numbers did count; the community could save itself by handing over a specific person demanded for a specific (and, some would add, a legitimate) reason. But not by handing over just anyone: the community could not "betray" one of its members, chosen at random, to save the others. David Daube, in an extended analysis of the passages reprinted here (*Collaboration with Tyranny in Rabbinic Law*, 1965), suggests that what was at issue was the "moral cohesion" of the community. There are other issues, obviously, including the survival of the members and the obligations of the leaders, but this one is sufficient to explain our inclusion of these painful discussions in this chapter. How was solidarity expressed when it was challenged in the most extreme way, when the *kahal* or even the whole of Kenneset Yisrael faced brutal tyranny and mass destruction?

Fate and Brotherhood

Shared Fate

1. Esther 4:5–16

The book of Esther provides a template for exilic politics. Esther (and to some extent her uncle Mordecai) is a model for future court Jews who run back and forth between their people and the non-Jewish government. The court Jew (for an extended discussion, see ¢28) occupies a highly privileged position, and his or her access to the non-Jewish environment is an option that ordinary Jews did not enjoy. But in a time of crisis, court Jews were as vulnerable as any other Jews.

[When Esther learned that the Jews of Shushan were fasting and weeping, she sent Hathach, one of her eunuchs, to Mordecai] to learn the why and wherefore of it all. Hathach went out to Mordecai in the city square in front of the palace gate; and Mordecai told him all that had happened to him and all about the money that Haman had offered to put into the royal treasury for the destruction of the Jews. He also gave him the written text of the law that had been proclaimed in Shushan for their destruction. [He bade him] show it to Esther and inform her, and charge her to go to the king and to appeal to him and to plead with him for her people. Esther told Hathach to take back to Mordecai the following reply: "All the king's courtiers and the people of the king's provinces know that if any person, man or woman, enters the king's presence in the inner court without having been summoned, there is but one law for him—that he be put to death. Only if the king extends the golden scepter to him may he live. Now I have not been summoned to visit the king for the last thirty days."

When Mordecai was told what Esther had said, Mordecai had this message delivered to Esther: "Do not imagine that you, of all the Jews, will escape with your life by being in the king's palace. On the contrary, if you keep silent in this crisis, relief and deliverance will come to the Jews from another quarter, while you and your father's house will perish. And who knows, perhaps you have attained to royal position for just such a crisis." Then Esther sent back this message to Mordecai: "Go, assemble all the Jews who live in Shushan, and fast on my behalf; do not eat or drink for three days, night or day. I and my maidens will observe that same fast. Then I shall go to the king, though it is contrary to the law, and if I am to perish, I shall perish."

We Are Brothers
2. Nehemiah 5:1–13

Biblical law set limits on the enslavement of "brothers" but apparently did not preclude the enslavement of debtors or their children. A definitive norm against such practices was established only through an intense class struggle in the early years of the Second Commonwealth (during the fifth century B.C.E.). The change was made by Nehemiah—a unique political leader, whose authority was based not only on his official position as peha *(governor) under the Persian Empire but also on his personal charisma and commitment. His words and actions are recorded in his memoir (the only autobiography in the Hebrew Bible). The controlling concept of this impassioned speech is the bond of brotherhood.*

There was a great outcry by the common folk and by their wives against their brother Jews. Some said, "Our sons and daughters are numerous; we must get grain in order that we may live!" Others said, "We must pawn our fields, our vineyards, and our homes to get grain to stave off hunger." Yet others said, "We have borrowed money against our fields and vineyards to pay the king's tax. Now we are as good as our brothers, and our children as good as theirs; yet here we are subjecting our sons and daughters to slavery—some of our daughters are already subjected—and we are powerless, while our fields and vineyards belong to others."

It angered me very much to hear their outcry and these complaints. After pondering the matter carefully, I censured the nobles and the prefects, saying, "Are you pressing claims on loans made to your brothers?" Then I raised a large crowd against them and said to them, "We have done our best to buy back our Jewish brothers who were sold to the nations, and will you now sell your brothers so that they must be sold [back] to us?"[1] They kept silent, for they found nothing to answer. So I continued, "What you are doing is not right. You ought to act in a God-fearing way so as not to give our enemies, the nations, room to reproach us. I, my brothers, and my servants, also have claims of money and grain against them; let us now abandon those claims! Give back at once their fields, their vineyards, their olive trees, and their homes. And [abandon] the claims for the hundred pieces of silver, the grain, the wine, and the oil that you have been pressing against them!" They replied, "We shall give them back, and not demand anything of them; we shall do just as you say." Summoning the priests, I put them under oath to keep this promise. I also shook out the bosom of my garment and said, "So may God shake free of his household and property any man who fails to keep

---

1. Nehemiah is here referring to his practice while still in exile to redeem Judean slaves transported from the land.

this promise; may he be thus shaken out and stripped." All the assembled an-swered, "Amen," and praised the Lord. The people kept this promise.

Individual Responsibility
3. BT Sotah 37a–b

We reprint this text from ¢1, §11, where it serves to indicate the centrality of covenanting in Jewish thought. We include it here because it also suggests the origins of the idea that every Israelite is responsible for every other.

Our rabbis taught: "Blessed" in general, "blessed" in particular; "cursed" in general, "cursed" in particular; "to study and to teach, to keep and to do"—these are four by four . . . which makes for sixteen. The same [took place also] at Sinai, and at the plains of Moab. . . . Thus there were forty-eight covenants for each *mitzvah* of the Torah. . . .

Rabbi Shimon b. Yehudah of Akko Village said in the name of Rabbi Shimon: With regard to each and every *mitzvah* of the Torah, there were en-acted forty-eight covenants by 603,550 [people].[2] [*Rashi:* For each one, as each became a guarantor on behalf of all his brothers.]

Rabbi [Judah the Prince] said: [This implies further that] for each and every Israelite, there were 603,550 [covenants].

What is the issue? Rav Mesharshia said, They disagree with respect to a guarantor for a guarantor. [*Rashi:* Rabbi is arguing that, according to Rabbi Shimon, who seeks to enumerate the covenants of guarantee . . . each of the 600,000 accepted [also] 600,000 covenants on account of the guaran-tees that his brothers had offered for their fellows.]

2. See ¢1, §11.

Common Fate

4. Joseph B. Soloveitchik, "The Covenant of Fate"

Fate and Destiny: From Holocaust to the State of Israel (Hoboken, N.J.: Ktav, 2000), pp. 46–53 (excerpts).

Soloveitchik's essay provides an internal orthodox argument for Jewish national unity intended to overcome profound disagreement as to the nature of religious obligation and/or commitment. Echoing the talmudic discussion of the conversion procedure (¢17, §9), he distinguishes the "covenant of fate" from the "covenant of destiny." The second of these, deriving from Sinai, centers on normative commitment, but it is preceded by the Exodus, which suggests that historical fate is the ground of Jewish solidarity.

The covenant of fate expresses itself . . . in positive categories which derive from the consciousness of a shared fate. There are four aspects to this rare mode of consciousness.

First, the consciousness of a shared fate manifests itself as a consciousness of shared circumstances. We all find ourselves in the realm of a common fate which binds together all of the people's different strata, its various units and groups, a fate which does not discriminate between one group and another group or between one person and his fellow. Our fate does not distinguish between aristocrats and common folk, between rich and poor, between a prince garbed in the royal purple and a pauper begging from door to door, between a pietist and an assimilationist. Even though we speak a plethora of languages, even though we are inhabitants of different lands, even though we look different . . . [and] live in varying and unequal social and economic conditions—one may dwell in a magnificent palace, the other in a miserable hovel—we still share the same fate. If the Jew in the hovel is beaten, the security of the Jew in the palace is endangered. "Think not with thyself that thou shalt escape in the king's house more than all the Jews" (Esther 4:13). . . .

Second, the consciousness of shared historical circumstances results in the experience of shared suffering. The feeling of sympathy is a fundamental feature of the consciousness of the unifying fate of the Jewish people. The suffering of one part of the people affects the people as a whole. The scattered and dispersed people mourn together and are comforted together. . . . The pleas that ascend from the abyss of affliction are not restricted to the suffering and pain of the individual supplicant. They include the needs of the entire community. When a person has a sick relative, he cannot pray for him alone, but has to pray for all the sick of Israel. If one enters into a mourner's home, and wipe away a tear from his grieving face, one directs one's words of comfort to all who mourn for Zion and Jerusalem. The slightest disturbance in the condition of a single individual or group ought to grieve all the various segments of the people in all of their dispersions. It is both forbidden and impossible for the "I" to isolate himself from his fellow and not share in his suffering. If the premise of shared historical circumstances is correct, then the experience of shared suffering is the direct conclusion of that premise. . . .

Third, shared suffering finds expression in the awareness of shared responsibility and liability. When Israel went forth from Egypt, Moses and Aaron fell down upon their faces, pleaded with God, and said, "O God, the God of the spirits of all flesh, shall one man sin, and will Thou be wroth with all the congregation?" (Num. 16:22). This prayer accomplished the aim intended for it by Moses and Aaron, the shepherds of their people, Israel; God agreed that they had acted properly in setting forth their plea and punished only the congregation of Korah. However, God's display of this particular mode of *hesed* was only temporary. On a permanent basis, the "I" is held responsible for the sin of his fellow if it was in his power to rebuke him, to protest against his behavior and induce him to repent. A collective ethico-halakhic responsibility devolves upon the entire Jewish people. The individuals coalesce into one ethico-halakhic unit, possessed of one conscience and an all-encompassing normative consciousness. The halakhah has already declared that all Jews are guarantors for one another. . . .

Shared responsibility is not only a theoretical halakhic idea; it is also a central fact in the history of the Jewish people in respect to its relationship to the nations of the world. Our neighbors have always condemned all of us for the sins of one of us; they have thereby transformed the rhetorical talmudic query, "Shall Tuviah sin and Zigud be punished?" (BT Pesahim 113b), into a daily reality that does not even surprise anyone. The identification of the actions of the individual with the deeds of the people is a fundamental feature of our history. Our enemies will not allow the individual Jew to remain isolated in his own private, separate sphere. They take him out of his four cubits into the public domain, and there they make use of him in order to level a harsh indictment against the entire community. . . .

Fourth, shared historical circumstances give rise to shared activity. The obligation to give charity and perform deeds of lovingkindness derives its force from the all-penetrating and all-encompassing experience of brotherhood. The Torah, in laying down these commandments, uses the term *akh,* "brother," instead of *re'ah,* "fellow." . . . "Thou shalt not harden thy heart, nor shut thy hand from thy needy brother. . . . Thou shalt surely open thy hand unto thy poor and needy brother in thy land" (Deuteronomy 15:7, 11). The confrontation with the people's strange and unusual fate-laden existence endows the Jew with a unifying consciousness in the field of social action.

Collective Responsibility

5. Emma Lazarus, *An Epistle to the Hebrews*

An Epistle to the Hebrews, introduction and notes by Morris U. Schappes (New York: Jewish Historical Society of New York, 1987), pp. 30–31, 42–43.

In 1881 a wave of pogroms, beginning in the Ukraine, swept across Russia. Lazarus's Epistle was written in response; it is a call for American Jews to rally to the aid of their brethren, accompanied by a new anxiety that life in the United States might weaken the brotherly (tribal) commitment.

"Tribal!" This perpetual taunt rings so persistently in our ears that most Jews themselves are willing to admit its justice, [despite] the fact that our "tribal God" has become the God . . . of Islam and Christendom, and that as a people we have adapted ourselves to the varying customs and climates of every nation in the world. In defiance of the hostile construction that may be put upon my words, I do not hesitate to say that our national defect is that we are not "tribal" enough; we have not sufficient solidarity to perceive that when the life and property of a Jew in the uttermost provinces of the Caucasus are attacked, the dignity of a Jew in free America is humiliated. We who are prosperous and independent have not sufficient homogeneity to champion, on the ground of a common creed, a common stock, a common history, a common heritage of misfortune, the rights of the lowest and poorest Jew-peddler who flees for life and liberty of thought from Slavonic mobs. Until we are all free, we are none of us free. But lest we should justify the taunts of our opponents, lest we should become "tribal" and narrow and Judaic rather than humane and cosmopolitan like the anti-Semites of Germany and the Jew-baiters of Russia, we ignore and repudiate our unhappy brethren as having no part or share in their misfortunes—until the cup of anguish is held also to our own lips. . . .

The fact that the Jews of America are civilly and religiously emancipated should be our strongest impelling motive for working towards the emancipation of our oppressed brethren. No other Jews in the world can bring to bear upon the enterprise such absolute disinterestedness of aim, such long and intimate familiarity with the blessings . . . of liberty. We must help our less fortunate brethren, not with the condescending patronage of the prosperous, who in self-defense undertake to conceal the social sores of the community by providing a remote hiding-place for the outcast and the beggar, but with the keen, human sympathy of . . . Jews who feel the sting of every wound and insult inflicted upon their blood-kindred. . . .

[A] wail of lamentation reaches us from distant countries, and to our grief and amazement we hear that other homeless and despoiled survivors of that wreck in which we suffered are subjected to renewed misery at the hands of powerful oppressors. Shall we remain deaf to their cry, or heeding the unanimous voice of friend and foe in counsel or in menace, shall we not rather exert ourselves to render feasible the only remedy applicable to the evil? A home for the homeless, a goal for the wanderer, an asylum for the persecuted, a nation for the denationalized. Such is the need of our generation.

Belonging and Including

Separation as Heresy

6. The Four Sons

A central feature of the Passover ritual dinner, the seder, is the recounting of the exodus, the community's founding myth, to the children at the table. In several passages, the Torah describes the (hypothetical) child's question, and the parent's reply, in various forms. Our text explains this variety as exemplifying educational attention to children's different capacities and attitudes.

The Torah relates to four children: one, wise, a second, wicked, a third, simple, and a fourth, [a child] that does not [yet] know how to ask.

What does the wise [child] say?

—"What mean the decrees, laws, and rules that the Lord our God has enjoined upon you?" (Deut. 6:20).

And you instruct him in the halakhot of Passover: "One may not conclude after the Paschal meal [by saying], 'Now to the entertainment!'"

What does the wicked [child] say?

—"What is this service to you?" (Exod. 12:26); [implying,] "to you," and not to him. Since he removes himself from the whole, he has denied the fundamental principle.[3]

You in return must set his teeth on edge, and answer him: "It is because of what the Lord did for me when I went free from Egypt" (Exod. 13:8); [implying], "for me," not for him. Had he been there, he would not have been redeemed.

What does the simple [child] say?

—"What is this?"

"And you shall say to him, 'It was with a mighty hand that the Lord brought us out from Egypt, the house of bondage'" (Exod. 13:14).

And with him who does not know how to ask, you yourself must

---

3. "Denying the fundamental principle [*ikar*]" in Rabbinic usage frequently denotes denying God.

take the initiative: "And you shall explain to your son on that day, 'It is be-cause of what the Lord did for me when I went free from Egypt" (Exod. 13:8).

The Severity of Withdrawal
7. BT Ta'anit 11a

In this homiletic passage, the Talmud engages in a critique of indifference and withdrawal in the face of communal grief and suffering. As is often the case, homiletic rhetoric yields an incisive phenomenology; here, of indifference and callousness.

Our Rabbis taught: When Israel experiences suffering and one [member] withdraws, the two angels of service that accompany a person come and lay their hands upon his head and say: "So and so who has withdrawn from the community—may he not behold the community's solace."

Another *baraita* teaches: When the community experiences suffering a person should not say, "I shall go home and eat and drink and [say to myself] 'Peace be unto you my soul.'" If indeed he does this, Scripture proclaims of him: "[My Lord God of Hosts summoned on that day to weeping and lament-ing, to tonsuring and girding with sackcloth.] Instead, there was rejoicing and merriment, killing of cattle and slaughtering of sheep, eating of meat and drinking of wine: 'Eat and drink, for tomorrow we die!'" (Isa. 22:12–13).

What writ follows?

"Then the Lord of Hosts revealed Himself to my ears: 'This iniquity shall never be forgiven you until you die'" (22:14).

All this is with regard to the average disposition, but [see] what is written with regard to the wicked disposition: "Come, I'll get some wine; let us swill some liquor. And tomorrow will be just the same or even much grander!" (Isa. 56:12).

What writ follows?

"The righteous man perishes, and no one considers; [pious men are taken away, and no one gives thought,] that because of evil the righteous was taken away" (57:1).

Rather a person should suffer with the community. For thus we have found with regard to Moses our master who suffered with the community; as written [in the story of the battle with Amalek], "But Moses' hands grew heavy; so they took a stone and put it under him and he sat on it" (Exod. 17:12). Now, was Moses lacking a pillow or a seat to sit upon? Rather, thus did Moses reason: "Given that Israel are experiencing suffering, I too will suffer with them."

And whosoever suffers with the community will merit to behold the community's solace.

—Now, should a person say, "Who will bear witness against me?"

—The stones of a person's home and the beams of his home bear witness against him, as written, "For a stone shall cry out from the wall, and a rafter shall answer it from the woodwork" (Hab. 2:11).

The school of Rabbi Sheila say: The two angels of service that accompany a person, they bear witness against him, as written: "For He will order His angels to you, [to oversee you wherever you go]" (Ps. 91:11).

Rabbi Hidka says: A person's soul, she bears witness against him, as written, "Be guarded in speech with her who lies in your bosom" (Mic. 7:5).

Congregating in Adversity

8. Maimonides, MT Laws of Fast Days 1:1–3, 17

The Code of Maimonides, Book Three: The Book of Seasons, translated by Solomon Gandz and Hyman Klein, YJS (New Haven: Yale University Press, 1961), pp. 431, 435.

Maimonides takes the previous selection's homiletic concern with regard to withdrawal a step further, articulating a communal norm of care, concern, and introspection.

1. A positive scriptural commandment prescribes prayer and the sounding of an alarm with trumpets whenever trouble befalls the community. For when scripture says, "Against the adversary that oppresseth you, then ye shall sound an alarm with the trumpets" (Num. 10:9), the meaning is: Cry out in prayer and sound an alarm against whatsoever is oppressing you, be it famine, pestilence, locusts, or the like.

2. This procedure is one of the roads to repentance, for as the community cries out in prayer and sounds an alarm when overtaken by trouble, everyone is bound to realize that evil has come upon them as a consequence of their own evil deeds, as it is written, "Your iniquities have turned away these things, and your sins have withholden good from you" (Jer. 5:25), and that their repentance will cause the trouble to be removed from them.

3. If, on the other hand, the people do not cry out in prayer and do not sound an alarm, but merely say that it is the way of the world for such a thing to happen to them, and that their trouble is a matter of pure chance [nikro nikret], they have chosen a cruel path which will cause them to persevere in their evil deeds and thus bring additional troubles upon them. For when scripture says, "But walk contrary [keri] to me; I will walk contrary to you in fury" (Lev. 26:27–28), the meaning is: If, when I bring trouble upon you in order to cause you to repent, you say that the trouble is purely accidental [keri], then I will add to your trouble the fury appropriate to such an "accident."

17. On each fast day undertaken by a community beset by troubles, the court and the elders should remain in session at the synagogue from the end of the morning service until midday, to examine into the conduct of the citizens and to remove the obstacles to righteous living provided by transgressions. They should carefully search and inquire after those guilty of extortion and similar crimes, in order to set them apart, and those who act high-handedly, in order to humble them, and after other such matters.

Do Not Withdraw

9. Mishnah Avot 2:4 and commentaries

In the following selections, our focus is on the admonition "Do not withdraw from the community [tzibbur]," which is the first of a string of adages by Hillel cited in tractate Avot. In Rabbinic usage, tzibbur denotes congregation, but in medieval or modern usages, it means community or public. Two commentaries follow directly. Mahzor Vitri

(France, c. 1100) interprets Hillel's injunction in terms of the medieval circumstances of exile. Joseph ibn Aknin (d. 1220, North Africa) addresses the challenge posed by an unworthy community. Drawing directly on Maimonides' formulation in MT Laws Concerning Character Traits 6:1, he raises the question whether withdrawing might at times be imperative. A further commentary on the same mishnah, by Menachem Meiri, is reproduced below (§13).

R. Hillel says:

> Do not withdraw from the community.
> Put no trust in yourself until the day of your death.
> Judge not your fellow until you stand in his place.

Sharing the Burden

Mahzor Vitri, *Commentary on Avot* 2:4

"Do not withdraw from the community": Rather, share in their burdens imposed by the government [*malkhut*], in their fasts, in their prayers. Thus indeed [the message that] Mordecai sent to Esther: "Do not imagine you, of all the Jews, will escape with your life by being in the king's palace . . . [see §1 above]." And we read in BT Ta'anit (11a), If one withdraws from the community, "the two Angels of Service who accompany a person . . . lay their hands upon his head and say: May So-and-so who withdrew from the community not share in the community's solace."

Withdrawing

Joseph ibn Aknin, *Commentary on Avot* 2:4

What happens when the community is morally corrupt? Can withdrawing be imperative?

A person should not maintain [character] dispositions far different from those of his community. But if he sees that the dispositions of the people of his city are corrupt, and he is worried lest if he remain with them he might adopt their course, walk in their evil ways, and thus be driven from the path of life, then he must leave their midst immediately, and go to another city the conduct of whose inhabitants is proper, whose dispositions are the just ones in accordance with the principle of the middle way. If he finds no such city close by, let him go to one far off. If he finds none, let him go off to the wilderness where there are no human beings, as Jeremiah, may he rest in peace, said: "Oh, to be in the wilderness, at an encampment for wayfarers" (Jer. 9:1).

Against Going It Alone

10. Maimonides, MT Laws of Repentance 3:11

Whosoever separates himself from the public practices, even if he does not commit transgressions but only separates from the congregation of Israel (*adat yisrael*), does not fulfill *mitzvoth* in common with them, is indifferent when they are in distress, does not participate in their fast, but goes his own way, as one of the gentiles of the land and does not belong to them—he has not portion in the world to come.

Community of Partners

11. Meir b. Baruch of Rothenburg (Maharam), *Responsa* (Lemberg) 108[4]

The complex economic conditions of Jews in medieval Germany revolved around their financial relations with the local nobility. Direct personal relations with a local lord could

---

4. We thank Joseph Isaac Lifschitz for his assistance with understanding this responsum and its historical background.

spell independence from the community and an unfair distribution of the tax load. The
community of Stendal was granted privilege of residence in 1267, and Meir was asked by
its leaders about various subsequent benefices granted to particular Jews. These ranged
from independent arrangements to special short-term tax reductions and incentives meant
to induce Jews to settle in central Germany. In his responsum he evokes the responsibility
of civic partnership in sharing the burden. He also makes use of the notion of "one union,"
which he took to be a constitutional principle of the kahal.

[Question:] Re'uven resided under the lord of a certain province and recently wished to leave and reside with Shimon and his fellows under the lord of their town. Before arriving he cut a deal with Shimon's lord [to pay] a certain sum [of taxes] per annum. He thus withdrew from the community, and refuses to participate with them in the tax [burden], claiming "I have already cut a deal with your lord, and I have nothing [to do] with you." Now Shimon and his fellows treat him as someone banned with a *herem* in accordance with the *takkanot* of the communities, because he did not participate in the [burden of the] tax. . . .

Inform us of your opinion: Who is in the right?

[Answer:] I hereby reply tersely due to the burdens of office. Regarding Re'uven, who has come to settle in a different town and who withdrew from the community, cutting a deal with the lord to pay taxes independently—it is not within his power to do this. For [following BT Bava Batra 8a (¢8, §§1–3)] all townspeople are partners for [the purpose of constructing the] wall, [maintenance of] a guard, a mounted guard, the town tax, the city gates, the charity fund and food-tray, and all similar matters such as taxes delivered to the lord of the town. The safekeeping of the town and its deliverance from [marauding] forces—this is [the lord's] responsibility, and this is similar to [the case of] a guard and a mounted guard [mentioned above]. And given that they are partners, it is established [as a point of law] that a partner cannot split [the assets of the partnership] without his fellow's consent. And even if it were not Torah law, since it is the custom [among the communities] throughout the kingdom to form partnerships, splitting off is not permitted.

For were they to split off, each individual on his own, they would come to evil consequences. For each one would shake off his yoke and lay the burden on his fellow, and the result would be grievous quarrels to no end. Would that we were one people and one union! And would that we could survive amongst our enemies!

Therefore Re'uven who wishes to split off ought to be chastised. Any one of the [towns]people may prevent it. If he complies—good, if not you have the authority to compel him by word, by whip, by *herem*, [or] by *niddui.* . . .

We thus agree with you. This is the law with regard to [those who split off]—all [of them] have to pay all taxes with you, and in all matters they are as you, one pocket for all. They are not permitted to split off unless you all consent.

Banning, Not Expulsion

12. Meir b. Baruch of Rothenburg (Maharam), *Responsa* (Sinai) 303

Sinai 5 (1942): 10–12, no. 303.

Whereas the previous responsum discussed the range of measures the kahal is at liberty to use against those who try to split off from the community, this responsum attempts to draw limits to their banishment. Someone who splits off, though his behavior is unacceptable, is nonetheless a member.

You asked with regard to Re'uven who is a splitter, and is divisive, yet has a share in the synagogue—can the kahal force him out, saying, "Depart from us! Pull out [yourself] or we will push you out"?[5]

Thus is my tradition: it is a herem of Rabbi Gershom the Light of the Exile of blessed memory, that no person is to be excluded from the synagogue nor driven out from sharing in the Lord's possession.[6] [A person may

---

5. Each partner in a partnership has a right to initiate a division of assets. One can demand of the other—"pull out and divide or I will do so." See BT Bava Batra 13a.
6. Paraphrasing 1 Sam. 26:19.

be excluded] only for a week or two, or a month, but not forever. . . . But if he is divisive and intolerable, the townspeople are authorized to impose punishment or a fine. If he does not heed them they have the authority to have him beaten by the gentiles till he agrees to obey what Israel demand of him.

Is it not the case that there are numerous violent and powerful [persons] who, if left to their own will, would seek exemption from the tax, but are compelled through the gentiles and by all manner of bans? So too in this case.

Responsibility

Protest or Assume Leadership
13. Menachem Meiri, *Bet ha-Behirah* Avot 2:4

After expressing his own view of the mishnah (§8 above), Meiri takes issue with a rival interpretation. The anonymous disputed view seems to be along the lines of spiritual self-preservation recommended by Joseph ibn Aknin (§9 above), a view Meiri refuses to endorse without an important qualification.

"Do not withdraw from the community," but rather share in their tribulation. This is to say that although one is able to be delivered from the tribulation independently, his sole and principle intent should be only the deliverance of the whole, himself being included. Otherwise his punishment shall be that the community will be delivered like a deer from the hands [of its hunters], while he will fall into the trap of his own iniquity. So have our Rabbis said,[7] Whoever does not share with the community, i.e. in their tribulation, will not share in the community's solace, as written, "Join in her jubilation, all you who mourned over her" (Isa. 66:10). The same notion [is expressed also in the verse]: "Relief and deliverance will come to the Jews from another quarter; while you and your father's house shall perish" (Esther 4:14).

7. Paraphrasing BT Ta'anit 30b.

There is another interpretation . . . [the quotation is not preserved—Eds.]. But this is naught, for . . . if they are evil [and] if he is worthy, he ought to rebuke them and lead them in the straight way. If he is unworthy, or unheeded, then he most certainly should withdraw from them, and even move away from their vicinity as far as is required to be [free from] their association, even if they are his relatives and companions; as written, "Go forth from your native land, and from your father's house" (Gen. 12:1).

If he fails to do so, let him fear for his life, lest he be swept away in the iniquity of the city.[8] With regard to human judgment, although his body will be spared, his property shall not—as explained in BT Sanhedrin (112a–b) regarding the seduced city, that the property of the righteous [among its inhabitants] is destroyed. What reason is given for this? "What caused them to live there? Their property [i.e., economic interest drew the righteous to settle in such an evil community]; therefore their property is destroyed."

Assume Political Responsibility

14. Joseph Alashkar, *Mirkevet ha-Mishneh* Avot 2:4

The mishnah we have been discussing is preceded by Rabban Shimon b. Gamaliel's statement, "Be wary of the government, for its [officials] draw a person near only for their own needs. They feign friendship when it benefits them and do not stand up for a person at his moments of distress." The statements in tractate Avot follow the linear chain of tradition. In the Kaufman manuscript, the saying is attributed to the third-century C.E. descendant of Hillel the Elder, and his namesake, R. Hillel, grandson of Judah the Prince. Many editions of the Mishnah simply attribute the saying to "Hillel," supporting the widespread attribution to Hillel the elder. Shimon b. Gamaliel, however, was Hillel the elder's sixth-generation descendant. Alashkar begins his discussion querying this temporal reversal.

8. Paraphrasing Gen. 19:15.

The reason the editor of the Mishnah introduced Hillel's statement here is that it further enhances Rabban Gamaliel's statement and expounds it. [He] admonishes persons to keep far from government, and we have already noted that whoever is [appointed] *parnas* must necessarily come close to the government. Hillel therefore means to warn such a person: Should [anyone] whom the *kahal* needs to be *parnas* over it say [to himself,] "Why do I need this trouble of being a *parnas* and having to turn on [the public's] behalf to the government? I will myself come close to the government and receive my own benefits from it, and I will not speak [on behalf of] the public at all." Hillel therefore comes and says, If it is the need of the hour, do not withdraw from the community, for the merit of the *kahal* will defend you.

Furthermore, it is possible that he means to admonish you—that even if you are close to the [rulers of the] kingdom and you are capable of distancing yourself from the [Jewish] community and all its affairs, even so, if they are suffering, be with them. If they give charity, give with them. If they make a payment to the kingdom, even though you are able not to contribute along with them, do not withdraw from their suffering.

Commentary. Why Choose Solidarity?

Hillel says: "Do not withdraw from the community." What does it mean to stand with one's community, and why is solidarity a good thing? Or, to put the question more precisely, is solidarity a good thing as such, or does its good depend wholly on the moral worth of the community it serves?

This question has its parallel, in the age of nation-states, in the question whether patriotism is a virtue independent of the ideals—such as freedom, equality, and respect for human rights—one's country may stand for. Clearly, it is good to love one's country and to contribute to its well-being insofar as it is just. But patriotism in this sense involves fidelity to principle, not communal obligation; the moral importance of my loyalty derives from the good things my country does, not necessarily from the good of standing with my fellow citizens and affirming our common identity.

In the case of the Jewish community, solidarity derives much of its moral weight from its role in creating conditions for the observance of divine commandments, so much so that it is unclear whether communal obligation has any other ground. Is the moral importance of community wholly derivative, or is solidarity a virtue for reasons independent of its role in promoting a righteous way of life?

It is clear that communal obligations go well beyond the obligations to fulfill divine commandments, and in this sense, solidarity is a good independent of religious observance. Jews must share in the burdens of government, pay taxes to the host government according to the assessments assigned by communal authorities, show concern to fellow members in distress, and join in the collective observance of fasts, festivals, and prayers. Maimonides writes that he who holds himself aloof from the congregation of Israel and goes his own way, as if he did not belong to the Jewish people, will be denied a portion of the world to come, even if he commits no (legal) transgression.

Although communal obligations go beyond the requirements of religious precepts, they are nonetheless enforced with the gravest of sanctions. The reason for enforcing communal obligations as if they were divine commandments must be that preserving the Jewish community is a necessary condition of observing the commandments, of living a Jewish life. In a twelfth-century responsa, Rabbi Meir of Rothenburg held that no Jew may pay his taxes directly to the overlord but must pay according to the assessments established by the Jewish community, which then pays the host government a collective sum. Any Jew who refuses the authority of the community and tries to make an independent deal with the overlord is subject to flagellation, ban, or excommunication. Rothenburg does not rest his conclusion on talmudic law alone but also on a practical political consideration. "If not for this rule, equitable distribution of the burden of taxation would be impossible and endless quarrels would ensue, endangering the position of the Jew among his neighbors." Holding the community together, and preserving such autonomy as it possesses vis-à-vis the host government, is an essential political condition for the observance of religious law.

The collective character of Jewish religious practice and the political vulnerability of Jewish communities in the diaspora may explain the importance of communal solidarity. Unless Jews displayed loyalty to their communities, an essential condition of the observance of Jewish law would be threatened. But if the preservation of Jewish religious life is the moral ground of communal obligation, then solidarity is a derivative good, not an independent one. Standing with one's community is not virtuous in itself but virtuous only to the extent that the community is worthy.

The notion that solidarity is a derivative good rather than an independent one is borne out by the fact that where Jewish communities fail to uphold religious precepts, the obligation not to withdraw ceases to hold. Indeed, in the case of corrupt communities, there may even be an obligation to withdraw. The twelfth-century commentator Joseph ibn Aknin writes that if a person sees that the dispositions the people of his city maintain are corrupt and is worried that he may fall into their evil ways, "then he must leave their midst immediately, and go to another city the conduct of whose inhabitants is proper. . . . If he finds no such city close by, let him go to one far off. If he finds none, let him go off to the wilderness where there are no human beings." Living with no community at all is better than standing by a corrupt one.

Rabbi Menachem Meiri, a thirteenth-century talmudic scholar, qualifies this view by insisting that, before withdrawing, a person should do his best to reform his evil brethren, to rebuke them and "lead them in the straight way." But if reform efforts fail, "then he most certainly should withdraw from them, and even move away from their vicinity as far as required to be [free from] their association, even if they are his relatives and companions." Where the community is unworthy, the obligation of solidarity gives way to an obligation to leave. So strong is the obligation to withdraw that a righteous person may be punished for living in an evil community even if he does not succumb to the corrupt ways of his brethren. Since only economic interest could explain his presence there, the possessions of the righteous resident of a corrupt community should be destroyed.

This reinforces the notion that community is a derivative good, not an independent one. Separation in defense of righteousness is no vice; solidarity in the face of transgression is no virtue.

Michael Sandel

Mutual Guarantors
15. BT Sanhedrin 27b

Communal responsibility is intergenerational. The decisions and actions of parents nec-
essarily implicate their children. Is this causal fact of moral significance? Does genealogy
imply culpability?

Our Rabbis have taught: "Parents should not be put to death for children"
(Deut. 24:16). What does [scripture] come to teach? If [it comes to teach] that
parents should not be put to death for the iniquities of children nor children
for the iniquities of parents, is it not already written "a person shall be put to
death only for his own crime" (Deut. 24:16)?

    —Rather, "Parents should not be put to death for children"—on
testimony of their children, "nor children be put to death for parents"—on
the testimony of parents.

    —But are children not to be put to death for the iniquities of par-
ents? Is it not written, "but visits the iniquity of parents upon children"
(Exod. 34:7)?!

    —[Scripture there refers to children] that hold fast to the deeds of
their parents.

    As it has been taught: "they shall be heartsick over the iniquities of
their fathers too" (Lev. 26:39)—that hold fast to the deeds of their parents.

    —So you say; yet perhaps it is not so, but true even if they do not
hold fast to the deeds of their parents?

    —Given that it is written, "a person shall be put to death only for his
own crime" (Deut. 24:16) [the previous verse must refer to those] that hold
fast to the deeds of their parents.

    —But is it not written, "they shall stumble over one another" (Lev.
26:37), [i.e.,] One [will stumble] over the sin of the other, thus teaching that
all are guarantors for one another?

    —That refers to those who had the ability to protest and failed to
do so.

Rebuke
16. Sifra Kedoshim parashah 2:8

The Holiness Code of the book of Leviticus is characterized by its unique conception that morality—not only cultic purity and integrity—is constitutive of holiness. The following midrash elaborates three consecutive injunctions of the code: "You shall not go up and down as a talebearer among your people: neither shall you stand idly by the blood of your neighbor; I am the Lord. You shall not hate your brother in your heart. You shall in any wise rebuke your brother but incur no guilt because of him" (Lev. 19:16-17). The midrash begins by querying the implications of the sequence. Why is the command forbidding gossip followed by a demand to take responsibility for the life of one's fellow? It teaches that giving testimony is not equal to talebearing.

8. And whence [have we learned] that if you know [what happened and can] testify, you may not keep silent?

    —We learn from what is written, "Neither shall you stand idly by the blood of your neighbor" (Lev. 19:16).

    Whence [have we learned] that if you see one drowning in the river or under attack by bandits or by a dangerous beast that you must save him?

    —We learn from what is written, "Neither shall you stand idly by the blood of your neighbor" (Lev. 19:16).

    Whence [have we learned] that in case of one who pursues his comrade so as to kill him, or after a male [to rape him] or a betrothed maiden [to rape her], you are obligated to save him [at the price of] his life?[9]

    —We learn from what is written, "Neither shall you stand idly by the blood of your neighbor" (Lev. 19:16).

    "You shall not hate your brother in your heart" (Lev. 19:17). Can it be [that this means only] "you shall not curse him, you shall not strike him, and you shall not slap him"?

---

9. See ¢23, §30.

—We learn from what is written, "In your heart" (Lev. 19:17). [This implies] "I have said so specifically with regard to hatred of the heart."

And whence do we know that if you rebuked four or five times, you should continue rebuking?

—We learn from what is written, "You shall in any wise rebuke" (Lev. 19:17).

Can it be [that this applies] even if you rebuke him and his face changes [color]?

—We learn from what is written, "But incur no guilt because of him" (Lev. 19:17).

Liability of the Righteous
17. BT Shabbat 54b–55a

The Talmud here continues developing the theme of the righteous being implicated in the evils of their society when they fail to protest and rebuke. In the chapter from Ezekiel invoked late in the discussion, which serves as the basis for the main midrashic argument, the righteous are expressly saved by a special mark. The Talmud, however, cites Rav Yosef's radical reinterpretation whereby the righteous were the first to be smitten.

Rav and R. Haninah, R. Yohanan, and Rav Havivah taught: . . . "Whoever can protest against [the sins of] his household and fails to do so is held [accountable] for his household; [if he can protest] against his fellow townsmen, he is held [accountable] for his fellow townsmen; [if he can protest] against the entire world, he is held [accountable] for the entire world."

Said Rav Papa: "The Exilarch's staff are thus held [accountable] for the entire world."

Said R. Haninah, "Why is it written, 'The Lord will bring this charge against the elders and officers of His people' (Isa. 3:14)? If the officers sinned, how have the elders sinned? Rather, the elders [are judged] because they did not protest against the officers."

Rav Yehudah was sitting before Shmu'el. There came a woman and cried before him, but he [Shmu'el] ignored her.

He [Yehudah] asked, "Is the Master not of the opinion [that] 'Who stops his ears at the cry of the wretched, he too will call and not be answered' (Prov. 21:13)"?

"O big teeth!"[10] he replied, "Your superior [will be punished] with chilled [water], but your superior's superior [will be punished] with scolding [water]! Is not Mar Ukva presiding over [the exilarch's] court?" As written, "O House of David,[11] thus said the Lord: 'Render just verdicts morning by morning; Rescue him who is robbed from him who defrauded him. Else My wrath will break forth like fire and burn, with none to quench it, because of your wicked acts,' etc. (Jer. 21:12)."

Rav Zera said to R. Simon, "Let the Master rebuke the exilarch's staff?"

He replied: "They do not accept."

He continued: "Even though they do not accept—rebuke them! For Rav Aha b. Haninah said: "Never did a favorable [decree] go forth from the mouth of the Holy One, which He [then] retracted for evil except for the following, where it is written, 'And the Lord said to him, "Pass through the city, through Jerusalem, and put a mark [taw][12] on the foreheads of the men who moan and groan because of all the abominations that are committed in it,"' etc. (Ezek. 9:4).

Said the Holy One to Gabriel, 'Go and register a taw of ink upon the foreheads of the righteous, that the destroying angels may have no power over them; and a taw of blood upon the foreheads of the wicked, that the destroying angels may have power over them.'

Said the Attribute of Justice before the Holy One, 'Sovereign of the Universe! Wherein are these different from those?'

He replied: 'Those are completely righteous, while these are completely wicked.'

10. Rav Yehudah's nickname.
11. The exilarchs continue the Davidic line.
12. The last letter of the Hebrew alphabet.

She said before Him: 'Sovereign of the Universe! They had the capacity to protest but did not.'

He replied: 'It was manifest and known to Me that had they protested, they would not have accepted [the protest].'

She said: 'Sovereign of the Universe! Although manifest to You, was it manifest to them?'

Hence it is written, '[kill off] graybeard, youth and maiden, women and children; but do not touch any person who bears the mark. Begin here at My Sanctuary [*mikdashi*]. So they began with the elders who were in front of the house' (Ezek. 9:6)."

Rav Yosef taught: "Read not *mikdashi* but *mekuddashay* [= My sanctified ones]: these are the people who fulfilled the Torah from *alef* to *taw*."[13]

Helping

"With You"

18. BT Bava Metzia 62a

What do we owe each other in case of extreme scarcity? Here is the classic debate regarding conflict of lives. This version presents R. Akiva as resolving the issue by recourse to Leviticus 25:36. In another version (Sifra Behar parashah 5:3 on this verse), Ben Patura presents his position as an interpretation of the same verse.

It has been taught: [In a case of] two [people] traveling on foot through the desert, one of whom possesses a pitcher of water — if both were to drink they die, if one was to drink he would reach civilization. Ben Patura expounded: Better that both drink and die and let not one behold the death of the other. Finally R. Akiva taught: "So that your brother may live with you" (Lev. 25: 36) — your life takes precedence over the life of your fellow.

---

13. From *a* to *z*.

Commentary. Life before Morality

This three-sentence story captures in a strikingly economic manner one of the deepest dilemmas in ethics: is it justified to save a person's life at the expense of another person's life. One should first notice the philosophical import of the extreme literary conciseness of the text. We are told nothing about the identity of the two protagonists, their age or other characteristics, nor do we know anything about their personal relations. More important, we do not know who is the legal owner of the pitcher of water (we know only that one of them "has it in his hands"). Of course, we have no indication whether one of the two is more responsible for the situation in which the two found themselves—stuck in the desert with no water. Was there some negligence? Was one of them a guide who (for example) was paid to lead the other safely through the desert?

The casuistic (or "particularistic") view in ethical methodology suggests that we tackle the talmudic problem only after learning more about the actual circumstances of the case. And the list of relevant questions about conditions, identity, expectations, and normative background, and then about the statistical chances of each possible scenario and the actual unfolding of events, could well be endless. So we would have to suspend judgment until more information is supplied. But the Talmud adopts a more ambitious method and raises the dilemma in its starkest form. It is an abstract thought experiment that lays bare the inescapable dilemma and blocks any attempt to evade the fundamental tension between the conflicting norms. Here exactly lies the philosophical beauty of the case.

The contemporary counterpart in moral philosophy to the talmudic story is the two-island dilemma: a lifeboat stationed onshore has enough time to reach only one of two islands that are under threat of flooding. On one island five people are waiting to be saved; on the other just one. Should the lifeguard head to the more populated island, saving more lives, or should he also give some chance of rescue to the unfortunate person on the other island? And in the latter case, what kind of chance? 1:1 (tossing a coin to choose among the islands) or 1:6 (casting a die, thus giving each person an equal chance)? There are also other solutions to this dilemma, combining utilitarian values (promoting the overall number of lives saved) and the values of justice or fairness (highlighting the principle of equality and the demand to accord equal respect and concern to each individual).

But despite appearances, the talmudic story is very different from the two-island dilemma. It involves the contemporary question "do the numbers count" in an even more extreme way, asking about the correct balancing, not between the many and the one, but between one and none. Thus, even if it makes sense to give 1/6 chance to each individual (and so probably saving five lives but without completely disregarding the principle of equal concern for everybody under threat of death), it seems irrational to give the two desert travelers the same chance to survive when we know that neither of them will! In other words, letting the two travelers share the pitcher of water cannot be regarded as an act of equal respect and concern since it would mean a conscious decision that they should both die.

But equal concern in the desert case could be achieved by lottery, as in the two-island case. The Talmud does not raise that option (although there is widespread appeal to lotteries as a decision-making procedure in both biblical and postbiblical writings). We could show equal concern for the lives of both travelers by tossing a coin and saving one of them. Such a procedure would respect both the principle of fairness (equal opportunity) and of utility (saving at least one life rather than none). Lottery is just a second-order procedure of egalitarian distribution in cases where the good to be distributed is itself indivisible. Rather than split the good into two, which would be destructive and wasteful, we split between the two the chances to get the entire good. The two contenders have an equally strong right to life. Ben Patura seems to conclude from their equal standing that the water must be equally divided between the two, even though this procedure would lead to the death of both. But a lottery can achieve the value of saving one life by shifting the distribution from the level of the good to the level of the chance to get it. Would not that be both fair and Pareto optimal?

The conspicuous disregard of the lottery as a possible solution to the talmudic dilemma turns our attention to a deep difference between the two stories. In the two-island case, the question is asked from the point of view of the lifeguard, whose survival is not at stake. The talmudic story, by contrast, is told from the point of view of one (or any) of the travelers for whom the question is literally "life or death." Can the shift from the impersonal perspective to the personal be made without some change in the reasoning and the criteria of the right solution? It seems that the whole point of morality is that this shift must not be made and that one should maintain the impersonal point of view even when one stands to gain or lose personally from the way a practical problem is resolved. One must be fair not only in making judgments about conflicts among other people but also when it comes to one's own interests. However, the desert story touches upon a unique limiting case, which casts doubt on the relevance of impersonal considerations to the personal decision—namely, the context of a direct and immediate threat to one's own life. It is an existential problem rather than one of the "tragic choices" widely discussed in bioethics or public policy.

Ben Patura believes that even in extreme cases of scarcity of the ultimate good (namely, life), the demands of egalitarian justice or fairness hold. The blood of one traveler is no redder than that of the other. Even a lottery would not show due respect to the idea of the sanctity of life and the equality of the value of each person. Better to share the water and let both live for a few hours (and then die) than to let one live "at the expense" of the other. This is the harsh but noble understanding of the moral imperative. Rabbi Akiva, on the other hand, holds that in such extreme situations morality loses its grip. Since no one deserves the water more than the other and since only one can survive, let it be me, i.e., the subject making the judgment from the first-person point of view (and the text implies that the addressee of Akiva's instruction is the person who actually is holding the pitcher). "Your life takes precedence over the life of your fellow" can only mean from your personal point of view, since from the impersonal perspective there are no criteria for establishing the priority of one life over another.

The grounding of Akiva's reasoning in the verse from Leviticus is itself interesting in the way it reverses the original meaning. "So that your brother may live with you" appears in the Torah as an explanation for the commandment to help the weak, the person in need, the stranger or sojourner. Akiva turns the reasoning on its head: he focuses on the life of the subject rather than of the other! The idea is not to follow the injunction so as to enable the other to live with you but to justify your own refusal to sacrifice yourself so as to let the other live. He interprets "so that your brother may live with you" as a conditional: if you do not live, there is no one with whom the brother could live, or to put it otherwise, you are bound to help your brother (or fellow) only on the assumption that you exist and that the act of assistance does not mean your own demise (which would mean that the brother would have no one to live with).

This is a bold interpretive move even if it isn't all that heroic from a moral point of view. For one could claim that the meaning of "so that your brother may live with you" implies that you should do everything possible to save his life (including self-sacrifice). And indeed such a supererogatory solution to the talmudic story should be considered as an option—namely, to go beyond the call of duty and heroically hand over the pitcher of water to your fellow traveler. That would be (again) both a rational solution (from a utilitarian point of view) and a moral one (actually, "supermoral" or saintly). And again, this supererogatory solution maintains the personal point of view since it deviates from the impersonal, justice-oriented view of a third-party judge who can recommend neither acting egoistically nor acting altruistically but only the impartial solution of a fair lottery (or the equal division of the water, as Ben Patura proposes).

However, Akiva's teaching, which has become the halakhic guiding rule, turns out to be bold in both its content and its justification. Life in a sense precedes morality. Indeed, your life is not objectively worth more than your fellow's life, but at least from your point of view, just because there is no relevant difference in right or desert between the two of you, you cannot be expected to act as an impersonal arbiter in matters pertaining to your own survival. Your life simply takes precedence. Watching the death of the other may be intolerable to you and cause lifelong guilt, as Ben Patura hints, but this cannot override the most fundamental, premoral drive (and maybe right!) to care for your own life first. This suspension of morality in extreme cases of life and death fits neatly into David Hume's doctrine of "the circumstances of justice." Justice, according to Hume, applies only when there is moderate scarcity of goods. In full abundance it is superfluous; in extreme scarcity it is impossible.

David Heyd

Permitted Rate for Ransoming
19. Mishnah Gittin 4:6, 9[14]

The destruction of the Judean state in the wake of the failed revolts against the Roman Empire led thousands into captivity. The dilemmas attending the burdens of pidyon — *literally redemption, primarily the ransom of captives — are here starkly presented. The commitment to redeeming captives is fundamental to the values of the Jewish community. The question of its boundaries tests the limits of mutual responsibility.*

6. . . . Captives should not be ransomed at more than their [market] value on account of social order [*tikkun olam*] and captives should not be aided in escaping on account of social order [*tikkun olam*]. Rabban Shimon b. Gamaliel says for the good [*tikkun*] of captives.

9. One who sells himself and his children to heathens should not be ransomed; but the children should be ransomed after their father's death.

Permitted Rate for Ransoming
20. BT Gittin 45a

The Talmud elaborates the criteria of the Mishnah. In Rashi's comment on the discussion we can sense the tragedy of medieval Jewish life in exile — namely, extreme vulnerability to abduction and violence.

The problem was raised: "on account of social order [*tikkun olam*]" — [does this mean] because of the burden on the public or perhaps it is so that the [captors] not seize them more often?[15]

14. For the talmudic discussion of this mishnah, see ¢15, §7.
15. *Rashi:* "There would be a practical difference [between the positions] when a captive has a wealthy father or relative who wishes to ransom him at a great cost that will not fall on the public."

Come and hear: Levi bar Darga ransomed his daughter for [a sum of] 13,000 golden dinars.

Said Abaye: "And who is to tell us that this was with rabbinic approval? Perhaps he did so without rabbinic approval!"

"Captives should not be helped to escape on account of social order [*tikkun olam*]. Rabban Shimon b. Gamaliel says, for the good [*tikkun*] of captives." What is [the difference] between them?

[Abaye refers to the] case where there is only one [captive].

[*Rashi:* The first *tanna* is concerned with the social order in the long run, [i.e.,] lest the captors treat future captives harshly, putting them in chains and harrows. R. Shimon's concern however relates only [to a case where] there currently are additional captives—lest the captors treat them harshly and torture them.]

Ransoming Captives

21. Maimonides, MT Laws Concerning Gifts to the Poor 8:10–15

The Code of Maimonides, Book Seven: The Book of Agriculture, translated by Isaac Klein, YJS (New Haven: Yale University Press, 1979), pp. 82–84.

Maimonides here underscores the commitment to ransom captives. Following the Talmud (BT Gittin 47a; ¢15, §7) he extends the duty to include any captive who is in mortal danger, despite the Mishnah's apparent rejection of responsibility for a person who brought about his own predicament.

10. The ransoming of captives has precedence over the feeding and clothing of the poor. Indeed there is no religious duty [*mitzvah*] more meritorious than the ransoming of captives, for not only is the captive included in the generality of the hungry, the thirsty, and the naked, but his very life is in jeopardy. He who turns his eyes away from ransoming him, transgresses the commandments "Thou shalt not harden thy heart, nor shut thy hand" (Deut. 15:7), "Neither shalt thou stand idly by the blood of thy neighbor" (Lev. 19:16), and "He shall not rule with rigor over him in thy sight" (Lev. 25:53). Moreover, he nullifies the commandments, "Thou shalt surely open thy hand unto him"

(Deut. 15:8), "That thy brother may live with thee" (Lev. 25:36), "Thou shalt love thy neighbor as thyself" (Lev. 19:18), "Deliver them that are drawn unto death" (Prov. 24:11), and many other admonitions like these. To sum up, there is no religious duty greater than the ransoming of captives.

11. If the people of the city, having collected money for the building of a synagogue, find themselves confronted with a matter of religious duty [*dvar mitzvah*], they must divert the money to the latter. If they had already bought stones and beams, they may not sell them in order to fulfill the religious duty, unless it be the ransoming of captives. Even if they have already brought in the stones and set them up, and the beams and planed them, and thus made everything ready for construction, they must nevertheless sell everything, but only for the ransoming of captives. If, however, they have already completed the erection of the building, they may not sell the synagogue, but should rather make a new collection from the community for the redemption of those captives.

12. Captives may not be ransomed for more than their fair value, for the sake of good world order [*tikkun ha-olam*], lest the enemies should seek them out in order to capture them. Nor may they be assisted to escape, for the same reason, lest the enemy should make their yoke heavier and guard them more vigilantly.

13. If a person sells himself and his children to heathens, or accepts a loan from them and is seized or imprisoned for his debt to them, the first time and the second time this happens it is a religious duty to ransom them; the third time, they may not be ransomed. The children, however, must be ransomed if their father dies in captivity. If the captors threaten to kill him, he must be ransomed even after several such captivities.

14. If a bondsman has been captured, he must be ransomed as if he were an Israelite, provided that he had been ritually immersed for the purpose of bondage and had accepted the commandments. If a captive has fallen into apostasy [*nishtamed*] by violating even no more than one commandment, as for example, by eating *nebelah* [carcasses] out of spite, or the like, it is forbidden to ransom him.

15. A woman takes precedence over a man as far as feeding, clothing, and redemption from captivity are concerned, because it is customary

for a man to go begging from door to door, but not for a woman, as her sense of shame is greater. If both of them are in captivity, and both are exposed to [abuse], the man takes precedence in being ransomed, [for this] is not customary for him.

Sharing the Expenses of Ransom

22. Meir b. Baruch of Rothenburg (Maharam), *Responsa* (Lemberg) 345, (Prague) 39

Here is a fuller account of the gloomy reality of medieval Jewish exilic life in the Rhineland only alluded to in Rashi's commentary. Like Maimonides, Rothenburg also extends the duty to redeem a captive who is in mortal danger. He goes beyond Maimonides in stressing that this is done even against the captive's will. It should be noted that Rothenburg spent his last years in captivity, probably in the tower of Ensisheim. He was incarcerated there by the Emperor Rudolf in 1286 following an aborted attempt to lead the Jews of his community out of Rudolf's jurisdiction. There seem to have been prolonged negotiations as to his ransom. Some traditions claim that he died before agreement was reached, whereas others claim that Rothenburg, following the Mishnah, refused to be ransomed at more than his market value (§19 above).

You asked concerning Reuven and Shimon who were abducted. Reuven was rich and Shimon poor. Reuven arranged a payment through messengers to his mother and had both of them released from captivity. Reuven is suing Shimon for [Shimon's] share in the payment, claiming that he acted on Shimon's express request. Shimon replies that he said nothing of the kind.

I have already been queried with regard to this case from Meideborg. I have also been asked with regard to a teacher who had a deposit held by his landlord and was abducted on trumped up charges. He commanded his landlord not to ransom him. I wrote back that he is to be ransomed against his will.

Support for this is in [BT Ketubot 48a]: "If one said, When I die, do not use my property to finance my burial, he is not heeded. Who is he to enrich his children and let himself fall on the public?"

Additional support comes from [the case of a maidservant whose father is to be coerced to redeem her]: If a father is coerced to redeem his daughter, how much more so is this one coerced to redeem himself! And [this is so] even when he cries out "Do not ransom me!" Certainly in the present case where he [Shimon] has said nothing. . . . How much more [is this necessary] so as to release him from the heathens, so that he should not assimilate among them or [so as to ensure that] they do not kill him or torture him by beating him without limit, which is more terrible than death, and due to the torture he may perhaps confess their [religion].

. . . Since he should be ransomed against his will, even if he cries out "Do not [do so on my behalf]," it follows that we need not seek his consent. The rule is that he must pay his share in proportion to his means.[16]

. . . Whosoever acts promptly to release him is deemed worthy and can collect what he provided for him.

It cannot be argued that perhaps the captors would eventually have released him gratis, for we do not speculate in [cases of] prospective mortal danger. Rather he is ransomed against his will. It is . . . well known that whoever falls into the hands of brigands cannot escape whole both in body and in property.

The Limits of Brotherhood
23. Eli'ezer b. Samuel of Metz, *Sefer Yere'im* 156

In his discourse on the commandment of "Lending to the Poor," Eli'ezer b. Samuel of Metz examines the concept of "brotherhood" and its application to various legal contexts. Drawing upon classic talmudic discussions of exclusion (¢15, §§6–7), he suggests the scope and limitations of Israelite brotherhood.

16. Maharam here refers to BT Bava Batra 7b (¢21, §3).

The Creator commanded, "If however, there is a needy person among you, one of thy brethren" etc. (Deut. 15:7). . . . But if he is a deliberate transgressor of any of the commandments promulgated in the Torah, and has not repented, one is not obliged to sustain him or give him a loan. For it is written, "So that your brother may live with you" (Lev. 25:37), and regarding lending, it is written "one of your brethren" (Lev. 25:35). Since he has intentionally transgressed, he is excluded from the category of brotherhood, as [observance of] the commandments is required for brotherhood. This follows from [the law established according to the majority of] the sages, maintaining that a slave has [the right to be paid indemnities for] shame, since "He is your brother with respect to the commandments" (BT Bava Kama 88a).[17] It was also taught (BT Makkot 23a), "'[lest being flogged further, to excess,] your brother be degraded before your eyes'[18] — once he has been punished he is your brother." This implies [that he is to be regarded again as a brother only] after suffering his sentence — but prior to that he is not your brother; hence we learn that an evildoer is excluded from the category of brotherhood.

Responsibilities of Loving-Kindness

24. Maimonides, MT Laws Concerning Mourning 1:1–3, 9–11; 3:8; 13:1–
2, 4; 14:1–4, 7–12

The Code of Maimonides, Book Fourteen: The Book of Judges, translated by Abraham M. Hershman, YJS (Yale University Press, 1949), pp. 164–66, 171–72, 200–202.

*One of the first institutions created by a Jewish community is a cemetery. The responsibility to the dead begins as a duty of loving-kindness [*gemilut hasadim*] toward the helpless other; its urgency takes precedence over the prohibition upon a priest to incur corpse defilement (Lev. 21:1–4). But it develops into a larger communal obligation where*

17. Against R. Yehudah in the mishnah BT Bava Kama 87a, who denies this right to slaves of alien origin, even though they are bound by (most of) the commandments — by virtue of their being barred from marrying into the ethnic brotherhood.
18. The verse concerns the administration of corporal punishment and is discussed in ¢6, §14; the midrash emphasizes that once punishment has been administered, the transgressor is fully readmitted to the community.

the community of the living is reflected in that of the dead, the two together serving as a
sign of collective continuity.

Chapter 1

1. It is a positive command to mourn for deceased relatives. . . . According to scriptural law, mourning is observed only on the first day, that is, the day of death, which is also the day of burial. Mourning on the other seven days is not of biblical origin. . . .

2. When does the observance of mourning begin? From the time that the top stone closes the grave. But before the body is buried, the near of kin is not prohibited from doing any of the things forbidden to the mourner. . . .

3. In the case of those [put to death by the kingdom and denied burial], the observance of mourning rites and the counting of the seven and the thirty days commence from the time that the relatives have ceased petitioning the government for permission to bury the bodies, even if they have not given up hope of stealing them.

9. [For all those put to death by the kingdom], although they are put to death by order of the king [*din hamelekh*], who is empowered by Scripture to do so, their relatives observe mourning and do not deny them any of the rites (preformed for the dead); their property goes to the king, and they are buried in their ancestral tombs. For those, however, who are [put to death] by the court, no mourning rites are observed; but the relatives grieve for them, for grief is a matter of the heart; they are not buried with their ancestors until their flesh has wasted away; and their property passes to their heirs.

10. As for those who [withdrew from the ways of the community]—that is, men who cast off the restraints of the commandments, did not join their fellow Jews in the performance of the precepts, observance of the festivals, attendance at the Synagogue and House of Study, but felt free to do as they pleased [as if they belonged to another nation], as well as *minim*, apostates [*meshumadim*], and informers—for these no mourning is observed. In the event of their death, their brethren and other relatives don white gar-

ments, and wrap themselves in white garments, eat, drink, and rejoice, because the enemies of the Lord have perished. . . .

11. For one who has committed suicide, no funeral rites are performed, no mourning is observed, no lamentation is made; but the relatives stand in line (to be comforted), the Mourner's Benediction is recited, and all that is intended as a matter for the living is done.

Who is regarded as a suicide? Not he who climbing up to the roof fell and died, but one who said: "Look! I am climbing up to the top of the roof." If he was seen ascending it, agitated by anger or fear, and then fell and died, the presumption is that he committed suicide. But if he is found strangled or hanging from a tree, or slain, or fallen upon his sword, his status is of that of any person who died. His obsequies are attended to, and none of the last rites is denied.

Chapter 3

8. If a priest finds a *met mitzvah* on the road, he must defile himself for him. Even the High Priest is bound to defile himself for him and bury the body.

What is meant by a *met mitzvah*? It is a body lying in the road with no one to bury it. . . . But if there are others who would respond, it is not deemed a *met mitzvah*. He [the priest] should call others to attend to the body.

Chapter 13

1. What procedure is followed in consoling mourners? After the body is buried, the mourners assemble and station themselves at the border of the cemetery. All those who have escorted the dead stand around them, forming themselves in rows, row after row, each consisting of no less than ten people, excluding the mourners.

2. The mourners stand on the left of the comforters, and all the comforters, one by one, pass by, saying to them, "Be ye comforted of Heaven." Then the mourners go home. On each of the seven days of mourning, condolence is tendered them, whether by the same visitors or new ones. . . .

4. If the deceased has left no near-of-kin to be comforted, ten worthy people come and sit in his place all the seven days of mourning and others come (to comfort them). If ten steady attendants are unavailable, the requisite number is supplied daily by those who volunteer their services. They come and they sit in his place.

Chapter 14

1. The following positive commands were ordained by the Rabbis: visiting the sick; comforting the mourners; joining a funeral procession; dowering a bride; escorting departing guests; performing for the dead the last tender offices; acting as a pallbearer; going before the bier; making lamentations (for the dead); digging a grave and burying the body; causing the bride and the bridegroom to rejoice; providing them with all their needs (for the wedding). These constitute deeds of loving kindness performed in person for which no fixed measure is prescribed. Although all these commands are only on rabbinical authority they are implied in the precept: "And thou shalt love thy neighbor as thyself" (Lev. 19:18), that is: What you would have others do unto you, do unto him who is your brother in the Law and in performing the commandments.

2. The reward for escorting strangers is greater than the reward for all the other commandments. It is a practice which Abraham, our father, instituted, and the act of kindness which he exercised. He gave wayfarers food to eat and water to drink and escorted them. Hospitality to wayfarers is greater than receiving the Divine Presence [see Gen. 18:1–2]. But escorting guests is greater than according them hospitality. Said the Rabbis: "Whoever does not accompany guests is as though he would shed blood" (BT Sotah 46b).

3. A person may be compelled to escort a visitor, just as he is compelled to contribute to charity. The court used to provide escorts for itinerants. If it neglected to do so, it was accounted as if it had shed blood. . . .

4. All are in duty bound to visit the sick person. Even a man of prominence must visit a less important person. The ill should be visited many times a day. The more often a person calls on the sick, the more praiseworthy

he is, provided that he does not inconvenience the patient. He who visits the sick is as though he would take away part of the sickness and lighten his pain. Whoever does not call to see the sick is as though he would shed blood.

7. It seems to me that the duty of comforting mourners takes precedence over the duty of visiting the sick, because comforting mourners is an act of benevolence [*gemilut hesed*] toward the living and the dead.

8. If one has a dead body to look after and a wedding to attend, he should let the wedding go by and tend the dead. For thus it is written: "The heart of the wise is in the house of mourning," [etc.] (Eccles. 7:4). If a funeral procession and a bridal procession meet, the funeral procession must make way for the bridal procession, and both of these make way for the king.

9. The study of the Law is suspended for the duty of joining a funeral procession or a procession conducting a bride to the canopy. This rule obtains only if there is not a sufficient number present (to pay the deceased their last respects), but if there is a sufficient number present, the study of the Torah is not to be interrupted. . . .

10. If a person dies, all the townspeople are forbidden to do work until the burial has taken place. But if there are others who will attend to the obsequies, they may carry on their work.

11. If a scholar dies, even if close to sixty myriads are present (to pay him the honor due him), study is interrupted for the duty of escorting the body; if, however, sixty myriads are present, study is not interrupted. But if the deceased was imparting instruction to others, there is no maximum limit. All must suspend their study in order to escort the body.

12. We bury the dead of the heathens, comfort their mourners, and visit their sick, [on account of the ways] of peace.

Burying the Righteous and the Wicked
25. Solomon b. Abraham Adret (Rashba), *Responsa* 5:237

Adret here attempts to draw the ultimate boundary of the community. Going beyond the discussions described in ¢15 above, he addresses the place in death of those individuals separated from the community in life, whether they were formally excommunicated or withdrew themselves.

You asked: A person who died when still under a ban—is there any indication that we ought not attend to his funeral arrangements? It is stated that the court stones his coffin (Mishnah Eduyot 5:6; ¢7, §4)—not that stones be heaped upon it [by the entire people], like the mound of Akhan (Josh. 7:10–26). There is no prohibition to be found regarding his funeral arrangements. A coffin and a burial are in any case [presumed even by the above law]. Moreover he can be hired or hire others during his lifetime, [and he is allowed] to benefit by this. Now would you claim that the comrades of someone under the *herem* are permitted [to bury him]? [The law] regarding such a one is more stringent, for he is not hired, nor can he hire. Could it be that perhaps in his lifetime [it is prohibited] because he benefits [therefrom], but not so after his death—or is there no difference?

Reply: I know of no stringency with regard to one under *niddui* beyond that mentioned with regard to the court. . . . We do, however, attend to his funeral arrangements and to all his needs. It may be assumed that we attend to all matters. For the stipulation that we do not attend to any of their needs holds for capital cases in court and in case of a suicide, and with regard to those who withdraw from the community and to informers. But the Rabbis did not say so with regard to one under *niddui* or even under *herem*. . . .

Nahmanides however, in his well-known book, *Torat ha-Adam,* wrote that [the law concerning] one under *niddui* is like [that regarding a person who committed] suicide. But I have written what seems right to me.

In any case, the prohibition applies only to one placed under *niddui* on account of impertinence, [i.e.,] disobeying the sages. But not on account of *mamona,* [in which case] as soon as he dies he is released from their ban; his coffin is not stoned and he is eulogized as befits him. In those cases where it is stipulated that "he is not to be attended" this does not apply to burial and shrouds; [it means] only that there is no rending of the garment and removal of shoes or eulogy. [Adret here cites the cases of suicide and capital punishments and argues:] It seems reasonable that even those placed under *niddui* or *herem* are buried in their ancestral plot. Otherwise, we would have to organize for them a third, or even fourth [burial ground], one for those placed under *niddui* and one for those placed under *herem*. For [the maxim is] "We do not bury a slightly wicked person near a seriously wicked one" (BT Sanhedrin 47a). Now, were you to say he is wicked, and "We do not bury a wicked person near a righteous one" (BT Sanhedrin 47a)! [Well then,] this could apply to other people as well, even an upright person beside one of the great of Israel.

"One who withdraws from the community"—this does not refer to one who withdraws from [paying his share of the] tax. For the latter is like an individual transgressor or a robber, as he steals his portion from the public. But not every robber of the public is considered to have withdrawn from the public. Those "withdrawers" referred to [with regard to exclusion from burial rites] are heretics, *mumarim,* and apostates; so too the informers and extortionists—these are not attended to in any way. Their brothers and relatives don white garments, and wrap themselves in white garments, eat, drink, and rejoice, because the enemies of the Lord have perished.

Crisis

Threatened Bodies: "Let Them Not Hand Over a Single Israelite"
26. Mishnah Terumot 7:11–12

Moments of acute crisis threaten to attenuate the communal bond. What are the limits of communal responsibility to an individual at such moments? The following three selections move from cases of threatened defilement by rape to threatened murder. The Mishnah addresses the case of rape and draws an analogy from the defiling of a holy portion, the terumah, *the priest's share of the crop.*

11. . . . If one were passing from one place to another carrying *terumah* loaves, and a heathen ordered him, 'Give me one of them and I will defile it; otherwise I will defile the entire lot'—R. Eli'ezer says: Let [the heathen] defile the whole lot, but let [the Israelite] not give him one of the loaves. R. Yehoshua says: Let [the Israelite] set one of the leaves before him on a stone.

12. Likewise, [in the case of] women ordered by heathens: "Give us one from among you that we may defile her; otherwise we will defile all of you"—let the heathens defile all of them, but let them not hand over a single Israelite person.

Threatened Lives: "Let Them Not Hand Over a Single Israelite"
27. Tosefta Terumot 7:20

The Tosefta takes the discussion a step further to cases of threatened murder. It seeks instruction from the biblical precedent recorded in 2 Sam. 20, concerning Sheva ben Bikhri's abortive uprising against King David. When soldiers loyal to David surrounded and threatened the walled city in which Sheva was holed up, a "wise woman" in the city spoke to Yoav, the commander of the Davidic forces, "You seek to bring death upon a mother city in Israel! Why should you destroy the Lord's possession?" (2 Sam. 20:19). Yoav asked only that Sheva be handed over, and the woman convinced her fellow citizens to kill Sheva and throw his head down to Yoav. The Rabbis debate the meaning of this precedent: is it enough that an individual has been singled out, or must he also be liable to die?

If a group of people are ordered by heathens: "Give us one of your number to be killed or we will kill you all"—Let them all be killed, but let them not hand over a single Israelite person. If, however, one of them is singled out, as was Sheva ben Bikhri, he should be given over so they should not all die.

　　Said R. Yehudah: This rule [that forbids handing over an individual unless he was singled out like Sheva ben Bikhri] only applies when the latter is inside [the city] and they [the heathens[19]] are on the outside. But if they are all together inside—since they will all be killed along with him, it is better that he should be given over so that they do not all get killed. Thus Scripture states: "The woman came to all the people in her wisdom, etc." (2 Sam. 20:

19. "They" here has been variously interpreted; we take it to mean that the enemies are outside and—at least as yet—are thus unable to kill their victim without Jewish cooperation.

22). She said to them: "Since [you] will all be killed along with him, give him over so that all of you will not be killed."

R. Shimon said: She said to them thus: "Whoever rebels against the House of David is liable to die."

Surrendering a Wanted Individual
28. JT Terumot 8:4 46b

The talmudic discussion emphasizes that difficult decisions in hard cases might leave the decisor with dirty hands.

If a group of travelers are accosted by heathens who ordered them "Give us one of your number to be killed or we will kill you all"—they should not hand over a single Israelite person even if they are all killed. [But if] one of them is singled out, as was Sheva ben Bikhri, he should be handed over so that all of them are not killed.

Said R. Shimon b. Lakish: [Only if] he is liable to die, like Sheva ben Bikhri.

R. Yohanan said: Even though he is not liable to die, like Sheva ben Bikhri.

Ulla bar Koshav was wanted by the kingdom [Rome] and fled to Lydda, the town of R. Yehoshua b. Levi. [The authorities] came, surrounded the city, and declared: "Unless you give him over to us, we shall destroy the city." R. Yehoshua b. Levi then went to him and persuaded him and then gave him over to them.

Up to that time, Elijah [the Prophet] of blessed memory had made regular visits to R. Yehoshua, but then he stopped. R. Yehoshua fasted repeatedly, and Elijah came to him.

"Do you think," he asked, "that I would reveal myself to an informer?"[20]

20. The Hebrew term for informer, *moser,* translates literally as "one who gives over"—thus denoting a collaborator.

R. Yehoshua replied: "Have I not acted according to the mishnah?"
Elijah answered: "But is this the mishnah of the pious?"

The Holocaust: Collaboration or Rescue

29. Ephraim Oshry, *Responsa mi-Ma'amakim*[21] 5:1

Oshry was the last remaining rabbi in the Kovno ghetto. As a disciple of the elderly Rabbi Shapira, head of the rabbinic court of Kovno, he recorded many of the horrific dilemmas arising from the extreme circumstances of the Holocaust and posed to rabbis by people seeking guidance. Oshry here discusses the talmudic precedents of Terumot but in a context where not just a group of people but an entire community is threatened.

Question: On 16 Elul 5701, September 8, 1941 according to the gentile calendar, the well-known destroyer of several ghettos, S.S. Oberfuhrer Goecke, came to Lithuania, eventually liquidating the ghetto of Kovno [Kaunas] too.

The abominable reputation of this evil, evil German—a bloodthirsty killer of the first order—preceded him, and the news of his coming stirred great panic among the imprisoned [inhabitants] of the ghetto, because immediately on his arrival a number of Jews were executed. Thus arose the question of the notorious white cards known as "Jordan."

Here is the tale: The German officer responsible for the ghetto, [Fritz] Jordan (may his name be obliterated), ordered the Council of Elders of the ghetto to distribute among the ghetto artisans 5,000 white cards that he presented them. Only those holding cards would be allowed to stay in the ghetto with their families—the rest would be liquidated.

At that time there were 30,000 Jews in the ghetto. Some 10,000 of them were artisans. It is impossible to describe the horror and panic that erupted among the artisans. Each wanted one of these white cards, knowing that if he did not obtain one, his and his family's fates were sealed.

They descended en masse on the Council of Elders seeking the

---

21. The title means: "Responsa out of the Depths," alluding to Ps. 130.

cards, and many just grabbed them forcefully. The commotion was greatest on Wednesday, 25 Elul, September 17, when it became known that the Germans had surrounded the ghetto on all sides, posted soldiers at all its entrances and ringed it with machine gun posts, while the accursed Germans and their Lithuanian collaborators stood at the ready to massacre the Jews.

It also became known that in the small ghetto armed Germans had burst into Jewish homes, chased out the inhabitants in murderous rage and driven them into the marketplace where they separated out those families who held the white cards from those who did not.

And so it was that in the midst of this panic and terror, I was asked a fateful question: Whether the Council of Elders is permitted to distribute the cards as commanded by this terrorizer of Jews, Jordan, inasmuch as with each card they distribute to one artisan they deny another, handing him over[22] to the accursed evil German regime to do with as they pleased, in effect setting aside one life for another. And who is to say that your life is dearer than the other's?[23]

Answer: [Oshry begins by citing JT Terumot and Tosefta Terumot §§27–28 above.]

Maimonides writes (MT Laws Concerning the Foundations of the Torah 5:5):

If gentiles say to them, hand over one of you to be killed or we will kill you all, they should all be killed rather than hand over a single soul of Israel. But if they singled out an individual, and he is guilty of a capital crime, as was Sheva ben Bikhri, they should hand him over. This however is [a last resort] and not ruled in the first instance, and if he is not himself deserving of death, they should all be killed.

Commenting on the passage in JT, [Moshe Margolis in his] *Mareh ha-Panim* [commentary] points out that Maimonides' source for this ruling appears to be Tosefta Terumot mentioned above. . . . This, he says, is difficult to reconcile with the fact that Maimonides adopts the opinion of R. Shimon b. Lakish ["provided that he be liable to die like Sheva . . ."] over that of R. Yo-

22. *Mosrim.*
23. See ¢11, §17.

hanan, contravening the general principle that in halakhic disagreements between the two, it is R. Yohanan's opinion that prevails. . . . Margolis concludes ". . . that Maimonides was working from a different version of the JT, in which the respective positions of R. Yohanan and R. Shimon b. Lakish were reversed."

[Joseph Karo in his commentary] *Kesef Mishneh* took a different view of Maimonides' position: "Maimonides indeed adopts the view of R. Shimon b. Lakish, even though ordinarily one would have ruled according to R. Yohanan, because this case presents [a judicial] uncertainty with human life hanging in the balance, and when that is true, we choose to err on the side of stringency—[which means] in this case, not directly to hand over an individual to his death. Moreover, there is support for this in the tannaitic statement 'like Sheva ben Bikhri,' indicating that had he not been liable to die in his own right, they would not have been allowed to hand him over. Our Rabbi [Maimonides] inferred from the fact that though the man handed over by R. Yehoshua b. Levi [as recounted in JT] had been liable to die like Sheva ben Bikhri, Elijah still stopped visiting R. Yehoshua—since the latter's act had not been 'a mishnah of the pious'—[indicating] that such a decision could only be taken as a last resort."

Now, Rema [Moses Isserles], commenting on *Shulhan Arukh* YD 157, wrote: "If Israelites are ordered by heathens, 'Give over one of your number to be killed or we will kill you all,' they should not give over a single one of them unless they singled him out saying, 'Give us so and so' (see Tosefta Terumot 7:20; §27 above; and Maimonides, MT Laws Concerning the Foundations of the Torah 5:5). Some say that even in such a case, he is not to be handed over unless he is liable to die like Sheva ben Bikhri (*Bet Yosef,* citing Rashi and Ran)."

. . . It is clear, at any rate, that all agree that no one Israelite is to be handed over unless he has been singled out. And even then, Maimonides, and the others cited by Rema, rule that [such a one] may be handed over only if he is liable to die like Sheva ben Bikhri. Otherwise, even if he was singled out, he may not be handed over. And even if he was singled out and he is liable to die like Sheva ben Bikhri, Maimonides is of the opinion that, although by law he may be handed over, this is not the first option. . . .

From all this it seems clear that the Council of Elders most certainly may not distribute these white cards. By distributing them they thereby hand over other Jews to death since the accursed Germans did not single out which Jews they want handed over to them. And even if they had singled out the Jews they want, those Jews are not liable to die like Sheva ben Bikhri. And thus, according to Maimonides and the minority opinion cited by Rema, not a single Israelite person is to be handed over, and how much more so not a large community, God forbid.

Prima facia it should therefore be ruled that the Council of Elders is forbidden to distribute these white cards and thereby hand other Jews over to death and torture at the hands of the Germans. Rather leave things as they are. . . .

However, on closer inspection, I found [Shabbetai b. Meir Ha-Kohen writing in his commentary to the *Shulhan Arukh*] Shakh, HM 163 n.18: "If a king or minister levies some exaction on one or two wealthy people and a well-connected Jew can successfully intercede at the court on their behalf, may he do so if it is quite certain that the exaction will then be placed on others? It is thus ruled in the Responsa of Rabbi Yosef ibn Lev (vol. II, 40): If the king has already levied the exaction on specific, known individuals [who are] already caught in his net, a ['court] Jew' may not work to extricate them in any matter that will certainly cause damage to others. But if a decree has been issued regarding two unspecified people, a [court] Jew may work to extricate anyone he wishes from its ambit, even though others will certainly end up taking their place."

Now the present situation seems exactly analogous to that described by R. Yosef ibn Lev, to wit, the Germans have not captured or singled out anyone in particular, but simply said that their decrees will apply to those not holding white cards. And so in our case the Council of Elders may work to save whomever they wish so that they not be included in the decree even though others will certainly take their place.

. . . I saw a similar case that came before the great sage Rabbi Abraham Dov Ber Kahana-Shapira of blessed memory, grand head of the rabbinic court of Kovno. On 6 Marheshvan 5702 [October 24, 1941,] the evil German authorities issued a decree to the Council of Elders, ordering them to post an announcement that on 8 Marheshvan (October 26, 1941), all those imprisoned in the ghetto—men, women, and children, the old and sick as well—were to gather in the well-known plaza known as "Democracy Place" and that not a single Israelite was to remain at home at that time.

The Council of Elders immediately sent a delegation of four men to the grand head of the rabbinic court of Kovno [Rabbi Shapira] with the desperate question whether to comply with the above mentioned German order, for according to the information in their hands, they knew that the great majority of those to be gathered in this plaza would be executed. The delegation arrived in the dead of night and Rabbi Shapira had already fallen asleep in his bed. And although Rabbi Shapira was an old man and not in good health, his wife woke him and informed him of the delegation's arrival. He sprang from his bed and, on hearing them out, began to tremble in sorrow, nearly fainted, and had to be revived with medication.

Rabbi Shapira was keenly aware of his tremendous responsibility to his flock and realized the awful significance of this decree. He told the delegation that while these sorts of decrees were not foreign to the long and blood-soaked history of the Jewish people, he [needed some time to think] and could not immediately deliver his opinion on this grave matter.

That night he did not return to sleep, [he stayed up all night] consulting the volumes in his library on this grave halakhic matter and after long deliberation rendered his decision in these words: "If a decree has been issued to destroy a community of Israel, God save us, and there is an option by resorting to various means to rescue some part of the community, then the heads of the community must summon up the courage to face their responsibilities and do what they can to save whatever can be saved."

And so in our case, where the decree has been imposed on the entire community, the leadership of the community must save as much as can be saved; and since a number of people may be rescued by means of these white cards, the Council of Elders should gather their courage and distribute these cards as they see fit. Since "rescue" is at stake, they must rescue by whatever means are available.

Commentary. The Price of Violation

If non-Jews threaten to rape each of a group of women unless they hand over one of their number, they are not permitted to "hand over a single soul of Israel." Why is it better to yield several souls, let us say ten, rather than one? One answer here is that if they were to comply, if they were to force the victim to yield, or at any rate not attempt to protect her, they would have collaborated in the crime, and they would have trusted in men rather than in God (trusted that the men will stop with one victim). One may say that if they collaborate, ten souls are lost from Israel, the bonds that tie the victim to the community are rent, and, having once betrayed a trust, henceforth the remaining women will be unable to trust one another.

If a group of men is similarly told to hand over one of their number to be killed, or else all of them will be killed, they are not permitted to hand him over *unless he is singled out like Sheva ben Bikhri.* In the latter case, they are to hand him over lest all of them die. How does the case of the women differ from that of the men? Why are there no exceptions to the prohibition in the case of the women? Here the answer must be at a minimum that while a person may have committed a capital offense, there are no offenses for which the legally prescribed punishment is rape. There cannot be, therefore, a woman who is singled out "like Sheva ben Bikhri" but for rape rather than for death. Still, one might raise this objection. Suppose that a specific woman is asked for *by name,* and suppose further that this woman has committed a capital offense, why then must she be protected from rape even at the cost of a significant number of other women? Here there are two possible answers, leading to different outcomes. On the one hand, the rabbis were concerned to uphold the dignity of human beings (for example, no man was to be beaten more than forty strokes) and rape is the ultimate indignity. Thus even someone deserving of death is not deserving of rape; the community's obligation to protect its members from dehumanizing experiences remains. On the other hand, were there such a woman, her case could be regarded as being like that of Sheva ben Bikhri; it would be required, or at least permissible, to hand her over. I am inclined to think that the first answer is closer to the spirit of the tradition.

Let us now turn to Sheva ben Bikhri. This case appears at first sight to be entirely beside the point of this mishnah. Sheva ben Bikhri was demanded not by non-Jews but by *the Jewish soldiers of the Jewish king David,* nor was he handed over by the people of the town in which he was hiding; they themselves executed him and then delivered his head to the Jewish general. The rabbis, therefore, must have meant to draw attention not to what the townspeople did to Sheva ben Bikhri but rather to what Sheva ben Bikhri himself had done. Sheva ben Bikhri had been the leader of an uprising *by Jews against the Jewish king;* he had done everything in his power to shatter the fragile, all-encompassing Jewish community that David had been at pains to establish. To cast out such a person is not to fracture the ties of community but rather to protect them.

The rabbis, I take it, are saying that no Jewish community, large or small, is required to risk its very existence for the sake of a person who himself threatens that existence from within. That leaves, however, the difficult question of what counts as threatening the existence of a Jewish community from within. The difficulty of that question is brought out clearly by the experience of Rabbi Yehoshua b. Levi, who persuaded Ulla bar Koshav to give himself up to the non-Jewish authorities who intended to execute him. We do not know whether the deed of Ulla bar Koshav was a crime only in the eyes of the gentile authorities or also in the eyes of the Jews. Let us consider both cases.

If Ulla bar Koshav committed a capital offense only in the eyes of the non-Jewish authorities, then he was not like Sheva ben Bikhri; he did not attempt to destroy the Jewish community from within, not even in the attenuated sense in which any criminal act against another member of the community is an act against the community as a whole. His case would be like that of Sheva ben Bikhri only in externals, only in that the town in which he lived was threatened because of his presence. The fact that Ulla bar Koshav let himself be persuaded to give himself up (unlike Sheva ben Bikhri) inclines me to the view that indeed he did not violate Jewish law. If so, we can well imagine that Rabbi Yehoshua's conscience would be troubled, that his appeals to the mishnah do not seem to settle the matter.

On the other hand, if Ulla bar Koshav committed a capital offense in the eyes of the Jews as well as the non-Jewish authorities, the event is to be interpreted rather differently. His action may now be seen as threatening the Jewish community from within as well as drawing calamity upon it from without. Rabbi Yehoshua's appeal to the mishnah is now entirely legitimate; why then is his conscience troubled? Why, on this supposition, is there a question whether appealing to the case of Sheva ben Bikhri is a teaching of the pious? Is this case analogous to that of Jews who commit crimes elsewhere and then flee to Israel? Are they to be sheltered even if their deed is a crime also by Israeli law?

I want to return to the first interpretation. On that interpretation the case of Ulla bar Koshav serves as a reminder that the exception to the mishnah is just that, an exception. The central point to be remembered is that Jews are not to betray their fellow Jews to the non-Jewish authorities. This basic principle makes the whole discussion relevant to the problems faced by rabbinical authorities in the ghetto; this is why it is considered with such care by Rabbi Ephraim Oshry. And yet, in the end, he found it not decisive. Appealing to authority, as he must, he ruled that attempting to save a remnant of a threatened community is permissible. How is this case different from the case of handing over a woman to be raped or a man to be killed? Do the numbers count, after all? I think not.

In the original cases, some men, or some women, hand over one of their number in an attempt to save *themselves*. Afterward, those saved will not be able to trust one another. No community is left, merely a group of isolated individuals. Rabbi Ephraim Oshry did not attempt to save himself (he did not say, "Give me a white card"), nor did he advise the members of the Council of Elders to save themselves; rather, he urged them to "gather their courage" and distribute the white cards "so as to save anybody they can."

We are not told how the cards were distributed or whether those who received them survived.

Ruth Anna Putnam

Contemporary Struggles

Introduction

"Choose this day which gods you are going to serve," Joshua told the elders assembled at Shechem, "but I and my household will serve the Lord" (Josh. 24:15). The biblical covenant was an association of "households" or families, spoken for by their male heads and pledged to divine service. This form of political organization was not superseded among the Jews for many centuries—not until the triumph of liberal individualism in the Western diaspora. We don't know the precise extent of the biblical household, but throughout the exilic years something very much like the nuclear family was the basic unit of the Jewish community. When the *kahal* was described as a partnership, what the writers had in mind was a partnership of fathers and husbands, not of solitary individuals. Women might sometimes be recognized as partners; in Roman times we know of women serving as leaders of synagogues and communities. But equality was probably more readily acknowledged in civil than in political matters (see ¢13, §6). In practice, throughout the Middle Ages and into the early modern period, men made communal decisions. Their wives and children were nonetheless "brethren," members of the community, with legal rights that the courts could, and sometimes did, enforce.

What is the nature of this family unit? How do its members relate to one another? When can or should the agents of the law—the court and the *kahal*—intervene in domestic affairs? These are the questions that we mean to address in the following two chapters, this one dealing with husband and wife, the founding members of the family, and the next one dealing with parents and children or, more generally, with the family as a transgenerational unit.

The Jewish family is formed by law rather than by nature: it is shaped by a divine command. Following the account in Genesis, the rabbis understand marriage as a human bonding divinely sanctioned and blessed, with two purposes, of which the first is, for most writers, by far the most important: procreation ("be fruitful and increase") and companionship ("it is not good for man to be alone"). It is, therefore, a holy union—though never quite a sacrament in the Christian sense. But this understanding is characteristically paralleled by another: marriage is at the same time a legal contract between two human beings. This contract is described variously in different times and places; initially, at least, it does not have anything like the reciprocity that we associate with contractual relations between equals. In what is probably its earliest version, marriage is an act of acquisition by the man, a kind of wife-purchase. But marriage is also, or the rabbis gradually turn it into, a consensual arrangement requiring the agreement of the woman and specifying a set of reciprocal obligations (which are set forth in a written document, the *ketubah*). We can see the obligations being worked out in the texts from Yevamot and Ketubot. The man's role is clearly dominant, as the idea of acquisition suggests, and it remains so to this day, but much of the halakhic literature is concerned to explain, and sometimes to expand, the reciprocal character of the contract and to determine the extent and means of its judicial enforcement.

Families stand under the law; their character and government are fixed by legal decisions. Though Maimonides says that the husband and father is "like a king," he does not have royal prerogatives. Nor is the political analogy at all common in the literature. The family is not conceived as a little state ruled by a patriarchal king; the state is not conceived (nor is the *kahal*) as a family writ large, ruled by a royal husband or father. As we saw in Chapter 17, this latter conception, pervasive in Western political thought until the seventeenth century, is largely absent from the Jewish tradition.

The kinglike authority of the biblical patriarchs over an extended household of wives and concubines was progressively restricted by rabbinic rulings. Maimonides himself is credited with banning concubinage, and the famous edict of Gershom b. Judah (the text of which has not been preserved) made monogamy the halakhic norm of Ashkenazic family life, ratifying what had probably been common practice in the Western diaspora for centuries before. There was some tension here with the commandment to "be fruitful and increase," which had been understood to allow, or even require, a man to take a second wife if his first was barren. Once monogamy became the norm, the commandment was understood to allow, or require, a divorce from the first wife: Maimonides says flatly of a barren woman that "she must be divorced without payment of the *ketubah*" (here, the dowry specified in the marriage contract). It follows, of course, that the man "must" marry again in order to have children. Procreation is an absolute command; the only exception is for a Torah scholar who fears that the obligations of marriage will distract him from his studies (and this exception holds only, according to Maimonides, "if his passion is not wont to overpower him." If his passion is indeed overpowering, he had better find a wife—this is the Jewish version of Paul's "It is better to marry than to burn").

But companionship can sometimes mitigate the severity of the command to procreate. Some rabbis were unwilling to require the divorce of a barren woman because they recognized the value of the existing union: divorce would be an act of cruelty. At the same time, and even though it was generally held (against the plain meaning of the biblical text) that women were not commanded to procreate, a husband's impotence might also be a reason for divorce. "He must divorce her," Maimonides says of a man who "does not eject with the force of an arrow," and "pay her the entire *ketubah*."

Even in the years before Gershom's ban on polygamy, however, no woman was allowed to take a second husband. Here reciprocity was definitely not a feature of gender relations in Jewish law. Sexual activity outside of marriage was possible for men, barred to women—with severe sanctions in the case of a woman's infidelity (even if she had been abandoned by her husband): any child born of such a union was stigmatized as *mamzer* (see ¢12, where we focus on this from the perspective of the injustice to the child). At the same time, the Talmud takes considerable care to specify the conjugal obligations of husbands to their wives. Women have at least a moral right to sexual satisfaction in marriage; radical dissatisfaction seems sometimes to have been a reason for a court-enforced divorce.

The obligations of the wife in the household are extensive, and they are worked out in the legal literature in great detail. Again, they are conceived not as natural duties but rather as work done in exchange for "sustenance." Here too the reciprocity is imperfect, but it does open some room for negotiation and freedom, as we can see in the texts in Ketubot. A wife who gives up sustenance (because she has money of her own or because of income earned outside the household) diminishes her household responsibilities. If, however, she simply refuses some or all of these responsibilities, she is called a "defiant" or "rebellious" wife. She is then subject, some writers think, to physical coercion by her husband—though Abraham b. David of Posquieres (Rabad), disputing Maimonides, says that "he never heard of such a thing" as a husband beating his wife. The practice was probably common enough; evidently Rabad meant to say that he had never heard of such a thing being justified (which is also unlikely). Still, the preferred practice was to turn to the court for counsel, admonition, and financial sanctions against the woman— the reduction or loss of her *ketubah* (dowry), which she would normally receive in case of divorce.

The property rights of a woman within the family, in relation to her husband, were extremely limited. She could hold property that she brought into the marriage, but her earnings were subject to the maxim, "Whatever a wife acquires is [straightaway] acquired by her husband" (or possibly not—if she gave up sustenance). There seems to have been some erosion of the husband's control over his wife's property in the course of the Middle Ages—

which is indicated in the responsum of Solomon b. Abraham Adret, in a case involving a widow and her husband's heir. Adret's ruling favors the widow and opens the way for women to assert their ownership rights.

In principle, at least, a husband could also be defiant or rebellious. The rabbis' commitment to the parallelism seems a bit halfhearted, but the husband, too, has legal obligations that he can fail to meet, and his wife can then appeal to the court for redress. The chief sanction that the court has in such a case, after private and public warnings aimed at shaming the husband, is to coerce him to divorce his wife, who departs with her *ketubah* payment. It is impossible to tell from the texts we have how often anything like this actually happened; we just don't know whether the courts were at all useful to women mistreated by their husbands. Certainly, there were cases that came to the courts—as the responsa reprinted here by Asher b. Yehi'el (Rosh) and Meir b. Baruch of Rothenburg (Maharam) make clear (see also the responsum of Simeon b. Zemah Duran, *Tashbetz,* quoted in the ruling of the Israeli Rabbinical Court, §33 below). The Geonim and Maimonides assert the wife's right to freedom ("She is not like a captive"), but Asher's insistence on patriarchal authority is probably the more common position in subsequent centuries. We take up some of the legal issues here; others are dealt with in Chapter 23, where coercion itself is our subject.

Strictly speaking, divorce is a male initiative. The biblical text (Deut. 24) sets a precedent that the rabbis follow: divorce requires a legal document (*get*) that the man writes and signs. Though the Bible gives only one ambiguous and much disputed reason for divorce—"because he has found in her a deed of indecency" [or, "because he has found anything disagreeable in her"]—some of the sages, including, most notably, Akiva, allow a man to divorce his wife for virtually any reason, hence, in effect, without reason. But this is only their original position—pure patriarchalism—and it was subsequently modified in three ways. First, the Rabbis invented the *ketubah,* which made divorce costlier to the husband and so provided some protection for the wife. Second, they (or, better, some of them) allowed the courts to coerce a husband to write a *get* in certain cases where the woman's need to escape from a disastrous marriage was acknowledged. And, third, an ordinance attributed to Gershom, and widely accepted, declared that husbands could not divorce their wives without winning their consent. Against a patriarchalist background, these are radical reforms, but they only modified, they did not overturn, the dominant role of the husband in the family. This was in any case reinforced by his dominant role in public and religious life outside the home (see ¢13 on the gender hierarchy).

The second of these reforms required a woman to appeal to the courts: she could not herself write a *get;* she had to persuade the judges to force her husband to do that, and they were often reluctant. Once again, we don't know how accessible or receptive the judges were to women in trouble. But they were, after all, husbands and fathers themselves with an interest in the familial status quo. Whether the husband could be physically coerced (by flogging) and whether a *get* written under coercion was legally valid—these remained open questions, which means that women who appealed to the courts were taking a chance, putting their well-being, such as it was, at risk. They were likely to do this only in extreme cases.

Still, the revision of the divorce laws, even though its extent was limited (and disputed even within its limits), makes it clear that the family was not pure private space. Public officials could intervene, when they wanted to, on behalf of the weaker members. Jewish men were not able to say, "My home is my castle," though it is likely that many of them lived that way, lords and barons (if not kings) in their families.

Because of the frequent unwillingness of the courts to coerce a *get* from unwilling husbands, and the oppressive condition of the "chained woman," some contemporary rabbis have looked for alternatives to a Jewish divorce. The most obvious alternative is judicial annulment, and there are some talmudic precedents for a procedure of this sort. First of all, marriages are performed "in accordance with the laws of Moses and Israel." Hence they are not, or not only, contracts between husband and wife; they are subject to legal validation—and then, in principle, to legal invalidation. Second, and perhaps more interestingly, they require, as we have seen, the agreement of the woman. But what if that agreement is unreasonable, or ignorant, or coerced? Then, perhaps, a court can step in, even long after the fact, and say that there never was the kind of agreement that the law requires and hence that there never was a marriage. But these seem like desperate measures, often urged, no doubt, on behalf of desperate women. Meanwhile, given the one-sided nature of Jewish divorce law, it is probably not a surprise that most divorces of Jewish couples in the contemporary Western diaspora are sought in and decreed by secular courts.

The alternative to annulment would be a radical revision in the character of Jewish marriage. This might take the form of a prenuptial agreement, which would affect not the ceremony itself but rather the understanding that bride and groom bring to it. Or one might go further and revise the ceremony, as Meir Feldblum suggests, giving up the idea that the woman is "acquired" and so, perhaps, making a *get* unnecessary if the marriage fails.

Marriage: Biblical Foundations

Fathers and Husbands: Controlling Women's Sexuality

1. Deuteronomy 22:13–29

These paragraphs set forth the patriarchal structure of the ancient Israelite family. A woman who engages in premarital sex (discovered after she has been betrothed by her father) is liable to be killed for violating paternal authority; female adultery, which violates the husband's right, is a capital offense for both the wife and her lover. In each case, the woman is not liable if she was taken by force. A husband's accusation that his wife was unfaithful could not, of course, be settled in the manner described here for a newlywed. Still, the matter was seen as too grievous to be left unresolved; hence the sotah *ordeal (Num. 5:11–31). Rabbinic* halakhah *introduced great changes in the rules of evidence in these matters and significantly reduced paternal authority over a grown daughter, but retained the legal conception of marriage as depicted here—subordination of the wife's sexuality to her husband's control.*

A man marries a woman and cohabits with her. Then he takes an aversion to her and makes up charges against her and defames her, saying, "I married

this woman, but when I approached her, I found that she was not a virgin."
In such a case, the girl's father and mother shall produce the evidence of the
girl's virginity before the elders of the town at the gate. And the girl's father
shall say to the elders, "I gave this man my daughter to wife, but he has taken
an aversion to her, so he has made up charges. . . . But here is the evidence
of my daughter's virginity!" And they shall spread out the cloth before the
elders. . . . The elders of the town shall then take the man and flog him, and
they shall fine him a hundred [shekels of] silver and give it to the girl's father;
for the man has defamed a virgin in Israel. Moreover, she shall remain his
wife; he shall never have the right to divorce her.

But if the charge proves true, the girl was found not to have been a
virgin, then the girl shall be brought out to the entrance of her father's house,
and the men of her town shall stone her to death, for she did a shameful thing
in Israel, committing fornication while under her father's authority. Thus you
shall sweep away evil from your midst.

If a man is found lying with another man's wife, both of them—
the man and the woman with whom he lay—shall die. Thus shall you sweep
away evil from Israel.

In the case of a virgin who is betrothed to a man—if a man comes
upon her in town and lies with her, you shall take the two of them out to the
gate of the town and stone them to death: the girl because she did not cry for
help . . . and the man because he violated another man's wife. Thus you will
sweep away evil from your midst. But if the man comes upon the betrothed
girl in the open country, and the man lies with her by force, only the man
who lay with her shall die, but you shall do nothing to the girl. The girl did
not incur the death penalty, for this case is like that of man attacking another
and murdering him. He came upon her in the open; though the betrothed
girl cried for help, there was no one to save her.

If a man comes upon a virgin who is not betrothed and he seizes her
and lies with her, and they are discovered, the man who lay with her shall pay
the girl's father fifty [shekels of] silver, and she shall be his wife. Because he
has violated her, he can never have the right to divorce her.

Marriage and Divorce: Taking and Sending Away
2. Deuteronomy 24:1–5

No procedure is described for "taking" a wife, but for sending her away, a "bill of sever-
ance" is specified. In both instances, biblical law makes no mention of her consent. It is not
clear whether the finding of "something obnoxious" (or: "indecent"—translations differ;
cf. §23 below) is intended as justification for the divorce; in any event, the divorcee's sub-
sequent marriage to another man "defiles" or disqualifies her for her first husband.

A man takes a wife and possesses her. She fails to please him because he finds
something obnoxious about her, and he writes her a bill of severance, hands
it to her, and sends her away from his house; she leaves his household and becomes the wife of another man, then the latter man rejects her, writes her a
bill of severance, hands it to her, and sends her away from his house; or the
man who married her last dies. Then the first husband who divorced her shall
not take her to wife again, since she has been defiled—for that would be abhorrent to the Lord. You must not bring sin upon the land that the Lord your
God is giving you as a heritage.

Against Divorce: Marriage as Covenant
3. Malachi 2:10–16

Malachi decries a general disintegration of social solidarity in the early decades of the Sec-
ond Commonwealth; within this context, he speaks bitterly of the tears of women di-
vorced by their husbands. The historical and literary contexts suggest that these wives were
sent away to make room for unions with gentile women, undertaken perhaps to cement
political or economic alliances (cf. ¢14, §4). In any case, Malachi's condemnation of di-
vorce represents a sharp contrast with the Deuteronomic view. Adducing divine affirma-
tion of the marital covenant, Malachi echoes earlier prophets' impassioned descriptions of
God's relationship with Israel in terms of a loving covenant between husband and wife.

Have we not all one Father? Did not one God create us? Why do we break faith with one another, profaning the covenant of our fathers? Judah has broken faith; abhorrent things have been done in Israel and in Jerusalem. For Judah has profaned what is holy to the Lord—what he desires—and espoused daughters of alien gods. May the Lord leave to him who does this no descendants dwelling in the tents of Jacob and presenting offerings to the Lord of Hosts. And this you do as well: You cover the altar of the Lord with tears, weeping, and moaning, so that He refuses to regard the oblation any more and to accept what you offer. But you ask, "Because of what?" Because the Lord is a witness between you and the wife of your youth with whom you have broken faith, though she is your partner and covenanted spouse. Did not the One make [all], so that all remaining life-breath is His? And what does the One seek but godly folk? So be careful of your life-breath, and let no one break faith with the wife of his youth. For I detest divorce—said the Lord, God of Israel.

Marriage: Basic Halakhic Conceptions

Acquiring

4. Mishnah Kiddushin 1:1; BT Kiddushin 2a–b

*Tractate Kiddushin defines the manner of effecting the marital bond. The verb used here is "acquisition," and the same term in the Mishnah's following clauses refers to gaining title to slaves, cattle, and real estate. The Bible speaks of a man "taking" a wife; in Rabbinic usage the same verb (l.q.h.) denotes buying, but the legal import of marital "acquisition" (q.n.h.) is that the husband acquires exclusivity of sexual intimacy. The tractate's following chapters consistently employ instead the term "consecrate" (*kiddush). *Although it denotes the same legal procedure and effect, "consecrate" carries different connotations (explored in the* sugya *here). Several modern scholars see in it a reflection of a more sacral conception of the marital bond.*

Mishnah Kiddushin 1:1

A woman is acquired in [one of] three ways, and acquires herself in [either of] two ways. She is acquired by money, by writ, or by intercourse. . . . And she acquires herself by a *get* [divorce writ] or by the death of the husband.

BT Kiddushin 2a–b

"A woman is acquired"—Why use specifically here [the term] "A woman is acquired," and why specifically there "A man consecrates [in person or through his agent; a woman is consecrated in person or through her agent]" (Mishnah Kiddushin 2:1)? Since [the mishnah] is about to use [the term] "money," it uses [the term] "A woman is acquired." . . .

Let it [then] use there [the term] "A man acquires"! At first, it uses the biblical term; then it goes on to use the Rabbinic term. And what is [the sense of] the Rabbinic term ["consecrate"]? That [the husband] renders her forbidden to all others, like [something] consecrated.

[Tosafot: The [formula recited by the bridegroom at weddings,] "You are hereby consecrated to me," [thus] means, "To be [exclusively] mine, consecrated vis-à-vis all others for my sake," just like "They are hereby consecrated to heaven" (BT Nedarim 48a) means: they shall be [exclusively] for heaven. The simple meaning of [the formula] "consecrated to me" is, however: dedicated to me, available to me.]

Let it [then] use here [the term] "A man acquires"!—Since it is about to teach in the second clause, "And she acquires herself," where she is the subject, it speaks of her as the subject in the first clause as well.

Let it [then] teach, "A man acquires . . . and delivers"!—[No,] for there is "death of the husband," where it is not he who delivers her; rather, she is delivered by heaven.

Or if you wish, I can say: If it had taught "[A man] acquires," we might think [it could be effected] even against her will; thus it teaches "A woman is acquired," [implying:] with her consent—yes; without her consent—no.

Wedding Benedictions

5. Traditional Wedding Liturgy

*The "consecration" (or acquisition)—identified with the biblical "betrothal" (erusin)—
was followed, in due course, by the wedding ceremony of the* huppah, *the bridal canopy,
initiating the couple's life together.*[1] *The ceremony includes reciting these seven benedictions, listed in the Talmud (BT Ketubot 7b); their full text appears in the earliest* siddur,
Seder Rav Amram Gaon (ninth century C.E.*). As in all components of Jewish liturgy,
there are numerous variations. For the most part, our translation follows the version found
in Maimonides' code (MT Laws Concerning Marriage 10:3). Celebration of the couple's
love and expected reproduction refers back to the First Wedding in Eden and looks forward
to the reunification of the "barren" Zion with her children.*

Blessed are You the Lord, our God, King of the Universe, creator of the fruit
of the vine.

Blessed are You the Lord, our God, King of the Universe, who has
created everything for His glory.

Blessed are You the Lord, our God, King of the Universe, maker of
the human.

Blessed are You the Lord, our God, King of the Universe, who has
made the human in His image,[2] the image of the likeness of His form, and set
up for him, from his self, in eternal reproduction. Blessed are You, the Lord,
maker of the human.

May the barren one rejoice and celebrate, when her children are
re-gathered with her in happiness. Blessed are You, the Lord, who causes
Zion to be happy in her children.

May You cause happiness to the beloved companions, as You caused

---

1. These two phases of entering into marriage—*kiddushin* and *huppah*—would normally be
separated by up to twelve months. In post-talmudic times they have come to be performed
together, as two items in a single ceremony.
2. The syntax is ambiguous: "his" here might refer either to the human or to God.

happiness to Your creature in former days, in the garden of Eden. Blessed are You, the Lord, who makes happy bridegroom and bride.

Blessed are You the Lord, our God, King of the Universe, who has created joy and happiness, bridegroom and bride, celebration and singing, delight and laughter, love and closeness, peace and companionship. May there soon be heard in the towns of Judea and in the outskirts of Jerusalem the sound of joy and the sound of happiness, the sound of bridegroom and the sound of bride,[3] the sound of bridegrooms' songs in their banquet and of youngsters making music. Blessed are You, the Lord, who makes happy bridegroom and bride.

Instructions to Husband and Wife

6. Maimonides, MT Laws Concerning Marriage 15:17–20

Chapters 14-15 in Maimonides' Laws Concerning Marriage discuss the legal obligations of conjugal sexuality. In these concluding sections, he moves to moral admonitions, drawing in part on Rabbinic teachings and describing what might be termed a benevolent patriarchy, which he regards as a recipe for marital harmony. A central theme here is control of female sexuality, including the wife's duty of "discretion" (tseniut), restraining various aspects of her behavior and expression. He begins by endorsing the practice of "warning against infidelity," a reference to the warning "Do not be secluded with X," which can initiate the sotah *ordeal (see Num. 5:11-31; Mishnah Sotah 1:2-5).*

17. It is the duty of every man to warn his wife against infidelity, and the sages have said, "A man should warn his wife only because the spirit of purity has entered into him." Nevertheless, he should not carry his jealousy of her beyond reason, nor should he compel her to have intercourse with him against her will. Rather, he should do it only with her consent, accompanied by pleasant discourse and enjoyment.

3. Cf. Jer. 33:9–10.

18. The sages have likewise ordained that the wife should behave with discretion within her house, and should not indulge in jesting and levity in the presence of her husband; nor should she demand intercourse by word of mouth, or keep talking about it. She should not deny herself to her husband merely in order to torment him, so as to make him love her all the more; she should rather submit to him whenever he desires. She should moreover be circumspect with his relatives and the members of his household, so that no spirit of jealousy should overcome him. She should keep away from anything unseemly or even approaching unseemliness.

19. The sages have likewise ordained that a man should honor his wife more than his own self, and love her as himself; that if he has money, he should increase his generosity to her according to his wealth; that he should not cast undue fear upon her; and that his discourse with her should be gentle—he should be prone neither to melancholy nor to anger.

20. They have likewise ordained that the wife should honor her husband exceedingly and hold him in awe, that she should arrange all her affairs according to his instructions, and that he should be in her eyes as if he were a prince or a king, while she behaves according to his heart's desire, and keeps away from anything that is hateful to him. This is the way of the daughters and the sons of Israel who are holy and pure in their mating, and in these ways will their life together be seemly and praiseworthy.

Divorce: By Husband's Writ
7. Maimonides, MT Laws Concerning Divorce 1:1–2

Listing the various requirements for a valid instrument of divorce (get), Maimonides distinguishes between certain formal requirements that are merely "scribal" (=Rabbinic) and the core elements of the biblically ordained mode of divorce. Prominent among the latter is the stipulation that the husband must freely grant the get: it is thus that he relinquishes his control over her, established when she agreed to be "acquired" as his wife. This is derived from the biblical account of divorce as a unilateral act by the husband.

1. A woman may be divorced only by means of a writ that reaches her, and this writ is called *get*.

There are ten rules that are basic to divorce, according to the Torah, and they are as follows:

1) That the man may not divorce his wife except of his own free will.

2) That he must divorce her by means of a writ, and not by means of anything else.

3) That the sense of the writ must be that he has divorced her and has removed her from his possession.

4) That its sense must be that it is an instrument which effects a severance between him and her.

5) That it must be written specifically for her.

6) That after the writing of it, no act must be lacking excepting only its delivery to her.

7) That he must deliver it to her.

8) That he must deliver it to her in the presence of witnesses.

9) That he must give it to her as an instrument of divorce.

10) That it must be the husband, or his agent, who gives it to her.

The other things that are involved in the *get,* such as the date, the signatures of the witnesses, and the like, are all of scribal origin.

2. And whence do we know that these ten rules are derived from the Torah? From the verse, "And it shall come to pass, if she find no favor in his eyes, because he has found some unseemly thing in her, that he shall write her a bill of severance, and give it into her hand, and send her out of his house" (Deut. 24:1). "If she find no favor in his eyes" implies that he may not divorce except of his own free will. If she is divorced against his will, she is not validly divorced. The woman, however, may be divorced with or without her consent.

Enforcing Divorce
8. BT Yevamot 106a; Mishnah Gittin 9:8; BT Gittin 88b

Even though only the husband may grant a divorce, Rabbinic law pronounces that in certain circumstances he is required to do so; sometimes coercion is explicitly mentioned. Hence the notion of a "forced get," which is introduced here through an analogy to a rule concerning an obligatory temple sacrifice—a context that likewise requires the subject's voluntary participation: "He shall bring it forth willingly" (see further ¢23, §§25-28). The sources in Gittin assert, however, that the forced utterance of consent is effective only if the coercion is properly authorized.

BT Yevamot 106a

A forced *halitzah* or a forced *get* is sometimes valid and sometimes invalid. It is valid if he said, "I consent," and invalid if he did not say, "I consent." As taught, "he shall bring it forth" (Lev. 1:3)—this implies that they coerce him [to bring the offering he has vowed]. Can it be [that it is valid] even against his will? We learn from what is written, "willingly." How so? They coerce him until he says, "I consent." The same is the case with regard to writs of divorce: They coerce him until he says, "I consent."

Mishnah Gittin 9:8

A forced *get*—if by Israelites it is valid, if by gentiles it is invalid. [A proper practice is that] the gentiles beat him, demanding: "Do what the Israelites are telling you!"

BT Gittin 88b

Said Rav Nahman, citing Shmu'el: A *get* forced by Israelites, if in accordance with the law [*Rashi:* as, for example, in the cases of which it was ruled, "he [must] divorce her and pay the *ketubah*," or in cases of a wife forbidden to this husband], is valid; if not in accordance with the law, it is invalid.

Man, Woman, and Procreation

9. Mishnah Yevamot 6:5–6; Tosefta Yevamot 8:7

The Mishnah frames the obligation to marry, and its specific requirements, in terms of the commandment to procreate: "Be fertile and increase" (Gen. 1:28). The Rabbis saw procreation as sustaining the divine image inhering in human beings. The Rabbis' discussion in the Tosefta regarding individuals who do not engage in procreation addresses their concern with the tension between marital commitment and devotion to Torah study.

Mishnah Yevamot 6:5–6

[5] An ordinary priest may not marry a sterile woman, unless he [already] has a wife and children. Rabbi Yehudah says: Even if he has a wife and children, he may not marry a sterile woman, for that is the "wanton woman" mentioned in Scripture (Lev. 21:7).[4] [But] the sages say: a "wanton woman" is only a convert, a freed slave, or one who was party to illicit intercourse.[5]

[6] A man may not desist from "being fertile and increasing," unless he has children. The School of Shammai says: Two male [children]; whereas the School of Hillel says: A male and a female, as written, "male and female He created them" (Gen. 1:27). If he took a wife and lived with her for ten years, and she did not give birth, he may not desist. If he divorces her, she may marry another; the second [husband] may live with her for ten years. If she miscarries, she counts from the time of the miscarriage. A man is com-

---

4. The Hebrew word is *zonah*, properly translated as "whore" or "harlot"; in Rabbinic usage, however, the root z.n.h. suggests more broadly any illicit intercourse.

5. Lit., "wanton intercourse." Regarding the convert and freed slave, Rabbinic law ascribes licentiousness to both heathens and slaves (cf. ¢14, §12; ¢16, §10); the stigma follows the woman in her new state.

manded with regard to "being fertile and increasing," but a woman is not. Rabbi Yohanan b. Beroka [however] says: Scripture refers to them both: "God blessed them and . . . said to them, 'Be fertile and increase'" (Gen. 1:28).

Tosefta Yevamot 8:7

[7] Rabbi Akiva says: Anyone who sheds blood thereby annuls the [divine] image, as written, "Whoever sheds the blood of man, by man shall his blood be shed; for in His image did God make man" (Gen. 9:6). Rabbi Elazar b. Azariah says: Anyone who does not engage in "being fertile and increasing," is considered by Scripture as having annulled the [divine] image, as written, "for in His image did God make man"—and [following immediately,] "Be fertile, then, and increase" (Gen. 9:6–7). Ben Azzai says: Anyone who does not engage in "being fertile and increasing," is considered by Scripture as having shed blood and annulled the [divine] image, as written, "for in His image did God make man"—and [following immediately,] "Be fertile, then, and increase" (Gen. 9:6–7). Rabbi Elazar b. Azariah retorted: Such words would be well spoken, were they to emerge from the mouth of one who lives up to them. Some preach well and practice well; others practice well, [though] they do not preach well; Ben Azzai preaches well, [yet] does not practice well! He answered: What can I do? My being craves Torah. Let the world be sustained by others.

Companionship and Procreation
10. BT Yevamot 61a–66a (selections)

The Talmud here emphasizes first the permissibility, and then the inherent value, of conjugal companionship independent of procreation. The ensuing discussion explores also the implications of the claim that women are exempt from "being fertile and increasing" and leaves unresolved the tannaitic dispute about that.

The exilarch said to Rav Huna: What is the reason [for the prohibition of marriage with a sterile woman]? [Surely] it is on account of "being fertile and increasing." But are only priests commanded [in this], and Israelites not? He responded: It is because [the mishnah's author] is about to continue, "Rabbi Yehudah says: Even if he has a wife and children, he may not marry a sterile woman, for that is the 'wanton woman' mentioned in Scripture"—and it is only priests, not Israelites, who are commanded regarding a "wanton woman." . . .

This [mishnah—§9, 6:6 above] implies that, if he has children, he may desist from "being fertile and increasing," but not from [living with] a wife. This lends support to the statement of Rav Nahman, citing Shmu'el: Even though a man has children, he may not remain without a wife, as written, "It is not good for man to be alone" (Gen. 2:18).

Some say: This implies that, if he has children, he may desist not only from "being fertile and increasing," but also from [living with] a wife— which would seem to constitute a refutation of the statement of Rav Nahman, citing Shmu'el!—No; if he has no children, he must marry a woman capable of [bearing] children; if he has children, he may marry a woman incapable of [bearing] children. . . .

What is the School of Shammai's reason? We learn [this] from Moses, as written, "The sons of Moses: Gershom and Eli'ezer" (1 Chron. 23: 15). And the School of Hillel? We learn from the creation of the world [Rashi: Adam and Eve]. Now the School of Shammai, let them learn from the creation of the world! One cannot draw conclusions . . . from [a setting in which there were] no [other] options. Now the School of Hillel, let them learn from Moses! One can retort: Moses acted on his own. As it was taught: "There were three actions that Moses took on his own, and [then] God concurred with him: [he] drew apart from his wife [lit., "from woman"], shattered the tablets, and added one day [to the people's preparation for Sinai]."

"He drew apart from his wife." Whence did he derive this? He argued: If regarding [the people of] Israel, with whom God spoke only at one instance, and [that] at an appointed time, the Torah said, "Do not go near a woman" (Exod. 19:15), how much more so regarding myself, as I am assigned [to hear] divine speech at multiple instances, with no appointed times! "And [then] God concurred with him"—as written, "Go, say to them, 'Return to your tents.' But you remain here with Me" (Deut. 5:27–28). . . .

Alternatively, it was taught: Rabbi Natan says, "The School of Shammai says: A male and a female; whereas the School of Hillel says: Either a male or a female." Said Rava: What is the reason for Rabbi Natan's version of the School of Hillel? As written, "He did not create it [the world] a waste, but formed it for habitation" (Isa. 45:18)—and [by producing] one child, he has effected "habitation." . . .

It was discussed: If a man had children, but they died—Rav Huna said: He has fulfilled [the commandment of] "being fertile and increasing." Rabbi Yohanan said: He has not fulfilled [it].

Rav Huna said, "He has fulfilled [it]"—[this is] based on the [teaching] of Rav Assi, for Rav Assi said: "The Son of David will not come until all the souls are gone from the 'body.'" [Rashi: That is to say, the purpose of "being fertile and increasing" is as explained by Rav Assi; and this individual, as he has created [certain] souls which have been removed from that treasure called "the body," has thereby fulfilled the [commandment].] . . .

Rabbi Yohanan said: "He has not fulfilled [it]"—"inhabited" is required, and has not [been achieved]. . . .

Against [Rav Huna, a baraita] was cited: "Grandchildren count as children. [But] if one of them died, or was found to be infertile, he has not fulfilled [the commandment of] 'being fertile and increasing.'" This [seems to be] a refutation of Rav Huna! [Indeed, it is] a refutation. . . .

It was taught: Rabbi Yehoshua says, If a person took a wife in his youth, he should [again] take a wife in old age; if he produced children in his youth, he should [again] produce children in old age. As written, "Sow your seed in the morning, and don't hold back your hand in the evening, since you don't know which is going to succeed, the one or the other, or if both are equally good" (Eccles. 11:6). . . .

Rabbi Tanhum said, citing Rabbi Hanilai: "Any person who has no wife exists without happiness, without blessing, without well-being." "Without happiness"—as written, "And you shall rejoice . . . with your household"

(Deut. 14:26). "Without blessing"—as written, "that a blessing may rest upon your home" (Ezek. 44:30).[6] "Without well-being [*tovah*]"—as written, "It is not good [*tov*] for man to be alone" (Gen. 2:18). . . . Rabbi Elazar said: Any person who has no wife is not [truly] a person [*adam*], as written, "male and female He created them . . . and named them *adam*" (Gen. 5:2).[7] . . .

From where does the [exemption of women from procreation] derive? Rabbi Ila said, citing Rabbi Elazar b. Shimon: Scripture says, "Fill the earth and master it" (Gen. 1:28); it is Man's manner to master, but it is not Woman's manner to master.[8] On the contrary, "master it" [as vocalized is in the plural], implying them both! Said Rav Nahman b. Yitzhak: The written form is [in the singular]. . . .

The [question of how to rule in the dispute over women's obligation to procreate] was discussed between Rabbi Yohanan and Rabbi Yehoshua b. Levi. One said that the law is according to Rabbi Yohanan b. Beroka, and the other said that the law is not according to Rabbi Yohanan b. Beroka.[9] . . .

Come and hear that which was said by Rabbi Aha b. Haninah, citing Rabbi Abahu, citing Rabbi Assi: There was a case [that came] before Rabbi Yohanan in the synagogue of Tsippori [*Rashi:* A wife demanded a divorce on the grounds of not having children], and Rabbi Yohanan ruled: "He must divorce her and pay her *ketubah* [money]."[10] Now if you suppose she is not commanded, what cause has she to [collect] the *ketubah?*—Perhaps she based her case on a [concrete] claim, like the [childless] woman who came before Rabbi Ami. She said to him: "Grant me my *ketubah!*" He replied: "Depart, you are not commanded." She answered him: "When this woman is old, what will become of her?" He [then] said: "In a case like this, we certainly compel [him to divorce her and pay the *ketubah*]."

---

6. The word *bayit,* translated as "household" or "home," is often used in Rabbinic Hebrew to refer to a wife.
7. NJPS: "and called them Man."
8. The verb (k.v.sh.) translated as "master" also means "conquer."
9. According to the standard talmudic approach, the law would not be according to the named *tana*, since the rival position (the *stam*) is deemed to represent the majority (cf. ¢7, §§2–3). In an exception to that rule, the debate is kept open by these *amora'im.*
10. Ruling, in effect, that the husband's putative infertility obliges him to divorce her.

A [childless] woman came before Rav Nahman; he told her, "You are not commanded." She answered him: "Does this woman not need a staff to [lean] her hand on and a spade for her burial?" He [then] said: "In a case like this, we certainly compel [him]."

Yehudah and Hizkiyah were twins; one was fully formed at the end of the ninth [month], the other was fully formed at the beginning of the seventh. [Their mother,] Yehudit, the wife of Rabbi Hiyya, experienced suffering at childbirth. She disguised herself and came before Rabbi Hiyya, and asked: "Is a woman commanded with regard to 'being fruitful and increasing'?" He told her: "No." She went and imbibed a concoction [inducing] infertility. Eventually, the matter was revealed. He said to her: "I wish you would have borne me one more [delivery of the] womb!"—for the master has taught, "Yehudah and Hizkiyah [were twin] brothers, Pazi and Tavi [were twin] sisters."[11]

But are [women] not commanded? Here, Rav Aha b. Rav Ketina said, citing Rav Yitzhak: "There was a case of a woman who was half slave and half free, and [the court] compelled her master to render her free." [*Rashi:* So that she could marry.] Rav Nahman b. Yitzhak explained: In that case, she had become the object of licentious behavior.

Valuing Male Domination

11. Abraham b. David of Posquieres (Rabad), *Ba'alei Hanefesh,* Introduction

Rabad's Ba'alei Hanefesh *had a tremendous impact on the mores of sexuality in the halakhic tradition. He begins this work by introducing his conception of the man-woman relationship. In this conception, the monistic exclusiveness of human male-female relations is tied to male dominance; this in turn is linked to a broader hierarchical scheme.*

---

11. Yehudit had borne two sets of (evidently remarkable) twins.

All creatures were created male and female, whereas Man was first created as a single [creature] and subsequently [God] created for him, from his very self, a fitting helper. . . .

Using my meager understanding, I propose that God created him thus, as a single [creature], for Man's advantage and benefit. For had [Man and Woman] been created from the earth, male and female, as in the creation of all the other creatures, the woman would stand in relation to the man just like the female animal to the male animal: she neither accepts his domination nor stays with him to serve him. Rather [the males] seize [the females] . . . and [afterward] any one of them can reject the other and go its own way. Indeed, they don't maintain any exclusive relationship, since from the beginning each was created separately. Therefore, giving consideration to Man's needs and benefits, He created him as a single [entity] and then took one of his ribs, fashioned the woman out of it, and brought her to the Man to be his wife and to stay with him to be his helper and provide support [for him]. For she is, in relation to him, like one of his limbs that were created to serve him, and he will rule over her as he rules over his limbs, since she will yearn for him just as his limbs yearn to be of benefit to him. . . .

God said, "It is not good that man be alone" (Gen. 2:18), meaning that it is not good that Man be separate, as with the animals, where the female has no exclusive [bond] to a [particular] male. Therefore "I will make a fitting helper for him"—I will create him in such a manner that she will be a fitting helper: "helper"—that she serve all his needs; "fitting"—that she be with him always. . . .

Therefore a man ought to love his wife as his own self, to honor her and have compassion toward her and protect her just as he protects any of his limbs. She too is obligated to serve and honor him and love him as her own self, for she was fashioned from him. Therefore the Creator commanded Man, with regard to his wife, "He must not withhold her food, her clothing, and her conjugal rights [onah]" (Exod. 21:10, see §16 below).

Now in order that Man know that his Creator rules over him, He established for him fixed rules regarding his sexual union with the woman.

The Value of Marriage: Family and Procreation
12. Jacob b. Asher, *Tur* EH 1; Yoel Sirkes, *Bayit Hadash* EH 1

*In Jacob's law code, "Four Columns" (*Turim*), the column devoted to marriage is named "Even ha-Ezer," alluding to the "fitting helper [ezer]" of Genesis 2:18. Following are the opening lines of the work, which stress the good of companionship as the foundation for the commandment to procreate. Commenting on this opening statement, Sirkes emphasizes the law's requirement that—subjective perceptions of interest notwithstanding—the law seeks to civilize human procreation by placing it within the institution of marriage.*

Jacob b. Asher, *Tur* EH 1

May the Holy One's name be blessed, who desires the good for His creatures; for He knew that it is not good for man to be alone, and therefore made for him a fitting helper. Furthermore, since the purpose of the creation of man is that he be fruitful and increase, which is impossible without this helper, He thus commanded him to cleave to the helper He had made for him. Hence every man is obligated to take a wife, so as to be fruitful and increase.

Yoel Sirkes, *Bayit Hadash* EH 1

It must be asked: To what purpose did [the author] place these introductory [words of] praise here at the beginning of this work, [considering] that they are irrelevant to the work's nature? For his purpose is solely to issue rulings, and he [thus] ought to have begun [simply]: "Every man is obligated to take a wife," etc. [The answer] seems to be that there are some people who entertain, in their confused minds, the idea that "since it is for my own good that [God] created the helper, as written 'It is not good for man to be alone, I will make a fitting helper for him' (Gen. 2:18)—well, I do not desire this good and prefer not to receive it." In his opinion, it is a greater good for him to live without a wife, and find a helpmate in a friend or relative whom he loves.[12] Therefore, to banish this mistake from the mind, [the author] said: "May the Holy One's name be blessed etc., for He knew that it is not good, etc." For He, may He be Blessed, knows what constitutes a helpmate, repudiating the thoughts of the person whose mind misleads him to find himself a helper of his desire. [The author] goes on to say, "Also, since the purpose of creation," etc., meaning: we must conclude that [the verse] "It is not good for man to be alone, I will make a fitting helper for him" does not mean that God's sole purpose was to provide a good for man by giving him a helper—in which case he could [indeed] assert that he prefers not to receive it. For if so, He need not have made [the helper] in the form of a woman, but rather should have created it in the form of another man! Rather, we must conclude that His purpose . . . in creating humans male and female and calling them "*adam,*" was specifically in order that the commandment "be fruitful and increase" be fulfilled . . . which cannot be fulfilled without the helper that God created for him.

[Furthermore,] the import is: Lest one entertain the notion that "being fruitful and increasing" is possible without marriage, by fornicating with women—[No,] it is not possible without a helper. . . . "He thus commanded him to cleave to the helper He had made for him," as our author states in his introductory remarks. This is the sense of "It is not good for man to be alone"—that is to say, it is not good that a man go off alone with a woman, like the animals who go off alone [sporadically, to mate], the females not being designated to particular males. Rather, He created for him a helper, designated to him and clinging to him, as written "a man . . . clings to his wife," that is, by way of marriage, not fornication. Our author [thus] states that from all this it follows that each man is obligated to take a wife, in order to be fruitful and increase . . . suppressing his will and opinion in the face of God's will, since it is an obligation and yoke upon man to take a wife and it is not—as a man might have thought—for his good alone. . . . Instead, it is an obligation, and he commits a transgression if he fails to take a wife.

12. Literally: "his soul is bound with his soul," suggesting platonic love.

Commentary. The Persistence of Patriarchal Marriage

The Jewish hermeneutical tradition is characterized by pluralism; there are few moral issues on which there is broad agreement among exegetes. As is evident from every page of this reader, there is almost no topic of discussion on which one cannot find a variety of moral stances and tensions between different world views, which are not always arbitrated by halakhic decisions. Some of them, on the contrary, continue to be reflected in contemporary halakhic literature.

This is not the case, however, with regard to the marital relationship and the family unit. Here is one of the few cases in which there is broad agreement among all the relevant sources: the marital relationship, as perceived in biblical, rabbinic, and later hermeneutical texts, to this very day, is fundamentally patriarchal in nature. The man is the one who "takes" the woman; it is he who "finds something indecent" in her and he who therefore sends her away. He is the active partner; she is passive. He controls; she is controlled. She is "acquired" in three ways. Even the ways in which she "acquires herself" are dependent not on her but rather on the death of her husband or his desire to divorce her. Similarly, sexual obligation within marital relations is expressly one-sided: the woman is obligated to sexual fidelity from the moment she is linked to a specific man, and whenever the man's exclusive rights over and access to his wife's sexuality are compromised, the woman (as well as the man with whom she has had adulterous relations) is punished with death. No parallel obligation and punishment for the married man exists. There is, therefore, no mutuality regarding the exclusivity of the marital sexual relation between man and woman. The wife is tied down; the husband is largely free to act as he wishes.

Some feminist critics attribute this patriarchal structure to monotheism. The belief in one God, these writers claim, creates a string of "truly frightening" beliefs, which are then translated from the theological plane to the level of man-woman relations, based on the understanding that "as God is to Man, so Man is to Woman." Thus, for instance, the unity of God is linked to his being "enough for Himself," a singular being who allows no competition from any other. God created the world and is responsible for it; he is hierarchically superior to humanity. He alone possesses complete knowledge and power. This kind of a God represents autonomy and strength. He is free, all-powerful; there is no law that restricts him in any way; he is the subject of adoration and worship. Humanity, on the other hand, represents weakness and sin and is therefore often perceived as "feminine." "What a nightmare!" writes Daphne Hampson. "God would seem to be the reflection of the male's wildest dreams."

In brief, monotheism makes for a gendered, hierarchical perception of reality.

There are those who would argue that this critique, which is, at its base, targeted at Christianity (although in many cases the blame is laid at Judaism's feet, as the root of Christianity), is incompatible with Jewish tradition. It is difficult, they say, to identify such clear-cut perceptions of male supremacy within Judaism, whereby man is seen as a Godlike figure for woman. But a look at the words of Rabbi Jacob b. Abba Mari Anatoli (¢13, §9) should be sufficient to establish the relevance of this critique for Judaism as well.

This source clearly points to hierarchical relations between husband and wife and to the man's constituting a kind of "God" for his wife, and it also highlights the more interesting point—in my opinion—that *God himself is a collaborator in this hierarchical scheme.* Since God understands and sympathizes with the man's soul, he releases the woman from some of her religious obligations in order not to cause conflict between the two hierarchical relationships in which she participates (between her and her husband and between her and God). No contradiction is perceived between these hierarchical relations and the peace of the Jewish home. Rather, it seems that this hierarchy enables the peaceful coexistence of husband and wife. As I will demonstrate later on, modern halakhic perceptions adhere to this view.

Feminist critics of monotheism are also critical of the notion of "covenant" as it is reflected in Scripture. They direct our attention to the fact that the biblical covenant is dissimilar to the liberal social contract, which is a pact made freely between individuals of equal worth. The biblical covenant, by contrast, is made between God and his people, between the strong and the weak. In this context it is appropriate to examine the words of the prophet Malachi, from which it appears that one can derive an egalitarian message.

Malachi reproves the man who breaks faith with the wife of his youth. The attitude reflected here views the relationship between husband and wife, the friendship and intimacy between them, as the purpose of the institution of marriage. This is a possible reading, but in light of the critique we have cited of the concept of covenant, it is clearly not a necessary one; nor is it common in the tradition.

The tension between readings that might be perceived as egalitarian and the prevalent patriarchal attitude is also evident in rabbinic literature. The sources included here reflect various opinions regarding the purpose of marriage and the marital relationship. Some see this relationship as stemming from considerations like the biblical dictum "It is not good that man should be alone." In other words, marriage is an end in itself, and not only a medium for the production of future generations. But others see it precisely and narrowly as an instrument with a central purpose, reproduction. This ambivalence is clearly reflected in the selection from BT Yevamot (§10).

The talmudic argument in Yevamot moves between two extremes: the value of fertility and the value of the marital relationship. It tends to place fertility ahead of the marital relationship on the hierarchical scale, with the marriage of a man to a woman who is incapable of childbearing serving as a test case. If we quantify the conclusion of the passage in economic terms, we find that a Torah scroll may be sold in order to fulfill the commandment "Be fruitful and multiply" but not in order to establish a sterile marital relationship. There is most certainly a value statement implicit in this. By contrast, in a later work, we find a certain reversal of this value hierarchy, which seems to view the marital relationship as a more important goal than fertility. Jacob b. Asher (§12) states that the dictum "It is not good that man should be alone" provides the primary reason for marriage and that the commandment to multiply is second to it.

But is there a connection between these different attitudes and our own understanding of the institution of marriage as a patriarchal or an egalitarian one?

The gap between hierarchal and egalitarian relationships is largely dependent on the ability to view the female marriage partner as a subject, possessing her own individual purpose and meaning. It seems self-evident

that within a framework that views the main purpose of marriage as the production of children, the potential for the perception of women as vehicles
of fertility is greater, and the likelihood of an egalitarian approach is diminished. If the vehicle does not serve the goal, she must be replaced. On the
flip side, the more value an approach places on the marital relationship, the
more likelihood there is that women will be perceived as subjects, a fact that
renders the patriarchal structure superfluous. This correlation, however, is
neither a causal nor a necessary one. One might presume that even if the purpose of marriage were believed to be the relationship between husband and
wife, its basic framework might remain patriarchal.

We can, if so, extricate from the sources a perception that views the
marital relationship as a goal in and of itself, and from there the distance to
a nonpatriarchal perception of the marriage institution is short. But there is
no point in holding early sources up to modern standards of equality; it is in
general preferable to identify within them the exegetical potential for, say, a
move toward an egalitarian understanding of marriage. I find it even more
interesting, however, to examine which exegetical choices are made by contemporary halakhic authorities, who are functioning in a time when world
views have undergone fundamental change. Again, the potential for egalitarian exegesis exists, even if it isn't necessary. But is it taken up? Unfortunately,
I must say that in most cases it is not. The dominant rhetoric, even if it doesn't
claim that the sole purpose of marriage is the fulfillment of the "Be fruitful
and multiply" commandment, is unwilling to give up the hierarchic underpinnings of this approach. According to this view, there is no contradiction
between hierarchical relations and love and intimacy. Not only can love grow
in a patriarchal framework, but there are those who will even claim that *only*
in this kind of framework, where each partner's "role" is clear, can a loving
and lasting relationship exist. This perception is not anomalous in contemporary halakhic writing; it is best summed up by Rabbi Eli'ezer Judah Waldenberg, one of the leading Israeli Orthodox halakhic authorities of the past
generation. After quoting Rabad (§11), Waldenberg says:

> According to this account, the *Prishah,* in *Tur Even ha-Ezer* 62:3, goes
> on to explain that that which we say in the marital blessing regard-

ing the creation of man in God's image, "and he instituted from him an everlasting building," points to Rabad's teaching. And it means that "from him" God created, from his body, so that he would rule over her in nature and this nature would exist forever, and this is "an everlasting building." . . . And thus this idea brings about true domestic peace and constitutes man and woman each in their rightful place, to know their duties in the shared and united home . . . (*Tsits Eli'ezer* 19:25).

Jewish tradition doesn't sanctify the written word. Bold exegetical moves have always been its life breath, and it is these moves that have, to a great extent, enabled its continued relevance in an ever-changing reality. Exegetical choices have always reflected, and continue to reflect, basic moral conceptions. In the overwhelming majority of cases, we are not dealing with bodies of halakhic precedents that are forced on the halakhic decisor and that determine a single decision. The question of which exegetical options halakhic leaders of our day choose is a crucial one, since their choices reflect the value system they have chosen to embrace. This is why I assume that so long as the moral ground that sanctifies the perception by which man "takes a woman," with all its patriarchal ramifications, does not change, we will not see radical changes in the area of marital and divorce law. Without exegetical moves that seek to view the marital relationship as egalitarian and not merely "respectful" of women, the existing state of affairs will continue to be problematic. To this it need only be added that, so long as those who (at least within the frame of Orthodox *halakhah*) are in charge of the exegesis and renewal of *halakhah* continue to be exclusively male, the chance for a change in perception remains extremely small.

It is fitting to ask out loud: Is it possible that the fortification of halakhic authority and its gendered confinement to men is wholly lacking in self-interest? Is it possible that there are those who gain personally from their control of the traditional patriarchal consciousness?

Ronit Irshay

Obligation to Marry, Restricting Polygamy

13. Joseph Karo, *Shulhan Arukh* EH 1:1–4, 8–11, 13; Glosses, Moses Isserles (Rema)

The Mishnah's insistence on a man's duty to procreate when his wife is presumed infertile does not necessarily imply a duty to divorce, given the option of taking another wife. Gershom b. Judah's eleventh-century ban prohibited polygamy in the Ashkenazic communities, as recorded here in Isserles's glosses. Karo's code reflects a similar tendency even in Sephardic communities, although they did not universally endorse the original ban. Hence, a central issue in the first section of Shulhan Arukh *EH is the possible conflict between monogamous companionship and the duty to procreate.*

The Laws of "being fruitful and increasing" and [the obligation] not to remain without a wife

1. Every man is obligated to take a wife, so as to be fruitful and increase. Anyone who does not engage in "being fruitful and increasing"—it is as though he sheds blood, and diminishes the [divine] image, and causes the *shekhinah* to depart from Israel.

Gloss: And anyone who has no wife lives without blessing, without Torah, etc. . . .

2. A Torah scroll may not be sold [for any purpose] save in order either to study Torah or to take a wife.

3. The mitzvah is incumbent upon every person to take a wife when he is eighteen years old; and taking a wife earlier, when one is thirteen, is the mitzvah in its best form. But one should not marry younger than thirteen, for that is like fornication. By no means may he go beyond the age of twenty without a wife. One who is past twenty years and does not wish to take a wife—the court coerces him to take a wife, in order to fulfill the commandment of "be fruitful and increase." However, one who is engaged in [the study of] Torah and involved in it, and is afraid to take a wife lest he will [have to] work for a living and be prevented from [studying] Torah, is permitted to delay.

Gloss: In these times, however, the custom is not to coerce in this matter. Likewise, one who has not fulfilled "being fruitful and increasing" and is about to take a wife incapable of [bearing] children (such as one who is sterile or old [i.e., postmenopausal], or a minor[13] [i.e., prepuberty]) because he desires her or because of her money—even though the law would require [intervention] to prevent him [*limhot*], it is now several generations that the custom is not to scrutinize the matter of mating. Indeed, even if one took a wife and lived with her for ten years [and she did not give birth], the custom has been not to coerce him to divorce her, even though he has not fulfilled "being fruitful and increasing." The same applies to [all] other matters of mating, provided that she is not forbidden to him.

4. But one whose very being craves Torah constantly, like Ben Azzai, and who clings to [the study of Torah] his entire life, and [thus] does not take a wife, he is without sin, provided that his inclination does not overcome him.

8. Even though he has fulfilled "being fruitful and increasing," [a man] may not remain without a wife. If he has the means, he should take a wife capable of [bearing] children, even if he already has several children. If he lacks the means to take a wife capable of [bearing] children without selling a Torah scroll, then if he has no children he should sell [it]. . . . But if he has children, he should not sell [it], but rather should take a wife incapable of [bearing] children. But [he should] not remain without a wife. Some, however, say that even if he has children, he should sell a Torah scroll in order to take a wife capable of [bearing] children.

Gloss: However, if he knows that he is no longer capable of [producing] children, i.e., he can no longer sire, he should take a wife incapable of [bearing] children. Likewise, if he has numerous children and is afraid that if he takes a wife capable of [bearing] children, discord and fighting will ensue between the children and his wife, he may take a wife incapable of [bearing] children. He is not permitted, however, to remain without a wife on account of this concern.

13. See ¢19, §4.

9. A man may take several wives, if he is able to provide for them. Nevertheless, the Rabbis proffered good advice, that a man should not take more than four wives, so that each receive consort [*onah*] once a month.[14] Yet in a location where the custom is to take one wife only, he may not take an additional wife.

10. Rabbenu Gershom instituted a *herem* against taking an additional wife, but did not apply this to a levirate. . . .

Gloss: . . . The same applies to any case where [Gershom's ban] would set aside an obligation [*mitzvah*], for example, in the case of one who has lived with his wife for ten years and she did not give birth. Some, however, disagree, holding that Rabbenu Gershom's ban applies even in the face of an obligation, including even levirate marriage. . . . In case the first [wife] cannot be divorced, as for example if she has become incompetent, or where the law mandates that she be divorced yet she refuses to accept a *get* from him, it is right to be lenient and permit him to take another wife. . . .

But [Gershom's] *takkanah*[15] did not take hold in all lands.

Gloss: Excepted are only locations regarding which it is known [definitely] that the *takkanah* did not take hold. Generally, it applies everywhere. . . .

[Gershom] set his ban only to the end of the fifth millennium [=1240 C.E.].

Gloss: Nevertheless, in all these lands the *takkanah* and custom are in force. It is not permitted to take two wives, and one who transgresses and takes two wives is compelled by means of *herem* and ban to divorce one of them. Some say that in these times coercion should not be used against one who transgresses against Rabbenu Gershom's *herem,* since the fifth millennium is past; but that is not the custom. . . .

11. It is good to establish a *takkanah,* by means of *herem* and ban, against anyone taking an additional wife.

13. A woman is not commanded with regard to "being fruitful and increasing."

---

14. Assuming the scholar's norm of conjugal relations once a week (see §18 below).
15. For the terminology and mechanism of such legislation, see ¢23, especially §16.

Gloss: Some however say that, to prevent suspicion, she ought not remain without a husband.

Gershom's Ban on Polygamy, and Its Purpose
14. *Otsar ha-Poskim* EH 1:61

*Halakhic literature uniformly attributes to Gershom b. Judah a dual ban (*herem*), forbidding both polygamy and unilateral divorce. There is, however, no extant text or traditional account of either the ban's original wording or the reasons for its institution. We reproduce here versions of these two as presented in the influential twentieth-century compendium* Otsar ha-Poskim. *One of the reasons cited ties this ban with Gershom's complementary* takkanah: *prohibiting a husband from divorcing his wife without her consent.*

a. The Ban's Wording

[The ban is cited in several early sources, including the following from Meir b. Baruch of Rothenburg (*Responsa* [Prague] 1022)]: [Regarding] the ban [*herem*] enacted by the communities, as established by Rabbenu Gershom, the Light of the Diaspora, to the effect that it is forbidden to take two wives, [an exemption] cannot be allowed other than by one hundred men from three [different communities], from three different lands. Furthermore, these [hundred] must not grant permission unless they find a clear-cut reason to do so; and [the first wife's] *ketubah* money must be set aside in trust, in [the form of] cash or in pawned objects.

b. The Ban's Reason

Various reasons have been postulated with regard to the ban. Some say that it was instituted in order to restrain wanton and unscrupulous [husbands] who mistreat their wives without justification [—as argued in a responsum attributed to Solomon b. Abraham Adret (Rashba) by Rabbi Joseph Colon (*Responsa,* #101), excluding from the ban a man whose wife had become insane]. Rabbi Nissim [Gerondi], in his responsum #48, discusses whether the ban was instituted solely for the benefit of women, or perhaps also for the sake of men, so that they not bring strife into their homes. . . .

Rabbi Meir of Padua [Maharim] (in section 14) wrote that the concern [of those who established the ban] was to protect the daughters of Israel, we being in exile, lest a man who takes many wives and produces many children will not be able to provide for them. Even Rava—whom the *halakhah* follows—who taught that a man may take several wives, added [the proviso] that this is only if he is capable of providing for them (BT Yevamot 65a). This was the concern of our predecessors [who established the ban], we being in exile, insecure and virtually destitute, since all our possessions are potentially fleeting. . . .

Another reason cited by Maharim is in order to avert harassment. Since [Gershom] decreed that a man cannot divorce his wife against her will, he feared that if [the husband] is permitted to take an additional wife, he will harass [the first wife] until she is forced to accept a *get*—and for that reason he decreed that a man cannot take an additional wife. . . . [Another reason cited in the name of Maharim] is based on the talmudic statement (BT Bava Batra 60b) that [in the wake of the destruction of the Temple] "it would have been appropriate for us to decree upon ourselves not to marry [at all] . . . but leave Israel alone; [it is] better that they act inadvertently than that they [sin] knowingly." Therefore Rabbenu Gershom forbade taking a second wife, since most people can make do with one wife.

Marital Relations: Obligations and Entitlements

Financial Entitlements and the Husband's Obligations
15. Mishnah Ketubot 4:4; BT Ketubot 47b–48a

The core financial components of the marital relationship are conceived as a set of entitlements and obligations falling upon the husband. In the mishnah here, these are defined by a comparison to the father's entitlements vis-à-vis his daughter. The verb "established" (tiknu—akin to takkanah) in the first part of the sugya clearly indicates that these are Rabbinic ordinances. Further on, however, some of the husband's obligations are de-

rived from the biblical law regarding the rights of a servant girl who has become a wife:
"He must not withhold her food [she'er], her clothing [kesut], and her conjugal rights
[onah]" (Exod. 21:10); thus intimate obligations are introduced into the discussion.

Mishnah Ketubot 4:4

A father is entitled, with regard to his daughter, to [give] her [away through] consecration by money, by writ, or by intercourse; he is entitled to whatever she finds, and to whatever she produces, and to annul her vows; and he receives her *get,* but is not entitled to usufruct [of her property][16] while she is alive. Once she is married, the husband—beyond [the above]—is entitled to the usufruct [of her dowry-property] while she is alive; and is obligated [to provide] for her sustenance, her redemption [from captivity], and her burial. Rabbi Yehudah says: Even the poorest Israelite must provide no less than two flutes and a lamenting woman.

BT Ketubot 47b–48a

Our Rabbis taught: [The obligation of] providing for a wife's sustenance was established in exchange for what she produces, and [for] burial in exchange for her *ketubah;*[17] therefore the husband is entitled to the usufruct.

"The usufruct"—whoever mentioned that? [Rather] the [received] text is incomplete, and should read thus: [The obligation of] providing for a wife's sustenance was established in exchange for what she produces, and [for] her redemption in exchange for the usufruct, and [for] her burial in exchange for her *ketubah;* therefore the husband is entitled to the usufruct. What is the meaning of "therefore"? You might argue that instead of taking the usufruct, he should set it aside, for otherwise he might fail to redeem her. [Against this the text] teaches us that it is better this way, for [what would be set aside] might not suffice, so [instead] he [is committed] to redeem her

16. E.g., an inheritance from her maternal grandfather.
17. When the husband outlives his wife, he inherits the property that was recorded as her dowry in the *ketubah,* which would revert to the wife on divorce or on his death.

using his own funds. And why not change the pairings? Said Abaye: The common was paired with the common, and the uncommon with the uncommon. [*Rashi:* A wife taken captive and a wife who brings in property as dowry are uncommon.]

Said Rava: The following *tanna* holds that [providing] for sustenance is required by the Torah [*de'orayta*], for it was taught: "Her flesh" [*she'er*] (Exod. 21:10)—that is sustenance, as Scripture states, "You have devoured My people's flesh" (Mic. 3:3); "her clothing" [*kesut*]—the meaning is plain; "and her needs" [*onah*]—that is the [sexual] cohabitation required by the Torah, as Scripture states, "If you treat my daughters harshly" (Gen. 31:50). Rabbi Elazar says: "Her flesh"—that is [sexual] cohabitation, as Scripture states, "None of you shall come near anyone of his own flesh to uncover nakedness" (Lev. 18:6); "her clothing"—the meaning is plain; "and her needs"—that is sustenance, as Scripture states, "He treated you harshly and caused you hunger" (Deut. 8:3). . . .

Rav Yosef taught: "Her flesh"—that is bodily contact, [teaching] that he may not treat her like the Persians, who keep their clothes on during intercourse. This supports Rav Huna, for Rav Huna said: A [husband] who declares: "I will not [have intercourse] unless we are both clothed" must divorce her and pay her *ketubah*.

Wife's Household Obligations
16. Mishnah Ketubot 5:5; BT Ketubot 61a

This mishnah specifies the full range of a wife's required service in the home. Included in the list, yet clearly distinct from its other items, is her obligation to spin wool—in antiquity, the most common form of the husband's entitlement to "whatever she produces," mentioned above. Significantly, the Talmud distinguishes the listed items from another class of services, those of an intimate nature.

Mishnah Ketubot 5:5

A wife performs the following labors for her husband: She grinds, bakes, launders, cooks, breastfeeds her child, makes up [her husband's] bed, and works the wool. If she brought along one slave woman, she need not grind, bake, or launder. If two, she need not cook or breastfeed her child. If three, she need not make up his bed or work the wool. If four, she sits in an easy chair. Rabbi Eli'ezer says: Even if she brought along a hundred slave women, he compels her to work the wool, since idleness leads to debauchery. Rabban Shimon b. Gamaliel says: Indeed, if a man makes a vow barring his wife from performing labor, he must divorce her and pay her *ketubah,* since idleness leads to ennui.

BT Ketubot 61a

Said Rav Hama (some say, Rav Shmu'el b. Nahmani): "brought along" should not be read literally; rather, [she is exempt] if she might bring along [slave women]. [*Rashi:* In case she brought a large dowry, such as it is appropriate to spend some of it to buy slave women to serve her. *Nahmanides:* The meaning is that the standard for women of her family is to bring along four slave women so that they need perform no labor.] It was taught: [She is exempt] whether she brought them along or saved from her own [allotment].

"If four, she sits in an easy chair." Said Rav Yitzhak b. Hanania, citing Rav Huna: Even though it was stated [that] "she sits in an easy chair," she still pours his cup, makes up his bed, and washes his face, hands, and feet. [*Rashi:*[18] The exemption above refers to making up the mattress and pillows, which is a burden, whereas the reference here is to spreading sheets and bedcoverings, which are acts of intimacy and are not burdensome.]

18. This comment of Rashi is cited in Tosafot Ketubot 4b, s.v. *ve-hatsa'at.*

Wife's Waiver of Sustenance
17. BT Ketubot 58b

In a bold reversal of the received teaching, the talmudic doctrine here—attributed to Rav, the great first-generation Babylonian amora—grants a wife the right to waive at least part of the arrangement described above.

Said Rav Huna, citing Rav: A woman may declare to her husband: "I will not receive sustenance, and will not produce [anything for you]." He holds that in the arrangement established by the Rabbis, the basic [component] is sustenance, whereas [the husband's entitlement to] what she produces is on account of [preventing] enmity. Thus if she declares, "I will not receive sustenance, and will not produce anything"—that is within her power.

Against this, [the following *baraita*] was cited: "Providing for a wife's sustenance was established in exchange for what she produces." Let me read instead, "[A husband's entitlement to] what his wife produces was established in exchange for [his providing for] her sustenance."

Required Cohabitation
18. Mishnah Ketubot 5:6

In Rabbinic times, vows were often employed not merely to reinforce personal commitments but as tools in interpersonal struggles. Thus a husband might make a vow prohibiting himself from enjoying intercourse with his wife; a similar move by a wife would be foiled by the husband's power to annul her vows (see §15 above). If the prohibition extends beyond a certain duration, it is cause for requesting divorce, as it violates the basic requirement of sexual cohabitation.

If a man introduces a vow barring his wife from intercourse [with him], the School of Shammai says: [She waits] two weeks; the School of Hillel says:

One week. Students may take leave in order to study Torah without [their wives'] permission [up to] thirty days; laborers, [up to] one week. The sexual cohabitation required by the Torah [is as follows]: men of leisure—every day; laborers—twice a week; ass-drivers—once a week; camel-drivers—once in thirty days; sailors—once in six months. Thus said Rabbi Elazar.

Service Owed by a Wife: Debating Modes of Compulsion

19. Maimonides, MT Laws Concerning Marriage 21:10; Gloss, Abraham b. David of Posquieres (Rabad)

There is no recognition here of the wife's right to opt out of the standard mutual obligations. Possibly, Maimonides holds that the option does not extend to her basic household duties. His endorsement of coercion does not make it entirely clear whether the husband himself may wield the rod or whether he must turn to the authorities for such enforcement. Rabad strongly disavows any notion of compulsion by physical punishment but shares the view that a wife can be made to submit.

A wife who refuses to perform any kind of work that she is obligated to do may be compelled to perform it, even by scourging her with a rod. If the husband claims that she is not doing the work, while she claims that she has not refused to work, another woman or some neighbors should be asked to stay with them. This matter should be handled according to what the judge may consider feasible.

  Gloss: I have never heard of disciplining women with a rod. Rather, [the husband] diminishes [his provision for] her needs and sustenance, until she submits.

Confirming a Wife's Property Rights

20. Solomon b. Abraham Adret (Rashba), *Responsa Attributed to Nahmanides 64*

Talmudic law assumes a society where the main property holders are men; marital law and the ketubah *stipulations reflect this assumption, while leaving room for exceptions and for private or familial arrangements. Similarly, the rule "Whatever a wife acquires is [straightaway] acquired by her husband" is already the subject of various qualifications in the Talmud. The gender gap in property rights was reduced somewhat further in medieval times, as indicated in Adret's responsum. The enhanced economic standing of wives was probably connected to the rise of an urban economy (for the Jews) based on money and commerce, where business was commonly conducted from the home by the husband and/ or the wife, with capital coming from both families of origin. The attempt in this case to deny the wife's rights is made by a son, heir to the estate of the deceased husband.*

Question: Reuven fell ill; his son Hanokh took him into his house and provided for his care. He died, and [Hanokh] buried him, making [provision] for all that is needed for the burial. Leah, Reuven's wife, had left items of value with Hanokh in safekeeping, and now demands from him the return of those items. Hanokh responded: "I had expenditures for [the care of] my father, and for the burial and shrouds; I am seizing these [items] on account of those expenditures." Leah argued: "Those items were my own [property], and you have no [right] to seize my property." Hanokh responded: "I do not know [for a fact] that they were your own. [Moreover], even if it were your own [property], 'Whatever a wife acquires is [straightaway] acquired by her husband.'" On whose side is the law?

Answer: The law is on Leah's side, for several reasons. With regard to her assertion that the items were hers, she is to be trusted, and he must return [them to her]; indeed [this would be the case] even if the husband were still alive, as taught, "If one received [an item in safekeeping] from the wife, one should return it to the wife" (BT Bava Batra 51b). Now this Hanokh does not know that [the items] are not hers, [in which case] he might seize them.

Rather, he argued that "I do not know [for a fact] that they were your own." With regard to his argument that 'Whatever a wife acquires is [straightaway] acquired by her husband'—that is nothing. For perhaps they were given to her [with the] stipulation that her husband shall have no right in them. That [possibility] is the basis for the aforementioned statement, "If one received [an item] from the wife, he should return it to the wife."

Besides, whatever a wife acquires is acquired by her husband only with respect to usufruct; it has the same status as her dowry-property, and if he dies, it becomes hers completely. Moreover, any items taken by Hanokh [from the estate] and used for his expenditures [in providing] for his father, even in providing for his burial, may be recovered by [the widow, if needed to secure her *ketubah* payment], provided that Reuven stipulated [in the *ketubah* contract that it can be collected] from movable as well as immovable [property].

Marital Breakdown: "Defiance" and Divorce

The Defiant Spouse

21. Mishnah Ketubot 5:7

The exact nature of spousal "defiance" in this mishnah is somewhat ambiguous, leaving ample room for talmudic debates (see §22 below), but the confrontation here has clearly moved beyond an isolated grievance. The asymmetrical structure of the marital relationship—the husband's power to grant or execute a divorce, and the wife's entitlement, after being divorced, to receive her ketubah *settlement—is reflected in the divergent mechanisms for financial sanctions. Still, it is striking that each partner can be deemed "defiant."*

If a woman defies[19] her husband, her *ketubah* is reduced by seven dinars a week. Rabbi Yehudah says: seven half-dinars. What is the maximal [total]

---

19. The Hebrew *mored/moredet* is often rendered "rebel," a word we used for *mamre* and *moré* (the rebellious elder and the wayward and rebellious son; see ¢¢7, 19).

reduction? The full sum of her *ketubah*. Rabbi Yose says: The reduction continues indefinitely, for perhaps she will receive an independent inheritance, and collection can be made from that. Likewise if a man defies his wife, her *ketubah* is increased by three dinars a week. Rabbi Yehudah says: three half-dinars.

Defiance: Definition and Sanctions
22. BT Ketubot 63a–64a

"Defies her husband"—with regard to what? Rav Huna said: With regard to intercourse. Rabbi Yose b. Haninah said: With regard to work.

The mishnah reads: "Likewise if a man defies his wife." On the view that [the defiance] is with regard to intercourse, this makes perfect sense; but on the view that it is with regard to work, is he bound to her? Indeed he is, in case he states, "I will give [her] neither food nor provision!" But note Rav's ruling, "[A husband] who states 'I will give [her] neither food nor provision' must divorce her and pay her *ketubah*." Still, is it not requisite to first consult with him?

Against [Rabbi Yose b. Haninah, the following *baraita*] was cited: "[The rule concerning defiance] applies . . . even if she is ill. . . ." On the view that [the defiance] is with regard to intercourse, this makes sense; but on the view that it is with regard to work, is an ill woman capable of work? Rather, with regard to intercourse all agree that she is considered "defiant." The dispute is only with regard to work: one master holds that she is not considered "defiant" on [account of refusing to] work, whereas the other master holds that on [this account] too she is considered "defiant."

[Returning] to the body [of the *baraita*], "If a woman defies her husband, her *ketubah* is reduced by seven dinars a week. . . . Our Rabbis subsequently voted that [instead of such an incremental reduction (Rashi)], a public announcement be made about her on four consecutive Shabbat days; and the court sends her a message: 'Be informed that, even if your *ketubah* is 100 *manè*, you will lose it.'"

. . . Said Rami b. Hama: The announcement is made only in syna-gogues and study-halls. Said Rava: This is indeed implied by the specific ref-erence to Shabbat days. Said Rami b. Hama: The court sends her its message twice, once prior to the announcement and once after it.

Rav Nahman b. Hisda expounded: The law follows the [teaching] of "Our Rabbis." Said Rava: That is unfounded. . . .

Rava, citing Rav Sheshet, said: The law is that she must be con-sulted. Rav Huna b. Yehudah said, citing Rav Sheshet: The law is that she need not be consulted.

What constitutes defiance? Said Amemar, it is in case she says, "I want him but will cause him suffering." But in case she says, "He is repellent to me," no compulsion is to be applied.[20] Mar Zutra [however] said: Coer-cion is applied. [Such] a case arose and Mar Zutra applied coercion, and [from that marriage] issued Rav Haninah of Sura. That, however, was a unique case, helped by divine providence.

Rav Zevid's daughter-in-law defied [her husband]; she had in her possession a silk garment. Amemar, Rav Ashi, and Mar Zutra sat to discuss this, and Rav Gamda was also present. Once seated, they pronounced: "A [wife] who defies [her husband] forfeits any items of clothing." Rav Gamda said to them: Is it because Rav Zevid is a great man that you favor him? For note, Rav Kahana said: Rava raised [this issue] as a problem and left it unre-solved.

Some say: Once seated, they pronounced: "A [wife] who defies [her husband] does not forfeit any items of clothing." Rav Gamda said to them: Just because Rav Zevid is a great man, you invert the law against him? For note, Rav Kahana said: Rava raised [this issue] as a problem and left it unre-solved. . . .

Delivery of the *get* is delayed for twelve months, and during that period she is not entitled to sustenance from her husband. . . .

Rav Hiya b. Yosef asked Shmu'el: What is the [reason for] the dif-

20. Our use of the passive here reflects the disagreement among medieval commentators re-garding the type and purpose of the compulsion under discussion and whether it is to be di-rected at the wife or at the husband ("at the husband" is a minority view, adopting a version with an additional letter *yud: leyh* rather than *lah*).

ference [in the incremental fine] between a "defiant" husband and wife? He answered: [One can] learn [the reason] by observing the prostitutes' district— who hires whom? Another explanation: The male's desire is external, whereas the female's desire is internal [*Rashi:* His erection is visible and he is shamed].

When Is Divorcing a Wife Legitimate?
23. Mishnah Gtitin 9:10; BT Gittin 90a–b

Tractate Gittin (plural of get) is dedicated to the laws governing the instrument of divorce and assumes throughout the husband's unilateral power to write and deliver a get. The tractate's concluding clause and sugya *give voice to a denunciation of divorce on moral/ religious grounds, citing the prophet Malachi's call (§3 above) for fidelity to one's "covenantal spouse." Still, the defining scriptural source is the basic passage from Deuteronomy (§2 above); most of the positions here are derived from that text—all from the husband's point of view. The grounds for divorce mentioned there (ervat davar— "something obnoxious") are rendered restrictively by the house of Shammai; the very same words, as rendered by the house of Hillel, provide a far more liberal teaching.*

Mishnah Gittin 9:10

The School of Shammai says: A man should not divorce his wife unless he has found in her [behavior] a deed constituting indecency, as written, "because he has found in her a deed of indecency [*ervat davar*]" (Deut. 24:1). But the School of Hillel says: Even if she [merely] burned his meal, as written, "because he has found anything disagreeable [=*ervat davar*] in her" (Deut. 24:1). Rabbi Akiva [however] says: Even if he has found another more appealing [woman], as written, "it happens that she finds no favor in his eyes" (Deut. 24:1).

BT Gittin 90a–b

Rav Papa asked Rava: If he found in her nothing indecent or dis-agreeable, what is [the law? [*Rashi:* In case he illicitly divorced her, do we compel him to take her back?] He replied: . . . What is done, is done.

Rav Mesharshiya asked Rava: What of [a husband] who intends to divorce [his wife], while she resides in his domain and sleeps with him?[21] He [responded by] citing the verse, "Do not devise harm against your fellow, Who lives trustfully with you" (Prov. 3:29).

It was taught: Rabbi Meir used to say: Just as there are different dis-positions regarding food, so it is regarding women. There is the kind of person who, if a fly falls into his cup, discards it—he will not drink it. Such was the practice of Pafos b. Yehudah, who would lock his wife up and go out. [Then] there is the kind of person who, if a fly falls into his cup, discards [the fly] and drinks. Such is the common practice among people, whereby a woman con-verses with her brothers, her neighbors, and her relatives, and [the husband] accepts this. [Finally], there is the kind of person who, if a fly falls into his dish, relishes and devours it. Such is the practice of an evil man, who sees his wife going forth with her hair uncovered, spinning [her yarn] in public, with both sides [of her garment] unfastened, and bathing with others[22] [—and does nothing]. One is commanded by the Torah to divorce such a woman, as writ-ten, "because he has found in her a deed of indecency" (Deut. 24:1).

"And [he] sends her away from his house; she leaves his household and becomes the wife of another man" (Deut. 24:1–2)—scripture calls him an "other," implying that he is unlike the first [husband]: That one expelled an evil woman from his home, whereas this one brought an evil woman into his home. If the second husband [accrues] merits, he divorces her, as writ-ten, "then this latter man rejects her"; if not, she buries him, as written, "or the man who married her last dies" (Deut. 24:3)—he is deserving of death, since [in contrast to the first husband, who] expelled an evil woman from his home, this one brought an evil woman in to his home. . . .

---

21. Lit., "resides under him and serves him."
22. The *sugya* interpolates: "Bathing with others—is that conceivable? Rather [read]: bathing in the same place as others" (i.e., where men bathe).

"For hated is divorce" (Mal. 2:16): Rabbi Yehudah says, If you hate her, divorce; whereas Rabbi Yohanan says, He who divorces is hateful. They do not disagree: One [statement] refers to a first marriage, whereas the other [statement] refers to a second marriage. For Rabbi Elazar said: Any man who divorces his first wife—even the altar sheds tears over him, as written, "And this you do as well: You cover the altar of the Lord with tears, weeping and moaning, so that He refuses to regard the oblation any more and to accept what you offer. But if you ask, 'Because of what?' Because the Lord is a witness between you and the wife of your youth with whom you have broken faith, though she is your partner and covenanted spouse" (Mal. 2:13–14).

A Woman Might Set Her Eyes upon Another
24. Mishnah Nedarim 11:12

Although divorce is in the hands of the husband, this source clearly assumes that there are circumstances where he is required to divorce his wife and, moreover, to pay the ketubah. But to generate such a legal requirement, the severe circumstances must be established by evidence; unilateral dissolution, by contrast, is a power reserved for the husband alone, as we saw in the previous selection. This mishnah denies the wife any similar option, recording—but then revoking—an early halakhic teaching, in which divorce accompanied with the ketubah payment was mandated upon the wife's affirmation that the marriage is untenable.

At first, the teaching was: Three women exit [their marriage] and collect their *ketubah*. She who declares, "I am defiled for you"[23] . . ."; [she who declares], "Let heaven be [a witness] between me and you"[24]; [and she who vows,] "I am hereby barred from all Jewish men."[25] Later, it was argued that

23. Implying adultery or perhaps rape.
24. Evidently, this means that she is asserting his impotency.
25. In making such a vow, she indicates that for her, sexual intercourse as such is disagreeable—perhaps painful.

a woman might set her eyes upon another and repudiate her husband. So instead, she who declares, "I am defiled for you . . ." must produce evidence for her claim. [She who declares], "Let heaven be [a witness] between me and you"—the [couple] should be given counseling. [And she who vows,] "I am hereby barred from all Jewish men"—he annuls [the vow] as it applies to him, and then, let her sleep with him[26] and [beyond that] be barred from all Jewish men.

Grounds for Demanding Divorce
25. Mishnah Ketubot 7:4–7, 9–10

A person cannot impose a vow upon another; yet a husband could in effect bar his wife from particular things, for example, by a conditional vow to forego intercourse should his wife perform some specified act. Such encroachments upon a wife's freedom can be causes for requiring divorce.[27] We reproduce here some of the instances listed in the Mishnah, along with other grounds for demanding divorce. A husband can unilaterally divorce his wife, but she forfeits the ketubah only if he has justified cause; when the wife has justified cause, the husband must divorce her and pay the ketubah. As we shall see below, medieval commentators debate whether the contrast between the language of the final clauses here ("is compelled to divorce") and that of the earlier clauses ("he [must] divorce her") signifies a difference in the measures that can be used against a recalcitrant husband.

[4] If a man makes a vow barring his wife from going to her parents' house — if the parents reside with her in the [same] town, [then] for the first month, he may keep her [as his wife]; in the second, he [must] divorce her and pay the *ketubah*. If the parents reside in another town, [then up to] the first festival, he may keep her; at the second, he must divorce her and pay the *ketubah*.

    [5] If a man makes a vow barring his wife from going to the house

---

26. Lit., "serve him."
27. For a vow directly prohibiting intercourse, see §18 above.

of mourning or to the house of [wedding] celebration, he must divorce her and pay the *ketubah,* since he [thereby] isolates her. If, however, he bases [the prohibition] on some specific grounds, he may [bar her]. If he demands of her: "You must tell X what you said to me," or "what I said to you," or "You must fill and spill out to waste"[28] — he must divorce her and pay the *ketubah.*

[6] The following are divorced, forfeiting the *ketubah:* She who transgresses the rule of Moses, or that of Jewish women. What constitutes [a transgression of] the rule of Moses? If she feeds him non-tithed [produce], or sleeps with him while she is *niddah,* or fails to set aside the *hallah* [from her dough], or makes vows and fails to observe [them]. What constitutes [a transgression of] the rule of Jewish women? If she goes out with her head uncovered, or spins [her yarn] in public, or converses with all [manner of] men. Aba Shaul says: Also she who curses his parents in his presence. Rabbi Tarfon says: Also she who is loud; that is, who speaks within her house and her voice is heard by her neighbors.[29]

[7] If one consecrates a woman on condition that she is not bound by any vows, and she is found to be bound by vows, she is not consecrated. If he consecrated her without stipulating, and she is found to be bound by vows, she may be divorced, forfeiting the *ketubah.* If one consecrates a woman on condition that she has no deformities, and she is found to have deformities, she is not consecrated. If he consecrated her without stipulating, and she is found to have deformities, she may be divorced, forfeiting the *ketubah.* All the deformities that disqualify priests, disqualify women.[30]

[9] A man in whom deformities appeared is not compelled to divorce [his wife]. Said Rabban Shimon b. Gamaliel: That apples only with regard to minor deformities; with regard to major deformities, however, he is compelled to divorce [his wife].

[10] [Any of] the following is compelled to divorce [his wife]: A leper, one who has polyps, a collector of dog droppings, a coppersmith, and

---

28. This can be interpreted as describing demeaning make-work; more likely, it refers to sexual behavior.

29. The Talmud suggests that speech here is a euphemism for intimacy.

30. A priest with a deformity is disqualified for temple service (Lev. 21:18–23); the deformities are specified in Mishnah Bekhorot 6–7.

a tanner. [This applies] whether these conditions obtained prior to the marriage or emerged subsequent to the marriage. Indeed, with regard to them all, Rabbi Meir said: Even if he stipulated with her, she can say: "I thought I could tolerate it, but now I cannot tolerate it." But the [other] sages say: With regard to them all, she must tolerate it without recourse, except for a leper, since [intercourse] causes deterioration. There was a case in Sidon, when a certain tanner died, and he had a brother who was [also] a tanner.[31] The sages said: She can tell him, "I was able to tolerate your brother, but cannot tolerate you."

The Medieval Debate: Freedom Versus Subjection

When Can a Wife Demand Divorce?
26. *Otsar ha-Geonim* Ketubot 190–91

With regard to a wife who unequivocally seeks to be released from her marriage, the upshot of the talmudic discussions (§§21–25 above) is unclear: Can her husband be compelled to divorce her, whether immediately or after twelve months? Is such compulsion restricted to the causes explicitly specified as grounds for enforcing a get, *and/or to her willingness to forfeit her* ketubah *payment? Among the Geonim, the prevalent position seems to have endorsed compulsion where the marriage was determined to be untenable. Moreover, gaonic* halakhah *here went expressly beyond talmudic law, establishing in effect a wife's right to divorce, as in the surrounding Islamic society.*

Rav Paltoy Gaon wrote: If [a couple] repeatedly quarrel, then if she is the instigator, she is deemed a defiant wife and is entitled to nothing. If he is the instigator, she is entitled to her full *ketubah* payment. If the instigators are members of the household, such as her mother-in-law or sister-in-law, he is required by law to relocate [his wife], since "No one lives in close quar-

---

31. Under the law of levirate marriage, if a man dies childless, his widow is bound to marry his brother unless he releases her through the *halitsah* ceremony (cf. Deut. 25:5–10 and ¢2, §1).

ters with a snake." If he fails to relocate her, he [must] divorce her and pay the *ketubah.*

> *Rav Sherira Gaon:*
>
> Regarding your question, "A woman living with [lit., "under"] her husband, who said to him: 'Divorce me, I do not want to live with you!'— Is he required to pay her any of her *ketubah,* or not? Is a woman such as this deemed a defiant wife, or not?" We conclude as follows. Initially, the law was that the husband was not required to divorce his wife when she requests a divorce, except for those cases of which the sages decreed that he is compelled to divorce her. A wife who refrains from intercourse and from the labors which she is obligated to perform for him—that is the defiant wife [here Sherira cites the mishnaic law and the several subsequent rulings as recorded in the Talmud regarding the sanctions imposed upon her, and then emphasizes:] Despite all this, they would not compel the husband to write her a *get;* [. . . rather], they ordered that she be made to wait twelve months with no divorce granted, in the hope that she will acquiesce. Once twelve months are up, the husband is compelled to write her a *get.*
>
> Later, after the time of the *savora'im,* [the rabbis] saw that Jewish women go and avail themselves of non-Jewish [courts], forcibly obtaining writs of divorce from their husbands, with the Jews writing the *get* under duress, [each of them] possibly constituting an "illicitly enforced *get,*" with disastrous results. A decree was therefore promulgated in the days of Mar Rav Raba and Mar Rav Hunay, as follows. A woman who defies [her husband] and demands divorce, [receives all the assets that she brought into the household, but nothing extra that he committed to pay her]. The husband is compelled immediately to write her a *get,* and she is entitled to her basic *ketubah* payment. This has been our practice now for more than three hundred years; you too should do the same.

She Is Not Like a Captive

27. Maimonides, MT Laws Concerning Marriage 14:8

Maimonides did not regard himself as necessarily bound by gaonic halakhah but often does follow the Geonim's teachings and enactments even when these depart from talmudic law. That is the case here; moreover, he adds a principled assertion of a married woman's right to personal freedom.

If a woman states: "He is repellent to me and I cannot consent to have intercourse with him," he is immediately compelled to divorce her, since she is not like a captive who must have intercourse with someone she hates.

Can the Husband Be Compelled?

28. Tosafot Ketubot 70a, s.v. *yotsi*

The recurring mishnaic phrase, "He [must] divorce her and pay the ketubah" (§25 above) is plainly meant as a legal norm, implying that in these cases the court will compel the husband to grant his wife a get—even though compulsion is mentioned explicitly in only two clauses. Isaac b. Samuel of Dampierre (Ri) offers ample talmudic support for this straightforward reading; the tosafist here tends to agree, but also cites an alternative ruling by Hananel b. Hushiel and goes on to raise the specter of an invalid or doubtfully valid get, thereby expanding the husband's power.

"He [must] divorce her and pay the *ketubah*": Rabbi Isaac holds that in all these cases where the Mishnah rules that "he must divorce her," he is to be compelled. . . . [This can be] further [proven] from the talmudic discussion below (BT Ketubot 77a): "Rav said, If a husband states, 'I will provide no food or sustenance,' he [must] divorce her and pay the *ketubah*." The [*sugya*] goes on to ask: "Instead of compelling him to divorce [her], let them compel him to provide [for her]!" This implies that the phrase "he [must] divorce her" indicates the use of compulsion. . . . Now you might ask, Why were these cases not included in the list of those who are "compelled to divorce" [Mishnah Ketubot 7:9–10, §25 above]? One can reply that that list only addresses cases like that of a leper or a man with polyps—conditions that come about involuntarily—but not cases like these, where the compulsion results from the husband's misbehavior.

Rabbenu Hananel, however, cited the Jerusalem Talmud to prove that in all these cases of which the Mishnah rules "he [must] divorce her," no compulsion is employed. . . . Hence he rules that compulsion can be used only in those cases of which it is explicitly stated that "he is compelled."

It seems more correct, however, that compulsion should be used in all these cases, as argued by Rabbi Isaac. The Jerusalem Talmud holds that compulsion can mean verbal pressure; whereas we [i.e., the BT tradition] hold according to the maxim that "A slave cannot be disciplined by words" [Prov. 29:19; cited to this effect in BT Ketubot 77a], and hence the instruction is to use the rod. The phrase "he [must] divorce" her implies compulsion, since he is wronging her. Still, this should not be put into practice—compelling a husband to divorce [his wife]—except on the basis of clear evidence. For [the Talmud (BT Gittin 88b, §8 above)] teaches that a *get* forced [even] by Israelites, [if] not in accordance with the law, is invalid, and a married woman should not be declared permitted [to another] where there is uncertainty.

Against Compulsion: Restraining Women
29. Asher b. Yehi'el (Rosh), *Responsa* 43:8

In the preceding selection we saw the hesitation among some of the tosafists to apply compulsion even in cases where the Mishnah rules that the husband must divorce his wife. When it came to interpreting the talmudic teachings about a wife who seeks divorce without specific grounds—simply because she does "not want him"—the dominant view in Ashkenaz was defined by Jacob b. Meir Tam's extremely conservative position. As Asher

explains here, this amounts to a reversal of the gaonic move, as codified in Maimonides'
assertion that a wife is "not like a captive" (§§26–27 above). Supporting the reversal,
Asher insists that it is crucial to keep wives in their place, "sitting under their husbands."

Answer: . . . With regard to compulsion to deliver a *get,* I found that our masters, the sages of Ashkenaz and France, avoid to the utmost extreme any manner of compelling the husband to divorce in the context of a wife's defiance;
for they find Rabbenu Tam's position and proofs to be correct and worthy of
being endorsed. Even if it were an open question [whether to endorse Tam's
position or that of the Geonim and Maimonides], one ought to steer clear of
[causing violation of] a possibly married woman and [thereby] proliferating
mamzerim in Israel.

Admittedly, in the generations following those of the talmudic
sages . . . the [leaders of the] Babylonian academies judged that the needs of
the hour in their days required departing from Torah law and constructing
a fence for prevention. They [therefore] established [*tikkenu*] that a man be
compelled to divorce his wife when she states, "I do not want this man," so
that she not avail herself of a non-Jewish [court, whereby] Israelite women
will fall into bad ways. They relied on the [talmudic dictum] "Every man who
consecrates [a woman] does so under the auspices of the rabbis" (BT Gittin
33a, §32 below), and the [Geonim] reached a consensus to annul the marriage
when a woman defies her husband. But that *takkanah* did not gain acceptance
in all lands. . . .

Moreover, I maintain that the Geonim who established this *takka-*
nah did so in accordance with [the circumstances in] that generation—what
they judged to be the needs of the hour with regard to Israelite women. At
present [however, consideration of] the issue leads to the opposite conclusion. Israelite women in this generation are haughty. If a woman is able to
release herself from under her husband by stating "I do not want him," no
daughter of Abraham will remain in place [lit., "sitting"] under her husband;
they will set their eyes upon others and defy their husbands. It is therefore
best to steer clear of compulsion.

Stranger still is Maimonides' position, that "If a woman states: 'He is repellent to me and I cannot consent to have intercourse with him,' he is immediately compelled to divorce her, since she is not like a captive who must have intercourse with someone she hates." What reason is this to compel the man to divorce and to render a married woman permitted? Let her not have intercourse with him, and be tied up all her life as a living widow. After all, she is not commanded to "be fruitful and increase"! Is it right that, as she follows her willful mind, having set her eyes upon another — preferring him to the husband of her youth — we should fulfill her desire and compel the husband, who loves the wife of his youth, to divorce her? God forbid that any *dayan* rule thus. Rabbi Meir [of Rothenburg] of blessed memory . . . would in general not apply the law of "He is repellent to me" unless she provides some basis for her statement, [explaining] why he is not acceptable to her. . . .

    In the case at hand, however, [the wife's] brother reported to me reasons that she has provided for her defiance. You are the judge in this; investigate the matter, whether there is anything to her claims. If [the husband] plans to leave her stranded [*agunah*], it is appropriate for you to rely upon your present custom, and compel him to deliver a *get* with a [future] date.

Coercing an Abusive Husband

30. Meir b. Baruch of Rothenburg, *Responsa* (Prague) 81

In the preceding selection Rothenburg was cited by Asher b. Yehi'el (his student) as rejecting a wife's right to no-fault divorce, requiring that she provide specific grounds. Here we see a prime example of such grounds. Although physical abuse is not explicitly mentioned in the Mishnah as a ground for compelling divorce, Rothenburg has no qualms in this case, penning the most forceful indictment of wife-beating among medieval Jewish halakhists.

Every member of the covenant is obliged to honor his wife more than his own person. . . ." [Woman] was given [to Man] for living, not for suffering" (BT Ketubot 61a). Let us learn from the text of the *ketubah* [where the bridegroom undertakes]: "I will work, honor, and provide." As for one who beats his wife, the tradition I received is that he should be treated more severely than one who beats his fellow, since he is not obliged to honor his fellow, whereas he is obliged to honor his wife. Such [behavior] is the manner of non-Jews; God forbid that any member of the covenant do this, and anyone who does should be banned, placed under *herem*, and punished by lashing and all manner of disciplining, and even have his hand cut off . . . if he does this regularly [Rothenburg cites some of the main talmudic sources for extralegal punishment; see ¢23]. If she wants to be divorced, he [must] divorce her and pay the *ketubah* [money].

Abuse Does Not Warrant Compulsion
31. David b. Solomon Ben Zimra (Radbaz), *Responsa* 4:157

Meir of Rothenburg's ruling in the preceding selection was attributed in some texts to Simhah of Speyer and serves as a foil for the contrary ruling here. Emphasizing the specter of mamzer offspring, Ben Zimra carries Jacob b. Meir Tam's position to the extreme and rejects compulsion even here—this is perhaps due to his peculiar view of spousal abuse. Nevertheless, he does not envision abandoning the wife to the power of her abusive husband: he is to be punished, severely if need be, though with regard to the get, *he retains unilateral power.*

Question: You asked me to tell you my view of a man who regularly beats his wife, constantly shaming her in public. How shall he be judged?

Answer: A text attributed to Rabbenu Simhah states that [such a husband] is compelled to divorce [his wife]; going far beyond [plausibility] so as to write that he should be compelled by the hand of non-Jews [who will demand,] "Do what the Israelites are telling you!" [cf. §8 above].

But I am perplexed at this ruling: since the *get* is forced, will not her offspring be *mamzerim?* How has her marital status been annulled? With regard to a man with polyps or the like, no such question arises, as the sages have verily assessed the universal mindset of women, [to the effect] that they cannot endure [such a husband], and therefore annulled her marriage through such a *get* [given under compulsion]. Here, however, at one time he beats her, and at another time he makes her happy; at one time he shames her, and at another time he honors her with fine garments. Compulsion by verbal pressure, or by making him pay the *ketubah* [money] or a fine, is acceptable; but as for compulsion with the rod by the hand of non-Jews—that should not be done! . . . Similarly, Rabbi Asher in a responsum wrote that there should be no compulsion with the rod. I therefore conclude that this ruling should not be relied upon. . . . Rather, what should they do? They order him on pain of being banned not to beat her. If he repents, well and good; if not, they pronounce him under a ban. If he then repents, well and good; if not, they fine him by [increasing] the *ketubah*. If he repents, well and good; if not, they subject him to corporal punishment, by the hand of non-Jews, since he has transgressed [the negative commandment], "lest he beat him excessively"[32] (Deut. 25:3), and they incarcerate him, since he has beaten her. [In all this] they make no mention of divorcing his wife. If he then goes ahead and divorces her because of [these] punishments, this does not constitute coercion, since he has by his own choice brought the coercion upon himself. Let him not beat her and not divorce her! But compelling him to divorce [her] by means of a ban or *herem* or corporal punishment—and certainly, by the hand of non-Jews—this I do not consider right and by no means endorse. It seems likely to me that the offspring [of this woman if she remarries, relying on such a *get*] is a *mamzer*.

Contemporary Struggles

Annulment: Consecration Is "Under the Auspices of the Rabbis"
32. Mishnah Gittin 4:1–2; BT Gittin 33a

As depicted above, halakhic marriage and divorce are conceived primarily as private transactions, albeit with social ramifications. Hence as a rule, any marriage properly executed

32. The received scriptural source for the prohibition on striking another person.

between the parties is valid, and even when the court holds that a marriage must be dissolved, it must enlist the husband's consent to deliver the get. *Yet there are a few exceptions: in specific circumstances, the Talmud is prepared to assert rabbinic control over marriage and its instruments, annulling the union retroactively. There are several talmudic pronouncements in this vein, each of which responds to an abuse of power by the husband. In our selection here, what is at issue is the husband's power to cancel a signed* get *up to the moment it is delivered.*

Might the application of annulment be extended beyond the specific talmudic precedents? Even those medieval authors who were willing to entertain this in theory were hesitant to follow through in practice—due to "the gravity of the issue" (see the responsum of Isaac b. Sheshet Perfet (Rivash) in ¢8, §12). This legacy is a challenge to efforts to use annulment as a solution to contemporary problems.

Mishnah Gittin 4:1–2

If a man sends a *get* to his wife, and then overtakes the messenger, or sends another messenger to overtake him, and tells him: "The *get* I handed you is hereby canceled!"—it is canceled. . . . Once the *get* has reached [the wife's] hands, he can no longer cancel it. At first, [the husband] would set up a court in another location and cancel [the *get* before its delivery, by means of a proclamation in their presence]. Rabban Gamaliel the elder ordained that this should not be done, on account of *tikkun olam.*

BT Gittin 33a

What is the issue of *tikkun olam* [here]? Rabbi Yohanan says: Redress for [potential] *mamzerim.* Resh Lakish says: Redress for [potential] chained women. Rabbi Yohanan says: Redress for [potential] *mamzerim* . . . as she might not learn of the cancellation and will unknowingly go ahead and get married, producing *mamzerim.* Resh Lakish says: Redress for [potential] chained women. . . . If she learns of the cancellation and thus knows [that she is not divorced] — [it is such a possibility that requires] redress for chained women.

Our rabbis taught: If he nevertheless canceled [a *get* from afar], it is canceled; those are the words of Rabbi [Judah the Prince]. Rabban Shimon b. Gamaliel says: He cannot cancel it . . . for otherwise, what is the effect of the court's authority?

Can it be that according to the Torah's law [*de'orayta*], the *get* is canceled, yet on account of "the effect of the court's authority," a married woman is rendered permitted to anyone?

—Indeed so; for every man who consecrates a woman does so under the auspices of the rabbis, and the rabbis [in such a case] annul the marriage.

Ravina said to Rav Ashi: This is plausible if he effected the consecration by [giving her] money; but if he effected the consecration by intercourse, what can be said?

—The rabbis render his intercourse an act of promiscuity.

Can the Husband Set Conditions for His Own Coercion?

33. Rabbinical Courts' Rulings, 1999–2000

Rulings by the Tel Aviv Regional and the High Rabbinical Courts (unpublished); Hadin Ve-Hadayyan (Ramat Gan: Rackman Center for the Advancement of the Status of Women, Faculty of Law, Bar Ilan University, 2003; Hebrew), 2:13.

In the state of Israel, religious courts have exclusive jurisdiction over marriage and divorce, though regular state courts retain jurisdiction in related matters of child custody and property. Members of Israel's Jewish majority are subject to the rabbinical courts, whose mandate is to rule according to Torah law. Hence, the reluctance of medieval rabbis to effect a get *against the husband's will produces numerous instances of "chained women" today. In the case at hand, most of the* dayanim *(rabbinical judges) acknowledged that there were grounds for coercing the husband to give a* get, *but a crucial block of judges adopted the sixteenth-century ruling of Samuel b. Moses de Modena (Maharshdam) — arguably, a minority view among rabbis — that allows even such a husband to impose "reasonable" conditions for his own compliance. Significantly, the condition imposed by the husband in*

this case was that the wife waive any entitlements accorded her by the (state) family court
and voluntarily subject all disputed matters to the rabbinical courts.

(Rabbinical court decisions are not usually officially published. The Rackman
Center collects the rulings — mainly from the parties' counsel — and publishes them in its
series Hadin Ve-Hadayan *(The law and its decisor: rabbinical court decisions in family*
matters), in either full or digest format. Our selections here follow the original rulings,
provided to us by the Rackman Center, except where we expressly indicate that we are
employing the digest.)

The facts [Hadin Ve-Hadayan 2:13, p. 9]:

At the time this petition was filed before the regional rabbinical
court, the couple had been married for twenty-four years but had been separated for the past eighteen years. The rabbinical court had already ruled that
the husband was required to divorce his wife by giving a *get*. The husband,
however, set conditions for doing so, demanding that all issues of property
and money — including sustenance for the wife and children already collected in the past — be transferred to the jurisdiction of the rabbinical court.
These issues had all been adjudicated in the civil court, which obligated the
husband to pay sustenance for the children, and also ordered dissolution of
the partnership in the jointly owned apartment. During all these years, the
wife collected the sustenance owed her through Social Security, but the husband still owed her considerable sums, in addition to his (resulting) outstanding debt to the Social Security Administration. The wife sought to collect
the husband's debt from his share of the apartment, so that he would end up
with no money from his half of the proceeds of its sale. The wife agreed that
the rabbinical court should adjudicate with regard to the outstanding debt
[to her] but not with regard to the sums she had already received from Social
Security.

Regional Rabbinical Court:

On November 21, 1999, this court ruled that the husband is required
to give his wife a *get* in accordance with the law of Moses and Israel. In fact,
to this day the husband has not divorced his wife.

Before this court now is a petition by counsel for the wife, requesting the court to apply sanctions in accordance with the *halakhah,* as expressed in the [state] law, so as to induce the husband to give the wife a *get.* . . .

In a session on July 4, 2000, the husband affirmed in court that he is willing to give his wife a *get* immediately in accordance to the law of Moses and Israel, but demands that all matters of property, money, sustenance for the wife both past and present, and past sustenance for the children, be transferred through the parties' consent to the authority of the [rabbinical] court, to render a decision about [all that] after the execution of the *get.*

[He] argued that he is not withholding the *get,* since he is prepared to give a *get* according to Torah law, on the condition that after its delivery it shall be the [rabbinical] court that will decide on all matters of property, money, and sustenance, according to Torah law.

Wife's counsel was prepared that the [rabbinical] court should, after the divorce, adjudicate the outstanding debt (presently in process of collection), but did not agree that the [rabbinical] court adjudicate with regard to money already received by the wife through the Social Security Administration.

The court hereby clarifies:

The husband's argument is valid. That is: even though the husband is required to give his wife a *get* (as we previously ruled), he should not be required to give a *get* so long as the wife is withholding money that is not hers in accordance with Torah law. It is the husband's right to demand that the [rabbinical] court adjudicate the matters of property and money. It is [thus] not the husband who is chaining his wife; rather, the wife is the one who is chaining herself by refusing adjudication in accordance with Torah law.

. . . [For] indeed, where both husband and wife want nothing but a divorce, there being no prospects for restoring peace in the home, each one of them should be required to [execute] a *get.* This is based on the following statement of Rabbenu Yeruham, citing his teacher Rabbi Abraham b. Ishmael, who reasoned as follows:

> If a woman says, "I do not want him, let him give me a *get* and the ketubah!"; whereas he says, "I too do not want her!"—yet is not

willing to give a *get*, it stands to reason that she should not be treated as a defiant wife, and [so she] loses nothing from the basic sum of her *ketubah* nor from her dowry. Still, we delay the *get* for twelve months in the hope that they change their minds, and at the year's end coerce him to divorce her, and she loses the additional sums.[33]

The sense of this ruling is that a person has a right not to be chained. This right and claim in itself constitutes grounds for requiring—even coercing—the other party to execute a *get*. . . . The very situation of a person being chained obligates the other party to grant a *get*. . . .

However [the court here cited several sources, including the following] Samuel de Modena (*Responsa* EH 41) wrote as follows:

. . . I reasoned that even [regarding] those of whom the Rabbis in the Mishnah taught "the following are coerced to divorce" etc., this coercion was undoubtedly ordained only in case he is completely unwilling to divorce [her]. If, however, he is willing to divorce [her], but [merely] seeks to impose some condition with respect to this *get*, surely they did not teach that he should be coerced to divorce without the condition. If anyone should employ coercion in such circumstances, I am almost prepared to conclude that he has stumbled into the pitfall of [illicit] coercion. . . . [With regard to] any condition that is easy [for the wife] to fulfill, undoubtedly one who coerces [the husband] to divorce without the condition [thereby] multiplies *mamzerim* etc. Thus it seems clear to me that he should not be coerced.

. . . Now [in the case before us] the sole basis for requiring [the husband to give] a *get* is the wife's right not to be chained. . . . The husband here is prepared to give a *get* immediately, but sets a condition in his demand that the wife accept the authority of the [rabbinic] court. . . . Since [he is willing] yet the wife is not, the [husband] should not be deemed as one who chains his wife; rather, it is she who is chaining herself. . . .

33. That is, she receives only the basic, minimal *ketubah* payment but forfeits any additional commitment undertaken by the husband in the *ketubah* contract.

This court hereby specifies that if, in spite of its ruling, the wife is granted by some other tribunal [extra] sustenance as due to a [wife who is] barred from remarrying by her [husband's obstinacy], this might produce doubts with regard to the [validity of any subsequent] *get*. This court will [then] be unable to facilitate execution of a *get* between these parties.

In light of the forgoing the court rules as follows:

We suspend [our] court's ruling from November 21, 1999. As of today, there is no requirement upon the husband to divorce the wife.

Rabbinical High Court—ruling on wife's appeal:

Chief Rabbi Eliyahu Bakshi Doron [*Hadin Ve-Hadayan* abstract]:

The dispute is about the [forum for further] adjudication regarding the sustenance received by the wife by reason of the [civil] court's ruling. Requiring the repayment of such sustenance, already spent by the wife—even if granted not in accordance with *halakhah*—is not within the authority of the [rabbinical] court. Nor should the requirement that the husband give a *get* be withdrawn, since they will then remain chained all their life, which is the very prospect [whose prevention] was grounds for the original requirement. The requirement should thus be reinstated, and then the accompanying issues should be addressed.

Dayan Avraham Sherman:

. . . Appellant's counsel argued that the regional court erred in holding that the wife's refusal to subject the monetary issues to Torah law [means] that she is chaining herself. He held, moreover, that making the requirement that the husband give a *get* dependent upon the wife's forgoing the rulings rendered by the [civil] court, constitutes an infringement by this lower court of the principle of mutual respect and recognition that should pertain between the civil and rabbinical courts. . . . The appellant objects appropriately, and within her legal rights, [to the proposal] that the rabbinical court should adjudicate all the issues that have already been adjudicated and decided by the [civil courts]. . . .

[As for the ruling by de Modena, the regional court itself cited dissenting rulings by other authorities, including the following by Simeon b. Zemah Duran (*Tashbetz*), *Responsa* part 4, *Hut ha-Meshulash* 1:6, sections a–b]:

Since this man is required by law to divorce her, for the reasons given, he cannot unilaterally impose upon her any condition attached to her divorce. Since the law requires [him] to divorce her, how can he force her [to accept] any condition? The law must bore through the mountain, and let him render a divorce in accordance with the law.

[Yet the regional court wrote:] "His language indicates that this applies only when the husband demands something to which he is not entitled by law. But when his demand is in accordance with the law and the wife refuses, it seems clear that [Duran] would agree that the wife is not to be deemed chained; rather, she is chaining herself." . . .

[Sherman emphatically rejects this reading, asserting that it goes against Duran's plain meaning. He continues:]

Indeed, [even the authors who allow a husband to pose a condition say this only with regard to a condition that can be easily fulfilled.] Thus in the case at hand, can it in any way be said that the condition posited by the husband—namely, that the wife forgo her entitlement to sustenance for herself and for the children, granted by the [civil] court and amounting to hundreds of thousands of shekels—can be fulfilled, [let alone that] she can easily fulfill it? Can the wife take [such] a great risk, that by transferring adjudication to the rabbinical court . . . she might come to owe enormous sums to the husband and to the Social Security Administration? . . . Hence the husband's condition is unacceptable, since the wife is unable to fulfill it. Therefore she should not . . . be deemed as chaining herself. Rather it is the husband who, by setting this condition, is the one who persists in chaining his wife. He must be required to give a *get,* and actions should be taken to compel him to do so.

Often, in cases where the husband chains his wife by withholding a *get* that he is required by law to give her, he argues before the [rabbinical] court that he is prepared to give a *get* on the condition that the wife transfer the children to his custody. The wife, however, refuses to part from her children. Now, even though the case may involve sons who have reached the age of education and of Torah study, and will perhaps not themselves be harmed by the change in custody, the husband's condition must not be accepted. . . .

For since [the wife's] heart is linked to her children, she is compelled by her emotions [to refuse]. The husband cannot justify [his failure to] execute the *get* . . . by her failure to fulfill the condition. He thus remains under the requirement to [give] a *get* and is liable to the imposition of sanctions [whether those provided for in Israeli law or those endorsed by] Rabbenu Tam,[34] so that he shall execute the *get* and release the woman from her state of being chained.

. . . In conclusion, the wife's appeal should be accepted; the husband is required to give his wife a *get* without any condition.

Dayan Zalman Nehemiah Goldberg:

[De Modena's position can be proven wrong from the Tosafot.]

This, however, applies only to cases where the husband seeks to impose a condition requiring [some action or restriction on her part]. But where the husband demands that she return what she has robbed from him, reason seems to indicate that he can withhold the *get* until she pays it back. . . .

Dayan Moshe Tufik:

After seeing the argument by Rabbi Sherman to the effect that the wife should not be deemed as chaining herself, since she is unable to return the money to the husband, it seems right to remand the case to the regional court. The court shall [then] summon the parties and examine the wife's capabilities, [i.e.,] what sums she is capable of returning to him in the eventuality that the court rules in the end that she must return them. . . . Alternatively, [the regional court] shall attempt to bring the parties to a compromise, [namely] that the wife pay the husband a one-time sum as [settlement for] his demands. Although in the past they [both] did not agree to this, they might now conclude that it is in both their interests to reach a resolution. For even if sanctions are imposed upon the husband, the wife cannot be sure that he will quickly give her a *get;* hence a compromise is good for them both.

Conclusion [by majority vote]:

The case is remanded to the regional court for further discussion,

---

34. As noted above (§29), Rabbenu Tam strongly opposed direct coercion of a husband to deliver a *get;* yet he endorsed the use of particular sanctions to put pressure on a recalcitrant husband.

to make a determination as described above or to bring [the parties] to an agreement.

Commentary. The Doomsday Weapon

This case stands as an antecedent to what has become the most alarming development in Israeli rabbinical courts' decision-making: allowing conditions to be set for the granting of a *get* even when it could legitimately be coerced, and then retroactively invalidating such a *get* if the conditions are violated. This is a "doomsday weapon" in more than one sense: when it is used, the battle is categorically over, with an indisputable victory for the husband, who regains control over his wife's freedom. No recourse to civil law is available to the woman, who now finds herself remarried to the husband from whom she believed herself to be divorced. The potential use of this tool has shifted gender power relations in this bitter field.

Before undertaking a legal analysis of this particular case, a preliminary question is necessary: Does the extreme position taken by the Regional Rabbinical Court and the majority in the Rabbinical High Court stem from the previous sources in this chapter? It is obviously not an easy task to summarize them all, and I shall not attempt to do that. Only an overview is possible here. Looking at the sources from §24 onward, which bring forth various facets of a wife's right to end the marriage, a clear struggle is evident between those who wish to expand women's options, even though the power of unilateral dissolution remains with the husband alone (Mishnah Ketubot §25; Otsar Ha-Geonim §26; Maimonides §27; Meir of Rothenburg §30; and Mishnah Gittin §32), and those who fear granting women such rights (Mishnah Nedarim §24; Tosafot Ketubot §28; Rosh §29; and Radbaz §31).

What is most striking is the explicit reference to political and social-psychological considerations beyond narrow halakhic ones. Perhaps the strongest expression of these, from the liberal side, is Maimonides' memorable statement that a married woman "is not like a captive who must have intercourse with someone she hates." But more surprising, and probably more far-reaching from the halakhic point of view, is the gaonic *takkanah* which went beyond talmudic law to establish a wife's right to what can be seen in modern terms as no-fault divorce. The explicit justification is national-political—the need to offer women solutions so as to stop them from turning to non-Jewish courts in their despair. The open accommodation to political reality appears not only in that original ruling but also in a later source retreating from it: Rosh admits that "the [leaders of the] Babylonian academies judged that the needs of the hour in their days required departing from Torah law." However, this open reliance on the "needs of the hour" is precisely what leads Rosh to overturn the *takkanah*: "At present [however, consideration of] the issues leads to the opposite conclusion. Israelite women in this generation are haughty."

What we see here is a fascinating move from national-political to overt gender-politics considerations. Rosh describes the alleged haughty nature of Jewish women in his time, who, if able easily to end their marriages, "will set their eyes upon others and defy their husbands." Consequently, "no daughter of Abraham will remain in place [lit., "sitting"] under her husband." This move to gender politics places Rosh's ruling in direct opposition to Maimonides. In fact, Rosh is the first to admit his disagreement and uses strong language to describe what he believes to be the proper fate of a woman seeking a divorce and threatening to go to a non-Jewish court: "Let her not have intercourse with him, and be tied up all her life as a living widow."

It is important to bear in mind this explicit resort to policy considerations, whether of a national-politics or gender-politics nature, when coming to discuss source §33. It is also important to note that even the extreme position taken by Rosh does not prevent him from recognizing the right of a wife to fault-based divorce—if she "provides some basis for her statement, [explaining] why he is not acceptable to her." In other words, while no-fault divorce (recognized by both the Geonim in their *takkanah* and Maimonides) was severely restricted, we can't find in any source a denial or restriction of a wife's right to divorce, provided she has valid grounds, as set forth in the Mishnah Ketubot (§25) and the literature that stemmed from it.

Let us now return to source §33 and its troubling argument. The first thing to note about this text, and the development it represents, is that it has nothing to do with *halakhah* and everything to do with religion/state politics, as reflected in the power relations between rabbinical courts and the civil legal system in the area of family law. Yet unlike the candid recognition of political considerations in the previous sources, the political motivation underlying this move is hardly ever admitted. The distressing reality in Israel is that divorce disputes take place on two battlefields: the first is the sad yet familiar one between husband and wife; the second is unique to the Israeli religious and civil legal systems. The "doomsday weapon" brings the two battlefields together: the rabbinical courts have sided with husbands in order to regain jurisdiction over issues they had previously lost to their civil rivals. They have done this by accepting (and sometimes even initiating) jurisdictional claims as conditions for the *get* and then retroactively invalidating *gittin* in cases where wives consented to these conditions yet afterward sought redress from civil courts.

To understand what is going on here, we need first to follow the halakhic reasoning, examine its (dubious) underpinnings, and analyze it within the context of the battle over jurisdiction between rabbinical and civil courts. We will then look into the timing of this development and trace its evolution through the High Rabbinical Court, and we will consider the practical outcomes of these rulings for women and men in divorce disputes.

As we have seen in this chapter (§§25–27), Jewish law recognizes a range of grounds for divorce that permit coercing a husband to divorce his wife, notwithstanding the basic requirement that the husband must consent of his own "free will" for the divorce to be valid. Clearly, if no such grounds exist, the man can set conditions as a prerequisite for granting the divorce. The question is whether this is allowed in cases in which there are grounds that would permit coercion. In theory, it is indeed possible to set conditions for the granting of a *get,* but since allowing husbands to condition divorce in all circumstances would make the recognition of grounds for divorce against men much more difficult and undermine the possibility of coercion, halakhic authorities have prohibited the execution of a conditional *get* or allowed it only in exceptional cases. Recall that one of the conclusions from my short survey of the earlier sources was that even the extreme position curtailing women's liberty never questioned the validity of fault-based divorce.

A conditional *get* and the invalidation of an allegedly "mistaken" *get* are in fact two sides of the same coin. Legally, if a condition written into the *get* was later on breached, this may theoretically raise a claim for voiding the *get*. But advancing such a claim is precluded by a clear halakhic instruction that strongly prohibits raising doubts as to the validity of a *get* after the fact — a prohibition that was attributed to Jacob b. Meir Tam. Thus, while introducing a condition into a *get* is only rarely permitted, the complementary practice of invalidating a "mistaken" *get* is clearly prohibited. Nevertheless, there have been a few exceptional cases permitting conditions in a *get* and even pronouncing a *get* invalid when such conditions were breached. The former is demonstrated in a sixteenth-century responsum by Maharshdam, which this rabbinical decision heavily relies upon and which has been followed by a growing number of rabbinical courts in the past decade, allowing for setting various conditions for granting *gittin,* even in circumstances where clear grounds for divorce exist and coercion could be employed. The latter is demonstrated in a seventeenth-century responsum by Meir b. Gedaliah of Lublin (Maharam of Lublin), relied upon by the Tel-Aviv Regional Rabbinical Court in a number of cases, similarly leading the way for more such decisions in the past decade, retroactively invalidating numerous *gittin*. Both these responsa addressed rather unusual sets of circumstances (notably, both involved different aspects of *halitzah*), and as was clearly shown in a number of law review articles, both were controversial from the outset and were clearly regarded as minority opinions as time went by.

And yet, in the twenty-first century we have witnessed an impressive resurrection of these contested responsa, in a series of rabbinical courts' decisions, led by a number of *dayanim*. The contemporary circumstances are obviously utterly different from the original settings. They typically involve demands that women give up rights that they may have gained in the civil courts and/or agree to adjudicate all aspects of the divorce dispute under the sole jurisdiction of the rabbinical court. Bear in mind the peculiar legal framework of divorce disputes in Israel, according to which marriage and divorce are under the exclusive jurisdiction of rabbinical courts, yet all other related matters (including child custody and support and distribution of marital property) are under concurrent jurisdiction of both civil and rabbinical courts (depending on where the claim was first brought). These two evidently reach different outcomes in identical cases, so this latest development will give the rabbinical courts unwavering jurisdictional powers.

The process is quite simple: if the rabbinical panel adopts the holding of Maharshdam, it will not entertain the woman's claim for divorce at all and will execute the *get* only if she concedes to her husband's demands. This is what took place in the case at hand (§33): in 1999, after twenty-three years of marriage, seventeen of them in separation, the regional rabbinical court accepted the wife's claim for divorce and ordered the husband to give her a *get*. In other words, there were clear grounds for divorce in this case. A year later, however, when the husband asserted his willingness to divorce on condition that his wife transfer to the jurisdiction of the rabbinical court all related matters (distribution of property and spousal and children's support, which had already been adjudicated and decided upon by the civil court), the same rabbinical court ruled that "The husband's argument is valid. That is: Even though the husband is required to give his wife a *get* (as we previously ruled), he should not be required to give a *get* so long as the wife is withholding money that is not hers in accordance with Torah law. . . . It is [thus] not the husband who is chaining the wife; rather the wife is the one who is chaining herself by refusing adjudication in accordance with Torah law." The result was that "as of today, there is no requirement upon the husband to divorce his wife." The Rabbinical High Court was unable to reach a decision on the wife's appeal, even after adding two *dayanim* to the original panel of three, and eventually remanded the case to the regional court for further discussion. Notably, only two of the five *dayanim* clearly ruled for accepting the wife's appeal and reinstating the *get*. Eventually the wife compromised, giving in to some of the husband's financial demands, and a second *get* was issued. Only then was she free.

Sadly, there is no other way to describe this but as extortion. Once the woman had conceded and the *get* was executed, she might retract and attempt to reclaim the rights she gave up, turning to the civil courts for redress. If the concessions related to the children, this might prove successful: under Israeli law, children are not bound by their parents' agreements unless their own interests were weighed independently. In such cases, if the rabbinical panel adopts the holding of Maharam of Lublin, it will simply pronounce the already executed *get* invalid, and the woman will be precluded from re-marrying unless a second *get* is issued. Obviously this will be done only if she withdraws her new claims in the civil system. In reality, the mere threat of invalidating the *get* is enough to make women turn back — or to not even seek redress in civil courts.

Let me be clear that the practical effect of this development is to undermine the whole system that recognizes grounds for divorce against men. The message is that any attempt by a woman to employ halakhically established grounds for divorce against her husband could prove to be futile, because her husband can condition his cooperation upon a series of demands, ranging from making monetary payments and concessions relating to marital property to giving in on child-related matters such as custody, visitation, and child support. Or the husband may simply demand that all divorce-related matters be adjudicated in the rabbinical court. Such demands, particularly the last, serve the interests of the rabbinical courts, which increasingly accept this tactic, taking the side of recalcitrant husbands, leaving the chained wives no option but to surrender to their extortion.

Anecdotally, the unequivocal adoption of Maharshdam's ruling may lead to such extreme holdings as the following obiter issued by Rabbi Izierer of the High Rabbinical Court in another case (in 2005): "We should further clarify that the right to impose conditions is not limited to monetary matters but also with respect to her behavior, i.e.: that she should refrain from eating certain foods, or from wearing certain clothes. Granted even a rabbinical court cannot hold the woman to these demands, but as conditions for granting a *get* they are valid and binding." Thus, the rabbinical courts have found the perfect method to regain the jurisdictional ground that they have been gradually losing, one that is completely immune from civil intervention, since matters related to the execution and validity of *gittin* are under the exclusive jurisdiction of the rabbinical system. The name "doomsday weapon" is thus entirely accurate.

This observation brings to the forefront the thesis with which I began. Policy considerations dealing with Jewish and non-Jewish politics have been replaced by the jurisdictional politics that plagues the Israeli legal system in the area of family law. If the Geonim were concerned about Jewish

women "avail[ing] themselves of non-Jewish [courts]," contemporary rabbinical courts are concerned about Israeli Jewish women preferring Israeli
civil courts. But whereas the Geonim's response to their fear of "illicitly enforced" *gittin* was a courageous move "departing from Torah law" (in the
words of Rosh) to constitute de facto no-fault divorce, contemporary rabbinical courts' response to their fear is a de facto restriction of fault-based divorce and a resurrection of the dubious tool of retroactive invalidation. And
even if one were to say that the Geonim's and Maimonides' arguments had
not become the accepted halakhic position, and that the concerns of contemporary rabbinical courts are closer to those of Rosh, whose position is viewed
as more mainstream, it should be remembered that at no point was Rosh
moving in the direction of restricting a wife's access to fault-based divorce.

It thus seems that the only way out of this doomsday bind is a dramatic external move that will challenge contemporary rabbinical courts in a
manner similar to the challenge their gaonic predecessors faced. Introducing
civil marriage and divorce in the state of Israel could be one way of doing
this. And this is only one more argument in support of this urgent move.

Ruth Halperin-Kaddari

Curtailing the Husband's Unilateral Power
34. Norman Lamm et al., Public Call and Prenuptial Agreement

*Whereas in Israel the rabbinic court often seeks to assert its independent authority vis-à-
vis the (secular) state court system—defending the husband's control of divorce—a rabbinical court in the United States can attain jurisdiction only through authority granted
by the parties and enforceable solely by state courts. Clearly the intent of this prenuptial
agreement is to employ the authority thus acquired in order to avoid cases of "chained
women," while evading the potentially invalidating claim that the get itself was illicitly
"forced" (see §8 above). A similar mechanism has been promoted in Israel by the feminist*

religious women's organization Kolech. With such an agreement, the wife's risk of being a "chained woman" (agunah) is significantly reduced, though by no means eliminated— for example, if the husband becomes incapacitated.

Public Call by Heads of Rabbi Isaac Elchanan Theological Seminary

A Message to Our Rabbinic Colleagues and Students—

The past decades have seen a significant increase in the number of divorces in the Orthodox Jewish Community. In the majority of these situations, the couples act in accordance with Jewish Law and provide for the proper delivery and receipt of a *get*. Each year, however, there is an accumulation of additional instances in which this is not the case.

We are painfully aware of the problems faced by individuals in our communities tied to undesired marriages. Many of these problems could have been avoided had the couple signed a halachicly and legally valid prenuptial agreement at the time of their marriage. We therefore strongly urge all officiating rabbis to counsel and encourage marrying couples to sign such an agreement.

The increased utilization of pre-nuptial agreements is a critical step in purging our community of the distressful problem of the modern-day Aguna and enabling men and women to remarry without restriction. By encouraging proper halachic behavior in the sanctification and the dissolution of marriage, we will illustrate *diracheha darchi noam v'chol netivoteha shalom*, all the Torah's paths are peaceful.

Signed by: [eleven prominent leaders of RIETS]

The Beth Din of America Binding Arbitration Agreement (excerpts)

This Agreement made on the _____ day of the month of _____ in the year _____ in the city/town/village of _____ state of _____

Husband-to-be _____ Residing at _____

Wife-to-be _____ Residing at _____

The parties, who intend to be married in the near future, hereby agree as follows:

I. Should a dispute arise between the parties after they are married, so that they do not live together as husband and wife, they agree to refer their marital dispute to the Beth Din of the United States of America, Inc. (cur-

rently located at 305 Seventh Ave., New York, NY 10001 . . . www.bethdin
.org), acting as an arbitration panel, for a binding decision.

II. The decision of the Beth Din of America shall be fully enforceable in any court of competent jurisdiction.

III. The parties agree that the Beth Din of America has exclusive
jurisdiction to decide all issues relating to a *get* (Jewish divorce) as well as
any issues arising from this Agreement or the *ketubah* and *tena'im* (Jewish premarital agreements) entered into by the Husband-to-Be and the Wife-to-Be.
Each of the parties agrees to appear in person before the Beth Din of America
at the demand of the other party.

VI. The decision of the Beth Din of America shall be made in accordance with Jewish law or Beth Din ordered settlement in accordance with
Jewish law, except as specifically provided otherwise in this Agreement. The
parties waive their right to contest the jurisdiction or procedures of the Beth
Din of America or the validity of this Agreement in any other rabbinical
court or arbitration forum other than the Beth Din of America. . . .

VII. The parties agree to appear in person before the Beth Din of
America at the demand of the other party . . . the Beth Din of America
may issue its decision despite the defaulting party's failure to appear, and
may impose costs and other penalties as legally permitted. Furthermore, the
Husband-to-Be acknowledges that he recites and accepts the following:

I hereby now obligate myself to support my Wife-to-Be from the
date that our domestic residence together shall cease for whatever reasons,
at the rate of $150 per day (calculated . . . adjusted annually be the Consumer
Price Index . . .) in lieu of my Jewish law obligation of support so long as the
two of us remain married according to Jewish law, even if she has another
source of income or earnings. Furthermore, I waive my halachic right to my
wife's earnings for the period that she is entitled to the above stipulated sum,
and I recite that I shall be deemed to have repeated this waiver at the time of
our wedding. . . .

However, this support obligation shall terminate if Wife-to-Be refuses to appear upon due notice before the Beth Din of America of in the
event that Wife-to-Be fails to abide by the decision of recommendation of
the Beth Din of America.

35. Meir Simcha Hakohen Feldblum, "The Problem of Chained Women and Mamzerim—A Proposal for a Comprehensive Solution"

Dine Yisrael 19 (1997-98): 203-16.

Feldblum, a rabbi and professor of Talmud, first at Yeshiva University in New York and then at Bar-Ilan University in Israel, was sympathetic to the efforts to employ prenuptial agreements but skeptical that they would constitute a satisfactory, across-the-board solution. He knew also of efforts by his elder colleague Rabbi Emanuel Rackman, who set up an unaffiliated rabbinical court and ruled in particular cases that a chained woman was free without need for a get, finding that her consent to an abusive marriage was invalid because based on substantive misrepresentation. Feldblum's thesis is more sweeping: modern women in general do not really consent to become "acquired."

The Problem of Chained Women and Mamzerim: A Proposal for a Comprehensive Solution (A Proposal for Halakhic and Value-Based Discussion)

The problem of chained women and *mamzerim* is constantly becoming more severe. The suffering and injustice caused chiefly to women and children, and the negative image [generated regarding] *halakhah* and the rabbinate, constitute a twisted thing that can hardly be made straight. . . .

Under Torah law, a *get* cannot be given except by the husband's free will; since Rabbenu Gershom's ban, the wife too may not be divorced against her will. In many cases the parties pose excessive demands, because of which one of the parties refuses to accede to a *get*. Even more difficult are cases where the husband leaves the home and his whereabouts are unknown, leaving the wife chained. Women who are not strictly observant—of whom there are unfortunately many—sometimes enter into a liaison with another man; the children born of such relationships are deemed *mamzerim* and bear the tragic consequences, as is well known.

This is not the place to enumerate the solutions proposed in the course of the ages, but these have not been deemed halakhically worthy by the majority of the authorities. Recently we have made progress through formulating prenuptial agreements that make it possible, when necessary, to employ financial pressure against the husband to give a *get.* For the time being, the practice of [signing] such agreements is not widespread. In any case, they will only solve a small part of the problem, since in cases where the husband is abroad, for example . . . such agreements will be of little avail. . . . The problem with most of the solutions proposed until now is the conviction held by the rabbinate (or by many [halakhic] authorities) that the rabbinate is not authorized to endorse radical solutions, such as would make it possible to pronounce a [married] woman permitted [to remarry] without a *get* . . . insofar as consecration has been properly conducted. . . . This necessitates searching for such a solution that might be accepted by the authorities, the *dayanim,* and the rabbis. . . . Which means pointing to existing facts, or even forging new conditions, that can fit existing forms and precedents . . . wherein it is possible to make do without a *get,* and the children are not *mamzerim.*

Perhaps the solution is already on the horizon, or even actually exists, requiring only that it be clarified, brought into focus, and carefully examined. . . .

The [marital] acquisition requires that it be made with the woman's full consent. . . .

[The author goes on to show that talmudic and medieval *halakhah* allowed for unions where valid consent is absent, since one or both of the parties are not legally competent. Dissolving such unions, called "marriage-like," does not require a *get.*]

In contemporary secular society, many women do not realize that the consecration [ceremony] involves an aspect of acquisition, that can [then] be cancelled only through the husband's consent. In light of women's contemporary striving for equality in all realms of life, a common postulate would be that . . . many women, were they to realize the above, would by no means consent to the consecration-as-acquisition—in contrast to the situation in the past. This postulate is further confirmed by statements by women who do realize the [nature] of consecration as acquisition, to wit, that they do not consent to this; their intention is only to enter a commitment of mutual fidelity. On this basis we can postulate that consent by the "seller" is absent. . . . These women are not a [meager] few, whose intention might be cancelled out [by the common understanding of the transaction]. Thus it is extremely doubtful whether the consecration in which they take part has any validity at all. . . . [The relationships thus instituted] should [rather] be accorded the status of "marriage-like" [unions]. . . .

I propose opting for the [alternative] formula "You are hereby designated [*meyuhedet*] unto me" . . . This formula will serve as a marker and statement that the [ceremony involves] a "marriage-like" [union] rather than traditional acquisition under Torah law. . . .

In summary: The proposed solution is guided by two principles:

1. [It is] a form of union found within the framework of *halakhah* and the Jewish tradition.

2. [It is] a form of union in which the woman is not deemed to be acquired and is not dependent exclusively upon the husband's goodwill in granting her a bill of divorce when the marriage comes to an end.

A "marriage-like" [union] as proposed, or something similar, would provide an appropriate solution for non-observant couples—and more generally, for all those women who do not consent that their freedom be dependent upon their husbands—without destroying the Jewish framework. Marriage in this form will solve the problem of chained women; and will reduce the instances of adultery and of *mamzerim*.

A Jewish Egalitarian Marriage

36. Rachel Adler, "*B'rit Ahuvim*: A Marriage Between Subjects"

Engendering Judaism: An Inclusive Theology and Ethics (Philadelphia: JPS, 1998), pp. 169–70, 190–94 (revised by the author); reprinted by permission of the University of Nebraska Press; copyright 1998 by Rachel Adler.

A contemporary feminist theologian proposes here an egalitarian form of marriage based on covenantal partnership. It is designed to be halakhically valid, yet its dissolution would not require a get. This final selection can also be read as a commentary on the classical marriage texts and on all earlier efforts to deal with the inequality they presuppose.

The book of Hosea illustrates a dilemma that haunts these texts on Jewish marriage: a husband who has appropriated a wife and assumed legal owner-ship of her sexuality finds that he wants not merely her fidelity, but fidelity freely given out of love. Possessing her is inadequate and, as it turns out, im-possible; his ownership does not preclude her infidelity. The prophet's text seesaws between the husband's rage at the woman as a defective possession and the painful tenderness he feels for someone whose will, desire, and feel-ings are distinct from his own. He does not see that his two desires—the urge to possess and control absolutely and the yearning for a loving, willing part-ner—are irreconcilable.

These unresolved tensions between woman as possession and woman as partner are embedded in the classical liturgy upon which all mod-ern Jewish wedding ceremonies draw. Two elements comprise this cere-mony: a legal transaction in which the bride is acquired by a declaration of exclusive possession and a ring, followed by a liturgical celebration (*Sheva Berakhot,* §5) that associates the new marriage with the covenantal reconcilia-tion of God and Israel and depicts it as a new Eden for "loving companions" to inhabit. If we unpack the definitions of marital relationships underlying these two components, however, we find that they are mutually exclusive. The legal definition, derived from talmudic property law, anachronistically categorizes women as a special kind of chattel over which the husband has ac-quired rights. In contrast, the metaphors that inform the *Sheva Berakhot* char-acterize marriage as a covenant between partners who choose each other, fail each other, even despair of each other, and yet return and renew their commitments. The traditional wedding ceremony, first treating the bride as a piece of property and then paradoxically depicting her as a covenanter, mirrors in its very structure the irreconcilable expectations implicit in patri-archal marriage.

To treat both parties consistently as persons rather than as property, we would have to reframe the legal portion of the ceremony in terms of part-nership law rather than property law as it is currently categorized. Only then would the ceremony's legal component accurately reflect the kind of mar-riage to which egalitarian couples mean to pledge themselves.

If *kiddushin* represents a sanctification through separation, then the *Sheva Berakhot* celebrate a sanctification through the holy coming together that is covenant. They celebrate the cosmic process of wedding that occurs at all levels of sacred time and sacred history: making one, making joy, making new. Wedding is the beginning and end of time shaped into a circle and wreathed around the bridegroom and the bride. Wedding is creation and redemption, the origin of all bonds and their perfect mending, the first encounter of lover-equals and Zion's reconciliation with the lover she will no longer call "my *ba'al* [owner]." This expansive metaphor of wedding strains at the limits of the *kiddushin* relationship it is meant to complement, and the strain cries out for relief. Either *kiddushin* must coopt the *Sheva Berakhot,* or the *Sheva Berakhot* must rise up and cast out *kiddushin.* This latter is the course I have chosen.

What are we to do when the words and gestures that effect marriage do not reflect but distort the event being celebrated in the life of the participants and their community? Under pressure from their constituents, nontraditional Judaisms and even modern Orthodoxy have sought to alleviate discomfort with the *erusin* portion of the wedding ceremony by liturgical innovations. These focus mainly upon the bride's silence and passivity in the traditional ceremony and the inability of the traditional *ketubbah,* the marriage settlement contract, to address the social reality of the relationship into which the participants intend to enter. These innovations include additional vows like those in Christian ceremonies, where the partners promise to cherish and protect one another. Or after the legal acquisition is concluded and the *ketubbah* has been read, the bride recites a verse from the Song of Solomon to her husband, sometimes accompanied by the gift of a ring. Creative *ketubbah* that articulate the couple's own visions of how the marriage is to be conducted supplement or replace the standard *ketubbah* form that attests the husband's responsibility to provide food, shelter, clothing, and sexual intercourse (*onah*) and records a financial settlement (now superseded by civil community property and inheritance laws) in the event of divorce or the husband's demise.

These innovations, however charming and individualized, are halakhically impotent. They leave the legal structure of *kiddushin* intact, and that structure with its implicit definitions of the marital relationship legally supersedes any personal statements the bride and groom make to one another. It is as if a man purchased a slave in accordance with laws governing the institution of slavery and then promised his purchase, "I'll always treat you like an equal." The slave's treatment would depend not upon any recognized legal standard, but upon whether his legal owner was an exceptionally nice guy.

This is not to belittle the serious efforts couples have made to renovate the wedding ceremony. Their alterations reveal an instinctive understanding that a Jewish marriage is a legal ritual, and therefore it is important that the words that specify the commitments being made be words that the participants intend to honor. Even though Jewish marriages are now performed solely by rabbis, Jewish marriage is not a sacrament effected by an anointed officiant with special powers. The couple themselves accomplish marriage by pronouncing and receiving the effectuating legal formula in the presence of witnesses. For this very reason, rabbinic law is at pains to establish the actors' intent to accomplish the condition the rabbis define as marriage.

One innovation that does reject the classical premises of *kiddushin* is the double-ring ceremony in which both partners make the traditional declaration of acquisition. According to classical halakhah, no *kiddushin* is effected, because equal exchanges cancel each other out. It is as if each participant had given the other a five dollar bill; their circumstances are precisely what they were before the transaction. From an ethical perspective, the double-ring ceremony is a dubious amelioration. The problem with marital *kinyan* (acquisitional) is not simply that it is unilateral, but that it commodifies human beings. The groom's commodification and acquisition of the bride is not rectified by the bride's retaliation in kind. *Kinyan* of persons violates values conscientious people have come to regard as moral goods. As the abolition of slavery and the institution of labor unions attest, ownership of another person's body or of another's alienated labor is no longer viewed as just. The vocabulary and constitutive assumptions of *kiddushin* cannot be made to reflect a partnership of equals.

Marriage, some wit once remarked, makes man and woman one—

and the man is the one. We have just reached a point in history where it is possible to envision, and sometimes to realize, marriages in which two remain two, marriages that are not incorporations but covenants. We need a wedding ceremony that embodies the partners' intentions to sustain and strive with each other all their lives, to endure like the protagonists of the stormy but ultimately redemptive covenant marriage of biblical prophecy. This intention is not reflected in an act of acquisition. It can only be expressed by an act of covenanting. Like all covenants, a marriage agreement must embody some of the characteristics of contracts, articulating standards for an ethical relation and laying out some of what the partners most need and want. The marriage agreement must specify the obligations that will form the fabric of the marriage. The partners must be able to make some promises to one another, even though promises are sometimes broken. And if a marriage loses its qualities as a *shutafut,* a partnership, people must be free to dissolve it.

For these reasons and others I will explain, partnership law, *hilkhot shutafut,* forms the legal basis for the contractual aspects of what I will call the *b'rit ahuvim* [covenant of lovers]. The model of a partnership reflects the undeniable fact that marriage is not only a social but an economic institution. But unlike the *ketubbah,* which presumes that most economic power and resources belong to the male, the *b'rit ahuvim* presumes communal resources and requires joint decisions about their distribution.

Partnership law embodies other desirable values as well. In halakhah, it mediates between the partners' needs for autonomy and their needs for interdependence. A partnership is formed by mutual agreement, and each party has the power to terminate it. In classical halakhah, a partnership is not an independent legal entity as a corporation is in modern Western law, nor are the identities of the partners submerged in it. They remain individually accountable. Because the laws of partnership developed out of the laws of joint ownership, the partnership is regarded as a kind of property in which the partners have invested. Consequently, each partner acquires legal obligations for maintaining the partnership and its projects.

The halakhic process of forming a partnership generally embodies three elements:

1. A partnership deed. Although from the tenth century on, verbal agreement was considered sufficient to contract partnerships, written evidence in the form of a deed seems to have been more usual.

2. A statement of personal undertaking in which partners committed themselves to certain acts on behalf of the partnership.

3. A *kinyan* or symbolic acquisition of the partnership. Partnerships were first understood as joint ownerships achieved by pooling resources. "Pooling resources" in talmudic idiom is *l'hatil b'kis,* to put into one pouch, and an ancient legal gesture for partnership acquisition was for each partner to put a sum into one pouch and to lift it up together. Lifting is one of the fundamental halakhic indications of taking something into one's domain. By lifting the pouch together, contributors would signify joint acquisition both of the money in the bag and the investment it represented. This special gesture was later abandoned in favor of a legal convention for ratifying all sorts of transactions, *kinyan sudar,* in which one party pulls a scarf or handkerchief out of the other's hand.

I have represented all three of these elements in the formation of the *b'rit ahuvim.* There is a partnership deed, which I have called a *shtar b'rit,* a covenant document, in recognition that this special partnership has the potential to be more than a contract (*shtar*). There is a verbal commitment by the partners during the ceremony. And, finally, there is a *kinyan* by means of which the partners symbolically acquire their partnership, not through the more common *kinyan sudar,* but through an adapted form of the more ancient pooling of resources in a pouch.

The *b'rit ahuvim* is not a private arrangement, but a commitment entailing communal responsibilities. While its stipulations can be tailored to the needs of particular couples, it embodies a standard of righteousness based upon how a conscientious progressive community interprets and lives out its Jewish obligations. As a *bayit b Yisra'el,* a household among the people Israel, *b'rit* partners share with other Jewish households a responsibility for the continuity and well-being of the people of Israel and for participating in its task of *tikkun olam,* repairing the world.

The *b'rit ahuvim* specifies both the standards of righteousness and the desires of the partners. But, as in classical covenants, the partners are committed ultimately to one another and not merely to the terms they have promised to fulfill. To the extent that this covenantal commitment is realized in the relationship, it can survive breaches in contractual obligations. Like the covenant between God and Israel, the *b'rit ahuvim is* a promise of exclusivity. The relationships it delineates are lasting, monogamous unions, whether heterosexual or homosexual.

The *b'rit* document should be written in Hebrew, because it is traditionally a language for learning, law, and sacred expression and because it is spoken as a living language by large communities of Jews in Israel and in the Diaspora. It records a commitment that affects not only individuals, but also *klal Yisra'el,* the collectivity of the Jewish people, and hence should be comprehensible anywhere Jews live. If Hebrew is not the primary language of the partners or those who will witness the wedding, the document should also be translated.

In the model of *b'rit ahuvim* I have designed, the *b'rit* document opens with two paragraphs rooting *b'rit ahuvim* in biblical covenant stories and identifying the relationship with the rabbinic ideal of holy companionship. The contractual stipulations follow. The specific stipulations I have recommended are: (1) a pledge of sexual exclusivity; (2) a commitment to the rights and duties of familial relationship; (3) an assumption of joint responsibility for children; (4) a pledge to live a holy life as a Jewish family; (5) a pledge to fulfill communal responsibilities; and (6) a pledge that either spouse will protect the dignity and comfort of the other in his or her dying.

Couples may wish to add or vary particular stipulations. For instance, blended families or noncustodial parents may have other arrangements about familial responsibilities. Stipulations such as these should be amendable upon mutual agreement.

A *b'rit ahuvim* is not a *kiddushin.* This is emphasized in the ceremony and in some *b'rit* documents. The couple have acquired, not one another, but the partnership itself. Perhaps they should state explicitly that they do not intend to have intercourse for the sake of establishing *kiddushin*. Since a *b'rit ahuvim* is not *kiddushin*, it should not require a Jewish divorce, a *get*, in which a man renounces ownership of his wife. Instead it can be dissolved like a business partnership, by one partner withdrawing from the partnership and, for purposes of documentation, assembling a *bet din* of three and informing them that the partnership is dissolved.

Halakhically, this account relies on one position in classical Jewish law that posits the existence of relationships that are neither *kiddushin* nor *z'nut*, promiscuity. Classical halakhists characterize these other relationships as *pilagshut*, concubinage, a disorderly catch-all category into which they throw the maidservant wives of the biblical patriarchs, the royal concubines of David and Solomon, the hetairas, amicae, and concubinae of Greco-Roman culture, and the mistresses of medieval Spanish Jewish aristocrats. These examples in turn served some legal authorities as models for civil marriage and other long-term non-halakhic relationships, which do not involve a *ketubbah* and do not require a Jewish divorce. This is the reason why some contemporary halakhists have suggested concubinage as an alternative for non-Orthodox couples who do not wish to deal with the possible consequences of *kiddushin*.

Kiddushin leaves the woman dependent on the man to grant her a divorce. It opens a door to blackmail, in which the husband demands money or property in exchange for divorce; he can simply withhold divorce indefinitely, rendering the woman an *aguna*, a chained woman. She may also be declared an *aguna* if the husband disappears and there are no eyewitnesses to his demise. An *aguna* is not permitted to remarry. If she does remarry, the children may be considered *mamzerim*, bastards, and not permitted to marry other Jews.

Having non-traditional couples contract concubinage relationships neatly solves these halakhic problems, but it offers women an insulting choice: either become a permanent possession or a long-term lease! I would argue that concubinage serves as a *placeholder* for categories of relationships that are neither *kiddushin* nor promiscuity, but not all such relationships are concubinage. Because rabbinic authorities lacked a concept of egalitarian relationships, they did not specify any, but we can remedy this omission.

B'rit ahuvim is an egalitarian alternative among the varieties of sexual relationships. It ensures that both partners are treated respectfully and offers a serious spiritual alternative to traditionalist discrimination and to soulless secularism. It is also an option for gay, lesbian, and transsexual couples who would not be eligible for *kiddushin* and provides them a legal means of establishing a *bayit b'yisrael,* a household among the people Israel.

NINETEEN   Parents and Children

Introduction

Parental Power and Its Limits

The Rebellious Son Put to Death
1. Deuteronomy 21:18–22

Revising the Biblical Law
2. Sifre Deuteronomy 218–20

Rebellious Sons Will Never Be Convicted
3. Mishnah Sanhedrin 8:4; BT Sanhedrin 71a

Father Effecting Marriage of a Daughter
4. Mishnah Kiddushin 2:1; BT Kiddushin 41a; Tosafot Kiddushin 41a, s.v. *asur*

Filial Autonomy: Choosing a Wife
5. Elijah Capsali, *Me'ah Shearim* 62

Filial Duties

Honoring and Revering Parents
6. Sifra Kedoshim parashah 1

Go Forth from Your Father's Home
7. Genesis Rabbah 39:7

Parental Authority and Leaving for the Land of Israel
8. Meir b. Baruch of Rothenburg (Maharam), *Responsa* (Berlin 1891) 2:79

Introduction

Transgenerational and intragenerational morality and law are necessarily different. Obligations of parents to children and of children to parents
are specified in the legal literature, but they are not contractual or reciprocal
in the same way as are the obligations of husbands and wives. This is so in part
because the two sets of transgenerational obligations don't coincide in time
and so are not subject to direct negotiation; there is no possibility of anything
like a *ketubah*. No Jewish writer imagined that parents were bound by contract to educate and maintain their children in exchange for care and main-

tenance in their own old age. John Locke, in his *Second Treatise of Civil Government,* suggests an exchange of just this sort: more or less "care, cost, and kindness" from the parents warrants more or less "respect, reverence, support, and compliance" from the children. But this hardly seems either wise or fair, since it leaves parents in their old age dependent on the perceptions and memories of their children. In any case, the two obligations are entirely independent in Jewish literature—which starts, it is important to remember, with an unqualified command addressed only to children: "Honor your father and your mother." There is no parallel command addressed to parents.

We begin this chapter with a critical test case of parental authority and filial obligation—the strange story of the "rebellious son." (Since it turns out, according to the Rabbis, that there are no "rebellious sons," it probably isn't too important that rebellious daughters—again, according to the Rabbis—are excluded. But the point is worth noting; some Rabbis contended that the exclusion made the law arbitrary and its enforcement problematic.) The Bible describes a son "who does not heed" his father and mother "even after they discipline him" and seems to permit his execution, though not by the parents themselves. By contrast, in Roman law, the *pater familias* (though not the *mater*) had a literal power of life and death over his children: like a king, he could punish rebellion capitally—even with his own hands. Deuteronomy 21 requires that the parents (father and mother together) deliver the "rebellious son" to the "elders of his city, and unto the gates of his place," a phrase commonly taken to designate the local court. He is then stoned by "the men of the city." No witnesses are required, which is unprecedented in capital cases. It isn't clear whether the execution depends on the judges or follows effectively from the parents' accusation.

The Rabbis don't explicitly resolve this last issue in their interpretations of the biblical text, but they place so many qualifications on the parental accusation, add so many defining conditions to the offense, and open so much room for judicial review as to make execution impossible. The biblical law is effectively repudiated (though it can't be repealed); it turns out that, when all its implications are fully grasped, "rebellious son" is a null category. While parents have great authority over their children, then, they have nothing like the power of life and death. Either the two of them will never fully agree on the rebelliousness of their child (and without the agreement of the two, there is no judicially recognizable rebellion), or the court will find some defect in the accusation or in the description of the "rebellion." The list of possible defects strongly suggests that the Rabbis believed the parents themselves were often at fault when their sons rebelled.

The discussions of the "rebellious son" in the Sifre and in tractate Sanhedrin provide yet another example of the interpretative freedom claimed and exercised by the Rabbis. They cannot have misunderstood what they were doing to the Deuteronomic law. But for our purposes here, the discussion is useful in another way. It illustrates the legal construction and reconstruction of the family, and it suggests the deep understandings that shape this process. The Rabbis are not able to imagine a "rebellious son" worthy of death. Unlike the Romans, they don't regard the family as a political unit; they read "rebellion" as gluttony and drunkenness, and they explain the biblical law as a preventive measure: the son is killed for the (nonpolitical) crimes he would have committed later in his life. Notice that they have no similar difficulty with subjects of the king or members of the *kahal*—even when they disagree about whether such people should actually be executed. "Informer," for example is not a null category; no effort is made to find defects in the charge or excuses for the crime.

Why are rebels in the family treated differently? Perhaps because the family is a holy union (as the political community is not), created first of all for the sake of reproduction and generational continuity: so one cannot allow the next generation to be killed off. Or perhaps, more simply, because the family is a set of relationships wholly different from political relationships. Individual well-being may hang on them, but not community safety.

Concern for individual well-being may also have played a part in arguments over the father's authority (here, the mother isn't in the picture) to choose marriage partners for his children. The father seems to have had near-absolute authority over his daughters in their minority and their maidenhood—though some Rabbis argued against this, holding that the father should wait to choose a husband for his daughter until she was old enough to say yes or no to the union. And when she was old enough, others argued, she should be allowed to see the man before agreeing to the marriage—as sons were required to do, lest they find the union intolerable. The Tosafot allowed the consecration of a minor daughter by her father—but only because of the exigencies of the Exile. The independence of men was more commonly defended, even in exilic conditions, though it too required a defense. In the sixteenth-century case that we have chosen, and probably in many others, rabbis allowed sons to defy their fathers, to follow the path of attraction and love and choose a wife for themselves. Not every rebellious son was a "rebellious son" in the legal sense of that phrase.

Still, a glance at the texts will suggest that there is nothing sentimental or romantic about the Rabbinic view of parent-child and child-parent obligations. Legal decisions about rebellion and marriage, and then about contract, reciprocity, and maintenance, have their own logic; they are often shrewdly responsive to social practicality, to human need and greed. But they are also governed by a divine ordinance and a theological purpose. The family, we said in Chapter 18, is the basic unit of the *kahal,* but it is also distinct from the *kahal.* It is a nonpolitical realm that the community is supposed to foster and protect.

As the biblical commandment suggests, the obligations of children are owed equally to both parents, and the Rabbis, in a midrashic exposition of Leviticus, argue that the obligations fall equally on sons and daughters. Still, the talmudic texts move pretty quickly to a discussion of fathers and sons. Married daughters have obligations to their husbands (see ¢18) that take precedence over "honoring" their parents. Widows, however, seem to have the same obligations as sons. What do sons owe? Deference and respect, above all, and these are described in fulsome terms, though they clearly have limits. One test of deference and respect, as we have seen, is the readiness to yield to paternal wishes when it comes to the choice of a wife. Another test comes with the choice of residence. It is impossible to pay a proper degree of deference and respect from a great distance. Can children choose to live far from their parents? Abraham did that, but his example was treated as the exception that proves the rule: children cannot move away and leave their (nonidolatrous) parents behind. But what if the children wish to make *aliyah,* to move to the Land of Israel? That question evoked sharp disagreements, which we represent here with both medieval and modern texts.

A third test of children's obedience to divine command is the care and sustenance of their aged parents: What is owed, and at whose expense must care be provided? There is an unusual disagreement between the Jerusalem and Babylonian Talmuds on this question: the Jerusalem rabbis say that the son must pay out of his own pocket for the care of his father; the Babylonian rabbis insist that the son is required to contribute only time and energy; he can pay for his father's care out of his father's pocket. Many efforts have been made to find some compromise between the two positions. The compromise that seems to command the most support holds that, although sons cannot be coerced to support their parents with their (the sons') own money, they can and should be shamed into doing so. This implies that there is a moral requirement of support whatever the financial resources of the father, but the law does not intervene in the intimate realm of parent-child relationships. Still, when a leading rabbi like Solomon b. Abraham Adret says in a legal responsa that "the son may not be compelled [to support his father but] the synagogue is closed to him and . . . he is to be shamed," the law has reached pretty effectively into the family. After all, the *kahal* was also, most often, a small and intimate community, and it would have been difficult to survive socially or economically under the pressure Adret prescribes. It is probably right to say that the community was committed to enforce mutual assistance within the family, even though there were disagreements about the proper enforcement measures.

What were the duties of parents? The education and maintenance of children was a legal obligation (like procreation itself) only of fathers— and education was due only to sons. Here again the background idea of the family was deeply patriarchal. Family law was focused first of all on education, and its requirements had a strict father/son form. Fathers were obligated to teach their sons how to earn a livelihood and also how to swim (imagined as a survival skill, not a recreation). They were also, and even more importantly, obligated to teach them Torah, so that they could study the law and observe it.

Curiously, the physical maintenance of children ranks below their education in importance; perhaps it was simply taken for granted (though it is rare that anything is taken for granted in halakhic discourse). Of course, there was no divine command. Would Jewish law have developed differently if God had added the words "Care for your sons and your daughters" to the two tablets? As it was, fathers were legally bound to maintain their children only for the first six years of their life; after that, until the children reached maturity, maintenance was imagined as *tzedakah,* charity. Think of the English maxim "Charity begins at home." Some of the rabbis seem to have held this position in its most literal sense, even though its likely effect is that, for many parents, charity would also end at home. So far as the father's own children are concerned, however, the maintenance-as-*tzedakah* rule makes little difference. The courts and the *kahal* could in fact require "charitable" giving, and so they could also force a father to provide for his children. Since the community as a whole would have to take responsibility if the father defaulted, it could legitimately intervene to prevent the default and save its own resources for children in more obvious need, whose parents were destitute or dead. The hard question—can fathers avoid supporting other people's children by calling the support they give to their own "charity"?—was much discussed among medieval and early modern rabbis. The next two chapters present the full range of arguments about communal provision and coercion.

Parents also care for their children by leaving them an inheritance. Many things can be passed on from one generation to another: culture, religion, a political system, a functioning economy, roads, and buildings. The education requirement encompasses what we might think of as cultural reproduction—though in fact much of the real work of cultural reproduction is done by women, who are not involved in the formal educational process. But it is the transfer of wealth, in both its movable and immovable forms, with which the law is most deeply engaged. The Bible specifies the precise distribution of parental resources in what is a fairly standard hierarchical order: the eldest son, the other sons, the daughters, and then other relatives—brothers and uncles. In biblical law, there is no such thing as a will; the dying father (or mother, though mothers had much less to leave) has no discretion. Deuteronomy goes out of its way to insist that he may not shift the distribution, choosing among his sons, favoring the child of his favorite wife. His wealth is not "his"; it belongs to his family, which has a structure he cannot alter.

The talmudic texts reveal the development of parental, most importantly paternal, discretion. The Rabbis seem to believe that individual property owners can do what they want with their wealth (so long as the statement of what they want does not literally contravene the biblical texts). Ideally, the wealth should remain in the family, but there is no legal means to prevent a father from disinheriting his children. If he leaves his property to "others," the act is valid: "What he has done is done," the Mishnah says, "however, the sages are displeased with him." Rabban Shimon b. Gamaliel thought that the disinheritance of a wicked son was commendable, but what about the son's son, who might turn out to be a pious Jew?

In subsequent years, the Rabbis looked for ways to encourage transfers from one generation to the next (and the next) in which they could take pleasure. The talmudic texts and the medieval responsa and *takkanot* that we include here suggest the general tendency of their efforts. They want fathers to endow their daughters handsomely (perhaps especially so when the sons of the Rabbis are suitors, as in the story in Ketubot), and so they seek to guarantee that some significant part of the money will be passed on to the fathers' grandchildren in the event of a daughter's premature death. The explicit aim is "that a person should be eager to give to his daughter *just as* to his son." In fact, however, the daughter never has actual control of the money; it passes through her, as it were, to her husband and her children. The Toledo ordinance splits the money evenly between those two. The share of female children consists in maintenance and dowry; they too are never in actual control of family wealth. Widows, however, could act independently in the economic sphere, accumulate wealth and spend it on their own, and unmarried women could do so too, in some times and places. But equality for women in inheritance is a modern secular creation; it is not yet halakhically vindicated, despite the efforts of Isaac Halevi Herzog, chief rabbi in 1948, who attempted to anticipate (and perhaps set limits on) the egalitarian enactments of the new state.

Parental Power and Its Limits

The Rebellious Son Put to Death

1. Deuteronomy 21:18–22

Unlike some other ancient legal systems, the Bible does not leave the fate of a rebellious child in the hands of the parents: they must bring him before the local authorities. In this discussion, the text begins with "a man" but immediately shifts to include the mother along with the father—an extension that the Rabbis make much of in the texts that follow.

If a man has a stubborn and rebellious son, who does not heed[1] his father or his mother and does not obey them even after they discipline him, his father and mother shall take hold of him and bring him out to the elders of his town at the public place [gates] of his community. They shall say to the elders of his town, "This son of ours is stubborn and rebellious; he does not heed us. He is a glutton and a drunkard." Thereupon the men of his town shall stone him to death. Thus you will sweep out evil from your midst: all Israel will hear and be afraid.

Revising the Biblical Law

2. Sifre Deuteronomy 218–20

Sifre, translated by Reuven Hammer (New Haven: Yale University Press, 1986), pp. 229–31.

This midrash is a classic example of the Rabbis' general policy of limiting the possibility of capital punishment (see ¢23 below). The limits are achieved here by a series of restrictive interpretations of biblical texts, starting with a constrained age span: the son must no longer be a minor, but also not yet an adult. Going beyond this, the Sifre reinterprets the biblical account of domestic chastisement as requiring an initial flogging before three

---

1. Here and below, "heed" is literally "listen to the voice of," and the Rabbis play on this meaning.

judges. This in turn lays the ground for an additional impediment to the death penalty: the
same judges who presided over the flogging must be present in the final stage of judgment.
Finally, the very fairness of capital punishment for such juvenile offenses is questioned,
but then justified, strikingly, as a preventive measure.

"If a man has a stubborn and rebellious son" (21:18): but not if a woman has
such a son. "A son," but not a daughter nor an adult son. A minor is exempt,
since he has not yet come under the rule of the commandments. . . .

"And though they chasten him, will not hearken unto them" (21:18):
showing that he is to be flogged in the presence of three [judges].

"Then his father and his mother lay hold on him" (21:19): this shows
that he is not liable unless he has a father and a mother; so taught R. Meir.
R. Judah says: if his mother was not fit for his father, he cannot be declared a
stubborn and rebellious son.

"And bring him out unto the elders of his city, and unto the gate of
his place" (21:19): this is a positive commandment specifying the elders of his
city and the gate of his place.

"And they shall say unto the elders of his city: this our son is stubborn and rebellious" (21:20): This is the one who was [previously] flogged in
your presence. Hence we learn that if one of the judges has since died, the son
may not be stoned. If one [of the parents] is an amputee, lame, mute, blind
or deaf, the son may not be declared stubborn and rebellious, since Scripture
says, "Lay hold on him"—therefore they may not be amputees—"and bring
him out" (21:19)—therefore they may not be lame—"and they shall say"—
therefore they may not be mute—"this our son"—therefore they may not be
blind—"doth not hearken to our voice" (21:20)—therefore they may not be
deaf. He should then be admonished in the presence of three [judges] and
flogged. If he misbehaves again, he must be judged before a court of twenty-
three [judges], but may not be stoned unless the original three judges are
present, since it is said, "This, our son"—this is the one who was flogged in
your presence.

"He is a glutton and drunkard" (21:20): a glutton in eating meat and
a drunkard in drinking wine. . . .

"And all the men of his city shall stone him to death" (21:21): . . .
R. Jose said: Should he be stoned to death just because he has eaten a *tarte-mar* of meat and drunk half a *log* of wine? Rather, the Torah foresaw what he will eventually come to do, and decreed that it is better for him to die while yet innocent than to die when guilty, for the death of the wicked [and the wicked-to-be] is beneficial for them and beneficial for the world, whereas the death of the righteous is bad for them and bad for the world.

Rebellious Sons Will Never Be Convicted
3. Mishnah Sanhedrin 8:4; BT Sanhedrin 71a

Here the Talmud extends, and perhaps completes, the project of making the conviction of a "rebellious son" impossible. Although the Mishnah (in an adjacent clause) repeats the Sifre's justification of capital punishment as prevention, the Talmud here offers a completely different answer to the question of unfairness. The radical move made in our text should be seen in the context of the Rabbinic efforts to curtail capital punishment or even to abolish it altogether in practice (see ¢23).

Mishnah Sanhedrin 8:4

If his father wants [to have him judged a stubborn and rebellious son] but his mother does not want to, or if his father does not want to but his mother does want to, he cannot be judged a stubborn and rebellious son, unless they both want it. Rabbi Yehudah said: if his mother is not fit for his father, he is not made a stubborn and rebellious son.

BT Sanhedrin 71a

What is [meant by] "not fit"? If you say [that it means that she is forbidden to him, and their relationship is] punishable by *karet* [extinction] or by capital punishment—after all, his father is his father, and his mother is his mother! Rather, [Rabbi Yehudah] is speaking of [similarity] to the father. It was likewise taught: Rabbi Yehudah says, if his mother is not the same as his father in voice, in appearance, and in height, he cannot be judged a stubborn and rebellious son. What is the reason? Scripture states, "he will not listen to our voice" (Deut. 21:20) [singular]. And since they must be the same in voice, they must also be the same in appearance and height. Whose opinion does the following *baraita* reflect: "There never has been a stubborn and rebellious son, nor will there ever be one. Why, then, was [this law] written? [So that you may] study it and receive [a] reward." Whose [opinion]? That of Rabbi Yehudah. If you wish I can say [it reflects the opinion of] Rabbi Shimon, as it was taught: Rabbi Shimon said, is it [possible that just] because he ate a *tartemar* of meat and drank a half a *log* of Italian wine his father and his mother will bring him out to be stoned? Rather, there never has been [a stubborn and rebellious son], nor will there ever be one. Why, then, was [this law] written? [So you may] study it and receive [a] reward. Rabbi Yonatan said: I saw such a one and sat on his grave.

Father Effecting Marriage of a Daughter
4. Mishnah Kiddushin 2:1; BT Kiddushin 41a; Tosafot Kiddushin 41a, s.v. *asur*

Drawing on a particular interpretation of the rules concerning male authority over the vows of daughters and wives, the Rabbis distinguished between three phases of female development. Before puberty, she is a minor, and her father has sole power to effect her consecration, whereupon she becomes the wife of the man he has chosen. There is then a short transitional phase when she is a "maiden," still under her father's power. Beyond puberty, a young woman is an adult and can only be consecrated and married[2] by her own consent.

2. For an exposition of marriage and its halakhic initiation by a man "consecrating" a woman, see ¢18, §4.

In relation to biblical law, the status of a legally independent adult woman seems to have been a definite innovation.

This mishnah discusses the capacity of a man or a woman to appoint an agent for the act of consecration, addressing also a father's power to effect this for his maiden daughter. The Talmud first notes the possible downside of entering marriage without face-to-face contact, and with regard to a minor daughter, it expresses reservations about the exercise of paternal power. Nevertheless, the power itself is not curtailed, and the tosafists demonstrate how it can gain renewed legitimacy under a patriarchal construction of gender.

Mishnah Kiddushin 2:1

A man can effect consecration whether in person or by his agent. A woman can become consecrated whether in person or by her agent. A man can effect consecration of his daughter, while she is a maiden, whether in person or by his agent.

BT Kiddushin 41a

Since he can effect consecration by his agent, what need [is there to say that he can do so] in person? Rav Yosef said: It is preferable that he do it in person, rather than by his agent. . . . Some say: This even involves a prohibition, as stated by Rav Yehudah, citing Rav: "A man may not consecrate a woman until he has seen her, lest he find some aspect of her [person] loathsome and [come to] loathe her, whereas the Merciful One has decreed, 'You shall love your fellow as your self' (Lev. 19:18)." As for Rav Yosef's statement, it was directed to the second clause: "A woman becomes consecrated whether in person or by her agent"—Since she can effect consecration by her agent, what need [is there to say that she can do so] in person? Rav Yosef said: It is preferable [*mitzvah*] that she do it in person, rather than by her agent. . . . Yet this involves no prohibition, in accordance with the [teaching] of Resh

Lakish. For Resh Lakish said: "It is better to reside, two bodies together, than to reside as a spinster."

"A man effects consecration of his daughter, while she is a maiden"— [Only] when she is a maiden, but not when she is a minor. This supports Rav, for Rav Yehudah said, citing Rav (or perhaps: Rabbi Elazar): A man may not effect consecration of his daughter while she is a minor, until she has grown up and declares: "It is X that I want."

Tosafot Kiddushin 41a, s.v. *asur*

"A man may not effect consecration of his daughter while she is a minor"—even though it was stated above that [consecration of a woman without her seeing the man] involves no prohibition, that applies only to an adult, for since she has consented there are no grounds for concern that she might regret [it]. But regarding a minor consecrated through her father, there are grounds for concern that had she been an adult, she would not consent [to marrying this man]. As for our present practice, namely, to effect consecration of our daughters, even while they are minors—that is because every day the Exile becomes more overpowering; if a man presently has the means to provide his daughter with a dowry, he might later lack the means, and thus his daughter would remain unmarriageable.

Filial Autonomy: Choosing a Wife
5. Elijah Capsali, *Me'ah Shearim 62*
Me'ah Shearim (Jerusalem: Ofeq Institute, 2000; Hebrew), pp. 273–75.

Capsali, a renowned Rabbinic leader in the Greek isles in the sixteenth century, devoted this book of a hundred sections to the details, the significance, and the limits of filial obligations—and thus also of the legitimate power of parents. Sections 61-62 reaffirm the Rabbinic teaching that parental authority must yield to divine commands (see §6 below). In section 61, the author cites Asher b. Yehi'el (Rosh, Responsa 15:5), who applied this

teaching to a case where a father instructed his son to remain an enemy of a certain indi-
vidual. Here this is extended to address a story the like of which can probably be told in
every language, in every religious community, and in every country: true love thwarted
by parental disapproval. A father's power over his minor daughter has no parallel regard-
ing his son, but he can still seek to control the son's choice of a mate. Capsali endeavors
to construct love-based marriage as a halakhic obligation. This enables him to invoke the
Rabbinic teaching that precludes obedience to parents when it would encroach upon divine
authority (and true love).

It once happened that Reuben fell in love with a young woman and wanted
to marry her. And Jacob, Reuben's father, disapproved of this young woman
and commanded him not to marry her. And [the father] arose in the synagogue and declared that [his son] would be under a ban if he married her. Tell
us, teacher, . . . whether Reuben is obligated by [Torah] law to obey Jacob, his
father, and to refrain from marrying her on account of the [commandments
to] honor and revere [one's parents]. And if he does marry her, does the ban
take effect or not? . . .

And I replied as follows: Indeed, [the value of] the commandment
of honoring and revering one's father and mother is greater than words can
express, wherefore Scripture equates honor due to one's father and mother
to the honor due to God; and likewise, Scripture equates reverence for one's
father and mother with the reverence for God, as the Rabbis taught in the
first chapter of [BT] Kiddushin [cf. §6 below]. And in the Jerusalem Talmud
[Tractate] Peah (1:1; 15d) [it is stated:] Rabbi Shimon b. Yohai said that honoring one's father and mother is so great that Scripture was stricter with it than
with honor due to God, etc.

Nevertheless, in my humble opinion if the young woman about
whom you ask is suitable for the aforementioned Reuben (I mean if there
is nothing in her or in her family that would disqualify[3] her [from marrying

---

3. The term employed here by Capsali is ambiguous: the criteria for disqualification may be
more or less objective.

him]), it does not appear to me that the commandments to honor or revere [one's parents] apply in such a case, and the son need not give her up on account of his father's pronouncement. For it seems that this father is like one who commands his son to transgress the Torah. [Capsali here reproduces the talmudic discussion in BT Kiddushin 41a (§4 above), which links personal choice of one's spouse to the biblical commandment "You shall love your fellow as your self'" (Lev. 19:18).] It is evident, then, that it is not appropriate for a man to consecrate a woman who is not attractive to him. If so, when the father commands him that he shall not marry the one he loves, it is as if he commanded him to transgress the Torah. And it is well known that a son should not obey his father in such a case. [Capsali here cites Sifra Kedoshim parashah 1 (§6 below)].

And one ought not distinguish between biblical commandments and Rabbinic commandments, since Maimonides has written in [MT] the Laws Concerning Rebels [6:12], with respect to [the obligation of] honoring one's father and mother: "If his father orders him to transgress a positive or a negative command of the Torah or even of Rabbinic origin, he should not obey, for it is written: 'You shall, each [of you], revere his mother and his father and keep My Sabbaths' (Lev. 19:3), that is, all of you are obligated to honor Me."

Therefore, even if you argue that the teachings of Rav Yosef and of Rav Yehudah citing Rav [advocating consecration in person] involve Rabbinic [laws], nevertheless, the son should not obey his father in a case such as this.

Filial Duties

Honoring and Revering Parents
6. Sifra Kedoshim parashah 1

The midrashic commentary on the verse in Leviticus that commands the Israelites to "revere" their parents addresses also the requirement to "honor" them in the Ten Commandments. Exegetical attention is given not only to the difference in verbs but also to the order in which the parents are mentioned and to the verse's second clause— "and keep My Sabbaths"; parental authority is likened, but also subjected, to divine authority.

"You shall, each [of you], revere his mother and his father" (Lev. 19:3). This might be thought to apply only to a man; whence [do we know that it applies also to] a woman? We learn from what is written, "you shall revere" [in the plural]. Why then say "man"?[4] It is just that a man has the capacity to act, whereas a woman lacks such capacity, since she is under the authority of another.

It is written: "You shall, each [of you], revere his mother and his father" (Lev. 19:3), and it is written, "Revere only the Lord your God" (Deut. 6:13). [Thus does] Scripture liken reverence for [one's] father and mother to reverence for God. It is written: "Honor your father and your mother" (Exod. 20:12), and it is written: "Honor the Lord with your wealth" (Prov. 3:9). [Thus does] Scripture liken the honor due one's father and mother to the honor due to God. It is written: "He who curses his father or his mother shall be put to death" (Exod. 21:17), and it is written: "Anyone who curses his God shall bear his guilt" (Lev. 24:15: "blasphemes" in NJPS). [Thus does] Scripture liken blessing[5] one's father and mother to blessing God. However, with respect to striking ["He who strikes his father or his mother shall be put to death" (Exod. 21:15)], it is impossible to utter that with regard to the Higher One. And [these comparisons] are proper, for the three of them are partners in [creating the child].

Rabbi Shimon said: The father as a rule comes before the mother. Can it be that honoring [one's] father has priority[6] over honoring [one's] mother? We learn from what is written, "You shall, each [of you], revere his mother and his father" (Lev. 19:3), which teaches that they are both equal. Still, the Rabbis have stated that the father generally comes before the mother, because both the child and his mother are obligated to honor his father.

4. The word rendered "each" is *ish*, lit., "man."

5. The use of the word "blessing" as a euphemism for "cursing" is common in biblical and Rabbinic literature, in particular toward the deity; see, e.g., Job 1:5, 2:9.

6. Lit., "comes before" [*kodem*].

What is "reverence" and what is "honor"? "Reverence"—he may not sit in his [father's] place, may not speak in his place, and may not contradict him. "Honor"—he must give him food and drink, clothe and cover him, bring him in and take him out.

Perhaps, then, "You shall, each [of you], revere his mother and his father" (Lev. 19:3) implies that if one's father or mother commanded him to transgress one of the Torah's commandments, he should obey? We learn from [the sequel], "and keep My Sabbaths" (Lev. 19:3)—you are all obligated to honor Me.

Go Forth from Your Father's Home
7. Genesis Rabbah 39:7

The Jewish tradition commonly traces its origin to God's call to Abraham to leave behind his country and his father's house and go forth to the promised land. The Midrash here suggests that such revolutionary severing of family roots may not be a model to be followed. The reference to Abraham's father, Terach, as "wicked" evidently draws on his standard depiction in Rabbinic discourse as an idolater.

What is written above? "and Terach died in Haran" (Gen. 11:32); "God said to Abraham: Go you forth." Said Rabbi Yitzhak: As for the reckoning [of Terach's years] up to this point, he still has sixty-five years to go!—Well, first of all one can explain that the wicked are deemed "dead" even while alive. [This was employed here] because Abraham was worried, reflecting: If I depart, I will cause desecration of the divine Name, [for people] will say: "He left behind his father in old age and went off." God said to him: I exempt you from honoring father and mother; but I do not exempt anyone else from honoring father and mother. Moreover, I will record his death prior to your departure. . . . "And Terach died in Haran," and then "God said to Abraham," etc.

Parental Authority and Leaving for the Land of Israel

8. Meir b. Baruch of Rothenburg (Maharam), *Responsa* (Berlin 1891)
2:79

Talmudic illustrations of the limitation upon parental authority are rather straightforward: one must disobey a parental order to flaunt a divine commandment. But what about religious values inherent in the broader features of a life plan? Among medieval Jews, living in the Land of Israel was acknowledged, at least in theory, as a religious ideal, although only a minuscule few tried to realize it (cf. ¢25). Here Rothenburg responds to questions about parents' opposition to their sons' aspiration to live in the holy land; it transpires that value judgments, even if clear-cut on paper, can be more ambiguous in practice.

With regard to your question, whether a father can bar his son from going up to the Land of Israel: Since it is established that going up is a *mitzvah,* it is written "I am the Lord" (Lev. 19:3)—implying that regarding a matter which is a *mitzvah,* the [son] should not obey [his father], for God's honor has priority. With regard to your question about a wife who does not want to go up, namely, whether the [husband] might be liable to [divine] punishment if he divorces her in order to go up—[well], if there were liability, the sages would not have permitted divorcing her while depriving her of the *ketubah!*

With regard to your question, whether I had heard why the great ones commanded their sons to return [from the Land of Israel]: I believe it is because no mercy whatever is shown over there [in the Land]. Also, it is not possible for them to occupy themselves with Torah, because they must work very hard to make a living. Also, since Torah [instruction] is not available there, they lack proper knowledge of the details of the commandments; this is what I have heard from their sons.

Reservations about Leaving Parents Behind

9. Eli'ezer Judah Waldenberg, *Tsits Eli'ezer* 14:72

Israel's chief Sephardi rabbi, Yitzhak Nissim, was asked by Shlomo Zalman Sheragai — a prominent leader and ideologue of the Mizrachi Party and its youth movements — about parental opposition to the movements' work abroad, which involved urging young people to make aliyah. *Nissim affirmed that "going up to the Land of Israel" — a divine commandment — has primacy over parental authority. Waldenberg, a longtime member of the High Rabbinical Court in Jerusalem, takes issue with this ruling. In sections of his argument not reproduced here, he explores the halakhic status of the putative mitzvah to move to the Land of Israel, echoing medieval discussions and in particular the debate about this in observant circles since the early days of the Zionist movement (cf. ¢25). But he also points to a major difference between this commandment and most others: it involves a permanent departure, "absconding" from filial duties altogether. Indeed Elijah Capsali, although expanding filial autonomy with regard to marriage, had expressly prohibited moving to a faraway location, leaving one's parents behind (Me'ah Shearim Section 16, citing some of the sources adduced here). Does it make a difference if the relocation is to the holy land?*

Whether It Is Permitted to Prepare and Train Youths to Go up to the Land of Israel against Their Parents' Wishes; [or] Does This Involve Infringement of the Commandment to Honor Father and Mother?

(a) I had the pleasant surprise of receiving yesterday from the post office your honor's [Rabbi Nissim's] gift of Torah, namely your valuable book Yen ha-Tov. . . . I enjoyed your fine discernment . . . illuminating the wise in issues pertaining to practice. . . . Now by way of cherishing that which is holy, I will offer a short comment regarding your argument in Part 2:7, relating to your response to a question . . . whether it is appropriate to instruct sons to go up to the Land of Israel against their parents' wishes.

Your honor cites the responsum by Mabit [Moses b. Joseph di Trani] 1:139, that one need not obey [a parental command against going to the Land of Israel], this being like that which the Rabbis derived from the verse "You shall, each [of you], revere his mother and his father, and keep My Sabbaths; I am the Lord" (Lev. 19:3) regarding all the commandments, since [the parents] too are obligated by the [same commandments]. Likewise, regarding the commandment to go up to the Land of Israel, the parents too are obligated to go up and settle therein. Additionally [you cite] R. Yehudah Ayyash (*Bet Yehudah* 1 YD 54), who also argued that one may go up to the Land of Israel despite opposition by his father and mother. From this you deduce, in conclusion, a ruling that youth movements abroad may educate and train youths toward going up to the Land of Israel even against the wishes of their parents, provided that the education is in accordance to Jewish tradition. . . .

[In (b) Waldenberg cites opposing sources, including Simeon d. Zemah Duran (*Tashbetz* 3:288), and continues:]

(c) Truly the great scholar [Pinehas Horwitz,] author of *Hafla'ah,* explicitly disagrees with di Trani as follows (*Panim Yafot* commentary on the Torah, at the beginning of Lekh-Lekha): "The Midrash here [says that God told Abraham], 'I exempt you [but not others] from honoring father and mother' [§7 above]. The meaning seems to be thus: If his father is abroad, the son's obligation to go up to the Land of Israel does not have priority over the obligation to honor his father. 'I exempt you [specifically]'—because Terach does not 'observe the people's practices,'[7] but as for other [sons], the obligation to go up to the Land of Israel does not have priority over the obligation to honor [parents]. . . . Still, if they were residents in the Land of Israel and the father moved abroad, the son is not obligated actively to transgress, leaving the Land of Israel to go abroad." . . .

(f) I should also point out that even the text of R. Yehuda Ayyash does not furnish clear proof that he permitted transgressing [the commandment of] honoring father and mother on account of the commandment to go up to the Land of Israel alone. For [in the course of his discussion] there he draws an implication to the contrary from the statement in [BT] Megillah (16b–17a): "Rav Yitzhak b. Shmu'el b. Marta said: Torah study is greater than

---

7. According to the Talmud a father, like others in positions of authority, loses his claim to obedience and respect once he is deemed a deviant; see BT Bava Kama 94b, relying on "among your people" (Exod. 22:27).

honoring father and mother, for Jacob did not incur [divine] punishment on account of all those years he spent [away from his parents, studying] in the House of Shem and Ever."[8] [Ayyash] wonders—What great [value] of Torah study does this show? For all other commandments are equally "greater than honoring father and mother"—[in the sense that] if one's father tells him to transgress even a Rabbinic commandment, one should not obey him! He therefore proposes (in the first of his two solutions) [the following distinction]. The general teaching that one should not obey one's father to transgress a commandment applies when observing that commandment will prevent honoring one's father only temporarily, after which [time] he will resume his normal obedience to the commandment [of honoring parents]. . . . In a case such as this, however, wherein Jacob abdicates from the commandment of honoring for an extended period—such as the fourteen years he was away [in the House of Shem and Ever]—he would not be entitled to such an extended exemption from honoring, except for the great [value] of Torah study.

Thus according to this solution, there is no permission to abscond from honoring one's father and mother for many years by going up to the Land of Israel. Indeed [Ayyash's] conclusion reflects this [argument], and his actual permission in the case at hand was based on the combined [value] of Torah study together with going to the Land of Israel, as stated there: "We thus can conclude as a ruling in the case before us, where there are two [valuable purposes, namely] studying Torah and going to the Land of Israel, that is, to Tsefat (may it be swiftly rebuilt in our time), that he clearly need not obey his father and mother, even though he [thereby] causes them great unhappiness." There is thus no proof that he would have granted a similar permission on account of going up to the Land of Israel alone. . . .

(h) From all the above it seems, in my humble opinion, that it not so straightforward to permit youth movements abroad to educate and train youths to go up to the Land of Israel against their parents' wishes. Rather,

---

8. Jacob's long, painful separation from his son Joseph is seen here as punishment for the equally long period Jacob spent away from his father, Isaac—not counting, however, the fourteen years he spent, by midrashic reckoning, in the legendary "study house of Shem and Ever" (the righteous son and grandson of Noah).

it is necessary to give serious consideration to the concern that this may involve infringement of the important commandment of honoring father and mother.

Going up to the Land: Religious Duty Trumps Parental Authority
10. Ovadyah Yosef, *Yehaveh Da'at* 4:49

Yosef served as Israel's chief Sephardi rabbi, and here takes the side of his predecessor Yitzhak Nissim, asserting that it is supported by the most authoritative traditional sources and offering an ingenious retort to the opposing argument from Genesis Rabbah (§7 above) cited by Eli'ezer Judah Waldenberg. Beyond this formal claim, he emphasizes the great value of settling in the Land of Israel for both the individual and the people, and the parents' own obligation to take part in this. Yosef recognizes the critical issue of mutually exclusive long-term commitments but insists that it is the Land of Israel that allows no more than temporary absence.

Question: Regarding a person whose parents live abroad, and command him to go down from the Land—should he obey his parents and go down in order to observe the commandment of honoring father and mother?

Answer: It is true that the commandment to honor father and mother is of [such] great import that Scripture equated it to the commandment of honoring the Holy One. . . . Nevertheless, the commandment to dwell in the Land of Israel takes precedence over the commandment to honor father and mother. . . .

The Talmud (BT Gittin 8b) states that one may, on Shabbat, instruct a gentile to purchase for him a dwelling in the Land of Israel, [instructing him also] to write and to transfer title in the gentile records, even though instructing a gentile [to perform a Shabbat violation on a Jew's behalf] infringes the Rabbinic definition of "rest" [*shevut*]. . . . Perfet (*Responsa* 387) pointed out that for the sake of performing circumcision—a commandment of great importance, involving thirteen covenants (Mishnah Nedarim 3:11) — infringing the Rabbinic definition of "rest" was not permitted. Yet such infringement was permitted for the sake of the commandment of settling the Land of Israel, because it is a commandment with lasting results, bringing benefit to all Israel, in that the holy land will not remain in the hands of gentiles. . . .

[Having established the importance of the commandment to dwell in the Land of Israel, Yosef cites the Rabbinic teaching that a son should not obey a parental command to transgress the Shabbat or any other commandment, and Meir of Rothenburg's application of that teaching to the issue of going to live in the Land of Israel (§§6 and 8 above), as well as several concordant sources.]

It is true that R. Simeon Duran wrote (*Tashbetz* 3:288) that it is impermissible to leave the Land of Israel except for the sake of the commandment of Torah study or for the commandment of honoring parents. Hence, even though on his view dwelling in the Land of Israel involves a scriptural commandment, it is nevertheless overridden by the commandment of honoring father and mother. However, even for the sake of the commandment of Torah study, leaving to go abroad was permitted only with the intention of returning to the Land of Israel. . . . This indicates that Duran likewise permitted leaving the Land of Israel to go abroad, for the sake of . . . honoring father and mother, only where the departure is accompanied with an intention to return. This is illustrated in the story of Rabbi Assi, who had an old mother abroad and asked Rabbi Yohanan whether he may depart from the Land of Israel to greet her (BT Kiddushin 31b). . . .

[Yosef now cites the contrary argument, based on the midrashic statement regarding Abraham and his father, Terach (§7 above), as set forth by Horwitz and others (presented in Waldenberg, §9 above). He asserts that those who hold so were not cognizant of the positions of Moses b. Joseph di Trani and of Rothenburg.]

Undoubtedly, had [they] known of Rothenburg's responsum they would retract [their teaching on this matter]. As for the proof they adduce from the midrash, it is possible to reply thus: The situation there was different, because the Land of Israel had not yet been consecrated until Abraham walked about its length and breadth, as written: "Up, walk about the land, through its length and its breadth, for I will give it to you" (Gen. 13:17). . . . That is why it was necessary for the Holy One to tell [Abraham] that He exempts him (but no other) from the commandment of honoring father and mother. . . .

In conclusion: The commandment of dwelling in the Land of Israel is of unique value, as it is equal in importance to all of the Torah's [other] commandments [combined]. This is especially so where the intention is to settle in the Land of Israel for the sake of the commandment, and to observe there all the commandments linked to the Land. Therefore if his father commanded him not to go up to the Land, he should not obey him. A fortiori regarding one who has [already] merited settling in the Land, and his father [then] commanded him to go down from the Land, he is certainly forbidden to obey him. For the commandment of dwelling in the Land of Israel takes precedence over the commandment of honoring father and mother, especially since the parents are themselves commanded to go up and settle in the Land. And may God, Blessed be He, gather in our scattered ones from the four corners of the earth.

Commentary. Individualism and Intimacy: God and Parents

At first glance, the biblical mitzvah of parental honor seems of a piece with other traditional patriarchal family practices. The prominence and centrality indicated by its inclusion in both accounts of the Decalogue (Exod. 20:1–14; Deut. 5:6–18) seem to announce unilateral deference and obedience to parents as an unequivocal cultural value. As in the case of the "rebellious son," however, talmudic and later Rabbinic interpretations complicate and subvert the absolute assertion of parental authority that seems to emerge from a plain reading of these verses.

The Talmud not only deconstructs the "rebellious son" law to the point of procedural absurdity (and thus practical irrelevance), it slyly inverts the value poles of the original. Where the Bible seems to prize filial obedience and parental honor above all—to the point of granting parents what amounts to an ownership claim, the power of life and death over their progeny—in the talmudic version, parents who bring this capital charge against their children are subject to social scrutiny and judicial suspicion. What emerges from some of the sources presented in this section is a similar, if perhaps subtler, transformation of the law of parental honor, which in turn may reflect a parallel evolution in the Rabbinic understanding of personal identity as it pertains to relationships with both parents and God.

The source from Sifra Kedoshim (§6) makes parental honor conditional in an important way—it must cohere with divine honor as reflected in the revealed commandments of the Torah. Parents, after all, are subject to God's authority no less than their children. Indeed, some biblical scholars hold that the passage from Leviticus quoted in this midrash is itself an interpretation of the Decalogue, which places the commandment of Sabbath observance before the commandment of parental honor. (This reading would also be supported by the traditional Jewish understanding of the first utterance, "I am the Lord your God," as one of the Ten Commandments, as opposed to its conventional Christian interpretation as an introductory statement.)

In the Rabbinic view of the mitzvah of parental honor, then, divine authority over parents ("you are *all* obligated to honor me") is emphasized as a mediating context for parental authority over children. However, reducing the discussion to a battle of competing authorities for obedience does not seem to capture the full sense of the tradition's take on this triangular relationship.

The richness of implication emerges poignantly in Elijah Capsali's handling of the father's attempt to interfere in his son's choice of a wife. In his response (§5), Capsali quotes the midrashic exception to the parental-honor commandment found in Sifra Kedoshim (via its codification by Maimonides as practical *halakhah*)—but does so in a way that radically expands its application. Since the wording of the original source suggests that its ruling should not be limited to the example provided (Shabbat) but extend equally to all commandments, Capsali further reasons that it must also apply to the commandment to "love your neighbor as yourself."

This logical step opens the exception to parental honor to a new dimension of personal discretion. Capsali invokes the "love your neighbor" commandment in the context of the talmudic opinion cited in tractate Kiddushin (§4), which prohibits a man from consecrating a woman to be his wife by way of an agent (i.e., without meeting her himself), since in doing so he might miss some core incompatibility and come to despise her, a clear violation of "love your neighbor." The talmudic discussion of the verse does not seems concerned with constructing (or nurturing) a positive sense of romantic or spiritual love as much as with identifying and avoiding what would be a clear violation of divine law. This is love as the absence of loathing.

By applying it to the case of the father and son, Capsali considerably expands the parameters of the Kiddushin ruling and of the "love your neighbor" imperative. Recognizing and affirming love's inherent subjectivity leads him to establish subjectivity itself (at least, as it applies to one's relational life) as a potent religious category—integral to the performance of what in the rabbinic imagination is one of the Torah's central commandments. Suddenly, God is on the side of love, such that "when the father commands him that he shall not marry the one he loves, it is as if he commanded him to transgress the Torah."

Here, then, is another instance of the tradition circumscribing parental honor and protecting the subjective integrity of children by linking it to the revealed will of God. What animates this mediating, mitigating voice? Its implications seem to transcend a simple assertion of divine authority over parents, a reminder of "who's really in charge." What looked in the midrash on Leviticus like an apparently straightforward, legalistic comparison of competing commandments—parental honor versus Shabbat—has expanded to make God an ally of subjectivity and an advocate of relationship.

To account for this powerful mitigating voice within the tradition clearly requires something beyond the legalist model. In its place, I would suggest a genetic model: that is, God as third parent. In other words, the limit on parental honor expresses not only an authority claim of God over parents but a parental intimacy between God and every human being. One of the first things the Bible establishes is humanity's creation "in the image of God," suggesting not only metaphorical resemblance but genealogy. Indeed, the Sifra Kedoshim justifies its own scriptural and halakhic comparison of a person's biological parents to God by explaining that "the three of them are partners in [creating the child]."

Parents naturally, if to varying degrees, seek to impress and impose their world view and values upon their children. The mirroring of parents is the earliest source of identity available to children, and it continues throughout life in children's attempts to mimic the particularities of the family culture, ideology, and norms, the parental "oughts" and "shoulds." The success of these attempts is determined by the extent to which they "make sense" to parents as legitimate expressions of themselves, which they can affirm and reinforce or reject, shaping their offspring's identity in their image.

Often, when parents object to their children's choice of a significant other, it is because that person does not fit in with their sense of the familial culture, identity, or destiny. In this context, the child's subjective experience is construed as unnatural or immoral, a perspective irreconcilably at odds with the experience of love. The children respond—as in the many familiar accounts—by protesting that their love is only conceivable as something God-given and intrinsic to their spiritual makeup and fulfillment ("If you really knew me, you would understand and support this"). In a forthcoming study of young Arab women in traditional Muslim communities, many of the young women my coauthor and I interviewed expressed their most intense feelings of betrayal toward parents who placed them in arranged marriages, forcing them to negate their profound inner knowledge of love and of themselves. The Capsali source would seem to suggest that this amounts to a negation of God as well.

God as third parent reminds us that although children do owe their biological parents deference and respect, the children are neither owned nor ultimately defined by their parents. For there is another source within each person, another image imprinted on the unique identity of every human being, another parent, acutely attuned to and affirming of an individual subjectivity that transcends biological parentage. So each individual is imbued with a unique inner voice that enables him or her to discern and desire. This tradition asserts, in other words, that even though we owe our parents respect and care, we do not owe them our identity or our particular destiny.

Against this theological backdrop, the answer to the question whether a person can move to Israel over parental objection may seem obvious. After all, living in the holy land is considered a *mitzvah:* both a legal obligation derived from a biblical verse and a spiritually enhancing life choice guaranteed to deepen one's relation with God. In the traditional imagination, the Land of Israel is a landscape infused with divine presence and love. Moreover, the choice of a home and the choice of a spouse would seem to be rooted in similarly subjective considerations: these are one-time acts; the stakes are high. These choices are also contexts—stamped with the imprimatur of divine affirmation by explicit reference in biblical verse—within which one's identity may be nurtured and shaped over time.

In this vein, it is not difficult to understand the positions cited in the sources expressing approval for going against parental wishes and moving to Israel. Meir of Rothenburg (§8) seems to construe the parental objection (to borrow from Capsali's formulation) as akin to a commandment to transgress the will of God. For him, the proximity of the proclamation "I am the Lord your God" to the commandment to live in Israel emphasizes God's authority over parents (as if in anticipation of just such a parental objection). It also recalls other sharp talmudic statements about the impossibility of having a true relationship with God outside of the holy land: "A person who dwells outside of the Land of Israel is like one who has no God"; "Whoever lives outside of the Land of Israel may be regarded as one who worships idols" (BT Ketubot 110a).

The more surprising ruling, in this context, is Eli'ezer Judah Waldenberg's (§9) solemn admonition that in the case of parental objection to moving to Israel, "it is necessary to give serious consideration to the concern that this may involve infringement of the important commandment of honoring father and mother." The earlier ruling that he invokes (which takes issue with the position expressed by Meir of Rothenburg above) is based on an intriguing and counterintuitive midrash on the founding moment of Jewish tradition: Abraham's decision to leave his father, Terach, to follow God. What is surprising is that the rabbis did not take the legitimacy of this decision for granted; on the contrary, it seems to leave them anxious about the precedential value of this portentous act by Judaism's founding father.

The Midrash here [says that God told Abraham], "I exempt you [but not others] from honoring father and mother" [§7 above]. The meaning seems to be thus: . . . 'I exempt you [specifically]'— because Terach does not 'observe the people's practices,' but as for other [sons], the obligation to go up to the Land of Israel does not have priority over the obligation to honor [parents].

The only justification this midrash can come up with to exempt Abraham permanently from the obligation to honor his parents is the worst offense against God known in the Bible: idolatry. The physical integrity of the family, the presence that makes relationship possible, emerges here as a core religious priority, trumping even the most divinely sanctioned desires and the most redemptive journeys, if such desires and journeys will remove a person permanently from the parental orbit.

Meir of Rothenburg wrote his responsum in the High Middle Ages, whereas Waldenberg, writing in the early years of the Jewish state, was responding not merely to the halakhic question at hand but to the phenomenon of Zionism itself and its impact on the Jewish family structure throughout Europe. Moving to Israel, in this context, connoted more than a change of location; it often came not only with a breaking of ties with tradition but with the family itself. For example, it was common practice for Zionist pioneers to change their name once they arrived in Israel. The price of *aliyah* was not only self-sacrifice but also sacrifice of the family. The dream of the Jewish state, which captured the imaginations of many young Jews, brought with it a grave loss, and this was partly by design. Nationalist movements often target the family structure as an obstacle to ideological purity, a "dual allegiance" deemed threatening to movement loyalty, and Zionism had an element of this as well.

Waldenberg takes pains to point out that this kind of break with the family contravenes one of Judaism's core values. Zionism demanded a different, less negotiable break from the past than love. Marrying someone against parental objections does not necessarily represent an exit from the familial fold. It is up to parents and children to resolve their differences and find their way to a life together. The subjective impulse to sever ties more radically, on the other hand, meets resistance from God as third parent, supporting biblical verse or not. Just as one's biological parents are never permitted to demand actions that might break one's relationship with God, so God is similarly protective of the integrity of the family relationship. The idea of exploding that unit is disturbing, no matter what the circumstance, no matter how seemingly justified. Not all forms of self-exploration are blessed with divine advocacy or protection.

Tova Hartman

Leaving Parents Behind to Build the Future

11. Avoth Yeshurun, "All Your Loved Ones"

Collected Poems, vol. 2 (Tel Aviv: Hakibbutz Hameuchad, 1997), p. 72.

Yeshurun was a powerful expressionist Hebrew poet living in Tel Aviv. He was born Yehiel Perlmutter, scion to an important Ukrainian hasidic family against whose traditions he rebelled. After experiencing the fate of a refugee as a child in the First World War, he immigrated as a young man to Palestine, leaving his family behind. As the years passed and the situation in Europe turned gloomier, and the possibility of facilitating his family's immigration became more and more remote, he experienced his own move as an abandonment. The experience of a redeeming immigration changing its hues is starkly encapsulated in this poem that speaks for an entire generation of youth leaving home for the utopian home of Zion.

All Your Loved Ones
I left his home
on my own.
To build him a home
on my own.

It has become clear
however that my father
remained alone
and abandoned
not on his own.

I was in motion toward my father.
I was escaping my father.
Every two pennies he sent me.
I for him a dollar.

All your loved ones. You should have
saved them.
And when the day of the moment arrived
I was no one to speak to.

My brothers I did not save.
Difficult—A writer of letters
am I. And when their letter and envelope ceased
I felt relief.

My father you are in my dreams. A moon fallen
asleep under cloud stone. You see
it repeats. Your life you repeat.
And life and love and death and me.

Caring for Parents
12. BT Kiddushin 31b–32a

The Talmud here focuses on "honoring" one's parents, interpreted above (§6) as an obligation to care for them and provide for their needs. Though the text speaks throughout of "him" and of one's "father," this is certainly an obligation owed to both parents. A central issue of contention here is whether this is a duty of personal care and service or also one of financial support.

What is "honor"?—One must give [his parent] food and drink, clothe and cover him, bring him in and take him out. The question arose, from whose [property are these things to be provided]? Rav Yehudah said, from the son's; Rav Natan b. Oshaia said, from the father's. The Rabbis rendered a decision to Rabbi Yirmiyah (others say it was to Rabbi Yirmiyah's son), in accordance with the one who said, "from the father's." Against this, the [following *baraita*] was cited: It is written: "Honor your father and your mother" (Exod. 20:12), and it is written: "Honor the Lord with your wealth" (Prov. 3:9). Just as in the latter case, "honor" means with financial cost, so too in the former case does it mean with financial cost. But if you say that [the provision is made] "from the father's" [property], what [financial] impact does it entail for [the son]?—The suspension of his work. . . .

Come and hear: Rabbi Eli'ezer was asked, How far must one go in honoring one's father and mother? He replied: To the point that [the parent] takes a purse and throws it into the sea in [the son's] presence, and [the son] does not berate him. Now if you say that [the provision is made] "from the father's" [property, and hence this must be the father's purse], what impact does it entail for [the son]?—This is [money] that he stands to inherit.

Providing for Parents

13. JT Kiddushin 1:7, 61a–c

The JT records the same debate about whether a son must use his own funds to provide for his father. In an initial section, paralleling the BT, a negative answer is defended; but the following discussions point conclusively in the other direction. A different analysis of the same biblical verses cited in the BT yields a requirement that children bear the financial

burden of parental support. Indeed, the burden is imposed even upon impoverished chil-
dren, who must beg for help from others in order to provide for their parents.

(61a) What is "reverence"? He may not sit in [the parent's] place, may not speak in his turn, and may not contradict him. What is "honor"? He must give him food and drink, clothing, covering, and shoes, bring him in and take him out. From whose [property are these things to be provided]? Huna b. Hiyya said, from the father's. Some wished to say, from [the son's; arguing:]—Did Rabbi Abahu not say, citing Rabbi Yose b. Rabbi Haninah: Whence do we know that even if his father said to him, "Throw this purse into the sea," he must obey him?—That refers to [a case] where [the son] has another [purse], and seeks to appease him [by throwing away an empty one].

(61b) . . . A saying of Rabbi Hiya bar Abba disagrees, for Rabbi Hiya bar Abba said, Rabbi Yudan, son of Rabbi Shimon b. Yohai's daughter, taught that Rabbi Shimon b. Yohai taught: "Great is the honoring of one's father and mother, for the Holy One extended [its demands] beyond those [involved in] honoring Him." It is written here, "Honor your father and your mother" (Exod. 20:12), and it is written elsewhere, "Honor the Lord with your wealth [with the best of all your income]" (Prov. 3:9). How do you honor [God] with your wealth? You set aside gleanings, the forgotten sheaf, and the corner of the field. You set aside *terumah,* first and second tithes, the poor's tithe, and *hallah.* You make a *sukkah, lulav, shofar,* phylacteries, and fringes. You feed the hungry and give drink to the thirsty. If you possess [property], you are obligated in all these [offerings], but if you don't, you are not obligated in any of them. However, when it comes to honoring your father and your mother, whether or not you have [property] you must "honor your father and your mother" even [if it requires you] to go [begging] from door to door. . . .

(61c) Rabbi Yanai and Rabbi Yonatan were sitting. A man came and kissed Rabbi Yonatan's feet. Rabbi Yanai said to him: What good turn of yours is he repaying? [Rabbi Yonatan] replied: He once complained to me, demanding that his son support him. I said to him, "Go shut [your son] out of the synagogue and shame him." [Rabbi Yanai] said to him: Why didn't you [simply] compel him [to support his father]? He replied: Can [children] be compelled [to support their parents]? Rabbi Yanai responded: You still question that? Rabbi Yonatan then reversed himself and established [this as] the tradition in [Rabbi Yanai's] name. Rabbi Aha b. Ya'akov [reported, citing] Rabbi Shmu'el b. Nahmani, in the name of Rabbi Yonatan: A son can be compelled to support his father. Rabbi Yose said: I wish all traditions were as clear to me as this one, that a son can be compelled to support his father.

Coercing and Shaming a Recalcitrant Son
14. Solomon b. Abraham Adret (Rashba), *Responsa* 4:56

The issue here—as in the previous selection—is whether the community can use its coercive powers to force a son to support his father, designated here as "Reuben." Adret argues that, even if compulsion is not warranted, there is room for employing social pressure. But when the father lacks resources and the son has means, support can be compelled as a form of tzedakah. This latter basis for communal coercion will be revisited in the next chapter (cf. also §§19-20 below). The father's attempt to place his son directly under a ban is deemed unauthorized, but it is not obvious that this would be so if such means of compulsion were warranted—that is, "if the son has means" that he refuses to use.

You asked about Reuben, who brought a charge at court regarding his son Hanokh, [demanding] that he support him. The son claims that he has children and must support them and, furthermore, that his father has debts [receivable] that would be sufficient to support him [if collected]. The father argues that these are doubtful debts, and that he would die of starvation before he could collect them. He remonstrated with his son, but [his son] paid no attention; he got angry at his son and pronounced a ban against him, forbidding his participation in prayers with ten [men in public] and in grace after meals with three [men], and compelling him to behave like a mourner,[9]

---

9. Lit., "cover his head"; all these are aspects of being under a formal ban (see ¢23, §16).

until he provides the support. Inform me whether or not the court ought to compel him to support his father.

Response: According to the conclusion of the [Babylonian] Talmud in the first chapter of Kiddushin, as a matter of law the son is not obligated to support his father. . . . However, the son may properly be shamed, and the synagogue services halted on his account[10] so that he will support his father. For we read in the Jerusalem Talmud: "Rabbi Yanai and Rabbi Yonatan were sitting . . ." (see §13 above). Hence, even according to the one who holds that the son may not be compelled [to support his father], the synagogue is closed to him and he is to be shamed. However, to pronounce a ban against him as Reuben did is not in accordance with the law. For . . . is this not the utmost compulsion? It is like "grabbing a man by his testicles so that he surrender his garment" (BT Shevuot 41b). And certainly if the father has debts [receivable] and the son wants to purchase [them] from him, or if the father could find someone to purchase [them] from him, the son is not obligated to support him at his own expense. Still, it stands to reason that if the son has means, we compel him to support his father at his own expense pursuant to the obligations of *tzedakah,* just as we compel the father to support his minor children pursuant to the obligations of *tzedakah,* as we read in [the Talmud]. . . ." [If the father] has means we compel him against his will, as in the [case] of Rava, who compelled Rav Natan b. Ami and extracted from him four hundred *zuz* for *tzedakah*" (BT Ketubot 49b, §19 below).

Protecting the Son's Financial Autonomy
15. David b. Solomon Ben Zimra (Radbaz), *Responsa* 2:663

For Jews of certain social classes, begging or hiring themselves out as day laborers was nearly unthinkable, and they would prefer making do with whatever meager resources they had. But is a man permitted to exercise such a preference when he has obligations

10. See ¢8, §8.

to others, or can he be compelled to resort to such means, even if unaccustomed, in order to pay creditors or fulfill his obligations toward his wife? In the previous selection, Adret ruled—following the BT—that a son can be compelled to support his father only if he has resources. The questioner here reports that a certain rabbi—echoing the JT—extended this to an obligation to go and earn, or beg for, the requisite resources. Writing in sixteenth-century Egypt, Ben Zimra strongly contests this ruling for the sake of the son's self-respect and self-sufficiency. Still, he employs the alternative JT tradition to preclude relegation of a parent to the status of a mere stranger.

Question: You have enquired from me regarding one of the *hakhamim* who ruled that a person is obligated to beg from door to door or to hire himself out in order to support his father; implausibly, he even [ruled] that [the son] must pay the king's tax, i.e., the poll tax, on [the father's] behalf. You wished to know whether or not it is proper to rely upon this ruling.

Response: This ruling is entirely wrong. The only question that arose [in the Talmud, see §12 above] was, From whose property should care be provided? . . . And the decision was rendered . . . that the law is in accordance with the one who said, "from the father's," and all the decisors have so ruled. [True], where the son has [resources] and the father has none, the son is obligated to support his father. . . .

[Ben Zimra cites the statement in the JT (§13 above) that the son must beg from door to door in order to provide for his father. He then cites various proposals to accommodate this statement—for example, that since the son is required to devote time to caring for his parents even if this involves suspending his work, this might lead him to destitution and so to beggary. But he concludes:]

From our [i.e., the Babylonian] Talmud one can deduce, however, that the law is not so. For the statement [in the JT, requiring the son to go begging] follows the view that support must be provided from the son's property, whereas we do not hold so. . . . Rather, it is [only] from the father's [property]. . . .

I conclude likewise from a close reading of the master's [Maimonides] language in the Laws Concerning Rebels: "What is 'Honor'—he must give [his father] food and drink, clothe and cover him—from the father's [property]. And if the father has no property and the son does, the son is compelled to support his father to the extent of his capacity" (MT Laws Concerning Rebels 6:3). We learn from his language that [the son] is not obligated to beg from door to door or to hire himself out in order to support his father. We further learn that if [the son] has abundant provision, he must provide abundantly for his father; and even if he has only bare provision, he must provide likewise for his father; this is implied in his language, "to the extent of his capacity." This diverges from the ruling of [Rabbi Joseph Karo in his] *Bet Yosef* (YD 240) [who rules that the son can be compelled to support his father only to the same extent as he would be compelled to support any other person in need].

It also seems to me, following the decisors, that if [the son] would have nothing to eat if he suspended his work, it is not in the father's honor that [his son] die of hunger or go begging from door to door at day's end. . . . And [this is certainly true] if the son has a wife, whom he is obligated to support! "The ways of [Torah] are the ways of pleasantness."[11] Rather, let him do his work [instead of personally caring for his father] and they will all be provided for equally. The Talmud's statement regarding suspension of work applies when he has [property]; in that case he is required to suspend his work [to care for his father] even though [this entails loss of income]. . . . That is the point of the master's writing, "to the extent of his capacity"—whereas if he has nothing, and his soul yearns only for his wages,[12] such a one lacks capacity. . . .

[Thus] even though the decisors have written that we collect from [the son to support the father] as *tzedakah,* [the father] is not exactly like other poor people. Rather, [the son pays] according to his income thus acting in righteousness [*tzedakah*] toward his father, as it is the way of the world to support [one's father] in accordance with one's income. This position is

---

11. This verse (Prov. 3:17) sometimes serves as a prooftext for the principle that halakhic norms must be interpreted so as to conform to what is appropriate and reasonable.

12. Paraphrasing Deut. 24:15—the prohibition on withholding the wages of a day laborer.

midway between [the teachings of] our [Babylonian] Talmud and the Jerusalem Talmud.

Support of Parents Trumps All Tzedakah

16. Moses Sofer, *Responsa Hatam Sofer* YD 2:229

In our discussion of welfare and of taxation in the following chapters, it is widely accepted that a person is required to give at least a certain portion of his income to tzedakah. This gives rise to the question here: If supporting one's parents is also tzedakah, can it be subtracted from what one would normally give to the community's fund or directly to the poor (the son's "regular tithe")? Sofer says yes, up to, and even beyond, the accepted limit on charitable giving. In ¢20, §30, Yehiel Mikhel Epstein gives a different answer to a related question, warning of the neglect of the community's poor that may follow if tzedakah is distributed entirely within the family.

This question was asked by a certain learned person, [a son] of honored, well-born parents who are in dire straits and cannot take their support from the [public] *tzedakah* fund. The son cannot afford to give them everything [to meet] their needs, for his children and the needs of his household are many. [The question is:] May he support them from the tithe that he regularly gives from his property [for *tzedakah,* thereby] giving to no other poor person, whether close or distant, until his parents are supported in honor and comfort?

[Response:] In my humble opinion, it is certainly permitted; indeed, there is an obligation [for the son to support his parents in this way]. He is not permitted to give his tithe to any [other] poor person unless his parents have enough for their own support. This can be established [as follows:] . . . The rule that honoring [supporting one's parents] is to be done from the father's [property] applies when the father has [resources], but when he has none, while the son prospers, the son is obligated to provide for his father.

This is derived also from the Jerusalem Talmud, where it is deduced from Scripture. Now the consensus of the decisors is that this is under the rubric of *tzedakah,* and compulsion should be employed, just as it is employed for *tzedakah,* as [stated] in [BT Ketubot 49b, §19 below] that a father is [likewise] compelled to support his [minor] children. . . . It is true that with regard to other poor relatives [who take precedence over poor persons in general], he should distribute [his *tzedakah* among them]; but to his father he must give everything. . . .

It seems clear that according to scriptural law, a person who has enough for his [immediate] needs of the day is required to give everything beyond that to the poor. It is true that his own life takes precedence;[13] but once he has enough for his needs that day, all the rest of his property should go to the poor in need. In Usha, however, it was ordained that one should not give away more than a fifth [of his money] (BT Ketubot 50a, ¢20, §33). . . . But this restriction was not [meant to] apply to honoring parents. Rather, here scriptural law was retained: as long as he is not forced to beg from door to door, but rather has enough to live on, anything beyond that should be given to his parents (Passover 5574 [1814]).

Parental Duties

The Obligations of Fathers
17. Mishnah Kiddushin 1:7; BT Kiddushin 29a—30b

The enigmatic mishnaic text, which we translate literally, is parsed in the talmudic commentary that follows: the mishnah refers to the obligations of parents. More particularly, it refers to the obligations of fathers to their sons. These begin with circumcision and with the ritual redeeming of the firstborn (see Maimonides, MT Laws Concerning First Fruits 11) and reach to a number of educational requirements. Regarding the obligation to provide for the son's marriage, the talmudic discussion extends this to daughters as well.

13. See ¢17, §18.

Mishnah Kiddushin 1:7

[With respect to] all obligations of the son on the father, men are
obligated and women are exempt. And [with respect to] all obligations of the
father on the son, both men and women are obligated.

BT Kiddushin 29a–30b

What [is meant by the phrase] "all obligations of the son on the
father"? If we say [that it means] "all obligations that the son is obligated to
perform toward his father"—Are women exempt? For it was taught, "'You
shall, each [of you], revere his mother and his father' (Lev. 19:3). This might
be thought to apply only to a man; whence [do we know that it applies also
to] a woman? The sequel, 'you shall revere' [in the plural] implies two." Rav
Yehudah said: [The mishnah] means: "All obligations of the son [that are in-
cumbent] upon the father" to do for his son, men are obligated and women
are exempt. This is in accordance with what our Rabbis taught: "A father is
obligated to circumcise his son, to redeem him, to teach him Torah, to take
a wife for him, and to teach him a craft. Some say [he is] also [obligated] to
teach him to swim. . . . Rabbi Yehudah said: Anyone who does not teach his
son a craft has taught him thievery." Can you really think [that he has taught
him] thievery? Rather it is as if he taught him thievery.

"To circumcise him." Whence do we know this? For it is written,
"And Abraham circumcised his son Isaac" (Gen. 21:4). And if his father does
not circumcise him, the court is obligated to circumcise him, for it is written, "Every male among you shall be circumcised" (Gen. 17:10). And if the
court does not circumcise him, he is obligated to circumcise himself, for it is
written, "Any male who is uncircumcised, who fails to circumcise the flesh
of his foreskin, shall be cut off" (Gen. 17:14). Whence do we know that she
[a mother] is not obligated? For it is written, "[And Abraham circumcised his
son Isaac . . .] as God had commanded him" (Gen. 21:4); "him" but not her.
We find an immediate [obligation]. Whence do we know it is for [all] generations? The School of Rabbi Yishmael taught: In every place that "command" is written [in Scripture], [the word] is there only to denote [that the

commandment is to be carried out with] zeal, immediately, and for [all] generations. With zeal, as it is written: "And command Joshua, and imbue him with strength and courage" (Deut. 3:28); immediately, and for [all] generations—as written, "from the day that the Lord commanded, and on through the ages" (Num. 15:23). . . .

"To teach him Torah." Whence do we know this? For it is written: "And teach them to your sons"[14] (Deut. 11:19). And if his father has not taught him, he is obligated to teach himself, as written: "Study them [the laws and rules]" (Deut. 5:1). Whence do we know that she [a mother] is not obligated [to teach her children]? For it is written (Deut. 11:19), "ve-limadetem" [and teach them], [which also reads] u-lemadetem [and study them], [hence] anyone who is commanded to study is commanded to teach, and anyone who is not commanded to study is not commanded to teach. And whence do we know that she [a woman] is not obligated to teach herself? For it is written, "ve-limadetem" [and teach them, which also reads] u-lemadetem [and study them]; hence, anyone whom others are commanded to teach is commanded to teach himself, and anyone whom others are not commanded to teach is not commanded to teach himself. And whence do we know that others are not commanded to teach her? For it is written: "and teach them to your sons" (Deut. 11:19)—and not to your daughters. . . .

"To take a wife for him." Whence do we know this? For it is written: "Take wives and beget sons and daughters; and take wives for your sons, and give your daughters to husbands" (Jer. 29:6). This makes sense regarding a son, for [taking a wife] is in [the father's] hands, but regarding [the giving of] a daughter, is it in his hands? This is what [the prophet] told them: Give her some [dowry], clothe her and adorn her, so that men will seek her.[15]

"To teach him a craft." Whence do we know this? Hizkiyah said that Scripture states, "Make yourself a living alongside[16] a woman that you love" (Eccles. 9:9). If "woman" is to be taken literally, [the import is that] just as one is obligated to take a wife for [his son], he is similarly obligated to teach

14. NJPS plausibly translates: "children."
15. See §24 below.
16. Idiomatically translated, this is: "Enjoy life with."

him a craft. And if [it] is [a metaphor for] the Torah, [the import is that] just as one is obligated to teach [his son] Torah, he is similarly obligated to teach him a craft.

"Some say [he is] also [obligated] to teach him to swim. . . ." What is the reason? His life may depend on it.

Commitments to Offspring in the Marriage Contract
18. Mishnah Ketubot 4:10–11, 6

The Mishnah attests to great variety in the clauses and wording of the marriage contract, and it aims to establish a core of "judicial stipulations" that bind the husband even if omitted. These include entitlements of the bride's future offspring after the husband's death (for implications regarding inheritance, see §24 below). As indicated in a previous section of this same Mishnah chapter (4:4, see ¢18, §15), it is only upon moving from her father's domain to that of her husband that a woman becomes entitled to sustenance, as emphasized here by Rabbi Elazar b. Azariah. Thus in our next selection, the Talmud explores a father's obligation to his children, both male and female.

10. If he omitted the clause "Male children that you shall bear me will inherit the sum of your *ketubah,* in addition to their shares among their [other] brothers"—he is [nevertheless] obligated, since it is a judicial stipulation.

11. If he omitted the clause "Female children that you shall bear me will reside in my house and be sustained from my estate until married to husbands"—he is [nevertheless] obligated, since it is a judicial stipulation.

6. A father is not obligated to [provide] sustenance for his daughter. This was derived by analogy by Rabbi Elazar b. Azariah before the sages in the Yavneh Vineyard: "The sons will inherit" and "the daughters will be sustained"—just as the sons inherit only after their father's death, so too the daughters are sustained only after their father's death.

Defining Child Support: Mitzvah *or Legal Obligation?*
19. BT Ketubot 49a–b

Seeking to explain why Rabbi Elazar b. Azariah (in §18 above) spoke only of sustenance
for daughters, the Talmud cites a baraita *in which two prominent teachers of the follow-*
ing (Usha) generation agree not only that a father must provide sustenance for children of
both genders but also that this mitzvah *does not give rise to a legal obligation. The* sugya
reports an Usha enactment of such an obligation but indicates that it was ultimately not
accepted. Elsewhere, sustenance for small children (up to the age of six) is subsumed under
the husband's obligation to provide for his wife (BT Ketubot 65b; see Maimonides' codi-
fication in the next selection).

[*Mishnah:* A father is not obligated to [provide] sustenance for his daughter.]
Gemara: It is his daughter for whom he is not obligated to [provide] sustenance—implying that for his son he is obligated to [provide] sustenance; and
[also that] even regarding his daughter, although there is no obligation, there
is a *mitzvah.* According to whom is this mishnah? Not Rabbi Meir, nor Rabbi
Yehudah, nor Rabbi Yohanan b. Beroka! For it was taught:

It is a *mitzvah* to sustain daughters, and even more so sons, who engage in Torah [study]; these are the words of Rabbi Meir. Rabbi Yehudah says:
It is a *mitzvah* to sustain sons, and even more so daughters, [to prevent] dishonor. Rabbi Yohanan b. Beroka says: There is an obligation to sustain daughters after their father's death; while he is alive, however, neither [sons] nor
[daughters] have [a claim] to sustenance.

[The *sugya* goes on to show how the mishnah's meaning can be variously construed in line with each of the three positions.]

Rabbi Illa said: Resh Lakish said, citing Rabbi Yehudah b. Haninah:
At Usha it was enacted [*hitkinu*] that a person must [provide] sustenance for
his sons and daughters while they are minors.

The question was raised: Is the law in accordance with him or is it
not? Come and hear: When [such a case] would come before Rav Yehudah,
he would say to them: The *yarod* [*Rashi:* a jackal, which is cruel to its off-

spring] has produced offspring and dumped them on the townspeople. . . . When [such a man] would come before Rava, he would say to him: Are you comfortable with your children being sustained from *tzedakah?* This only applies, however, if he is without means, for [if the father] has means we compel him against his will, as in the [case] of Rava, who compelled Rav Natan b. Ami and extracted from him four hundred *zuz* for *tzedakah.*[17]

Child Support: Between Pressure and Enforcement

20. Maimonides, MT Laws Concerning Marriage 12:14–15

The Code of Maimonides, Book Four: The Book of Women, translated by Isaac Klein, YJS (New Haven: Yale University Press, 1972), pp. 76–77.

This chapter of the Mishneh Torah sets out the core of the standard requisite marriage contract and then goes on to detail the man's obligation to "maintain" his wife—i.e., to provide sustenance. In this context, Maimonides codifies not only the talmudic teaching about sustaining small children but also the requirement to sustain older children, which is not, strictly speaking, enforceable—unless the father has means (cf. §§14 and 19 above).

14. Just as a man is liable for the maintenance of his wife, so is he liable for the maintenance of his minor sons and daughters, until they reach the age of six years. After that, he must provide them with food until they grow up, according to the enactment of the Sages. If he refuses, he should be reprimanded, shamed, and importuned. If he still refuses, a public announcement should be made as follows: "So-and-so is a cruel man and refuses to maintain his children." He is worse therefore than an unclean bird, for it feeds its young. He may not be compelled, however, to maintain his children after the age of six.

       15. When does this apply? When the man is not reputed to be of means, and it is not known whether or not he is able to give *tzedakah.* If he is reputed to possess enough means to be able to afford *tzedakah* sufficient to

17. BT Bava Batra 8b; cf. ¢20, §27.

cover his children's needs, the corresponding amount should be forcibly collected from him, under the heading of *tzedakah*, and the children should be maintained until they grow up.

Extending Parental Obligation: Support for Adolescents

21. Explanatory Statement of 1944 Enactment of the Council of the Chief Rabbinate

Jewish Law: History, Sources, Principles, translated by Bernard Auerbach and Melvin J. Sykes, vol. 2 (Philadelphia: JPS, 1994), pp. 831–32; reprinted by permission of the University of Nebraska Press; copyright 1994 by Menachem Elon.

This takkanah *requires that parents support their children until age fifteen—and that they do so as a legal obligation (*tzedakah *is not mentioned). It was drafted by the Chief Rabbinate of the Land of Israel, which had been constituted under the British Mandate and viewed itself as one of the institutions of the emergent Jewish state. The argument here thus conveys a sense of reclaiming the authority to right an age-old wrong. Eventually, Israeli state law mandated support of minors up to the age of eighteen.*

Previously among the Jewish people, although under strict law a father was compelled [by the court] to support his minor children from his assets only up to the age of six, he would be shamed and publicly excoriated in order to compel him to support them until they became adults. However, in our times, the generation is deficient, to our sorrow, and such moral pressure is not at all effective.

This is a matter for great shame and anger. Whoever looks at this fairly will conclude that the situation requires appropriate remedial legislation. In our time, even adolescent children (girls as well as boys) under the age of fifteen face serious moral dangers if their support is not assured on a legal basis. There is no need to elaborate on a matter that is understood by anyone whose eyes are open to the present situation.

There is only one way to overcome the confusion and complications, namely, to adopt an all-inclusive enactment that will apply universally;

and after this enactment is adopted by the Chief Rabbinate of the Land of Israel and its expanded Council and by the rabbinical courts and the rabbis who function in the communities (under the sanction of the Chief Rabbinate) and with the approval of the communities through their councils and committees, this enactment will have full force and effect to the same extent as the enactments of "Shum,"[18] Toledo (see §23 below), the Council of the Four Lands, and so on.

It will be law in the full and strict sense of the term. It will be the basis of decision by the Jewish courts in the entire holy land. In a case of noncompliance, the governmental courts will necessarily rule in accordance with this enactment; and this enactment will apply both prospectively and retroactively.

God forbid that we compare ourselves to our rabbis, the Geonim of blessed memory. However, Jephthah in his generation is equal to Samuel in his generation;[19] and enactments were adopted in every generation to counteract wrongdoers, to promote the public welfare, and to maintain the rule of law. Why should we be deficient when the time requires such action, especially when this enactment will also be a communal enactment?

It is for this reason that we have adopted this general enactment for the entire Land of Israel. Just as from ancient times until today a Jewish court has had the power to impose on a father the full legal obligation to support his children up to the age of six years and to enforce this obligation against his property and through all possible legal means, so from this time forward it will have the power to impose upon him the full legal obligation to support his sons and daughters up to the age of fifteen years and to enforce this obligation against his property and through all possible means.

18. This represents the Hebrew acronym for the leading Jewish communities in the Rhine valley during the High Middle Ages.
19. See BT Rosh Hashanah 25b.

Inheritance

Biblical Law of Succession

22. Numbers 27:8–11; Deuteronomy 21:15–17

These are the crucial biblical texts dealing with inheritance (for the full context of the first section, allowing for succession by a daughter in the absence of a son, see ¢13, §§4–5). Although the second text here speaks of the father's action in distributing his property to his sons, no room is allowed for a "will" reflecting individual preference. The kinship system wholly determines the transfer of property across generations.

Numbers 27:8–11

Further, speak to the Israelite people as follows: "If a man dies without leaving a son, you shall transfer his property to his daughter. If he has no daughter, you shall assign his property to his brothers. If he has no brothers, you shall assign his property to his father's brothers. If his father had no brothers, you shall assign his property to his nearest relative in his own clan, and he shall inherit it." This shall be the law of procedure for the Israelites, in accordance with the Lord's command to Moses.

Deuteronomy 21:15–17

If a man has two wives, one loved and the other unloved, and both the loved one and the unloved have borne him sons, but the first-born is the son of the unloved one—when he wills his property to his sons, he may not treat as first-born the son of the loved one in disregard of the son of the unloved one who is older. Instead, he must accept the first-born, the son of the unloved one, and allot to him a double portion of all he possesses; since he is the first fruit of his vigor, the birthright is his due.

The Gift and the Will
23. Mishnah Bava Batra 8:5

Here the Rabbis begin the complicated legal process of establishing the right to make dis-tributions, departing in effect from the biblical laws of inheritance (while formally respect-ing scriptural authority). The father can leave his property to persons not authorized in the biblical texts to receive it; he can do this in writing or by an oral deathbed testament, so long as he does not use the language of inheritance. It seems probable that the Rabbis are recognizing a process that began independently of their initiative—and perhaps try-ing to set limits on it. The effort to set limits, to regulate cross-generational transfers (and protect the sons' entitlements from arbitrary parental power), is reflected also in the texts that follow this one.

One who says: "So-and-so, my firstborn son, shall not collect a double por-tion," or "So-and-so, my son, shall not inherit with his brothers"—has said nothing, for he has stipulated against what is written in Scripture. One who distributes his property to his sons by oral testament, giving more to one and less to the other or equating the firstborn to the others—his words are valid. But if he declares [this as a division] by way of inheritance, he has said noth-ing. One who writes, whether at the beginning, the middle, or the end [that this is a division] by way of gift—his words are valid. One who says: "So-and-so shall inherit from me" while he has a daughter, [or] "My daughter shall inherit from me" while he has a son—has said nothing, for he has stipulated against what is written in Scripture. Rabbi Yohanan b. Beroka says: If he says this regarding one who is eligible to inherit from him, his words are valid, but if [he says this] regarding one who is not eligible to inherit from him, his words are not valid. One who [conveys] his property to others and leaves out his sons—what he has done is done; however, the Sages are displeased with him. Rabban Shimon b. Gamaliel says: If his sons had been behaving improp-erly, he is to be commended.

Endowing One's Daughter

24. Mishnah Ketubot 4:10; BT Ketubot 52b–53a

As we saw in ¢18, the term ketubah *denotes not only the contract accompanying marriage but also the sum to which the wife is entitled in case of divorce or her husband's death. This sum consists of a fixed minimum, often enhanced by a much larger dowry given by the bride's father. Among the nonnegotiable "judicial stipulations" (see §18 above), the mishnah here designates this sum to this wife's sons, excluding the husband's sons from any other wife. As pointed out in the ensuing talmudic discussion, this restriction on a husband's power to distribute the property under his control may induce fathers to increase their daughters' dowries, partly offsetting the effects of male priority in inheritance.*

Mishnah Ketubot 4:10

(10) If he omitted the clause "Male children that you shall bear me will inherit the sum of your *ketubah,* in addition to their shares among their [other] brothers"—he is [nevertheless] obligated, since it is a judicial stipulation.

BT Ketubot 52b–53a

Said Rabbi Yohanan, citing Rabbi Shimon b. Yohai: Why did [the sages] establish [*hitkinu*] the *ketubah* [clause regarding] male children? So that a person should be eager to give to his daughter just as to his son.

But is such a thing possible, that God has said that a son shall inherit, and a daughter not inherit, yet the sages came [along] and enacted that a daughter shall inherit?—This too is [grounded] in Scripture [*de'orayta*], as written: "Take wives and beget sons and daughters; and take wives for your sons, and give your daughters to husbands" (Jer. 29:6). There is no difficulty regarding the sons, for [initiating their marriage] is in [the father's] hands; but as for the daughters, is it in his hands? The [text's] meaning is, that [the father] should clothe her and adorn her and give her some endowment, so that men should be eager to come and marry her. How much [should one give a daughter]? Rava and Abaye both said: up to a tenth of one's property.

If [that is the reason], let [the male children] inherit the father's [part, i.e., the dowry] but not the husband's [part of the sum stipulated in the *ketubah*]. Were that [the law], the father too would refrain from giving [*Rashi:* He would say: "Since he [the husband] is so niggardly and refrains from bequeathing to my daughter's sons, I too will refrain from giving him an extensive dowry."]. . . .

Rav Papa was negotiating the marriage of his son to [a daughter of] the House of Abba Sura'a, and was on his way to the writing of her *ketubah*. Yehudah b. Meremar heard [of this] and came out to meet [and accompany] him. When they reached the entrance, he started to take his leave; [Rav Papa] said to him: "Let [your honor] come in with me." He noticed that [Yehudah] was uncomfortable, and asked him: "Are you troubled on account of what Shmu'el said to Rav Yehudah, 'Sharp one! Do not be present at the transfer of an estate, even from a bad son to a good son, for one cannot know what [kind of] offspring he [the bad son] might produce'? [And] how much more so regarding [a transfer] from a son to a daughter!—[Well,] this too is a Rabbinic *takkanah,* as stated by Rabbi Yohanan, citing Rabbi Shimon b. Yohai." He answered: "That refers to [whatever the father gives her] on his own; does it also [allow] putting pressure on him?" [Rav Papa] responded: "Have I asked you to come in and put pressure on him? What I asked is for you [just] to come in, without putting pressure on him." He responded: "My coming in constitutes pressure"; [yet Rav Papa] forced him to come in. [Yehudah] came in and sat silently. [The father] thought: "He must be very annoyed [with what I am proposing to give her]," and gave her all he had. Finally, he said to him: "Even now his honor refuses to speak! On his honor's life, I have left nothing for myself!" [Yehudah] answered: "For my part, I would not endorse your giving her [so much]." He asked: "Then may I now retract it?" He answered: "Suit yourself; I did not say you should retract."

Protecting a Wife's Heirs: The Toledo Takkanah
25. Asher b. Yehi'el (Rosh), *Responsa* 55:1

The dowry provided to a daughter is retained by her offspring under the Mishnah's judicial stipulation (see the preceding selection) only if she is survived by male children. Otherwise, under talmudic marriage law, her husband is her sole heir (see ¢18, §15). In the social and economic context of medieval Jewish families (see ¢18, §20 headnote), this was often deemed unacceptable; hence enactments such as the Toledo takkanah, *adopted sometime in the late thirteenth century (other enactments are discussed in our next selection). We know it chiefly from early fourteenth-century texts like this one, where Asher quotes and interprets its provisions. It greatly restricts the traditional rights of the husband but, as Asher argues, does not give the wife control over her estate during her lifetime; in particular, she is barred from making a will in favor of her husband, negating the* takkanah.*

Question: The case [involves] a woman who bequeathed to her husband the half [of her estate] that her heirs were entitled to take pursuant to the Toledo *takkanah*. Is this a [valid] gift or not?

This is the text of the *takkanah*:

If the wife dies during the lifetime of her husband, and if she is survived by living offspring from him, whether a son or a daughter (the phrase "living offspring" means a child who was alive during the mother's lifetime and who continues living past her death for at least thirty full days), then all that remains of her estate — that is, the clothes or land of her dowry — shall be divided equally between the husband and the living offspring. And if she is not survived by living offspring as defined above, all her remaining estate as described shall be [divided] between the husband and the one who is entitled to inherit apart from him. The aforementioned half [of her estate] shall be diverted from the husband, who is entitled to inherit it according to the law, to the one who is, legally, first to inherit from among her heirs, as if the husband had predeceased her. For this purpose it shall be deemed as if the husband predeceased the wife, so as to accord to the rightful heir (apart from the husband) the half of her remaining estate, namely her dowry, whether land or movable items, whereas the second half shall be left for the husband.

If the wife is survived by her mother, and it is clearly established that the property in the wife's estate was brought in [to the marriage] and given to the wife by her mother, such as [in a case] where the mother is a widow or divorcee, and she married off her daughter and gave her land or clothing that belonged to her, and [it is recorded] in the *ketubah* that [the wife] is entitled to that which was given by so-and-so the mother; or where it is clearly established in any similar manner that certain land belonged to the mother, or that certain clothes were purchased from [the mother's] property, if the daughter then predeceases her mother with no living offspring, as defined— [under these circumstances] all that remains from that property shall be returned to the mother, who gave it to her daughter. It shall not be inherited by the daughter's heirs, leaving the mother none of it, which would fulfill the [ominous] words of the prophet (Deut. 28:31): "Your ox shall be slaughtered before your eyes, but you shall not eat of it." Rather, the half shall be returned to her, and the other half shall remain with the husband.

Answer: It appears from the language of the *takkanah* that its purpose is to ensure that the inheritance of the wife's relatives not be diverted to the husband. It thus was decreed that half of her inheritance shall remain in the hands of her heirs, and the inheritance of the husband, the one entitled to inherit according to Scripture, was uprooted and was given to the wife's heirs after her death. However, during her lifetime she does not have dominion over half of the property, to give it to whomever she wants, for this is not at all indicated from the language of the *takkanah* . . . for if the wife should have the power to give it to whomever she wants, they would have accomplished nothing with the *takkanah,* because the husband would implore her every day to bequeath it to him after her death, and since no person can live with a snake,[20] she would heed him more than all her relatives! And thus the text states: "The aforementioned half [of her estate] shall be diverted from the husband, who is entitled to inherit it according to the law, to the one

20. This phrase is from BT Ketubot 72a.

who is, legally, first to inherit from among her heirs, as if the husband had predeceased her. For this purpose it shall be deemed as if the husband predeceased the wife, so as to accord to the rightful heir (apart from the husband) the half of her remaining estate." This implies that it is specifically for this purpose that the husband is deemed to have predeceased his wife, so that those who are entitled to inherit shall inherit after her death; however, during her lifetime the husband's power [over the property] was not nullified at all. Therefore, her sale and gift during her husband's lifetime is null; rather, exactly as set forth in the *takkanah,* the one entitled to inherit shall inherit. Indeed, the authors of the *takkanah* were meticulous, intending that it be carried out exactly as written. Note, then, that they wrote: "And if she is survived by living offspring *from him,* whether son or daughter" [then the children inherit half the property]—implying that if she has children from a different husband, they have no portion in the inheritance.

Thus, the inheritance in no way derives from any power she has to vest property in all of her heirs; rather, as explained in the *takkanah,* [its authors] uprooted the inheritance of the husband, the one who is entitled to inherit according to Scripture, and conveyed it as they saw fit. But they did not confer any power on the wife during her lifetime. And if, during her lifetime, she [purported to] divide her property equally between her offspring with this husband and the children she had from [a previous] husband, her words would have no import. For if she had the power to do this, she would always give preference to the children from the [deceased] husband who would [upon her death] become orphans from both father and the mother, and in this would undermine the purpose of the *takkanah*. . . . Rather, it is certain that the wife has no power to depart in any wise from that which is written in the *takkanah,* for [its authors] meticulously [formulated] every detail in light of their purpose. They even transferred the inheritance from [the wife's] heirs and gave it to her mother, who is not entitled to inherit, because the property originated from [the mother]. Therefore, the entire *takkanah* must be implemented exactly as written.

Modern Israel: An Attempt at Revision

26. Isaac Halevi Herzog, "A Proposal for Enactments Regarding Inheritance"

"Hatsa'at Takkanot bi-Yerushot," *Talpioth* 6 (March 1953): 36–37;[21] *Talpioth* 9 (November 1964): 11–26.

In medieval and early modern times, various measures were adopted by some individuals or communities seeking to go beyond the Toledo enactment and to secure greater property rights for daughters and for wives. Immediately after the establishment of the state of Israel, the chief Ashkenazi rabbi, Isaac Halevi Herzog, submitted a proposal on inheritance — an optional contract, granting daughters succession rights and permitting a wife's heirs to retain half of her property, rather than the husband inheriting all of it.

Although he realizes the necessity for substantive revision, Herzog goes out of his way to emphasize the great difficulty of "uprooting" Torah law, especially in the realm of inheritance (see ¢10, §2). While he acknowledges that husband and wife, in modern times, are coproducers of property and that many of his contemporaries are calling for greater equality between them, he regards this as a falling off from an earlier and better time— "the decline of the generations." He defends his own proposal only as a way of avoiding strife in Israel; it seems designed to ward off more radical revisions by the secular state. The Rabbinical Council did not accept Herzog's proposal, and Israel's Knesset passed a gender-egalitarian law of inheritance in 1965.

In 1949, I wrote a monograph, "a proposal for enactments regarding inheritance," which I submitted to the members of the Council of the Chief Rabbinate of Israel. I outlined the widest and most extreme perimeters for possible enactments, and the Council could have chosen to accept the proposal in whole or in part, or to reject it completely. The matter never came to a vote, but it was clear that most of the rabbis on the Council were not inclined to adopt any enactment. One who was the most extreme in his opposition

---

21. Translation of the opening remarks from Menachem Elon, *Jewish Law: History, Sources, Principles*, vol. 3 (Philadelphia: JPS, 1994), p. 1494 n. 124.

argued that the proposal, even in its mildest form, would not satisfy the Government. The end was that the matter was shelved, and the Government did what it did (there is no need for me to go into the sad details); and a law providing for total equality was passed, contrary to Jewish law. . . . It may well be that some of the members of our Council now regret what happened. At the time, not one of them offered any halakhic objection to my proposals, except for one prominent rabbi whom I answered. . . . At any rate, some record should remain for posterity of my efforts in this matter, which were truly for the sake of heaven.

. . . Moses Isserles wrote (Gloss to *Shulhan Arukh* EH 53:4): "Rabbenu Tam and the scholars of France enacted that, even after the father has delivered the dowry, if the wife or husband dies within the first year without enduring offspring, it all reverts to the father or [if deceased] to his heirs [rather than going to the husband or to his heirs]. Some say that even in the second year, half of the dowry must be returned." . . . This [essentially] is the custom of the Ashkenazi communities in Jerusalem, who record in the *ketubah* according to the enactments of [the medieval Rhine valley communities]. Still, this rule requires a reason: On what grounds can the court establish such an enactment, which involves uprooting a biblical norm?

Now, regarding the [talmudic] enactments [stipulating] sustenance for daughters (§§18–19 above), and the inheritance for a woman's male offspring (§24 above), the enactment was established as a stipulation by the court, which amounts to an order to distribute one's property as a gift; and the instrument of the *ketubah* is sufficient to effect such gifts. Thus there is no uprooting of inheritance; and therefore the court is indeed authorized to expropriate [property] and transfer it even to one who is not entitled to it (see BT Gittin 30a and Bava Metzia 13b). Even so, this is [justified] for the sake of attending to the daughters' needs until they grow up, and in order that a person should be eager to give to his daughter just as to his son. Regarding inheritance by the husband, however, what reason did the scholars have to uproot the husband's [entitlement] to inherit [his wife's property] . . . ? This should not be done except in the face of absolute necessity, as in the case of providing the daughters with sustenance and marriage prospects.

Taz [David Halevi, commentary on *Shulhan Arukh* EH 118:8] noted this problem and wrote . . . that Rabbenu Tam's enactment was made in order to [avert] the [unacceptable outcome expressed in the] biblical curse, "And your strength shall be spent in vain" (Lev. 26:20).[22] . . . For when a dowry is provided by the [bride's] father or by any of her paternal relatives, it is plausible to posit that they are providing it in order to give their relative the benefit of conjugal life with her husband. Her death then constitutes a double curse, as they lose both their daughter (or relative) and the property to which they would be entitled through the father, who, being his daughter's heir, passes her portion to his sons upon his death. . . .

This however cannot explain the [above-mentioned] enactment, which requires that half the property be returned within two years of the marriage. . . . Which way would you have it? If we say that by the second year of the marriage the father (or any other provider) is satisfied that the daughter has benefited in her [more than a year of] marriage, then why uproot half of the husband's inheritance? If, however, the father (or provider) is not satisfied [with such a short marriage], then why uproot half the inheritance of the dowry [that was provided in the expectation of a long marriage]? . . .

Moreover, in matters of inheritance an enactment by rabbis ought not be followed—even if they [seek to] rely on the power of expropriation—wherever the enactment resembles the teaching of the Sadducees of other religions. . . .

The principle "Israel's custom is Torah" does not apply here, for it does not hold where they have adopted a custom in opposition to the Torah. This follows from the statement by Asher b. Yehi'el in his *Responsa:* "This is not a custom that can be relied upon to collect money [from anyone]; thus even if it was practiced for several generations and established by the earlier [leaders], it is a mistaken custom and should be canceled, since it involves transgressing the Torah's law and transferring the inheritance [away] from him who is entitled to receive it—unless through the power of the court to expropriate" (Asher b. Yehi'el, *Responsa* 55:6). From this you can see that Israel's custom does not constitute Torah, even in laws pertaining to money

22. KJV; the verse is interpreted along these lines in an early Rabbinic midrash; cf. Sifra Behukotai 2:5.

[as distinct from ritual or other religious matters], whenever it involves up-rooting Torah law. True, Asher's statement implies that expropriation by the court can be effective even where it involves uprooting Torah law, but this is only where there is reason amounting to [true] necessity, as in the cases of the Rabbinic enactments regarding *prosbul,* sustenance for [minor] daughters, and inheritance for a wife's male offspring. Absent such [compelling] reasons, the court cannot establish enactments that amount to uprooting a Torah law. Thus the question stands, What is the reason for this enactment, that uproots inheritance by the husband, which is his entitlement by Torah law? . . . In-deed, even where there is no [direct] uprooting of Torah law, the rabbis may not instruct the people to act in a way that [through circumvention] leads to uprooting the Torah's law, as written by the tosafists regarding *prosbul* (BT Gittin 36a, s.v. *mi ika*).[23] Now God showed me the light, as I found [an expla-nation of a similar enactment in Castile] in Adret's responsum (3: 432). . . .

It emerges that all such enactments are founded on the principle of "ways of peace." For as the generations have declined, matters of inheritance have become an issue of contention and strife between father and sons and between husband and wife. It seems to me that Rabbenu Tam's enactment was also similarly motivated; for the greater the bitterness over the [death] of the deceased [woman], the more jealousy and antagonism it induces in [the hearts] of her relatives . . . which in turn leads to strife. [This is the reason], rather than [simple] compassion, for we have no reason to be more compas-sionate than the Compassionate One who gave us the Torah, nor than our predecessors who refrained from any such enactment. For in their times, Torah law was lovingly accepted; whereas with the decline of the genera-tions, jealousy and enmity have come to prevail, and the rabbis of those gen-erations and communities were required [and therefore also authorized] to make enactments because of the ways of peace (see BT Gittin 59a–b).

[Herzog proceeds to cite and discuss the Toledo enactment (see §25 above) and a variety of similar enactments, covering a broad geographical and historical range.]

---

23. Hillel's enactment of the *prosbul* instrument, circumventing the biblical law of debt remis-sion, is discussed above in ¢6, §15; we there present Rashi's more radical interpretation, rather than the tosafist's more conservative account favored here by Herzog.

In light of the above discussion, let us now address the enactments that we need to establish in order to provide a portion of a wife's property to her heirs. . . . The only way to do this is to instruct [the people regarding a contract they ought to sign], along the lines of the *prosbul* enacted by Hillel. This [route] however, brings us up against the problem of effecting transfer of property not yet in existence at the time that the deed is made.

Still, we are not permitted to disregard entirely the demand by a large portion of the community, in accordance with contemporary conditions, where the wife works alongside her husband, and property is produced by combining her work [with his]. Now if upon her death without enduring offspring from him, everything is transferred to her husband, while her children (whether from this husband or from another) or her paternal heirs have no portion nor share in their mother's property and in the fruits if her work—this causes strife within Israel and [consequently] transfer of jurisdiction in matters of inheritance to civil courts [which rule] according to alien laws, adopted from outside. In such a situation, it is our obligation to remove the stumbling-block from our people's path, and clear away all causes of stumbling and strife; following in the footsteps of our great, angel-like predecessors, our teachers and luminaries, such as Hillel the Elder. . . .

Now all previous enactments did not accord any part of the inheritance to daughters when there are [any] sons. This, however, is the [very] matter that is the focus of contention in these our times, which requires correction [*le-takken*] in order to remove strife and to prevent, in a manner permitted by the Torah, any turning away from the Torah's laws. . . . I thus propose that a writ of obligation be signed [at the time of marriage], wherein the husband will undertake [the following] toward his wife:

> I hereby undertake that upon my death that, if you _____ at that time be my wife (rather than my divorcee or a declared "defiant wife"[24]), then your children by me who survive you, or your [other] heirs, . . . shall receive half of all the property in your possession at the time of your death . . . to be equally divided among male and

24. See ¢18, §§21–22.

female children. The other half shall go to me and (after my death)
to my heirs, in equal parts to males and females.

[By virtue of] being attached to the *ketubah,* this deed applies [to
future property as well]. And in this manner, we steer clear of anything even
close to uprooting Torah law, since the Torah has granted permission to every
man or woman, while alive, to dispose of his or her property at will. . . .

This deed is optional rather than obligatory; hence regarding all
those who do not so obligate themselves, inheritance will proceed according
to Torah law and rabbinic enactments.

Commentary. The Laws of Inheritance: Liberty, Equality, and
Circumvention

Laws of inheritance, as discussed in these texts and more generally,
establish rules governing the transfer of a deceased person's property to the
person's heirs. The function of these laws varies from one society to another,
but they are usually connected to mechanisms that preserve economic power
in society; they facilitate the transfer of property acquired by one generation
to its successors. Thus, the laws of inheritance represent and reflect distinctly
political positions, such as the attitude toward private ownership. The specific issue is this: Does the property a person accumulated in the course of a
lifetime go to his or her offspring, serving to perpetuate social disparities? Or
does it revert (in full or in part) to society as a whole, effecting a redistribution of acquired wealth and providing incentives to individuals to rely more
on their personal efforts and less on capital acquired without effort?

Even if absolute precedence is given to private ownership (precluding possible encroachment by society, e.g., through an estate tax), there remains a question regarding the nature of the laws of inheritance. Are they
cogent, inalterable rules determining the details of inheritance, or are they
dispositive rules, allowing full freedom to create contrary arrangements
through individual stipulation? Thus, for example, European legal systems,
as the result of a long struggle between absolute monarchs and the old feudal

aristocracy, do not grant a testator full freedom to dispose of his or her property at will. Some portion of the estate is preserved for the deceased's legal heirs—in particular, his or her offspring—and he or she is not authorized to stipulate otherwise regarding that portion.

By contrast, the English common law tradition recognizes the principle of freedom of bequest, under which a testator has unfettered freedom to bequeath his or her property as desired, by means of making a will. The common law system regards the testator as the focal point of the legal arrangements, whereas the continental approach sees an additional focus of attention in the offspring, with their expectation to inherit.

Either way, legally defined rules of inheritance crystallize social conceptions of the desirable social order. There is thus undoubtedly a link between the laws of inheritance and family law. One manifestation of this link is in that the right to inherit is one of the primary markers of the parent-child relation, expressing the idea that the continuity of parents after their death is through their offspring. Moreover, in a traditional society these laws might represent a hierarchical structure expressing the supremacy of men over women, of sons over daughters, or of the firstborn over other sons or daughters. Of course, where these laws are (only) dispositive, an individual can stipulate otherwise and put in place, for example, an egalitarian arrangement. In reality, however, even a dispositive rule has very great value, as on the one hand it spares most individuals the costs of making their own arrangements, and on the other hand—absent stipulation to the contrary— it enables society to realize its desired normative arrangement. In order to establish this desired arrangement, it is not necessary to ban any testator's stipulations against the legally decreed rules of inheritance. It is possible to grant formal recognition to the individual's freedom to bequeath while acting indirectly to thwart it through impeding the making of wills. This might be achieved by dictating a painstaking formality, any departure from which—even in the minutest detail—renders the will void, reinstating the legal rules of inheritance.

The opposite is also, of course, possible: a society might grant decisive weight to the wishes of the individual, and even posit that "it is requisite to uphold the words of the deceased"—as in BT Ketubot 70a. Such an ap-

proach opposes any attempt to thwart these wishes through formal requirements, sets up an array of means for making a will, is prepared to validate a
will despite formal defects as long as its authenticity is assured, and is ready,
moreover, to reshape the legal rules of inheritance themselves. This liberal
and individualistic approach foregoes dictating a normative arrangement; it
simply attempts to assess the testator's wishes (this approach inspires most details of Israeli inheritance law). True, it is undesirable to grant the court full
discretion to assess the wishes of each individual testator. But it is possible
to look for standard rules, whose aim is to find the proper balance among
people's various wishes, and make it easy to stipulate accordingly through a
will. These measures can fully and truly respect the testator's liberty to escape
any normative system that might apply to his or her estate as a default option
in the absence of a will.

The freedom to bequeath also frees the testator from possible subjection to his or her own prior wishes. A will is subject to the testator's continuing wish to maintain it: it was established by his or her speech alone and
by that speech alone it can be canceled. Simply by remaining silent and refraining from canceling it, the testator as it were renews the will every day,
up to the day of death, when it receives the final seal of approval.

Against the background of these characterizations of inheritance
law from a comparative perspective, let us now examine inheritance law in
halakhah. The law here indeed represents a hierarchical conception of social
relations, wherein daughters do not inherit when there are sons, the firstborn
son inherits a double portion, and a husband inherits from his wife but a wife
does not inherit from her husband. The crucial question is then whether it
is possible, by means of contrary stipulation, to replace this hierarchical approach with an egalitarian approach, granting, for example, equal rights to
daughters and sons. At first glance, a negative answer seems indicated, since
the halakhic laws of inheritance are presented as cogent rules that may not be
escaped through contrary stipulation. As stated by the Mishnah (§23): "One
who says: 'So-and-so, my son, shall not inherit with his brothers,' . . . [or]
'My daughter shall inherit from me' while he has a son—has said nothing, for
he has stipulated against what is written in Scripture." Likewise, Maimonides ruled (MT Laws of Inheritance 6:1): "A person cannot convey his inheri-

tance to someone not eligible to be an heir, nor can he deny it to a [rightful] heir, even though it is an issue of property [*mamon*], since it is written in the section regarding inheritance 'it shall be unto the children of Israel a statute [*hok*] of judgment' (Num. 27:11), signifying that this statute is inalterable, and stipulation directed at it shall be of no avail."

The laws of inheritance are thus an exception to the principle that in matters concerning property (*mamon*) a person can stipulate against Torah law (cf. ¢9, §12). This exception might be explained both in light of the close link between the laws of inheritance and the laws of lineage, and in light of an aversion to transfer of property from one family to another. Still, there is — despite all this — no absolute bar to stipulating against Torah law. This can be achieved by writing a will formulated in terms of a gift, employing the halakhic mechanism of "a gift conferred in good health" (the term is meant to exclude a deathbed gift). In this mechanism, a person conveys his or her property "as of now, but after my death," which means that the abstract title is conveyed at present, but the actual right to possess the property, to use it and enjoy its fruits, is retained by the testator and is only conveyed a moment before death. The formal, legal construction of this deed is as a gift, but its legal and social function is that of a will that puts in place an arrangement contrary to Torah law. In other words, Jewish law is prepared to allow circumvention of the Torah's laws by means of a legal fiction, which continues to show symbolic respect toward the laws of inheritance but in fact curtails their reach. It is fair to note that there are significant legal distinctions between a gift and a will: a person cannot, for example, cancel a gift once made, whereas a will is liable to cancellation as long as the testator lives. This distinction can, however, be overcome by retaining, in the document conferring the gift, the power to cancel it whenever desired. Introducing such a condition brings this kind of gift ever closer, in practice, to a will.

Why is Jewish law prepared to accept what is in effect a will that entirely undercuts its seemingly cogent laws of inheritance? Why is determinative weight given to distinctions in formulation, if in essence there is no real difference? Evidently, uprooting the laws of inheritance directly and explicitly constitutes an affront to the symbolic value attached to lineage and family institutions; that is unacceptable in halakhic discourse. As mentioned above, conveying an inheritance to a person's son is conceived as a central indicator that this is indeed the son of that person. But when affront to the symbolic value is avoided—by refraining from employing the language of "inheritance"—there is halakhic willingness to accept results that were not originally seen as the desired arrangement. In this, Jewish law, like other traditional legal systems, differs from modern systems that often disregard the formal shape of transactions, focusing instead on their substantive, actual essence. The same mishnah thus goes on to state: "One who [conveys] his property to others and leaves out his sons—what he has done is done; however, the sages are displeased with him" (Bava Batra 8:5). The issue here is exclusion of the sons from the inheritance through conveying gifts—while the father is alive—to unrelated individuals; this is morally condemned but legally let to stand. The Babylonian Talmud extends the moral condemnation to cases that do not involve outward transfer of familial property, applying it also to intrafamilial transfers, where the father prefers one son over another on grounds of moral merit or endows a daughter with property instead of allowing the son(s) to inherit it: "Shmu'el said to Rav Yehudah, 'Sharp one! Do not be present at the transfer of an estate, even from a bad son to a good son, for one cannot know what [kind of] offspring he [the bad son] might produce.' [And] how much more so regarding [a transfer] from a son to a daughter!" (BT Ketubot 53a, §24).

Despite this moral condemnation, the Talmud itself expresses a positive view of a person having equal regard for daughters and sons, explaining the purpose of the *ketubah* clause "regarding male children" (cf. §24 headnote): "so that a person should be eager to give to his daughter just as to his son" (BT Ketubot 52b, §24).

In a similar vein, medieval Jewish practice saw the establishment of a "half-male deed," whereby a father grants his daughter, upon her marriage, a deed entitling her to receive, when he dies, half of the share inherited by each of his sons. This grant is accomplished through the (common) device of an "attestation" by the father that he owes his daughter the sum in question (Moses Isserles, Gloss to *Shulhan Arukh* HM 281:7). Likewise, many *poskim* permit a person to convey his property to [unrelated] others, as long as he leaves "a significant portion" for his heirs. In fact, this is no more than a symbolic sum, which by being bequeathed suffices to forestall the moral condemnation attached to denying the legal heirs their inheritance. The picture is clear: as long as there was no alteration of the symbolic value attached to the halakhic principles, there has been halakhic willingness to allow its circumvention through practical arrangements. The idea seems to be that there is educational value in retaining the symbol as such; indeed, the effort invested in its circumvention may even bolster the recognition that the symbol must be given due respect. By contrast, any attempt to alter the symbol itself produces opposition. This can serve to explain why Rabbi Herzog's proposals—that the Rabbinate should enact *takkanot* aiming to bring egalitarian initiatives regarding inheritance law within the ambit of halakhic discourse— failed to gain acceptance. As a result, a secular law was passed by the Knesset (the Law of Inheritance, 1965) that is essentially foreign to Jewish law.

Evident here is a commitment to preserve halakhic rules as a dispositive arrangement, in the sense that allows contrary stipulation by means of wills formulated as gifts—and only in this way to attain an egalitarian arrangement between sons and daughters or between the firstborn and other sons. This has the effect of avoiding a principled effort to establish a cogent egalitarianism regarding inheritance, resembling the continental systems that preserve a portion of the estate, to be equally divided among the legal heirs. The dispositive arrangement accepts in fact the transfer of property away from the family, even where this does not involve noble purposes such as charitable contributions but only a passing whim or a thoughtless act of the testator. The result is an abandonment of the moral spirit of the religious law, which regarded inheritance laws as cogent rules. It has become necessary to circumvent them because of their failure regarding equality, in particular their failure from the outset to care properly for daughters. The circumvention could not be avoided, so long as halakhists refuse to recognize the principle of equality itself.

Pinhas Shifman

TWENTY

Welfare

Introduction

The Question of Ownership

Apportioning the Land
1. Numbers 26:1–5, 51–56

"The Land Is Mine"
2. Leviticus 25:1–14, 20–24

Communal Property
3. Rule of the Community (1QS) 1:1–15

The Essenes' Community
4. Josephus, *Wars of the Jews* 2:120–29

Private Ownership
5. Mishnah Avot 5:10

The Justice of Private Ownership
6. Judah Loew (Maharal of Prague), *Derekh ha-Hayyim* Avot 5:10

Joint Ownership as Utopian Ideal
7. Jacob Emden, *Lehem Shamayyim* Avot 5:10

Joshua's Stipulations: The Public and the Private
8. BT Bava Kama 80b–81b

Ownership and the Political Order
9. Maimonides, MT Laws Concerning Original Acquisition and Gifts 1:1–2, 14–15
   Commentary. Bonnie Honig, "By the Numbers"

Commentary. Fania Oz-Salzberger, "*Tzedakah,* Zionism, and the Modern Jewish Citizen"

Introduction

The chapters on welfare and taxation form a pair. Though welfare provision was often described as a charitable activity, charity, as the Hebrew word *tzedakah* suggests, was always thought of as a matter of justice [*tzedek*]. Maimonides says flatly that members of the community can be "compelled to contribute to charity." This is probably a normative, not a descriptive statement: some communities used whatever power they possessed to collect the charity fund; in many others contributions were entirely voluntary. Still, Maimonides' claim suggests that *tzedakah* is at least a distant cousin to taxation. We separate the two topics, though the separation is a little arbitrary, taking up in this chapter the range of services that individual men and women are supposed to provide for their fellows, examining how individual responsibilities are determined by degrees of fellowship, and then looking at the process through which provision becomes a collective enterprise, either of the *kahal* as a whole or of specially formed fraternities, "holy societies."

First, however, we need to address the critical background condition of both charity/welfare and taxation—that is, the property system. If property were widely and equally distributed, there would presumably be no need for charity; and if property were not privately owned, there would be nothing to tax. So we begin with the legitimacy, extent, and conditions of ownership; the first unit in this chapter serves also as an introduction to the chapter that follows.

The literature on property has a twofold character that is probably not unusual in discussions of distributive justice. It offers on the one hand a highly idealized, even utopian, picture of a just society and, on the other, a set of pragmatic and down-to-earth rules about social practices and arrangements. The utopia is mostly biblical; the rules are mostly Rabbinic. It is useful to ask, when reading the selections that follow, whether biblical utopianism had any effect on later practice.

The utopia is itself defined in two ways. There is first of all a historical account, looking back to Joshua's egalitarian distribution of the land and assuming a nation of (male) freeholders — none of whose members are either enslaved or in debt. The laws of the sabbatical and jubilee years require a periodic restoration of this original condition, which is obviously unstable. Alongside this history, there stands what might best be called an economic version of theocracy, enshrined in the claim of Leviticus: "the Land is Mine." As with the political version of theocracy, it is not entirely clear what follows from this claim. The Essene practice of communal ownership may be one of its products. More generally, it seems that God's ownership casts a shadow over private ownership (much as God's kingship casts a shadow over monarchic rule — see ¢3) without, however, abolishing or replacing it. One gets some sense of the shadow in the text from Avot, which has been much commented upon, not only in ancient and medieval but also in modern times. The suggestion that medieval rabbis found so strange, that private property was an institution appropriate to the city of Sodom, perhaps had its greatest influence in the twentieth century.

Over most of its history, however, despite original equality and the role of God as ultimate landlord, the Jewish tradition has been overwhelmingly sympathetic to private property. Considerable energy has been spent explaining the necessity of ownership and denying that it has a shadowy side: the commentary by Judah Loew of Prague (Maharal) on Avot is a nice example of the dominant view. Earlier on, the talmudic discussion in Bava Kama, which starts from a tannaitic account of the conditions that Joshua imposed on private ownership, is mostly concerned to reduce the impact of those conditions, to set owners (almost) entirely free. For similar pragmatic reasons, the Talmud works hard to ensure that the market in money and also, though with greater constraints, in agricultural produce will remain open even in sabbatical and jubilee years; the Rabbis obviously mean to escape the radical consequences of biblical law. And, again, Maimonides' description of acquisition in the state of nature suggests no limits at all on the extent of what can be taken; there is no anticipation here of John Locke's proviso that "as much and as good" must be left for those who come after.

Given the scope of the inequalities that Jewish writers were prepared to allow or, at least, to accept, charitable giving and the provision of welfare become enormously important. There are sure to be people in need: How should they be helped? Once again, the argument begins from the Bible, in this case from the claims of "brotherhood" as they are described, chiefly in Deuteronomy, also in Exodus and Leviticus; these texts resonate through the ages. It is harder to gauge the impact of the more radical prophetic writings, like the extraordinary Isaiah 58, which are often evoked by religious reformers and political radicals in modern times. Isaiah 58 is used as a proof text in Bava Batra, in a passage just before the one we reprint here, and is elaborated, its radicalism mitigated, in the classic midrash to Leviticus. But this prophetic text and the many others like it don't figure much in medieval writings on *tzedakah*.

What brotherhood required, or seemed to require, from every Israelite was an unstinting commitment to the welfare of the community and to all its members: "you must open your hand" (Deut. 15:8; the King James Version better captures the intensifying effect of the Hebrew, where the verb "open" is doubled: "thou shalt open thine hand wide"). In the Bible, this sentence refers to loans, which must be made (without interest) to one's "brothers." The Rabbis turned the sentence into a general injunction to charitable giving. The brotherhood doctrine, as we suggested in Chapter 17, helps to explain the solidarity of the *kahal*. But just how (wide) open the hands of the brethren were supposed to be was the subject of ongoing debate; the Rabbis, unlike the biblical writers, were ready to acknowledge and even to specify practical limits.

The biblical understanding of welfare provision, systematized in the Mishnah, is adapted to the needs of an agricultural society without a strong central government—indeed, without a government that takes any active interest, except through its courts, in the fate of the poor and the weak. Provision is a matter for individual charity. But charity is governed in detail by religious law. Unlike alms-giving in much of the world, little is left to the feelings of the giver. We have to stress again that charity is closer to justice than to love. This closeness is especially apparent in the general rule that the giver must absent himself from his gift. The stress is on *leaving behind* (the corners of the field, the forgotten sheaf, the gleanings of the vineyard) rather than on *handing over*. Indeed, the very act of handing over and, even more, any exercise of discretion in deciding what to hand over to whom, is viewed as vainglorious on the part of the prosperous farmers and humiliating for the landless poor. In the mishnaic texts, especially, it is clear that the gift relationship is designed to protect the self-respect and independence of the recipients. But it may also reflect the understanding, most clearly expressed by Moshe Alshekh, that the goods left behind for the poor belong in fact to God—whose decree it is that they be left behind. They are not "gifts" at all.

All this is not to say that the Rabbis reject the social hierarchy. They require, indeed, that charitable gifts should aim at matching the status expectations of people suddenly fallen on hard times. Some of the Rabbis were critical of grandiose expectations; still, tractate Ketubot tells us that Hillel himself served (briefly) as a slave for a poor man of good family, whose previous life had led him to expect the services of slaves. The talmudic authors or editors are expressing concern here for the individual and his "honor" rather than endorsing hierarchy as such. The needs of the poor are defined not only by their physical condition but also, to some degree at least, by their social experience and by the needs and tastes that it produced. It is as if there was no way to repair the injuries of sudden poverty and radical dependency except by respecting, at least symbolically, the old status hierarchy and the expectations it produced. Among theorists of distributive justice today, the question of what society owes to people with expensive needs or tastes, however these were formed, is still being debated.

Even when welfare provision was an individual matter, left in practice to the will of the giver, it was not a personal or discretionary matter: it was not supposed to depend upon noblesse oblige or good feeling or a sense of pity. In principle, at least, the poor were not left to the tender mercies of the rich and powerful. Nor were the rich and powerful allowed to glory in the value of their gifts. Though pledges of charitable gifts were often made in public, in the synagogue, Jewish charity tended from the beginning to set a high value on anonymity. Maimonides' twelfth-century codification, re-printed below, probably reflects actual practice in some times and places; it certainly reflects ideals established early on.

The most useful contrast here is with Greece and Rome, where phil-anthropic giving was closely connected to and legitimately motivated by the pursuit of glory. The "princely gift" has come to have a place in twentieth-century Jewish life, but it doesn't figure significantly in ancient and medieval texts. Wealthy Greeks and Romans, by contrast, competed with one another for recognition as philanthropic princes: a large benefaction for some pub-lic purpose was a step on the road to renown and, often, to office and power. Among the Jews, too, wealth and the willingness to use it—particularly at critical moments when it was necessary to ransom captives or bribe gentile overlords—were often a means to power in the *kahal*. But Jewish doctrine emphasized day-in, day-out routines of giving and offered no special recog-nition to large gifts or rich givers.

What seems crucial in Rabbinic writings is the obligation to give and not the value of the gift. How one gave was at least as important as how much one gave (indeed, Rabbis set limits on how much one could give, so that philanthropic spendthrifts should not bankrupt themselves and their children). But there were standards built into both categories—the giving and the gift—and the fact that so little was left to the discretion of the giver must have made the shift from individual to communal provision easier than it might otherwise have been. It was nonetheless only gradually (and in-completely) that the officers of the *kahal* took control, mobilizing whatever coercive powers they possessed to collect the necessary funds and claiming the right to use even donated money for communal purposes rather than for purposes specified by the donors.

One of the most interesting and revealing debates among the medi-eval Rabbis concerns this last point. It has its secular parallel in the modern state's claim to "break" the will of a deceased philanthropist who has left his money to some charitable purpose that now seems outdated, irrelevant, or irrational. At stake here is the community's ability to determine, within whatever limits, what constitutes a reasonable use of charitable funds. The money was given for such and such a purpose, narrowly defined, but that purpose has now been met, or more money has accumulated than it requires, and meanwhile new and urgent needs have arisen. Must the *kahal* consult the donor or his or her heirs? Or can it simply redirect the funds, assuming that its officers represent a kind of general will, which incorporates the will of the donor? The partnership model of communal life (see ¢17) suggests that the first question must be answered affirmatively: each partner has to be consulted. The brotherhood model invites an affirmative answer to the second question: the band of brothers can act collectively.

But the *kahal* was often too weak to play much of a part in welfare provision, and it wasn't, it couldn't be, the only communal agency of charity and welfare. At some point in the Middle Ages, early on in Spain, much later in Germany, many welfare needs were taken over by "holy societies"— voluntary associations dedicated to a specific social purpose. The classic *hevra kadisha* was and is the burial society, but in fourteenth-century Spanish towns, and in Provence, too, there were many others, providing education for poor boys and dowries for poor girls, ministering to the sick, offering hospitality for travelers, and much more.

The development of the *hevrot* may be a sign of growing complexity and social differentiation, but it also reflects the difficulties that the *kahal* had in collecting money and organizing services. At the same time, there is a sense in which the voluntary character of the charitable associations fits nicely with the original spirit of *tzedakah* (the same fit between caritas and voluntary association helps explain the Catholic confraternities, which may have provided a model for the *hevrot*). Each *hevra* was governed by a book of rules drawn up and sworn to by the founders—a kind of constitution (which the kahal never had): we have included an example from sixteenth- and seventeenth-century Kraków. The *hevrot* also functioned as religious congregations, meeting for services, annual banquets, and sermons. Some of them had women's groups attached (to visit the female sick, for example, and prepare the bodies of the dead). In some places, women organized *hevrot* of their own. Given the size of the Jewish communities, the large number of holy societies could not have been sustained unless many people belonged to more than one of them. The kahal had a limited set of officers, but the *hevrot* had many more. What their existence and activities suggest is that the kahal should not be thought of as a little welfare state but as a welfare society in which many individuals participated through a variety of associations.

It is clear, then, that the commitment of the *kahal* to the welfare of its members was never meant to replace, and never could or did replace, individual charity. The *kahal* supplemented and regulated what its members did singly or in association. It was certainly something more than an agent of last resort. But the rabbis always insisted that individuals had charitable obligations in addition to, even in a sense prior too, the contributions (and the taxes) that the *kahal* collected. They were bound, first of all, to help their relatives (before seeking help for them from the community: see the selection from the *Tur*) and also to lend money to friends and business associates in trouble, to respond positively (if also discreetly) to beggars at their door, and finally to do all the things that the *hevrot* did. And they were also bound to take their turn collecting and dispensing the communal funds. Their time and energy, as well as their money, were in some sense, and always within limits, owed to their brethren, whether or not the giving was coerced by the *kahal*.

Since the *kahal* turned both collected and donated funds to its own use, its members and officers had to argue about priorities. Sometimes the argument was settled in accordance with the stated preferences of wealthy individuals, as in the dispute adjudicated by Nissim Gerondi (Ran) between two *hevrot* in Perpignan contending for the money of a deceased donor. But often the argument was more general and more substantive: What were the primary needs of the community? This is the stuff of political controversy in modern democratic welfare states; it also figures prominently in the legal literature of medieval and early modern Jews. Ransoming captives took first place, as we have seen. It appears that education ran a close second, and it will provide our illustrative material both in this chapter and the next one. Schooling for the poor was often supported by a *hevra kadisha* (as in the Perpignan and Kraków examples), but the single most remarkable educational program of the Jewish Middle Ages was financed, or was supposed to be financed, through taxation. So we will have more to say about these questions of priority and funding in the next chapter, where we also consider the nature and extent of coercive "takings."

A number of modern commentators have argued that there is nothing in these discussions (after biblical utopianism has been left behind) that marks a commitment to income or resource redistribution—no commitment to economic equality. That seems right, though it has to be noted that welfare provision is always in fact redistributive. Its point here, clearly, is to bring the poor up to some minimal standard, not to make them the equals of the rich. But the relevant standard is not merely one of subsistence; it has to do also with independence and membership. Equality figures importantly in these texts, but it is an equality of attention and respect rather than of wealth. The poor are "brothers," that is, full members of the community; they need to study, celebrate the holidays, marry, earn a living, and provide in turn for people poorer than themselves. The consistent purpose of both individual charity and communal provision is not to maintain them at the margins of society but to pull them back into mainstream religious and economic life.

How successfully did the *kahal* do this? Given its limited governmental powers and its often meager resources (and the power of the rich within the communities—see ¢22), it was never entirely successful, and it was radically ineffective in the face of mass poverty, especially in early modern times, as communal institutions declined. The literary convention of the Jewish *schnorrer* undoubtedly reflects a disturbing reality. The boldness of the *schnorrer* suggests a sense of entitlement that our selections help to explain, but his ubiquity is a sign of communal failure. At the same time, it has to be said that begging is a recognized feature of Jewish life across the ages, attested to in many of the texts in this chapter. Beggary and *tzedakah* are part of the same universe. Twentieth-century Zionism and socialism aimed to transform this universe, drawing inspiration for their effort not only from modern secular, but also from ancient religious versions of utopianism. In our final section, two early Zionist texts illustrate this combination; our last text, from the United States, suggests a more circumscribed and moderate version of the argument, designed for a diaspora setting.

The Question of Ownership

Apportioning the Land

I. Numbers 26:1–5, 51–56

In preparation for entering the promised land, the Israelites are here instructed to take
a census. This would serve as the basis for apportioning the land among the tribes, their
subdivisions ("ancestral houses"), and so on, down to individual freeholders. The mode of
distribution shows a commitment to egalitarianism, at least among all military-age men
(for the women, see ¢13, §4).

The Lord said to Moses and to Eleazar son of Aaron the priest, "Take a census of the whole Israelite community from the age of twenty years up, by
their ancestral houses, all Israelites able to bear arms." So Moses and Eleazar
the priest, on the steppes of Moab, at the Jordan near Jericho, gave instructions about them, namely, those from twenty years up, as the Lord had commanded Moses.

The descendants of the Israelites who came out of the land of Egypt
were:

Reuben, Israel's first-born. Descendants of Reuben . . . [The text reports the specific numbers for each of the twelve tribes and their individual
families.]. This is the enrollment of the Israelites: 601,730.

The Lord spoke to Moses, saying, "Among these shall the land be
apportioned as shares, according to the listed names: with larger groups increase the share, with smaller groups reduce the share. Each is to be assigned
its share according to its enrollment. The land, moreover, is to be apportioned by lot; and the allotment shall be made according to the listings of
their ancestral tribes. Each portion shall be assigned by lot, whether for larger
or smaller groups."

"The Land Is Mine"

2. Leviticus 25:1–14, 20–24

According to Genesis (chapters 1–2), the seventh day is consecrated for rest following God's creation of the world in six days and his resting on the seventh. Here the idea of the Sabbath is extended from weeks to years in (probably utopian) legislation emphasizing divine ownership of the land. The law of the "sabbatical year," calling for a suspension of property rights and a shared consumption of whatever the land produces, is examined in greater detail below (see §10 and the reservations expressed in §12). The jubilee, which sets a limit to land acquisition, is apparently directed against the kind of feudal oppression depicted in Isaiah 5:8: "Ah, those who add house to house and join field to field / Till there is room for none but you to dwell in the land!"

The Lord spoke to Moses on Mount Sinai: Speak to the Israelite people and say to them:

When you enter the land that I assign to you, the land shall observe a sabbath of the Lord. Six years you may sow your field and six years you may prune your vineyard and gather in the yield. But in the seventh year the land shall have a sabbath of complete rest, a sabbath of the Lord: you shall not sow your field or prune your vineyard. You shall not reap the aftergrowth of your harvest or gather the grapes of your untrimmed vines; it shall be a year of complete rest for the land. But you may eat whatever the land during its sabbath will produce—you, your male and female slaves, the hired and bound laborers who live with you, and your cattle and the beasts in your land may eat all its yield.

You shall count off seven weeks of years—seven times seven years—so that the period of seven weeks of years gives you a total of forty-nine years. Then you shall sound the horn loud; in the seventh month, on the tenth day of the month—the Day of Atonement—you shall have the horn sounded throughout your land and you shall hallow the fiftieth year. You shall proclaim liberty[1] throughout the land for all its inhabitants. It shall be a

---

1. NJPS, perhaps more precisely: "release."

jubilee for you: each of you shall return to his holding and each of you shall return to his family. That fiftieth year shall be a jubilee for you: you shall not sow, neither shall you reap the aftergrowth or harvest the untrimmed vines, for it is a jubilee. It shall be holy to you: you may only eat the growth direct from the field.

In this year of jubilee, each of you shall return to his holding. When you sell property to your neighbor, or buy any from your neighbor, you shall not wrong one another. . . .

And should you ask, "What are we to eat in the seventh year, if we may neither sow nor gather in our crops?" I will ordain My blessing for you in the sixth year, so that it shall yield a crop sufficient for three years. When you sow in the eighth year, you will still be eating old grain of that crop; you will be eating the old until the ninth year, until its crops come in.

But the land must not be sold beyond reclaim, for the land is Mine; you are but strangers resident with Me. Throughout the land that you hold, you must provide for the redemption of the land.

Communal Property

3. Rule of the Community (1QS) 1:1–15

The Dead Sea Scrolls: Hebrew, Aramaic, and Greek Texts with Translations, vol. 1: *Rule of the Community and Related Documents,* edited by J. H. Charlesworth et al., translated by E. Qimron and J. H. Charlesworth (Tübingen: J. C. B. Mohr; Louisville, Ky.: Westminster John Knox Press, 1994), p. 7.

The sect of Qumran, which left us the "Dead Sea Scrolls," flourished during the last few centuries of the Second Commonwealth; most scholars link it to the Essenes described by Josephus. One feature common to both groups is the renunciation of private property. The Qumranites defined themselves as the "Council of God," sharply distinguished from the rest of humanity, the "Sons of Darkness." The "Book of the Rule of the Community," which provides detailed rules for government and daily life, opens with a list of purposes, introduced with the repeated phrase: "In order to . . . ." The list includes the pronouncement that, among the "Sons of Light," everything was to be shared.

The Book of the Rule[2] of the Community. In order to seek God with all the heart and soul, doing what is good and right before Him, as He commanded through Moses and through all his servants and prophets; and in order to love all that He has chosen, and to hate all that He has rejected, keeping away from evil and adhering to all good works; and in order to perform truth and righteousness and justice upon the earth, to walk no longer with the stubbornness of a guilty heart, and [no longer with] lustful eyes doing all evil; in order to receive all those who devote themselves to do the statutes of God into the covenant of mercy, to be joined to the Council of God, to walk perfectly before Him [according to] all revealed [laws] at their appointed times; and in order to love all the Sons of Light each according to his lot in the Council of God, and to hate all the Sons of Darkness each according to his guilt at the vengeance of God;

[A]ll those devoting themselves to His truth bringing all their knowledge, and their strength, and their property into the Community of God in order to strengthen their knowledge by the truth of God's statutes, and discipline their strength according to the perfection of His ways, and all their property according to His righteous counsel; and in order . . . not to turn aside from His true statutes [by] walking either [to] the right or [to] the left.

The Essenes' Community

4. Josephus, *Wars of the Jews* 2:120–29

The Famous and Memorable Works of Josephus, trans. Thomas Lodge (London, 1620), pp. 614–15 (spelling modernized).

Before the discovery of the Dead Sea scrolls, the contemporary testimony of Josephus was the chief source for knowledge about the Essenes. His admiring account was preserved both in the original Greek and in the medieval Hebrew book Josippon *and was an in-*

2. These opening words, and also the words "all the heart and soul" in the following phrase, are reconstructed because the main manuscript is damaged.

spirational source, much later, for several visions of communal life, including the Israeli kibbutz.

They condemn riches, and all things with them are common, and no man among them is richer than [another]. And they have a law among themselves, that whosoever will follow their sect, he must make his goods common to them all: for so neither any among them shall seem abject for poverty, nor any great for riches' sake, but they have as it were all equal patrimonies like brethren. They account it a shame to use oil: and if any man against his will be anointed therewith, they use all diligence to wipe it away: for they account homeliness best; and all their clothes are white. They have among them procurators, to oversee and use all things for their common benefit, and everyone seeks the good of all, who are chosen from among them by a common consent.

They have not one certain city, but are in many cities: and if any of their sect come unto them from another place, they give him anything they have, as if he himself were owner thereof. And in brief, they go boldly into those, whom they never in their lives did see before, as though they were very familiarly acquainted with them: and therefore when they take a journey, they only arm themselves against thieves, and carry nothing else with them. In every city there is one of them appointed, whose office is to have a care of the guests, and see that they neither want clothes nor anything else necessary for them. All children under [their] government, brought up by them, go appareled alike, and they never change their apparel, nor shoes, except they have clean worn their first apparel, or that by reason of long wearing they will do no more service. They among themselves neither buy nor sell: but every man that has anything that another wants, gives him it, and takes that of him which [he] needs: yet every one of them may take anything he has need of from whom he pleases, without any charge.

Above all, towards God they are very religious: for before the sunrise they have no profane talk, but they make certain vows and prayers after the custom of their country, as it were, praying that it may rise upon them. After this, everyone is dismissed to practice the art he knows: and when everyone has diligently labored till five o'clock, they all gather themselves together again, and being covered with linen clothes, so they wash their bodies with cold water: and having thus purged themselves, they have a secret assembly, unto the which no man that is not of their sect is admitted: and so they come into the refectory as into a holy temple, all sitting down with silence, and the baker sets every man in order a loaf, and the cook every man a mess of pottage of one sort. Then before meat the Priest gives thanks, and no man may taste any meat before they have made their prayers unto God. Likewise when dinner is ended, they pray again: for both before and after they give thanks unto God the giver of all, and then putting off that apparel as sacred, they apply themselves unto their work till evening. This done, they do as before, causing their guests to sup with them, if by fortune any come. Their house is never troubled with cries or tumults, for everyone is appointed to speak in his turn: so that they who are without the house esteem their silence as some sacred mystery. The cause hereof is their continual sobriety, and that everyone is limited in how much he should eat or drink.

Private Ownership
5. Mishnah Avot 5:10

*This mishnah classifies various kinds of people according to their stance with regard to property. Its condemnation of the "ignoramus" (*am ha-aretz*) apparently presents the Essenes' communalism as misguided rather than wicked.*

There are four kinds [*midot*] of people.
One who maintains, "Mine is mine, and yours is yours"—that is an average kind. Some say: That kind is of Sodom.
[One who maintains,] "Mine is yours, and yours is mine"—is an *am ha-aretz;*
"Mine is yours, and yours is yours"—is pious (*hasid*);
"Mine is mine, and yours is mine"—is wicked.

The Justice of Private Ownership

6. Judah Loew (Maharal of Prague), *Derekh ha-Hayyim* Avot 5:10

Loew's interpretation of mishnah 5:10 shows him to be a staunch defender of private prop-
erty, which is, in his view, required by reason. Although generosity is commendable, any
far-reaching surrender of property rights is an instance of false piety. The Hebrew midah,
translated above as "kind," also means disposition, especially a virtuous one. Loew's in-
terpretation assumes this meaning of the term.

"There are four kinds [*midot*] of people, etc." . . . One may ask with regard to
the statement "'Mine is yours, and yours is mine' — is an *am ha-aretz*," why is
this kind of person considered an *am ha-aretz?* Why is he not an average kind,
like "One who maintains, 'Mine is mine, and yours is yours'"?

  The explanation . . . is that when he maintains "Mine is yours" this is
not due to the virtue [*midah*] of generosity and kind-heartedness. For the generous [person] does not ask for anything from others, and it is as if he [the *am
ha-aretz*] is saying, "mine is yours in order that yours [then] be mine, in order
that my property be your property and your property mine." This kind is declared to be an *am ha-aretz,* for were he rational,[3] he would know that reason
demands that whatever belongs to a person is his. This [kind of person], "who
maintains mine is yours, and yours is mine," and does not demarcate between
his property and the property of others but rather equates them, is certainly
irrational. For wisdom measures everything according to what ought to be,
[thereby] demarcating it. . . .

  [The mishnah] further states that ["One who maintains,] 'Mine is
mine, and yours is yours' — that is an average kind." It is virtuous not to crave
another's property, yet not wishing to do good to others is a vice, therefore
he is an average kind. . . . Furthermore, he is punctilious with regard to the
right [*din*]: He does not go beyond the right, as would a *hasid,* yet does not
detract from it as would a wicked [person]. He is therefore considered an
average kind. . . .

3. *Sekhel ve-hokhmah,* lit., "[if he had] intellect and wisdom."

"Some say: That kind is of Sodom." These [sages] are of the opinion that . . . the reason he says, "yours is yours," is so that he will be able to say, "mine is mine." A person maintaining [such an attitude, would find] it impossible to say, "Mine is yours, and yours is mine"; he therefore says, "yours is yours," so that "you will not be able to ask of mine." This kind is certainly of Sodom. For [the people of Sodom] did not want to benefit others from their [property] at all. They were so concerned to avoid benefiting others that they preferred not to gain any benefit from others, for they feared that then those others would come seeking benefit from them.

This is the disagreement [between the two positions]: According to the first position, he who maintains, "Mine is mine, and yours is yours," does not say, "yours is yours," so that others should come and benefit from him, etc., but rather [only because] he does not wish to benefit from others. Would his friend ask for something in such a manner "that one gains and the other does not lose,"[4] he would comply [with his friend's request]. However, according to the [second position], he would not comply [with the friend's request], for the reason he maintains that "yours is yours" is so that no person should come to benefit from him. . . . He would not wish others to benefit from him at all even in a manner that would cause him no loss. . . .

[The mishnah] further states: "'Mine is yours, and yours is yours'— is pious." Some ask: How can one who maintains, "Mine is yours, and yours is yours," be considered pious, seeing that he has no regard for his own, giving it all to others? They have labored to find solutions [to this difficulty]. But all this is not serious. For the sages are certainly not speaking of someone who gives away too much, as they have already said, "One who gives [his money] away, should not give away more than a fifth, lest he becomes [himself] dependent on people" (BT Ketubot 50a, §33 below). Their statement here [regarding] the pious is that in such a case he gives away up to a fifth or as [much as] he considers appropriate. But it is not their intention to say that he maintains ["Mine is yours, and yours is yours"] with regard to all his possessions, for this is certainly an inappropriate position. This is clear and does not merit a lengthy [discussion].

4. See BT Bava Kama 20a.

Joint Ownership as Utopian Ideal
7. Jacob Emden, *Lehem Shamayyim* Avot 5:10

The Essenes' norm of communal ownership, which may have been the original foil of the Mishnah, is revived by Emden, centuries later, but only in a parenthesis. It can have, he insists, no legal effect. The tenor of the law, he argues, shows that the discussion in the Mishnah should be treated as ethical, not legal, in character.

"That kind is of Sodom." . . . It is certainly inconceivable that the Rabbis would have obligated a person to relinquish his property to others and to his companions. (Nonetheless, there is no doubt that joint ownership would be very beneficial for the perfection of political society [*tikkun ha-kibbutz ha-medini*], since jealousy and hatred would no longer exist among people. Therefore among the earlier generations of Israel, pietistic sects were found all of whose property was [owned] in partnership; no one would have a particular right beyond his companions in any possession, but all would be sustained from the common [property]. This is recorded in *Josippon*.) For if you were to say [that property should be relinquished] you would [in effect] void the entire portion of *mishpatim* (Exod. 21–23) and the [mishnaic] order of torts [Nezikin] and civil law generally. The issue under discussion here is therefore certainly not any of this, but is rather concerned with acts of kindness [*gemilut hasadim*].

Joshua's Stipulations: The Public and the Private
8. BT Bava Kama 80b–81b

Although Moses conducted the preparatory census (§1 above), he did not enter the promised land; it was his disciple Joshua who led the conquest and then apportioned the land to the Israelites (Josh. 13:1–7, 18:1–10). The Rabbis ascribe to him a set of "conditions" attached from the outset to tribal and individual holdings, so that private ownership is qualified by extensive provisos for use by others. The force of the provisos is not limited to the Land of Israel or to Joshua's age; according to Shmu'el, they are inherent to property relations everywhere and in all times.

Our rabbis taught:

Joshua stipulated ten conditions [when apportioning the land]:

That it be permitted to graze in the woodlands, and to collect firewood from the fields, and to collect grass from anywhere except from a field of clover, and to cut shoots [for planting] from anywhere except from the small olive stumps, and that any new spring be for the use of the [nearby] town, and [that it be permitted] to fish in the Sea of Galilee, provided that one does not cast the large net . . . ,[5] and to relieve oneself behind the fence [of another's field]—even in a field planted full of saffron, and to walk in paths through others' property until the second rain falls, and to move off the road to avoid potholes, and that one who is lost among the vineyards may remove branches high and low [to find a way out], and that a dead [person] whom it is incumbent to bury acquires that place [for burial].

"To graze in the woodlands"—Said Rav Papa: This applies only regarding small [cattle] in large [woods].[6] But small [cattle] in small [woods], or large [cattle] in large [woods]—and certainly large [cattle] in small [woods]— [are] not [permitted]. . . .

[The Talmud goes on to treat similarly the other clauses, for the most part restricting the permissions and expanding the rights of private owners.]

"To move off the road to avoid potholes"—Shmu'el and Rav Yehudah were walking along a road; Shmu'el would move off the road. Rav Yehudah asked: "Joshua's stipulations—[do they apply] even in Babylonia?"[7] [Shmu'el] replied: "Indeed, I maintain [that they apply] even abroad." . . .

---

5. This, the most efficient mode of fishing—dragging ashore a large, U-shaped net—was reserved for the local tribe of Naphtali; cf. M. Nun, *Ancient Hebrew Fishery* (Hakibbutz Hameuchad, 1964; Hebrew), pp. 98–111.

6. Commentators differ as to whether "large" here refers to the size of the trees or of the forest or, perhaps, to its density.

7. A few of the ritual laws applying to the Land of Israel were extended also to the large Jewish center in Babylonia.

I say, "ten"—but these are eleven!

—[The permission] "to walk in paths through others' property" was established by Solomon. As it was taught: "If one's crop has been collected from the field, yet he bars people from entering his field, what do people say about him? 'What advantage does X attain [from this]? What harm would people cause him?' Of him Scripture says . . . "Do not withhold good from one who deserves it[8] / When you have the power to do it [for him]" (Prov. 3:27).[9]

Ownership and the Political Order

9. Maimonides, MT Laws Concerning Original Acquisition and Gifts 1:1-2, 14-15

The Code of Maimonides, Book Twelve: The Book of Acquisition, translated by Isaac Klein, YJS (New Haven: Yale University Press, 1951), pp. 110, 113.

Maimonides codified "Joshua's ten conditions" and affirmed their worldwide application (MT Laws Concerning Damages 5:3-6). Here he provides a more abstract account of property, which begins not from a historical moment but from an ahistorical "state of nature" where resources are ownerless (hefker) and hence available for appropriation. He concludes the chapter with an assertion of the king's right to define modes of acquisition, citing the general authority of the king's law ("law of the land") in civil matters (mamon; see ¢9, esp. §9).

1. Whoever takes possession of ownerless property acquires title to it.

Thus also in the case of deserts, rivers, and streams, the law is that whatever is in them, as for example, plants, trees, and the fruits of the trees of the woods, has the status of ownerless property, and whoever is first to take possession of them acquires title to them.

2. If one has caught fish in seas or rivers, or if he has caught birds or any species of beasts, he acquires title to them inasmuch as they have no

---

8. Lit., "from its owner."
9. The book of Proverbs begins with an explicit attribution to Solomon.

owners, except that he should not catch them in another's field. If he does catch them there, however, he acquires title to them.

If the fish are in fisheries owned by someone, also if the animals and birds are similarly enclosed in special enclosures, then the law is that though these enclosures are so large that game within them has to be hunted, they belong to the owners of the enclosure and whoever catches anything in them is considered a robber.

14. If a heathen sells movables to an Israelite or buys movables from him, he acquires title by performance of the act of drawing[10] and transfers title by the vendee's performance of the act of drawing or by his payment of money.

Title to land, however, which he buys from an Israelite or sells to an Israelite passes only by a deed because he relies only on a deed. . . .

15. This rule applies only where there is no established law of the land.

But where there is an established law to the effect that only he who writes a deed or pays the price or does anything similar acquires title to real property, we follow the law of the land because in all such matters we abide by the law of the land.

Commentary. By the Numbers

Every ten years in the United States, there is a census, and the act of counting invariably calls out a politics: How will the count be conducted? Will its procedure capture or obscure the presence in the country of immigrants, undocumented workers, citizens and residents living in substandard housing, slave labor hidden in the interiors of nice homes and dark workplaces, the homeless, the nomadic? How will the numbers be interpreted? Will they license new distributions or safeguard old ones? Will they confirm or challenge established self-understandings of American identity?

---

10. When transferring movables, a formal act of drawing, pulling, or lifting is required for the transfer of ownership to take place.

There is a politics in the biblical census as well, but in this parsimonious and elusive text we need to read closely.

The count of the Israelites called for in Numbers 26 is the prelude to the Israelites' entry to the promised land. But the count does not only look forward; it also looks back. It occurs, as we are told in Numbers, "after the plague" (25:19). Rashi says the census count is like what the shepherd does after his flock is attacked: he counts his flock, lovingly, to see how many are left. But God's love is more complicated than that of Rashi's shepherd, since it is God himself who harmed his flock. The plague is the latest in a series of God's wrathful responses in the desert to the Israelites' unruliness. This time, God might well have wiped out his flock altogether, he says, were it not for the disturbingly redemptive passion of Phinehas, after whom this portion of the Torah is named (Num. 25:11; ¢23, §33). The plague ends when Phinehas kills an Israelite man and a Moabite woman, Zimri and Cozbi, for what an American Conservative commentary calls their "flagrant immorality" (*Etz Hayim* commentary on 25:11, 918). Phinehas's violent act is decried quietly, if at all, in the Bible: Rashi notes that the reward offered to Phinehas for his act—the high priesthood for him and his line—is not simply a reward. The priesthood will teach Phinehas to cool his temper, provide the discipline he lacks.

Some hasidic commentaries introduce a more radical interpretation of this story: Zimri and Cozbi are cosmic soulmates, and their joining together across lines of difference is part of a mystical process of *tikkun,* world-healing or correction, which can take many forms, including that of a masculine and feminine erotic union. Phinehas missed this because he was so focused on the rules forbidding the union that he could not see beyond them. It can be a mistake, on this view, to take the rules too seriously, to get stuck on them. Since the rules multiply as the Israelites move toward and enter the land, it is worth keeping this possible mistake in mind. And indeed, something like this concern about the promise and limits of rules is discernible, I think, in the treatment of the census and the distribution of land called for in the portion that bears Phinehas's name.

After the plague, after Phinehas's violent act of moral outrage, God calls for the count that will mark his and the people's new beginning together. To stand up and be counted on this occasion means in part, surely, to be thankful one is still alive.

But it means still more. Only men of age to bear arms are to be counted. Based on their numbers, each tribe will be given a piece of land in the promised land. Since women, children, and old men are not counted, it seems that the aim here is not merely to provide space as needed but to sign men up for service and to promise recognition to each tribe for its contribution to the collective fighting force that will be needed to take the land. Here ownership has martial roots as, indeed, it may always have.

But recognition's rationality is interrupted by chance. The count—rational and distributive—is not the only mechanism of land assignment. The count assigns to each group a "share," but which specific piece of land each will get as its share will be decided by lot, a second principle of distribution that introduces contingency into the system. "Each [group] is to be assigned its share according to its enrollment" (54). And "each portion shall be assigned by lot" (56). Combining these two incommensurable principles of distribution—the count and the lot—the procedure here speaks to the promise and limitations of private property as such. Is not each tribe told by way of this procedure: Your assigned share is yours but not yours? Or insofar as it is yours, it is yours as a matter of both numerical recognition and lottery, rationality and luck, system and chance? Surely private property is both stabilized and destabilized by such a combination.

This doubleness is embedded in Israelite temporality as well, by way of sabbaticals and the jubilee. These interrupt the sovereignty of human agriculture and seek to establish a more egalitarian communality among people hierarchically divided by the institution of private property. When private landowners give the land a rest, the people too get a rest. Rather than master nature, for that year they are made vulnerable to it: they may eat only what happens by chance to grow or what has been set aside. The sabbatical year exposes everyone to the vagaries of contingency. Rendering the powerful and the vulnerable dependent upon chance, the land sabbatical highlights some of the costs of the institution of private property—that it makes domination a habit for some and relegates others to poverty.

When God says, "The land is Mine," he underscores the real object lesson: when the Israelites enter the land, the land must also enter them. They may work it, but they must also allow it to work on them. The sabbatical requirement is not merely a rational precursor to crop rotation—allowing the earth to replenish itself. The sabbatical also replenishes the people who normally take their livelihood from the earth but for one year, every few years, must receive its bounty as an unearned gift. The unearned gift is like the result of the lottery by which the land is distributed. The years of labor are like the rational distribution of shares, reflecting the needs and contributions of each group. The philosopher John Rawls unknowingly extended this line of thought when he grounded his theory of justice as rational distribution in an affirmation of radical contingency. Rejecting desert or deservingness as the basis of distributions, Rawls argued that although some may work harder or be smarter or sing better than others, these traits are not themselves deserved; they are ours as a result of our good fortune in what we might now call the genetic lottery. Thus, Rawlsian justice combines the rational, justifiable counting of distributive justice with an acknowledgment of the world's fundamental, unjustified and unjustifiable contingency.

Between the count and the lot, the rules and their suspension, the rational and the contingent, the Jewish tradition's commentators enter to provide the rationales and justifications that firm up the ground beneath our feet. What is allowed in the name of private property is expanded. But we should not think that rules as such necessarily pile up on the side of the realities of private property, whereas exposure to contingency must stand with the more abstract ideal of equality. Not at all. The highly regulated life of the radically egalitarian Essene community suggests otherwise.

In the Essene community, members are watched for any hint of vanity, self-importance, or individuality. Their communal form of life is thoroughly regulated to guard against infection by inequality. The Essenes leave nothing to chance, and so their form of life seems lifeless. As is often the case with zealots, the Essenes as Josephus depicts them are so identified with godliness that they seem not open to divinity. The doubleness of Numbers—its impossible combination of contingency and distribution—finds no expression here. The Essenes are all controlled distribution, no contingent lottery. In rejecting property and ownership, they reject vulnerability and exposure in a way that is uncannily like those whose property-based system of inequality they oppose. If the Essenes achieve equality, they do so by way of practices no less committed to controlling chance than the private property regime they reject.

The *schnorrer* is the Essenes' opposing self. He mirrors them. By contrast with their overregulation, he lives a life that is unregulated. Where the Essenes go to great lengths to insulate themselves from contingency, he lives his life exposed to it. They are independent and inward looking; he is heteronomous, dependent on others, always looking out. Both of these, the cultish community and the wandering beggar, are among those who often go uncounted in the official censuses of modern states. By means of their very existence, both the radical egalitarian community and the outcast poor reproach the institution of private property for its institutionalization of inequality, from which the sabbaticals and the jubilee promise some reprieve but to which they do not provide an alternative.

Even as a political tradition, Judaism is always pointing beyond mere politics to something more. We can see this in theological terms. But we need not do so. As it happens, this orientation to "something more" is itself a sort of *political* orientation, the best sort, for it prescribes openness to the other, scripted here as divinity, land, or contingency. Such openness is difficult to practice, and those who practice it are often punished by censors and zealots like Phinehas. Still, as Machiavelli knew, politics is never just about counting, ordering, and rule-making or rule-following but also always about *fortuna,* contingency, and the call of the other. The uncounted, the uncountable, the one who refuses to be discounted, is one on whom we can always count to overturn our plans and undermine our human-all-too-human aspirations to sovereignty. Sometimes, in community service, tending to the other's needs as members of a *hevra kadisha,* or other local or transnational groups, we enlist ourselves into the service of the count and the lot. Acting with others in the tension between the two incommensurable principles of allocation—distributive and contingent, rational and vulnerable—

we may even elicit from the institution of private property, and in spite of it, the justice it promises and maybe even a bit of that something more.

Bonnie Honig

Sabbatical Year: Utopia and Reality

Sabbatical for the Land

10. Exodus 23:10–12

This passage from the so-called Book of the Covenant provides the core idea of the laws of the seventh year as expounded in Leviticus 25 (§2 above) emphasizing its character as a Sabbath. It requires that the land be "forsaken," implying a suspension not only of cultivation but also of any rights of ownership.

Six years you shall sow your land and gather in its yield; but in the seventh you shall let it rest and forsake it.[11] Let the needy among your people eat of it, and what they leave let the wild beasts eat. You shall do the same with your vineyards and your olive groves. Six days you shall do your work, but on the seventh day you shall cease from labor, in order that your ox and your ass may rest, and that your bondsman and the stranger may be refreshed.

Debt Remission and a Duty to Lend

11. Deuteronomy 14:28–15:11

The Deuteronomic system of distribution envisages a tithe allocated to the needy every third year. Deuteronomy's sabbatical year also reshapes the distribution of capital (as well

---

11. This is the general meaning of the Hebrew verb; NJPS translates, "lie fallow."

as the control over land). The text enjoins the remission of debts — and then immediately confronts the problem raised by such an injunction. Providing loans to the needy, it insists, even knowing that they might never be repaid, is a definite obligation. Note the inconsistency as to whether the poor are always with us (Sifre Deuteronomy, §22 below, recognizes the contradiction and tries to explain it).

Every third year you shall bring out the full tithe of your yield of that year, but leave it within your settlements. Then the Levite, who has no hereditary portion as you have, and the stranger, the fatherless, and the widow in your settlements shall come and eat their fill, so that the Lord your God may bless you in all the enterprises you undertake.

Every seventh year you shall practice remission of debts. This shall be the nature of the remission: every creditor shall remit the due that he claims from his fellow; he shall not dun his fellow or kinsman, for the remission proclaimed is of the Lord. You may dun the foreigner; but you must remit whatever is due you from your kinsmen.

There shall be no needy among you — since the Lord your God will bless you in the land that the Lord your God is giving you as a hereditary portion — if only you heed the Lord your God and take care to keep all this Instruction that I enjoin upon you this day. For the Lord your God will bless you as He has promised you: you will extend loans to many nations, but require none yourself; you will rule over[12] many nations, but they will not rule over you.

If, however, there is a needy person among you, one of your kinsmen in any of your settlements in the land that the Lord your God is giving you, do not harden your heart and shut your hand against your needy kinsman. Rather, you must open your hand and lend him sufficient for whatever he needs. Beware lest you harbor the base thought, "The seventh year, the year of remission, is approaching," so that you are mean to your needy kinsman and give him nothing. He will cry out to the Lord against you, and you will incur guilt. Give to him readily and have no regrets when you do so,

---

12. This is a change from the JPS translation, which says "dominate" (Hebrew: *timshol*).

for in return the Lord your God will bless you in all your efforts and in all your undertakings. For there will never cease to be needy ones in your land, which is why I command you: open your hand to the poor and needy kinsman in your land.

The Dangers of Common Use: Protecting Private Property

12. Abraham b. David of Posquieres (Rabad), *Commentary on Mishnah Eduyot* 5:1

Rabad cites Mekhilta Derabbi Yishmael, *which candidly explains how the Rabbis shied away from the radical suspension of property rights during the seventh year. He identifies this stance with the School of Hillel's insistence on an owner's control over access to his field. Indeed, the Mishnah in tractate Shevi'it contains several additional examples of preserving the owner's (noncommercial) use of the seventh year's fruits.*

Mishnah, Eduyot 5:1: The fruits of the seventh year may be consumed with or without [the landowner's] consent — according to the School of Shammai. But the School of Hillel says: They may be consumed only with [his] consent.

Rabad: It seems to me that the School of Hillel's reason for prohibiting [unrestrained access] on the seventh year is their concern regarding the other six years, lest people become accustomed to entering their fellow's field, or garden, or orchard without his consent. Under Torah law, however, it is certainly permitted, as written, "but in the seventh you shall let it rest and forsake it" (Exod. 23:11, §10 above). The *Mekhilta* (Kaspa 20) comments: "This teaches that he must make breaches in [the fence around] the field; the Rabbis, however, made a hedge [around the law, and suspended this requirement] for the sake of *tikkun olam*."

Prosbul: *Circumventing the Rule of Remission*
13. Mishnah Shevi'it 10:3–4

A fuller account of the prosbul, *from BT Gittin 36a–b, can be found in ¢6, §15, in the discussion of rabbinic authority. Here we mean only to illustrate the Rabbis' determination to keep the market in money open and credit available.*

3. [A debt secured by] a *prosbul* is not remitted. This is one of the things enacted by Hillel the Elder. He saw that the people refused to make loans to each other, thus transgressing against that which is written in the Torah: "Beware lest you harbor the base thought 'The seventh year, the year of remission, is approaching,' so that you are mean to your needy brother and give him nothing" (Deut. 15:9). So he arose and enacted the *prosbul*.

4. The text of a *prosbul* runs thus: "I, X, hereby consign to you, the judges at location Y, that any debt owed me by Z may be collected at any time I see fit." And the judges or witnesses sign below.

Edges and Gleanings

Edges
14. Leviticus 19:9–10

This text and the next one provide the crucial biblical limits on the prerogatives of the landowner. The size of the "edges" and the amount of the leavings are not specified and will be elaborated in the Mishnah.

When you reap the harvest of your land, you shall not reap all the way to the edges of your field, or gather the gleanings of your harvest. You shall not pick your vineyard bare, or gather the fallen fruit of your vineyard; you shall leave them for the poor and the stranger: I the Lord am your God.

Gleanings
15. Deuteronomy 24:19–22

When you reap the harvest in your field and overlook a sheaf in the field, do not turn back to get it; it shall go to the stranger, the fatherless, and the widow—in order that the Lord your God may bless you in all your undertakings.

When you beat down the fruit of your olive trees, do not go over them again; that shall go to the stranger, the fatherless, and the widow. When you gather the grapes of your vineyard, do not pick it over again; that shall go to the stranger, the fatherless, and the widow. Always remember that you were a slave in the land of Egypt; therefore do I enjoin you to observe this commandment.

The Extent of Edges
16. Mishnah Peah 1:1–2

Here in the Mishnah, and then in the Tosefta (§17 below), the Rabbis ponder the significance of a commandment to give that lacks precise measure.

1. The following things have no [fixed] measure: *peah* [edges], first-fruits, appearing [at the temple],[13] loving-kindness, and Torah study. The fruits of the following things one enjoys in this world, while the capital [reward] remains intact for him in the world to come: Honoring father and mother, [deeds of] lovingkindness, and producing peace between a person and his fellow; and Torah study is equal to them all.

2. The *peah* [left unharvested] should be no less than a sixtieth—even though it has been taught that *peah* has no [fixed] measure. It all de-

13. This can mean either the *mitzvah* of appearing in the Temple (pilgrimage) or the offering brought on that occasion.

pends on the size of the field, on the number of the poor, and on the extent of piety.[14]

Rationale of Edges
17. Tosefta Peah 1:1, 6

The distinction between allocation as a private endeavor and as a public institution is suggested in the Mishnah but explicitly elaborated here.

1. Things which have no fixed measure: *peah,* first-fruits, appearing [in the temple], deeds of loving-kindness, and Torah study. *Peah* has a minimal [fixed] measure, though not a maximal [fixed] measure. Yet one who dedicates his entire field as *peah*—it is not *peah.*

6. Rabbi Shimon said: There are four reasons for the Torah's stipulation, that one must leave the *peah* only at the edge of his field:[15] [to prevent] robbing the poor, [to prevent] wasting the time of the poor, [to maintain] appearances, and [to obstruct] cheaters. [To prevent] robbing the poor—lest he seek a moment when no one is present and say to his poor relative: "Come collect this *peah!*" [To prevent] wasting the time of the poor—so that the poor [need] not wait idly all day, saying, "Now he will give *peah!* Now he will give *peah!*" Instead, as it is given from the edge, a poor person can go about his work and in the end come and collect it. [To maintain] appearances—lest the passersby say: "Look how X has reaped his field without giving *peah*"—since the Torah stipulated "the edges of your field." [To obstruct] cheaters—so that they cannot say: "We have already given!"

Another opinion: lest he keeps the better [crop] and leaves the worse.

14. The Hebrew word *anavah,* translated here as "piety," is uncertain with respect to both its received spelling and its meaning; the phrase might signify instead "extent of their poverty" or "size of the yield."
15. The Mishnah (Peah 1:3) records an argument on this point: Rabbi Shimon's view is preceded by a more liberal interpretation, which allows the owner free choice regarding the section of his field to be designated as *peah.*

Manner of Distribution
18. Mishnah Peah 4:1–4

Distribution implies the authority of the distributing agent, which the biblical texts seem intended to deny. So peah *is not to be allotted by the owner but rather taken by the poor. Hence they may "loot" as it were the produce set aside—it is not distributed. The only check upon this is in case of possible harm to the collectors due to the height of the trees or the sharp implements used for reaping.*

1. *Peah* is given while [the crop] is [still] connected to the soil. In [case of] a trellised vine or a palm tree the owner takes down [the produce] and distributes it to the poor. Rabbi Shimon says: Also in [case of] smooth nut trees.

Even if ninety-nine say, "Distribute!" while one says, "Loot!"—he is heeded for he spoke the *halakhah*.

2. This is not so in [case of] a trellised vine or a palm tree: Even if ninety-nine say, "Loot!" while one says, "Distribute!"—he is heeded for he spoke the *halakhah*.

3. If [one of the poor] seized a bit of *peah* and threw it upon the remainder he has no claim at all. If he fell upon it or spread his cloak upon it, he is removed from it. So too with regard to gleanings and leavings.

4. *Peah* may not be harvested [by the poor] by scythes nor uprooted by spades so that they do not strike their comrades.

Defining Need
19. Mishnah Peah 5:4

Immediate need determines what a person may glean, but actual wealth determines his long-term entitlements and obligations.

If a homeowner who was traveling from place to place were in need of taking gleanings, the forgotten-sheaf, *peah,* or the poor's tithe, he may take them.

But when he returns home, he should pay [them] back.[16] This is the view of Rabbi Eli'ezer; but the sages say, He was poor at that time.

All God's Sons Should Share His Blessing
20. Moshe Alshekh, *Commentary on the Torah*, Leviticus 19:9–10

Alshekh's homily takes the commandment in Leviticus to leave the gleanings of the harvest to the poor as a point of departure. He assumes here the stipulation of the Mishnah (Peah 5:4, §18) that gleanings cannot be distributed to the poor by the landowner and weaves together notions of responsibility, dignity, shame, and economic interdependency to shape an ethics of sharing.

Discussing Deuteronomy 14:22, our sages taught in the Pesikta: "God, as it were, says, 'One who brings a sharecropper into his field lets him keep a half or a third or a quarter even though all his labors, his tilling and planting, would come to naught if I did not blow the winds or bring the rain or lay down the dew. In fact, I do everything, and yet I ask for even less than does a sharecropper—a tithe.'"

Thus God here says: "Of the peace-offering[17] that you bring Me as a gift you may eat most of what is offered on the supernal table. Now, by this reasoning you should, by rights, give most of your harvest—all derived from Me—back to me for the poor of My people, yet all I ask from you are the leftovers [of your harvest]."

[The verse reads:] "When you reap the harvest of your land, you shall not reap all the way to the edges of your field, or gather the gleanings of your harvest" (Lev. 19:9), i.e., that which falls away during the harvest and the clusters of grapes [that fall to the ground of the vineyard]—all of meager value to you.

16. That is, make donations to the poor equal in value to what he took.
17. A sacrifice offered in the Temple, lit., "*shelamim*," which in an untranslatable Rabbinic pun is said to indicate both that the animal is sacrificed and that it brings peace—*shalom*—to the world since God, priest, and everyman alike share in it. See Rashi to Lev. 3:1, s.v. *shelamim*.

"And let not the thought cross your mind that what you give to the poor comes from yours, or that My not having provided for the poor man as I have for you is because of My rejection of him—for he is My son just as you are. Rather, his lot is in your crop, and it is for your own benefit that I have arranged for his portion to come from you. . . ."

Hence [the verse] "When you reap the harvest of your land, you shall not reap all the way . . ." begins in the plural and shifts to the singular.[18] It begins in the plural, "your harvest" to indicate landowner and "the poor and the stranger" (Lev. 19:10), because in truth it derives from the common [weal], the latter's part included. This is even more true [when one realizes] that the landowner's hired hands are usually drawn from "the poor and the stranger." [The verse] addresses the landowner and the harvesters [in the plural] and then turns to the landowner, addressing him in the singular: "you shall not reap all the way [to the edges of your field]"; rather you, the landowner [must leave some of the harvest] for the poor man included with you earlier in the verse. The verse then emphatically says *ta'azov:* "You shall leave them," even though it would have sufficed simply to say something like "It will be the poor man's and the stranger's."

It may be argued, "If everything belongs to you, God, why leave such a small amount for your poor?" Scripture therefore says, "You shall not reap all the way to the edges [of your field, or gather the gleanings of your harvest]." . . . [God says]: "From all that I have grown and given you, all your wheat and vineyards and olive groves, all I ask is the edge of the field and the gleanings that fall away, provided that they are given in a respectful manner. Do not gather in the edges of your field and hand the wheat to the poor man, for you will embarrass him. Rather, leave the edges and the fallen gleanings [on the ground] and the grapes [on the floor of the vineyard], and the poor will come and gather them as their own harvest with dignity. . . ."

In an [alternative but] similar vein: He, may He be exalted, wanted to teach the value of a discreet gift that will not embarrass the recipient. His message here would then be: "See, I have given you your harvests with-

18. In Hebrew, the second person singular and plural pronouns are different words, unlike English, in which "you" suffices for both.

out your feeling that you are receiving them, but rather as if they are, [as the verse says,] "the harvest of your land" though it is I who have given you everything. So too you should be careful not to make it look as though you are giving him something. Instead, just leave the edges and the fallings [on the ground] and the grapes [on the floor], and they will come later once the landowners have gone."

The meaning of the verse "when you reap" is that I will look upon it as if you were giving of your own harvests, even though "the land is Mine" (Lev. 25:23). . . . First He gives you "the harvest of your land" and then you can go ahead and perform the *mitzvah* of "You shall not reap all the way to the edges, etc."

Moreover, giving to the poor man in a respectful manner will cause the poor not to resort to theft to fill his hunger. Otherwise he might say to himself, "Better that I steal into the field in the darkness of the night, not seen by anyone, rather than shamefacedly entreat the rich man to . . . give me the edge of the field or two fallen gleanings or clusters of grapes." And sometimes he will endure this shame gratuitously and come away empty-handed with the rich man saying that he is giving to another. This will be cause to steal. The rich man will thus be an unwitting accomplice in the poor man's theft. And this is why the very next verse says, "You shall not steal" (Lev. 19: 11), again in the plural, that is, "If you act the way I told the two of you in the previous verse, you will not steal; and if you don't heed me, then both of you—rich man, poor man—will end up stealing."

The Basics of Tzedakah

The Full Scope of Moral Obligation
21. Isaiah 58:1–12

This famous text is commonly read as a critique of the ritual observances of "pious" men and women who have no compassion for others and no commitment to moral practice. Less noticed is the extraordinary extent of the commitment that the prophet demands.

Cry with full throat, without restraint;

Raise your voice like a ram's horn!

Declare to My people their transgression,

To the House of Jacob their sin.

To be sure, they seek Me daily,

Eager to learn My ways.

Like a nation that does what is right,

That has not abandoned the laws of its God,

They ask Me for the right way,

They are eager for the nearness of God:

"Why, when we fasted, did You not see?

When we starved our bodies, did You pay no heed?"

Because on your fast day

You see to your business

And oppress all your laborers!

Because you fast in strife and contention,

And you strike with a wicked fist!

Your fasting today is not such

As to make your voice heard on high.

Is such the fast I desire,

A day for men to starve their bodies?

Is it bowing the head like a bulrush

And lying in sackcloth and ashes?

Do you call that a fast,

A day when the Lord is favorable?

No, this is the fast I desire:

To unlock fetters of wickedness,

And untie the cords of the yoke

To let the oppressed go free;

To break off every yoke.

It is to share your bread with the hungry,

And to take the wretched poor into your home;

When you see the naked, to clothe him,

And not to ignore your own kin.

Then shall your light burst through like the dawn
And your healing spring up quickly;
Your Vindicator shall march before you,
The Presence of the Lord shall be your rear guard.
Then, when you call, the Lord will answer;
When you cry, He will say: Here I am.
If you banish the yoke from your midst,
The menacing hand, and evil speech,
And you offer your compassion to the hungry
And satisfy the famished creature—
Then shall your light shine in darkness,
And your gloom shall be like noonday.
The Lord will guide you always;
He will slake your thirst in parched places
And give strength to your bones.
You shall be like a watered garden,
Like a spring whose waters do not fail.
Men from your midst shall rebuild ancient ruins,
You shall restore foundations laid long ago.
And you shall be called
"Repairer of fallen walls,
Restorer of lanes for habitation."

Not to Harden the Heart

22. Sifre Deuteronomy 116–18

Sifre, translated by Reuven Hammer, YJS (New Haven: Yale University Press, 1986), pp. 161–64.

This interpretive reading of the Deuteronomic text is the most extensive Rabbinic discussion of charitable giving, focused chiefly on the manner, but also on the nature and extent, of the gift. Note the dramatic shift in its reading of Deuteronomy. The biblical injunction "to open one's hand" is now taken to refer to charity rather than to a loan. Like other Rab-

binic texts, Sifre Deuteronomy is multilayered, and the modern editors of such texts have
traditionally marked interpolations here indicated by double brackets.

116. . . . "If there be among you"—not among others—"a needy man"—
the one most needy takes precedence—"one of thy brethren"—your brother
on your father's side, takes precedence over your brother on your mother's
side—"within any of thy gates"—the inhabitants of your own city take precedence over the inhabitants of any other city—"in thy land"—the inhabitants of the (Holy) Land take precedence over those who dwell outside the
Land; when Scripture says, "within any of thy gates," it means that if he resides in one place, you are commanded to support him, but if he goes around
(begging) from place to place, you are under no obligation to support him—
"which the Lord thy God giveth thee" (15:7)—wherever that may be [even
abroad].

"Thou shalt not harden thy heart"—there are persons who agonize
over whether they should give or not—"nor shut thy hand"—there are some
who first extend their hand but then withdraw it and shut it—"from thy
needy brother" (15:7): If you fail to give to him you will end up by having to
beg from him. Whence do we learn that having opened (your hand) to him
once, you must continue to do so even a hundred times? From the verse, "But
thou shalt surely open thy hand unto him, and shalt surely lend him" (15:8).
"Thou shalt surely open"—open first with words, for if he is ashamed, you
should say to him, "Do you need a loan?" Hence the Sages have said: Charity
should be extended the same way as a loan. [["And shalt surely lend him"—
you should first give him (what he needs), and then suggest that he deposit
a pledge (with you); so taught R. Judah. The Sages say: You may say to him,
"Bring a pledge," in order to encourage him.]]

"Sufficient for his need"—you are not commanded to make him
rich—"in that which he wanteth" (15:8)—be it even a horse or a slave.

[The Sifre now cites the story of Hillel that is reproduced below, BT
Ketubot 67b, §25.]

117. "Beware" (15:9): [Be careful not to withhold mercy, for whosoever withholds mercy is analogous to transgressors and throws off the yoke

of heaven, as is indicated by the following "base thought" (be*liya'*al), meaning "without the yoke (*beli 'ol*)"] Another interpretation: "Beware" signifies a negative commandment, and the following "lest" also signifies a negative commandment (thus emphasizing the gravity of the command).

[["Lest there be a base thought in thy heart, saying" (15:9): Such thought is termed idolatry, since base is used here and also in "Certain base fellows are gone out" (13:14); just as "base" there refers to idolatry, so base here refers to idolatry. . . .]]

"And thine eye be evil against thy needy brother, and thou give him naught; and he cry unto the Lord against thee" (14:9). . . . One might think that if he cries out against you, a sin is charged against you, but if he does not cry out against you, no sin is charged against you; therefore the verse goes on to say, "And it be sin in thee" (15:9)—in any event. If so, why does the verse end with "And he cry unto the Lord against thee"? Because I (the Lord) will exact punishment more quickly in response to the one who cries out than to the one who does not cry out. Whence do we learn that even if you had already given once, you must continue to give even a hundred times? From the following verse, "Thou shalt surely give him" (15:10)—it is (an obligation) between you and him. Hence the Sages have said: That is why there was a Chamber of Secrets in Jerusalem.[19]

"Because that for this thing (the Lord thy God will bless thee in all thy work, and in all that thou puttest thy hand unto)" (15:10): If a person had said that he would give and then gave, he would receive one reward for the saying and another reward for the act of giving. If he had said that he would give but was then unable to do so, he would receive a reward for the saying equivalent to the reward for the act of giving. If he did not say that he would give but told others to give, he would receive a reward for that, as it is said, "Because that for this thing." If he neither said that he would give nor told others to give, but comforted the donee with kind words, whence do we learn that he would receive a reward even for that? From the statement, "Because that for this thing the Lord thy God will bless thee in all thy work."

118. "For the poor shall never cease out of the land" (15:11): Earlier,

19. See Mishnah Shekalim 5:6.

Scripture has said, "Howbeit there shall be no needy among you" (15:4). How can both these promises be fulfilled? So long as you perform God's will, there will be poor only among others, but when you do not perform God's will, the poor will be also among you.

"Therefore I command thee, saying—therefore means for this reason; I command thee, saying" means I am giving you good advice for your own benefit—"Thou shalt surely open thy hand unto thy poor and needy brother" (15:11): Why are all of these specified? To indicate that one should give bread to the one who requires bread, dough to the one who requires dough, a *ma'ah* coin to the one who requires a *me'ah* coin, and even actually feed by mouth one who requires such feeding.

Assuming Responsibility for the Poor
23. BT Bava Batra 10a

The theological assessment of poverty plays an important role in all conceptions of divine providence and justice. The following debate concerning the poor is cast in the form of a clash of civilizations between Rome and Israel. Rome here is typologically represented by Tinneius Rufus, sent by the emperor Hadrian to be governor of Judea to quell unrest in the province. His policies and his corruption ultimately sparked the Bar Kochba revolt. Israel is represented by Rabbi Akiva, traditionally known as a supporter, and ultimately martyr, of the revolt. The story, one of several in Rabbinic literature depicting a confrontation between the two figures, begins with the fate of the poor, but the clash between a Jewish sense of election and Roman power and oppression is a steady undertone.

The following question was put to Rabbi Akiva by the wicked Tinneius Rufus: "If your God loves the poor, why then does he not provide for them?"

He replied: "So that we [will] be saved by them from damnation in Gehenna!"

He retorted: "[On the contrary,] this condemns you to Gehenna!

Let me offer you a parable. To what might this be compared? To a king of flesh and blood who was angered with his servant [*avdo*] and he threw him into prison, commanding . . . that he be given neither food nor drink. There came a certain person who fed him and gave him drink. When the king hears of this, is he not angry with him? And you [Israel] are called 'servants,' as written: 'For it is to me that the Israelites are servants' (Lev. 25:55)."

Rabbi Akiva said to him: "Not so! Let me offer you a parable: To what might this be compared? To a king of flesh and blood who was angered with his son and he threw him into prison, commanding with regard to him that he be given neither food nor drink. There came a certain person who fed him and gave him drink. When the king hears of this, does he not send him a gift? And we are called 'sons,' as written: 'You are sons of the Lord your God' (Deut. 14:1)."

[Tinneius] replied: "You are called 'sons' and you are called 'servants.' When you do God's will, you are called 'sons'; when you do not do God's will, you are called 'servants.' And presently you do not do God's will."

[Akiva] replied: "Nevertheless! [Scripture states:] 'It is to share your bread with the hungry, And to take the wretched poor into your home' (Isa. 58:6, §21). When is it that [one is commanded] 'to take the wretched poor into your home'? Now! [i.e., given the condition of homeless people right now]. And [Scripture goes on] to say: 'share your bread with the hungry.'"

Degrees and Dilemmas of Receiving and Giving

24. Maimonides, MT Laws Concerning Gifts to the Poor 10

The Code of Maimonides, Book Seven: The Book of Agriculture, translated by Isaac Klein, YJS (New Haven: Yale University Press, 1979), pp. 89–93.

This is the final chapter of Maimonides' discussion of the many laws concerning "gifts to the poor"—all discussed in the texts printed above. Previously, Maimonides had declared, "We have never seen nor heard of an Israelite community that does not have a tzedakah fund" (9:3). In this chapter, he presents the "degrees of tzedakah" and defines them. Though faithful to the spirit of the tradition, the ranking is his own and has played

an important role in shaping Jewish philanthropy. It is preceded here by a very strong read-
ing of the meaning of biblical "brotherhood," coupled with a prejudicial view of those who
are not "brothers"—the cruel and presumably uncharitable heathen. For Maimonides'
account of those charitable acts of kindness that require face-to-face engagement and that
cannot be performed anonymously, see ¢17, §24.

1. It is our duty to be more careful in the performance of the commandment
of *tzedakah* than in that of any other positive commandment, for *tzedakah* is
the mark of the righteous man who is of the seed of our father Abraham, as
it is said, "For I have known him, to the end that he may command his children, etc., to do righteousness" (Gen. 18:19). The throne of Israel cannot be
established, nor true faith made to stand up, except through *tzedakah,* as it is
said, "In righteousness [*tzedakah*] shalt thou be established" (Isa. 54:14); nor
will Israel be redeemed, except through the practice of *tzedakah,* as it is said,
"Zion shall be redeemed with justice, and they that return of her with righteousness [*tzedakah*]" (Isa. 1:27).

2. No man is ever impoverished by *tzedakah,* nor does evil or harm
befall anyone by reason of it, as it is said, "And the work of righteousness [*tzedakah*] shall be peace" (Isa. 32:17).

He who has compassion upon others, others will have compassion
upon him, as it is said, "That the Lord may . . . show thee mercy, and have
compassion upon thee" (Deut. 13:18).

Whosoever is cruel and merciless lays himself open to suspicion
as to his descent, for cruelty is found only among the heathens, as it is said,
"They are cruel, and have no compassion" (Jer. 50:42). All Israelites and those
that have attached themselves to them are to each other like brothers, as it is
said, "Ye are the children of the Lord your God" (Deut. 14:1). If brother will
show no compassion to brother, who will? And unto whom shall the poor
of Israel raise their eyes? Unto the heathens, who hate them and persecute
them? Their eyes are therefore focused solely upon their brethren.

3. He who turns his eyes away from *tzedakah* is called a base fellow,
just as is he who worships idols. . . .

4. He who gives *tzedakah* to a poor man with a hostile countenance

and with his face averted to the ground, loses his merit and forfeits it, even if he gives as much as a thousand gold coins. He should rather give with a friendly countenance and joyfully. He should commiserate with the recipient in his distress, as it is said, "If I have not wept for him that was in trouble, and if my soul grieved not for the needy?" (Job 30:25). He should also speak to him prayerful and comforting words, as it is said, "And I caused the widow's heart to sing for joy" (Job 29:13).

5. If a poor man asks you for *tzedakah* and you have nothing to give him, comfort him with words. It is forbidden to rebuke a poor man or to raise one's voice in a shout at him, seeing that his heart is broken and crushed, and Scripture says, "A broken and contrite heart, O God, Thou wilt not despise" (Ps. 51:19), and again, "To revive the spirit of the humble, and to revive the heart of the contrite ones" (Isa. 57:15). Woe unto him who shames the poor, Woe unto him! One should rather be unto the poor as a father, with both compassion and words, as it is said, "I was a father to the needy" (Job 29:16).

6. He who presses others to give *tzedakah* and moves them to act thus, his reward is greater than the reward of him who gives [*tzedakah* himself], as it is said, "And the work of righteousness shall be peace" (Isa. 32:17). Concerning *tzedakah* collectors and their like, Scripture says, "And they that turn the many to righteousness (shall shine) as the stars" (Dan. 12:3).

7. There are eight degrees of *tzedakah,* each one superior to the other. The highest degree, than which there is none higher, is one who upholds the hand of an Israelite reduced to poverty by handing him a gift or a loan, or entering into a partnership with him, or finding work for him, in order to strengthen his hand, so that he would have no need to beg from other people. Concerning such a one, Scripture says, "Thou shalt uphold him; as a stranger and a settler shall he live with thee" (Lev. 25:35), meaning uphold him, so that he would not lapse into want.

8. Below this is he who gives *tzedakah* to the poor in such a way that he does not know to whom he has given, nor does the poor man know from whom he has received. This constitutes the fulfilling of a religious duty for its own sake, and for such there was a Chamber of Secrets in the Temple, whereunto the righteous [*tzaddikim*] would contribute secretly, and wherefrom the

poor of good families would draw their sustenance in equal secrecy. Close to such a person is he who contributes directly to the *tzedakah* fund.

One should not, however, contribute directly to the *tzedakah* fund unless he knows that the person in charge of it is trustworthy, is a Sage [*hakham,* wise], and knows how to manage it properly, as was the case of Rabbi Hananiah ben Teradion.

9. Below this is he who knows to whom he is giving, while the poor man does not know from whom he is receiving. He is thus like the great among the Sages who were wont to set out secretly and throw the money down at the doors of the poor. This is a proper way of doing it, and a preferable one if those in charge of *tzedakah* are not conducting themselves as they should.

10. Below this is the case where the poor man knows from whom he is receiving, but himself remains unknown to the giver. He is thus like the great among the Sages who used to place the money in the fold of a linen sheet which they would throw over their shoulder, whereupon the poor would come behind them and take the money without being exposed to humiliation.

11. Below this is he who hands [*tzedakah*] to the poor man before being asked for [it].

12. Below this is he who hands [*tzedakah*] to the poor man after the latter has asked for [it].

13. Below this is he who gives the poor man less than what is proper, but with a friendly countenance.

14. Below this is he who gives [*tzedakah*] with a frowning countenance.

15. The great among the Sages used to hand a *perutah* [groat] to a poor man before praying, and then proceeded to pray, as it is said, "As for me, I shall behold Thy face in righteousness" (Ps. 17:15).

16. He who provides maintenance for his grown sons and daughters—whom he is not obligated to maintain—in order that the sons might study Torah, and that the daughters might learn to follow the right path and not expose themselves to contempt, and likewise he who provides maintenance for his father and mother, is accounted as performing *tzedakah*. Indeed

it is an outstanding act of *tzedakah,* since one's relative has precedence over other people. Whosoever serves food and drink to poor men and orphans at his table, will, when he calls to God, receive an answer and find delight in it, as it is said, "Then shalt thou call, and the Lord will answer, etc." (Isa. 58:9).

17. The Sages have commanded that one should have poor men and orphans as members of his household rather than bondsmen, for it is better for him to employ the former, so that children of Abraham, Isaac, and Jacob might benefit from his possessions rather than children of Ham, seeing that he who multiplies bondsmen multiplies sin and iniquity every day in the world, whereas if poor people are members of his household, he adds to merits and fulfillment of commandments every hour.

18. One should always restrain himself and submit to privation rather than be dependent upon other people or cast himself upon [the] public, for thus have the Sages commanded us, saying, "Make the Sabbath a weekday rather than be dependent upon other people" (BT Pesahim 112a). Even if one is a Sage held in honor, once he becomes impoverished, he should engage in a trade, be it even a loathsome trade, rather than be dependent upon other people. It is better to strip hides off animal carcasses than to say to other people, "I am a great Sage, I am a priest, provide me therefore with maintenance." So did the Sages command us. Among the great Sages there were hewers of wood, carriers of beams, drawers of water to irrigate gardens, and workers in iron and charcoal. They did not ask for public assistance, nor did they accept it when offered to them.

19. Whosoever is in no need of [*tzedakah*] but deceives the public and does accept [it], will not die of old age until he indeed becomes dependent upon other people. He is included among those of whom Scripture says, "Cursed is the man that trusteth in man" (Jer. 17:5). On the other hand, whosoever is in need of [*tzedakah*] and cannot survive unless he accepts [it], such as a person who is of advanced age, or ill, or afflicted with sore trials, but is too proud and refuses to accept [it], is the same as a shedder of blood and is held to account for his own soul, and by his suffering he gains nothing but sin and guilt.

Whosoever is in need . . . but denies himself, postpones the hour, and lives a life of want in order not to be a burden upon the public, will not die of old age until he shall have provided maintenance for others out of his own wealth. Of him and of those like him it is said, "Blessed is the man that trusteth in the Lord" (Jer. 17:7).

Commentary. What Is *Tzedakah?*

Chapter 10 concludes Maimonides' exhaustive treatise on laws concerning gifts to the poor. *Tzedakah* is commanded by Torah, and Maimonides opens with a striking declaration: it is our duty to perform *tzedakah* with greater care than any other commandment! He closes with stern admonitions to avoid becoming dependent on *tzedakah,* by working and maintaining one's relatives. Maimonides' instructions on giving, "eight degrees of *tzedakah,*" is the central portion and the author's invention. It is often read today as a freestanding teaching about *how* charity should be performed. But in the context of the chapter as a whole it does more: it underscores the fact that *tzedakah* is not a personal transaction but a communal one.

Tzedakah was a familiar element of living according to Torah, and Maimonides cites the reward of righteousness: "the Lord may . . . have compassion unto thee." He does not dwell on scriptural promises, though. "Eight degrees" addresses those who do not need to be exhorted to give but who do require guidance; his concern is less obdurate omission than failing to understand and perform *tzedakah* well. *Tzedakah* is complex because, as we have seen, it takes many forms; "degrees" encompasses direct giving (inviting the poor to a meal, offering alms to beggars) along with regular collections for charitable funds. *Tzedakah* is complex too because it rests on a specific historical and philosophical understanding of need; it demands judgment about what is "fitting" and what provision meets a person's "lack." *Tzedakah* requires proportioning one's contributions to one's means and identifying minimums and maximums—a floor that mandates some contribution from everyone and a ceiling that prevents both self-impoverishment and domination. Finally, the manner of giving matters.

Maimonides' ranking is sometimes referred to as the "ladder of charity." That is the perspective from the bottom, lowest to highest. On this view, the ranking is aspirational and the pinnacle of the arduous climb is virtue or righteousness. Many religious and philosophical (especially Platonic) traditions of self-perfection employ the image of stages of ascent. In other writings Maimonides himself speaks of perfection of the soul and of the few pious men, the "great among sages," whose performance of *tzedakah* allows them to behold the face of God (*Guide of the Perplexed,* part 3, ch. 52–53). "Eight degrees" rejects stringent regimens of self-perfection and transcendence, however; here, Maimonides sets out a simpler pedagogy directing concrete, day-to-day performance by all Jews.

Aristotle provided other terms for focusing on the character of the giver. The virtues of liberality and magnanimity represent giving as part of the care of the self. In other philosophical works Maimonides reflects on and employs these ideas, but there is no trace of classical virtue here or of measured giving as therapy for conquering pride or prodigality. Because Maimonides' ranking is not oriented toward the effects of *tzedakah* on the giver, "degrees" applied to acts of *tzedakah* is preferable to "ladder" applied to character. There is no reason to think that all of a person's gifts to the poor could (or should) occupy just one rank, and Maimonides reminds us that acts of giving are constrained by circumstances such as the presence or absence of a well-managed *tzedakah* fund and of trustworthy leaders to oversee collections.

"Eight degrees" is oriented to the effects of giving on the poor. In contrast to the perspective of personal ascent up the ladder of *tzedakah,* Maimonides *starts* at the top. The highest form addresses dependence and makes the recipient self-sufficient with a gift or loan, a partnership or employment. It comes closest to fulfilling the injunctions of Isaiah and Job to avoid shaming or dishonoring the poor. For this reason, too, Maimonides' ranking gives preference to preserving the anonymity of both giver and receiver through donation via the charity fund. If direct personal assistance is necessary, the next best is to give anonymously, and below that to protect the anonymity of the recipient. When Maimonides ranks giving before being asked above giving in response to a needy person's plea, and giving less than is appropriate in a friendly manner above giving the appropriate gift grudgingly, the aim is to shield recipients from injurious rebuke, to protect their dignity.

Tzedakah requires more than a respectful stance: "to revive the spirit of the humble" is also imperative. *Tzedakah* comprises money and goods but also care and consolation. Giving joyfully and "compassionately" is what makes it a "gift." Together, the effect of solicitude for recipients' dignity and comfort is to inspire hope, to enable the poor to overcome paralyzing helplessness and a crushed heart so that they can join in community life, including contributing to *tzedakah* themselves.

Anonymity, which is so central to this ranking, serves an overarching purpose on my view: to underscore that *tzedakah* is not a personal moral interaction but a communal one. The heart of *tzedakah* is reciprocity. Everyone must contribute, even the poor who rely on alms. Anyone is liable to become needy and claim assistance. Certainly, everyone will suffer "sore trials" and require comfort and consolation. Cautions against giving too much aim at avoiding destitution; they argue for securing provision for one's own family. They have a second communal aim: ceilings on giving shield the community from undue dependence on the wealthy and from their claim to superiority and influence. *Tzedakah* is the defining act of recognition of community, and with "degrees" Maimonides outlines the basis for a righteous community.

This concern with dignity and reciprocity may incline us to think of *tzedakah* as a source in Jewish law of moral egalitarianism, in particular the value of respect for the dignity of all persons. The resonance is surely there, but several things strain a humanist reading. Maimonides' purpose is to show the reasonableness of the true foundations of dignity, which are, first, scriptural/spiritual: the capacity to worship God and fulfill the commands of Torah; and, second, historical: debased by Christians and Muslims, Jews must not inflict shame or cause desolation to one another. His purpose is not to show that Torah is congruent with a universal ethic discovered by independent reason.

Moreover, when it comes to the actions *tzedakah* prescribes, supplying a poor man "according to his dignity," Maimonides does not anticipate egalitarian accounts of justice. Dignity is understood here to be tied to the social structure of the community. The command is "to give alms to the poor of Israel, according to what is fitting for them" (7:1), where "fitting" is not an estimate of rationality or desert but a social judgment. *Tzedakah* is corrective: to restore a person to his accustomed place, to "strengthen his hand."

Maimonides introduces one startling exception to this socially conservative teaching. He employs the example of talmudic sages ("hewers of wood") and implicitly the authority of his own active life to oppose public support for rabbis. His demand that they take up "even a loathsome trade" defies a tradition of entitlement and the accepted view that Torah would be neglected were scholars not salaried at community expense. His challenge to the rabbis' claim to support (and prestige) may reflect principled opposition to an institutionalized, subsidized class of scholars or contempt for his contemporaries' pedantry and insular disregard for the complementarity of Talmud and philosophy.

Maimonides surrounds "eight degrees" with commentary and citation. His purpose is to provide a foundation for his guide to giving, a compressed teaching about *why* "it is our duty to be more careful in the performance of the commandment of *tzedakah* than in that of any other positive commandment." *Tzedakah* is simultaneously philosophical and theological, its significance both holy and practical. In this context Maimonides chooses to make *tzedakah* comprehensible less by suffusing it with theology or philosophy than by explaining why it is indispensable to the social well-being of Jews.

Tzedakah is a command of God, which Jews should perform for its own sake with the purpose of worshiping God through fulfillment of the law, *and* it is the specific command whose fulfillment is necessary to preserve Jewish autonomy and solidarity. The narrative of Jewish history shows a vulnerable people dependent on one another to restore again and again the conditions for the existence of their communities of belief. Certainly for medieval Jews in exile among "the heathens, who hate and persecute them," self-preservation is a stark necessity. (We can see *tzedakah* as a piece with the priority assigned funds to ransom captives.) Maimonides calls *tzedakah* "the mark of the righteous man who is the seed of our father Abraham" to underscore the plain fact: "if brother will show no compassion to brother, who will?" As a matter of experience, not intrinsic defect, heathens can be expected to be cruel; in any case they are under no obligation to support Jewish life. Thus, Maimonides says that the genealogy of Jews who fail to perform *tzedakah* is open to suspicion because it is inconceivable that they would willfully reject Jewish law and threaten Jews with social death. For Maimonides there is no more forceful way to make the point that abrogation is nonetheless a moral choice and that the stake is Jewish survival: he who *"turns from"* *tzedakah* is as base as he who worships idols, an abomination. He adds a twist to drive the point home; a person who refuses to accept *tzedakah* out of pride is the "same as a shedder of blood": he deprives the community of a faithful member.

Linking *tzedakah* to Jewish identity and survival, Maimonides enlists poetry and authority. He opens with a remarkable, lyrical passage that evokes the prophetic language of the Bible: "The throne of Israel cannot be established nor true faith made to stand up, except through *tzedakah*." In addition to the individual rewards of righteousness, he recalls God's promise to the Jews as a nation in Isaiah: "Zion shall be redeemed with justice, and they that return of her with righteousness."

Tzedakah emerges as a comprehensive arrangement of institutions and coordinated practices comprising both organized collections (often with penalties attached) and personal donations and acts of care, all having the same character and purpose. *Tzedakah* encompasses both justice and charity, things that are sharply distinguished in contemporary moral discourse. True, in the larger context of discussions of justice or righteousness the Rabbinic literature sometimes employs separate terms. But the discourse of *tzedakah,* and certainly Maimonides on my reading of these passages, does not draw the distinction that is standard in moral and political thought today. Contra Maimonides, contemporary philosophers labor to cordon off justice and what can be claimed as a right from the vicissitudes of voluntarism said to define charity, just as they work to protect charity from being tainted by determinate standards of contribution coercively enforced. If we accept the congruence of justice and charity and take these prescriptions to be meaningful apart from Torah and life in autonomous Jewish communities, "eight degrees" offers a critical perspective on contemporary welfare and philanthropy.

Consonant with reciprocity, public welfare should be funded by universal contribution proportioned to means and organized to protect the dignity of those in need. Welfare should aim at securing independence through loans and suitable work. The manner of provision should not be demeaning, and recipients' anonymity should be preserved. Qualification for assistance should not require the poor to give up assets that are the mark of respectable social standing. For Maimonides, *tzedakah* aimed at restoring each person to his or her accustomed place in the social community. The admonition carries a less conservative, more egalitarian thrust today. But the heart of Maimonides' standard nonetheless applies: need extends beyond basic minimums to include the social goods and opportunities indispensable to participation in the activities that signal membership. In practice, social welfare often falls short of the standards of *tzedakah*.

For its part, contemporary philanthropic practices plainly violate Maimonides' guide to giving. Philanthropy today does not value anonymity, solicits donations through competition for public recognition, and typically prizes extraordinary gifts over contributions from everyone. Moreover, philanthropy fails to accord with *tzedakah* because it is not congruent with justice: it is not oriented to "human services." This can be charged to misplaced confidence in public welfare to provide for needs and to a deliberate turning away from the command to comfort and console those who suffer "sore trials"—the sick and sorrowful, elderly and young. In addition, the disjuncture between justice and philanthropy can be charged to the legal framework of giving. For even if, contra *tzedakah,* the mark of charity is voluntarism, public policy defines, regulates, and subsidizes individual and organized giving. In the United States, policy invites "charitable contributions" in support of a vast range of personal projects; it assigns no priority to gifts to the poor. And instead of encouraging universal contribution by providing equal benefits to all donors, public policy favors high-income taxpayers. Once again, reciprocity, the heart of *tzedakah,* disappears from view.

If contemporary welfare and philanthropy did conform to Maimonides' guide to giving, could we then say that ungrudging contribution to social welfare as citizens and as donors to Jewish and non-Jewish organizations and causes *just is tzedakah?* For Maimonides *tzedakah* was inconceivable except as obedience to Torah and with the aim of preserving the autonomy and solidarity of the Jewish community; his negative answer is clear. The answer I take from this reading is still "no." Jews are citizens of wide political communities; their welfare is bound up with "brothers" and "heathens." On this extension of Maimonides' reasoning, the beneficiaries of *tzedakah* today should include everyone with whom the peace and well-being of Jewish life is bound up. However, *tzedakah* applies only to contributions *by* Jews, and only if giving is understood to serve justice and charity in Judaism's unique terms. By themselves bare acts of giving (however attentive to "degrees" and to the requirements of justice), care and compassion do not define *tzedakah*. Contributions constitute *tzedakah* only if they are mediated and understood as living according to Torah and preserving Jewish life. This understanding is elusive for secular Jews like me, who see piety exclusively as ritual and prayer and do not see "gifts to the poor" as a form of observance. Secular Jews are unable to translate taxes and contributions from the ethical to the sacred realm. But we do approach *tzedakah* if we acknowledge our contributions as elements of living Jewish law and tradition. More, over time, our experience of giving may come to be imbued with this distinctive end and worth. Then, following Maimonides, we can say that *tzedakah* insures Jewish survival.

Nancy L. Rosenblum

Welfare Organization in the Community

Communal Responsibility: Defining Needs

25. BT Ketubot 67a–b

The Mishnah (Ketubot 6:5) defines fifty zuz *as the proper sum a father should give his daughter as a dowry. The same amount is set as the minimum for an orphan whose dowry is provided from "the purse" — a* tzedakah *fund; if additional resources are available, she should be provided for "according to her status." This serves as a point of departure for an extensive talmudic discussion incorporating elements from the Sifre (§22 above) regarding distinctive needs and the limits of responsibility.*

Our rabbis taught: If an orphan boy and an orphan girl ask for provision, provision is made [first] for the orphan girl and [only] then for the orphan boy, because it is a man's practice to go seeking, but it is not a woman's practice to go seeking. If an orphan boy and an orphan girl ask [for support in order] to get married, [arrangements are] made [first] for the orphan girl's marriage and [only] then for the orphan boy's, because a woman's shame is greater than a man's.

Our rabbis taught: If an orphan boy asks [for support in order] to get married, [the officers] rent him a home and set up a bed and all [necessary] utensils, and then [arrange] for him to marry a woman. As written, "lend him sufficient for whatever is needed for him"[20] (Deut. 15:8): "sufficient"—that is a home; "whatever is needed"—that is a bed and table; "for him"—that is a wife, as written, "I will make a fitting helper for him" (Gen. 2:18).

Our rabbis taught: "sufficient"—you are obligated to provide for him, but you are not obligated to make him rich. "Whatever is needed for him"—even a horse to ride and a slave to run before him. It was said of Hillel the Elder that he provided for a certain [impoverished] person from a good family a horse to ride and a slave to run before him. Once he was unable to provide a slave to run before him, so [Hillel] ran before him for three miles.

Our rabbis taught: It once happened that the people of Upper Galilee bought, for a certain poor [person] from a good family in Tsippori, a pound of meat every day. "A pound of meat"—What is the big deal?[21] Said Rav Huna: A pound of fowl's brains. If you wish, I can say: A pound's worth of meat. Rav Ashi said: It was a small village, and every day they would waste an animal on his account.

A [poor] person came before Rabbi Nehemiah [asking for provi-

---

20. More properly translated by NJPS as "whatever he needs" (as in §11); altered here to explain the midrash below.
21. This question—and the answers that follow—reflect a great difference in the price of meat between Palestine and Babylonia.

sion]. [Nehemiah] asked him: "What is your [accustomed] dinner?" He answered, "Fat meat and old wine." "Do you wish to share my fare of lentils?" He shared his fare of lentils and [presently] died. A cry went up: "Woe to this one, who was killed by Nehemiah!" But should it not be, "Woe to Nehemiah, who killed this one"?—It was he who ought not to have pampered himself to such an extent.

A [poor] person came before Rava [asking for provision]. [Rava] asked him: "What is your [accustomed] dinner?" He answered, "A fattened chicken and old wine." [Rava] inquired, "Have you no concern for the burden upon the community?" He replied, "Does what I eat come from them? It comes from God, for it was taught, 'The eyes of all look to You expectantly, and You give them their food when it is due' (Ps. 145:15) . . . implying that God makes provision for each and every individual when it is due." Meanwhile, Rava's sister—who had not seen him for thirteen years—came and brought him a fattened chicken and old wine. [Rava] remarked: "What is this here? I concede, go ahead and eat."

Our rabbis taught: "One who has nothing yet refuses to receive provision—[the officers] give him [money] as a loan, and then give [it] to him as a gift; thus says Rabbi Meir. The [other] sages say, they give him [money] as a gift, and then give [it] to him as a loan." ". . . As a gift"—but he refuses to take! Said Rava: [The point is] that they should first offer [it] as a gift. "One who has [resources] yet refuses to [spend for his own] provisions—[the officers] give him [money] as a gift, and then [later] collect from him." "[They later] collect from him"—but then he will no longer take! Said Rav Papa, [They collect] after he dies. "Rabbi Shimon says: One who has [resources] yet refuses to [spend for his own] provision should be ignored." . . .

Mar Ukva had a poor man in his neighborhood, to whom he would send 400 *zuz* every [year on the] eve of the Day of Atonement. Once he sent [the money] over by [the] hand of his [Mar Ukva's] son, who returned and said: "He does not need [it]." He asked him: "What have you seen?" "I saw them sprinkling old wine before him." [Mar Ukva then] remarked, "Is he so pampered?" He doubled the sum and sent it over.

When he was about to die, he said: Bring me my *tzedakah* tally. The total recorded was 7000 gold dinars. He said: "The provisions are meager and the journey far!" He arose and gave away half his property. How could he do so? For see, Rabbi Ila'i has said, "At Usha it was ordained: One who gives away [his property] should not give away more than a fifth."—That rule [applies only to gifts] while one is alive, lest he become impoverished and dependent upon [others]; but [regarding a gift to be bestowed] after death, we are not concerned.

Rabbi Abba would enfold coins in his cloak, throw it over his back, and locate himself among the poor while keeping an eye out for deceivers.

Rabbi Haninah had a poor man, to whom he would send four *zuz* every [week on the] eve of Shabbat. Once he sent [the money] over by [the] hand of his wife, who returned and said: "He does not need [it]." He asked her: "What have you seen?" "I heard them asking him: What will you use for dinner, the silver utensils or the gold utensils?" [Haninah] said: "This illustrates the saying of Rabbi Elazar: "Let us be thankful to the deceivers, for were it not for them we [who do not respond to every request for charity] would sin each day, as written, 'He will cry out to the Lord against you, and you will [thus] sin' (Deut. 15:9). . . ."

The Mishnah elsewhere states: "He is not required to sell his home or his utensils" (Mishnah Peah 8:8, §26 below). Is he not? For see, it has been taught: "If a [person seeking assistance] had been using gold utensils, he should change to silver utensils; if silver utensils, he should change to copper utensils." Said Rav Zevid: There is no difficulty; one [text] refers to bed and table, and the other [text] to cups and bowls.

Charity Fund
26. Mishnah Peah 8:7–9

Most of tractate Peah is focused on the agricultural setting. Its last chapter shifts to an urban setting. We are introduced to the tzedakah fund, which provides—primarily on a weekly basis—money for two meals a day (and an additional meal on Shabbat); and to the daily "food-tray," from which prepared food is dispensed. These two institutions are

further described in the following selection (§27), which also considers the coercive au-
thority of the charity collectors.

7. A transient poor [person] must be given no less than a loaf costing a *pundiyon,* assuming 4 *se'ah* [of wheat] cost a *sela* [such a loaf suffices for two meals].
If he stays the night, he must be given a bed and bed clothing. If he stays for
Shabbat, he must be given food for three meals. One who has food for two
meals, should not take from the food-tray; [one who has] food for fourteen
meals should not take from the [*tzedakah*] fund. The fund is collected by two
[officers] and dispensed by three.

8. One who has 200 *zuz* should not take gleanings, forgotten
sheaves, edges, or the poor's tithe. If he has 199 [*zuz*], even if one thousand
[individuals] give to him at the same time—he may take. If [any of his 200
zuz] are pledged to his creditor or to his wife's *ketubah,* he may take. He is not
required to sell his home or his utensils.

9. One who has fifty *zuz,* which he uses for doing business, may not
take. Whoever does not need to take but does take, will not pass [away] from
the world until he becomes dependent on [other] persons. Whoever needs
to take but does not take, will not die of old age until he provides for others
out of his own [property]. Of him Scripture says, "Blessed is he who trusts in
the Lord, whose trust is the Lord alone" (Jer. 17:7).

Commentary. Justice, Charity, and Indulgence

What are we to make of the famous story about Hillel related in Ketubot 67b? According to this story, Hillel provided an impoverished gentleman with a horse and a slave to run ahead of him, and when the slave failed
to show up one day, Hillel took his place and "ran before him for three miles."
The story is puzzling in several ways. One obvious question concerns how
Hillel happened to be in such great shape that at a moment's notice he could
manage a three-mile run. His remarkable physical condition is intriguing. I
shall devote my attention here, however, to other aspects of the story.

The story is often cited as though the conduct and character it attributes to Hillel are exceptionally admirable, perhaps even saintly. But despite his immense prestige, I do not believe that the story is to his credit. What it represents him as doing does not constitute, to my mind, a worthy moral paradigm. Moreover, the texts before us reveal that at least some of the Rabbis had similar misgivings.

What a person needs is whatever he or she must have to avoid harm. The Jewish understanding of charity and welfare is not limited to a concern with physical harms and material needs. Individuals and communities are required not only to help the poor to stay alive in reasonable health and comfort. They are also enjoined to provide for their spiritual needs and to enable them to maintain their dignity.

Thus Mishnah Peah stipulates: "If [a poor wanderer] stays for Shabbat, he must be given food for three meals." Two meals a day are ordinarily enough, but it is a religious duty to eat three meals during the Sabbath. A poor wanderer who lacked the wherewithal for three Sabbath meals would not be punishable for failing to eat them, of course, but he would be spiritually diminished by his inability to accept the obligation. He must be protected from this harm. It is not to be allowed that a person might be too poor to be Jewish.

Further: marriage grants are to be provided to an orphaned woman before being provided to an orphaned man, because being unmarried is a greater shame for a woman than for a man. The welfare of an orphaned woman takes precedence generally, in its claim on the community's charitable resources, over the welfare of an orphaned man. Men can go begging, after all, while it is not normal or fitting for a woman to pursue that alternative.

And: when a female orphan marries she is not only to receive a basic allowance in cash; if it is financially possible, she is to be fitted out in accordance with the dignity of her position (see §25). The basic biblical injunction concerning charity states: "If there is a needy person among you . . . you must open your hand and lend him sufficient for whatever he needs" (Deut. 15:7–8). A person's needs are not construed as including only what is indispensable for bare survival. They also include what he or she requires in order to live a religious life, to avoid unfitting behavior, and to maintain the dignity of his or her position.

Charitable giving to meet these needs is not left to the adventitious impulses of donors. It is subject both in the large and in detail to social and legal regulation. These regulations nonetheless leave it unclear just what is behind Jewish concern for the poor. Are the community and its members interested in helping the poor because they feel pity for those who suffer, because they are moved by love of their fellow human beings, or because they desire to promote communal solidarity in the face of economic discrepancies? Or are they motivated to be charitable by a conviction that the poor are, as a matter of justice or fairness, entitled to support?

Charity appears to have little if anything to do with distributive concerns: seeing to it that people have rightful shares is not its point. Hillel's conduct is plainly not motivated, in any case, by a refusal to tolerate injustice. The impoverished gentleman is not entitled to a horse and a servant, either as a matter of fairness or by any other reasonable conception of what is his due. Nor does he require these luxuries, as the poor wanderer or the orphaned bride require certain goods, in order to engage fully in religious life or in basic social practices. Going about like a rich man is neither a religious requirement nor a communal norm. The warrant for Hillel's conduct cannot be, then, that it enables the impoverished gentleman to participate in the activities or in the style of life that are standard in his community.

Perhaps what moved Hillel to help the impoverished gentleman was simply love—love of humanity. Love does motivate people, of course, to promote and to protect the interests of others. But is it truly in the interest of the impoverished gentleman to have what Hillel gives him? It is doubtless possible to imagine unusual circumstances in which a poor man would be at a substantial additional disadvantage unless a horse and a servant were at his disposal. However, no such circumstances are part of our story; therefore, they cannot be essential to its point. The horse and servant must be regarded as having no more than the function they are most naturally taken to have: they serve to support or to restore the impoverished gentleman's pride.

Now what sort of pride is at stake here? A person can legitimately take pride in his or her character and accomplishments, and in living honorably, but horses and servants have nothing to do with that. What they support is a pride in one's status rather than in oneself. Hillel's charity enables the impoverished gentleman to imitate his lost opulence by providing him with luxuries that are specifically for enjoyment in public. Thus, the pride Hillel facilitates is based on illusion; and it is, at least in part, a pride in ostentation.

Someone might nonetheless maintain that this sort of pride is better than nothing and that it is indeed in a person's interest to enjoy it. But no such claim could be countenanced by Hillel. He is on record, after all, as having declared: "My self-abasement is my exaltation; my self-exaltation is my abasement" (*Midrash Rabbah* Leviticus 1:5). Now it is obviously not a favor to anyone to encourage him to harm himself. Hillel thinks that it is very important to be humble, and he regards self-exaltation as abasing. It could hardly be love that moves him, accordingly, to feed the impoverished gentleman's pride.

While he was wealthy, the impoverished gentleman developed expensive tastes. Being unable to gratify these tastes would naturally be difficult for him. It might even be genuinely painful, causing him to suffer so intensely that sensitive and well-meaning people would be aroused to pity him. But pity could not justify what Hillel did. Pity makes a person want to help, and it may justify that impulse. What the person does to help, however, is another matter.

Suffering that is caused by ungratified desire can be alleviated in two quite different ways: by giving the sufferer what he or she wants, or by inducing the sufferer to stop wanting it so much. Suppose that what motivated Hillel's charity was, in fact, sensitivity to suffering. Then, rather than indulge the impoverished gentleman's factitious need for comfort and prestige, he should have helped him to develop a more realistic appreciation of his position and a deeper understanding of what is truly important in life. That, too, would have eased the pain of frustration. It would also have made the impoverished gentleman a better person, and it would have provided a better example for others. Hillel's way of alleviating suffering fosters illusion; and it caters unnecessarily to false values, which he himself did not accept. This is not moral depth. It is merely sentimentality.

The Hillel story is directly followed in the text by three other stories dealing with expensive tastes: a tannaitic account, and then two non-tannaitic cases. All three concern the provision to poor people of costly food. It may be that this selection of illustrative material in itself makes a point about Hillel. Since a person has to eat something, expensive food differs from the luxuries Hillel provided in that it meets an indisputably fundamental need. Furthermore, eating well is not an essentially public activity; and giving a person food, unlike running three miles in front of a horse, does not require the donor to display himself. In focusing on expensive tastes in food, perhaps the Rabbis were seeking to avoid aspects of the Hillel case that they found somewhat dubious.

The first story plainly supports Hillel. After relating that the people of Upper Galilee bought a pound of meat every day for "a poor member of a good family," it assures us that this charitable provision was not just costly but wastefully extravagant. There is no moral analysis. It appears to be simply taken for granted that the indulgence in question is admirable. The story does no more than echo the Hillel story, by describing another situation in which people went to remarkable lengths to gratify a poor person's expensive taste.

The second story is more complicated. Rabbi Nehemiah induces a poor man to give up expecting expensive meals and to live instead, as Nehemiah does, on lentils. On that diet, the man dies. This does not make it easier than in Hillel's case to justify indulgence. It is true that while Hillel's protégé might have been miserable without a horse and servant, the deprivation would not have killed him. On the other hand, however, Nehemiah could not reasonably have anticipated that a diet of lentils would be fatal. So the decision concerning indulgence, as he faced it, did not really differ in this respect from the question Hillel faced.

We are told that Nehemiah felt sorry for the dead man but that he should have felt sorry only for himself. The death naturally causes him to suffer, since it was his lentils that killed the man. But his conduct was not blameworthy. It is the dead man alone who is to be blamed and who deserves no sympathy; for he "ought not to have pampered himself to such an extent." Nehemiah refused to indulge those habits. He rejected Hillel's example and, in effect, adopted the alternative I have recommended. Despite the drastically undesirable outcome, there is no suggestion in the story that Nehemiah did anything wrong.

In the third story, a poor man asks Rava for costly food. When Rava suggests that it is not fair to ask the community to support his extravagant diet, the man replies that he does not expect this. He expects what he wants to be provided by God; for, he says, "God makes provision for each and every individual when it is due." Thereupon, lo and behold, the costly food miraculously arrives and the poor man ends up getting what he wants.

The point of the story, as I read it, is that the expensive tastes of a poor man may be indulged if this can be accomplished at no cost. Hillel goes out of his way to see to it that the impoverished gentleman has a horse and a servant. Rava takes no initiative, and he expends no charitable resources. Turning over the food his sister has brought is just a matter of transmitting something that, in the circumstances, he can regard only as a gift to the poor man from God. The propriety of cooperating in the execution of God's specific intention goes without saying; it does not need to be learned from Hillel.

If God wishes to indulge the expensive tastes of the poor, who can argue? By no means, however, does the story endorse the claim that such indulgence is God's general policy. That claim is enunciated and endorsed only by the beggar, and it is palpably false, as Rava implies when he says, "What is this here?" thus characterizing what has happened as a remarkable incident.

Unquestionably, the dignity of the poor must be maintained. But this injunction does not require that the yearnings of the poor must be supported insofar as they pertain merely to considerations of status or to luxurious habits or tastes. There is a critical difference between what people need and what they want, even when doing without what they want will make them suffer. It may occasionally be appropriate to indulge an expensive habit or taste for a limited time, on an emergency basis, to assuage intense suffering until the frustrated desire can be foresworn or reduced. Otherwise, as in Hillel's case, indulgence has little to be said for it and much against.

Harry Frankfurt

Collection, Dispensation, and Management
27. BT Bava Batra 8b

This discussion explores the authority of the officers entrusted with the collection and dis-
tribution of tzedakah. To enforce payment they may seize a "pledge"—that is, a valu-
able object to be held until remittance is made. As for dispensing the funds, the question
is raised whether they are authorized to redirect funds from one communal purpose to
another.

Our rabbis taught: The [*tzedakah*] fund is collected by two [officers] and dispensed by three. "Collected by two"—for authority over the public must
not be wielded by less than two; "and dispensed by three"—since it is like a
civil procedure. The food-tray is collected by three [officers] and dispensed
by three—for its collection and dispensation run together. The food-tray [is
operated] every day; the [*tzedakah*] fund [is dispensed] every Friday.[22] The
food-tray [serves] the poor at large, the [*tzedakah*] fund [only] the poor of that
town. The townspeople are authorized to convert [money from] the [*tzedakah*] fund to the food-tray, or [from] the food-tray to the [*tzedakah*] fund, and
to redirect them for any purpose they see fit. . . .

What "authority" is there [in *tzedakah* collection]? [That reflected in]
the statement of Rav Nahman, citing Rabbah b. Avuha: ". . . for a pledge is
seized to secure *tzedakah* [owed], even on Friday."—Is that so? But it is written, "And I will deal with all his oppressors" (Jer. 30:20), and Rav Yitzhak b.
Shmu'el b. Marta commented, citing Rav: "[This refers] to *tzedakah* collectors!"—There is no difficulty: [taking a pledge] relates to a person of means,
while [the warning against "oppression"] relates to a person without means.
For example, Rava coerced Rav Natan b. Ami and extracted from him four
hundred *zuz* for *tzedakah*. . . .

Said Abaye: At first, my teacher would not sit on the mats in the
synagogue [*Rashi:* Since they had been purchased from the [*tzedakah*] fund].
Once he learned the [*baraita*], "[The townspeople are authorized] . . . to re-

22. Lit., "eve of Shabbat."

direct them for any purpose they see fit," he would sit [on them]. At first, my teacher set up two purses: one for the poor at large and one for the poor of the town. Once he learned of Shmu'el's instruction to Rav Tahlifa b. Avdimi, "Set up a single purse and [publicly] stipulate [that the funds may be redirected]," he too set up a single purse and stipulated about it.

Rav Ashi said: I do not even have to stipulate, for all that comes [in], comes [in] under my auspices, and I may do with it as I wish.

28. Isaac Or Zaru'a, *Or Zaru'a*, part 1, Laws of *Tzedakah* 4

Is tzedakah *a matter of individual charity or of communal redistribution? This hinges, in part, on the legitimacy of exercising coercive authority in its collection. The case of Rava and Rav Natan b. Ami in the previous selection provides a talmudic precedent that would support coercion and so bring* tzedakah *close to taxation. Isaac Or Zaru'a begins his discussion by questioning this precedent, citing a talmudic principle that seems to exclude certain commandments, including* tzedakah, *from human jurisdiction. A particular strand within halakhic thinking, identified with Jacob b. Meir Tam (cf. ¢8, §10), resisted any attribution of coercive authority to the* kahal.

This poses a difficulty, for it is stated that "A positive commandment whose reward [is pronounced] alongside it [in Scripture] is not [committed to] the *bet din*'s responsibility" (BT Hullin 110b). Now, [with regard to *tzedakah*,] it is written, "You must open your hand to [the needy], for in return the Lord your God will bless you in all your efforts and in all your undertakings" (Deut. 15:8–10). [How then did Rava coerce Rav Natan b. Ami to pay 400 *zuz*?]

Rabbenu Tam interpreted "coercion" here as verbal coercion.[23] . . .

23. I.e., exhortation. This is supported by a reference to BT Ketubot 53a. Talmudic and halakhic sources reflect arguments on employing outright coercion versus social or emotional pressure in other contexts, such as the financial obligations between parents and children; see ¢19, §§15–16, 21–22.

Yet this interpretation is difficult [to accept], for [the Talmud] concludes that a pledge is seized [to secure *tzedakah*] from a person of means as in the case in which Rava coerced Rav Natan. It follows that the case involved a clear exercise of coercion.

Rabbenu Tam argued further that townspeople may certainly not coerce an individual [to give] *tzedakah,* nor [may they resort to coercion] for any purpose other than [the enforcement of] town ordinances [*takkanah*]. [So] the case of Rava coercing Rav Natan b. Ami involved a prior agreed-upon stipulation and fixed determination on which [Rav Natan] subsequently reneged. Therefore, [Rava] coerced him.

At [other] times, Rabbenu Tam explained [instead] that Rav Natan's townspeople [originally] accepted upon themselves the coercive authority of the officers [*gabba'im*], and for that reason Rava coerced him.

Rabbi Yitzhak b. Avraham (Ritzva) has written a responsum as a "ruling for practice"[24] that a person refusing to contribute to the *tzedakah* fund may be coerced by the townspeople [to do so], citing the case of Rava, who coerced Rav Natan b. Ami, extracting from him four hundred *zuz* for *tzedakah*. It is true that "A positive commandment whose reward [is pronounced] alongside it [in Scripture] is not [committed to] the *bet din*'s responsibility." He however adopts the interpretation of Rabbi Yitzhak b. Shmu'el, that *tzedakah* involves [not only the positive commandment of "open your hand" but also] the negative commandment "Do not harden your heart and shut your hand [against your needy kinsman]" (Deut. 15:7).

Moreover, he explained, and his brother Rabbi Shimshon [of Sens] agreed, that even with regard to "a positive commandment whose reward [is pronounced] alongside it [in Scripture]," coercion may be applied [to enforce compliance]. It is just that [the court] is not punished [by Heaven] should it fail vigorously to apply coercive [force] to the point of [the deviant's] death. [This is] unlike [the case of] one who fails to build a *sukkah* or to preform *lulav,* who is flogged to the point of death (cf. BT Hullin 132b). Hence, [the Talmud states that it] "is not [committed to] the *bet din*'s responsibility," i.e., they are not punished.

24. *Halakhah le-ma'aseh*—as opposed to a theoretical ruling.

Precedence of Relatives and Neighbors
29. Jacob b. Asher, *Tur* YD 251

The dispute concerning coercion in tzedakah *was reflected in the varieties of communal practice. But whether the* tzedakah *fund was provided by voluntary donation or by enforced collection, it normally sufficed for not much more than a certain minimum. This left ample scope for individual giving and, hence, individual discretion among prospective claimants. It thus also enabled the recognition of special obligations to one's family and neighbors. At the communal level, too, local priorities compete with universal obligation.*

Anyone who puts out his hand to beg is given; even a gentile. For "the heathen[25] poor should be provided for along with the Israelite poor . . . on account of the ways of peace" (¢16, §15).

Rabbi Eli'ezer [b. Samuel of Metz] has written that [the commandment] "Let him live by your side as your brother" (Lev. 25:36) does not apply to a poor [person] who transgresses any of the commandments. There is no obligation to give him *tzedakah* until it is established that he has repented.[26]

One who gives to his grown sons and daughters—whose sustenance is not his duty—in order that the sons study Torah and that the daughters be guided in the straight path; and equally one who gives gifts to his father and mother, when they [indeed] need them—all this falls within the definition of *tzedakah.* Moreover, he ought to give them precedence over others (cf. ¢19, §16). This applies even [in giving] to one who is not his son nor his father, but simply his relative: he should be accorded precedence over any other person. The poor of one's household take precedence over the poor of one's town; and the poor of one's town take precedence over the poor of another town.

[A responsum:] Re'uven had many poor relatives in town, while his neighbor Shime'on did not. Re'uven wished to appropriate a large sum for distribution among the poor of the town, diminishing the allowance for

---

25. *Goyim.* In the original Rabbinic context this meant idolators, hence the translation "heathen" in ¢16, §15; here the reference is to any non-Jew.
26. Jacob b. Asher is succinctly summarizing Eli'ezer b. Samuel of Metz's position, ¢17, §23.

other poor people who come by, for, he argued, "The poor of your town take precedence." But Shime'on opposed this.

Rabbi Isaac b. Baruch wrote: Re'uven should not be heeded. For the rule "the poor of your town take precedence" means that we should not send [funds] to another town; but regarding those who come to the town—we do not apply the rule "The poor of your town take precedence." Rather, they should diminish [the provision] for the poor of this town, and give the [itinerant] poor whatever they can.

[Author's comment:] This seems wrong to me, for surely the poor of your town take precedence.

Rav Saadiah [Gaon] wrote: One should accord precedence to his own provision over any other person, and one has no obligation to give *tzedakah* unless he has provided for himself; as written, "So that your brother may live with you" (Lev. 25:36)—your life takes precedence over the life of your fellow (BT Bava Metzia 62a, ¢17, §18). Thus said the woman of Zarephath to Elijah: "so that I can go home and prepare [food] for me and my son"—first for me, and then for my son; and Elijah agreed with her, saying: "then make for yourself and [then for] your son" (1 Kings 17:12-13). After providing for himself, providing for his father and mother should be accorded precedence over providing for his children; after that, he should provide for his children. If one's father and son are captive, and he has not sufficient [funds] to ransom them both, he should ransom his father, leaving the son. After children come brothers, and after brothers, [other] relatives. After his relatives come his neighbors, and after them his townspeople; after his townspeople, captives from other lands.

Restricting Exclusionary Commitments
30. Yehiel Mikhel Epstein, *Arukh ha-Shulhan* YD 251:4–5

Criticizing the previous text in his important commentary on the Shulhan Arukh *(in the form of an elaborate reworking of the classic work), Epstein acknowledges the priority ranking formulated by R. Saadiah but emphasizes the danger of abuse—above all, the*

neglect of the poor that would follow if these priorities were strictly applied. Yet he fails
to address the respective responsibilities of the public funds and of private contributors.

4. Now we have already explicated (in section 248:3) that [the rule] exempting one from giving *tzedakah* unless he has [enough] to provide for himself
relates only to regular contributions, a tithe or a fifth; while fulfilling the
[minimal] obligation of *tzedakah*—a third of a *shekel* each year—is required
of every person, even of a poor [person] whose provision is from *tzedakah*.

However, I find the very principle extremely problematic. For if it
is taken literally, that "these are prior to those, and [further] these to those,"
meaning that one should give nothing at all to the rung below—well, it is
known that every rich person has many poor relatives! The problem is even
more pronounced regarding an [ordinary] head of the household, whose
[funds for] *tzedakah* are limited. It would follow that those of the poor who
lack rich relatives will perish of hunger—how can one maintain such a position?

Therefore it seems clear to me that the matter must be explicated
as follows. Certainly anyone giving *tzedakah,* whether an [ordinary] householder or a rich person, is obligated to give some portion to poor people not
related to him; but he should give more to his relatives—and similarly down
the line.

So too regarding [the rule that] "his own provision takes precedence
[over providing for others]." Were it to be taken literally, most householders
would be totally exempt from [giving] *tzedakah* (except for the annual third
of a *shekel*). For it is well known that most Jews can hardly make ends meet;
thus they would all be exempt from *tzedakah* except for the extremely rich!
In localities where there are no [such] rich persons, the poor will perish of
hunger! How can one maintain such a position? Nor is this the custom.

5. Therefore it seems clear to me, that the Gaon's statement about
the priority [of providing for oneself] relates only to a person whose income
suffices only for scant bread and scant water. . . . But a person who earns the
living of a respectable householder, who consumes properly both bread and
meat and cooked dishes, and covers himself with proper garments is surely
obligated to give a tenth or a fifth of his income for *tzedakah*. The greater

measure of this he should give to his relatives and to the poor of his own town; yet a small [measure] must be given also to non-relatives and to the poor of other towns. Otherwise, a town of poor people would—God forbid—perish of hunger.

This must certainly be true, for otherwise what limit might be set on one's "own provision"? Everyone will declare "To provide for myself, my entire income is required"—for there is no limit to spending, as is well known. Rather it is surely as I said, that [the rule of precedence] relates only to one who barely has the bread necessary to keep himself alive, along with his wife and small children.

Against Redirecting Charity Funds
31. Joseph ibn Migash, *Novellae on Bava Batra* 8b

Ibn Migash provides a narrow interpretation of the baraita *allowing the redirecting of money "from the [tzedakah] fund to the food-tray." The distributive agencies of the community serve as a conduit for charitable contributions, but the funds are not considered as communal revenue subject to discretionary reallocation. Funds earmarked for the poor may be redirected only for the needs of the poor.*

"To convert [money from] the [*tzedakah*] fund to the food-tray or [from] the food-tray to the [*tzedakah*] fund." If they collected a surplus for the [*tzedakah*] fund but [the collection for] the food-tray did not suffice, they may use the surplus of the [*tzedakah*] fund to buy the necessary [provisions] for the food-tray. So too if they collected a surplus for the food-tray but lacked [funds] for [*tzedakah*], they may sell the remainder of the food-tray to make up the necessary [funds] for [*tzedakah*]. [Money from] the [*tzedakah*] fund may only [be transferred] to the food-tray, and vice versa, for both are needs of the poor. But it is forbidden to transfer [money from either of] them to other purposes that are not [related to the] needs of the poor, as this constitutes robbing the poor.

Thus we read, "Surplus from [a collection for] the poor to the poor, and from [a collection for] the captives to captives" (Mishnah Shekalim 2:5). We also read [that Abaye] made a single purse for collecting *tzedakah* [only after explicitly] stipulating [with the public that he can dispense the funds to any needy person]. Hence we surmise that the stipulation is the reason [that he was able] to redirect funds from the local poor to the poor in general. Now, if funds may be transferred even to purposes that are not [related to] the needs of the poor, then Abaye, as head of the town, could certainly have redirected them to the poor in general without stipulation! [As this is not the case] one infers that the clause "to redirect them for any purpose they see fit" applies to the needs of the poor, but they may not redirect anything to purposes that are not [related to] the needs of the poor. [This is the case] even if this *tzedakah* [contribution] was made by the townspeople, and how much more so if it was made voluntarily by an individual. For even according to those who mistakenly interpret the clause "to transfer them for any purpose they see fit" as applying to purposes that are not [related to] the needs [of the poor], this is so only with regard to [an enactment] the townspeople imposed upon themselves. But they have no authority at all to redirect a contribution imposed by others or [stipulated in] an individual gift. Even if the name of the original donor had long since been forgotten, for example, if he dedicated real estate for the poor . . . , the townspeople have no authority to redirect it to a purpose that is not [related to] the needs of the poor.

We read regarding "an Israelite who has donated a *menorah* [candelabrum] or a candle to a synagogue" (BT Arakhin 6b), that even if the name of the original donor has not been forgotten, it is permitted to redirect it to an obligatory purpose [*mitzvah*], but not to optional activities. This case however differs [from that of *tzedakah*] because the original dedication was to the synagogue, and the synagogue falls under the needs of the townspeople and is subject to their authority. Is it not the case that they have the authority to sell it even to drink beer?[27] But whatever has been originally dedicated to the poor, the townspeople have no authority whatsoever to sell or to redirect to another purpose, given that these poor are their responsibility. . . . Further-

27. See JT Megillah 74a; ¢8, §4.

Welfare Organization in the Community   293

more, the poor prefer to have [this surplus handy] as their own—funds [avail-able to them] that are not in need of collection.

Allowing Redirecting of Charity Funds
32. Meir b. Baruch of Rothenburg (Maharam), *Mordechai* Bava Batra
485–86

In contrast to the position of Joseph ibn Migash in the previous selection (§31), Rothen-burg, speaking for the kehillot *of thirteenth-century Germany, rules that funds allo-cated to the community and its officers for distribution are a form of communal revenue; he therefore accords the town officers broad discretionary authority.*

Rabbi Meir was asked about [the case of] Re'uven who had bequeathed his property to *tzedakah* saying, "This property should be invested. The *kahal* should use the gains to hire a rabbi whom they consider fit, but the capital should remain intact." This man "was gathered to his kin" and died, and after that the *kahal* hired a certain rabbi who was related to [some of] them. Now there is another rabbi available too, who is a son-in-law of the deceased and who is equally learned. Is the [position of] Rabbi Shimon b. Menasya on as-sessing [the donor's intentions] applicable here too?[28]

He replied: It is my opinion that as [Re'uven] bequeathed [the prop-erty] to the *kahal,* and it has already been handed over to the officers, his chil-dren and heirs have no more claim than do the rest of the *kahal.* The *kahal* should do "what is good and right in the sight of the Lord" (Deut. 12:28) and of man.[29]

For whatever comes into [the hands of the officers] comes under

---

28. The Talmud attributes the position that we follow the donor's intentions to Rabbi Shi-mon b. Menasya: "If one's son went abroad and [the father] heard that he had died and willed his entire property to another, his bequest holds. Rabbi Shimon b. Menasya says it does not hold, for had he known that his son was alive, he would not have bequeathed [his property to another]" (BT Bava Batra 146b).
29. Cf. Sifre Deuteronomy 79.

their discretion. [Rothenburg cites the case of Rav Ashi, §27 above.] For this reason, too, it was Rabbenu Tam's custom to divert tributes to [pay the] town guards.

So long [however], as [the money] has not reached the hands of the officer, one may certainly give it, at one's pleasure, to one's own poor relation. One may even decide to transfer this property to another *mitzvah*. Thus too we read: Rabbi Hiya bar Abba went to Babylonia and was given coins to dispense to orphans and widows. He went out and dispensed them to scholars. Must he apportion other funds in their stead [to orphans and widows as was originally intended]? . . . Rabbi Ya'akov b. Aha and Rabbi Yose and Rabbi Elazar [citing Rabbi Haninah] say, "[Regarding] all coins [contributed]— before they are handed over to the treasurers you may redirect them [for other purposes]; once they are handed over to the treasurers you may not redirect them" (JT Megillah 74a). But the *kahal* may do whatever they wish with [the money] once it is handed over to the officer, and he is to follow their orders, as I have explained.

Moreover, even if a live donor notified the *kahal* [that he is hereby donating] a certain sum to be given by the officers to the poor of the town and then [lost his remaining money and] became poor [himself], even he cannot withhold [such] funds for his own purposes. . . . For as he proclaimed in the presence of the *kahal*, "I pledge to hand over to the officers a certain sum for the poor of the town or for the general poor," this is tantamount to its coming into the officer's hand and [the donor] cannot retract. For we are the proxy[30] of the poor. We are obliged to coerce him [the donor] to fulfill his vow and give the officer [funds] to dispense to the rest of the poor. Is the fact that he has become impoverished [sufficient grounds] for not fulfilling his vow? . . . So too regarding a poor [person] who sets aside the poor tithe. He cannot withhold the funds for [his own use]; if he acts thus he does not fulfill his obligation of giving. How much more so regarding the case at hand as [the funds] have [already] been handed over to the officer! His children have no special right [in the funds] over and above the other poor. Rather,

30. Hebrew: *yad*, lit. "hand."

all depends on the discretion of the officer and the *kahal*. For it is under their auspices that the donor bequeathed, as I have explained.

A Limit on Charitable Giving?

33. BT Ketubot 50a

In formal terms, the one-fifth limit established here applies to giving and not to taking (taxation). However, as the next selection makes clear, the limit holds for coerced tzedakah *and so also for the communal allocation and collection of taxes.*

Rabbi Ila'i said: It was ordained at Usha that one who gives [his money] away should not give away more than a fifth. Likewise it was taught: One who gives [his money] away should not give away more than a fifth, lest he becomes dependent on [other] people.

It once happened that a man wished to give away more than a fifth, but his colleague did not allow him. Who was it [i.e., the colleague]? Rabbi Yeshevav. Others say: it was Rabbi Yeshevav whose colleague did not allow him; and who was [the friend]?—Rabbi Akiva.

Rav Nahman (or as some say, Rav Aha b. Ya'akov) said: What verse [supports this rule]?—"And of all that You give me, I will set aside a tithe[31] for You" (Gen. 28:22).

But the second tenth is not equal to the first!—Rav Ashi replied: I will . . . give the tenth of it [i.e., the repeated term] implies, "I will make the second like the first."

---

31. The Hebrew employs here an emphatic construction by repeating the root a.s.r. as a verb and as an infinitive absolute—*asser a'asserenu*. The KJV translates it as "I will surely give the tenth." The construction is construed by the Rabbis to imply two-tenths.

Exceptions to the Limit
34. Yehiel Mikhel Epstein, *Arukh ha-Shulhan* YD 249:1–5

Here Epstein reviews the literature on the one-fifth limit. Much of his discussion deals with charitable gifts, but the limit here is also a limit on taxation, except in cases of extremity, "involving danger to life"—then both giving and taking are unlimited until the danger is past. Note that the power of the kahal *to tax its members had largely disappeared by the time Epstein wrote. Still, a prevalent and broadly recognized halakhic norm requires a tithe from one's yearly income for the poor.*

1. The *Tur* and *Shulhan Arukh* write:

> The measure for giving *tzedakah* is this: if one has the capacity, he should give according to the needs of the poor. . . . If his capacity does not extend that far, then the finest *mitzvah* is that he give up to a fifth of his possessions; [giving] a tenth constitutes middling virtue; while less than this constitutes stinginess. The said fifth means: in the first year a fifth of the capital, and from then onward a fifth of one's annual profit.

The same obviously holds with regard to the tenth. And our master Moses Isserles (Rema) writes:

> One who gives [his money] away should not give away more than a fifth, lest he becomes dependent on [other] people (BT Ketubot 50a). This applies only during one's lifetime; upon his death, he can give to *tzedakah* as much as he wishes.

[Yet] the talmudic discussion implies that upon his death one may give away up to a half of his possessions but no more. The reason is clear: so that he not radically dispossess his heirs. Up to a half he may give away, for this is as though he is splitting with [them]: one half for himself, [i.e.,] for his soul, and one half for [them].

2. Now the statement of the *Tur* and *Shulhan Arukh* calls for clarification: What is the point of their stipulation that "if one has the capacity, he

should give according to the needs of the poor"? Since one is required to give a fifth or a tenth, and is not permitted to give more than a fifth—then it follows automatically: If he is very rich, so that his tenth or fifth suffices for the needs of all the poor, let all their needs be provided for! While if it is insufficient, what [more] is he to do? They should rather have written that every person is required to give a fifth or a tenth; from these [collected funds], we provide for the poor.

This is how (it seems to me) this statement should be interpreted. The measures of a tenth and a fifth are not part of Torah law, but are merely Rabbinic [stipulations] that were attached to the verse "And of all that You give me, I will set aside a tithe for You" (Gen. 28:22), implying two tenths, as explicated in BT Ketubot (Gen. 28:22). The tenth ordained by Torah law is only the tithe of the crop, which does not go to the poor; rather the First Tithe goes to the Levites, and the Second Tithe is consumed by the owner in Jerusalem. Only once in three years is there a Poor-Man's Tithe, decreed by the Torah, which is clearly no substitute for *tzedakah*.

3. The obligation in respect to *tzedakah*, on the other hand, is stated explicitly by the Torah in several verses. . . . The measure for this is: however much the poor person needs, as it is written, "sufficient for whatever he needs" (Deut. 15:8, §11). Nevertheless, it is obvious that the Torah would not command one to give away to the poor all that he has, making himself poor—for "Her ways are pleasant ways" (Prov. 3:17).[32] Truly, when Israel was in the land [of Israel] and their condition was good, the poor being few, they were capable of fulfilling "Sufficient for whatever he needs," etc. But now that we have been exiled from our land, the poor have multiplied while the rich have become few. Even were the rich to give away all their money, it would not suffice to fulfill the needs of all the poor. Therefore the Rabbis have ordained as upper limits the tenth and the fifth. This is along the lines of Rava's statement (BT Ta'anit 20b), "I am capable of fulfilling all [the commandments] except for opening the door and announcing "May anyone who

32. This verse is traditionally understood to be expressive of the teleology of the Torah as divine law; see BT Sukkah 32a–b and Maimonides, MT Laws Concerning Megillah and Hanukkah 4:14.

is in need come and eat," for the populace of Mahuza are numerous"—i.e., the poor there were many, and he would be wiped out. . . .

4. This then is how it should be interpreted: if one has the capacity, i.e., if he is very rich and the poor are few, he should give according to the needs of the poor, even if this comes neither to a fifth nor even to a tenth—for this is the basic requirement in *tzedakah:* to give "Sufficient for whatever he needs." But if he lacks the capacity—i.e., either he is not so rich or the poor are numerous—then he should give up to a fifth or a tenth; and even if this does not constitute "Sufficient for whatever he needs"—well, no more can be done. Now, even one who does not give a tenth, he has fulfilled the *mitzvah* of *tzedakah,* but not properly. . . . A similar position is implied in Maimonides' phrasing at the beginning of MT Laws Concerning Gifts to the Poor 7:1, 5:[33] "It is a positive duty to give alms to the poor of Israel, according to what is fitting for them, if the giver can afford it," etc. . . . "You are commanded to give the poor man according to what he lacks," etc. "If the poor man comes forth and asks for enough to satisfy his want, and the giver is unable to afford it, the latter may give him as much as he can afford. How much is that? In the best performance of this religious duty, up to one fifth of his possessions," etc.—clearly, just as we have stated.

5. The upshot of our investigation supports the view of those eminent scholars who hold that the "Tithe of Monies" has no biblical foundation. Some have sought proof from here [i.e., from the measure set for *tzedakah*] that the Tithe of Monies is biblical; according to our investigation, the contrary is proven. . . .

It seems to me that for ransoming captives, one is allowed to exceed [the said limit of] a fifth, and equally so for [the care of] the hungry, the thirsty, and the like; in any matter involving danger to life, one is obligated to give more.

---

33. *The Code of Maimonides, Book Seven: The Book of Agriculture,* pp. 77–78.

Holy Societies

The Founding Agreements
35. Nissim Gerondi (Ran), *Responsa* 1

The immediate issue in this text, involving a dispute between two "holy societies," is whether a deathbed will supersedes previous oaths and documentary stipulations. But our interest is in the description provided here of the formation of these charitable associations and the obligations accepted by their members. Among these is the hekdesh, *a consecrated donation or fund. It is also important to note, first, how the synagogue functions as the place where commitments are made and, second, how the courts and the officers of the* kahal *interpret and enforce these commitments.*

You asked about the following: a few years ago, some of the town elders united to form a society for a religious purpose[34]—to support and visit indigent Israelites who are ill. And all the members of the Society drew up and signed a document, as is the practice in every religious society, which mentioned all the agreements and stipulations to which they were bound. . . . The document began as follows: "We, the undersigned, hereby agree and have sworn in the name of the Lord, God of Israel, while holding a [holy] object, in accordance with God's determination, and in accordance with the public's determination, with no basis for release or retraction, to fulfill all of the conditions written below, with no evasion whatsoever."[35] Afterward, the document listed certain agreements and stipulations with respect to the appointees of the Society, its officers, the visiting of the sick, and other matters. Some of the agreements [had this form]: "We agree to do such-and-such, and we accept upon ourselves, and are bound by the aforementioned oath, to do such-and-such." Some simply stated, "We agree to do such-and-such" without mentioning the oath. Also included was an agreement that stated: "We also agree that, with respect to any pledge that any of us will make in the synagogue (with the exception of pledges to the funds for lamp oil), half

34. Lit., an obligatory purpose, *mitzvah,* as opposed to optional activities, *reshut.*
35. Cf. ¢1, §12.

of the amount pledged will be given to this *hekdesh* and half will go to the [particular] recipient designated by the donor [at that time]. The donor shall pay the half owed to this *hekdesh* within thirty days to the selectmen [*berurim*]; however, the selectmen shall have the power to defer payment as they see fit."

After some time, a Society for Torah Study was [also] created. [Recently], one of the [signatories of the founding document] of the *Hekdesh* Society for the Sick arose in the synagogue in this town, and pledged a certain sum to the Society for Torah Study. He made no mention of his earlier stipulation, or of any stipulation, when making this pledge. Thereafter, he died. At the time of his death, he commanded his son in accordance with the (most recent) pronouncement, to give from his property the amount pledged to the managers of the Society for Torah Study. In his statement, he did not explain whether or not, when pledging to [the Society for] Torah Study, he recalled the document he had signed [earlier]. Now the financial managers of the *Hekdesh* for the Sick are suing the son for one half of the pledge amount, even though it was assigned to the *Hekdesh* for Torah Study, because his pledge was preceded by the stipulation set forth in the document that one half of every synagogue pledge would go to that *hekdesh*. Moreover, as stated in the Society's document, [the donor] swore that he would fulfill all the stipulations, and this is certainly one of them.

The managers of the Society for Torah Study are suing the son of the donor to recover the total amount pledged, as his father had vowed. [Gerondi here cites the detailed legal arguments of the sides.] The son, the heir, asserts a claim as well. He states: "I will give half of the amount pledged to [the Society for] Torah Study, and I will keep the second half due to its doubtful status. . . ."

Answer: The law is on the side of the Society for Torah Study. . . . If, at the time of his second oath, he did not remember his first oath, the first oath did not take effect. . . . Since it is possible that he did not purposely violate his first oath, and this appears to be the case, we undoubtedly assert this. . . . [Hence the claim of the Society of the Sick is definitely rejected. The heir's attempt to retain half the sum claiming doubtful ownership is also rejected.] This is all the more so because the heir states that his father commanded him, at the time of his death, to provide the officers of the Society for Torah Study with what he had pledged from his property. There is no doubt that this [last command] is not nullified at all by his earlier stipulation, for he only stipulated there with respect to pledges made in the synagogue. Here, it is as if he retracts and makes a new pledge commanding his son at the time of his death. And the heir's credibility on this matter is stronger than that of a hundred men. [The money must all revert to the Society for Torah Study.]

The Workings of Holy Societies

36. Record-Book of the Non-Profit Society for Torah Study in the Holy Community of Kraków, 5311–99 (1551–1639)

Jewish Autonomy in Poland and Lithuania until 1648 (5408) by Shmuel A. Arthur Cygielman (Jerusalem: n.p., 1997), pp. 234–38.

These texts show how the holy societies went about their work and how the members understood their project. We don't know, of course, if the teachers actually performed as required, but the members of the society obviously believed that "he who pays the piper calls the tune," and they carefully laid out the course of study in the schools they were subsidizing. Interestingly, they prescribed a curriculum that included secular and well as religious subjects. The money required came from a variety of sources, mostly charitable in kind, but note the rule that at every circumcision ceremony, the infant's father should make a "voluntary contribution" to the society and that at every wedding the bride's and groom's families should be asked for contributions. The amount isn't fixed, so this is still tzedakah, *but it definitely isn't voluntary! In an important sense, these societies carry out the work of the community much as do nongovernmental organizations in contemporary civil society.*

a. Regulations and Curriculum

1. The Non-Profit [Charitable] Society (*Hevra Kaddisha*) in question was established in order to supervise Torah study in general, including all the teachers here, whether elementary schoolteachers or [advanced] teachers

of Talmud, lest they neglect their duties. Each week, some members of the Torah Study [Society] shall go to listen to the students in the teacher's presence, to verify that they have been taught properly, each student according to his own intelligence.

2. Heaven forfend that any teacher teach Pentateuch with any commentary other than [the ancient Yiddish language commentary] *Be'er Moshe,* which is [in] our language [Yiddish], in which we speak, in order that each youth know the proper commentary. And even with a student sufficiently intelligent to understand Rashi's commentary, he shall not study any commentary other than Rashi's, which is the correct explanation according to the plain meaning of the Bible and according to the truth.

3. It is forbidden for an elementary schoolteacher to keep in his *cheder*[36] more than forty children, and he shall employ two teaching assistants for them, to study with them, and [a junior] teaching assistant to bring them to school. Similarly, it is forbidden for a [Talmud] teacher to keep more than twenty-five [students], and he shall employ two teaching assistants to study with them and bring them to school.

4. Heaven forfend that a teacher should encroach on his fellow teacher's livelihood in the middle of the term, taking a student from the latter to his own *cheder.* Moreover, at the end of the term no teacher may go to a householder to persuade him to take his son, a student of another teacher, and transfer him to [his] school. Only if the householder should come himself and bring his son to study with him, then is the teacher permitted to take him into his *cheder*-school. All this shall be supervised by the members of the Society for Torah Study.

5. The members of the Society for Torah Study shall make it their business to hire a proper, God-fearing teacher, to study with the children of the poor and with orphans who are brought to the youths' study-house that was prepared for that purpose. They shall also hire a teaching assistant according to the number of children who come.

6. The teacher and teaching assistant . . . shall study with the children brought to the youths' study-house: alphabet with vowels, *siddur* (prayer

36. Lit., "room," i.e., classroom—the traditional Ashkenazi term for elementary school.

book), and Pentateuch, specifically with the *Be'er Moshe* commentary, and also with Rashi's commentary, and the order of prayers in their proper time, good manners and proper behavior, with each and every one according to his intelligence and level. They shall also study with them foreign [language] letters in their tongue so that they should be able to read in them and [acquire decency and] manners and proper behavior, and they should also study with them writing in the script and usage of [the foreign] language in which we speak. Also, with the more intelligent of the students they shall study the table of [Hebrew] verbs, so that they should know the essence of the holy tongue—past, present, future, singular, plural, second person, third person, regular and irregular verbs. . . . Also, they shall study with them arithmetic—addition, subtraction, multiplication, division. And if one of the students be an intelligent boy and capable of achieving the study of laws of forbidden foods, etc., he shall begin [to study] . . . Talmud, with the commentaries of Rashi and the Tosafoth.

b. Income and Officers

1. They shall receive from all synagogues and study-houses and other *minyanim* one sixth of the income accrued from the rounds [of the charity box at services] each week on Monday and Thursday.

2. At every circumcision ceremony, the circumcisor shall receive a voluntary contribution from the infant's father and from the dinner guests and shall hand it over to this Society.

3. At every wedding, two members of this Society shall go to the groom's side and to the bride's side to solicit voluntary contributions to the Society, and during the wedding feast, too, this Society shall send a sealed box to one of the guests, who shall place the box on the table, and whichever of the guests desires to throw a donation into the box shall do so, and at the end of the feast the selected guest shall count the contents of the box in the presence of the bride's and groom's families and deliver the contents to the Society.

4. The *gabba'im* [officers] shall give to this Society one tenth of the contents of the ["anonymous alms" box][37] in each synagogue.

37. See Maimonides, MT Laws Concerning Gifts to the Poor 10:8 (§24).

Officers will be appointed as stipulated by three persons elected by lot from the members of this Society, and those elected will appoint three *gabba'im* and three deputies, and one treasurer, and a deputy treasurer, through whom expenses will be paid and money collected, and four supervisors to watch over all things, whether they have been done properly and honestly, and to hold the treasurer to account that everything has been done truthfully and honestly. No person aged less than thirty-six years shall be appointed to hold office in this Society. Moreover, they [the officers] should be proficient in Torah, knowledgeable, and prominent persons.

Caring for the Poor and Sick

37. Contract of Dr. Abraham Kisch with the Holy Brotherhood for the Care of the Sick, Breslau, 1767

Jacob R. Marcus, *Communal Sick-Care in the German Ghetto* (Cincinnati: Hebrew Union College Press, 1947), pp. 242–44.

We see here how the community's obligation to provide health care to its members was understood: caring for the sick was a "holy task." The holy society looked for piety and religious learning as well as medical competence in its search for a communal physician. The "Jewish hospital" in Dr. Kisch's community seems to have been maintained independently of this society.

When the princes of the people of the God of Abraham, the chiefs and heads and leaders of the Holy Society of Those who Visit the Sick, gathered together in this place, Breslau, they carefully took thought of the poor sick here, to provide for their care, and to concern themselves with their cure. At their head stood the leader and chief in all things religious, that lion of our society, that guide under all circumstances, our master and teacher, the great and distinguished scholar, our judge and the academy head of our community and province, the honorable Joseph Teomim (May God preserve him and deliver him).

And they found it advisable to invite a sage from among our own people, one who is distinguished in righteousness, who is upright in heart, fears God, and is an expert in medicine. The purpose of this is that he may take care of the poor sick in the spirit of his knowledge, and that he may comfort them upon the bed of sickness, as is customary in the other holy communities of Israel.

And behold God has brought to them the distinguished scholar and the competent graduate doctor of medicine, who also happens to be a Jewish doctor, Abraham Kisch, a man in whom there reposes the spirit of wisdom and understanding and all the above-mentioned virtues. Then the two sides spoke to one another, in the presence of the rabbi, and they agreed to the following:

1. The fortunate society has accepted the learned Dr. Kisch for the above-mentioned office for three successive years, beginning in the month of *Tebet* coming, 5528 (December 22, 1767). And he has cheerfully agreed to accept this holy task for the period agreed upon with all the binding power as hereinafter stipulated, and now this is the nature of his ministry, this is what has been agreed upon between the two parties:

2. He is to visit the poor sick in the local Jewish hospital twice daily, as well as the other poor sick found among those who live in our community. Moreover, he shall treat anyone who presents an authentic statement to him signed by the Officer-of-the-Month of our society certifying that he belongs to our community, that he is poor, and that he requires help.

3. All payments for medicaments required for the cure of the poor are to be taken care of by the doctor out of his own pocket and to be given for nothing. The society assumes no responsibility with respect to this for the entire period indicated.

4. As payment for all this, the Brotherhood gives him from their treasury, as compensation for this holy work and for the medicaments, all told, annually, 399*Rt.,* cash, paid in two portions, at the end of each half-year. It is upon the above-mentioned conditions that the two contracting parties have agreed. On his part, the doctor has solemnly agreed by oath not to retract, nor to change, nor to withdraw from this service during this period. If he does transgress he has to pay 200 specie ducats fine to the royal authorities.

May He who is "the physician of those who are broken hearted and who binds up their suffering" (Ps. 147:3) remove all sickness from the midst of His people and help them to escape from their perils. May He "send His word and heal them, and bring them out of all trouble" (ibid. 107:20). Thus sayeth the two honorable contracting parties who sign today, the 12th of *Elul* 527 (1767), here in Breslau.

Beyond Tzedakah: *The* Kibbutz *and the Welfare State*

Overcoming Pauperism

38. Theodore Herzl, *Old-New Land,* book 3, chapter 6

Old-New Land (1902), translated by Lotta Levensohn (New York: Bloch, 1941), book 3, ch. 6, p. 176.

Herzl views pauperism to be endemic to Jewish diasporic existence. Only a state that can ensure civic status and opportunity could alleviate this poverty that tzedakah *merely prolongs.*

Then, all the great Jewish philanthropic associations pooled their resources. They had been burdened with the co-religionists forced to wander from one country to another under the pressure of persecution and poverty. When the destitute Jews of some East European country could endure their lot no longer and set out on their pathetic journeys, their brethren in the remoter communities had to extend a helping hand. They gave and gave to the wandering beggars, but it was never enough. Vast sums were spent without opportunity to investigate the merits of individual cases. There was, therefore, no way to make certain that only the deserving would receive aid. The result was that misery was not alleviated even temporarily, while pauperism was fostered.

The Zionist idea provided a base on which all humanitarian Jewish effort could unite. Jewish communities everywhere colonized their own poor in Palestine, and thus relieved themselves of these dependents. This method was cheaper than the former planless sending of wanderers to some foreign land or other; and there was the certainty that only willing workers and the deserving poor were receiving assistance. Anyone who wished to do honest work was certain of an opportunity in Palestine. If a man declared that he could not find work even there, he thereby stamped himself as a ne'er-do-well deserving of no sympathy.

Critique of Tzedakah

39. Kaddish Luz, "On the Spiritual Sources of the *Kevutzah*"

"Limkorotehah ha-ruhaniyim shel ha-kevutzah," *Adam Va-derekh,* edited by Mordechai Sever (Deganya: n.p., 1974), pp. 62–64.

Luz succinctly describes the social and spiritual forces that animated the kibbutz *movement. (He uses the synonymous* kevutzah. *The term* kibbutz *was originally coined for a commune that combined agricultural and industrial work and only later became the general name for all communal settlements.) His critique of charity motivated by mercifulness, and of private property generally, gains its special character from its messianic combination of both socialist and hasidic motifs.*

The primary factors acting upon the people who embarked on the construction of new life forms were the same factors that gave birth to the world's great social and religious movements. It is the absolute moral imperative dwelling in a person's heart, it is . . . attentiveness to that which occurs deep in one's heart and the constantly reiterated inner demand for self-realization. When these transcend the boundaries of individual experience and become the possession of . . . [people] united in a movement, such causes have the power to produce great events. No doubt, there were other factors that shaped the character of our novel village. The fact that it was founded at the beginning of Zionist realization [*hagshamah*] was of enormous significance. The ideas of the [founding] generation were highly influential, as was the revolutionary ferment in Russia. But the primary [cause] . . . [lies in the] hearts of the people. Hundreds and thousands of young people were moved by deep moral yearnings, sublime cravings for human redemption [and for the redemption of] the people and the land, for the revitalization and perfection [*tikkun*] of life, and for an elevation of human relationships. *Aliyah* to the land and the revolution in one's way of life shook the human psyche [and] transformed the heart's imperatives from a [state of] potentiality to actuality, from theory to realization.

We draw our nourishment from the religious-national movement of our people. The novelty of our movement is in . . . [our readiness] "to force the end."[38] Zionism is the final link, indeed the most radiant link, in the chain of messianic movements. And socialist-Zionism brings together national and social messianism. We believe that if there is [any] hope of realizing the vision of the end-of-days, then there is a possibility of its realization in our lives too. . . .

The fundamental characteristic of the commune revolution is the combination of the individual moral imperative with the creation of an objective framework for a life of justice and love. Human beings have various dispositions: violence, lawfulness, mercy, justice, love. The disposition to act lawfully is but a moderated version of the disposition to violence; violence is always more comfortable when it dons the mantle of law. The virtue of mercy entices the heart so! But it involves terrible injustice. For mercy presupposes the existence of the powerful and the weak, the wealthy and the poor. Do the weak and the impoverished have mercy—in real life, not in metaphysical life—upon the powerful and the wealthy? Mercy presupposes the existence of violence as a permanent feature of this world.

Mercy will not suffice for the repairing and perfection [*le-takken*] of human relationships. Let us choose then the virtues of justice and love. But to enable love to reign in human relations, the unassailable existence of justice as an objective factor—independent of the will, whims, and wavering mercifulness of the individual—must first be insured.

So long as human society sustains the right of private property, which must always be defended against the other, the virtue of love will depend on miracles for its existence. Even the love between father and child can turn into hatred when private property stands between them. That is why the

---

38. For "force the end," see Midrash Rabbah Lev. 19:5: "Rabbi Yehoshua b. Levi said: It refers to such, for instance, as would force the [coming of the] 'End' too soon"—in other words, end the exile before the time deemed right by God (see also BT Ketubot 111a, ¢26).

family should not be an economic unit. It ought to desist from any economic function, even from the distribution of food and allowances. In the commune, the family is the elemental unit of love—the love of man and woman and [the love] of parents and children. [The family] . . . is liberated from the struggle for survival, from distribution of material benefits and from provision of material needs. . . .

Whatever the numerical [scope of its membership], the *kevutzah* must [be sure] to retain its capacity to fulfill the communal rule, "From each according to his means, to each according to his needs."

Private Property Is Incompatible with Righteousness

40. Yeshayahu Shapira, "Do What Is Right and Good"

"Ve-asita ha-Yahar veha-Tov," in *Yalkut Ma'amarim al Ra'ayon ha-Torah va-Avodah,* edited by N. Aminoah and Y. Berenstein (Jerusalem: Tenu'at Torah va-Avodah, 1931), pp. 38–43.

Aware of the central role of private property in the halakhic tradition, Shapira's attempt to provide Orthodox backing for the kibbutz *appeals to religious and ethical arguments and to the morality of aspiration rather than to strict duties. His critique of private property also undercuts, though he does not say so, the possibility of individual charity.*

There are many who contest the attempt to combine "Torah" and "labor." Between the two, they contend, there is no connection. From the Torah's point of view, no difference exists between the laborer and the merchant, and those who seek to combine "Torah" with "labor" are grafting a foreign implant onto the vine of the House of Israel. Proof of the matter [they contend, is the fact] that the *Shulhan Arukh* includes no explicit clause requiring individual labor, hence implying that this is not one of Judaism's demands. Moreover, *halakhah* includes many clauses regarding business transactions and claims, proving that, according to Judaism, business is permitted.

They also say that Judaism has taken no position with regard to the question of [private] property: neither for nor against. Its only demand is that life be ordered in a just manner.

The demand to adduce proofs of the value of labor from the *hala-khah* would be appropriate were we maintaining that labor is a halakhic obligation. This however has not been maintained by any of us. . . . We maintain only that labor and toil are an aspiration of Judaism, and that beside the value of labor for *tikkun olam* and civilizing society [*yishuv ha-olam*], Judaism sees in labor the only possibility for a completely just life. Regarding the aspiration of Judaism, one may infer not only from *halakhah* but from *aggadah* and from all our ancient literature. The aspiration finds expression not only through the law [*din*] but especially through [imperatives that are] beyond the rule of [strict] law ["*lifnim mi-shurat ha-din*" (BT Bava Metzia 30b)].

According to Nahmanides, the numerous laws of the Torah cannot ensure that an Israelite person will truly live in accordance with the spirit of the Torah.[39] A person may be a "scoundrel with the Torah's permission." He may be completely immersed in appetite for things permitted to him, be a kosher glutton, and find legal loopholes for swindling his companion without transgressing any explicit prohibition. Therefore the Torah has commanded "You shall be holy" (Lev. 19:2) so as to say that it is wrong to restrict [observance] to the law alone . . . : but rather, as Maimonides has said, [one ought] "to pursue the purpose of the Torah" (paraphrasing *The Guide of the Perplexed* 2:25), or as the Rabbis have said, "sanctify yourself in that which is permitted to you" (BT Yevamot 20a).

Whoever wishes perfectly to fulfill the Torah . . . must not only keep in mind the right and good in his own eyes but "the right and the good in the eyes of the Lord" (Deut. 6:18). . . . [Now although] the purpose of the entire law is to show a person the right path, there are a number of deeds [formally] permitted by the law that are specifically prohibited by [the commandment] "You shall do what is right and good in the eyes of the Lord." . . . For Judaism is not satisfied with restricting evil deeds alone but also aspires to uproot potential evil from the human psyche. Therefore one finds special commandments regarding internal tendencies that are the roots of various crimes. The Torah is not satisfied with "You shall not steal" (Exod. 20:13) but demands also "You shall not covet" (20:14). Whoever restricts the require-

39. See Nahmanides, *Commentary on the Torah* Lev. 19:2.

ment only to "You shall not steal" might still find a possibility for [what is but] the "residue" of stealing[40] within [the boundaries of] the Torah's permission. But whoever aspires to fulfill "You shall not covet," whoever is cautious not only of touching his companion's penny but of coveting it in any form whatever, is the only one who . . . thereby observes "You shall not steal" also in all the depth of the significance ascribed to it by the Torah.

. . . Individuals existed in all generations . . . who devoted themselves to sublime sanctification and purification, but the public was mired in the difficult subjection [of the Exile], and the effort to keep its essence and identity, so as not to assimilate among the nations and learn from their ways, was hard enough. But now, as we return to our land, wishing to create here an authentic Jewish [way of] life, it is incumbent upon us to set ourselves again this goal of the holiness of life in all its depth and scope. We must create here a form of life that would be permitted not only by law but [by such general norms] as "You shall be holy" and "You shall do the right and the just," too. Judging matters from this vantage point we will see that Judaism is in no way supportive of private property but rather opposes it.

If Judaism has any place for those who maintain that "Mine is mine, and yours is yours," which is the foundation of private property, are "the kind of Sodom" (§5 above), it certainly does not tend toward [a celebration of private] property. True, this is only the opinion of "some," but on all accounts this maxim is not [adopted by people of] pious virtue [*midat hasidut*]. The pious virtue, that is to say the ideal virtue of Judaism, is "Mine is yours, and yours is yours," which rejects the foundations of private property.

The Torah clearly hints at its position regarding this question. The reason given by the Torah for the *mitzvah* of jubilee, "for the land is Mine; you are but strangers resident with Me" (Lev. 25:23, §2 above), expressly indicates the Torah's attitude to property and to private ownership in general. It follows from [this verse] that man has no ownership in the entirety of creation, for God owns it all, and we are but strangers and residents. The sole right we possess is to work the land and consume its fruits—all of us

---

40. This metaphor denotes behavior falling just outside the formal boundaries of a transgression. Regarding the "residue" of stealing, see, e.g., MT Laws of Repentance 4:4.

equally—but we have no right to consider ourselves masters of the land and its owners. . . .

It would thus seem that according to the outlook of Judaism, the only thing a person owns in the world is labor. Only an object gained through labor is his. For the capacity to work was not given in partnership to the entirety of creation but individually to each person. Indeed, regarding this too we must bear in mind that it is God who gives "you the power to get wealth" (Deut. 8:18). Therefore too, when one assists his fellow, giving from one's own money, he must constantly remember that "You and yours are His. So too is it written with regard to David, 'All is from You, and it is Your gift that we have given to You' (1 Chron. 29:14)" (Avot 3:7).

The commandment of debt remittance also contradicts [the institution of] private property. . . . From the perspective of individual human justice founded upon "Mine is mine, and yours is yours"—whose main concern is . . . the sanctification of the "mine" and the "yours"—there is an injustice here with regard to the affluent. But from the perspective of divine justice, derived from the view that "All is from You" (1 Chron. 29:14), the *mitzvah* of remittance is the most sublime expression of equity and justice.

Jews in the American Welfare State

41. I. M. Rubinow, "What Do We Owe to Peter Stuyvesant?"

Trends and Issues in Jewish Social Welfare in the United States, 1899-1958, edited by Robert Morris and Michael Freund (Philadelphia: JPS, 1966), pp. 288–96; reprinted by permission of the University of Nebraska Press; copyright 1966 by the Jewish Publication Society of America.

This is the diaspora version of Kaddish Luz's argument that welfare is a general social obligation and not a matter for private philanthropy. Speaking to Jewish social workers in 1930, in the early years of the Great Depression, Rubinow is more sober and pragmatic than Luz and Yeshayahu Shapira. With a combination of realism and foresight, he anticipates the social legislation of the New Deal and calls for Jewish support for a welfare state committed not only to the relief of poverty but also to its prevention. The well-being of the Jewish poor could no longer depend on the charitable giving of pious Jews.

In 1652, Peter Stuyvesant, Governor of New Amsterdam, now New York, received a promise from the Jews who came to settle there that they would care for their own poor. Ever since then, the Jews of this country have prided themselves that this sacred promise, which the first Jewish settlers in America made, has never been broken. . . .

[But] if we are proud, is the pride justified? Have we, as a matter of fact, always taken care of our poor in this country? If we have made the promise, can we really claim to have kept it? Far be it from me to deny the well-known generosity of Jewish philanthropy in this country, as judged by comparison with other groups. The facts and figures are available. . . . The average family supported by Jewish philanthropic relief agencies receives about twice as much . . . as non-Jewish families from non-sectarian agencies. I believe that in every city where Jewish philanthropic Federations exist side by side with non-sectarian Community Chests, the per capita contribution for the Jewish population is considerably higher than for the general population. . . .

And of these things we Jews are proud, perhaps justly so. I say "perhaps" deliberately . . . for it has not yet been established with an equal degree of statistical accuracy that on the whole the Jewish voluntary contribution to public and social needs is in excess of what would be their fair proportion, according to their population and economic resources. . . . Is it necessary to remind the professional worker that the Jews have not built their own insane asylums? Nor have Jews refused to accept treatment in non-Jewish hospitals, whether public or private. . . . Nor have we worried very much . . . that thousands and tens of thousands of our students in colleges, mostly poor, were being maintained partly out of State funds and partly out of philanthropic contributions of non-Jews. And let us come somewhat more closely to the specific problem of relief. Injured Jewish workmen receive large amounts through compensation legislation. Jewish widows are on the lists of most widows' and mothers' pension funds. Presumably, among the 50,000 men and women over seventy years of age who have been put on the roster of the New York Old Age Security scheme, there is no dearth of Jewish names. The plain, unadorned truth, therefore, is that the Jews, as a separate group, have not singly and entirely supported their own poor.

. . . The promise itself may have been not only diplomatic, but fair and just in its own day. . . . It was based upon a . . . social philosophy which, like all other social philosophies, derived its strength from a certain social structure. Two hundred and fifty years ago, and perhaps even fifty years ago, poverty may have been primarily a result of individual factors or, at most, group factors. Perhaps the shrewd business people who signed that blank check 250 years ago had good reasons to believe that the amount [needed] would never become a very heavy burden. But conditions have changed. Very much so! Instead of a quarter of a million Jews scarcely a generation ago, we have four million and a quarter. Instead of being a country of small individual enterprise, we have become the greatest industrial country in all the world and in all history. . . .

Why, then, under these conditions, do we have this somewhat naive, antiquated emphasis upon isolation in philanthropic work, in dealing with the problems of economic distress? . . .

If we give due consideration to American economic problems, surely the pragmatic bent of our thinking, for which we Jews are so known and of which we may be justly proud, should have convinced us . . . that for all the publicity given to or purchased by private philanthropy in this country, it is a very [inadequate] method of meeting the problems which it claims to meet. . . . Limiting ourselves to American conditions, how pitiful, how tragically pitiful, are the figures of private philanthropy and relief as compared with public resources already made available. A year or two ago, our professional journal announced, with a great beating of drums and sounding of trumpets, that Community Chests were collecting the fabulous sum of some $60–$65,000,000 per annum. How much . . . publicity was necessary to obtain this amount? How much flattery was poured out before the generous givers? Yet, at the same time, how many of you remember that for the government relief of only one group of cases—namely, industrial accidents, a comparatively minor cause of poverty and distress in the experience of social agencies—for that group of cases alone, $250,000,000 are paid out each year through the instrumentality of workmen's compensation laws, and the amount is annually rising. Some fifteen years ago, when the mother's pension movement first came up for discussion, the leaders of our profession fought against it on the ground that private philanthropy was amply able to handle the situation and could do it in a more scientific way. And already, some $50,000,000 a year are distributed in mothers' pensions from public funds.

. . . If it be the purpose and the duty of organized society to eliminate suffering and distress by undertaking the painstaking task of preventing its causes, then "private philanthropy" cannot do it, while public relief and a social policy of compensation and insurance can and does.

[But] today my purpose is a more circumscribed one. I am dealing primarily with the problems confronting the Jewish social worker and Jewish social service. My thesis may perhaps be best summed up in the following statements:

Jewish poverty is not a result of intra-group conditions. It is part and parcel of the whole economic and social problem of wealth, production, and wealth accumulation of the country as a whole. The expectation that the problem of Jewish poverty can be met individually and eliminated irrespective of those general economic forces is an expression of excessive group pride uncontrolled by scientific research and thinking. The sermon [about] independent group responsibility becomes a definite anti-social force if it destroys Jewish . . . interest and Jewish participation in national progressive social movements.

Commentary. *Tzedakah,* Zionism, and the Modern Jewish Citizen

It is fair to claim, generalizing as it may sound, that Zionism vehemently rejected the concept of *tzedakah,* as it was understood in the nineteenth century—halakhic-inspired personal and voluntary almsgiving. From Theodore Herzl's program of sovereignty-based economic sustainability, through the alternative Passover *hagadot* written in the *kibbutzim* and extolling a life of independent communal labor, to recent Israeli debates on the merits and demerits of external and internal philanthropy, this Jewish idea seems particularly antagonistic to the fundaments of modern Jewish statehood.

The word *tzedakah* has not disappeared from modern Hebrew and from public discourse. It resonates in two main ways. *Tzedakah* either maintains its traditional meaning, the halakhic imperative exercised within the segregated Jewish community, or it takes on the modern sense of philanthropy, along with its civil society and global aspects. Neither usage represents an original Israeli version of the concept. The reason for this is simple: modern Israel was not intended, by any of its visionaries and founders, to stand in need of *tzedakah*. The word evoked the *kahal* in its decadence, the *shtetl* landscape of people mired in perpetual poverty and constantly needy of alms provided by individual donors obeying religious commandments or following the sentimental call of pity.

In medieval and early modern times, *tzedakah* still carried a double sense of charity and justice. Writers like Maimonides argued that this kind of giving was not only morally required but could be legally enforced; it hardly differed, as earlier texts in this chapter suggest, from taxation. But the early Zionists encountered a very different Jewish world: the challenge to autonomy by the modern state, the growing weakness of the *kahal,* and the economic upheavals of the nineteenth century transformed the communal version of *tzedakah* into an individualist version—almsgiving simply. And such an institution could have no future, Zionists believed, in the modern state of the Jews.

Herzl's economic analysis of the situation of Europe's Jews and his ensuing vision for modern Jewish statehood, seen here in the selection from *Old-New Land,* required the transformation of Jewish charity into Zionist sustainability. Herzl was not opposed to charity, as long as it was duly acculturated: in his utopian novel, discussants in the *Ship of the Wise* tackle "the establishment of a truly modern commonwealth, education through art, land reform, charity organization, [and] social welfare for workingmen," among other aspects of "civilized society" such as the role of women and the progress of applied science. In Jerusalem, the three great religions freely and equally run their institutions, charities included; but these were not part of Herzl's civic vision.

Mainstream Zionism followed Herzl's aversion to poverty-perpetuating almsgiving. Pauperism and *schnorring* were among the most hated features of the atavistic *shtetl* mentality. Zionism was conceived as a

collective move to abandon the shameful practices produced by the abnor-
mal, unproductive economy that characterized contemporary eastern European Jewish life and, Zionist writers claimed, almost two millennia of "extra-
historical" Jewish existence.

A poignant early example of the Zionist transformation of *tzedakah*
into collective state-building effort is the famous "blue box." Born together
with the Jewish National Fund (Keren Kayemeth LeIsrael) in 1901 and deliberately modeled on the old Jewish charity boxes, it displayed a blue-and-
white map of the Land of Israel. This highly symbolic instrument of the Jewish people's collective enlistment to the cause of a nation-state was patently
intended to make its predecessors obsolete. The money was collected to "redeem the soil" of the ancestral homeland and make it available to Jewish agriculture and industry, thus obliterating the very need for *tzedakah*.

The absence of *tzedakah* from Zionist discourse is tellingly revealed
through a search for the term in the excellent Israeli website Zemereshet,
which has made available online most of the Hebrew songs composed since
the late nineteenth century. *Tzedakah* and its synonyms appear in this immense collection of lyrics in only a handful of liturgical texts set to music.
The single exception is one of the earliest and best-known Zionist hymns,
"Se'u Tziyonah Nes va-Degel" (Carry the flag to Zion) written by Noah
Rosenblum and the cantor Noah Zladukovsky. "Dress us with the spirit of
Joab," it goes, "The spirit of heroic justness (*tzedakah*) / For our people, for
our country / Be strong and let us get stronger!" Like the transformed charity
box, *tzedakah* is here redeployed in the tenor of Zionist self-help. It is also
re-biblicized, rolled back into its earlier sense of justice and coupled with
biblical heroism.

Socialist Zionism, which set both the political and ideological tone
from the early pre-state phase (the "new *yishuv*") through the first three decades of the young state, offered the most practical alternatives to the charity-
based community. As early as 1903, a meeting in Zichron Yaakov, headed by
Menachem Ussishkin, called for a new union of Zionist laborers who would
live by their labor and receive no *tzedakah*. At that stage, only a teachers'
union was launched. Later waves of socialist immigrants in the second and

third *aliyot* established several practical versions of the principle: the *kibbutz* and *kevutzah,* which shunned all private property; agricultural smallholders' communities; organized labor unions in cities and in the countryside; self-defense organizations; and above all the Histadrut (founded in 1920), still active today as Israel's major national workers' union.

This major branch of Zionist thought is represented here by the secular *kibbutz* member, Mapai politician, and later Knesset speaker Kaddish Luz (1895–1972) and by the "pioneer rabbi" and religious labor leader Yeshayahu Shapira (1891–1945). Luz's discussion of the "spiritual sources" of the *kevutzah,* a smaller version of the *kibbutz* devoted to agriculture and intimate communal existence, is in some ways as religious as Shapira's alignment of socialism and Jewish orthodoxy. Luz's "deep moral yearnings" of the heart, the "sublime cravings for human redemption," were typical of the secular religiosity of many early labor Zionists. Even the impressive, Marxist-inspired pragmatism of the early kibbutzniks is conceived in the quasi-mystical terms of "realization" (*hagshamah*), spiritual mending (*tikkun*), and "transformation to actuality." Luz therefore felt a need to justify the banishing of mercy, a laudable sentiment of the heart, from its time-honored spiritual pedestal by showing its necessary link to the cruelties of social inequality. The combination of justice, a social and political value, and love, the most elevated denizen of the heart, were called upon to trump mercy. Work and solidarity, not *tzedakah* and mercy, were the true vehicles of human and national redemption.

Shapira, too, must justify the socialist values of work, self-sufficiency, and solidarity, but without Luz's "absolute moral imperative dwelling in a person's heart." The religious labor movement, under the motto "Torah and Work," confronted the traditions of the *shtetl* as well as the old *yishuv,* where orthodoxy trumped modernization, where talmudic scholarship was valued far more than working for a living, and where *tzedakah* was internalized as a legitimate, indeed necessary and laudable, source of subsistence. While admitting that labor (the original Hebrew text has "self-labor," emphasizing individual duty) is not a halakhic obligation, Shapira nevertheless links it with two values that had become central for modern Jewish orthodoxy: setting the world to rights (*tikkun olam*) and civilizing the world (*yishuv olam*). Shapira's bold claim that "Judaism sees in labor the only possibility for a completely just life" is not made in terms of halakhic law, where it is absent, but in terms of "Jewish aspiration." Incorporating the revolutionary stance of religious Zionism, a movement aiming to modernize and normalize Jewish existence without secularizing it, this early text clearly anticipates an ongoing and highly politicized debate between the ultraorthodox and the national orthodox in Israel today.

Shapira's critique of private property revisits the Mosaic limits on all human ownership ("for the land is Mine; you are but strangers resident with Me") with a Marxist twist: "the only thing a person owns in the world is [his] labor." This resonates of Moses Hess, the pre-Zionist socialist thinker, whose writings may well have been familiar to Shapira. In the world of Israel's national orthodox today, the battle against private property is long lost. But the case against the ultraorthodox living by charity, the battle for "self-work" and sharing in civil and military burdens, is very much alive.

Interestingly, the concepts developed by the labor movement for institutionalizing social solidarity were taken from the Jewish tradition and recontextualized. Mutual help (*ezra hadadit*) and mutual responsibility (*arvut hadadit*) both served as mottos for the legal and practical structures aimed at abolishing poverty within the communal frameworks of organized Zionism. Thus, during the 1920s, the Labor Battalion (Gdud Ha'avoda) and the emerging *kibbutzim* movements enacted several versions of these principles: full economic equality and "equal living conditions" within each group of pioneers, and differing levels of mutual support among worker groups, *kevutzot* and *kibbutzim* belonging to the same movement. On a higher level, the Histradrut set up an unemployment fund as early as 1923. The economic crisis of the late 1920s triggered institutional provisions of homes and food for unemployed workers, equal allotment of available work, "initiated labor," and collective fundraising among paid laborers. In 1927 a new fund was established for direct financial aid, and employers were made to contribute to it.

It is important to note that these enacted and on-the-ground arrangements were often quite successful, not so much in obliterating poverty — since most of the pioneering groups and settlements were initially very poor — but in abolishing the reliance of needy individuals on the generosity of their wealthier brethren. In their early years, when private property was thin on the ground anyway, the *kibbutzim* could truly claim to have built a system that demands "from each according to his capabilities" and gives "to each according to his needs."

Even today, after a dramatic process of economic liberalization, some strands of socialist justice-seeking are still part of Israel's public sphere. Since the establishment of Israel, the Histadrut was instrumental in combating unemployment by practical means and pressing for legal remedies — especially during the tough 1950s and 1960s, and still today. The *kibbutzim*, too, have always maintained some degree of mutual support within and among the communities. In recent years, when both equality and communality have largely been abandoned, a basic level of mutual support remains the norm. In other words, the concept of *tzedakah* as voluntary charity has been anathema to the Zionist labor movement from its early beginnings to the present-day *kibbutz* and workers' unions.

After the establishment of Israel in 1948, the government included a Support (*sa'ad*) Ministry and a Labor Ministry, which later became the Ministry for Work and Welfare. There was a near-general agreement that social aid, incorporating the crucial value of labor, is now a matter for the state, led by a socialist ruling coalition and egged on by the Histadrut (which functioned as a weighty extra-parliamentary opposition whenever the government appeared to pursue other priorities). We can see a connection here to I. M. Rubinow's call to American Jews to support "organized society," the welfare state in the making, and recognize the insufficiency of the time-honored system of private philanthropy. In one sense, Rubinow's attitude is more sober and realistic than the utopian dreams of socialist Zionism, which hoped to turn the whole Land of Israel into a poverty-free, perhaps even private-property-free, zone. On the other hand, the thrust of Rubinow's argument would not have been necessary in the young state of Israel.

Rubinow's proposed leap from private philanthropy to civil support of state-run welfare has no equivalent in early Israeli discourse, because Zionism eschewed private philanthropy half a century before the state came into being. Herzl's *Judenstaat* is a nascent welfare state, where institutions of settlement (the "Society of the Jews") pay salaries to pregnant women and provide everyone with sickness, injury, and death insurance. However, the unemployed capable of labor are to be offered "initiated work" ("labor aid," in Herzl's terminology) rather than rely on charity or welfare. The young state of Israel followed these guidelines almost to the letter. The language of mutual aid, gleaned from Zionist socialism, translated easily into the new governmental order. What kept the original utopia at bay was the sheer numbers of poor immigrants, refugees, and Holocaust survivors that tripled the country's population within a decade.

This human influx, and the young country's meager resources, created a far more complex reality. Although *tzedakah* may have been absent from Israeli discourse, philanthropy was always a mainstay of Israel's existence. By 1948 it was clear to all, David Ben-Gurion strongly included, that the young state had little chance of survival without a great deal of external support, from gentile governments and from Jewish donors. To be sure, the crushing weight of the Holocaust and the imperative of allowing all Jews into the new state—more than a million penniless refugees—were not a fair burden for the proudly self-sufficient labor Zionism of old (whose members made up less than half of that number). Furthermore, national fundraising among diaspora Jews could be seen as an extension of the old "blue box," an act of civil participation and self-redemption.

In recent years, a rising number of Israeli intellectuals and opinion makers (alongside a very few politicians) have voiced their distaste for the Israeli courtship of overseas charity, from Jews and non-Jews alike. Although most of these commentators agree that American military aid cannot be given up and that philanthropy-targeting public institutions are legitimate players in a global setting, Israel is increasingly seen as capable of fending for itself.

Neither *tzedakah* nor philanthropy is absent from modern Israeli life. There are probably more old-fashioned collection boxes around the country today, especially those circulated by religious institutions, than Jewish National Fund "blue boxes." Well-to-do Israelis are increasingly involved in local and global philanthropic projects. But these concepts, which hail respectively from the Jewish tradition and from international modern culture, never took on a specific Israeli character. They are significantly absent from the unique vocabulary of a society that had attempted to free human beings from the need to seek the voluntary or religiously instructed generosity of their peers.

Fania Oz-Salzberger

TWENTY-ONE Taxation

Introduction

Principles

Temple Tax: Equality
1. Exodus 30:11–16

Partnership: The Caravan in the Wilderness
2. BT Bava Kama 116b

Security, Taxation, and Exemptions
3. Mishnah Bava Batra 1:5; BT Bava Batra 7b–8a

The Injustice of Tax Avoidance
4. Rabbi Nathan, Responsum

Criteria of Just Taxation

Property and Profits
5. Joseph b. Samuel Bonfils, Responsum

Taxation According to Means
6. Joseph ibn Migash, *Novellae on Bava Batra* 7b

Calculation of Taxes
7. Meir b. Baruch of Rothenburg (Maharam), *Responsa* (Cremona) 228

Beyond Proportionality
8. *Sefer Hasidim* 1046

Guard Duty
9. Meir b. Baruch of Rothenburg (Maharam), *Mordechai* Bava Batra 475

323

Renewing the Educational and Scholarly Institutions
20. Valladolid Synod of 1432

Introduction

Taxation is the other side of welfare provision: the communal taking that makes communal giving possible. But from whom should we take? And how much should we take? In accordance with what criteria? The Bible provides less help with regard to these questions than it does in the case of *tzedakah.* There is the poll tax described in Exodus 30, the same for everyone, devoted to the costs of the sanctuary and the service. The priestly writers add to this a tithe for the Levites (Num. 18:21), which is reassigned in Deuteronomy (26:12) to "the Levite, the stranger, the fatherless, and the widow." But this is not a tax that is actually collected by communal officials; nor is anything said about how, exactly, it was to be distributed. Some medieval writers found a precedent here for proportional taxation by the *kahal;* it is a weak precedent, however, for the biblical equivalents of the *kahal*'s selectmen, the king's officers, had nothing to do with the priestly or the Deuteronomic tithe.

Insofar as there is a biblical view of taxation (where the taxes are *collected* by state officials), it is the highly negative view expressed by Samuel, when he warns the people against the establishment of monarchic rule. Samuel describes another tithe, which will be "taken" by the king to pay his officers and servants. We can assume the reality of the taking (1 Kings 7 ff. lists Solomon's tax collectors), even though the Bible provides no information as to how much was collected or by what methods. The most important royal tax, also foreseen by Samuel, was the tax on labor, which made Solomon's building program possible. Both the royal tithe (if that's what it was in practice) and the corvée were bitterly resented, providing the immediate occasion for the northern revolt. Hence they don't make useful precedents for the *kahal*—which did, nonetheless, tax both resources and bodily service (for guard duty, for example: see the second selection from Meir of Rothenburg, §9 below).

Samuel's warning seems to imply that if there were no king there would be no taxes or, at least, no secular taxes. But though this is a view that reappears in political history—as a criticism of government generally or of too much government or of particularly corrupt governments—it is certainly wrong. Nor, in fact, did any of the rabbis doubt that the Jewish communities needed money for their proper functioning and had a right to collect it from the members. The parallel right of non-Jewish rulers was more likely to be doubted, particularly when the rulers were oppressive and their taxes arbitrary. Within limits, though, the maxim "*dina de-malkhuta dina*" sanctioned these taxes, too (see ¢9). In any case, the same questions arose with regard to the *kahal* and the gentile state within which it was located: How were the burdens to be distributed? What made for justice in taxation?

Though the responsa literature dealing with these questions is extensive, the Rabbis were often reluctant to assert their authority in matters of tax policy. Taxes fell within the realm of *mamona,* where local custom and the decisions of the "good men" were permitted great latitude. Even gentile rulers, as we saw in Chapter 9, had latitude here, subject only to certain formal constraints. Nonetheless, Rabbinic guidance was sought whenever the rules or the criteria of taxation were disputed—and these disputes were as common in the *kahal* as in any other political community.

Three different criteria figure significantly in the Rabbinic discussions. The first is simple uniformity—a fixed sum from each member of the *kahal*—which was commonly favored, for obvious reasons, by the wealthier members. Given the limited resources of the poor, it would have set tax rates at a very low level. The Rabbis tended to oppose this, arguing from the requirements of justice (though they could as easily have made an argument from necessity). In particular cases, with reference to particular taxes, however, some of them defended uniformity, invoking the second criterion.

Second, derived from the partnership model, this was also a justice-based standard: members should contribute in proportion to the benefits they could reasonably be expected to receive from whatever service the community was providing. (Certain sorts of contemporary taxes, assessments for sidewalks and sewers, for example, follow this standard.) The rich had a greater stake, say, in the defense of the community against marauders and thieves; moreover, it was their wealth that attracted these (and other) predators; so they should pay a greater share of the costs of security. When it came to hiring a cantor, by contrast, everyone had the same stake and should share equally in the costs. But the partnership model was never fully accepted in taxation cases: it seems to have been universally agreed, for example, that childless members of the *kahal,* and also members whose children were fully grown, should be taxed like everyone else for the support of the educational system. And the charity fund obviously worked on something other than the partnership model.

Third, most of the Rabbis favored taxation according to means: a fixed percentage rather than a fixed amount. They thought that uniformity and relative benefit were legitimate criteria only insofar as these two were mixed with or supplemented by a means test. The argument that *those who had more owed more* did not derive, like some of its modern versions, from a theory about the communal production of wealth (but see the selection from Moshe Alshekh in ¢20, which hints at such a theory: the harvest is the joint product of landowner and fieldworkers). It was drawn, instead, from a closely parallel religious doctrine, which also held that wealthy men and women were not the sole authors of their good fortune or, more specifically, of their large fortunes. Wealth was God's gift and was never given entirely into the hands of the wealthy to spend as they wished. The common view, which we discussed in Chapter 20, held that God always remained the ultimate owner. His gift did not allow the full and exclusive possession that we associate with capitalist ideology and law. As in medieval Christian thought, the rich were understood to be stewards rather than owners of (at least some portion of) their riches. And even after they were taxed according to a fixed percentage, they were expected to be generous with what remained.

A refusal to pay taxes or give charity was therefore something more than an offense against the *kahal.* The money belonged to God, who had assigned some of it to the poor. Nonpayment was a form of robbery from God or, more directly, as Rabbi Nathan argues in the text reprinted here, from the poor themselves. It was like withholding wages from a hired servant (see

Deut. 24:15): as the money was in principle already his, so in the case of taxation and *tzedakah*, the money was already theirs—an entitlement that, in this latter instance, did not have to be earned.

What was owed to the poor was a fixed percentage: beyond this the Rabbis don't seem to have ventured. There are occasional texts that hint at something more like progressive taxation, and we have included one such from the fourteenth-century *Sefer Hasidim*. But the subterfuge suggested there points to the limits of the traditional debates. Perhaps these limits reflect the power of the wealthy within the *kahal*. Perhaps they reflect some lingering uncertainty about the legitimate extent of communal coercion: a Davidic king or a Sanhedrin meeting in the Land of Israel might have undertaken a more far-reaching tax. But it also seems true that, for many of the Rabbis, despite the stewardship doctrine, the rich were held to deserve their riches.

There was no animus in medieval Judaism toward the pursuit of wealth. It isn't only because of their exclusion from land owning or their social marginality that Jewish merchants were protocapitalists. The sense that it is a good thing to make money, so long as some proportion of it is given away, must also have played a part in fostering their activity. It certainly figured in the tax debates. The Rabbis were even ready to set limits on how much could rightly be given away (or, a fortiori, taken by the community for its normal activities): as in the discussions of *tzedakah* in the last chapter, 20 percent is the usual maximum, with exceptions for both communal emergencies and individual cases of hunger or homelessness (and, standardly, for bequests to the *kahal*). Fortunes should not be dissipated through excessive piety. It is unclear whether this argument reflects a commitment to individual "property rights," as some contemporary libertarians have claimed, or a belief that the long-term interests of the *kahal* were best served by the presence and security of wealthy members. Riches, on the latter view, are the legitimate good fortune of the individual who possesses them—but also of his friends and neighbors. This seems the more likely Rabbinic opinion: if wealth had been understood as a right, the wealthy would presumably have been allowed to keep their money, or spend it or give it away as they pleased, without moral or legal constraints.

The level and reach of taxation will seem to us the most important issues in these discussions, but in the Talmud and among medieval rabbis, they may well have run second to the issue of exemptions. In all European countries, feudal law exempted the aristocracy from most of the king's taxes. Jewish law exempted scholars—the aristocrats of Israel-in-exile—from both royal and (significant aspects of) communal taxation. The exemptions have a threefold explanation: first, because scholars don't require the protection that the community provides—they are protected directly by God; second, because it was not the scholars but ordinary Israelites who were responsible for the exile and subjection of Israel—if they all joined in the study of Torah, the day of deliverance would be at hand; and third, because scholarship was taken to be a labor of love, without economic reward. For all these reasons, differently emphasized by different writers, the *kahal* commonly paid what would have been the scholars' share of the king's levies (Nahmanides tried to set limits to this practice: see the selection below and Menachem Meiri's response) and also freed them from the burdens of security—not only personal guard service but also any taxes connected with the building of walls and towers and the paying of guards. They were not freed from the laws of *tzedakah* and so not, presumably, from the taxes necessary for welfare and religious services, though little is said about this liability in our sources.

Perhaps scholars were meant to be the objects rather than the agents of charitable activity, much like the landless Levites in Deuteronomy. The socioeconomic character of their work was the subject of a long and intense debate among the scholars themselves, focused on the deepest questions of identity and status. On one view, championed by Maimonides, the ideal scholar would never seek to "benefit from the Torah" (but see too our discussion of scholarly elitism, ¢12, §13). He would earn his own living, on the side, through one or another trade—a scant living in most cases, because study would naturally take up most of his time. On another view, this very preoccupation ruled out economic activity entirely or almost entirely, and it then followed, given the importance of study, that the community should offer scholars a regular stipend, as Joseph Karo argues against Maimonides (§14 below). Whether or not stipends were provided as a general rule, most writers thought it both necessary and right to pay salaries to scholars serving as rabbis and judges, even if this allowed them to benefit from (their knowledge of) the Torah—and some would then have taxed these salaries like any other income.

This debate is more intensely focused on the question: Can scholars take money (stipends or salaries) from the community? than on the question of immediate interest here: Can the community take money (taxes) from scholars? As we have seen, this latter question was answered by arguing for the rightness of the exemptions on something like the partnership model: the scholars were not responsible for the plight of the exilic communities; they did not need the security the *kahal* struggled to provide; and they were in any case without significant resources. When the scholars were in fact prosperous, members of leading families, these last two arguments were likely to seem hypocritical and false, as David b. Solomon Ben Zimra (Radbaz) argues below (§15). But even if they held, weren't the scholars also members of the *kahal,* bound not to separate themselves, accountable for their fellows? So the exemptions were also defended by an argument, more often implied than explicitly stated, that set the "good" above the "right." Even wealthy scholars were exempt, Maimonides insisted: the value of their religious studies was apparently more important than the justice of their financial contribution. Of course, this value was fixed by the scholars themselves, but they were able to fix it so high only because of the respect they commanded among the people.

Ordinary Israelites were also supposed to devote some part of every day to Torah study. Perhaps the many who did not or could not do this thought of the scholars as surrogates for themselves. Providing for them or, at least, not taking from them was a vicarious fulfillment of their own duty. Had all Israel become a "nation of priests," the priestly tithe would presumably have been unnecessary. Had all Israel become a nation of scholars, the exemptions would have disappeared. In the messianic age, taxes will be abolished or, alternatively, the burden will fall equally on everyone (but will we still have to argue about what that means?).

Exemptions are an issue again in the modern state of Israel, though only with regard to bodily service. In the exilic communities, scholars were generally exempt from guard duty, and rabbis in Israel have claimed the same exemption from military conscription for themselves and their students.

They make the familiar arguments about the value of Torah study and the protection God provides for those engaged in it. We reprint here a strong response to these arguments that appeared during the 1948 Independence War.

The respect for scholars is a function of the general importance assigned to education in the Jewish tradition. Schools were doubly supported, through both *tzedakah* and taxation. We included in Chapter 20 a text describing a *hevra kadisha* for the support of Torah study in sixteenth-century Kraków, whose income was drawn from the dues and gifts of members but also from levies that resemble taxes. Clearly, education did not depend entirely on charitable giving—or, again, this kind of "giving" was also, as we have seen again and again, a kind of "taking." In any case, schools were a communal obligation: the establishment of an educational system was legally required according to the texts from Bava Batra and Maimonides (§§17–18 below). And among all the other communal obligations, education had a high priority, perhaps second only to the rescue of captives. Thus, it ranks first among the ordinances enacted by the Valladolid Synod in 1432: all Jewish communities in the kingdom of Castile "shall be obliged to establish and provide a Voluntary Fund" for the school system. Obliged to act voluntarily: here again is the familiar paradox of charity/taxation. The synod then went on to describe a set of levies that are not in any sense voluntary. Schools had to be supported, because study was the "work" described in the maxim of Mishnah Avot (2:21): "You are not obligated to complete the work; nor are you free to desist from it" (quoted by Maimonides in §13 below). Children had to be prepared for that work, and its support required both giving and taking.

Principles

Temple Tax: Equality
1. Exodus 30:11–16

The uniform payment of a half-shekel is portrayed here as a one-off "ransom," protecting each man from an unspecified mortal danger connected to the census ("enrollment"). At

*the beginning of the Second Commonwealth, its members voluntarily pledged a yearly
"third of a shekel" to provide for the temple service (Neh. 10:33, ¢1, §6). In Rabbinic law,
the annual nationwide collection of the half-shekel before Passover is the main form of
universal participation in the temple's service and upkeep (cf. Mishnah Shekalim 1:1–4,
2:3, 3:1–4:4).*

The Lord spoke to Moses, saying: When you take a census of the Israelite
people according to their enrollment, each shall pay the Lord a ransom for
himself on being enrolled, that no plague may come upon them through their
being enrolled. This is what everyone who is entered in the records shall pay:
a half-shekel by the sanctuary weight—twenty *gerahs* to the shekel—a half-
shekel as an offering to the Lord. Everyone who is entered in the records,
from the age of twenty years up, shall give the Lord's offering: the rich shall
not pay more and the poor shall not pay less than half a shekel when giving
the Lord's offering as expiation for your persons. You shall take the expiation
money from the Israelites and assign it to the service of the Tent of Meeting; it shall serve the Israelites as a reminder before the Lord, as expiation for
your persons.

Partnership: The Caravan in the Wilderness
2. BT Bava Kama 116b

*Travelers in the desert or on the high seas are not fellow citizens, and they share only the
obligations arising from their situation. The baraitot here deal with the just distribution
of burdens, based on the extent of each individual's exposure to risk or on his or her causal
responsibility for any shared danger.*

Our Rabbis taught: If a caravan was traveling in the desert and a band threatened to attack it, [the payment for buying them off] is calculated by value [of
merchandise] rather than by [number of] persons. But if they hire a guide to

lead them, [his fee] is calculated also[1] by [number of] persons. However, they should not deviate from the custom of ass-drivers. . . .

Our Rabbis taught: If a ship was sailing on the sea and a storm threatened to sink it, and they jettisoned [some of] its cargo, [the losses] are calculated by weight rather than by value.[2] However, they should not deviate from the custom of mariners.

Security, Taxation, and Exemptions
3. Mishnah Bava Batra 1:5; BT Bava Batra 7b–8a

The tannaitic context of this mishnah and its ramifications for the townspeople's political authority were elaborated above (¢8, §2); for its implications with regard to tzedakah *collection, see the talmudic discussion cited in the previous chapter (¢20, §25). Our interest here is the restriction of the public's authority to tax individuals to the provision of public works related to security. The talmudic discussion focuses on taxation and explores principles for distributing the burden, closely echoing those cited in the context of the convoy (§2). The grounding of obligation in the receipt of benefits provides a justification for certain exemptions, notably of "scholars"—strikingly equated here with "the righteous." (We have discussed the status of scholars in ¢12 above.) As is not uncommon in the Talmud, an aggadic sequel seems to suggest a critique of the "official" position.*

Mishnah Bava Batra 1:5

They compel him [to share] in [the cost of] building an antechamber and door for the courtyard. Rabban Shimon b. Gamaliel says: Not every courtyard requires an antechamber. They compel him [to share] in [the cost of] building a wall and gates for the town and [providing] a bolt for the gates.

---

1. "Also" is missing in JT Bava Metzia 11a.
2. For the sake of a just distribution, no matter whose cargo was jettisoned in the joint emergency.

Rabban Shimon b. Gamaliel says: Not every town requires a wall. How long shall one reside in a town to be considered a townsman? Twelve months. If, however, one acquires a residence there, one is considered a townsman immediately.

BT Bava Batra 7b–8a

"They compel him [to share] in [the cost of] building a wall and gates for the town and [buying] a bolt for the gates." It was taught: Rabban Shimon b. Gamaliel says, "Not every town requires a wall; a town that is near the frontier requires a wall, but a town that is not near the frontier does not require a wall." And [why do] the [other] sages [require a wall for every town]?—Occasionally, a roving band might invade.

Rabbi Elazar inquired of Rabbi Yohanan: Is the payment [for the wall] collected in accordance with [number of] persons or value [of possessions]? He replied: It is collected by value; and Elazar, my son, establish this ruling firmly!

According to another version, Rabbi Elazar inquired: Is the payment collected by proximity [of each house to the wall] or by value? He replied: It is collected by proximity; and Elazar, my son, establish this ruling firmly!

Rabbi Yehudah Nesi'a collected [payment] for a wall from the scholars [*rabbanan*]. Said Resh Lakish: Scholars do not require protection, as written, "I count them—they exceed the grains of sand"[3] (Ps. 139:18)—"Count" whom? If one says [it is] the righteous, well, regarding the whole of Israel it is written [that they shall be] "as numerous as . . . the sands on the seashore" (Gen. 22:17), so how can the righteous exceed the sand?—Rather, it means to say: "I shall count the deeds of the righteous, and they shall exceed the sand." Now [one may argue] a fortiori: If the grains of sand, [despite] being fewer, protect [the land] against the sea, certainly the deeds of the righteous, being more numerous, protect them! . . .

3. A prevalent midrashic interpretation reads the previous verse, "they were all recorded in Your book," as referring to a book God showed Adam, listing the leaders—or, according to some sources, the righteous—of all future generations (see, e.g., Genesis Rabbah 24:2–3).

Rav Nahman b. Rav Hisda collected a poll tax from the scholars. Rav Nahman b. Yitzhak said to him: You have transgressed against the Torah, the Prophets, and the Writings. Against the Torah, as written: "Lover, indeed, of the peoples, their hallowed are all in Your hand" (Deut. 33:3)—Moses said before the Holy One: Master of the world, even when You love the [other] peoples [allowing Israel's subjugation], let all [Israel's] hallowed ones be [protected] in Your hand. [The verse proceeds,] "They followed in Your steps, taking on Your teachings," [and] Rav Yosef taught: These are the scholars [talmide hakhamim] whose steps carry them from one town to another and from one land to another, to give and take in God's teachings.—Against the Prophets, as written, ". . . if they yetanu[4] among the nations, I will promptly gather them up, and . . . partly diminish from the burden of king and princes" (Hos. 8:10), [on which] Ulla commented, This verse is written [partly] in Aramaic: "If all [Israel] study [tanu] among the nations, I will promptly gather them up [out of their exile]; whereas if [only] some part [engage in Torah study], they shall be free from the burden of king and princes."—Against the Writings, as written, "It is not permissible to impose tribute, poll tax, or land tax [arnona] upon [any priest, Levite, . . . or any servant of this House of God]" (Ezra 7:24). . . .

Rav Papa imposed [payment for the] digging [of a well] upon orphans[5] [too]. Rav Shesha b. Rav Idi queried Rav Papa: Perhaps no water will be found? He replied: I collect from them; [then,] if water is found, I will spend [the money], and if not, I will refund it.

Rav Yehudah said: Everyone [must share in the cost] of doors for the town gates, even orphans; but not scholars, since scholars do not require protection. Everyone [must share in the cost] of excavating [for] the square—even the scholars. If, however, they all march out [to work], it is not appropriate for scholars to march out.

During years of drought, Rabbi [Judah the Prince] opened [his] storehouses, proclaiming: "Let those enter who have studied Scripture, or Mishnah, or Talmud; but the ignorant [amme ha-aretz] may not enter!"

---

4. Meaning of the Hebrew is obscure; JPS: "are courting."
5. I.e., from an estate held under guardianship for minors.

Rabbi Yonatan b. Amram pushed his way in and said, Master, provide for me. [Rabbi] asked him: Have you studied Scripture?

He replied, No.

—Have you studied Mishnah?

He replied, No.

—So by [virtue of] what shall I provide for you?

He answered, Provide for me like a dog or a raven.

So he gave him provisions.

When he had exited, Rabbi sat and complained: Woe to me, for I have given of my bread to an *am ha-aretz!* Rabbi Shimon, Rabbi's son, said before him: Perhaps it was Yonatan b. Amram, who refuses to benefit from the Torah's honor? Inquiries were made and this was confirmed; whereupon Rabbi proclaimed: Let everyone enter.

Rabbi's [original action] was in accordance with his position that "Calamity occurs solely on account of *amme ha-aretz.*" Once, a levy for the crown was imposed upon the inhabitants of Tiberias. They came before Rabbi and said to him, "Let the scholars contribute along with us."

He replied: "No."

—"Then we will flee!"

—"So flee."

Half of them fled; half [of the levy] was lifted. The other half [then] came before Rabbi and said to him, "Let the scholars contribute along with us." He replied, "No."

—"Then we will flee!"

—"So flee."

They all fled. One fuller remained; [the levy] was then imposed upon the fuller. The fuller [then] fled, and the levy for the crown was retracted. Thereupon Rabbi said: "As you have seen, calamity occurs solely on account of *amme ha-aretz.*" . . .

Rav Assi further said in the name of Rabbi Yohanan: Everyone [must share in the cost] of the town walls, even orphans; but not scholars, since scholars do not require protection. Rav Papa said: For the repair of the walls, for the horse guard, and for the keeper of the armory, even orphans [must share the cost]. The general principle is: Any [expenditure] that involves protection is imposed even [upon] orphans. Rabbah imposed *tzedakah* upon orphans of the estate of Bar Merion. Abaye said to him: Has not Rav Shmu'el b. Yehudah taught that assessment for *tzedakah* is not to be imposed upon orphans, even for the redemption of captives?—He replied: My purpose is to enhance their prestige.

The Injustice of Tax Avoidance

4. Rabbi Nathan, Responsum

Irving A. Agus, *Urban Civilization in Pre-Crusade Europe: A Study of Organized Town-Life in Northwestern Europe during the Tenth and Eleventh Centuries Based on the Responsa Literature*, vol. 2 (New York: Yeshiva University Press, 1965), p. 431.[6]

This responsum of an unidentified scholar whose name was Rabbi Nathan vividly portrays the internal politics of the kahal *in eleventh-century France. Some of its members enjoy a direct connection with the gentile rulers and seek to avoid the taxes imposed upon the community. Working out the criteria for a just distribution of the tax burden leads to a clarification of what goods are taxable and to a ruling that tax avoidance is robbery.*

Question: If indeed it is as written: there are some who own no vineyards, but who buy grapes from the gentiles and fill storerooms and vats with such fruit. These men are subject to your tax. There are others who hail from [elsewhere], who never before participated with you in the payment of your taxes, but who now [reside among you] permanently. They married local women and thus acquired [real] property through their wives, or through defunct mortgages. Both the former and the latter residents, however, refuse to [partake in the payment of the present special tax; but rely on the protection of the overlord.]

   Answer: This is my opinion: The law requires that you appoint three persons who are specialists in taxation [matters], and that they fix [the tax] on each [resident of your town] according to his wealth. Whoever possesses land, the value of that land shall be taken into account. Whoever possesses no

6. Slightly amended.

vineyards and no land, but has guldens with which he trades or buys grapes from the gentiles, that money shall be taken into account and shall be subject to the tax. They, however, must follow the custom of your place, [i.e.,] the custom of your forefathers heretofore, to levy [a certain amount] on a person who owned one-hundred-gulden-worth of real property, and a [different] amount on a person who owned one-hundred-gulden-worth of merchandise. They cannot change the custom of the early settlers [of your town]; for the sages have ruled that a custom has [legal] status.

Should the dealers in merchandise claim that the owners of houses or of land have hidden money, [or] that they trade with merchandise [the value of] which is unknown, in contrast to themselves who deal in merchandise [the value of] which is well known—the law requires that a *herem* be pronounced against anyone who has any hidden assets, such as coins, merchandise, silver, gold, or vessels, [and does not declare them] so that they become publicly known to the above-mentioned three appointees, called "sergents Messiliers." The appointees will then levy the tax in proportion to the amount each person admits [to own].

Should the above-mentioned residents fail to act in this manner [and should they persist in] relying on the rulers—as they do according to your letter—they would absolutely be guilty of felonious possession. To them applies the Scriptural verse: "The spoil of the poor is in your houses (Is. 3:14)." They are to be compared to those who withhold a hired man's wages or who defer payment of such wages; for such practices are absolute robberies. Thus it is stated [in the Talmud, BT Sukkah 29b]: "People eventually lose their possessions for committing the following four wrongs: for withholding a hired man's wages, for deferring payment of such wages, for removing the yoke [of taxation] from their own necks and placing it on the necks of their neighbors, and for rude haughtiness, which is the worst of all." Nothing, however, is more serious than robbery. Thus our sages said: "The verdict of the generation of the flood was not sealed until they committed robbery (BT Sanhedrin 108a)." They also stated: "He who robs a pennyworth from his fellow is as guilty as if he took his life, for Scripture states: 'He taketh away the soul of the owners thereof'" (BT Bava Kama 119a). Note, therefore, how severe is the punishment for this crime.

Criteria of Just Taxation

Property and Profits

5. Joseph b. Samuel Bonfils, Responsum

Irving A. Agus, *Urban Civilization in Pre-Crusade Europe: A Study of Organized Town-Life in Northwestern Europe during the Tenth and Eleventh Centuries Based on the Responsa Literature,* vol. 2 (New York: Yeshiva University Press, 1965), p. 438.[7]

This eleventh-century French responsum is characterized by Bonfils's meager use of tal-mudic precedent, coupled with his insistence that taxation be subject to criteria of fairness: this, he claims, constitutes "the Jewish way" entailed by the biblical maxim of loving one's neighbor and Hillel's version of the golden rule: "Whatever is hateful to you, you should not do to your fellow" (BT Shabbat 31a).

Question: In order to collect the king's tax, the townspeople levied on every man and woman, while under a decree of *herem*, a fixed amount per pound of value of his or her money, merchandise, and other saleable possessions, in ac-cordance with their estimation [of the value of such possessions] and depend-ing on the exigencies of the moment. Leah possessed [several] vineyards. She was requested by the townspeople to pay the fixed amount upon every pound of value of her vineyards, [and in addition, of] her harvested grapes, and her other possessions—as they similarly requested from one another, since the vineyard was worth money independently of the grapes. . . . They claimed the vineyards were in the same category as the capital of a loan, while the harvested crop was equivalent to the interest. One derived no benefit from the vineyard itself, nor from the capital of the loan, during the first half year or year of its investment. Since they paid taxes from both the capital and the interest of their money investments, from their merchandise as well as from its profit, they held that Leah should do likewise. Leah, on her part, argued that a vineyard could not be compared to the capital of a loan, nor even to merchandise; for a vineyard required a heavy yearly investment in money and effort as well as a great deal of expensive labor in upkeep and in harvesting its crop. In a vineyard a person invested a great deal of labor and money, but was rarely sure of his profit. Moreover the lords of the land came every year and

7. Slightly amended.

carried away their fat portions. Sometimes the crop was completely burnt and the cultivator received no return whatever for all his invested money and labor. Money lent at interest, on the other hand, or invested in merchandise, constituted a much safer and more convenient [enterprise]. The creditor held on to his pledges, while his capital constantly increased with the passing of time. He reaped his profit without investing labor and expense and without [the danger attending] display [of wealth]. Whenever he needed his money, he could make use of it. Thus they argued back and forth.

Answer: In view of the written statement of the facts, it seems to me that Leah's claims are valid. For her occupation is not as convenient as merchandizing, nor is its profit as easily available or as little troublesome as money lent at interest. These are self-evident facts. Moreover the usurers make a mockery of Moses and of his Law. They say: "Had Moses known that there was profit in usury, he would not have forbidden it." All merchandizing is convenient and profitable; for the merchant always holds securely in hand either his money or the merchandise he bought for that money. He even dispenses with an agent, since his money speaks for itself and attracts his customers. A cultivator of the soil, on the other hand, is not so fortunate; for he must depend on an *aris* [a sharecropper] who receives half of the fruit; and his crop is exposed to many dangers. Sometimes the weather is too hot, sometimes too cold. Sometimes there is too much rain, at other times too little; and sometimes the plants are struck by hail or consumed by several kinds of locust. He cannot hide his trees nor protect them as effectively as he can other kinds of merchandise. . . . How, then, can one compare a toilsome and wearying occupation that produces little profit, with a comfortable, secure, and highly profitable type of business? If we uphold the view of the towns-people and allow them to take away the painfully acquired small profit and to tax even the land itself—they would thus consume the capital as well as the income and the owner of the land would be left with nothing. Heaven forfend! Such [an injustice] shall not be practiced in Israel! For this is a practice typical of Esau: . . . He ['Esau,' that is, the gentile overlord] imposes the *arnona* [land tax] on Israel; before Israel succeeds in paying it, he is confronted with the poll-tax; and before that is paid, the burghers come with their oppressive demands. That is not the way of Israel. Rather they carefully consider their actions and equitably allocate all costs on themselves in accordance with the individual's ability to pay. One should not seek clever arguments and press shrewd claims that would result in divesting a person of his capital; one should act in accordance with the principle: "Love thy neighbor as thyself."

The following is the manner of Israel, as well as the accepted custom of the communities: Prudent men are selected [as tax-assessors]; . . . men who carefully examine each case, and, in strict honesty and justice, levy the tax on each individual in accordance with his labor and his expenses. They consider the interests of their brothers as if they were their own interests — in accordance with the principle: "Whatever is hateful to you, you should not do to your fellow" (BT Shabbat 31a). [It is unjust] to levy the same tax on a pound-worth of merchandise as on a pound-worth of land, since the income from the latter is so much smaller than from the former. The following is the usual practice of the wise men of the communities: they estimate how light the tax on land must be, and [often] completely free it from taxation. For were they to tax both the land and its produce, its owner would lose his livelihood. . . . For the Torah never taxes Israel's land, only the produce. The claim of the townspeople that even immediately after the harvest the vineyard still has a certain market value [that is] independent of its crop and should, therefore, be taxable — this is not valid. For that value stems from the vineyard's potential to produce a crop. There would otherwise be no end to it. The vineyard is to be compared to the tools and equipment acquired by a person to produce his income. Are these tools and equipment taxable? Such is not the case! People . . . roam around in search of income; and when they earn their living, they pay their share of the taxes according to [the success of] their business. But that individuals should be singled out for oppression and attack: I have never heard [of such behavior on the part of townspeople]!

6. Joseph ibn Migash, *Novellae on Bava Batra* 7b

This is ibn Migash's commentary on the talmudic discussion above (§3). Although commenting on the talmudic cases, the issues he addresses are central also to medieval disputes. Should tax assessments depend on benefits received or on wealth and possessions? Ibn Migash's interpretation places the greater emphasis on wealth.

"Rabbi Elazar inquired of Rabbi Yohanan: Is the payment [for building] a [town] wall with double doors and a bolt or for a gatehouse and courtyard door collected in accordance with [the number of] persons or the value [of the property]?" The latter suggestion—assessment based on property value— is explained by the fact that the purpose of the collection is to protect property, not lives.

There are those who say that what Rabbi Elazar inquired of Rabbi Yohanan was whether the assessment is made according to property value *alone* or whether, perhaps, they also base the assessment on the proximity of the houses [to the town wall].

According to both versions [of the question], the assessment is based on the value of possessions. What the latter version adds is that the calculation of value should be adjusted according to proximity. This must be so, for if there are two houses near [the wall] that are not equal in possessions, the assessment will certainly be made on the basis of the value of possessions. Alternatively, if there is a house close [to the wall] that contains no possessions whatsoever, it would never occur to anyone to collect anything therefrom; since it has no possessions, what is there for its owner to fear? . . . This teaches that the value of possessions is the critical issue.

And what is this factor, "according to the proximity of the houses" which was mentioned? It means "also according to proximity." Thus, initially we examine who has more possessions and who has less. Afterwards we examine whose house [from among the wealthy] is close to the source of [potential] harm, and whose is distant, and the assessment is made accordingly. This is the *halakhah*.

Rabbenu Hananel ruled in the matter of courtyards that the assessment is based on the value of possessions; he considered proximity to be irrelevant. His view makes sense, because a rule to attend to proximity would only apply in a town, where there are courtyards that are closer to and farther from [the outer wall]; but within a courtyard . . . even if one house is closer [to the wall] than another, this distinction is an insignificant matter that makes no difference whatever. And this stands to reason.

All the above applies only in time of peace, when there is fear of [i.e., respect for] the governmental authorities, and the only threat is from highwaymen coming to rob or from random incidents. However, during time of war, when rulers are in conflict with one another, it makes sense that the question of proximity of houses is of no concern whatsoever, since to a legion conquering a city near and far are all the same; accordingly, the assessment is made solely on the basis of the value of possessions. If an assessment concerns matters of human life, [the number of] people should also be taken into account since both possessions and lives are at stake.

Calculation of Taxes

7. Meir of b. Baruch Rothenburg (Maharam), *Responsa* (Cremona) 228

Rothenburg here proposes a mode of calculation that takes into account both life and possessions as combined factors each of equal weight. The number-of-lives component has the uniformity of a poll tax. The value-of-possessions component functions as a progressive corrective.

Maharam explicated [Rabbi Yohanan's reply (BT Bava Batra 7b) that payment for the wall is collected by value of possessions to mean] *also* by value of possessions. For example, [imagine a case] where Reuven and Shimon are obliged to pay £1 . . . which is collected according to [both the number of] persons and the value of possessions. Now, if we were to collect according to persons each would give half [i.e., 10 d.]. Now let us make the other calculation, according to value of possessions. If one has £1 and the other £19 the former would pay 12 pennies [= 1 d.] and the latter 19 d. Now combine the two sums: The former would thus pay 11 d. (10 d. originally and now [an additional] 12 pennies [i.e., 1 d.]). The latter would pay 29 d. (10 d. originally [+ 19 d.]). But all we need from them together is £1 and now we have two calculations that, combined, make £2. Let us therefore halve each of the contributions. The outcome is [thus]: The one who has £1 shall give 5.5 d. and the one who has £19 shall give 14.5 d. . . . . This constitutes "also by value of possessions," i.e., according to [both the number of] persons and the value of possessions.

Beyond Proportionality

8. *Sefer Hasidim* 1046[8]

Sefer Hasidim is a major work of religious ethics compiled in twelfth-century Germany, traditionally attributed to Rabbi Judah the Hasid. Here the author argues against a blanket exemption of the poor from taxes, fearing that people of means would feign poverty to avoid taxation. Everyone is subject to scrutiny and assessment, and it appears that everyone pays the same percentage of his or her assessed value; but then the poor are secretly reimbursed.

The Torah established a fixed measure because of the human capacity [to make excuses and exploit loopholes]. It told the rich and the poor to give tithes, *terumot,* and [other] priestly gifts. If there is a poor Israelite and a rich priest, how can it be that the poor shall give to the rich? Nevertheless, the Torah commanded everyone, poor and rich, so that the rich might not say: "I am poor, and how can I give to a rich priest?" And even to a poor priest, he will say: "You are rich!" Therefore Scripture makes no distinctions.

　　Similarly, when the *kahal* has to provide for *tzedakah*—even though

---

8. The section number follows *Sefer Hasidim,* ed. Re'uven Margaliot (Jerusalem: Mosad ha-Rav Kuk, 1957).

among the townspeople there are poor who barely get by—they proclaim a *herem* [requiring everyone] to give [uniformly], so much from every pound. Truly, it is not right that a poor person give for the sake of other poor people, and sometimes the person who gives is poorer than the recipient—yet they have to impose the *herem* on everyone because of the bad ones. For if this poor person is not included in the *herem,* many others will also not be included; as a result, many poor people will lose, and the whole business of the *kahal* will be nullified. Therefore it is better that they [i.e., the poorer towns-people] too should give and should join the *herem.* If, however, the bad ones were to obey the good ones, they would not put pressure on the poor.

And they [i.e., the officers of the *kahal*] should secretly return to the poor all they have given, without the knowledge of the bad ones. And do not say: "Is the collection not for the poor?"—implying that they should be given no more than any of those for whom the collection was made. [Instead, the poor who were unjustly compelled to contribute should be fully reimbursed].

Guard Duty

9. Meir b. Baruch of Rothenburg (Maharam), *Mordechai* Bava Batra 475

Time and effort are taxed as well as money, and the appropriate criteria for personal service are not the same as for wealth. Here is one of the earliest (thirteenth-century) discussions of the difference between the two. The rule of strict equality in personal service still figures in our contemporary debates, as it does here, but Rothenburg (as in his previous responsum, §7) argues for a more progressive distribution of financial burdens.

Re: the town guard. At first, all [all members of the *kahal*] participated in person in the night guard. The *kahal* later reached an agreement [with the town to make instead] a fixed annual payment. [How should the burden be divided?]

Rabbi Meir replied that given [the fact that] the guard [duty] had been reorganized in accordance with Torah law—for BT Bava Batra chapter 1 (7b) states that calculation follows the value of possessions—the present [arrangement] is to be followed, even though they had originally [divided] guard duty equally, rich and poor [serving] alike. And though originally, when the gentiles were in charge of the guard, they deviated from the Jewish practice [dat yehudit] of making rich and poor equal, now that they have transferred [the responsibility] to us we ought not to deviate from the practice of the Torah [mi-dat torah]. For any matter that depends upon possessions is calculated in accordance to possessions. When they served in person, it was clearly reasonable that guard duty be [divided] equally, for it is each body that serves, and the poor man's body can guard just like the rich man's body. Indeed—even better! But now that the contribution is a fixed sum, one cannot claim that since the sum is in place of the original guard duty, [then] "the rich shall not pay more and the poor shall not pay less" (Exod. 30:15).

[Rothenburg cites the talmudic discussion (§3) to the effect that "everyone [must share in the cost] of excavating [for] the square—even the scholars. If, however, they all march out [to work], it is not appropriate for scholars to march out." And he continues:] The scholars cannot claim that since, if the townsmen had marched out to work, we would have been exempted, so too now [that only a levy has been imposed] we should not give anything. . . . This matter is clear.

Rich Versus Poor

10. Solomon b. Abraham Adret (Rashba), *Responsa* 3:380–82

These three responsa address disputes about taxation in late thirteenth- or early fourteenth-century Spain. The first deals with a community where the wealthier members defend old-fashioned tzedakah, *which in practice if not in principle maximizes their discretion, whereas (what we would call) the middle class defends taxation and communal provision. Adret supports the second group: the communal response to hunger must be through taxation, with the wealthy giving more. In the last paragraph, however, he admits that*

door-to-door begging is not likely to be eliminated, perhaps expressing a tacit concession
to the very rich. But the second responsum is a further indication of his commitment to
the principle: from each according to his wealth. In the third responsum, Adret applies in
practice Joseph ibn Migash's interpretation of Bava Batra (§6 above) spelling out its im-
plication in detail.

380. You asked [the following question]: the poor of the town are numerous, and the [burden of] the kingdom is costly. As a result, a dispute has arisen among the wealthy. The very wealthy say "Let [the poor] go from door to door [collecting charity], and we will all give them bread every day in order to sustain them, since the law also demands of the moderately wealthy that they give bread to all the poor daily, just like us." And the moderately wealthy argue that this is not what the law dictates; [it demands], rather, that [the poor] should remain in their homes and should not go from door to door, "for they are our brothers, our flesh. Let [the responsibility for] their support be borne by the public. We shall all pay according to our wealth, with the court enforcing the assessment, as in the case of Rava."[9] Inform me, with whom does the law agree?

Answer: Justice demands that we follow the view of the moderately wealthy, for [obligations of] charity and sustenance for the poor are in proportion to [one's] wealth. It is like the case where Rava coerced Rav Ami and extracted 400 *zuz* in charity from him; so the [weight of the] burden is according to [the strength of] the camel, and the key to preserving one's money lies in [the performance of acts of] *hesed*.[10] It has already been said regarding Nakdimon Ben-Gurion that even though he gave much charity, because he did not do so appropriately, he lost all his wealth [cf. BT Ketubot 66b–67a].

Each and every poor person is to be given sustenance according to what he [needs]. It has already been stated that even one who does not want to be supported, if he does not have [enough to sustain himself], he should be given [money] cunningly, in the guise of a loan, and then [the debt should be] revoked, rendering it a gift; or [the money] should be offered to him as a

9. Cited below in the reply.
10. Lit., compassion is the pickling salt for money.

gift at the outset, and then given as a loan if he will not accept [the gift] [cf. BT Ketubot 67b, ¢20, §25].

Each and every person should be given [sustenance] according to his status, such that if he is from a wealthy family, we add [more for] him . . . as stated [BT Ketubot 67b, ¢20, §25]. A fortiori, he should not go from door to door [begging]. Whether he has [already] imposed himself upon the [*tzeda-kah*] officer (like the poor person from a wealthy family for whom the people of the Upper Galilee would collect a pound of meat every day, in spite of the fact that it was a small village [BT Ketubot 67b, ¢20, §25]), or whether, before imposing himself upon the officer, he is supported by an individual (as in the case of Rava, who sustained [such a poor person] with a fattened chicken and old wine in order to fill his need),[11] it has certainly been written: "and You give them their food when it is due" [Ps. 145:15], teaching that the Holy One gives to each and every person according to his need for sustenance. It is as stated there.

However, this generation has become impoverished, and there is no wealth, whether in the pocket or in understanding, and in any event, everywhere [the practice is to] support [the poor] from the communal fund and according to monetary [need]. And if, beyond that, they [the poor] go from door to door [seeking charity], let them do so, and let each person give according to his understanding and inclination.

381. You have also asked whether the cantor's[12] salary ought to be paid from the communal fund, for although he fulfills his duty for the poor and the rich alike, the poor cannot afford as much as the rich. In all matters of the public good requiring funds, contribution must be made according to financial means. In most places, there are designated sources for paying cantors. In some places [their salary] is supplemented from the communal fund. And if you disagree and say that rich and poor should contribute equally because they benefit equally, should we then say that the illiterate should make all the payments, since the cantor [recites the prayer for] the illiterate, thus fulfilling their duty to pray, while he fulfills no such duty for the literate?

---

11. BT Ketubot 67b, see ¢20, §25.
12. Lit., "emissary of the community"; the leader in public prayer.

382. You also asked whether [the cost of] guarding the town at night ought to be [assessed] according to property value or divided nightly according to [the number of] people. The wealthy say to the poor, "You must protect your wives and your children as we do." And the poor contend that when an army comes to town, they seize the wealthy in order to extract money from them. Accordingly, the wealthy ought to supply protection for ten nights and the poor for one night. The wealthy argue [in response] that the army also kills human beings, both rich and poor alike. With whom is the right?

Answer: It all depends on what is at stake. How so? If what you fear is an enemy coming to rob and plunder, collection is to be made according to property and according to proximity of the houses [to the outer wall]. How so? Because of his proximity, the wealthy person who is closer [to the wall] pays more than the equally wealthy person who is farther away. In any event, the wealthy person who is distant [should] always pay more than the poor person who is near, for what is there to collect from the poor person? Moreover, the poor person does not greatly fear the plunderers because, in comparison to a wealthy person, he does not have as many possessions.

The "property" according to which we said [the assessment is measured] is specifically movable property, not immovable property, because the plunderers will only take movable property. However, if they come to conquer the town during a time of warring kings, the assessment should also be made on the basis of real property since all [property] is in jeopardy. In any event, [the assessment is] always proportionate to property value, and the wealthy person [pays] more than one who is not as wealthy, even though the latter's house is closer [to the wall]. It goes without saying that the wealthy pays more than the poor since, while they are both in a state of risk, the wealthy person is more at risk because of his wealth.

[Adret ends by citing BT Bava Batra 8a, §3 above; and Joseph ibn Migash, §6 above.]

Commentary. Distributing the Burdens of Taxation

The arguments here are entirely familiar. Not only the poor, but the rich as well, are "always with us," and they appear here, as in every time and place, to have nerve endings in their pocketbooks. As reported in these medieval texts, the rich argue in favor of a system of taxation that is uniform for rich and poor: everyone pays the same (small) amount, as with the biblical half-shekel. Or they favor unregulated *tzedakah:* let the poor come begging, and we will give them what we like.

But, contrary to Karl Marx's maxim that the ruling ideas of the age are the ideas of the ruling class, the Rabbis' rulings don't endorse the claims of the rich. Of course, they have their own interests, which some (but not all) of them defend with vigor—as we see in the texts that deal with tax exemptions. But in the texts before us here, the Rabbis act in the name of an objective justice. They argue, and they rule, that the needs of the community and the demands of the gentile overlords should be met by the members of the *kahal* in accordance with their resources. With regard to the internal life of the community, they come very close to the maxim "From each according to his ability, to each according to his needs," though with some small qualifications having to do with relative risk (proximity to the wall). So elements of the partnership model are incorporated into the brotherhood model, which is clearly dominant.

It isn't only helping the poor that is at issue here. Solomon b. Abraham Adret asserts a more general principle: "In all matters of public good requiring funds, contribution must be made according to financial means." A given public good may benefit everybody equally, but that isn't a reason for uniform contributions. The wealthy pay more simply because they have more—Adret seems to consider this an obvious requirement. Meir b. Baruch of Rothenburg's argument about guard duty makes the same point. When bodily service is required, every (adult male) member of the *kahal* serves for the same time in the same way: each man has only one body. When guards are hired, the cost is distributed differently because the members don't have, so to speak, the same purse. Difference in wealth makes a difference, and again the point seems obvious. Rothenburg rejects the argument of the wealthy that equality in guard duty requires that the cost of hiring guards also be shared equally. This is a claim, he says simply, that "cannot" be made.

The Rabbis were not protosocialists; they had no theory of class struggle, of exploitation, or of surplus labor. With regard to *tzedakah,* there were theological arguments for a kind of redistributive justice, but we should note that God was equally responsible for the wealth of the wealthy and for the entitlements of the poor. Both of these were thus accorded divine legitimacy. With regard to taxation, Rabbinic arguments seem to have more to do with fairness among brethren than with obedience to God's commandments. But I think that it isn't only fairness but also necessity that drives their arguments. Without a heavier tax on the wealthy members of the *kahal,* the resources of the community would be woefully inadequate to meet communal needs. And the Rabbis clearly believed (whatever they thought about their own possible contributions) that there were centrally important communal needs. The *kahal* was not an association of individuals each of whom was concerned only with personal good; the partnership model provided a partial account of the religious/moral reality of the Jewish community—but no more than that. There were "public goods" that had to be provided (like a cemetery and a synagogue), and there were also brotherly responsibilities, requirements of mutual aid that had to be met.

With regard to these two, I would suggest that nothing has changed, not even in our modern secular communities. Fairness and necessity still require taxation "according to financial means."

Michael Walzer

Exemptions

Rabbis and Scholars: The Scope of the Exemption

11. Menachem Meiri, *Bet ha-Behirah* Bava Batra 8b

Rabbis and scholars claimed to be exempt from many taxes (§3 above), and the legitimate scope of this claim was the subject of frequent disputes in the medieval period. For Meiri the political authority of the local rabbi derived solely from his appointment by the townspeople. Here he argues, against many other decisors, that taxes levied on individuals as

individuals (the poll tax) or taxes on personal property must be paid by rabbis and schol-
ars along with everyone else.

It seems to me that this exemption for scholars applies only in the case of "the king's portion," . . . a known and established tax imposed on the public at large [*karga*]. This is the law regarding all types of levies and conscriptions that are imposed on the community: the public must pay the scholars' shares. However, regarding a poll tax, which is specifically affixed upon each and every individual, and *arnona,* which is the tithing of one's crops and cattle, the words do not seem to dictate that others are required to pay what [the scholar] owes as an individual. Even though it says, "Do not impose [tribute, poll tax, or land tax on any priest, Levite, . . . etc.]" (Ezra 7:24), with respect to all [these taxes, King] Darius was the one who ordered that their obligation be waived. Only "the king's portion" is mentioned here, and this is the law with respect to any [obligation] imposed on the [community as a] whole.

This seems clear to me; yet [Maimonides] has written in one of his works [*Commentary on the Mishnah* Avot 4:7, §12 below] that the public is required to pay for [scholars] even with respect to these [individual taxes]. And he averred, in the name of his master [i.e., Joseph ibn Migash], that this was put into practice. But the matter appears to be as we have written. In any event, even with respect to the [exemption from individual taxes], the great decisors [i.e., Isaac Alfasi] have written that [it applies] only to a scholar who is not occupied at all with needs of the world and for whom the [study of] Torah is his entire occupation. But the other scholars, who participate in worldly matters alongside their studies, do not fall within this rule.

Not to Benefit from Torah
12. Maimonides, *Commentary on the Mishnah* Avot 4:7

The question whether scholars may derive economic benefits from their study of Torah is different from the question whether their wealth, however derived, can be taxed. Still the two issues are usefully discussed together, as they are in this selection. Maimonides strictly prohibits scholars from seeking benefits from Torah study. Despite his perfectionist and hierarchical attitude regarding the status of the learned vis-à-vis the am ha-aretz *(¢12, §13), he does not claim that the latter owe sustenance or support to the former. Note, however, that he supports a strong version of the exemptions.*

Mishnah: Rabbi Zadok says: Do not fashion [the Torah] into a crown with which to aggrandize yourself, nor into a spade with which to dig. Thus Hillel used to say, "And he who makes use of the crown will perish." Hence you may deduce [that] whoever derives benefit from matters of Torah removes his life from the world [i.e., will perish].

     Maimonides: I had thought that I would not discuss this instruction because it is clear, and also because I know that my statements concerning it will displease most, if not all, of the great sages of the Torah law. Nevertheless, I will speak, and I will not pay attention to or worry about the ancients or my contemporaries.

     Know that his statement, "Do not fashion the Torah into a spade with which to dig," means do not consider it an implement for earning a livelihood. [The Mishnah] explains that anyone who benefits in this world from the Torah's honor cuts his soul off from the life of the world to come. People have blinded themselves to [the meaning of] this clear language, and they have cast it away. They fixated upon external meanings [of Scripture and of Rabbinic statements], which they did not understand and which I will explain. And they established rights for themselves, which devolved upon individuals and upon communities. They converted [halakhic] law into the rules of [extortionist] tax collectors; and they exploited people by means of this complete deception . . . that it is obligatory to support scholars and students and people who are engaged in the law and for whom the Torah is their art.

     All this is in error, with no foundation in the law and no legs to support it whatsoever. For when we examine the legacy of the sages, may their memories be blessed, we do not find that they collected money from people, nor did they gather contributions for esteemed and honored academies, nor for exilarchs, nor for judges, nor for disseminators of the Torah, nor for any of the appointees, nor for any other person. Instead, we find that there were among them some who were completely destitute, as well as some who were extremely wealthy. God forefend that I should say of [the community] that they were not generous and charitable. For indeed, had the poor [scholar] stretched out his hand to receive, they would have filled his abode with gold and pearls. Yet he did not do so. Instead, he occupied himself with a craft from which he could support himself, whether in abundance or in scarcity, and he spurned people's handouts because the law precluded him from [accepting them].

You already know that Hillel the Elder was a woodcutter by profession. He chopped wood, and he studied under Shemayah and Avtalyon, and he was utterly poor. His achievement was famous and, indeed, his students were compared to Moses and Joshua, the least among them being Rabban Yohanan b. Zakai. No intelligent person would doubt that if he had been willing to permit people to help him, they would not have allowed him to chop wood.

And Haninah b. Dosa, about whom it is proclaimed that "the entire world is sustained only because of my son Haninah, and Haninah my son is satisfied with a *kav* of carobs from one Shabbat eve to the next (BT Berakhot 17b)," requested nothing from other people.

And Karna, a judge throughout the Land of Israel, was a water drawer. When litigants came before him, he said to them, "Either provide someone who can draw water in my place while I am busy with you, or compensate me for my lost wages, and I will serve as judge for you."

And the Israelites living in the generations of these and other [Rabbis] were neither cruel nor ungenerous. Nor have we found a single impoverished Sage who rebuked the people of his generation for not helping him. God forbid. To the contrary, they themselves were virtuous, believers in the truth for its own sake, they had faith in God and in the law of Moses our master, through which a man will find [a place] in eternity. And they did not permit themselves [to request money from people]. They saw in this a profanation of God's name in the eyes of the people, who would come to believe that the Torah is a trade like any other trade by which one can support oneself, and it would become despicable in their eyes. One who does this has "despised the word of God" (Num. 15:31).

Those who deny the truth and this clear language, and who take people's money either with or without their consent, mistakenly rely on cases found in the Talmud involving the physically impaired, or the elderly, who are unable to work. They have no recourse but to accept [money from others]; for what are they to do, die? The law does not require this.

And you will find that the case in which the proof text, "She is like the merchant ships, she brings her food from afar" (Prov. 31:14),[13] was adduced involved an individual who was physically impaired and unable to work. But for one who is capable [of working], there is no legal basis [for accepting money] in this way.

Rav Yosef, peace be unto him, used to carry wooden beams and say, "Great is labor for it warms those who perform it," i.e., when his limbs, honored be their resting place, toiled in carrying the heavy beams, his body was undoubtedly warmed, and his will was satisfied and joyous. He was thus content with his lot in virtue of his self-sufficiency.

I have heard the simpletons who rely on the saying: "One who desires to derive benefit should derive benefit, like Elisha; and one who desires not to derive benefit let him not derive benefit, like Samuel the Ramahite" (BT Berakhot 10a). This is in no way comparable. To me this is nothing other than a distortion of this source, since it is clear, and there is no room for error. Since Elisha would not accept money from people, a fortiori, he would not solicit from them or impose obligations upon them, God forbid. Rather, he would accept only [gestures of] respect, such as when someone would give him lodging while he was traveling—he would sleep at [the house of his benefactor], eat [with him] that night or that day, and then proceed with his affairs. [By contrast,] Samuel would not enter any person's house, nor would he eat from anyone's food. In regard to such cases, the sages said that if a scholar wishes to emulate [Samuel] to the point of not entering anyone's house, he is permitted to do so, and if a scholar [wishes to] lodge with someone in a situation of necessity while traveling on the road . . . he is permitted to do so. They have already cautioned against eating [at someone's house] except at a time of necessity, and they have said that all scholars who readily eat

13. Rabbi Elazar b. Shimon quoted this verse when receiving a gift; see BT Bava Metzia 84b.

meals in all places [will inevitably suffer great harm] (see BT Pesahim 49a). And they said, "scholars are prohibited from accepting dinner invitations except for religious celebrations" (BT Pesahim 49a).

Why do I need to go on about this? I will simply recount the incident that was related and expounded in the Talmud, and the person who wishes to argue and disagree will do as he likes. It happened that a certain man had a vineyard into which thieves would enter. Every day that he visited [his vineyard], he found that grapes were missing. He was sure that one of the thieves was targeting [his vineyard], and he was distressed about this throughout the entire grape season. [The time came when] he gathered from it what he could gather, laid [the grapes] out until they dried, and then he gathered the raisins. It is usual when people gather raisins that they drop some and [anyone] is permitted to eat them because they are "ownerless," as their owners have already abandoned them because they are insignificant in number.

One day Rabbi Tarfon came upon that vineyard by chance. He sat down to gather some of the raisins that had fallen, and he began eating them. Along came the owner of the vineyard, who thought that this was the person who had stolen from him all year long—for though he knew Rabbi Tarfon by reputation he did not recognize him [in person]. He hastened toward him, overpowered him, put him into a sack, and ran, with him on his back, in order to throw him into the river. When Rabbi Tarfon saw that he was lost, he shouted, "Woe to you, Tarfon, that this is your killer, for you are done." When the vineyard owner heard this, he left him and fled, realizing that he had committed a great sin.

From that day on, Rabbi Tarfon was regretful and distressed over that event, because he had rescued himself through the honor of the Torah. For he was a rich man, and he could have said to [the vineyard owner], "Put me down and I will give you such and such [an amount] of *dinars*," and he would have given it to him. He would not have had to make known that he was Tarfon; he would have saved himself with his money and not by means of the Torah. They said that this righteous man was distressed over this matter throughout all the days of his life, saying, "Woe to me that I made use of the crown of the Torah, for anyone who makes use of the crown of the Torah is uprooted from the world." . . .

[Maimonides here cites the story of Rabbi Judah the Prince and his student Yonatan b. Amram, §3 above.]

These two incidents will silence all who would wish to argue with regard to this subject. But the law does permit scholars to invest money in another's business [with the owner having full control]. If the business yields a profit, this can fill the pockets of scholars. [Regarding scholars who engage in trade,] their goods should be sold before those of other sellers, and [the merchants] must give them the first option for goods in the market. For God has established these privileges for them, just as He established the portions for the priest and the tithes for the Levite according to what has come [down to us] in the tradition. For these are two practices that merchants sometimes do for one another out of respect, even though it is [not in honor] of wisdom, and a scholar should at least be treated like an *am ha-aretz* who is given respect.

The law has exempted all scholars from all governmental dues, such as levies, land taxes, and special personal taxes—those which are called "poll taxes." [All of these] must be paid by the community, including [taxes for] the building of walls and the like. Even a scholar who is a man of great financial means is not to be held liable for any of these.

Our rabbi Joseph Ha-Levi [ibn Migash] already ruled in this matter concerning a man in Andalusia who had gardens and orchards that were worth thousands of gold pieces. Ibn Migash ruled that he was exempt from any assessment because he was a scholar, even though the poorest Israelite was paying [his] levy. Thus the law rules, just as the law exempted the priests from the half-shekel, as we explained ad loc, and from all matters that are similar to this.[14]

14. See *Commentary on the Mishnah* Shekalim 1:4. Maimonides apparently changed his mind on this matter, cf. MT Laws of Shekalim 1:7.

No Benefits, Codified

13. Maimonides, MT Laws of the Study of Torah 3:6, 10

In his code, Maimonides reiterates his position forbidding scholars from receiving financial support. Here his position is prefaced by a description of the ideal of Torah study as a path of total dedication, renouncing all earthly acquisition.

6. Whoever desires to fulfill this commandment properly, and to become adorned with the crown of the Torah, must not divert his thoughts to other matters, nor set his heart on acquiring [the knowledge of] Torah and wealth and honor simultaneously. The way [leading to the knowledge] of Torah is as follows: "You shall eat a morsel of bread with salt and drink a small quantity of water, and you shall sleep on the ground and live a life of suffering while you labor in the Torah." You are not obligated to complete it, nor are you free to desist from it [cf. Mishnah Avot 2:21]. If you increase your [study of] Torah, you increase your reward, as the [amount of] reward is in accordance with the [amount of] pain.

10. Whoever sets his heart on pursuing Torah study, while doing no work and supporting himself through charity, has blasphemed God's name and degraded the Torah, extinguished the light of religion, caused evil [to be brought] upon himself, and has deprived his life of [its share in] the world to come. For it is forbidden to derive benefit in this world from the words of Torah. The sages have said, "Whoever derives benefit from the words of the Torah removes his life from the world" [Mishnah Avot 4.7]. They also commanded, saying, "Do not fashion [the words of Torah] into a crown with which to aggrandize yourself, nor into a spade with which to dig" [Mishnah Avot 4.7]. They also commanded, saying, "Love work and hate mastery" [Mishnah Avot 1.10]; "All [study of] Torah that is not accompanied by work will end in futility and will become the cause of sin" [Mishnah Avot 2.2]. Such a person will end up as a robber of the people.

Critique of Maimonides

14. Joseph Karo, *Kesef Mishneh,* MT Laws of the Study of Torah 3:10

Many scholars found Maimonides' demand that scholars abstain from any benefit what-

soever, including salaries or stipends, impossible to accept. Karo's critique is located in his

commentary to the MT, but he focuses on Maimonides' elaboration in the Commentary

on the Mishnah. *He argues not only against the force of the particular proof texts cited*

by Maimonides but adds the realistic argument that no serious scholarly pursuit of Torah

would be possible were we to follow his ruling.

In his Commentary on the Mishnah . . . our Rabbi [Maimonides] spoke derisively
. . . about financial support given to students and rabbis. It appears from his
statements that most, if not all, of the great Torah scholars at that time [of
the Mishnah], supported themselves [by labor or trade] in the manner he described. Here, too, he follows the same reasoning.

There [in his *Commentary on the Mishnah*] he brings proof from the
fact that Hillel the Elder (BT Yoma 35b) studied and was also a woodcutter. This provides no proof, as it relates specifically to the beginning of his
studies. Since there were tens of thousands of students at that time, perhaps
[financial support] was provided only to the famous among them, or perhaps
it was the case that anyone who was able to forgo deriving benefit [from
Torah] did so. In any event, once [Hillel] had attained wisdom and was transmitting it to the people, would it even occur to you that he chopped wood?

Nor does his citation of Haninah ben Dosa (BT Berakhot 17b) constitute proof. For if he had wanted to become rich, he would not have had to
ask other people; it would be granted to him directly from Heaven, as stated
(BT Ta'anit 25a). However, he did not want to derive benefit from this world,
whereas we are speaking only about those who do wish to derive benefit
from this world, albeit in a manner that is not prohibited.

Karna (BT Ketubot 105a) made money by examining stores of wine
to see which [wine] was worth keeping. This was a good trade that did not
require much exertion. There is no doubt that whoever has been endowed
by God [with the ability] to support himself from his work is not permitted

to take [from others]. Rav Huna was a water drawer who, according to Rashi, drew water to irrigate his own fields, and there is no impropriety in this. Furthermore, according to this, he already had land and had no need to take [from others].

[The story] regarding Yonatan ben Amram (BT Bava Batra 8a, §3 above) is proof of the opposite. Our holy Rabbi [Judah the Prince] said that only scholars were permitted to come and take sustenance from his [wheat]. If it is prohibited [to derive benefit from Torah study], how could he have caused scholars to transgress? . . . If [a scholar] does [need to] derive benefit, he should manufacture all possible excuses so [it appears that] he is doing so in the capacity of a poor person, as in the case of Yonatan ben Amram.

Furthermore, it should be stated that anyone who is impoverished is permitted to derive benefit [from Torah study]; Yonatan ben Amram's behavior was supererogatory. As [they] said [to Judah the Prince:] "Perhaps it was Yonatan b. Amram, who refuses to benefit by [virtue of] the Torah's honor?" (§3 above) demonstrating that it was Yonatan in particular who refused to derive [any] benefit, whereas others were willing to derive benefit. For if this were not so, they should have said to him, "Perhaps it is some scholar who will not benefit [by virtue of] the Torah's honor." Moreover, if it is [indeed] prohibited, how is it that we do not find a single person who strictly upheld Torah law except Yonatan ben Amram?

. . . The general rule that emerges is that anyone who has no other means of support is permitted to collect payment from teaching, either from the pupils themselves or from the public. One is similarly permitted to collect payment for judging, either from the public or from the litigants, when done in compliance with the conditions set forth in [MT] Laws Concerning Sanhedrin.

Having determined all this, it is possible to say that what our Rabbi [Maimonides] meant is that one should not cast off the yoke of work so as to be supported by other people, in order to study. Instead, he should learn a trade with which he can support himself. If it provides sufficient means, that is well and good. If it does not, he can collect financial support from the community, and there is nothing [wrong] with that. This is what [he meant when] he said, "Whoever sets his heart, etc." (3:10). He also cited a few *mish-*

nayot which taught that it is fitting to learn a trade. Yet even if we are to maintain [instead] that our Rabbi's [Maimonides'] real opinion is reflected in his statements in his *Commentary on the Mishnah,* the rule is that any time the law is unclear one follows custom. And we have seen that it has been customary for all scholars of Israel, both before and after Maimonides' time, to collect their pay from the public. Alternatively, even if the law is as Maimonides states, perhaps the scholars of all generations have collectively enacted [otherwise], on the basis of [the principle] "It is a time to act for the Lord—they have violated Your teaching" (Ps. 119:127).[15] If students and teachers were not readily provided with financial support, they would not be able to dedicate themselves properly to the Torah, and the Torah would be forgotten, God forbid. With the provision of financial support, they are able to pursue [Torah study], and "magnify and glorify [His] Teaching" (Is. 42:21).

Self-Serving Sages
15. David b. Solomon Ben Zimra (Radbaz), *Responsa 752*

Here is a critique of rich rabbis whose claim to be exempt from taxation seems obviously exploitative. Ben Zimra, writing in sixteenth-century Palestine, speaks (bravely, perhaps, but also cautiously) on behalf of the ordinary members of his community, against his fellow scholars.

You have asked for my opinion regarding the disagreement that has arisen in Jerusalem between the householders and the scholars [*hakhamim*] over how to pay the neighborhood guards.

Now, you know that we read in BT Bava Batra 8a (§3 above): "Rav Yehudah said: Everyone [must share in the cost] of doors for the town gates, even orphans; but not scholars, since scholars do not require protection."

15. Reference to this verse invokes the legal principle whereby the rules of the Torah may be altered to meet the "needs of the hour," which is the Rabbinic term for crises or emergencies. See Mishnah Berakhot 9:5 and BT Berakhot 63a.

That is agreed to without objection. But the subject of disagreement is a per capita (poll) tax: Must the community pay for [the scholars] or not? And it has become accepted to follow the lenient view, so [the community] pays the entire tax.[16]

In the case at hand, however, even those who say that the scholars do not have to pay a per capita tax would agree that they must pay for guards. It is one thing when the king or the local authority orders guards to be posted in every city, or when they [the residents] guard in person, one a night—in that case the scholars are exempt, for they do not require protection. And if the guard duty is personal the [townspeople] should fulfill it and not the scholars for "it is not appropriate for scholars to march out" (§3 above). The same holds where the king neither orders nor compels them, but rather the townspeople themselves need to hire guards—the scholars are exempt, as I have written.

It is another thing in our case, where the [local] householders say, "We are poor and do not need watchmen!" while the scholars are pressing them to engage watchmen, and are thus admitting that they do need protection. Can justice or any other argument imply that the householders should be compelled to appoint watchmen without any participation by the scholars? Certainly, to compel the householders to pay under these circumstances is simply unheard of! Indeed, even if someone were to say [that they should], we would not listen to him; it would be a perversion of justice. But they can be compelled to appoint guards if there is a need, and all will pitch in, as stated in the Mishnah that the residents of a town may compel each other, etc. (§3 above).

And even though I know that there are scholars who dispute this, it is their own interest that they seek, and they should not be heeded.

Do not, however, misunderstand me; what I say applies to these circumstances, wherein the householders argue that they will do without watchmen unless everybody pitches in, and the scholars say that no matter what, watchmen should be hired. It is in this case that I say the former can

16. The per capita tax for the rabbis is covered by the community; this ruling is called the more "lenient" in the sense that it permits the rabbis a greater exemption.

compel the latter. There is [also] an independent reason, inasmuch as it is questionable whether nowadays there is anyone who can be said not to need protection. At any rate, I will not engage now in this investigation, since my words will undoubtedly pain some of the scholars, and so silence is preferable to speech. . . .

If, however, it is evident that the householders too are in need of protection, and are only claiming [that they are not] so that the scholars will participate, while the scholars say they do not need protection or are silent, it is clear that they need not participate. But if [the scholars] admit that they do need protection, and are pressing for watchmen, it is clear to me that they must participate, inasmuch as "the admission of a disputant is worth a hundred witnesses." . . .

This is especially true regarding the situation that I see in Jerusalem, where the thieves are setting their eyes on the scholars, who dress differently than the householders and appear more dignified. All the more so if, as is well known, there is danger to life at stake; there should not be any negligence in this matter.

I have written what seems [true] to my feeble intellect. And Rashba [Adret] wrote in a responsum regarding one who was exempt from taxes and duties, that he was nonetheless obligated to help pay for the upkeep of the city walls, since he was in need of their protection; so too here, even though the scholars are exempt from taxes and duties, if they are in need of protection they are obligated to help pay for the upkeep of the city walls.

Against the Exemption from Military Service

16. Shelomo Yosef Zevin, "On the Drafting of Yeshiva Students"

Tradition: A Journal of Orthodox Jewish Thought 21, no. 4 (Fall 1985): 52–55; the article was translated by David Wachsman.

The following pamphlet was published anonymously in besieged Jerusalem in the midst of the 1948 Israeli War of Independence. It was written in response to a da'at torah *(Torah view) published a short time earlier by rabbis in Jerusalem opposing the recruitment of yeshiva students. From the halakhic point of view, Zevin asserts, the War of Independence, since it is defensive, is an obligatory war (¢26). Therefore, taking part in this war is also obligatory, tantamount to the obligation to save someone else's life, binding even (or especially) on scholars. Yet between the lines of this erudite ruling, Zevin repeatedly levels at the new evaders of army service an ancient and poignant moral accusation: "Who is to say that your blood is dearer?" (BT Sanhedrin 74a; ¢11, §17).*

The deepest respect and admiration is due the rabbis and learned scholars of our holy city, but the question may nonetheless be asked: Teach us, our masters, how can this be justified?

What is the source for exempting yeshiva students and Torah scholars from an obligatory war fought to defend Israel from those who come to destroy her, God forbid? How can you pass it off as if it were *halakhah* or the *da'at torah* that yeshiva students need not register or serve? Have we not learned that when it comes to saving a life—not many lives, just one—"these things are done by the leaders of Israel" (BT Yoma 84b; MT Laws of Shabbat 2:3) and by the scholars (MT Laws of Shabbat 2:3) "in order to teach the *halakhah* to the nation"? (*Turei Zahav* to *Shulhan Arukh* OH 328:5). Was any distinction made [as to] whether . . . it is time learning Torah that is to be lost? If this is the case in the saving of one life, how much more so in the saving of tens of thousands of Jews?

Perhaps a distinction should be made as to whether one must endanger himself in order to save someone else's life. Could we go so far as to say that if one's own life would be threatened, he has no obligation to save other people? If so, where does the Torah differentiate between the self-sacrifice of the highest of the high and that of the lowest of the low? If a person should not have to be drafted because of the danger involved, all Israel is exempt! Why have you excused only the yeshiva students? "Who is to say that your blood is dearer?" (BT Sanhedrin 74a). There is no distinction to be made between the blood of a Torah scholar and that of a common man. The rule that "one life is not set aside for another" (Mishnah Ohalot 7:6) applies even to a day-old baby! It is clear that up to now there had only been controversy as to whether the principle that one must put his own life in danger to save another's applies only to saving an individual's life — or perhaps the lives of many individuals. But there is certainly no disagreement when it comes to saving Israel as a whole [klal yisrael] — surely there is no need to review the unanimous opinion that a defensive war fought to save Israel from her enemies is an obligatory one (MT Laws of Kings 5:1) of which it has been said, "All must go, even a bridegroom from his room and a bride from under her canopy" (BT Sotah 44b; MT Laws of Kings 7:4). How have we arrived at the conclusion that scholars are not included in this obligation? If our generation merited everyone studying Torah, would we allow our enemies to ravage our land and kill our people without taking up arms to defend ourselves? We were not worthy, but thank God that there are people ready to stand firm and fight! What source have we for a hierarchy of obligation regarding participating in a war to save Israel from its enemies?[17]

But we have found sources expressing a totally opposite position. The Captain of the Lord's host admonished Joshua before the battle of Jericho, saying, "You have not made the afternoon sacrifice, and now you abolish the study of Torah" (BT Megillah 3a), and Rashi explained, "Now that it is night you should be involved in studying Torah because you do not fight at night." This is very explicit: "You do not fight at night!" In times of war, the Torah is pushed aside if there is a need for it.

In the Jerusalem Talmud it is written, "And Asa the king called all of Judah to his army without exception . . . not even a teacher or his student was exempt" (Sotah 8:10). And while the Babylonian Talmud says that Asa was punished for this (BT Sotah 10a), Samuel Edeles explained that this was a voluntary war, because in an obligatory war certainly even a Torah scholar must fight. The *Arukh Dictionary* explained how Asa could call the Torah scholars to war, because when it was said "without exception" it means "even a bridegroom from his room and a bride from under her canopy," so the scholars too must be included (*Arukh Dictionary*, s.v. *angaria;* BT Sotah 10a). From here

17. There is a possible answer: see the rules of priority among claims for assistance that appear in Mishnah Horayot 3:8, ¢4, §15.

we learn that if in an obligatory war a bride and groom must go, so must the rabbis! In the war against Midian we read that Moses sent a thousand from each tribe to the army along with Phinehas, and the Sanhedrin was included (BT Sotah 43a).

Indeed, are we dealing with saving others? Every one of us is in mortal danger, as are our families and everyone dear to us. Is it right for the scholars not to save themselves, but to place the obligation upon others? Is this the *da'at torah*? Where have we seen such a thing?

Doesn't the Torah protect her scholars? On the contrary! Let the scholars fight at the front and the merit of their learning Torah will defend them and their comrades! "If you follow in my statutes"—this requires the study of Torah, not simply doing the *mitzvot* (*Torat Kohanim*, Rashi to Lev. 26:3) And what is the promised reward for this? "You will chase your enemies and they will fall by the sword before you." Yes, "they will fall," but "you will chase!" The Tanna Devei Eliyahu says: "God said, I did not write so in my Torah, but even if Israel were not absorbed in the study of Torah and kept only the *mitzvah* of common decency [*derekh eretz*], the *shekhinah* [divine presence] would be with them and the promise of 'five chasing a hundred and a hundred chasing ten thousand' would be fulfilled. If they fulfilled the Torah and *mitzvot* one would chase a thousand and two would put to flight ten thousand" (11:3).

"Scholars do not require protection" (BT Baba Batra 7b, §3)? God Almighty! When actual lives are at stake may we rely on miracles? In 1929 at Hebron (such a calamity should never occur twice!) didn't young students of the yeshiva, whose holiness shone like stars in the sky, fall before the malicious enemy? Please, did these martyrs need protection or not? And those same murderous Arabs are still the enemy today! If you understand that the scholars need no protecting in relatively peaceful times and are exempt from building the protective walls, what consequence has this when compared to a life-and-death struggle, a war which is a *mitzvah* and in which all are obligated? The defense authorities ordered everyone to cover all windows as protection against shattering glass in case of an air raid. Would anyone think that some rabbis will not do so, claiming, "Scholars do not require protection"? Did anyone absorbed in Torah study exempt himself from this? Why did rabbis leave areas under enemy fire along with the rest of the general population? Why did they not rely on this maxim? Is this the *da'at torah?* They took this Torah concept out of context and used it improperly, while if it were used in its proper context it would be a valuable pearl. I understand the feelings of Neturei Karta who are unalterably opposed to the state of Israel. They oppose the war because they feel that we should surrender. Even according to these ideas, there is no difference between the yeshiva students and the common people. Anyone who subscribes to this philosophy must be against the conscription of anyone in Israel, whoever he may be. Luckily, very few people feel this way. Our entire nation, in Israel and in the Diaspora, eagerly risk their lives in this defensive war which has been thrust upon us. They understand well that there is no future for the *yishuv* here or for the refugees waiting in the Diaspora without our own independent country, one that would be open to accept our bloodied brothers who wander in the burning *galut.* God, Israel, and the rest of the world know that we are not the aggressors. We do not want war, and we are not gladdened by the spilling of blood. But if our enemies fall upon us in a mad killing frenzy, we must defend ourselves. And you, our *geonim,* admit the dire necessity of this obligatory war. Many of you have sent blessings and words of encouragement to our valiant soldiers. It is your obligation to encourage young and healthy scholars to fight. Will you send your brothers to war, and yourselves sit at home?[18]

A practical fear has been expressed that if the students go to war, all the *yeshivot* will become depleted and who knows what will happen to Torah in Israel. It would be possible to arrange a mutually agreeable accommodation and as far as I know the draft offices are willing to negotiate this. But to decide in the manner of *halakhah* not to participate at all—how can you possibly justify this?

Many yeshiva students are standing at the front even now, sanctifying God's name. With one hand they are turning the pages of a Bible or Talmud, and in the other hand they hold their rifles. Their spirit of Torah and belief in the Almighty strengthen their comrades and influences them in the

18. Paraphrasing Num. 32:6.

ways of Torah. Most respected rabbis, are you not obligated to encourage others to follow in their footsteps?

The opinion of the Torah? It is clear and explicit: "Those who act quickly when lives are at stake are to be praised and do not require the permission of Bet Din" (BT Yoma 84b; see MT Laws of Kings 5:2). "For the Lord thy God goes with you to fight against your enemies and save you!" (Deut. 20:4).

Commentary. On Scholars and Soldiers

In the ideal state, according to Plato's *Republic,* every philosopher is a veteran soldier, for military service is a necessary stage in the process of training the philosopher-king. Excellence in battle against another person demands excellence in battle against one's self, and self-discipline is a necessary condition, though not a sufficient one, for anyone who endeavors to manage affairs of state in the name of truth.

In the Jewish state, however, even in the ideal Jewish state, the relationship between scholar and soldier is more complex. On the one hand, the Messiah King, at least in Maimonides' utopian account, is a scholar who fights God's wars. On the other hand, no one ever asserts, or even suggests, that a scholar must be a soldier or, at least, a veteran soldier. The brutality of the soldier presumably distances him from the scholar. So writers in the Jewish tradition looked with suspicion at the scholar-soldier.

The central question for Jewish writers is not whether scholars ought to be soldiers but whether, under what terms, and to what extent they can be *required* to be soldiers. The issue they consider is not excellence, as with Plato, but merely taxation—for military duty is regarded as a tax imposed by society on the individual's body and time (rather than on his property).

No society is without taxation. No taxation is without exemptions. No exemptions are without grounds. Different grounds create different relations between those who are exempted—individuals or groups—and those who are not. If we are to understand the exempt scholars' place within society, we need to consider the particular grounds for their exemption. Concerning a defensive war, classified by the *halakhah* as an obligatory war, there are four grounds for exemption from military duty—and therefore four models of the relation between scholars and the society they live in.

Model A. Citizens Defend Scholars. The basis of this model includes various versions of the following argument: study of the Torah is society's overriding ultimate good, and this study requires absolute devotion on the part of the scholars. Scholars conscripted into the city's defense forces, let alone exposed to the enemy, will be forced to abandon their study of the Torah. Hence, scholars must not be conscripted or exposed in battles with the enemy. In other words, scholars must be protected.

In this, as in other regards, the scholars wish to fill the social position left void by the Levites after the Temple's destruction. To my mind, this social position is fashioned with remarkable clarity at the beginning of the book of Numbers. On the one hand, the book's first chapter states that the carrying of the Tabernacle exempts the Levites from carrying arms. But, on the other hand, according to the second chapter of the book, God does not protect them because they are carrying the Tabernacle. Rather, they need, and get, special human protection. That is also the organizing principle of the Israelites' journey in the wilderness; whether in motion or at rest, the various tribes take care to protect the Levites by surrounding them physically, placing them in the center of camp, keeping them as far as possible from the line of battle.

Model B. Scholars Defending Citizens. Here the relationship between scholars and citizens is inverted. Scholars are presented not as needful of the citizens' protection but, on the contrary, as those who themselves defend the citizens.

This defense might be construed as supernatural, miraculous protection, yet it may also be considered natural, ethical protection. On the first view, the study of the Torah has, as does prayer, a magical effect that ensures the city's protection: "As long as Jacob's voice pipes in synagogues and houses of study Esau's hands have no hold on him (according to Lamentations Rabbah, proem 2)." On the second, more worldly view, a city with scholars is stronger than a city without them because scholars concern themselves with a systematic examination of the organizing principles of the city and with how it is actually managed. The *Bet Ha-midrash* is where the city contemplates itself. The external robustness of the city is the result of constant self-examination. Scholars, therefore, are the most effective barrier between Israel and its opponents. The home front is the true front.

A radical version of this standpoint was adopted, according to the JT (Hagigah 76c), by Rabbis Hiyya, Assi, and Ami. These sages were delegated by Judah the Prince to visit the various small cities of the Land of Israel with the purpose of setting up teachers of Scripture and teachers of Mishnah. They come upon a place devoid of such teachers. "Bring us the guards of the city [*neturei karta*]," the delegates request. When the local people present the city's bailiffs before them, the disappointed delegates retort: "Are these the guardians of the city? Nay, they are its destroyers." When the locals asked in surprise who may the true guardians of the city be, the delegates reply, "The teachers of Scripture and teachers of Mishnah. As Scripture says, 'Unless the Lord builds the house, [its builders labor in vain on it; unless the Lord watches over the city, the watchmen keep vigil in vain]'" (Ps. 127:1).

Model C. Cooperation and Mutual Protection. The two previous models are opposed to each other but do not necessarily contradict each other. The assertion that scholars defend the city does not entail the assertion that the city bailiffs destroy the city. And vice versa, the assertion that the bailiffs, guardians of the city, actually do protect it does not entail the assertion that scholars weaken the city by opting to study rather than fight.

The model of cooperation unifies the two previous models. Now the citizens and the scholars are seen as two groups that mutually protect each other. One holds the sword while the other holds the book in order to defend the city. The latter type of defense can be understood, again, either in terms of a natural-ethical or a supernatural-magical protection—and even as a combination of these two.

Rabbi Shelomo Yosef Zevin demands that scholars be enlisted in the army. But his argument may also fit the model of cooperation:

> "If you follow my statutes"—this requires the study of Torah, not simply doing the *mitzvot* (*Torat Kohanim*, Rashi to Lev. 26:3). And what is the promised reward for this? "You will chase your enemies

and they will fall by the sword before you." Yes, "they will fall," but "you will chase!" (§16).

In order to defeat the assailing enemy, the Israelites are required both to study Torah and to engage in battle. Complete and efficient fulfillment of this dual mission, according to the model of cooperation, requires that, as part of society's general division of labor, some citizens specialize in study and some focus on warfare. The former provide the city with *religious-ethical* protection, whereas the latter provide the city with *military* protection. Cooperation here is ensured through the realization that protection singularly provided by either of the two is indeed necessary, yet not sufficient. Each group realizes that in order to protect itself it must protect the other. Defending the city, according to this model, necessitates cooperation, yet presumably, this necessity will give rise to mutual understanding and appreciation between scholars and other citizens.

Model D. Separation: "Scholars do not require protection." The three previous models exempt scholars from army duty based on relations of dependence between scholars and the general public. According to the first model, the scholars depend on the public; according to the second, the public depends on the scholars, whereas according to the third, the two groups depend on each other. Conversely, the fourth and final model bases the exemption of the scholars on their complete separation from society.

The assertion here is that in contrast with the other city residents, scholars are provided with God's direct protection. Therefore, they are exempt from the need to defend themselves or to pay for the defense of others. This was Resh Lakish and Rabbi Yohanan's argument against the city walls tax imposed on the scholars by Rabbi Yehudah Nesi'a (grandson of Judah the Prince; BT Bava Batra 7b, §3). Scholars, so they claimed, simply do not benefit from the city's defense services and should therefore be exempt from paying for them.

But this is not merely a matter of benefit. The scholars, in claiming that in matters of life and death their destiny is not that of the general public, sever themselves from the society of the city. In their singular standing before God, they establish for themselves a city within the city. The walls of the scholar's city are not made of stone, nor do its towers rise high. Instead, as Rabbi Yohanan explicates the verse from the Song of Solomon, "I am a wall and my breasts are like towers": "'I am a wall'—that is the Torah, and 'my breasts are like towers' (8:1)—those are the scholars" (BT Bava Batra 7b, §3).

Rabbi Yohanan's explication presents a radical version of the separation model. He rejects the commonly accepted argument, presented by Resh Lakish on the same matter, which holds that the Song of Songs describes the relationship between the people of Israel and God. Instead, he maintains that it describes the relationship between the scholars and God. The scholars are presented here, in a clearly sectarian way, as the "true Israel." They see themselves as extrinsic to their time and place. Their textual city is the true city and their "everyday" is the Age of the Messiah. In the same way, some yeshiva scholars in the modern state of Israel perceive themselves as living in a city of refuge within the larger, hedonistic city, whose sons are conscripted into the army. According to this view, the soldiers of the Israel Defense Forces, precisely because of their proximity to God's city and their radically different life-style, jeopardize God's city even more than its distant and alien enemies.

The counterargument, in this perennially engaging Israeli polemic, contends that the people threatening Israeli society from within are precisely the yeshiva scholars who shirk their military responsibility. For no society can long maintain its basic cohesion while an entire sector within it refuses its share of the burdens essential to routine social functioning. After decades of war, Israeli society is plagued by bereavement, and it demands in the name of justice that all its sectors bear their equal share of bereavement.

In contemporary Israeli society, Torah scholars have lost their elite status, which in the past had underwritten their exemption from monetary and/or corporal taxation for the purpose of defending the city. Scholars no longer serve to focus communal identity, and the sentiment that they study Torah on behalf of the general public is no longer widely felt. The persuasive power of the traditional reasons for exemption is nearly completely exhausted. Outside the world of yeshivas, few nowadays are of the opinion that scholars should be exempt from military service because they are protected by God, as Resh Lakish and Rabbi Yohanan asserted (§3). Similarly, few would be ready today to accept an argument in the vein of that presented by Rabbi

Judah the Prince, that "calamity occurs solely on account of *amme ha-aretz*" and therefore *amme ha-aretz,* and solely *amme ha-aretz* should bear the burden of calamities, including the wars that may fall upon the state of Israel. Moreover, because defense tax in Israel is corporal, not monetary, scholars' economic difficulties no longer serve them as grounds for exemption.

Yet contemporary voices that call for the immediate military conscription of yeshiva scholars don't come from only one direction. Some, indeed, come from Israelis who wish to distance themselves—sometimes to the point of complete alienation—from Jewish tradition. But another, significant number come from those who wish to maintain and cultivate the Jewish tradition. In any case, it is remarkable to note that all the different voices, consciously or not, echo the traditional arguments against the granting of exemptions.

The common claim, for example, that abuse of exemptions by imposters is sufficient reason for canceling them is remarkably referred to already in *Sefer Hasidim* (§8). Even though the context there is different— exemption from taxation for the poor rather than exemption from military duty for scholars—the argument is the same: exemption must be canceled because it is abused by imposters, whether the wealthy pretending to be poor in twelfth-century Germany or laypeople posing as yeshiva scholars in twenty-first-century Israel. However, in the case of yeshiva scholars in modern Israel, it would be difficult to parallel the medieval Hasidim's method of coping with imposters: cancel the exemption, and then return the tax covertly to the (truly) poor.

The critique of the scholars as flagrantly hypocritical is also very old. On the one hand, they claim complete independence of the city's defense services since "God is our refuge" (Ps. 46:2); they have no need for these services, and therefore they are exempt from participating in them. At the same time, they actively take refuge under the protection provided by the city's citizens—and even blatantly interfere with its management. Different versions of this argument were presented in varying contexts in Jerusalem, four hundred years apart, by two scholars perturbed by the way their peers dishonestly took advantage of their status. David ben Zimra, writing in the mid-sixteenth century, doubts "whether nowadays there is anyone who can be said not to need protection" (§15). But he has no doubt that wealthy scholars' use of the motto "Scholars do not require protection" is commensurate neither with *halakhah* nor with common sense. For despite it being *their* initiative to appoint city guards to defend their property and their lives, they seek to impose all the costs of defense on poor homeowners, claiming their own exemption. In a similar way, Zevin, who anonymously published a pamphlet in besieged Jerusalem during the 1948 War of Independence, also doubts the sincerity of yeshiva scholars who demand exemption on the grounds that, as scholars, they are directly protected by God. The same scholars abandoned the frontier neighborhoods of Jerusalem when they were hit by snipers, according to Zevin, exactly as all the other residents did. "Doesn't the Torah protect her scholars? On the contrary! Let the scholars fight at the front and the merit of their learning Torah will defend them and their comrades!" (§16). But the greatest scandal, many argue after Zevin, is that political representatives of scholars shirking military service sit in the government and take part in declaring wars and deciding on their course and on the terms for their cessation.

Still, the most potent traditional argument in the Israeli context is not political but legal; it comes from *halakhah*. The wars of Israel are defensive wars, and as such it is required that all participate. As Zevin says, "There is no distinction to be made between the blood of a Torah scholar and that of a common man" (§16). For "there is certainly no disagreement when it comes to saving Israel as a whole [*klal yisrael*]—surely there is no need to review the unanimous opinion that a defensive war fought to save Israel from her enemies is an obligatory one (MT Laws of Kings 5:1) of which it has been said, 'All must go, even a bridegroom from his room and a bride from under her canopy' (BT Sotah 44b; MT Laws of Kings 7:4)" (§16).

So cancellation of the current scholars' exemption is commensurate not only with popular opinion in modern Israel but also with the fundamental standpoint of the Jewish tradition over the generations. Nevertheless, except for extreme cases where the state of Israel is in immediate danger (as in the War of Independence), my own suggestion is to cancel only the current form of the exemption, not the exemption itself. Instead of cancellation, what is required is to reform the exemption by adopting *cultural excellence* as its organizing principle. The commitment to excellence will ensure a significant reduction of the number of exemptions granted to scholars, and the commitment to culture will ensure a widening of the circle of entitlement.

Adoption of a criterion of excellence will end the current indiscriminate granting of exemptions to an entire sector of the population, which causes a dangerous split in Israeli society. Granting exemption to a *very* small group of *outstanding* scholars may significantly lessen the mutual alienation between orthodox Jews and the rest of the citizens in Israel—if it is coupled with a parallel exemption granted to young Israelis who are outstanding achievers in science, the arts, and sports.

A decent respect for the different sectors of Israeli society necessitates such a widening of the scope of exemption. Yet it is not only decency that necessitates it but also culture's fundamental importance to the state. Culture in its wider sense is what gives value to the state and justifies the state's maintenance and its defense. Even if the state is a product of culture, it has no value in itself. The state is intended to serve culture, and not vice versa. And as the state is able to accommodate the demand that for the sake of culture's advancement and well-being, a limited number of citizens be granted exemption from military service, it is the state's obligation to do so. And if this is true of states in general, it must also be true of the relation between culture and state in Israel.

The recognition that the Jewish religion does not delineate the boundaries of Jewish culture (as Rabbi Saadiah Gaon asserted) but is merely one of the *regions* of Jewish culture (as Ahad Ha'am asserted), is one of the most important steps taken by Jewish consciousness in the transition from the Middle Ages to the modern era. In order to sustain that advance, the state of Israel, as a modern Jewish state, must include in any exemption from military service based on excellence not only yeshiva scholars but also young scientists, artists, and athletes who contribute significantly not only to Jewish Israeli culture but to human culture in general.

Yuval Jobani

Education and Scholarship

Establishing a School System

17. BT Bava Batra 21a

This is the earliest account of the Rabbinic decision to require the establishment of a school system "in each and every district." According to this account, initially, fathers were responsible for the education of their sons; it was the plight of the fatherless that prompted the creation of what are in effect public schools. Presumably, fathers with money had to pay school fees, but it is clear from this text that public expenditure was also necessary, and so public funds had to be collected (not until medieval times do we get clear accounts of how that was done—see §20 below). The specific context of the discussion below is the rule restricting business initiatives that are a nuisance to the courtyard neighbors. An exception is mentioned with regard to children.

Rava said: [The special exception regarding children refers to a school,] following the *takkanah* of Yehoshua b. Gamla. As Rav Yehudah said, citing Rav: Indeed, blessed is the memory of that man, namely, Yehoshua b. Gamla, for were it not for him, the Torah would have been forgotten from among Israel. For at first, [a child] who had a father would be taught Torah by his father, while one who had no father would not study Torah. . . . It was therefore ordained that schoolteachers be established in Jerusalem. . . . Still, [a child] who had a father would be brought up [to Jerusalem] by his father to study, while one who had no father would not come up to study. It was therefore ordained that schoolteachers be established in each and every district. [The youngsters] would be brought in at the age of sixteen or [even] seventeen, and whoever was scolded by his teacher would spurn him and walk out. Finally, Yehoshua b. Gamla came [along] and ordained that schoolteachers be established in each and every city and town, and that [the students] be brought in at the age of six or seven.

  Rav instructed Rav Shmu'el b. Shelat [who was a schoolteacher]: "Do not take in [a child] under the age of six. From [that age] upwards, take [him] in and feed him [i.e., teach him] like an ox." Rav [further] instructed

Rav Shmu'el b. Shelat: "When you strike a child, do so only with a shoelace. Whoever studies will study; and whoever does not study, let him be a companion to the other." . . .

Said Rava: From the *takkanah* of Yehoshua b. Gamla onward, a child may not be transported from town to town [for schooling]; but [he may be] transported from one [neighborhood's] synagogue to another. Across a river, transportation is forbidden; if there is a wide bridge, it is permitted; if a [mere] plank, it is not permitted.

Rava further said: The [proper] number [of students] per schoolteacher is twenty-five. If there are fifty, two teachers are established; if there are forty, a helper is appointed, paid for by the town.

Rava further said: If there is a schoolteacher who is knowledgeable and another [i.e., a prospective teacher] who is more knowledgeable—he should not be replaced, lest [the new teacher, through haughtiness,] become careless. Rav Dimi of Neharde'a said: On the contrary, [he should be replaced,] since this will improve study! For "the jealousy of scribes increases wisdom."

The School System

18. Maimonides, MT Laws of the Study of Torah 2

Codifying talmudic teachings, Maimonides here provides a comprehensive regulation for the school system. This includes a conception of the process of socialization and regimentation of the young. His medieval sensibilities are reflected in the role he ascribes to corporal punishment as well as in the strict insistence on what he takes to be appropriate gender roles. Ultimately this system would feed into the more advanced forms of scholarly pursuit and excellence reproducing the Rabbinic elite of the community.

1. Teachers of young children are to be appointed in each province and city. If a town has no children's school [*tinokot shel bet rabban,* "children of the house of rabbis"], its inhabitants are placed under a *herem,* till such teachers have

been engaged. And if they do not [appoint any], the city is destroyed, for the world exists only by the breath of *tinokot shel bet rabban*.

2. Children enter [school] to study at the age of six or seven years, according to the strength of the child and its physical stature. But no child enters [school] under six years [of age]. The teacher may strike his pupils to inspire them with awe. But he must not do so in enmity and cruelty. Accordingly, he must not strike them with whips or sticks, but only use a small strap. He is to teach them the entire day and part of the night, so as to educate them to study day and night. And there is to be no idleness except on the eve of Shabbat or eves of festivals, toward the close of the day, and on festivals. On Shabbat, pupils are not taught a new lesson, but they review what they had already previously learned, even if only once. Pupils must not be dismissed from their studies, even for the building of the temple [in Jerusalem].

3. A teacher who leaves the children and goes out, or does other work while he is with them, or is negligent in teaching, falls under [the scriptural admonition] "Cursed be he that doeth the work of the Lord with a slack hand" (Jer. 48:10). Hence, it is not proper to appoint anyone as teacher unless he is God-fearing and well versed in reading and in grammar.

4. An unmarried man should not teach children because the mothers come to see them. Nor should a woman teach children, because the fathers come to see their sons.

5. Twenty-five children may study with one teacher. If the number [in the class] exceeds twenty-five but is not more than forty, he should have an assistant appointed to help with the instruction. If there are more than forty, two teachers must be appointed.

6. A child may be transferred from one teacher to another who is more competent in reading or grammar—only, however, if both [the teacher and the pupil] live in the same town and are not separated by a river. But the child must not be taken to school in another town nor even across a river in the same town, unless it is spanned by a firm bridge, not likely soon to collapse.

7. If one of the residents in an alley or even in a courtyard wishes to become a teacher [and to open a school], his neighbors cannot protest this. Nor can [one] teacher, [already established, object] to [a second] teacher

opening another [school building] next door to him, either for new pupils or even with the intention of drawing away pupils from [the existing school], for it is said, "The Lord was pleased for his righteousness' sake, to make the Torah great and glorious" (Is. 42:21).

Priority of Education and Care for the Sick
19. Simeon b. Zemah Duran, *Tashbetz* 3:190

In the case at hand a woman proposed to disinherit her offspring by transferring her fortune to the tzedakah *fund or synagogue maintenance (both publicly funded). Duran addresses the question of the "transfer" of an estate and the heir's rights (on this, see ¢19, §§23–24). But the deciding factor in disallowing the bequest lies in its grossly misplaced priorities. Family resources must be preserved for such purposes as supporting scholarly pursuits or facilitating marriage (cf. ¢20, §§29–30). More generally, highest priority is accorded to caring for the sick and providing scholarships.*

You further asked: A certain woman owns property, and has fallen ill. She proposes to transfer her estate from the relatives who are her proper heirs under Torah law and dedicate her property [instead] to the poor or to the synagogue. The relative who [would be] her heir has sons who are scholars and a daughter who needs to be married [off]; he is forced to travel from his town to beg from the [various] communities to [provide for] his daughter's marriage. [Now,] is the *hekdesh* [endowment] that this woman proposes acceptable to the sages, or not? This is the gist of the question.

Answer: Everyone is familiar with the talmudic statement, "Do not be present at the transfer of an estate, even from a bad son to a good son—and even more so, from a son to a daughter" (BT Bava Batra 133b). If this is what they stated regarding [persons who can be] proper heirs, how much more so regarding those who cannot be proper heirs at all, such as the *hekdesh* or the synagogue! For an endowment for the synagogue is used for its upkeep, or for the provision of oil for lighting, or for other requirements.

These things are the public's obligation, and one who dedicates his property to this is simply releasing the public from their obligation. He thus in effect transfers the estate from persons who can be proper heirs to those who cannot be proper heirs. The same is true in the case of dedicating [money] to the poor . . . since he [in effect] releases the public from an obligation incumbent upon them. . . .

All this, however, cannot [furnish grounds] for voiding the gift once it is made—rather [only for asserting] that it is improper to make it. It can, however, be voided on the basis of the statement in JT Peah (21b): "Rabbi [Judah the Prince] showed Rav a synagogue gate that [his family] had built, and exclaimed: 'How much money my ancestors invested here!' He replied: 'Rather, how many lives have your ancestors invested here! Was there no person studying Torah [whom they might have supported], or sick people lying in a dump?' He referred him to the following verse, 'Israel has ignored his Maker and built temples'" (Hos. 8:14).

This implies that it is a greater obligation to [finance the] education of students and to provide for the poor than to build a synagogue; the same has been maintained by several early authors, of blessed memory. Now since this comes under "Israel has ignored . . . ," and the law is that if a person on his deathbed ordered that a transgression be committed with his estate, he shall not be heeded (see Maimonides, MT Laws Concerning Original Acquisition and Gifts, chapter 9). It follows that this dedication is void, and her relative shall inherit her estate. A midrash states: When building the temple, Solomon used none of the [materials] dedicated by his father, David (cf. 1 Chron. 28–29), [for] he said: There was a famine in my father's time, lasting three years (2 Sam. 21:1); he should have spent all those dedicated [resources] to sustain the poor ones of Israel.[19]

19. The closest extant source seems to be Midrash Zuta Ruth 2:13.

Renewing the Educational and Scholarly Institutions

20. Valladolid Synod of 1432

Louis Finkelstein, *Jewish Self-Government in the Middle Ages* (New York: Jewish Theological Seminary, 1924), pp. 350–55.

The persecution and pogroms of 1391 began the long decline of the Jews of Christian Spain. In 1432, a synod of community leaders met in Valladolid in an effort to repair and renew communal institutions. These are the takkanot *they adopted for the educational system; it is doubtful that the new rules were ever successfully enforced. Note the effort to ensure the independence of the advanced scholar and teacher from the leaders of the community, so that "he may reprove them."*

The first of our decisions and the beginning of our *takkanot* has for its object the maintenance of the students of our Torah. For it is upon the Torah that the world is founded, as the Sages say. "On three things the world stands, on the Torah, on Divine Service, and on acts of kindness" [Mishnah Avot 1:2]. Whereas we saw that the hands of the students of the Torah have slackened in most places, and that they obtain their livelihood only with extreme pain, and that for this reason the pupils are becoming constantly fewer, and even the children of the primary schools are idle in many places because their parents cannot afford to pay the salary of those who might teach them the Torah, and the Torah will almost have been forgotten in Israel because of these reasons, [therefore] in order to "bring back the crown to its ancient glory" and so that there may be found scholars in Israel and students may increase in the Communities, we ordain that each of the Communities of the entire kingdom of Castile shall be obliged to establish . . . a Voluntary Fund for Talmud Torah [elementary school] in the following manner. For every head of large cattle which is slaughtered as *kasher* among them and for them, they should pay for Talmud Torah five *maravedis* [Iberian coins of gold or silver]; for every calf or heifer that weighs one hundred pounds, which are equivalent to twenty-five *arreldes,* they should pay for Talmud Torah two *maravedis;* and for each head of small cattle, a *wether,* a sheep, a he-goat, or a she-goat, they should pay one *maravedi.* For each small goat or sheep weighing less than four *arreldes,* they should pay for Talmud Torah one *conrado* [copper coin equaling one-sixth of a *maravedi*]. If it weigh four *arreldes* or more, they should pay five pence. For each jug of wine which is sold at retail—if more than five jars are sold at one time, it may be considered wholesale—they should pay to the Talmud Torah three pence per jar. If over five jars are sold, whether to individual Jews or to Jewish muleteers and traders, they should pay to the said Talmud Torah two *dinars*. But of the wine that is sold to Christians, they should pay half a penny for each jar to the Talmud Torah.

Whoever makes a wedding shall pay ten *maravedis* within the wedding week. For a circumcision they shall pay to the Talmud Torah ten *maravedis* as soon as the child reaches the stage when he is no longer to be considered a *nefel*.[20] If one of either sex dies above the age of ten years, his or her heirs shall give to the Talmud Torah the dress which was worn above the under-shirt or ten *maravedis,* as the heirs may choose. Whoever gives more than the above amount deserves a blessing. The tax is to be paid in the coins current or in use at the time of payment. The above-mentioned payments of the bridegroom or of one celebrating a circumcision or in the case of death are not to be collected from such as derive their maintenance from charity or such as are fit to receive charity in the opinion of the treasurers who are appointed over these taxes.

We ordain that each community shall be obliged to assemble by announcement according to their custom, ten days before the expiration of the terms of the farmers of the wine and meat tax. And they shall not disband until they have let out the tax for the Talmud Torah Fund, so that through their hands there may be accomplished whatever the Rabbi of the Court may ordain or command in regard to it.

In those places where there is no tax on meat and wine, we ordain that within thirty days after the day when this ordinance is shown to them, they shall assemble by announcement as has been mentioned and establish an ordinance in regard to the Talmud Torah in accordance with what has been set forth above.

Moreover do we ordain that in those places where there are less than ten families, there shall be established the said Talmud Torah Fund as in all

20. An infant who dies before the age of thirty days is called a *nefel;* no formal burial is required.

the other communities in the manner described. That amount they shall be obliged to deliver each year so long as this ordinance is in force to the treasurers of the Community to whom they pay ordinary taxes and they shall take a receipt for the amount which they have given.

In those places where there are ten families or more, although they pay taxes to another community, they shall be obliged to name among themselves a treasurer in whose hands they shall entrust the Talmud Torah Fund and they shall keep the money until the Rabbi of the Court shall give orders as to how it should be used, so that the said Talmud Torah Fund may be in general use throughout the Communities of the Kingdom of Castile.

And we ordain that neither a community nor any individual shall be authorized to use the funds of the Talmud Torah, even a single *maravedi* of it, for any need that may arise whether public or private, either as a loan or in any other way, but that all the money should rather be in cash ready to be used for the purpose which the Rabbi of the Court shall order.

But in those places where there are Rabbis teaching the Torah appointed over the Community, they may give and pay to the said Rabbi or to the pupils their maintenance from the said Talmud Torah Fund; after the above mentioned amounts have been paid, [the fund] shall be kept for use as the Rabbi of the Court will ordain, as has been said.

Moreover, we ordain that if the Rabbi of the Court sees fit he may ordain that such communities as have a Rabbi shall pay him his salary in a different manner and should not use for that purpose the funds of the Talmud Torah. They shall then pay the salary of the Rabbi from the taxes on meat and wine or from the income of the *hekdesh* or rents from houses and the like if they have any.

PRIMARY SCHOOL TEACHERS

Every community of fifteen families shall maintain a proper teacher for the children of primary school age, who shall instruct them in Scripture. They shall allow him a reasonable salary according to his needs. The fathers of the children shall pay the teacher each according to their means, and if the amount paid by the fathers is insufficient for the maintenance of the teacher, the community shall be obliged to pay the remainder necessary for his livelihood.

RABBIS

A community having forty families or more shall be obliged to endeavor so far as possible to maintain among themselves a Rabbi who will teach them Halakhot and Aggadot. The community must maintain him reasonably. His salary shall be paid from the income of the tax on meat and wine and the income from the *hekdesh,* if there is any, or from the Talmud Torah Fund, so that he should not have to beg his livelihood from any of the leaders of the Community, so that he may reprove them and guide them in all things which pertain to the service of the Creator, blessed be He. If the community and the Rabbi can come to no agreement as to the amount of the salary they shall be obliged to give him the income of the Talmud Torah of the locality and then to increase the amount as may be ordered by the Rabbi of the Court.

TALMUDIC ACADEMY

Moreover we ordain that each Rabbi shall maintain a Talmudical academy where those desirous of learning may study the *halakhah.* He shall lecture at such hours as the Rabbis are wont to lecture.

NUMBER OF PUPILS PER TEACHER

Whereas according to the Talmudic law no teacher is permitted to teach more than twenty-five pupils, unless he have an assistant, therefore we ordain that no teacher shall teach Scripture to more than twenty-five children, but that if he have an assistant he may teach forty in accordance with the law of the Talmud. A community having fifty children shall be obliged to maintain two teachers; the same law applies to any number above forty.

TWENTY-TWO Communal Government

Introduction

Majority Rule

Excluding the Unworthy Heir

1. Isaac b. Yeda'ayah, *Commentary to Midrash Bamidbar Rabbah* 1:26

The Quorum

2. JT Megillah 74a

Unanimity

3. Jacob b. Meir Tam, *Mordechai* Bava Batra 480

The Majority of the Taxpayers Rules

4. Meir b. Baruch of Rothenburg (Maharam), *Responsa* (Prague) 865

Majority Rule

5. Asher b. Yehi'el (Rosh), *Responsa* 6:5

The One, the Few, and the Many—Which Majority?

The Few as the Majority

6. Asher b. Yehi'el (Rosh), *Responsa* 7:3

One Man—One Vote

7. Elijah Mizrahi (Re'em), *Responsa* 53

The Plutocratic Argument

8. Moses Isserles (Rema), *Shulhan Arukh* HM 163:3

The Few and the Many: Mutual Veto

9. Joshua Falk (Sma), *Sefer Me'irat Einayim, Shulhan Arukh* HM 163:2 n.14

385

Introduction

If the *kahal* was something like the Jewish polis, what was its appropriate regime? And how was this regime supposed to function? These are the questions we mean to pose in this chapter. In Chapter 8, on the "good men of the town," we were concerned with the nature, extent, and legitimacy of secular authority—the position of the political leaders of the *kahal* vis-à-vis the custodians of divine law. What was the relative force or the proper domain of political decision, on the one hand, and of legal interpretation, on the other? This has always been an issue in Judaism, taking many different forms, and we will see it again in Chapter 24, which is focused on the rabbinic and lay courts. But here our concern is with the course of political decision-making. We need to know how the process worked, what were its procedural rules, what was its preferred setting, and who were its leading participants— and we also need to know how all these issues were understood and argued about (they were understood in part, of course, by analogy with the law).

In many historical periods and in many parts of the Diaspora, the political regime under which the Jews lived was imposed from outside the Jewish community, by gentile rulers pursuing their own interests and working from their own ideas about political order. Jewish participation was largely a matter of lobbying (as we would call it) in the king's court—and, often enough, bribing the king's officials or the king himself. Obviously, only the most wealthy and powerful members of the *kahal* could engage in such activities, though these people were occasionally challenged by representatives of less wealthy members, banded together to defend their interests. The politics of the court Jew, what was later called *shtadlanut,* will be taken up in Chapter 28, where we will treat the experience of the *shtadlan* as a key to understanding the meaning of exile. Here we are concerned with the internal politics of the Jewish community. Of course, the positions taken outside, the arrangements negotiated with gentile overlords, still had to be defended inside, and if the arguments made to the king were directed largely to his sense of prudence and self-interest, the arguments made to fellow Jews appealed also to traditional conceptions of what was right.

Hence what we may call the constitutional question, the nature of a just regime, was widely debated: Who governs? The form of the debate is familiar, since it involved, first of all, the hereditary principle, common throughout feudal Europe and often criticized by religious writers—by ecclesiastical reformers in the Christian world, by rabbinic pietists and meritocrats among the Jews. Our first selection, from Isaac b. Yeda'ayah, reflects a challenge of this sort, made in the course of a long political struggle among Spanish Jews. But the debate was not only or most importantly about who should hold office; it was also about who should vote: Who were the effective citizens of the *kahal?* Who (and how many) were the "good men of the town"?

Here the rabbis reiterate in their own idiom the Greek argument about the one, the few, and the many. As with the Greeks, the rule of one—philosopher-king or preeminent sage—is largely confined to the ideal realm. In practice, Jewish writers usually require that the local sage, the "prominent person" (*adam hashuv*), be consulted; they disagree about whether (or with regard to what issues) his views must be accepted. But in most secular matters, and especially in monetary matters (*mamona*), controversy among laymen was entirely legitimate and best resolved by "following the majority." But what sort of majority was this, whose members were entitled to rule the *kahal?* A majority of whom? It is possible to produce a majority, after all, among any number of people greater than two. The production need not lead to anything like a democratic government; it could as easily make for a government representing the greater number of oligarchs.

But the idea of *producing* a majority either of oligarchs or of democratic citizens is probably alien to Jewish, as it was to Greek, writers. Today we think immediately of the shifting coalitions and ever-new alignments of our own political life, the results of endless bargaining and debate. But the modern version of this kind of politics, the version we are familiar with, grows out of a new pluralism of religions, ideologies, and ethnicities that, along with the old pluralism of social classes, divides society in multiple and crosscutting ways. In ancient and medieval communities, by contrast, one division was paramount, reflected everywhere in the literature: this was the division between rich and poor or between the few and the many. (Some of our texts refer to a middle group, which has not yet emerged, however, into full visibility.) Religion and ethnicity did not divide but rather united the old communities: thus the *kahal* itself, entirely Jewish, segregated within Christendom; and thus the various ethnic *kehillot* within a single city in the years after the exile and dispersion of the Spanish Jews. Individuals and families might feud, but the basic and constant social cleavage in these communities was economic in character.

The most commonly used Hebrew terms for the many and the few are *rov minyan* and *rov binyan*. *Rov* means "majority," so what we have here are two different majorities. The second of these was more often dominant. Literally translated, *rov binyan* means "structural majority"—the phrase describes the rule of the weightier or more powerful or wealthier (*rov mamon*) members, conceived as a stable and unified group. These Jewish oligarchs were commonly a coalition of the wealthy and the learned: plutocrats and aristocrats, often from the same families. We will refer to them as the "majority of substance." *Rov minyan* describes the numerical majority (also *rov nefashot*, "majority of persons")—which is only sometimes discovered by counting heads after a public debate, as the responsum by Elijah Mizrahi (Re'em) seems to call for. Most often, the many are conceived as a stable, coherent, preexisting group, whose position is known, because its interests are known, in advance of any political process.

So the issue in the rabbinic writings is whether the *kahal* should be ruled by a majority of substance or a majority of numbers—or by the two together, each with authority in a different area or with a veto over the decisions of the other (see the arguments of Joshua Falk [Sma] and Menahem

Mendel Krochmal, §§9–10). In practice, of course, once either (or both) of these "majorities" was in place, the members turned out to disagree among themselves, and sometimes, at least, they settled their disagreements by voting and "following the majority." In moments of political decision, there must have been majorities and minorities within the two "majorities." But the Rabbis focus less on the actual decision process than on the social character and political rights of the participants.

The argument for the *rov binyan* followed most naturally from the partnership model: these people were entitled to rule because they paid most of the taxes, dealt with the non-Jewish overlords, and (given their learning as well as their wealth) filled most of the offices of the *kahal*. The argument for the *rov minyan* followed from the brotherhood and covenantal models: all Israel had stood at Sinai, accepted the law, and so constituted themselves as a community of brethren, responsible for one another (see ¢1, §12). There was also a practical argument, advanced on behalf of the many, as it had been on behalf of the plebes of ancient Rome: without them, the community could hardly survive. If we deny the vote to the many, wrote Menahem Mendel Krochmal in one of the selections included here (but he calls them *am ha- aretz,* "the ignorant," since he saw no problem about enfranchising the relatively small number of learned poor), they will simply walk away and set up a community of their own!

Despite this possibility, it was most often the oligarchs who ruled: the "good men" were men of substance. But the synagogue was a democratic assembly, and some issues of common interest were discussed there (it was there, too, that individual members of either "majority" could, and frequently did, interrupt the service to protest communal decisions). When the rabbis wrote about the decision process, they seem to have had this assembly or something like it in mind, though they often understood the assembly, as we have already suggested, in terms derived from arguments about the courts. The texts reprinted below by Solomon b. Abraham Adret (Rashba) and Solomon b. Abraham Hakohen (Maharshakh) (on the courts) and by Benjamin Aryeh Hakohen Weiss (on assemblies and "parliaments") describe a public discussion where the attendance and participation of the relevant people—in the case of the assembly, all the male members of the *kahal*—are required (see §§11–13). Indeed, the descriptions have a normative purpose: the authors suggest that the participants must argue actively with one another. Weiss, interpreting a talmudic passage rarely cited in this context, insists that every decision must be opposed: unanimity is the sign of a missing argument. We have here a Jewish version of what the contemporary philosopher Jürgen Habermas has called an "ideal speech situation" in which, over an indeterminate range of opinions, the reasons of each speaker are accorded equal and respectful attention—so that the best reasons will carry the day.

But arguments like Weiss's are relatively rare in rabbinic writings; he reads secular treatises on "politics," which very few of our authors do (Shimon b. Wolf [Wolfowicz] is probably another). The crucial procedural issue in the literature of the kahal was how to deal with conflicts of interest, not how to deal with political disagreements. The text from Kraków suggests the lengths to which medieval and early modern Jews were prepared to go to make sure that kinship ties and private "deals" did not determine communal policy. But a strong sense of the value of debate and deliberation in the assembly (as opposed to the *bet midrash,* the study hall) is not evident among the rabbis or in the *kahal* documents.

It is uncommon, in fact, in Jewish literature generally, from its biblical beginnings. Deliberation is defended in the early wisdom writings: "In the multitude of counselors, there is safety" (Prov. 11:14). But the prophets are critical of counsel, and when the rabbis call themselves wise, it is not political wisdom (prudence, discretion, calculation) that they have in mind but rather their knowledge of Torah. Of course, any defense of secular authority or of the need to act beyond or even against the Torah in order to meet "the needs of the hour" implies the importance of prudential considerations. But how these considerations are actually to be *considered*—with what procedural safeguards, say—is not a major issue (see Nissim Gerondi, *Derashot* 11 [¢3, §16], and Menachem Lorberbaum's accompanying commentary, "The Price of Politics"). Insofar as it is discussed at any length, the reference is to the courts rather than to the *kahal,* as we will see in the next chapters.

The *kahal* is the assumed, sometimes the explicit, political unit in these texts. But in fact its independence is an issue that diaspora Jews had to confront again and again. Very small *kehillot* were often ruled by some larger and more powerful neighbor—though the justice of this sort of rule was sometimes disputed (see ¢8, §11). And in some communities important decisions were made by different ethnic congregations rather than by the *kahal* as a whole. In Poland and Lithuania, prompted by their gentile rulers, the Jews experimented with a large-scale federation of communities, the Council of the Four Lands (Va'ad Arba Aratzot). From the mid-sixteenth until the mid-eighteenth century, the leading *kehillot* sent representatives to provincial and then to national assemblies, where they debated a wide range of issues and made binding decisions on questions of taxation, commerce, consumption, book publishing, education, and other civil and also ritual matters. The federal regime, like most of the *kehillot,* was strongly oligarchic: recent historical work suggests that fewer than 5 percent of Polish Jews voted for their representatives. There was probably opposition to the oligarchs, but we have only meager records of what went on when representatives were chosen and in the assemblies where they met and deliberated. Nathan Hanover's description of the council is highly idealized and, characteristically, does not raise questions about representation, suffrage, or decision procedures.

The rise of the modern state brought an end to Jewish autonomy (the Council of the Four Lands was abolished in 1764) and opened the possibility of emancipation and citizenship in the larger political community. Many Jews embraced this possibility, responding in part to the parochialism of the *kahal* and in part to its oligarchic character. The appeal of Shimon b. Wolf [Wolfowicz] for the dissolution of Jewish self-rule, written in 1789, suggests the influence of revolutionary ideas about equality and church/state separation (§20). For Shimon, the *kahal* is the appropriate unit only for decisions about religious matters (which were, however, more extensive in his mind than they would be for a contemporary secular political theorist); decisions about civil matters belonged to the (gentile) state. Simon Dubnow tried to revive both the idea of self-rule (fully democratized now) and the federalist model in the early twentieth century; his "autonomist" doctrine was meant to serve as a diasporic alternative to Zionism (§21). The destruction of European Jewry doomed that idea, which no sovereign state is likely to have accepted in any event. The American Jewish "federations" represent a very partial realization of Dubnow's vision. Morris Loeb invoked the U.S.

constitution rather than the Jewish tradition when he first proposed a federalist governing structure for welfare and philanthropy (§22), but federalism,
as Daniel Elazar has demonstrated, has a long Jewish history. And the debate
about whether the federations should be run by the few or the many is also a
recurrent feature of American Jewish politics.

Majority Rule

Excluding the Unworthy Heir

1. Isaac b. Yeda'ayah, *Commentary to Midrash Bamidbar Rabbah* 1:26

This sermon criticizing a midrashic interpretation of primogeniture and hereditary rule
takes as its point of departure the story of Nadab and Abihu's death by a fire that "came
forth from the Lord" (Lev. 10:2). Scripture says that the two sons of Aaron brought an
"alien" offering in the Tabernacle—for which they are duly punished. Later on, the book
of Numbers (3:4–5) states that as "they left no sons . . . Eleazar and Ithamar [their
brothers] . . . served as priests" in their stead. The midrash takes the verse to emphasize
that the younger brothers assumed the priesthood because the older ones were found un-
worthy of office and thereby removed. In typical sermonic style, Isaac strings together cita-
tions and paraphrases of biblical verses.

"So it was Eleazar and Ithamar who served as priests" (Num. 3:4)—"since
whoever has precedence in inheritance takes precedence in honors, so long
as he behaves in accordance with the traditions of his forefathers" (*Midrash
Bamidbar Rabbah* 1:26).

It is a convention among every nation, "each people in its own language" (Esther 1:22), to give honor to the eldest son "that his mother and
father have borne" (Zech. 13:3), "and on the day that a man passes his legacy
on to his sons" (Deut. 21:16), "the rich man in his riches" (Jer. 9:22) will give
his firstborn "ten measures" (2 Sam. 19:44) and to the rest of his sons will
give legacies according to his wealth, "whether great or small" (1 Sam. 14:6).

Now kings pass on the monarchy to their eldest sons—even if he is "a foolish firstborn" (BT Bava Batra 126b), "bereft of [the] wisdom" (Prov. 30:2) to rule over his people. The father does not "withhold any good" from him (Jer. 5:25 and Prov. 3:27), and will even ask the nobles to give his son the kingship (cf. 1 Kings 2:22); he will "establish it in his eldest" (Josh 6:26) and parade him on the royal steed "at the king's behest" (Jon. 3:7) during the old king's lifetime to show the people that his son is to rule after him (after 1 Kings 1:13), when his father dies, even if the firstborn is not worthy to be king. . . . And the king appoints [as] local governors "men of truth . . . who will judge the people" (Exod. 18:21–22) so that "their ways will not become corrupted" (Joel 2:7).

Here, "giving wisdom to the simple-minded" (Prov. 1:4), the eldest son inherits in place of the father who died while his own aged father was yet alive and inherits the portion of his grandfather's estate that was due his father—thus precluding his uncles and cousins. And this principle holds true with regard to succession in high office as well, if his father "was priest to the High God" (Gen. 14:18) or *nasi* of a tribe with coercive power over his people, "and dies in his prime" (Job 21:23), the son will succeed his father regarding every holy matter and minister in his father's place, provided that he will truly take his father's place in worthiness and greatness, and be wiser than his father's brothers, and know the Most High's counsel. And if his uncle is worthier in the eyes of God "and is greater in wisdom" (Prov. 9:9), he will take precedence to wear the best clothes, the priestly robes (after Lev. 21:10) while the eldest son of the deceased will return "unto his people" (Ezek. 18:18) like one of them; "his head shall be uncovered" (in mourning) (Lev. 13:45). He will wear neither "the crown of priesthood" (after Mishnah Avot 4:13) nor "the crown of monarchy" (Esther 2:17) that he had sought. . . .

This intended goal, as mandated by the Torah, is the opposite of that which obtains among every other nation, who honor the eldest son above the rest—even if he is "a foolish son" (Prov. 17:25), a simpleton who knows nothing—because God does not choose "the fool [who] walks in darkness" (Eccles. 2:14) "to do him honor" (Esther 6:6). Not like those "who are wise in their own eyes" (Isa. 5:21), our kinsmen who seek the Torah without preparation, [without] the rational insight that brings "truthful understanding,"[1] who "walk in the ways of the gentiles" (Lev. 20:23). They bring the sons of the *nesi'im* in place of their fathers "who acted rightly" (Eccles. 8:10) "and call them by their father's title" (Gen. 48:16) as *nasi,* even if the son "is panting after the wind" (Jer. 2:24) from morning to night and his heart has not in all his days "seen or sought wisdom and understanding" (Eccles. 1:16), [even if he] arises to play at the gaming tables,[2] "from night to night" (Ps. 19:3), and looks for his salvation to worthless things (after Exod. 5:9). And yet he is called *nasi* among his people because his father was "the *nasi* of God" (Gen. 23:6) on account of "the wisdom and greatness that were his own strength" (Eccles. 7:19). . . . And now when it comes to his son who rises after him, "who makes his company" (Job 34:8) with men who have neither reputation nor heart,[3] they will "teach their tongues to lie" (Jer. 9:4) and call him *nasi;* because the title of *nasi* brings with it greatness and elevation over one's peers, and if those attributes are not present, how in truth can he be called *nasi?* "Honor does not well suit the fool" (Prov. 26:1). Nowadays the Shabbat and Scroll of the Torah are profaned by him, inasmuch as he is called to the Torah by the leader of the services "in front of all the people" (Exod. 19:11), "the *nasi* of the day" (Num. 7:11), and "blesses God" (Job 1:5) "and makes light of Him—as one makes fun of a man" (Job 13:9), by honoring with the Torah one whom God despises, who has not filled his parent's empty place.

Regarding this matter, Moses "enlightened every blind eye" (Isa. 42:7) when he said of Phinehas that "he had been zealous on God's behalf" (Num. 25:13) and mindful of his Creator's honor. He thrice repeated his praise and mentioned Phinehas's forebears, Aaron and Eleazar, who had raised him to resemble them "to follow after God" (1 Kings 11:6), and so he was chosen "to minister after his forebears" (Lev. 16:32) in "the King's sanctuary" (Ps. 45:12). And he [Moses] taught the people by God's command that the son of the priest or the prophet will be called by his father's title if he "walks in righteousness" (Prov. 10:9) before God; then he may justly rule in his father's place because he is suited to it.

1. Prov. 22:21, i.e., philosophical insight.
2. After Exod. 3:26 and Mishnah Sanhedrin 3:3.
3. A composite reference to Num. 16:2 and Job 30:8.

From the positive we see the negative and understand well from "the Torah that enlightens simpletons" (Ps. 19:8) that the son born to a priest or prophet [who] is not worthy of their position "will not enter His sanctuary" (Ezek. 44:9). "The King has no desire to see him elevated" (Esther 6:6), because the priest is chosen not according to his impressive stature or handsomeness but for his wisdom—if it has stood him in good stead, is well in his hand, [and if] "he has feared God from his youth and avoided evil" (Job 1:1).

The Quorum

2. JT Megillah 74a

This talmudic discussion refers to the mishnah authorizing the sale of public property (including a synagogue) by the "townspeople" (¢8, §4). But who are the townspeople whose consent is necessary to validate the sale?

Three of the synagogue [members] are equal to the [entire] synagogue; seven of the townspeople are equal to the [entire] town.

What is the case? If they accepted [these three or seven] over themselves—even one [should suffice]! If they did not accept [them] upon themselves—even many [should not suffice]!

Rather, the case is one in which [the scope of their authority] was not specified.[4]

---

4. I.e., a body of three or seven individuals was appointed for overseeing collective affairs, but the terms of appointment did not specifically authorize the sale of such public assets as holy objects.

Unanimity
3. Jacob b. Meir Tam, *Mordechai* Bava Batra 480

Tam was the strongest advocate of the partnership model of the kahal: *the partners, on his view, could not collect money from one another, spend it for any common purpose, or sell or buy property except by unanimous agreement. Only leading halakhic figures (such as himself in his generation) are empowered to expropriate.*

Attributed to Rabbenu Tam: "The townspeople . . . are authorized to enforce their decree" (BT Bava Batra 8b, ¢8, §§2–3) . . . i.e., in the case of a preexisting stipulation among themselves; however, if they did not stipulate [their readiness to accept the decrees] from the outset, the townspeople have no power to force one of their townsmen to act in accordance with their will. And regarding the maxim "The court has the power to expropriate," it is stated (BT Gittin 36b, ¢6, §15) that this applies [only] to courts like those of Rav Ami and Rav Assi who have the power of expropriation. [Should you ask, is it not stated: "'You shall appear before the priests [that shall be in those days]' (Deut. 17:9) — Would it even occur to you that [one should go to a judge who is not in those days? This shows that you must be content to go to the contemporary judge . . .]" (BT Rosh Hashanah 35b)? This applies so long as there is no one as great in the later generation. However, even if there are [judges] as great in the later generation, they [the townspeople] are not empowered to expropriate.

The Majority of the Taxpayers Rules
4. Meir b. Baruch of Rothenburg (Maharam), *Responsa* (Prague) 865

Here the rule of the majority is firmly established, though only taxpayers are allowed to vote in the kahal's *assembly. There is no need for unanimity — but note that the initial question establishes that there is also no possibility of unanimity. The* kahal *is no longer a small "partnership" whose participants can negotiate until they reach a consensus. It is now a complex political community.*

You have asked: Strife runs high in your community, and [the members] can come to no agreement and cannot unanimously elect their leaders. One says one thing, another says something else. Because of this disagreement, the daily service is interrupted; the rule of law is impaired; neither truth, nor judgment, nor peace prevails in this town or throughout the kingdom in its wake. What shall be done?

In my opinion, the taxpaying householders should be convened, and each of them should commit by oath [to the following]: that he will express his opinion [and be motivated] solely for the sake of heaven [with no ulterior motives but only] to further the well-being [*takkanah*] of the community. The householders should follow the majority to select their officers, and the officers shall . . . build or destroy [aught] in the synagogue, add or subtract in acquiring a [community] wedding hall or guild house, or institute . . . any other communal needs, acting in accordance with the householders' directives [and all their pronouncements should be treated in good faith by the minority]. Should the minority refuse stubbornly to keep [the directives] and perform them, this majority, or its appointed leaders, is empowered to coerce or to force them, whether through Israelite judges or the judges of the nations, until they say, "We consent." . . .

Should anyone refuse to express his opinion under the aforesaid oath, his opinion is null, and the majority of those who have taken the oath shall be followed.

To sum up: "The townspeople," says the Tosefta (Bava Metzia 11:23), may force one another to provide for [the public needs of their town]. This even if they are not urgent needs; how much more so with regard to matters that are necessities!

Majority Rule
5. Asher b. Yehi'el (Rosh), *Responsa* 6:5

Following earlier writers, Asher (re)constructs Exodus 23:2 to provide a proof text for majority rule. The verse reads, "You shall not follow the majority to do evil." The Rabbis took this to mean that you should follow the majority to do good, and on the assumption that good was being done, formulated the maxim "Follow the majority." The Hebrew word rabim *means both "many," in the sense of "the public," and "majority," and this duality is central to the argument.*

You asked whether two or three average members of the town can remove themselves from any communal agreement[5] or from a decree of excommunication issued for any cause. Know that with respect to the public (*rabim*) business, Scripture states, "Follow the majority" (*rabim*) (Exod. 23:2). And with respect to any matter about which the *kahal* needs to reach agreement, we follow the majority; individuals are required to fulfill whatever [obligations] the public (*rabim*) has agreed to with respect to them. For if this were not so, that is, if individuals had the power to nullify [collective] agreements, the *kahal* would never reach agreement. For this reason, the Torah states that in all cases where the public (*rabim*) has to agree, the rule is to "follow the majority" (*rabim*).

The One, the Few, and the Many—Which Majority?

The Few as the Majority
6. Asher b. Yehi'el (Rosh), *Responsa* 7:3

It turns out that there are two majorities or, better, two groups (the taxpayers alone and the taxpayers with everyone else) out of which majorities can be formed—and each ma-

5. Heb., *haskamah*. In medieval texts the word means either enactment or agreement.

jority has, so to speak, its own jurisdiction. But the crucial decisions about raising and spending money are made by the first majority.

Question: When a *kahal* imposes a ban, is it dependent on a majority or can it be rescinded by a minority? And are we to follow the majority even if the matter involves money and the rich are the minority?

Answer: [With respect to] the imposition of a *herem* by a *kahal*, if it has to do with financial matters we follow the majority of money [*rov hamamon*]. It is similar to the [case of the] caravan traveling through the wilderness that is threatened by a band of robbers [—with respect to which it was decided, in BT Bava Kama 116b (¢21, §2), that] the contribution to be paid [by each person for buying off the robbers] is apportioned in accordance with the amount of each person's possessions [rather than by all persons equally]. Here, too, since the *herem* relates to monetary needs, we follow the majority of money. It is unreasonable that the majority of persons who contribute the minority of taxes should [be able to] decree a *herem* upon the wealthy as they see fit.

One Man—One Vote

7. Elijah Mizrahi (Re'em), *Responsa 53*

Jewish Law: History, Sources, Principles, translated by Bernard Auerbach and Melvin J. Sykes, vol. 2 (Philadelphia: JPS, 1994), p. 701; reprinted by permission of the University of Nebraska Press; copyright 1994 by Menachem Elon.

Writing in Constantinople in the late fifteenth or early sixteenth century, Mizrahi argues against the two-majorities-for-two-jurisdictions doctrine. He seems to support a democratic decision process, a rare position in his time and place.

The community as a body is denominated a court in these [communal] matters. Its members are like judges at a session of court, who may not shirk their judicial responsibilities notwithstanding a difference of opinion as to whether something should be declared pure or impure or whether the defendant should be found innocent or guilty. They must cast their vote; and the decision of the majority governs, in accordance with the instruction of our holy Torah to "follow the majority" (Exod. 23:2). Hence, one who refuses to follow the majority is considered a sinner. It makes no difference whether the majority consists of the wealthy, the poor, the scholarly, or the unlettered, because the entire community is denominated a court in dealing with matters of communal interest.

The Plutocratic Argument

8. Moses Isserles (Rema), *Shulhan Arukh* HM 163:3

In his authoritative glosses on the Shulhan Arukh, *Moses Isserles adopts the argument of Asher b. Yehi'el (Rosh), in effect codifying it and creating the foundation for the ensuing arguments.*

With respect to all [payments] that are assessed on the basis of money, we follow the majority of money, and the wealthy people, who represent the minority of persons, are considered the majority in these issues.

The Few and the Many: Mutual Veto

9. Joshua Falk (Sma), *Sefer Me'irat Einayim, Shulhan Arukh* HM 163:3 n.14

Falk was a student of Moses Isserles (Rema), whose text he is here interpreting and revising. He was also active in the Council of the Four Lands during the first century of its existence, and so his effort to work out a compromise between the few and the many may reflect his actual political/legal work.

"And the wealthy people, who represent the minority of persons [are considered the majority]." An examination of the responsum by Rosh (§6 above) shows that these words [cited by Isserles] are not without context; rather, he responded [specifically] to the question put to him, as to whether a *herem* imposed by a *kahal* is considered a majority [vote] if the minority—the wealthy—contests it. He replied, "Since the *herem* relates to monetary needs, we follow the majority of money. It is unreasonable that the majority of persons who contribute the minority of taxes, should [be able to] decree a *herem* upon the wealthy as they see fit." It could be argued that what Rosh [meant] was that we follow the majority [of money] only in cases where the majority of other members of the *kahal* seek to issue decrees oblivious of their [the wealthy members'] position. However, he did not state that the wealthy minority is considered a majority [of money—and is thus empowered] to impose a *herem* on the majority of the *kahal*. It could further be submitted that he reasoned that the [two groups] are each considered [the equivalent of] half [the *kahal*], and that they must compromise with each other in matters such as these.

Reasoned Argument for the "Two Majorities"

10. Menahem Mendel Krochmal, *Responsa Zemah Zedek 2*

Like Joshua Falk, whose position he defends, Krochmal had attended the Council of the Four Lands (in the 1630s). This responsum is one of several, written later in his life when he was chief rabbi of Moravia, in which he rules on issues of communal organization. Krochmal here addresses the attempt to shift the power of decision from the entire body of taxpayers to an aristocracy of the plutocratic and learned. Class distinction, he argues, is not grounds for procedural predominance. The competing claims of the specific classes, the rich and the poor, wealth and exertion, respectively, cancel each other out and so make for equality.

I was asked by a *kahal* whose long-standing custom has been to make all agreements of the *kahal*, [including] the appointment of the rabbi, the cantor, and the *shammash,* by the agreement of all taxpayers. Similarly, the leaders and good men of the town, the officers, the judges, and the *shammashim* are selected by [a committee of] selectors from among all taxpayers by lottery. Now some of the honorable [members of] the town wish to initiate a new custom whereby, from now on, all matters of public needs will no longer be in the hands of the taxpayers generally, small and large, as established heretofore. Instead, they will be in the hands of those [members] of [financial] stature who pay a large amount of taxes or have stature [as scholars] of Torah.

[Krochmal continues to detail the minimum criteria, tax payments, and/or learnedness, said to be necessary to hold public office or serve on a selection committee.]

They reason thus: Since most of the needs of the *kahal* relate to the business of financial expenditure, how is it possible that the opinion of a poor man [should] be equal to the opinion of a rich man? How too is it possible that the opinion of an *am ha-aretz* [should] be equal to that of a *haver*—even if the latter has no wealth? A further plea they put forth for their proposal is that it is the norm[6] of all the great and important communities. . . .

And the poor, a multitude of people, raise an outcry: Why should their rights be diminished, given that they are among the taxpayers who pay their part! And even though the rich pay more, the small [amount] they pay is more difficult for them than is the greater [amount] paid by the rich. Also, the custom [*minhag*] of their fathers has been in place forever, since the early days, and custom [is so strong that it] even overrides *halakhah.* How can [the rich] be permitted to change the custom?

Our teacher, instruct us, with whom is the law?

Answer: It appears that it is not right to act this way, to reject the poor who give a small amount. Proof of this lies in the mishnah at the end of [tractate Menahot (13:11): "[Scripture] refers to a sacrificial offering of an animal as 'an offering by fire, of pleasing odor [to the Lord]' (Lev. 1:9), and to a sacrificial offering of a bird as 'an offering by fire, of pleasing odor [to the Lord]' (Lev. 1:17), in order to teach that those who give more and those who

---

6. Heb., *nohagim,* translated here as a noun not a verb. It may also be rendered "customary."

give less are the same. . . ." It is thus expressly explained that the small amount given by a poor person is equal to the large amount given by the rich person.

Moreover, [it can] even [be said] that [the contribution of the poor person] is greater on the basis of what is written in connection with a meal offering: "When a person [nefesh] presents an offering of meal to the Lord. . . ." (Lev. 2:1). [Commenting on this verse,] our Rabbis . . . said, "The word 'soul' [nefesh] was not used in connection with any voluntary offering except the meal offering. Who usually offers a meal offering? A poor person. God said: 'I consider it as if he had offered his soul'" (BT Menahot 104b). . . . This is because a poor person must labor strenuously[7] to earn what he brings as a meal offering. Scripture therefore states 'soul.'" This is also written in connection with the person [collecting] laborer's wages: "[You must pay him his wages on the same day . . .] for he is poor and his soul [nafsho] depends on it" (Deut. 24:15)—this is not the case with regard to a wealthy person, who brings [a sacrifice] from what is for him ready at hand, with no exertion.

It is for this reason that the Mishnah states, "Those who give more and those who give less [are the same]" (Menahot 13:11). There is no reason for this statement other than to tell you that the one [who gives] less is like the one [who gives] more "so long as [his intent is for the sake of Heaven." This, in turn, must be stated because] there is reason on both [sides of the argument]. There is a reason to say that the donation of the wealthy person is more desired because it is greater, and there is a reason to say that the donation of the poor person is more desired, even though it is smaller, because it is harder for him [to give this smaller amount]. For this reason, [the Mishnah] states that "those who give more and those who give less [are the same]" (BT Menahot 110a)—both are equal. In other words, the donation of the wealthy person is no more satisfying because of its greater amount, as you might have thought, and the donation of the poor person no more satisfying because of [his] exertion, as you might have thought. . . .

The argument of the poor is therefore a worthy argument.

[Krochmal proceeds to consider the positions of Asher b. Yehi'el (§6) and Joshua Falk (§9), emphasizing the latter.]

---

7. Lit., "with his soul."

[Falk] explicitly wrote that the wealthy may not [issue a] decree against the poor, [who are] the majority of the *kahal,* just as the majority [of the *kahal*]—the poor—may not [issue a] decree against the wealthy, [who are] the minority. This is because there are two majorities [to be considered]: the majority of persons and the majority of wealth, and the two are equal. The custom has therefore been established in most *kehillot* in this land that, for appointing the rabbi, cantor, and *shammash,* a majority is not considered to exist unless there is an agreement of both the *rov binyan* and the *rov minyan*—"*rov minyan*" is the majority of persons, and "*rov binyan*" is the majority of wealth—because these two [majorities] are considered equal. Were we to follow the majority of persons, would they not be canceled out by the . . . majority of money? Were we to follow the wealthy, are they not canceled out by the poor, who represent a majority of persons? Therefore, both [majorities] are needed. . . .

Their desire to reject [the poor] because they are not learned in Torah is also not right. Support for this is found in [BT] Haggigah 22a. . . . "R. Papa said: On whose authority do we accept today the testimony of an *am ha-aretz?* This is the opinion of R. Yose. . . . And R. Yose's reason is to prevent each and every individual from going and erecting his own altar." This explains that even testimony is accepted from the *am ha-aretz* out of a fear of enmity,[8] [for] if they see that they are rejected, they will split off from the community.[9] How much more so in the case at hand! If the *amme ha-aretz* are rejected to such a degree that they are barred from all participation in the agreements of the *kahal,* it is certain that they will feel hatred and will erect their own alter and separate themselves from the community, with the result that dissension will be multiplied in Israel, God forbid.[10] Therefore, it is definitely not right to act this way.

8. See ¢16, §§15, 17.
9. Lit., "build their own altar."
10. See ¢6, §10.

Decision Rules

The Importance of Deliberation
11. Solomon b. Abraham Adret (Rashba), *Responsa* 2:104

This extraordinary defense of deliberation ("give-and-take") may derive from the experience of the talmudic academies and the medieval yeshivas, where argumentation was the key means of halakhic learning. Or it may derive from Adret's extensive experience in Hispano-Jewish politics. In any case, it seems to be a new position; the earlier defenses of majority rule in the kahal *do not explicitly consider a deliberative decision process.*

You asked: two litigating parties designated ten men to oversee their case to its solution, whether through adjudication or compromise. They swore to uphold whatever those ten men say and decree, with the proviso that if [the arbitrators] could not agree unanimously, they would follow the majority, which is Torah law. As things turned out, one of the ten refused the designation and would not issue his opinion on the matter at hand. Are the disputants obligated to accept the opinion of the remaining nine (or the majority thereof), or has the departure of the one invalidate the entire [procedure]? For a disputant could argue that had my missing designee been present, he could conceivably have provided the best argument for my rights, on my behalf?

Answer: It is clear that had these ten been designated as judges, and one of them had absented himself, [the panel] is dissolved; and what's more, even if [the tenth man had remained, but] said, "I do not know [how to decide]," the remaining nine may not judge nor deliver decision. For we do not follow the majority unless the majority (whatever its direction) established itself through a [deliberative process] of give-and-take involving them all. But when the minority is [simply] absent, we do not [follow the majority], for if it had been present, it might have overturned the consensus with a contrary argument bringing about their concession; and so too with one who says, "I don't know how to decide." As the Mishnah states: "Even if two [out of three judges] vote for acquittal or conviction, and one [of the three] says, 'I don't know'—more judges shall be added [to the panel]" (Sanhedrin 3:6).

And the case is the same if one of the judges absents himself, the [remaining] two judges acting by themselves may not render judgment. . . .

The same applies to arbitration—for what is the difference? Given that we never [recognize] a majority of an entire [body] unless it is [produced] through a [deliberative process of] give-and-take. But a majority that has set itself apart, that judges or arbitrates unto itself without engaging the whole in give-and-take, [arguing only] in their absence, has done nothing at all.

The Importance of Deliberation: Rejecting the Secret Ballot
12. Solomon b. Abraham Hakohen (Maharshakh), *Responsa* 2:109

The understanding of the "small town" discussed here was that the maxim "follow the majority" means: be it as it may—rich or poor. No regard was to be given to the kind of majority at hand, numerical or substantive. Yet the deliberative process in this community was remiss: "For they do not say let us band together in one convocation and examine the majority opinion thereby nullifying the minority . . . Rather they convene in the absence of the minority, and when they seem to have established a majority amongst themselves they follow their heart's desire, the minority knowing nothing of the matter." The immediate issue is the repeal of a prior communal agreement. Hakohen cites precedents by Solomon b. Abraham Adret (Rashba) and Isaac b. Sheshet Perfet (Rivash) and then delivers his main argument:

In the case at hand, the community's agreement is not abrogated, notwithstanding the majority's decision to do so, because when we say that a majority is empowered to enact against the will of the protesting minority, that is only if they were all together in the same convocation, and they [deliberated], engaging in give and take, and then the majority consensus emerged in favor of abrogation. In such a case we say that the majority rules. But in the case at hand, where they did not all convene in the convocation, but rather the *shammash* went from individual to individual separately, as mentioned in the query, and as was reported to me orally, then definitely in such a case it is clear that the majority decision to abrogate ought not have any effect. . . .

And there is a good reason for my opinion, because it is possible that if they had all convened together, many of those who opted for abrogation might have been swayed by the arguments of those who opposed it, or that in their assemblage, the opponents would have outnumbered the proponents.

And so it is not right to say that the greater number outweighs the lesser unless they are assembled together and argue by give-and-take and through that process the agreement of the majority emerges, whether for or against. Only then is it really considered a majority. But with respect to things done covertly, outside a general assembly, as in the case at hand, they do not have the status of a majority, such that it would outweigh the minority.

All I have written applies even when the minority [that was not consulted] consists of common people of no noted excellence and importance. How much more so in our case, where the agreement disregarded the opinion of men of stature and excellence.

The Need for Parliamentary Opposition
13. Benjamin Aryeh Hakohen Weiss, *Even Yekarah* 20

Weiss, a rabbinic judge in Chernowitz (in the Austro-Hungarian Empire), here documents a remarkable discussion of parliamentary and judiciary majorities with a "learned gentile" that is informed by Weiss's reading of the works of "gentile sages" about politics. Weiss argues that unanimity is the sign of a faulty deliberation.

I was asked by a learned gentile about the passage in BT Sanhedrin (17a) that says that if [in a capital case] all the judges vote to convict, the defendant is acquitted, a result that seems to fly in the face of reasoned, logical judgment. Thus, for example, if in a Sanhedrin of 71 judges, a simple majority of 37 over

34 voting to convict would result in a conviction, a decision by all 71 to convict would result in an acquittal!

I answered that he was quite right [about the talmudic ruling]. According to what was said in a book by one of the ancient gentile sages, in the part discussing state government, any assembly that does not have an opposition, a minority opposed to the majority, does not fulfill its calling, and should be dissolved and new assemblymen appointed. Because in the nature of things, every man is capable of error—and not only individuals; in any given matter, large groups can err as well. And so there is a need for sifting the truth from conflicting arguments, as the holder of each respective opinion strives to establish his view through arguments and analogies and thus vanquish opposing views. And if, after the airing of differing views, the majority chooses to accept one of them, it is clear that that is the true one. But this is not the case if only one view is presented without opposing evidence and arguments, [for] that does not create the debate necessary for determining true views. After all, all their intellects could have been captivated by error, thus being mistaken in judgment, and so the assembled group has not fulfilled its required goal.

Thus the words of our sages are quite just. For the Sanhedrin was a gathering of sages with the responsibility to adjudicate matters of life and death: whether to afflict or to show mercy. Hence, if with regard to a given matter, some moved to convict and others to acquit, there was then a genuine debate necessary to arrive at the truth. Then, if after [the debate], the majority of sages gathered there agreed to convict the defendant standing before them, their judgment is free of doubt, and the defendant is definitely guilty, and their decision is true and their judgment just. But if there were only judges voting to convict, with nobody to contest their view, no one working to demonstrate the truth of alternative reasoning, it is only natural that they may all have erred, and thus that they will spill an innocent's blood. And so their words are just, [namely] that if all of them vote to convict, the defendant shall go free and not be condemned by the judgment of this panel, which may simply be seeing things incorrectly.

And my wise interlocutor saw my point [about our sages] and proceeded to sing their praises.

Commentary. The Meaning and Value of Deliberation

Deliberation in public life is often associated with judicial proceedings in which arguments are aired by parties on opposing sides of an issue, after which judges render reasoned decisions in light of the arguments. These three texts transplant the deliberative model from courts to politics more generally and in so doing argue that in legislative politics a majority produced by deliberation is more legitimate than any other majority, even more legitimate than unanimity.

Solomon b. Abraham Adret considers a controversy in which the disputants agree to abide by the will of the majority of arbitrators. Why, in light of their agreement, is majority rule not a sufficient standard for a binding decision? If majority rule were valued as a normatively neutral procedure that moves a collective body in the direction determined by the greater force of the greater number, then counting votes would be sufficient for a legitimate outcome, regardless of the number of participants or the quality of the discussion.

Adret rightly suggests that the purpose of collective decision-making is typically more than determining a direction in which to move. The purpose is to arrive at a substantively good decision that can be publicly justified before the opposing parties to a dispute. At least, this moral purpose makes sense of Adret's two provisos on majority rule, that it is legitimate if and only if: (1) all those responsible for arbitrating a dispute actually take part in the decision, voicing an opinion on the matter; and (2) each engages with all the others in a deliberative process of give-and-take. Solomon Hakohen extends the same argument to legislatures, also emphasizing the importance of a give-and-take discussion among the entire group and the illegitimacy of mere majority rule.

Let's consider the two provisos separately. Why do abstentions or absentees call the legitimacy of a decision into question? Because any abstention or absentee potentially deprives the other decision-makers of an argument or point of view relevant to the decision. Doesn't this answer fall prey to the foolishness of believing that a stipulated number of decision-makers guarantees a good outcome? Decision-makers may after all abstain, as Adret recognizes, because they don't know how to decide, or because they don't have an opinion on the disputed matter, or because they have an interest in the outcome of the dispute. Surely it's better that they abstain than fabricate an opinion or argue their own interest. Were they to offer an opinion under these circumstances, the decision would be worse, not better. So more opinions are not necessarily better. They are better only if all the decision-makers actually have views worthy of consideration or are replaced by others who do.

The first proviso also depends on a distinctive conception of public justification, a conception at the heart of the social contract tradition in political philosophy. Were a good decision justifiable apart from the process that produced it, then Adret's idea that a missing opinion destroys the legitimacy of a decision would be mistaken, if not downright foolish. But good decisions in public life are typically not justifiable simply on their merits, because reasonable people disagree on the merits of most cases that appear before courts, arbitration panels, and legislatures. All the more important, therefore, that public institutions designate some set number of opinions that must be obtained before a decision can be publicly justified, both to the parties to a dispute and to those directly affected by the decision. Public justification often depends on authorities being able to say not that the decision is correct beyond a reasonable doubt but that the disputed matter has been given the benefit of full discussion by the same number of reliable people that is afforded every such dispute. Under these circumstances, it would be unreasonable for any interested party to deny the legitimacy of the outcome, even if he does not agree with it. Subjective agreement on, or objective proof of, the merits of most disputed cases is typically too much to reasonably expect in politics. To hold out for the clearly correct outcome is unreasonable in those situations where reasonable disagreement brought the matter into the realm of public adjudication or decision-making in the first place.

This claim brings us to the second proviso: each decision-maker must engage in the give-and-take of argument with every other. Why bother deliberating if reasonable people disagree and subjective agreement or objective proof is generally too much to expect? Why not just have every decision-maker vote, tally the votes, and be done with it? Because it is reasonable to believe that the give-and-take of argument will move decision-makers toward a better view of the matter, even if not to an obviously correct view, than that held by a majority before the deliberations begin. Mere majority rule, absent deliberation, yields less-legitimate decisions by virtue of not taking account of arguments that could have changed the minds of the deliberators or brought better resolutions to light than are obvious to the majority at the outset. The likelihood that better arguments will emerge also helps explain what's wrong with secret deliberations among a subsection of legislators. Secret deliberations interfere with the full give-and-take of argument. It is not just ordinary citizens deliberating together, as Aristotle argues, but also public officials—judges, arbitrators, legislators, "learned men"— deliberating who are more likely to arrive at better decisions than any single person or subgroup judging alone.

These two provisos on majority rule make it something considerably more than a mere procedure. A legitimate majority represents more than the power of numbers alone. The political legitimacy of majorities, on this deliberative model, presumes that the greater number reflects the legitimate moral judgment of reasonable people who have engaged open-mindedly in the give-and take of argument among themselves. The moral force of the greater number is contingent on the give-and-take of argument among all the deliberators, who are presumed to be reasonable and open-minded. Deliberation is the politics of persuasion.

The juxtaposition of mere majority rule with a real majority resembles Jean-Jacques Rousseau's distinction between the will of all and the general will. Rousseau, however, enlists the distinction to make the opposite argument: the general will is more likely to emerge without communication, when each citizen thinks "only his own thoughts." Why? Because communication in politics, on Rousseau's understanding, offers opportunities to create factions that close men's minds to considerations of the common good. Adret and Solomon Hakohen make communication crucial to just decisions presumably because they don't have in mind decision-makers who are prone to vote their economic or other factional interests against the merits of the case or the common good.

Suppose we take into account Rousseau's concern for factionalism as an obstacle to the common good. We still might ask whether deliberation among all legislators conduces to more or less destructive factionalism. And we might surmise that the particular interests of legislators are less likely to interfere with their full consideration of the merits of a case in a deliberative forum, where all are obligated to participate in the give-and-take of argument, to make their case before the entire group, and to render a reasoned decision. Granting that politics is about power, not just persuasion, deliberation may still be the most effective antidote to the exercise of power on behalf of factional interests. Factions are likely to operate more effectively against the common good when legislative bodies do not deliberate or when a subgroup secretly deliberates. The moral norms of genuine majority rule, as captured by Adret and Solomon Hakohen, provide some unintended protection against the invidious effects of factionalism that, pace Rousseau, cannot effectively or justly be submerged by stifling discussion. Deliberation cannot guarantee unanimity, but it can expose bad arguments that serve interests antithetical to justice.

A paradox now emerges from the arguments favoring public deliberation, which Benjamin Weiss's responsum directly addresses. If deliberative give-and-take is designed to bring the best arguments to light, and the decision-makers are reasonable people, then why not conclude that the more unanimous the decision, the better. If a majority decision favoring x is authoritative, then how can one reasonably conclude that a unanimous decision favoring x is illegitimate? Weiss does not doubt that the decision-makers are reasonable people; the learned men of the Sanhedrin inspire this deliberative model. If ten, twenty, or a hundred reasonable people agree, isn't that a reason to be more, rather than less, confident that the decision is justified?

Weiss dissolves the paradox by arguing, in the spirit of John Stuart Mill, that all people, even the wisest, are prone to error, that conflicting arguments often contain partial truths that need "sifting," and that the give-and-take of conflicting arguments therefore creates the "debate necessary for determining true ideas." But this sound Millean argument yields something less than Weiss's conclusion concerning the illegitimacy of unanimous decisions. A deliberative forum that does not deal thoroughly with conflicting arguments is unreliable, and its decisions ought to be suspect. And for decision-makers to deal thoroughly with conflicting arguments, they must begin by disagreeing. But the deliberative model still does not render a unanimous decision suspect unless the process that yields the decision is bereft of conflicting perspectives and the give-and-take of argument among all the participants. We can also surmise that a decision-making body that begins with full debate among conflicting views is unlikely to end with a unanimous decision. But if it did, and if its deliberations were known to satisfy the two provisos, then, far from being suspect, the unanimous decision would be a testimony to the power of reason. Whereas unanimity at the outset of deliberations is generally a bad thing, unanimity in the end may be a symptom of the success, not the failure, of deliberation. The diagnosis must depend on the nature of the deliberations.

With this qualification, Weiss's critique of unanimity is an important antidote to the conventional Rousseauean assumption that the more unanimous the decision, the more reliable. Drawing upon the deliberative model, Weiss rightly deems unreliable a unanimous decision that follows from consideration of "only one view without opposing . . . arguments."

Weiss, however, joins Rousseau in the mistaken conclusion that a legitimate decision is necessarily a true one, "free of doubt." Deliberation may be the most legitimate way to make political decisions, but even the fullest deliberation does not guarantee that ideas free of uncertainty will emerge. Under the best of circumstances, deliberation is an error-reducing, not a truth-guaranteeing or a certainty-producing, process. In politics, where binding decisions must be reached, deliberation can yield legitimate decisions, even if not true or certain ones. The antidote to error and uncertainty in politics is typically not truth and certainty but more and better deliberation.

Amy Gutmann

Tacit Consent of Absentees

14. Moses Sofer, *Responsa Hatam Sofer* HM 116

The principle of tacit consent is invoked here to permit community leaders to carry on the public's business—in this case, by overriding the interests of a few wealthy members. Was it customary for "only some thirty people" to show up at the kahal's general assembly? And were these thirty the effective rulers of the kahal or just a random sample of its members? In any case, the others are represented as choosing not to speak; and so they are legitimately spoken for.

The selectmen of a community wishing to allocate among individuals the burden of the latest exaction imposed by the lord announced several times that all individuals should attend the selectmen's assembly to oversee the manner of allocating the said exaction. In the event, only some thirty people [lit., "householders"] showed up, and they agreed to appoint [a committee of] nine members, three members each from the upper, middle, and lower classes, respectively, who would, along with the selectmen, oversee what is to be done and how it is to be done. This joint committee all agreed to tax one particular form of business, for a reason known to them. The matter also became known publicly and no one protested. Only one wealthy member of the committee objected, insofar as the taxed activity happened to concern him directly. He is contesting the [decision] with the community. [His protest was] joined by one of the selectmen, who was similarly affected. They are litigating and wish to be directed by the law of the holy Torah: Can the community impose upon them against their will?

[Reply:] Prima facie it would seem that the majority are not empowered to cause loss to individuals by imposing upon their businesses, inasmuch as Rabbenu Tam, cited by Mordechai [b. Hillel's codification] in the first chapter of Bava Batra (§3 above), [argued that in order for a community's levy to be binding,] it must originally be enacted unanimously.

[Sofer goes on to discuss at length the opinion of Eli'ezer b. Yoel Halevi ("Avi ha-Ezri"), cited along with Jacob b. Meir Tam in the same discussion of *Mordechai,* who grants the majority greater leeway in allocating tax burdens on unwilling individuals.]

We see, then, that "Avi ha-Ezri" was willing to grant the majority greater authority only to the degree that they are constituted like the leadership of a synagogue, who may go ahead and sell the premises because they were unanimously appointed for that express purpose. In this case, they [the selectmen] had not been appointed for this express purpose, for we see that they made this announcement, inviting all the members to discuss the matter. In fact only some thirty members of the community participated, while the overwhelming majority—four times that number—was left out. Only the thirty who showed up at the meeting vested the committee of nine with authority, and the committee was not even unanimous: the eight are opposed by one. In this sort of case, a majority will not suffice, but rather they must all agree. . . .

Nevertheless, it seems to me that in this case the community has the better of the argument. True, only thirty people came to the assembly, but it is nonetheless clear that once it was publicly announced that all should gather on such and such a day to oversee this particular matter, those who did not show up in effect gave their power and authorization to those who did [to decide on their behalf.] There is a clear proof text for this in BT Ketubot 94a, where it says that if one of two brothers or partners submits a disputed matter to judgment, the other [brother or partner] cannot say: "I am no party to this litigation." The Talmud concludes there that if [the second brother or partner] was in town on that day he was obligated to come, which is to say that he must now accept the ruling against his will. Since he did not arrive [at the discussion, we presume that] he realized and accepted [the consequences of his absence]. And this is the decision of all the *poskim.*

And *Hagahot Maimoniyot* (MT Laws of Agency and Partnership 3:4) writes that this also applies to one who disputes another's right of residence . . . implying that once the townspeople heard [the announcement] and failed to come, they lost their rights, and whatever is decided and imposed on them by the judgment [is their own responsibility.] And so it is in this case and in all similar ones; and all the more so when no protest was ever raised about the decision by the thirty people mentioned who appointed the committee of nine. On the contrary, it suited all members of the community. And even this individual who now protests initially accepted their selection. The upshot is that these nine men have been specifically designated from among all members of the community to handle the matter [on behalf of the others], and their decisions are considered to be like those of the seven good men of the town in the presence of all the townspeople.[11] For "in the presence of all the townspeople" means that they heard and did not protest—and here too no one has protested, except for the two who contested the decision, while all the other townspeople, or most of them, are satisfied.

Conflict of Interest

15. The Holy Community of Kraków: Regulations, 5355 (1595)

Shmuel A. Arthur Cygielman, *Jewish Autonomy in Poland and Lithuania until 1648 (5408)* (Jerusalem: n.p., 1997), pp. 56–59.

Kraków in the late sixteenth century was one of the larger Jewish communities in Poland, with six or seven synagogues and several thousand members. These rules are for the community as a whole, and they reflect the great concern of the "good men of the town" to avoid corruption and nepotism—not easy to do given what appears to be a fairly small governing class.

The procedures for appointment of *primores* (*rashim*) and *boni viri* (*tovim*) and *kahal* and judges (*dayyanim*) and accountants (*ba'alei cheshbonoth*) on the Intermediate Days of Passover shall be as follows. The *primores* and *boni viri* and [the] *kahal* . . . shall convene and undertake, under oath, in the name of God and in the name of the people, without subterfuge and without deception, that no person should have concluded a deal or should conclude one [in the future] in the matter of the aforementioned elections with any person outside the *kahal*, whether with individuals or with a group. The election of these persons shall be exclusively for the sake of heaven and for the public

11. See ₵8, §4.

good, as they are instructed from heaven, not for their own good, but so that they shall serve others, and not to arouse anyone's wrath—to elect persons who are generally considered worthy and honest, who will act for the public good and for the sake of heaven.

And this is the manner of their election. The *primores* and the *boni viri* and the *kahal* . . . may each place in the [ballot] box the name of one person in order to choose a member of the election committee, the latter having no family ties with the person whose name has been placed in the box. By family ties the following is meant: second cousin, husband and wife, former relative, father of son-in-law or father of daughter-in-law, and two friends or partners, most of whose business is done with one another—it is forbidden to place [the names of] any of these in the box. It is permitted to place the name of a person from the *kahal* or outside the *kahal* in the box. The names of the *primores* may not be placed in the box. The . . . beadles (*shammashim*) shall draw [the names of] nine men, who must be eligible for one another according to the Torah.[12] The first whose name has been drawn disqualifies any relative whose name may be drawn from the box after his.

Immediately after [the names of] the nine men have been drawn from the box, they shall take an oath before the open Holy Ark and in the presence of the beadles . . . to the effect that they shall elect five intelligent and knowledgeable persons, including in the oath [an undertaking] that none of them shall conclude a deal, not even two together. And these shall be men well acquainted with the needs of the communal leadership . . . and who are worthy and fit to elect, for the benefit of the community, *primores* and *boni viri* and *kahal* . . . and three tribunals, as mentioned previously, and three accountants, who shall sit with the *boni viri*. They shall elect all those listed above in accordance with their oath, with the Holy Ark thrown open, in the presence of the *primores* and the *boni viri* and the beadles . . . not for the benefit of any individual, but for the benefit of the community to the best of their knowledge. And those five, not even two of them, shall not conclude a deal with others, and in the name of God, without any trick or deception whatsoever;

---

12. The criteria are of those eligible [*kosher*] for marriage according to Jewish law. The reference here is to heads of families whose members are permitted to marry one another.

[moreover,] of the aforementioned nine, at most two may be chosen (for the committee), but not all five.

. . . Those five men, after taking the oath, shall be locked up[13] until they appoint the *primores* and the *boni viri* and the kahal . . . and magistrates and accountants as described above, and affix their signatures and the seal, and deliver (the documents) to one of the beadles, and that beadle shall hold them until [the *wojewoda*'s (provincial governor's)] approval has been secured.

. . . It is forbidden for the above five men, in the name of God, blessed be He, and in the name of the public, on pain of punishment in view of the gravity of the oath, to divulge whom they have elected, not even so much as a hint, until the community leaders shall make it public as is customary.

The five chosen individuals [electors] should be eligible [as witnesses] to one another, having no [family] ties [kin relations] with one another, that is, even second cousins, husband and wife, close or former relative, father of son-in-law or father of daughter-in-law, and two partners—all such [relations] disqualify one another.

Similarly, the *primores* and magistrates of each tribunal elected by the five men, they too should be eligible relative to one another and have no connection with one another, as mentioned. The *boni viri* elected for the above term of office shall also be eligible relative to one another and to the *primores,* as required by the law of the Torah. . . . But if they wish to elect some who are not eligible for one another [with regard to] marriage, or for *primores* and *boni viri,* even according to the Torah, then, nevertheless, when the business of the *kahal* is in progress, the two mutually ineligible members shall be reckoned as one opinion [one vote] and need not absent themselves.

13. Yidd., *ainshlissen,* i.e., locked up in a room without food, to force them to complete the proceedings on the same day.

No Taxation Without Representation

16. Ezekiel Landau, *Responsa Noda Bihudah* I, HM 20

We excerpt here a responsum sent from Prague to Bamberg in 1761 in which Landau navigates carefully between the claims of the litigants in a difficult tax case. Jacob Eiger, a wealthy and learned communal leader, refused to heed a communal decision to extend the tax assessment to house rentals, an ordinance enacted without his knowledge or participation—and therefore, he claimed, invalid. Landau's argument clearly favors Eiger's position that all members of the kahal must be represented at any meeting where taxes are levied (and especially those members in the highest tax bracket).

Question: I have been asked [the following] by the esteemed Torah scholar, distinguished and honorable, our teacher and rabbi Jacob Eiger of the holy community of Bamberg. He presented his case in litigation against the honorable leaders and functionaries of his community who passed an inequitable [decision] against him. Not only did they wish to change matters with regard to tax payments and to introduce the novelty of taxing house rentals—something completely unheard of hitherto—but they also changed the ancient custom pertaining to the manner of oaths [regarding assessment and disclosure], and they did all this without his knowledge and did not include him [in the discussion, in order] to hear his opinion regarding the said *tak-kanah*. According to his claim, the committee includes neither a majority of persons nor a majority of [substance]. Moreover, they [publicly] declared a ban on him and three days later imposed a *herem* upon him in the synagogue. He cries out, what sin or crime has he committed to be publicly humiliated [in this manner]—and he is a scholar [too]!

Answer: . . . I say that when the good men of the town wish to enact a novel ordinance regarding tax issues they have no elevated [status] due to their being officers and good men of the town. And even though the good men of the town are equal to the High Court, still with regard to issues of tax payment they have no greater authority or power than the rest of the people. This is not only the case with respect to the positions . . . that maintain that the good men of the town may only enforce an ancient custom but may not introduce any novelty with regard to "matters of loss to one and gain to an-other" without the consent [of the relevant parties]. Even if the good men of the town were not a party to the dispute (e.g., if they had their own tax arrangement), still, they may not impose a *takkanah* on the public regarding tax payments. For in all these matters what benefits one causes difficulty for another. But even according to the ruling of Rema [Moses Isserles] that the good men of the town are empowered to enforce such [novel enactments] where it is customary, still this custom must be publicly established in the town. A practice is termed a custom only if it is common and is performed many times. The practice of the aforementioned community must be investi-gated with regard to this matter. The burden of proof [however] is upon the good men of the town to establish that this is indeed an established custom in their town—[and only then will they] have the upper hand in a "matter of loss to one and gain to another."

Now even if the investigation has shown that this is indeed the cus-tom, in any case where they themselves are an interested party, they are not considered "the good men of the town." Would it occur to you that the good men of the town are fit to sit in judgment with regard to themselves? Now with regard to tax issues, they too are an interested party. It is clearly stated in [the *Shulhan Arukh* HM] 163 in [Isserles's] gloss, that regarding all public matters in which agreement cannot be reached, all the taxpaying heads of households are convened [to discuss and decide the matter by majority vote]. And according to the esteemed Rabbi Jacob, [this meeting] was convened to consider the enactment without him. And even if they had a majority of persons or a majority of wealth without him, and even if his own dissenting opinion would have been voided by the majority that would be valid only if they had heard his words and his stated opinion. But as they did not include him in their meeting and did not hear his reasoning at all, it is absolutely clear that there is no basis to claim that he is canceled out as a minority. They must reconvene and vote again, and anything done without him is void.

[This is especially clear] if the committee did not include a majority of persons or a majority of wealth, i.e., of those paying the greater sums of money, the major part of the tax . . . and if [it is the case], as the esteemed Rabbi Jacob claims, that they acted against the previously established *takka-*

not of the town, which expressly state that the officers are not empowered to innovate except in conjunction with members of the highest [tax] brackets and [payers] of the greatest sums and in the presence of former public appointees. He [Rabbi Jacob] is in the high [tax] bracket, and he has already had a high appointment in the town and was a leader of the community. Nevertheless, they innovated all this without him. As their actions are void, he may rightfully refuse [their enactment] and is under no obligation to heed them. Clearly they may not fine him or ban him [*lenadoto*] for his refusal.

Defining the Self-Ruling Community

Communal Independence

17. Samuel b. Moses de Modena (Maharshdam), *Responsa* YD 153

Salonika, where de Modena lived, had taken in large numbers of refugees from Spain and Portugal, who formed many separate congregations, each one following the customs of the old country (or the old city). This pluralism was the practice in many communities but was here contested in the community of Patras by some congregations who called for a united leadership. The native congregation of Patras feared that this would create a situation whereby they would become a permanent minority, and their positions would constantly be overruled by the newfound majority of immigrant communities. The disputants turned to de Modena, who clearly articulates the pain of the outsider lured into the internecine fray of communal politics. Still, he recommends maintaining the status quo. This ruling put him at odds with Joseph Formon, rabbi of nearby Lepanto, who took Patras to be under his "jurisdiction" and who supported the merger.

God, the creator of the universe, to whom all mysteries are transparent, will comprehend [the truth behind] the impure occurrence, the withdrawal and controversy, that occurred in Patras. They inquired of us whether three *kehillot*—two being Sicilian and one Sephardic—have the power to force the *kahal* of [original] residents to join with them as one inclusive political government [and] to follow the opinion of the majority of officers from them all. Apparently, the [original] residents rejected this [idea] because they saw that their opinions would forever be null, as the Sicilians, who are the majority, would forever govern the town.

We responded in purity of heart and mind that there is no doubt that unity and concord are good for the righteous, yet the law is as clear as the sun that each and every *kahal* is considered to be a town unto itself, as has been expressly written by Adret and by Rabbi David Katz, who [originally] "reigned" [as rabbi] in those localities and who wrote this clearly, bringing proof from the city of Salonika as he stated.

We were [originally] of the opinion that [Katz's ruling and our verbal support] would suffice and there would be no need to respond in writing as the issue was elementary. Our words however did not savor sweetly to the palate of the esteemed *haver,* our teacher Rabbi Joseph Formon may God keep him and guard him. He placed the [original] residents under extreme pressure, treating them as separatists and dictating that no one shall do business with them. Thus were the people of Israel made a mockery and an embarrassment among the gentiles. The bitterness continued . . . until both parties sent agents here to Salonika to ask our opinion [with all the relevant rulings and documents].

We will consent to inform them of our opinion but under condition that both parties commit themselves to uphold our decree—for if not, why should we labor in vain?

[De Modena continues to depict the unwillingness of Formon's representatives to concede to his condition and the resulting bitterness of the dispute that spilled over to Salonika. The Sicilian community there engaged in violence and excommunications and involved the non-Jewish government against individuals connected with the other communities of Patras. The events led to a visit to Salonika by Formon that ended badly for de Modena, who had naively consented to extend his hospitality to the pugnacious guest. After a detailed account of all this, de Modena elaborates his position.]

The issue is whether the three *kehillot* in Patras may God protect them can force the *kahal* of [original] residents . . . to join with them so that the political government would be [administrated] by the majority of officers of each of the *kehillot* [combined] and not by the majority of each of the independent communities. The [original] residents opposed [the union] because they saw that they would always have the weaker hand and the government would be by the Sicilians, and the opinion of the residents would be null since the Sicilians are the majority. They resemble a lion ravaging them. . . .

[Formon brought] two arguments [on behalf of the union]. One is that separation is [prohibited by] "You shall not cut yourself up" (Deut. 14:1), for as it says in the Talmud (BT Yevamot 14a), Israel is not meant to be in factions.[14] A second argument is this: "The Torah said, 'Follow the majority,' and in all differences among [the people of] Israel the basic dictate of the Torah is to act in accordance with the position of the majority. Since [here] the majority says that the officers together and the political government should follow the majority, the residents are obligated to follow their words." These are his arguments. My fellows and I say that the law is with the [original] residents. I would not have to [discuss] this at length, except [in order to] explain how to respond [to these arguments]. . . .

Even with regard to a matter of *issur*, [if there is a town where] some have one custom and some have a different custom, where there are two courts, this does not constitute [a violation of] "You shall not cut yourself up" (Deut. 14:1). For the conclusion of the Gemara (BT Yevamot 14a, ¢7, §14) is that the School of Shammai acted in accordance with their own rulings [and the School of Hillel followed their own rulings]. . . . And in [the case of] a town with two *kehillot*, all the wise [decisors] have unanimously written that [the two *kehillot*] are as two courts.

[De Modena goes on to cite both contemporary and earlier rulings to this effect among them rulings by Rabbi Katz, mentioned previously, and by Solomon b. Abraham Adret and Elijah Mizrahi (cf. ¢8, §§11 and 13).]

It now remains for us to expound [on the second argument]. It is conceded that there is [in this case no violation] of "You shall not cut yourself up," but there is still the fact that in all places the Torah says, "Follow the majority."

14. See ¢7, §18 (BT Yevamot 14a), where the Rabbis interpret the phrase "You shall not cut yourself up" (Deut. 14:1) to mean "You shall not become divided into factions."

This question also is a simple matter seeing too that all the rabbis mentioned sought only to solve [the issue of] "You shall not cut yourself up," but they had no concern with [the issue of] "Follow the majority." . . . I will preface my remarks by stating that all [pluralist] positions [must] face this question. For it is written in the Gemara, "In the locality of R. Eli'ezer they used to cut wood to make charcoal for making iron on Shabbat. In the locality of R. Yose the Galilean they used to eat chicken with milk" (BT Shabbat 130a); And it is later written, "There was a town in the land of Israel where they followed R. Eli'ezer, and they died in their time [rather than being struck down by God]. One wonders how it is possible that one lone town used to behave differently from all of Israel [with respect to] violating Shabbat. For one would assume from [BT] Yevamot that all [of Israel] would be considered as one town with respect to Shabbat because of its [importance and the] severity [of its laws]. As if this was not enough, they were rewarded too ["they died in their time"]. One must therefore say that there is no question if the towns are separate. And if that is so, we return to the principle that two distinct synagogues are each considered as a town unto itself. . . .

We therefore should say that [the rule] "follow the majority" is a binding norm only in cases that are analogous to the Sanhedrin, where [the members] are gathered in one place and convened for a specific ruling—then they are to carry out the words of the majority. But in a case where they did not convene to debate together, each one can, in his locality, do as he understands. . . .

The Sicilians are the majority, and they will always have the upper hand, for good or for bad. If [that is allowed], it will turn out that [the town] will always be led by the Sicilians, with "the natives [i.e., the residents who arrived in the land first] on the bottom and the strangers on top."[15] . . .

The matter is clear, that the law is with the [original] residents for all the reasons mentioned [above], and I have signed my name, the young Samuel de Modena.

15. See BT Yoma 47a.

Single Community Subject to Three
18. Moses b. Joseph di Trani (Mabit), *Responsa* 3:77

This responsum continues to address the strife in the Patras community. Apparently, over the years agreement was achieved for a united government. But the arrangement proved precarious and was still contested. Although a native of Salonika, di Trani does not follow the custom there; he supports Formon and argues for the supremacy of the town over its constituent communities. It appears from the case described here that pluralism (the control of each synagogue/kahal over its own members) worked in favor of the rich, whereas the town's majority was more likely to defend what it took to be the common interest.

Question: I was asked about a town with four synagogues, which operated according to an agreement [*haskamah*] established by four great rabbis . . . that whosoever should transgress a prohibition or an enactment [*haskamah*] would be judged, punished, and fined by the officers of the [united] four *kehillot*. [Di Trani describes an infringement of the agreement by one of the subcommunities and continues:] The said sages passed away, and there came to that city a [new] sage who taught much Torah and founded a yeshiva, and in his time the four *kehillot* came together as partners as they were originally. For the sage mentioned observed in the communal ledger of agreements and enactments this agreement, [namely] that they would be judged by the officers of the [united] four *kehillot*. . . . Sometimes they would consult the sage — for their condition for accepting him was that when they imposed punishment, they would consult if they so wished. During this time, a wealthy man committed an infraction and was banned unanimously by the officers of the four *kehillot*. In response, he, his friends, and his relatives claimed that he had been punished excessively because of the exclusive involvement of the other three *kehillot* and that had [the decision] been [made] by the officers of his *kahal* alone, they would not have been as harsh with him. This appealed to all other kehillot — that every man should wield authority in his own [particular] community[16] — and especially to the rich. The said sage protested on the

---

16. A pun on Est. 1:22: "that every man should wield authority in his own home."

basis of the agreement he had seen written in the *kahal* ledger. Whereupon they concealed that agreement, and wrote a [new] agreement according to which anyone [seemingly] deserving of punishment would be judged by the officers of his [own] *kahal*. Controversy then abounded, and the [view of] the wealthy [individual and his friends and relatives] prevailed. The sage also signed onto this view. It was known that the sage was upright, so they [the rich] wrote that the officers alone would impose fines and punishments; the sage would not deal with these [cases].

The [town] acted in accordance with this agreement for a number of years, during which time most of the Jews fled from Patras to Lepanto [because of the war]. [The practice] among those who remained [was that] sometimes punishments were imposed by all the *kehillot,* and sometimes by the officers of [a single] *kahal.* After the Venetians had made peace with the Turks, everyone returned to Patras. When they [the returnees] reviewed the judgments of the *kehillot,* they saw that [in fact] the officers of each *kahal* would overturn [judgments] so as to favor their own individual members. They initiated an annulment of the [second] agreement, and a [return to] the original agreement, according to which a transgressor is judged and punished by the majority of the officers of all the *kehillot,* for favoritism would not be so rampant if all rulings were made by one united community.

Moreover, the original agreement from thirty-three years ago has been found [again] in the book of the *kehillot,* and so the crown [of the law] has been returned to its glory. Even the officers who leaned toward voiding the original agreement [now accept it], for they have seen the original of thirty-three years ago. They annulled the agreement made seven years ago, even though the sage said that it was never legally effective and that it did not need to be annulled.

One *kahal* does not want to be part of this [original] agreement, because they say that a sage in their *kahal* exempted them [at the time it was made]. The [other] three *kehillot* assert that the exemption was not [lawful].

[Di Trani begins his reply by quoting approvingly Rabbi Joseph Formon's responsum to the parties in the spirit mentioned in the previous selection. He elaborates different points of law and continues:]

With regard to the issue of three or four synagogues in one town, can the majority of numbers [*rov minyan*] or majority of substance [*rov binyan*] of the synagogues force the minority—even if [the said minority] is one [integral] *kahal*—to accept upon themselves the stipulation agreed [*haskamah*] upon by the majority of *kehillot?* [Rabbi Formon] has written extensively and decisively that the majority of *kehillot* in one town can force another *kahal* in the town to agree with them [when it concerns] erecting a fence to [preempt transgressions of] a prohibition [*issura*]. It seems to me that the law agrees with him.

With respect to what Adret and Duran have written[17]—that one *kahal* may not force another *kahal* to agree to their stipulation—it appears that the "one *kahal*" here is [the name given to] the townspeople of one town, as the sage has written in his responsum: "However, [with multiple] synagogues in one town, the majority can compel the minority to accept upon themselves matters that pertain to erecting a fence to [preempt transgressions of] a prohibition. [This follows] the plain meaning of the *baraita* in the first chapter of [BT] Bava Batra [8b, which states,] "The townspeople are authorized to stipulate . . . and to enforce their decrees."[18] Similarly, all the decisors have written that "The townspeople are authorized, etc.," meaning thereby the members of one town, regardless of whether it has within it one *kahal* or a number of *kehillot*. The breaking up into two, three, or four *kehillot* is only due to lack of space in the synagogue that cannot contain the many [congregants] . . . and each and every neighborhood needs its own synagogue. But this is no reason for them to be separate in their enactments; rather, they are all one union and one heart for [the purposes of] erecting a fence to [preempt transgressions of] a prohibition. Indeed, Jerusalem, the city of a mighty nation, had as many synagogues as the fullness of its laws, yet it was said, "Such was the custom of the people of Jerusalem, etc." (BT Sukkah 41b). It seems that such was the custom of all synagogues in the city. . . . So should we surmise in our times too with respect to all town matters, that they should be one union in one town . . . as they are united in one God, one Torah, and one law. This should also be the case with enactments erecting a fence. . . . The minority is

17. See, e.g., ¢8, §§11–12.
18. ¢8, §2.

obligated to follow the majority in all these matters, even if there are multiple synagogues in one town. The majority [rov minyan] of the significant[19] men in the town, and rov binyan of the synagogues, can force the minority when it appears necessary to them, according [to the needs of] the time, to enact an ordinance and to erect a fence, so as not to touch a biblical prohibition or infringe upon a rabbinical one, if they see that the possibility of violating it is too great. . . .

What does need to be explored in this case is the following: Given that the three kehillot can force the single kahal to enter into their agreement to chastise the transgressors, what if they say, "We agree [to be bound by] your enactments and stipulations, but we want to punish the transgressors [from our kahal] as we see fit? Are they also forced [to follow the majority] with respect to the [imposition of] punishment, such that all punishments are to be [dictated] jointly, by the officers of all the kehillot (as the sage wrote—for the power of the many is better suited to punishing the felons and criminals than is that of the smaller number, the officers of his kahal)? For his kahal and its officers do have some reason to say that he should be punished by them—that it is more likely that he will obey them when they tell him that he is being punished not for revenge but for his own good, seeing that he transgressed the general agreement of all the kehillot of the city and that they do not want to embarrass him before the officers of all the kehillot.

It is doubtful that they ought to be forced also with respect to this [matter of punishment], as opposed to the simple acceptance of the agreement, as originally set forth. However, after some years have passed in which . . . the officers of all the kehillot punish the violators jointly, one kahal thereafter cannot, on its own, deviate from this [agreement] and declare that they will punish the transgressor from their kahal [on their own]. How much more so given that, as described in the question, the agreement was undertaken originally in accordance with all the important sages of the town, and [was endorsed by] those who came later as written [above] in the query. It is obvious that they cannot [deviate from the agreement].

19. Hashive—we take this to mean not the "important" but simply the taxpaying members.

Federalism: The Four Lands

19. Nathan Hanover, *Abyss of Despair (Yeven Metzulah)*

Abyss of Despair (Yeven Metzulah [Venice, 1653]*)*, translated by Abraham J. Mesch (1950; reprint ed., New Brunswick, N.J.: Transaction Books, 1983), pp. 119–20.

Nathan Hanover's chronicle of the Chmielnicki pogroms of 1648 includes this brief description of the federated Jewish communities of Poland and their governing council. During the years that the council flourished, Hanover assures us, no Jew ever brought a dispute before a gentile court, and every Jew who did that was severely punished. The contradiction points to the idealized form of the narrative. Still, Hanover provides one of the few descriptions of what was in fact a major political achievement.

The Pillar of Justice was in the Kingdom of Poland as it was in Jerusalem before the destruction of the Temple, when courts were set up in every city, and if one refused to be judged by the court of his city, he went to the nearest court, and if he refused to be judged by the nearest court, he went before the great court. For in every province there was a great court. Thus in the capital city of Ostrog, there was the great court for Volhynia and the Ukraine; and in the capital city of Lwow, there the great court for [Little] Russia. There were thus many communities each of which had a great court for its own province.

   If two important communities had a dispute between them, they would let themselves by judged by the heads of the Council of the Four Lands (may their Rock and Redeemer preserve them), who would be in session twice a year. One leader would be chosen from each important community; added to these were six great scholars from the land of Poland, and these [representatives] were known as the Council of the Four Lands. They would be in session during every fair in Lublin between Purim and Passover, and during every fair in Jaroslaw in the month of Ab or Elul. The leaders of the Four Lands were like the Sanhedrin in the Chamber of Hewn Stones. They had the authority to judge all Israel in the Kingdom of Poland, to establish safeguards, to institute ordinances, and to punish each man as they saw fit. Each difficult matter was brought before them and they judged it. And the leaders of the Four Lands selected judges from the provinces to relieve their burden, and these were called judges of the provinces. They attended to cases involving money matters. Fines, titles, and other difficult laws were brought before [them]. Never was a dispute among Jews brought before a Gentile judge, or before a nobleman, or before the King, may his glory increase, and if a Jew took his case before a Gentile court he was punished and chastised severely, to observe: "even our enemies themselves being judges" [Deut. 32:31; NJPS: "For their rock is not like our Rock, In our enemies' own estimation"].

Separation of Communal Government and Religion

20. Shimon b. Wolf [Wolfowicz], Dissolution of the *Kahal*

Israel Klausner, "Ha-Ma'avak ha-penimi be-kehilot Rusyah ve-Lita' ve-hatsa'at R' Shim'on ben Volf le-tikunim," *He-'Avar* 19 (1972): 64–73.[20]

This letter from prison is the only lasting literary product of a decades-long dispute in the Vilna kahal between rival rabbis and their supporters and also, more important, between representatives of the "multitude," complaining of heavy and unjust taxation, and the kahal plutocrats. It is also one of eleven petitions addressed to the Seym of Poland on the eve of a debate on "the Jewish question." These petitions mark the first appearance of French revolutionary ideas in the Jewish communities of eastern Europe. Shimon argues for a radical separation of the religious and political authority that the kahal *had commonly combined. Of course, Jewish writers always recognized that what we might call "the king's business" was in fact something separate—and that the king's law was law:* dina de-malkhuta dina. *But Shimon wanted to move far beyond the traditional meaning of that maxim; he would have handed over all matters of property, taxation, and distributive justice to the Polish state. He sought state protection against the exploitative practices of the Jewish oligarchs. His assumption, premature, to say the least, was that the Polish state in 1789 was committed to the well-being of all its members, the Jews included.*

20. This article includes a Hebrew translation of the Polish original. We reproduce an English translation based on the Hebrew text but checked against the original.

The Prisoner in Nieswicju to the Seym now in session, regarding the need for Reform of the Jews

The period of my imprisonment in Nieswicju, now twenty months, has been long enough to bemoan my bitter lot, to describe the cruelty of my treatment, to realize that I am innocent, and also to contemplate the question: What [kind of community] are the Jews and what is the jurisdiction that rules us?

We two, representatives of the Jewish multitude in Vilna, as well as two [members of] that multitude [Shimon's fellow inmates], have been for too long bearing the weight of [our] chains, the instruments of shame and punishment, without thinking ourselves guilty of any crime save that of bringing a suit against the Vilna *kahal*—even worse, of having prevailed in this suit, both at the King's Court and at the Commission of the Lithuanian Treasury. We have neither freedom nor security, even while universal enlightenment argues everywhere for [the cause of] humanity, and even though the supreme national government . . . could have taken note of this oppression of innocence.

The period of captivity, so prolonged, has begun to remove from my heart any hope of freedom, so long as no one with feeling and loving kindness arises [who can] prevail with the Seym on behalf of oppressed innocence. [But] this protracted captivity cannot uproot my loyalty to the country in which I was born and raised. Because of this [loyalty], I have decided to present to the exalted Seym my comments regarding Jewish [self-]government, knowing that the state, deliberating on the happiness of its people, and encompassing all aspects of government, cannot in the current Seym forget the Jews. The exalted Seym, which in its wisdom prepares for all a better fate . . . will not wish to leave our Jewish people behind, in its present condition of disorder. On the contrary, will it not inscribe in the holy book of laws whether we shall be happy and useful to the country, or not?

The case, exalted Seym, is as follows. The Jews in Poland are an independent people or, rather, a state within a state [*status in statu*]. The fault for this lies both in the neglect of the Jews by the country's government and in their own aspiration not to be subject to [any] government save their own. . . . On the one hand, the writs of privileges they received, and on the other, their abuse of these privileges, have placed insurmountable obstacles in the path of reform. Only the Seym can bring relief, for the benefit both of the state and of the Jews.

The independence of the Jewish people is expressed most clearly in their difference [from other subjects of the state] regarding religion, civil [status], enforcement of jurisdiction based on their own laws, language, and dress. In the present context, all this should be reduced to two categories, namely, religion and civil government.

Religion should be left to the Jews, since toleration brings great blessings to a free people. Jewish civil [government], which in effect constitutes a state within a state, should be abrogated, and this abrogation should not be achieved by means of small corrections, which would serve only as temporary remedies; rather, [Jewish civil government] must be destroyed from its very foundation.

It has always seemed as though religion is linked to civil [affairs] to such a degree that any reform of the Jewish people is impossible. But at a time when separating civil [affairs] from religion is not so difficult, the current Seym can attain glory by making the Jews both a happier people and [one] more useful to the state.

Let us examine this separation.

Religion cannot include anything other than prayer and those practices belonging to religion, that is, circumcision, marriage, divorce, *tzedakah* for the poor, *kashrut,* true loving kindness [burial], and observance of the holidays.

For all these, there is no need for a head of the *kahal,* nor for the institution of a communal court.

Regarding prayer, each Jew prays on his own behalf, each is a priest to himself, bringing his own offering; when ten Jews gather, they can celebrate [even] the most important holidays. Although each Jew is obliged to know the commandments of his religion, not all are equally experts therein; hence a rabbi is needed. The people should elect as rabbi he who is most learned, for he must teach Torah in the synagogue, examine the *hazanim,* and issue them certificates attesting to their knowledge. The *kahal* never intervenes in these matters.

Circumcision may be performed by any Jew, provided that he knows how to do it. The father can appoint anyone he wishes to perform the circumcision, as this constitutes an honor both to that individual and to the person who holds the baby. This practice thus has no connection to the government of the *kahal*.

Marriages are effected by the mutual consent of the two parties, with their parents' permission. Two friends, appointed by the fathers of the young man and woman, lead the young man to the canopy. The blessing for the couple, which is written in a book, is recited by a man upon whom the groom's father wishes to confer this honor. Organizing the practices of marriage thus has nothing to do with the government of the *kahal*.

Writs of divorce [*gittin*] are easily arranged, but they must go through the religious court. They do not require involvement by the *kahal* or its permission.

The laws of *kashrut* are clearly established in the books. A rabbi, or his deputy, provides confirmation with respect to *kashrut*. This he does without any connection to the *kahal*.

Regarding the holidays, the Jews observe them strictly. It is impossible to demand any kind of change pertaining to the holidays or *shabbat,* since these are determined by religious commandments and honored by tradition.

Caring for the sick, the poor, and the dead is ordained by religion; this is performed not by the *kahal* but by special associations that are independent of it. Nearly all Jews join and pay membership dues to the associations for sick care [*bikkur holim*] and true loving-kindness [burial]. The heads of the burial society collect from [the heirs of] every deceased person a payment in accordance with his property; the members of this association, selected by ballot, perform the functions connected to the burial of the dead. Only one-third of the sums collected from burials remains in this association's fund for [financing] its needs and for the grand annual dinner it conducts. The other two-thirds are given over to the poor fund, administered by four *gabba'im*. In order to provide [further support] for the poor, significant sums are collected in the synagogue [as donations] from individuals called up to the Torah and by means of a special box for collecting *tzedakah* [affixed near the synagogue's entrance]. The association for the care of the sick has its own funds and [collection] boxes. Even the lighting in the synagogue is specially provided for, so that the *kahal* does not participate in any expense.

This exhausts the Jews' obligations toward [their] religion, as pertains to its practices—from which it is evident that the Jewish religion [can] exist without a *kahal* and that the religion and the practices connected to it cannot be considered [to constitute] a state within a state.

Let us now consider, What is the Jewish civil government? In what manner do the politics of the *kahal* leaders, and their extensive abuse of their liberties, create a special estate within Poland, whose seat is the *kahal* and whose fortress is its juridical authority (the *bet din*)? I grant that my assessment is based on the Vilna *kahal,* presuming that all *kahal* governing bodies are alike. But if some have not reached this level, who can guarantee that they are not headed the same way, or shall not attain the same measure of ambition and violence?

Fourteen men, who are elected for a year and must then step down, constitute the *kahal.* Twelve men, similarly elected each year, constitute the communal—or religious—*bet din.*

The *kahal* adopts various resolutions and imposes regular taxes (a function that ought to be granted solely to the country's legislative branch) and thereby becomes master of the citizens' property. The money it extracts from the multitude is used to pay its own salaries, and what remains it spends and wastes as it sees fit. Can this have anything at all to do with religion?

The *kahal* sells *hazakot* [franchises][21] for money, thereby causing definite harm to the owners of inns in the villages and to the owners of houses and castles in the towns, since no Jew is allowed to lease—or even make a bid for—an inn [whose owner has] a *hazakah,* without first buying the *hazakah* from the [owner]. . . . In the towns, first, no Jew can become an agent, tailor, furrier . . . unless he has a *hazakah* on a house, or on the person of the landlord himself. Second, no Jew who has not first paid for the *hazakah* may buy from this house or from this landlord. Third, when a Jew resides in a house

---

21. *Hazakah* (pl. *hazakot*), lit., "holding"; an exclusive franchise to deal in particular goods or with a particular establishment or individual.

whose *hazakah* the *kahal* has sold, he must pay for the *hazakah* a third of the sum that he pays as rent to the landlord; if he leaves the apartment, he must bring in his stead another Jew, so that a Catholic Christian not come to reside there, and so that the *hazakah* income not be diminished. What connection is there here to religion?

Whenever the *kahal* desires money, it obtains it with ease, though this places a great burden upon the multitude and upon particular individuals. The *kahal* does this as follows: it records a resolution, that "the bearer of this document" (no name is ever specified) hereby lends to the *kahal* the sum of, say, one thousand gold coins; and the *kahal* orders the *shammash* that, as security for said bearer, ten writs of debt be drawn up [naming] ten individuals—e.g., Abraham, David, and so on—as owing the bearer one hundred gold coins each. All these individuals . . . know nothing, yet when they are sued before the religious *bet din* by a *rodef ne'elam,* that is, by a secret suit, wherein it is forbidden even to enquire as to the plaintiff's identity, they . . . must pay the debt imposed upon them. The signing of the debtor's name by the *shammash* is binding as though the debtor had signed with his own hand. If they fail to appear, the *bet din* issues a judgment in absentia and records [them as owing] the original sum, [plus] interest and fines, and immediately executes this judgment. If anyone dares resist . . . [the court] issues a [request for action] "by the Courts of the Gentiles," i.e., a certificate of resistance or failure to appear, on the basis of which the governor's official sends military assistance. Thus Abraham, David, and so on—who owed no money, signed no writ of debt, and had no way of knowing the identity of the bearer in whose favor the court ordered the payment—see their merchandise and movable property confiscated and transferred. And sometimes they themselves end up in prison. Can religion require such injustice or approve of it? . . .

In addition to regular taxes, called *korovkas,* the *kahal* imposes various levies and collects them by threat of *herem.*

The *kahal* restricts trade within the country, since it collects taxes both from the townspeople—according to their trade or profits, however these are produced—and from visiting merchants, who must pay both from merchandise sold and from merchandise bought in the town. . . .

The *kahal* [governing] committees cannot be trusted in any matter, since they suffer no rulers above them, for they wish to exercise [unlimited] power. In seeking to ensure their power in the future, they adopt resolutions, enact *takkanot,* and issue decrees. The heads of the *kahal* do not step down from their position until the new heads confirm the actions of their predecessors and undertake to carry them out. Proof of this [can be seen] in Vilna, where the community board elected for one year has not handed over its position for five years, because it lacks faith in its successors' will or capacity to carry on according to its desires. . . .

The fortress of the *kahal*'s arbitrary [power] is the judicial authority, divided between the *kahal* and the religious *bet din.* The *kahal* improperly holds in one and the same hand [the powers of] legislation and judgment. It imposes corporal punishments and fines. The religious—or communal—*bate din* judge in suits involving inheritance, obligations, deeds, trade, and matters of property.

These two magisterial powers often judge without summons, [or] on the basis of investigations that are not conducted in the presence of the parties. Their rulings are written without setting out the reasons for their decision. The [rulings] are not recorded in the ledgers, and [the judges] forbid by [threat] of *herem* filing an appeal against them [even though] this is permitted by the laws of the state with respect to rulings of the [royal] court— in order that the state government not . . . alter the rulings. The rulings are therefore quickly enforced—even assessing and confiscating property or placing the person [found guilty] in prison. This is assisted by the *namiastnik* [governor's official] employing soldiers from the fortress garrison. . . . Can such violations of the laws of the state and its judges be a religious concern?

The Jewish judicial authority, which is the fortress of their arbitrary political power, applies the *herem* with the utmost severity, thereby giving force to all [their actions]. Every Jew must perforce fear the *herem,* for it is forbidden to sell bread or meat to a person under *herem;* the *shohet* will not slaughter a chicken for him; the doors of the synagogue are closed to him; he loses his right to participate in the [elective] assembly and any positions he [might have held, and] his seats in the synagogue. He is denied access to the cemetery and burial. Anyone may, without being punished, wrong him . . . and confiscate his property. There is no justice for him, and toward him it is permitted to engage in lying, libel, perjury, and false oaths. Once a Jew has been listed in the black ledgers, he loses his membership in the congregation of the living and the dead. . . .

I would not wish that my voice, raised herein to the Seym, have only the character of an indictment of my people or of hatred toward the heads of the *kahal,* who have brought about my captivity these twenty months. On the contrary, I wish that the Jewish people be useful to the country that not only tolerates them but supports through the produce of its land such a great number of Jews and permits them various benefits. I wish that this country might feel greater trust toward the Jews and think better of them. This it will do once it sees greater adherence on our part to the laws and the judicial authorities of the state and finds our morality improved through honest behavior toward the Christians, which will be a necessary result of the uniformity of law, sovereignty, and civil government.

These ends will be perfectly attained by separating the civil [affairs] of the Jews from their religion. Religion should be left to the Jews alone, but civil [affairs] must be placed under the laws of the state. . . .

The conclusion from all this is that authority to order a ban, a *herem,* or a listing in the black ledger should never be solely in the hands of the rabbi. The *rodef ne'elam* form of filing suit—the secret filing, with no [specified] plaintiff . . .—must be forbidden, on pain of punishment against the rabbis. This punishment will be imposed by the state. . . . Neither the rabbi nor any Jewish association or assembly shall be authorized to enact any *takkanot,* on any pretext whatever, or to impose any kind of payments—and certainly not to enforce them. They will not [be authorized] to take an interest in the property of private citizens, under any pretext whatever—and certainly not to demand payments from such property—on pain of liability of their own property and loss of their positions. In case there is an unexpected need to collect money for a religious purpose, the rabbi shall announce this need in the synagogue. He shall not be able to coerce anyone to make an obligatory contribution . . . but rather shall place a box in the synagogue into which each Jew shall insert money in accordance with his graciousness, capacity, and goodwill.

Autonomy Revived

21. Simon Dubnow, "Autonomism, the Basis of the National Program"

Letters on Old and New Judaism (1897–1907), Fourth Letter, in *Nationalism and History* by Simon Dubnow, edited by Koppel S. Pinson (New York: Atheneum, 1970), pp. 136–39; reproduced by permission of the University of Nebraska Press; copyright 1958 by the Jewish Publication Society of America.

Dubnow rejects the political argument of the previous text, though he doesn't address, and perhaps didn't know, Shimon b. Wolf's pamphlet. He probably would have thought Shimon one of those assimilationist Jews who rush into the arms of their "liberators." His own plan for national autonomy for the Jews of central and eastern Europe would never have received the sanction of the nation-states of the region. Interestingly, though, Dubnow argues that considerable autonomy can be achieved without state sanction, through purely voluntary association—and points to the United States as a place where this more limited autonomy might be realized.

The more complex and original the historical development in question, the stronger is the force which leads it to "laws of its own" (this is the meaning of the word "autonomy") and to resistance to "alien laws" (or heteronomy) that force it to accept the substance and form of alien development. Autonomy as a historic claim is thus the firm and inalienable right of each national individuality; only its forms depend on the status that a nationality has within a multi-national state. . . . In view of its condition in the Diaspora, Jewish nationality cannot strive for territorial or political isolation [separation], but only for social and cultural autonomy. The Jew says: "As a citizen of my country, I participate in its civic and political life; but as a member of the Jewish nationality I have, in addition, my own national needs, and in this sphere I must be independent to the same degree that any other national minority is autonomous in the state. I have the right to speak my language, to use it in all my social institutions, to make it the language of instruction in my schools, to order my internal life in my communities, and to create institutions serving a variety of national purposes; to join in the common activities with my brethren not only in this country but in all countries of the world, and to participate in all the organizations that serve to further the needs of the Jewish nationality and to defend them everywhere."

During the "period of isolation" [i.e., before emancipation], the Jews enjoyed in great measure the right of national autonomy, although in outmoded forms, but they lacked civic and political rights. During the "period of assimilation," they began to participate in the civic and political life of the countries in which they lived, but many became alienated from the chosen inheritance of the nation, from its internal autonomy, which, in their limited view, did not accord with [the] civic emancipation already granted or about to be granted by law. In this manner old Jewry sacrificed its civic rights for its national rights, and new Jewry [sacrificed] its national rights for its political or civic rights. The period of autonomy now approaching does not tend to either of the two extremes of the previous epochs, which had rendered the life of the Jewish people defective and impaired. The new epoch must combine our equal civic and political rights with the social and cultural autonomy enjoyed by other nationalities whose historical conditions resemble our own. The Jews must demand simultaneously all civic, political and national rights, without renouncing one for the other as . . . in the past.

The chief axiom of Jewish autonomy may thus be formulated as follows: Jews in each and every country who take an active part in civic and political life enjoy all rights given to the citizens, not merely as individuals, but also as members of their national groups.

Now that we have succeeded in establishing the principle of autonomy, we must analyze the problem of how it can be realized under the conditions in which the Jewish nationality finds itself. Here we have to differentiate between two kinds of national minorities in a multi-national state: (1) a territorial minority, which is a minority as compared with the total population of the commonwealth, but which constitutes a majority in its own historical state or province; (2) a non-territorial minority, scattered over various provinces without being a majority in any. Nationalities of the first kind require regional autonomy where they are settled; nationalities of the second kind must have communal and cultural autonomy.

Up to the nineteenth century, the community (*kahal*) was the basis of Jewish autonomy in the lands of the Diaspora. . . . Since all our social and private life in those days was dominated by laws that operated with religious sanctions, the administration of the community also took on a religious form. The order that turned all Jewry into a type of religious nation created also the type of religious community; and in practice the nationality as a whole fulfilled tasks under the rule of religion that transcended the sphere of religion, so that all the tasks of secular organization were fulfilled in the "religious" community. The *kahal* took care of matters of communal welfare, supervised economic life, education, and tax collection for the government, while the rabbinic tribunals adjudicated cases involving family and financial matters. . . . The synagogue and the rabbis occupied the central position in all these institutions in name only; in practice the community was a kind of Jewish city within the Christian city. Up to the period of emancipation, communal Jewish autonomy as described above served as a substitute for government, for a state, and for citizenship, which under the old order were completely absent from Jewish life.

What, then, should modern Jewry have done after it had received its civic freedom in the West or, already before then, after it had absorbed the spirit of European culture? It should have adapted its autonomy to modern ideas, to the way of life of free citizens. Judaism, too, was now subjected to the general European process of secularization that separated the social from the religious elements. In its communal organization it, too, should have separated the core of nationality from its heavy religious shell. Even after the extent of self-administration had diminished under the influence of emancipation, a wide area of social and cultural autonomy still remained inside the community and outside — in the political associations dedicated to the ordering of the general affairs of Jewry. . . . All this, however, the assimilationist Jews forgot as they rushed into the (not always open) arms of their "liberators." The emancipated, who rejected the secular national idea and who attached to Judaism the unhappy label of a "religious group," retained only the symbols of the former autonomy: the synagogue, the rabbinate and, to a small degree, the welfare fund; everything else they assigned to the control of the state. Thus was created in Germany and Austria a greatly restricted organization that rested, not on the free national community, but on the religious community, the association of worshippers in the synagogue (*Synagogenge-*

meinden, Cultusgemeinden). . . . For many, membership in the community was merely a fiction, since by conviction they were distant from religious service; others severed this link as well and proclaimed themselves to be without any religious affiliation (*Konfessionslos*), thereby being freed also from the requirement to pay the communal tax. . . .

The fiction of the "religious community" was bound to be destroyed together with the fiction of the "religious society," not in the sense of a disruption of the religious service, but of a removal of the religious label from secular institutions. It is necessary to reconstruct the shattered autonomy in forms . . . adapted to modern social conditions. In countries of German culture, the nationalist Jews must convert their religious communities into national communities (*Volksgemeinden*). Even before such a change can be effected officially, with the approval of the government, it is possible, on the basis of the existing laws guaranteeing freedom of association, to widen perceptibly the circle of activities of the communities, and, at the same time, to wage a parliamentary battle for the recognition of the fullest measures of secular national communal autonomy. . . . Real and broad autonomy is especially possible in countries in which the principle prevails that the government does not interfere in the private lives of its citizens, and where authoritarian governments or exaggerated concentrations of power do not exist. In such countries, especially in the United States of America, Jews could enjoy even now a large measure of self-administration if only they were willing to advance beyond the confines of the "religious community."

American Federalism

22. Morris Loeb, "Federation or Consolidation of Jewish Charities"

Trends and Issues in Jewish Social Welfare in the United States, 1899–1952, edited by Robert Morris and Michael Freund (Philadelphia: JPS, 1966), pp. 136–37; reprinted by permission of the University of Nebraska Press; copyright 1966 by the Jewish Publication Society of America.

This text, though it deals only with the organization of welfare services and the collection of funds, is aimed at something like Dubnow's autonomy without state support. Loeb's federation of Jewish charities, modeled, he says, on American federalism (it probably de-

rives from his own experience of communal politics), has actually been achieved, more or less as he imagined it. It is doubtful, though, whether this federation lives up to Dubnow's hopes.

As a remedy for the evils, material and moral, which I have sought to recall to you ["waste of money, misdirection of energy, and deterioration of the communal spirit"], two methods present themselves: (1) consolidation, or (2) federation of the existing Jewish charitable societies in a single city. Both plans have their advocates, and both are being tried more or less thoroughly, here [in New York City] and elsewhere. While I consider complete consolidation preferable to complete individualization [i.e., every Jewish organization on its own], it appears to me that difficulties are . . . likely to imperil its success. . . . The chief objection to complete consolidation arises when we consider the probable relation of such an amalgamated society to the general [Jewish] community. It would be inevitable that the directorate would become somewhat autocratic, somewhat opinionated, somewhat self-satisfied. Healthy criticism from outside sources would become more difficult; dissatisfaction could only make itself felt in a falling off of the revenues for the entire system. It would be difficult to persuade a large [communal] corporation, proverbially ultraconservative, to take up new lines of work, to venture upon new philanthropic experiments. If an independent organization were formed for such a purpose, it would either be crowded out or, if it succeeded, it would gradually bring back the old state of individualization. . . .

To secure freedom of movement in all essentials, coupled with a unity of purpose and concentration of effort whenever needed, and healthful supervision without arbitrary domination, our charities should follow the example of our country; they should adopt a system of federation with sufficient elasticity to meet the wants of the large as well as the small organizations. No organization should be called upon to surrender its charter or its property; in fact, as an inducement for all organizations to join the federation without hesitation, it should be clearly stipulated that any member may withdraw if dissatisfied with the arrangement after giving reasonable notice, without forfeit of any kind. This, I believe, is generally known as the Liver-

pool plan, since it either originated in that English city or has been most successfully tried there.

As modified to suit the wants of an American Jewish community,
this plan might advantageously take the following form. The various cooperating societies, whether incorporated or not, would retain their respective
entities, no attempt being made to induce them to surrender their property,
or their individual subscribers, [or their] form of management, etc. They
would agree, however, to place the task of the solicitation of funds from the
Jewish public into the hands of a general committee, say of fifty or one hundred, chosen perhaps for the larger part from among their own directors. This
committee would publish annually a report stating briefly the purposes and
methods of the constituent societies, their financial condition, etc., and end-
ing with a list of all the subscribers and the amounts of their respective donations. The committee would solicit, either by circular or through personal
appeal, the contribution of an aggregate sum sufficient for the regular annual
expenses of all the constituent societies. The subscribers would be asked to
make annual, semi-annual, or quarterly payments to a central treasurer, but
the subscription blanks would be so worded that the donation might indicate
to what extent each particular charity was to benefit; while the subscriber
could, if he desired, put a part or the whole of his subscription into the hands
of the central committee for appropriate distribution.

Commentary. Autonomy and Cultural Reproduction

Living in exile under gentile rule posed two closely related political
questions for the Jews. The first had to do with the obligation to obey gentile
law, the limits on that obligation, and the remaining jurisdiction of Jewish
courts. The second had to do with the organization of Jewish life, the degree
of communal autonomy claimed by, or accorded to, the *kahal*. Both questions
became more difficult after emancipation. The achievement of full and equal
citizenship was undoubtedly a Jewish victory, but it was one of those victo-
ries that brings new problems in its wake.

The first question was originally dealt with by the maxim *dina de-*

malkhuta dina, which was already, before emancipation, a far-reaching concession to gentile rule and which reached even farther after Jews became citizens—and especially after they became citizens of democratic states. For then the "law of the kingdom" was the law that they gave to themselves; it was their own law, as much as Jewish law was, and for most Jews it pretty much limited Jewish law to questions of religious practice. Submission to the legal rulings of a *bet din* became an entirely voluntary matter.

But the impact of emancipation on the *kahal* was even greater, for citizenship in the larger community meant the end of autonomy in the smaller one. The French revolutionaries were explicit about this: everything for the Jews as individuals, nothing for the Jewish nation. Shimon b. Wolf [Wolfowicz], writing in 1789 from a Vilna prison (§20), hadn't heard about the revolution in Paris, but he had heard the good news of "universal enlightenment." Though Polish Jewry was not yet emancipated, he writes in (bold or naive) anticipation of a Polish state that will be equally committed to "the happiness of [all] its people." His is the first Jewish voice in eastern Europe calling for the end of the *kahal* and the full integration of the Jews into the secular state.

Shimon would retain for the Jews only the religious functions of the old communities. All matters of civil status and civil government would be transferred to the state—this includes the power to tax, to distribute the burdens of the state's taxes, to grant licenses for various economic activities, and to regulate those activities in the name of the common good. And as these powers were surrendered, Wolf insisted, the *kahal* would also be required to give up its right to enforce its rulings with the *herem.* So his critique of the Vilna oligarchs led him to defend a transfer of all coercive power to the state and a division of functions between state and synagogue that is essentially the modern division.

But there is one striking omission in Shimon's argument: he has nothing at all to say about education. He doesn't treat the establishment of schools (for boys, in the old days, and now for girls as well) as a religious obligation, which is the way it was always treated in the Jewish world, but he also fails to include it in the jurisdiction of the secular state. Who will educate the next generation of Jews? Shimon probably just assumed that the cultural reproduction of the Jewish community would go on more or less as it always had—it wasn't yet an urgent issue. But this is really the central issue posed by emancipation.

Another Shimon, writing a little more than a hundred years later, recognized the importance of education and the need, therefore, for some degree of communal autonomy even after emancipation (§21). For Simon Dubnow, emancipation was a fact of life. At least, he writes about it in the present tense: "As a citizen of my country, I participate in its civic and political life." But he wants to establish, or better reestablish, another sphere of participation—the self-government of the Jews as a recognized national minority. And one of the first things that government would include is control over education: "I have the right to speak my language . . . [and] to make it the language of instruction in my schools." The language was Yiddish, and that language has been lost, but I want to stress Dubnow's other possessive pronoun: "my schools." He was right, I think, to call Jews like Shimon b. Wolf, who forgot about the schools, assimilationists; they rushed too quickly "into the (not always open) arms of their 'liberators.'"

Dubnow wanted political and legal equality together with social and cultural autonomy. He would like the autonomous regime to be recognized by the secular state; he favors a kind of corporatism. The problem with this idea is that the Jewish community, even in Dubnow's time and much more today, isn't a single corporation; it is fragmented politically and, with the rise of denominationalism, religiously too. Dubnow's "schools" were already many different schools: Zionist, socialist, orthodox—and more. It is possible to imagine a secular state licensing these schools and even helping to pay their costs, but this was never likely in eastern Europe; nor was it likely that Poland or (czarist or Bolshevik) Russia would permit the flowering of an independent Jewish school system. So Dubnow looked across the Atlantic to an America where voluntarism prevailed and where it was possible to achieve "a large measure of self-administration" without the help or interference of the state—if only the Jews understood themselves as a nation and not simply a "religious community."

It is hard to tell from the text reprinted here (§22) how Morris Loeb imagined the American Jewish community. But he speaks of a "Jewish public" whose interests clearly reach beyond religion, and perhaps that is enough to make him a follower of Dubnow. His concern is with the funding of the range of activities in which this public is engaged. He argues for one fund-raising agency that would allocate money to many different federated organizations. He doesn't mention schools, but the book from which our selection is taken deals extensively with Jewish education (its main interest, however, is social welfare and the integration of immigrants and refugees). Loeb's federation exists today; the activities and institutions it funds are less extensive than those that Dubnow envisaged, but they do include Jewish day schools and other educational programs.

Zionism became—perhaps it already was, in Dubnow's time—the primary expression of Jewish nationalism. Dubnow argued, against the Zionists, for the primacy of diaspora nationalism, expressed in autonomous institutions that would organize, shape, and sustain the cultural life of the Jews. He thought that cultural autonomy was the key to Jewish survival, and he also thought that this autonomy was consistent with, and could be realized alongside of, democratic citizenship in non-Jewish states. Today, many Zionists, looking at the Jewish world from their own sovereign state, have learned the value of a vibrant Jewish life abroad. Some might even describe themselves as Dubnovians for the diaspora.

Michael Walzer

TWENTY-THREE   Enforcement and Coercion

Introduction

Punishment: Foundations and Transformations

Theory of Punishment
1. Maimonides, *The Guide of the Perplexed* 3:41

Principle and Application: *Lex Talionis*

Lex Talionis
2. Exodus 21:18–20, 22–26

Retaliation Versus Restitution
3. Leviticus 24:17–23

Assault and Injury: Affirming and Justifying Monetary Sanctions
4. Mishnah Bava Kama 8:1; BT Bava Kama 83b–84a

Compensation
5. Judah Halevi, *The Kuzari* 3:46–47

Karaite Position on Lex Talionis
6. Aaron b. Elijah, *Sefer ha-Mitzvot* Gan Eden
Commentary. Daniel Greenwood, "Justice in Heaven, Peace on Earth"

Corporal and Capital Punishment: The Law

Corporal Punishment
7. Deuteronomy 25:1–3

Lashing
8. Mishnah Makkot 3:10–15

Introduction

The distinction that we mean to draw between law enforcement or punishment, on the one hand, and coercion, on the other, is a conventional one in Western law, and although it doesn't appear explicitly in Rabbinic literature, it is equally apparent in Jewish law; it divides the material in an obvious and useful way. Punishment is a response to crimes already committed: it takes place not only "after the fact" but also after some procedural appraisal of the "fact." Coercion describes all forceful attempts to prevent crimes or to interrupt them, whether by concerned citizens, "zealots," or public officials; these officials can also use coercion in a positive way—to compel people to do what the law or the courts require.

With regard to punishment, we have chosen a nonstandard beginning for this chapter: not the usual biblical texts but a strong summary statement, a theory of punishment, from Maimonides' *Guide of the Perplexed*. Here we find the tradition revised, as it were, by philosophy. Maimonides clearly looks back to and draws on the Bible (though not, in this case, on the

Talmud), but he is also a participant in contemporary philosophical debates about the purpose of punishment and the justice of specific penalties. The debates still go on, and the list of purposes has not changed much (the terms we use here, however, are modern): retribution, deterrence, social condemnation, individual reformation. Maimonides defends the biblical *lex talionis*—setting aside its rejection by the Rabbis—as a kind of ideal justice, retributive in form. But his practical argument is radically focused on deterrence: the character and extent of the punishments are carefully calculated, in ways that anticipate Jeremy Bentham's utilitarianism, with this purpose always in mind.

The biblical writers seem to have had a wholly different conception of punishment: in their eyes, it had as much to do with God and the cosmic order as with men and women and the social order. They were not unaware of punishment's deterrent effects. Recall the line from Deuteronomy 21 on the stoning of the rebellious son (¢19, §1): "all Israel will hear and be afraid." But this same text (and many others too) expresses another very different idea: that the criminal must be cast out of Israel; the community must be purged so as to maintain its holiness and its moral integrity—"thus you will sweep out evil from your midst." "Evil" here is some kind of embodied entity that can literally be removed. Maimonides avoids this idea, and it has no place in later philosophical discussions.

Nor is the *lex talionis* philosophically defended in the biblical texts. (Michael Fishbane discusses the Rabbinic debate about *talion* in his introductory essay to Volume I, "Law, Story, and Interpretation: Reading Rabbinic Texts.") It can readily be explained, as by Maimonides, in retributive terms—and as readily in deterrent terms. But the Bible hardly offers any explanation beyond the implicit idea of symmetry—as if criminal acts violate the cosmic order and symmetrical punishment restores its integrity. At the same time, bodily assault and murder seem also to have been understood as crimes against God, the creator of the body. Thus the original statement of the *talion*: "Whoever sheds the blood of man, by man shall his blood be shed: for in His image did God make man" (Gen. 9:6). Presumably, deterrence is one of the ends in view here, but the plain meaning of the text is that murder is an affront to God, which must be avenged.

This line from Genesis, however, provides a highly subversive rationale for "shedding man's blood." Since the criminal also bears God's image, killing him might be called a second affront. Some such view probably accounts for Rabbi Akiva's opposition to capital punishment. The general Rabbinic assault on the *talion* may be similarly motivated, though it is differently defended: the Rabbis rule out mutilation as a punishment on the grounds that it can never achieve a genuine symmetry (this is the strongest argument in BT Bava Kama, though it is formally rejected). Except in capital cases, they require monetary compensation—which serves a purpose that is also largely ignored in later philosophical discussions: benefiting the victim. In contemporary terms, they replace criminal with civil law, and they then provide a detailed and lively account of the victim's right to be compensated not only for the lost limb but also for pain and humiliation, as well as for short-term consequences of the injury, such as lost work time or the costs of medical care. Their arguments represent a classic example of interpretive revision. They were apparently so persuasive that even the Karaites, for all their biblical literalism, abandoned the *lex talionis* in most cases. In medieval communities, mutilation was sometimes employed as a punishment—it was common in the surrounding Christian and Muslim societies. But it was defended as an emergency measure, designed to meet "the needs of the hour" (and used chiefly against "informers," who were perceived as deadly threats to the safety of the *kahal*), rather than as a divinely ordained, symmetrical response to ordinary crime.

Punishment itself is a problem for the Jews after the loss of statehood and sovereignty. The Rabbis continually insist that their courts, meeting in exile, have no authority to administer corporal punishments or even, in most cases, to impose fines. And yet, as we will see in the next chapter, they do contrive to punish criminals in both these ways, relying on a variety of legal fictions or appealing to the "needs of the hour"—which means appealing also to the community whose needs these were. In fact, their ability to punish in any of the conventional ways depended as much on the allowance of gentile rulers as on their own standing in the Jewish community. By and large, gentile rulers claimed the right of capital, and often of corporal, punishment exclusively for themselves—though they might well act at the behest of Jewish courts. It doesn't appear that medieval Jews were all that reluctant to yield the right: if killing or maiming was necessary, many of them seem to have thought, it was better that the gentiles do it. But in some parts of the Diaspora (in Spain, especially), in some periods, the *kehillot* administered the full range of punishments through their own officials.

The Rabbis seem to have been especially uneasy with capital punishment (Maimonides did not entirely share their unease). Though tractate Sanhedrin provides an extraordinarily detailed account of the four methods of execution, the discussions there, and in the Tosefta, have the effect of making the actual use of any of these methods virtually impossible. Since death is an approved punishment in the Bible, the interpretive work here focuses on procedural issues—first, on the biblical requirement of two eyewitnesses in criminal cases and, second, on the Rabbinic ruling that individuals about to commit a crime for which death was the prescribed penalty (other crimes also, though the Rabbinic arguments are focused on the capital cases) must be alerted to that fact, explicitly warned by one or another (or by both!) of the witnesses. Though the method is indirect, these two together effectively abolished capital punishment as a possible verdict of a Jewish court. But even the radical remark attributed to Akiva and Tarfon in tractate Makkot, to the effect that no court in which they participated would ever vote for capital punishment, does not quite come to an explicit abolitionism.

In the *kahal,* the punishments most readily available to the authorities, and therefore the most common punishments, were the fine and the ban; flogging and mutilation were also used, with permission or assistance from gentile governments. Given the talmudic arguments, we might describe the first two of these as the preferred punishments, despite the obvious constraints under which they were chosen. But we really don't know how the Jewish law of punishment would have developed in a sovereign state. The fine and the ban worked well enough in the *kahal,* a small and tightly knit community, whose members knew one another's business and were dependent on one another's support.

A banned individual was not only socially ostracized but also cut off from every sort of economic cooperation and denied access to the synagogue, that is, to worship and study and to all ritual observances that required the participation of fellow Jews. Even if the ban was enacted only by the *bet din* or the selectmen, it was understood to rest upon a religious duty of each and every member of the community: to have no dealings whatsoever with the condemned individual. But no mere ordinance could cut someone out of the "brotherhood" of the *kahal.* The extraordinary exactitude of Nahmanides' analysis of the imposition and release of the ban demonstrates its seriousness: as God was once immanent in the Chamber of Hewn Stones, so he was invoked now in the *herem.* Unless the condemned person converted or fled to a distant Jewish settlement (before Baruch Spinoza's time, there were no other options), he would have to seek some relief from the ban. And this, of course, was its purpose; as in earlier Rabbinic texts (see §8 below), individual reformation is a central goal of punishment. The ban was not commonly described in the literature of the *kahal* as a way of casting the evildoer out of the community. It aimed instead at producing compliance—and bringing the culprit back in.

But whenever Jewish writers thought about a political order larger than the *kahal,* or whenever they had to address the long-term necessities of the order that actually existed, they were driven back from fines and bans to the question of capital punishment. And many of them, it seems, were then prepared to acknowledge the worldly inadequacy of the talmudic arguments about witnesses and warnings and to argue, audaciously, that it was sometimes necessary to act outside or even against the divine law. We have already seen this argument in Nissim Gerondi's authorization of kings (¢3, §16), and Solomon b. Abraham Adret's and Isaac b. Sheshet Perfet's authorization of the *kahal* (¢8, §§11–12), to meet what were taken to be the requirements of public order. The texts from Sanhedrin on capital punishment are central to all descriptions of the Torah as an "ideal law" that can't be allowed to govern the everyday life of the community or that must, at least, be set aside in emergencies. How extensive was the use of emergency punishments? We have no statistics, only scattered stories about cases and many arguments about principles. But it seems likely that the "needs of the hour" were in fact the needs of many hours. Some of the rabbis (see especially the text from Joseph ibn Migash) strove to limit the scope of emergency so as to hold open room for the idealism of the Torah. By contrast, Meir b. Gedaliah of Lublin, perhaps reflecting the conditions of his own time, seems to have abandoned any effort to restrict the emergency powers of the *bet din*. Other writers, like the pseudo-Ran, preferred to turn to the gentile king rather than to the Jewish authorities for permission to kill and mutilate Jewish criminals. But for most of the rabbis, the necessary self-defense of the community against traitors and "informers" overrode all reservations about corporal and capital punishment and about their own legal powers.

The Rabbis were wrestling here with one of the central issues of political life and political theory: the relation of justice and prudence, eternal principle and everyday practice, ends and means. "Building a fence for the Torah" is a Rabbinic doctrine that parallels the "needs of the hour" but allows us a more direct access to the basic argument. Building a fence is the means; a life in accordance with the Torah is the end. Sometimes the fence does no more than thicken the laws, especially the negative commandments, adding new prohibitions, so that pious men and women never even get close to the originally prohibited act. (Or, in the alternative imagery of contemporary moral philosophy, they never slide down the slippery slope that starts with trivial but leads inexorably to serious violations of the law.) But sometimes the fence and the laws are contradictory: the Rabbis break the law in order to protect it. There is nothing strange here; it is easy to find modern examples—as when a liberal and democratic state curtails civil liberties or bans antidemocratic political parties, defending its existence by violating its principles. This is to address the "needs of the hour" by "building a fence." What is fenced is what is most valued. But it is always a question whether the value will survive the fencing.

Throughout most of Jewish history, as throughout most of history generally, it was assumed that there was no effective deterrence without the threat of death. Today, however, many states have abolished the death penalty in all or most of the cases to which it once applied. Immediately after the founding of the state of Israel, a similar abolition was debated and enacted—the age-old reluctance of the Rabbis was finally given political expression and practical effect. The arguments in the Knesset draw heavily on the tradition and also on the modern Western debates about the legitimacy and value of capital punishment.

The courts and the *kahal* did not exist only to punish criminals—

though this was often taken to be the central activity of the political order. As in other religious cultures, the function of government was also to sponsor, and sometimes to impose, a common morality and a life of ritual observance. The brief selection from BT Sanhedrin (§34) suggests, however, that the sages were reluctant to authorize the kind of zealotry that such an imposition would require. Even Maimonides, who doesn't seem to feel the same reluctance, sends out his morality patrols only on holidays. It is not clear whether these patrols would be authorized to interfere only with illicit conduct already in progress or to take steps to prevent such conduct before it started. But it is hard to imagine agents of this sort who would not set themselves the second goal. If that is right, then the patrols are simply and unapologetically coercive, rather in the style, say, of John Calvin's Geneva and later puritanical regimes in England and New England or, in today's world, in the Islamic Republic of Iran.

But coercion to act rightly, in accordance with moral or religious law, is more of a problem than Maimonides' text suggests, and the discussions of its role in the marketplace and (especially) in divorce law sound very much like the debates about "positive freedom" set off by Jean-Jacques Rousseau's *Social Contract*. The problem is this: there are many cases in which free choice is necessary to the moral, and even the social and economic, effectiveness of individual action. But how can individuals be said to act freely when they are forced to act in certain ways?

Obviously, this is a problem only for writers who set a high value on acting freely. We have already seen that value expressed in the accounts of the acceptance of the law at Sinai and again in the description of the conversion ceremony (¢¢1 and 14). Now it is repeated in the conditions of everyday life—where the paradigmatic free individual is the male patriarch in his relations with women. Divorce, on the biblical account, is wholly in his hands (see the texts in ¢18). In order to provide at least minimal protection for married women, the Rabbis permit them to initiate divorce proceedings and allow the courts to require an actual divorce, that is, to force the man "willingly" to write a *get*. "We beat him until he consents." But, again, how can this "consent" possibly meet the requirements of the law?

Two different answers to this question are suggested in our texts, both of them familiar from later philosophical literature. The first holds that doing what the law (or the court) requires is the very definition of freedom, for we violate the law only when we are the slaves of our passions. So the husband, though coerced, nonetheless acts freely, at least in some ideal sense. The second answer is more obviously focused on individual consent: when we choose to live within a community, we willingly accept its laws, and then the enforcement of those laws cannot be called coercive. Here the husband is forced to act like the good Jew he surely means to be. It is interesting to ask whether these arguments were carried over from the familial to the communal setting. The *kahal* also rested, in part at least, on the agreement of its members, and the extent to which these members could be coerced was, as we have seen, a matter of intense debate. But the reference to a higher or prior individual will was not explicitly made in these debates—except when Jews were reminded that they were "already under oath from Mount Sinai" (¢8, §7).

The divorce arguments, however problematic, at least assume a legal/political procedure of some sort. But it is in the nature of a religious code claiming to shape and control every aspect of ordinary life that violators will commonly escape official surveillance. Hence there is room for "zealots," who take it upon themselves, without any specific legal sanction, to enforce the law. Zealotry in religious cultures is something like the idea of "citizen's arrest" in republics—where the claims of *civisme* are almost as extensive as those of divine law. Citizen's arrests, however, are relatively rare: republican zeal is unlikely to outlast the revolutionary founding of the republic. After that, citizens reach some sort of *modus vivendi* with their wayward fellows and leave law enforcement to the police.

Religious zeal is probably no more long-lasting. Phinehas, the biblical prototype of the zealot, is a figure of the wilderness period. Later on in the Bible, the zealot is effectively replaced by the prophet, who castigates evildoers but does not assault them. The discussion of zealotry in tractate Sanhedrin suggests the hesitations and ambiguous feelings of the sages— though Phinehas is not exactly repudiated. The zealot does not figure at all in the literature of the *kahal,* where Rabbinic arguments are focused (see ¢8) on admonition and protest, not physical interference. But, once again, Maimonides provides a telling illustration of the continuing attraction of a kind of institutionalized zealotry—if only as a way of suggesting that the law of the Torah takes precedence, every day, everywhere, over friendship and human dignity and the forms of courtesy they require. Later rabbis, confronting the same issues, gave greater weight to human dignity.

Punishment: Foundations and Transformations

Theory of Punishment

1. Maimonides, *The Guide of the Perplexed* 3:41

The Guide of the Perplexed, translated with an introduction and notes by Shlomo Pines (Chicago: University of Chicago Press, 1963), pp. 558–60.

Maimonides here develops a philosophical theory of punishment. It is a unique theoretical text in a casuistically inclined legal tradition. True to his declared focus on biblical theology, Maimonides does not address the Rabbinic critique of capital punishment. Instead he provides a philosophical commentary on the biblical lex talionis *as the axial notion of retributive justice (but Maimonides' own argument focuses on deterrence).*

The punishment meted out to anyone who has done wrong to somebody else consists in general in his being given exactly the same treatment that he has given to somebody else. If he has injured the latter's body, he shall be injured in his body, and if he has injured him in his property, he shall be injured in his property. The owner of the property may be indulgent and forgive. To the murderer alone, however, because of the greatness of his wrongdoing, no indulgence shall be shown at all and no blood money shall be accepted form him: "And the land cannot be cleansed of the blood that is shed therein, but by the blood of him that shed it" (Num. 35:33). Hence even if the victim remains alive for an hour or for several days, speaks, and is in full possession of his mind and says: Let him who murdered me be dismissed; I have forgiven and pardoned him—this cannot be accepted from him. For necessarily there must be a soul for a soul—the young and the old, the slaves and the free, the men of knowledge and the ignorant, being considered as equal. For among the crimes of man there is no greater than this.

And he who has deprived someone of a member, shall be deprived of a similar member: "As he hath maimed a man, so shall it be rendered unto him" (Lev. 24:20). You should not engage in cogitation concerning the fact that in such a case we punish by imposing a fine. For at present my purpose is to give reasons for the [biblical] texts and not for the pronouncements of the legal science. Withal I have an opinion concerning this provision of legal science, which should only be expressed by word of mouth. A fine was imposed in the case of wounds in requital of which exactly similar wounds could not be inflicted: "Only he shall pay for the loss of his time, and shall cause him to be thoroughly healed" (Exod. 21:19).

He who has caused damage to property shall have inflicted upon him damage to his property up to exactly the same amount: "Whom the judges shall condemn, he shall pay double unto his neighbor" (Exod. 22:8)— that is, the thing taken by him and an equal amount taken from the property of the thief. . . .

Similarly the law concerning false witnesses is that the thing that they wished to be done unto another shall be done unto them: if they wished the one they bore witness against to be killed, they shall be killed; if they wished him to be flogged, they shall be flogged: and if they wished him to be fined, they shall have a similar fine imposed upon them. In all this the intention is to make the penalty equal to the crime, and this too is the meaning of the expression: righteous judgments. . . .

Introduction. Know that whether a penalty is great and most grievous or small and easy to bear depends on four things being taken into consideration. The first is the greatness of the crime: for actions for which only small and slight harm results entail but slight penalty. The second is the frequency of the occurrence of the crime: for a crime that occurs rather often ought to be prevented by means of a heavy penalty, whereas a slight penalty suffices to prevent one that is rare in view of its rarity. The third is the strength of the incitement: for a man can be made to give up a thing toward which he is incited—either because desire draws him strongly toward it or because of the strength of habit or because of his feeling great hardship when refraining from it—only by fear of a heavy penalty. The fourth is the ease with which the action can be committed in secret and in concealment, so that the others are unaware of it: for the deterrent for this can only be the fear of a great and heavy penalty.

After this introduction has been made, you should know that the classification of punishments, according to the text of the Torah, comprises four degrees: (1) that which entails death by order of a court of law; (2) that which entails being cut off—that is, being whipped, the crime being believed withal to be a great one; (3) that which entails being whipped, but the crime is not believed to be a great one, but a mere transgression, or entails death at the hands of Heaven; (4) that in which there is only a prohibition the transgression of which does not even entail flogging.

Principle and Application: Lex Talionis

Lex Talionis

2. Exodus 21:18–20, 22–26

A central theme in these passages is the distinction between monetary compensation for financial loss and punishments wrought upon the body, mandated whenever permanent harm was perpetrated against human life or limb (strikingly excluding miscarriage). The formula "x for x" seems entirely unambiguous, yet regarding injuries there was great reluctance in later generations to take it literally, supported perhaps by the biblical language in our next selection.

When men quarrel and one strikes the other with stone or fist, and he does not die but has to take to his bed—if he then gets up and walks outdoors upon his staff, the assailant shall go unpunished, except that he must pay for his idleness and his cure. When a man strikes his slave, male or female, with a rod, and he dies there and then, he must be avenged. But if he survives a day or two, he is not to be avenged, since he is the other's property.[1]

---

1. Evidently, the time-lapse indicates that the beating was not with an intent to kill but was rather within the owner's prerogative of chastising his slave. See Moshe Greenberg, "Some

When men fight, and one of them pushes a pregnant woman and a miscarriage results, but no other damage ensues, the one responsible shall be fined according as the woman's husband may exact from him, the payment to be based on reckoning. But if other damage[2] ensues, the penalty shall be life for life, eye for eye, tooth for tooth, hand for hand, foot for foot, burn for burn, wound for wound, bruise for bruise. When a man strikes the eye of his slave, male or female, and destroys it, he shall let him go free on account of his eye. If he knocks out the tooth of his slave, male or female, he shall let him go free on account of his tooth.

Retaliation Versus Restitution

3. Leviticus 24:17–23

Here killing a human being is contrasted with killing a beast; the "life for life" stipulated for the latter mandates restitution rather than retaliatory harm. The immediately following "eye for eye" mandated for maiming a person could thus be perceived as also calling for restitution. The sequel seems, however, to demand instead a literal application of the lex talionis — *though the concluding contrast focuses narrowly upon fatal outcomes.*

If anyone kills any human being, he shall be put to death. One who kills a beast shall make restitution for it: life for life. If anyone maims his fellow, as he has done so shall it be done to him: fracture for fracture, eye for eye, tooth for tooth. The injury he inflicted on another shall be inflicted on him. One who kills a beast shall make restitution for it; but one who kills a human being shall be put to death. You shall have one standard for stranger and citizen alike: for I the Lord am your God. Moses spoke thus to the Israelites.

Postulates of Biblical Criminal Law," in *Studies in the Bible and Jewish Thought* (Philadelphia: JPS, 1995), 25–41.

2. Heb., *ason,* alternatively translated as "serious injury."

Assault and Injury: Affirming and Justifying Monetary Sanctions

4. Mishnah Bava Kama 8:1; BT Bava Kama 83b–84a

Despite the biblical mandate of "eye for eye"—and its own endorsement, at least in principle, of both corporal and capital punishment (cf. §§9-10 below)—the Mishnah specifies a set of monetary sanctions for assault and battery. The Talmud boldly asks about the warrant for deviating from Scripture's plain meaning, but the sages represented in this compendium of justifications clearly assume the monetary option as the bottom line. The contrary view of Rabbi Eli'ezer (who is often a lone voice defending ancient traditions) is recorded at the sugya's conclusion, but met with incredulity. Several of the justifications question whether "eye for eye" can ever represent an actual equality, so that the victim and the perpetrator are injured in exactly the same way. The first baraita, however, emphasizes a substantive contrast with homicide.[3]

Mishnah Bava Kama 8:1

One who [assaults and] injures his fellow is liable on his account for five things: for [physical] damage, for pain, for healing, for loss of time, and for humiliation. How [is] "damage" [appraised]? If he blinded his eye, cut off his hand, or broke his leg—[the victim] is deemed as a slave put up for sale: How much was he worth, and how much is he worth [now]? How is "pain" [appraised]? If he burned him with a skewer or [stabbed him] with a nail, even upon his fingernail where no wound is produced—an appraisal is made: How much would a person like this agree to receive in order to suffer such pain? . . .

3. For further discussion see Michael Fishbane's introductory essay on reading Rabbinic texts in Vol. I.

BT Bava Kama 83b–84a

Why [so]? It is "eye for eye" that God stated (Exod. 21:24; Lev. 24: 20), [so] I say [he must lose] an actual eye! One cannot suppose so, for it was taught:

"Can it be that, if a person blinded [his fellow's] eye, his eye is blinded; if he cut off his hand, his hand is cut off, or if he broke his leg, his leg is broken? We learn [otherwise] from what is written, 'One who strikes [a person]' and 'One who strikes [a beast]' [reasoning by association]:[4] just as one who strikes a beast [makes] monetary payment, so too one who strikes a person [makes] monetary payment.

"Or if you prefer, it can be argued [thus]: [Scripture] states, 'You may not accept ransom for the life of a murderer who is guilty of a capital crime' (Num. 35:31), [implying that] it is [only] for the life of a murderer that you may not accept ransom, whereas you may accept ransom for principal limbs, [though] they do not grow back." . . .

What [calls for the statement], "Or if you prefer, it can be argued . . ."? The *tanna*'s difficulty [with the first argument] was as follows: What [is the sense in] drawing [an association] from [the law governing] the striking of a beast? It should [rather] be drawn from [the law governing] the striking of a person [i.e., homicide]! [Well,] it is appropriate to compare damages to damages, rather than damages to a fatality.—On the contrary, it is appropriate to compare human [victim] to human [victim], rather than human to beast!—This was [indeed the point of the alternative argument introduced by] the statement "Or if you prefer, it can be argued."

Since it was written, "You may not accept ransom [for the life of a murderer]" (Num. 35:31), [with the said implication], what need is there for the proof [by association of] "striking" and "striking"?—From the [said implication alone], I might have said that [it is optional:] if he wishes his eye will be taken, whereas if he wishes the value of his eye [will be taken]. [This

---

4. The language indicates the midrashic mechanism of *gezerah shavah,* which expounds a link between two instances of the same term. The talmudic discussion (not reproduced here) labors to determine specifically which of several verses with the term "striking" are intended, focusing on Lev. 24:17–21 (above, §3—where the verb is translated as "kill").

therefore] is precluded by "One who strikes [a person]" and "one who strikes [a beast]"—just as one who strikes a beast [makes] monetary payment, so too one who strikes a person [makes] monetary payment.

It was taught, Rabbi Dostai b. Yehudah says: "Eye for eye" [means] money [payment]. You say money, but perhaps [it means] actually an eye?— Indeed? Then suppose the eye of one was large and the eye of the other small; How can I apply here "eye for eye"? Whereas the Torah stated, "You shall have one standard" (Lev. 24:22), [implying that] the law should be equal for all. I say: What is the difficulty? Perhaps [in exchange for the] eyesight [that was] taken from [the victim,] God said eyesight is to be taken from [the offender]! For otherwise, how could capital punishment be applied in the case of a large person who killed a small person? . . . [Thus "life for life" must mean that in exchange for] the life that was taken from [the victim,] God said life is to be taken from [the offender]. Here too, [in exchange for] eyesight taken from [the victim], God said eyesight is to be taken from [the offender].

Another [*baraita*] taught: Rabbi Shimon b. Yohai says: "Eye for eye" [means] money. You say money, but perhaps [it means] actually an eye? Indeed? Then suppose a blind person blinded [another person], or an amputee cut off the limb [of another], or a lame person made [another person] lame. How can I apply here "eye for eye"? Whereas the Torah stated, "You shall have one standard" (Lev. 24:22), [implying that] the law should be equal for all! I say: What is the difficulty? Perhaps where it is possible [to carry out actual maiming] it is possible, but where it is impossible, it is impossible, and [the offender] is [simply] released. . . .

Abaye said: [That "eye for eye" means money] can be derived from the teaching of the School of Hizkiyah. For the School of Hizkiyah taught: "'Eye for eye,' but not 'life and eye for eye.'" Now should you suppose [it means] actually an eye, sometimes [what is taken] will be life and eye for eye: while [the offender] is being blinded, his soul departs from him. [But] what is the difficulty? Perhaps [the court] must arrange an assessment: if the offender is [deemed] able to survive [the maiming], it is done to him, but if he is not [so deemed], it is not done. And if the assessment was that he is able to survive it, yet when it was done his soul departed from him—if he dies, he dies. For was it not taught regarding lashes: "[If after] he was assessed . . . he died under the hand [of the officer of the court, the officer is] exempt [from liability]"? (Mishnah Makkot 3:11–14, §9 below).

Rav Zevid said, citing Rava: "Scripture states, 'Wound for wound' (Exod. 21:25)—[this] mandates [payment] for pain [even] where [payment is also made for] damage." Now, if you suppose that actual [maiming is meant], just as [the victim] suffered pain, [the offender] would also suffer pain [obviating justification for a separate recovery for pain]! . . .

Rav Papa, citing Rava, said: "Scripture states, 'He must pay for his cure' (Exod. 21:19). [This] mandates [payment for] healing [even] where [payment is also made for] damage." Now, if you suppose that actual [maiming is meant], just as [the victim] needed a physician, [the offender] would also need a physician, [obviating justification for a separate recovery for healing]! . . .

It was taught: "Rabbi Eli'ezer said: 'Eye for eye' [means] actually [an eye]." Do you suppose he [truly upholds] "actually [an eye]"? Does Rabbi Eli'ezer disagree with all these *tanna'im* [cited above]? Said Rabbah: [He] means to say that [in assessing "damage," the victim] is not appraised as if he were a slave. Abaye said to him: Like whom [else could he be appraised]? Like a free man? Does a free man have a monetary value? Rather, Rav Ashi said: [He] means to say that the appraisal is not of [the eye of] the victim but of the offender.

Compensation

5. Judah Halevi, *The Kuzari* 3:46–47

Translated by Barry S. Kogan, forthcoming in the YJS (New Haven: Yale University Press).

This section of The Kuzari *focuses on refuting Karaite positions. The sage argues for the primacy of faith and tradition over independent interpretation of Scripture's apparent meaning. Yet, pressed by his royal interlocutor, he is prepared to provide justifications for some salient Rabbinic departures from the literal sense of biblical commandments. First and foremost among these is "eye for eye."*

(3:46) The Khazar said: Isn't retaliation in kind clearly expounded in the Torah, when it says, . . . *eye for eye, tooth for tooth. The injury he inflicted on another shall be inflicted on him?* (Lev. 24:20).

(3:47) The sage said: But didn't it say right after that, *One who kills a beast shall make restitution for it: life for life . . . ?* (Lev. 24:18; cf. Exod. 21:24; Lev. 24:21). Isn't this monetary compensation? [If it actually intended retaliation in kind,] why didn't it say, "Whoever kills your horse, kill his horse"? But [in effect, this is what] it said: "Take his horse, since there is no benefit to you in killing his horse." In the same way, if someone cuts off your hand, then take the monetary equivalent of his hand in compensation, since there is no benefit to you in cutting off his hand, especially when something that the intellect opposes is implied by these precepts [being taken literally], to wit, *wound for wound, bruise for bruise* (Exod. 21:25). How can we possibly decree that, when sometimes one of the two has died from his wound, while the other has not died from a wound just like it? Moreover, how can we assume that something like it can even be appraised? Again, how can we put out the eye of a man who is already blind in one eye for what is owed to someone who has two eyes, so that the one will be left totally blind, while the other will be blind in one eye only, when the Torah says, *the injury he inflicted on another shall be inflicted on him?* (Lev. 24:20; BT Bava Kama 84a). Indeed, why do I need to dispute with you about these particulars, after I have already established the need for relying upon authoritative tradition [based upon faith] in conjunction with the trustworthiness, superior standing, knowledge, and diligence of those who are to be accepted as authorities?

Karaite Position on Lex Talionis

6. Aaron b. Elijah, *Sefer ha-Mitzvot* Gan Eden

Sefer ha-Mitzvot ha-Gadol: Gan Eden (Israel: n.p., 1972), pp. 179–80.

Here is a Karaite argument that supports, but only in part, a literal interpretation of "eye for eye." Aaron b. Elijah is well versed in Rabbanite sources, and his rhetoric is carefully crafted. He eschews the Rabbanites' style of branding their opponents heretics and care-

fully considers the opposing interpretation of the Rabbis—which he presents first in an inclusive manner: they, too, are among the wise.[5]

Laws of Maiming

With regard to the laws of maiming and the Torah's statement, "life for life, eye for eye, tooth for tooth"—the wise are in dispute. There are those among them who say that Scripture wishes to impose monetary compensation for [such injuries]. This is because they have found Scripture prohibiting compensation in case of death [murder] while passing over in silence compensation for maiming. It is therefore to be deduced, they say, that Scripture supports compensation for maiming. And others say that Scripture states "life for life, eye for eye"—and just as there is no substitution for a life, so too there is no substitution for maiming [and just as a soul cannot be substituted for by compensation, but rather murder must be punished by retribution. so too in case of maiming.] And this seems [to be right].

The former respond to the latter by argumentation—some by saying that if an adult knocked out a child's tooth, how could the adult's tooth be knocked out [as retribution]? For a child's tooth will be replaced, not so an adult's! Or in case [the assailant] was blind in one eye, and he blinded his fellow, how can we put out his one eye! And if he had no eyes, how could we implement "eye for eye"? And in case of a partial reduction of sight, what would be [a precise measure], not more or less? And [what of a case] where imposing upon the assailant the same [bodily] damage [that he has caused] would endanger his life—how ought we to go about that?

The respondents say that if the assailant has no eye, we should incapacitate another sense. Should we fear that injuring him in this place or that one is dangerous [to his life], we should do it elsewhere. . . .

The followers of Scripture dispute the followers of Talmud with regard to liability in case of unintentional maiming or assault. The difference is [as follows]: The followers of [Rabbinic] tradition impose [monetary] compensation for maiming.

---

5. For the Karaite-Rabbanite controversy regarding the authority of talmudic interpretations, see ¢6, §§16–18.

[Aaron cites the talmudic discussion in BT Bava Kama (§4 above) and Abraham ibn Ezra's commentary on the Torah. After critically considering their interpretations of Scripture, he concludes:]

It should [rather] be maintained that [in case of] unintentional maiming [the assailant] makes no compensation whatsoever, and in case of intentional [maiming] too, there is no compensation but rather an actual eye for an eye.

The followers of [Rabbinic] tradition disagree [among themselves]. Some say that there is compensation for maiming whether [it is caused] intentionally or not. Rabbi Eli'ezer however says, "'Eye for eye' [means] actually [an eye]."

On this matter Maimonides has made an absolute pronouncement:

> And he who has deprived someone of a member, shall be deprived of a similar member: "As he hath maimed a man, so shall it be rendered unto him" (Lev. 24:20). You should not engage in cogitation concerning the fact that in such a case we punish by imposing a fine. For at present my purpose is to give reasons for the [biblical] texts and not for the pronouncements of the Talmud.[6]

We may thus learn from the words of this sage that Scripture has not empowered them [the Rabbanites] to [determine the] punishment for maiming.

Now seeing that our Torah provides for a just governance, we must turn to investigate its crafted words.

. . . Scripture states an "Eye for eye" [*ayin tahat ayin*] (Exod. 21:24) and it states "An eye by an eye" [*ayin be-ayin*] (Deut. 19:21). The reason is [to indicate by the latter] that the [loss of the] right eye [finds its retribution] by the [loss of the] right eye. And in case of a tooth for a tooth, an analogy is to be drawn from the eye. Just as an "eye" does not grow again, so too with regard to a "tooth"—one that does not grow again. If an adult knocked out the tooth of a child, he gives monetary [compensation].

6. *Guide of the Perplexed* 3:41; §1 above. Maimonides employed the Islamic jurisprudential term for "legal science"; Aaron is using Samuel ibn Tibbon's Hebrew translation, which renders this as "Talmud."

So too [Scripture's] stating, "An eye by an eye," indicates that if the wound is in a dangerous place and the harm [caused by retribution] will not [be equal] in measure to the harm caused [by the assailant] but will be greater, the law is that monetary [compensation] is to be given so that the assailant not be endangered more than the danger he caused. So too in case the assailant caused a loss of a third of the [victim's] sight . . . and if the assailant has no eyes, or only one eye, he is to pay ransom [i.e., monetary compensation].

Commentary. Justice in Heaven, Peace on Earth

Eye for eye, tooth for tooth, hand for hand, foot for foot, burn for burn, wound for wound, bruise for bruise: in concrete and brutal symmetry, the text insists, as Leviticus explicitly glosses, "as he has done so shall it be done to him." The poetry raises but does not resolve basic arguments about punishment, the purposes of criminal and tort law, and the nature of justice itself.

"As he has done so shall it be done to him" could pass for an abstract epitome of justice that could motivate a criminal law system. Aristotle taught that justice is treating equals equally; Maimonides states that punishment should be exactly the same as the offense (§1). By doing to the offender as he has done, we restore precisely the balance of the status quo ante; equals have been treated equally and justice is done. But the claim undermines itself. If an eye for an eye is justice, it is the justice of poets, not the justice of law in our world.

We are mere humans, not God. For us, restoration is impossible; as *The Kuzari* emphasizes (§5), cutting off an offender's hand does nothing to restore the victim's. Nor is the equality of balance any easier. If justice is founded on equal treatment of equals, the problem is that—as R. Dostai b. Yehudah and R. Shimon b. Yohai point out in the Bava Kama excerpt (§4)— eyes and limbs are never equal. Some eyes are highly trained, others see little; destroying the eye of a one-eyed man is vastly different from removing the eye of a two-eyed or blind man. And there is the Shylock problem, explicated by both Abaye and *The Kuzari:* the principle is "an eye for an eye," not "an eye and a life for an eye." It is almost as difficult to extract an eye as a pound of flesh without collateral damage. Mere humans can never attain the level of precision of an eye for an eye; the wound we make in retribution will always be different from the one it is meant to offset. Our punishment will never truly fit the crime.

Justice requires justice. If what is done to the criminal is not "as he has done," then judicial violence is just violence. The criminal has been wronged, and this version of the eye for an eye principle suggests that yet more violence is necessary to restore the balance. Indeed, the Bible itself is aware of this problem, as we see in its very first allusion to the "life for a life." After Cain murders Abel, God's punishment fits his crime in a symbolic, not literal, way: Cain, the settled farmer, is condemned to wander in place of his murdered brother, the shepherd. Cain, however, immediately assumes that people will apply the *lex talionis* more literally: "anyone who finds me will kill me" (Gen. 4:15). Violence, that is, will beget violence in a never-ending cycle, made worse by God's proposed solution, "If anyone slays Cain, he shall be avenged seven times." Five generations later, Lemekh understands the full logic of this system: he kills a man for wounding him, a child for his bruise—and vows that if anyone responds in kind he shall be avenged seventy-sevenfold (Gen. 4:23–24). This route leads to war without end, the world that could be cleansed only by the Flood.

But the postbiblical argument does not focus on the instability of regimes of retaliation. Instead, the later texts assume a state or statelike adjudicator whose actions, just or unjust, do not demand revenge. Private revenge has been transformed into a communal system of mixed criminal and tort law.

In this statelike system, the central problem is not violence without end but hubris: humans pretending to be gods. A criminal law meant to restore the cosmic balance of a mythological status quo ante, to achieve justice by doing to the offender what he sought to do to his victim, or to appease vengeful victims by allowing them to take what they lost, is basically beyond the capacity of a human legal system. To be fair, it must restore what cannot be restored and measure the incommensurable.

Determining the sanctions for assault, in short, raises exactly the same problems as criminal law generally: a just system of adjudication requires a level of knowledge, empathy, and moral certainty not possible in human systems. In the Talmud, the ultimate expression of these requirements appears in discussions of capital punishment. The talmudic texts (see, e.g., §§9–10, 12 below) describe the requirements for an ideal criminal law system: seventy wise judges, speaking every language in the world so that they will not be tripped up by translations, able to prove the purity of an impure "swarming thing" despite Leviticus 11:29 so that they know the limits of legal logic, parents so that they can empathize with the frailties of flesh, speaking in reverse order of seniority to avoid peer pressure, waiting overnight before conviction to allow arguments to ripen, ready to revisit any conviction at any time over any new evidence so that procedural finality does not interfere with the pursuit of truth, acquitting on a unanimous vote of conviction since such agreement must indicate a failure of independent thought, requiring two reliable and religiously observant eyewitnesses for each crime without inferences or circumstantial evidence, duly warned of the gravity of the enterprise, making sure that the accused had acknowledged the wrongfulness of the action immediately before doing it, and so on.

But this is a system for poets, not attorneys. If it is law, it can only work as law administered directly by the Court Above. As the Rabbis emphasize, this system will never generate human convictions or human punishment. It must rely, instead, on the king's less just law (see §§13–15 below) or on "snakebites" (cf. BT Sanhedrin 37b) to punish the guilty. Only God can enforce his rules.

Paradoxically, the argument from the pursuit of justice leads to the inescapable conclusion that we should, instead, pursue something less. Perhaps, prefiguring later liberal arguments, human institutions ought to be based on the lesser virtue of peace—preventing people from "eating each other alive."

Still, even if the goal is civil order, not absolute justice, ideals remain critical. Systems based merely on deterrence—simple fear of negative consequences—are likely to be both violent and ineffective. People react quite differently to negative consequences depending on whether they interpret them as hostile oppression or deserved punishment. The norms of the oppressor we resist if we are brave and subvert if we are not.

Accordingly, the first task of a criminal justice system is to convince the population to adopt a particular understanding of what is right and what is wrong: that murder is wrong, and so is beating women into miscarriage, beating slaves to death, killing for family honor, warring on neighbors to steal their property. Only if criminals accept that their actions were crimes will they agree that the state's violence is punishment rather than oppression or mere random fate. So, although an actual criminal law system need not be absolutely just, if it is to be effective it must persuade its subjects that it is at least reasonably legitimate.

Thus, the unenforceable, uninstitutionalized system of poetic justice exists to educate, to structure debates about how people should act that will help those of moderate goodwill conform their behavior to social expectations. That educational system is the primary source of social control. Only when it fails do we move to more conventional criminal law. There, instead of justice, the first goal should be reducing crime; punishments should be judged by whether they in fact reduce crime. Creating superegos or deterring violence, not restoring balance, is the primary point.

This seems to be Maimonides' view in this excerpt from *The Guide of the Perplexed* (§1). He begins by giving a straightforward philosophical account of the principle of proportionality. But at the point marked "Introduction," he switches mode entirely. Discussing appropriate penalties, he abandons the equality principle and, instead, gives an account of punishment that would be familiar to any Benthamite: punishment should be calibrated to prevent crime, with harsher punishments for more common, more highly motivated, or more easily concealed crimes regardless of exact fit or abstract justice.

Our primary talmudic text, by contrast, does not discuss deterrence at all. The Mishnah lists the types of injuries that must be compensated to make a victim whole. The focus is on redress of injury, not with Maimonides' concerns of keeping the peace or deterrence or the eye-for-an-eye principle's goals of restoring cosmic balance or retribution. In modern terms, this is tort, not criminal law (although some medieval commentators blur the distinction by treating the Mishnah's compensation as a sort of fine, just as some modern lawyers construe tort liability as stigmatizing rather than compensatory). As Rav Papa points out, the principle of an eye for an eye would reject compensating a victim for the costs of medical care if the offender will also need (after retribution) care as well.

The Gemara seeks to reconcile the Mishnah with the biblical text through its discussion of how to monetize eyes. Consider the last paragraph of our excerpt. The immediate question is what Rabbi Eli'ezer could have meant by contending that "eye for an eye" means "actually" an eye for an eye. All the discussants agree that he couldn't have meant actually poking eyes out. Although perhaps that is exactly what he meant, the *amora'im* are committed to the Mishnah's position that simple literalism won't do: multiplying blindness would require ignoring the biblical text's basic emphasis on re-creating balance in the world. Rabbah contends, instead, that Eli'ezer's disagreement was over the issue of valuing a freeman based on the slave market. The measure of a free man (or his body parts) is not merely his price in the resale market. Abaye counters that this could not explain Eli'ezer's dissent: everyone agrees that freemen are not for sale. Rav Ashi gives us the solution: Eli'ezer must have agreed that compensation is the basic remedy and compensation must be based on the slave market, since there is no other way to price eyes. But even if it is reasonable to equate the value of an eye with the marginal market price of slaves, the problem of varying eyes remains. Eli'ezer disagreed with the Rabbis only about whether the eye that should be compared to the slave market was the victim's or the perpetrator's. In any event, in nonstandard markets such as the market for eyes, there may not be a single market clearing price. All tort lawyers understand, implicitly if not explicitly, that the price a tort victim would pay to restore his lost eye is far lower than the price he'd have demanded to sell it in a voluntary contract, and neither is likely to be closely related to the increment in wage-earning capacity associated with a working eye.

But the Gemara seems to overlook an important analytic distinction. The biblical eye-for-an-eye principle is a criminal law concept. The simplest resolution of its seeming tension with the Mishnah's compensation principles is to limit the principle to the heavenly criminal justice system where it originated, leaving the Mishnah's compensatory rules free to govern in tort and even the king's deterrence-based criminal law. Can we learn something from the Gemara's commitment to apply the biblical law even to a tort context where the focus is on the victim rather than the offender?

The *Kuzari* offers one possibility. Judah Halevi contends that "cutting off his hand does not profit you." But this claim ignores the pleasures of schadenfreude, let alone revenge. Perhaps the Gemara is countering by misdirection the claim of an honor culture that destroying the offender's bodily parts reduces the victim's humiliation and thus is a form of "compensation." Its detailed debate over whose eye is to be valued, what valuation methods are appropriate, and whether the victim is entitled to medical costs seem too picayune to leave room for grand questions of revenge. In the discussion of prayer (3:19), *The Kuzari* contends that a prayer can be granted only if it "benefits the world without damaging it in any way." On this view, just as we know that oppressing our fellow human is wrong (*The Kuzari* 3:7), just as we doubt the justness of a God who makes the rabbit the carnivore's prey (*The Kuzari* 3:11), so we should know that revenge for its own sake is also wrong. *The Kuzari*'s refusal to allow harm for the greater good is the core of Halevi's concept of divine justice, but it leaves criminal law in an awkward bind. If humans cannot restore the divine balance, and revenge and retribution do not "profit you," deterrence is an empty threat. An eye for an eye teaches that the criminal deserves punishment but denies that a human court or family has the right actually to impose it. Not every wrong has a remedy.

Finally, a life for a life—as opposed to an eye for an eye—raises a distinct issue. The texts resist equating one eye with another: each eye's specificity gives it its own value. In contrast, they accept that, at least in principle, specific eyes can be priced in money. But none of our texts makes the analogous argument for lives. No one suggests that the individuality of human beings means that some souls are worth more than others. Similarly, no one suggests pricing specific lives, although one could get prices as exact as the prices for eyes by looking to the slave market or a freeman's earning power. Indeed, our Gemara passage goes so far as to quote Numbers to explicitly reject the usual revenge culture notion that money (*damim*) can atone for blood (*dam,* or in the Cain story, *damim*) as a synecdoche for life. Life, it maintains, is incommensurable with money. (My dictionary indicates that the two *damim* are etymologically independent, and the use of *damim* for money is postbiblical. Still, the pun cannot have gone unnoticed.)

Conversely, all lives are treated as equally valuable. As Maimonides puts it: "Necessarily, there must be a soul for a soul—the young and the old, the slaves and the free, the men of knowledge and the ignorant being considered as equal." Equal in what?, Aristotle might have asked. After all, if eyes differ in their abilities and monetary value, so do lives. Or so one might imagine a believer in natural aristocracy and the inferiority of the barbarians arguing.

Genesis responds in one of the most important myths of the biblical corpus. Each child of Adam is a unique creation of a single God and equally a descendant of his creation Adam, "so that no man might say my father is better than yours" and the death of a single individual must be seen as the destruction of an entire world (cf. Mishnah Sanhedrin 4:5). We are equally humans, equally made in the image of God. Maimonides' pointed examples emphasize Genesis's egalitarian ethos: age and knowledge would be the markers of an Aristotelean natural aristocracy in a society that valued scholars above all.

The claim of fundamental equality regularly conflicts with convenient prejudices; its victory is never obvious or final. Biblical law applies it to foreigners—"You shall have one standard for stranger and citizen alike: for I the Lord am your God" (Lev. 24:22)—even though it does not fully apply it to slaves, ruling that a master who beats his slave need not be treated as a murderer if the slave survives for a few days. But the principle ultimately is more powerful than the prejudice: slaves are also unique creations of a unique Creator. Impressively, Maimonides recognizes the contradiction, using the very same example of a man who is beaten and survives for a few days to illustrate the importance of actual capital punishment only a few lines away from his statement that slave souls are equal to free ones. The same logic should apply to require a fundamental equality of men and women, Jews and gentiles, citizens and aliens, even criminals and victims.

Neither eye for eye nor life for life ultimately serves as a principle of vengeance or criminal law. In those spheres, the slogan reminds us that true justice is out of our reach; we have neither the knowledge nor the skill to match wound for wound, punishment for offense. Instead, we must temper our aspirations: real criminal law (the "law of the king") can be justified only by the more modest goal of actual effectiveness in reducing crime. Eye for eye and life for life, then, are primarily rhetorical tropes to teach basic principles of fairness—turnabout is fair play, what's sauce for the goose is sauce for the gander—and equality. Our eyes may not be equal, but our souls are, in the simple sense that we are all fellow humans, none of us more alive than the others. Basic decency requires that we respect this basic equality.

Daniel Greenwood

Corporal and Capital Punishment: The Law

Corporal Punishment

7. Deuteronomy 25:1–3

This biblical text is the basis for the later Rabbinic discussions of corporal punishment. A crucial idea here is that the guilty person is still a "brother" who must be respected even in the act of punishment.

When there is a dispute between men and they go to law, and a decision is rendered declaring the one in the right and the other in the wrong—if the guilty one is to be flogged, the magistrate shall have him lie down and be given lashes in his presence, by count, as his guilt warrants. He may be given up to forty lashes, but not more, lest being flogged further, to excess, your brother be degraded before your eyes.

Lashing
8. Mishnah Makkot 3:10–15[7]

In the Deuteronomic text, corporal punishment in the form of lashings serves as a sanction for interpersonal wrongdoing. Departing from the plain meaning, the Rabbis construed the wrongdoer here as a person convicted of transgressing any of the Torah's negative commandments. Lashing thus became the standard punishment for noncapital sins; for the more severe of these, it is here said to ward off the divinely imposed karet, *"extinction." The mishnah begins with a dispute over the exact sense of the biblical limit of forty and goes on to lay down the basic rules for the infliction of corporal punishment. First among these is an (evidently medical) "assessment" of the number of lashes this individual can bear without risk of death.*

(10) How many [lashes] are inflicted upon him? Forty less one, as written, "by count [as his guilt warrants . . . up to] forty" (§7 above), a number short of forty. Rabbi Yehudah says, a full forty [lashes]. And where is the extra [fortieth lash] inflicted? Between his shoulders.[8]

(11) He is assessed [a count] of lashes that is divisible by three.[9] If he was assessed to receive forty [lashes], and after some were inflicted upon him, they said he cannot bear [the entire] forty, he is exempt [from the remainder]. If he was assessed to receive eighteen [lashes], and after they were inflicted upon him, they said he can bear [the entire] forty, he is exempt [nevertheless from any additional lashes].

If he committed a transgression that violated two prohibitions, and they imposed one [overall] assessment [for both transgressions, say forty-two lashes (thirty-nine plus three)], the [specified amount of lashes] is inflicted him and he is exempt [from any more, even though he suffered only three for the second count]. But if no [combined assessment was made], the [specified amount of] lashes is inflicted upon him; he then heals and [fol-

---

7. Here and below slight amendments to the printed text follow the Kaufmann ms.
8. See clause 13 below; for this first clause, cf. ¢6, §14.
9. I.e., if he was assessed to be capable of bearing twenty lashes, he receives eighteen.

lowing an assessment for the second transgression, lashes are] inflicted upon him again.

(12) How is the lashing administered? His two hands are tied to the post on either side; the communal officer seizes his clothes—if they are torn they are torn, and if they become unstitched they are [left] unstitched—until his chest is exposed. Then the stone is placed behind him, upon which the communal officer stands. A calf [leather] strap is in his hand, folded first into two and [again] from two into four, and two straps rise and fall in it [the fold].

(13). Its handpiece is one handbreadth and its width is a handbreadth and its end must reach up to his navel. And he hits him by [laying on] one-third [of the lashes] in front of him [on his chest], and two-thirds behind him [over his shoulders]. He is not hit standing or sitting, but bending over, as written, "and the magistrate shall have him lie down" (§7). And the hitter hits using one hand with all his strength.

(14) And the reader recites [these verses while the lashes are in-flicted,] repeating them again from the beginning [as needed]: "If you fail to observe faithfully [all the terms of this Teaching that are written in this book, to reverence this honored and awesome Name, the Lord your God,] the Lord will inflict extraordinary plagues upon you and your offspring, strange and lasting plagues.[10] . . . [Therefore observe the words of this covenant, etc.]" (Deut. 28:58–69). If he dies under his hand, he [the communal officer] is exempt; [however,] if he added [even] one extra lash and he died, he is exiled [to a city of refuge] on his account.[11] Should he be soiled by excrement or water, he is exempt. Rabbi Yehudah said: a man by excrement and a woman by water.

(15) All who are liable to karet who have [had lashes] inflicted upon them are exempt from their [penalty of] karet, as written, "[Lest] your brother [ahikha] be degraded [niklah] before your eyes" (Deut. 25:3; §8)—once he has been lashed [lakah] then he is like your brother. Thus said R. Hanania b. Gemaliel.

---

10. Here and above, makot; this is the same word translated as "lashes" in §7 above, the equiva-lent of the Rabbinic malkot, and is the name of the tractate.

11. The standard sanction for negligent manslaughter; see Deut. 4:41–42.

Procedure in Capital Cases

9. Mishnah Sanhedrin 4:5–6:4

The continual shift between past and present tenses in this selection conveys the sense of a report on actual practice (cf. ¢4, §13), though by the time of the compiling of the Mishnah, Rabbinic courts had long lost the authority to administer capital punishment. The discussion assumes that capital punishment is an actual possibility and that some defendants are in fact found guilty and executed. Witnesses are exhorted to come forward on that assumption: it is a good thing, they are told, that the wicked perish. And yet the procedural rules seem designed to make that outcome virtually impossible—a goal stated explicitly in the next selection. The bias against capital punishment is clear, even though the only alternative suggested here is acquittal. In case the defendant is condemned, the witnesses themselves are charged with the execution (see Deut. 17:7).

Chapter 4

(5) How are witnesses admonished in capital cases?

They would bring them in and admonish them, "Perhaps you give your account on [the basis of] an assessment, or hearsay, [or] testimony from another witness, or [perhaps you will say,] "we heard it from the mouth of a trustworthy person," or perhaps you do not know that we will eventually subject you to [a thorough] investigation and inquiry? You should know that capital cases are not like monetary [civil] cases [*mamonot*]. In a monetary case, a person pays money and [thereby] achieves atonement; in a capital case the blood [of the executed person] and the blood of his [potential future] offspring are [the witness's] responsibility, until the end of the world. For so we find in the case of Cain, who killed his brother [Abel], as written, "your brother's bloods[12] cry out to Me [from the ground]" (Gen. 4:10)—it does not say, "your brother's blood," but rather "your brother's bloods": his blood and the blood of his [potential] offspring. . . .

12. The Hebrew is literally in the plural: *demey*.

Therefore Adam[13] was created alone, to teach you that whoever destroys a single life is deemed by Scripture as if he had destroyed a whole world; [conversely,] whoever saves a single life is deemed by Scripture as if he had saved a whole world. . . .

Now should you say, "Why do we need this trouble [of testifying]?"—Is it not already written, "Although able to testify as one who has either seen or learned of the matter—[if] he does not give information . . . he is subject to punishment"? (Lev. 5:1).

And should you say, "Why should we become culpable for [the defendant's] blood?"—Is it not already written, "When the wicked perish there are shouts of joy"? (Prov. 11:10).

Chapter 5

(1) They would examine [the witnesses] with seven investigations [regarding the event. They would ask:] In which seven-year cycle [of the jubilee cycle], in what year, in what month, on what date in the month, on what day [of the week], in what hour, [and] in what place? . . . [They would further inquire:] Do you recognize him? Did you warn him? In case of an idol worshipper: What did he worship, and in what manner did he worship?

(2) Any [judge] who engages in extensive examinations is to be praised. Once [Rabban Yohanan] ben Zakai examined [the witnesses] regarding the stems of figs. . . . [And] if the witnesses contradict each other [in any detail], their testimony is nullified.

(3) If one [witness] says, "on the second of the month," and one says, "on the third of the month," their testimony stands, since [we can assume that] one knows of the intercalated month[14] and the other does not know. If one [witness] says, "on the third [day of the month]," and one says, "on the fifth," their testimony is nullified. . . .

(4) They would then bring in the second [witness] and examine him. Should the words [of the two witnesses] be found congruent, [the

13. Translated here as a proper name. The word's alternate sense, as a common noun meaning person, resonates with the previous sentences: the first man represents Humanity.
14. He knows that the previous month had thirty days, not twenty-nine.

judges] commence [discussion with arguments] for acquittal. If one of the witnesses said, "I have an argument for his conviction," they silence him. If one of the students said,[15] "I have an argument for his acquittal," they bring him up [to the dais] and seat him among [the judges], and he would not go down the entire day. If there is substance in his words, they heed him. And even if [the accused] said, "I have an argument for my own acquittal," they heed him, provided there is substance in his words.

(5) If they found [grounds for] his acquittal, they release him; if not, they adjourn until the following day. They would pair up, eat little food, and refrain from drinking wine the entire day, and deliberate the matter thoroughly throughout the night. They arose early the following day and came to court. Each one in favor of acquittal would say, "I favored acquittal [yesterday] and I maintain my [vote for] acquittal." Each one in favor of conviction would say, "I favored conviction [yesterday] and I maintain my [vote for] conviction." One who argued for conviction may argue for acquittal, but one who argued for acquittal cannot retract and argue for conviction. If they erred in this matter, the scribes of the judges remind them.

If they found [grounds for] his acquittal, they release him. If not, they tally the vote: [if] twelve [vote to] acquit and eleven to convict, he is acquitted. [If] twelve convict and eleven acquit, or even if eleven acquit and eleven convict and one says "I don't know"; or even if twenty-two acquit or convict and one says "I don't know"—they must add judges. How many do they add? Two at a time, up to seventy-one. [If then] thirty-six acquit and thirty-five convict, he is acquitted. [If] thirty-six convict and thirty-five acquit, they must reason with each other until one favoring conviction comes around to the view of those favoring acquittal.

Chapter 6

(1) Once the verdict has been rendered, they take him out to stone him. The place of stoning was outside the court, as written, "Take the blasphemer outside [the camp]" (Lev. 24:14).

15. Cf. ¢7, §5.

One [person] stands at the entrance of the court with a scarf in his hand; and [another sits on] a horse a way off but within sight. Should someone say, "I have an argument for acquittal," he waves the scarf, and the horse runs and stops him. And even if [the condemned person] says, "I have an argument for my own acquittal," they bring him back, even four or five times, provided there is substance to his words.

If they found [grounds for] his acquittal, they release him, and if not he is taken out to be stoned. A crier goes out before him [proclaiming,] "So-and-so son of so-and-so is being taken out to be stoned because he committed this-and-this transgression, and so-and-so and so-and-so are his witnesses. If anyone knows [an argument for] his acquittal, let him come and argue it."

(2) When he was ten cubits from the place of stoning, they say to him, "Confess, for it is the manner of those to be put to death to confess, for all who confess have a portion in the World to Come." . . . And if he does not know how to confess, they say to him, "Say [as follows:] May my death be an atonement for all my sins." . . .

(3) When he was four cubits from the place of stoning, they strip off his clothing: a man is covered in front, a woman is covered [both] in front and behind. Thus says Rabbi Yehudah, but the sages say: a man is stoned naked but a woman is not stoned naked.

(4) The place of stoning was double the height of a person. One of the witnesses pushes him [off] by his back;[16] [after] he landed on his chest, he turns him on his back. If he died, [the witness] fulfilled [his obligation]. If not, the second [witness] takes a stone and places it[17] on his chest. If he died thereby, [the witness] fulfilled [his obligation], but if not, his stoning [is carried out] by all Israel, as written, "Let the hands of the witnesses be the first against him to put him to death, and the hands of the rest of the people thereafter" (Deut. 17:7). All who are stoned are [then] hanged. Thus says

16. The Rabbis transformed biblical "stoning" into pushing off from a (moderately) high place; likewise, the biblical "burning" was transformed into forcing the condemned person to swallow molten lead (see Mishnah Sanhedrin 7:2). Evidently, these modifications were designed to preserve as far as possible the integrity of the body.
17. I.e., drops it.

Rabbi Eli'ezer, but the sages say: No one is hanged except the blasphemer and the idol worshipper.

Repudiating Capital Punishment: A Debate
10. Mishnah Makkot 1:10; BT Makkot 7a

This is the classic tannaitic debate on capital punishment. It is placed as the final section of the Mishnah's discussion of laws of testimony, which in turn conclude its discussion of capital punishment. The blanket repudiation of capital punishment by Rabbis Tarfon and Akiva indicates a principled stand and seems to have guided the construction of halakhic capital law; their victory is most clearly revealed in the selection from the Tosefta below (§12). And yet as we have seen in previous chapters (¢3, §16; ¢8, §11), Shimon b. Gamaliel's retort guided the political practice of medieval Jewish communities and underlay the arguments about "the needs of the hour."

Mishnah Makkot 1:10

A Sanhedrin that executes once in seven years is called a destroyer. Rabbi Elazer b. Azariah says, "once in seventy years." Rabbi Tarfon and Rabbi Akiva say, "Had we been in a Sanhedrin, no person would ever have been executed by it." Rabban Shimon b. Gamaliel says, "They, too, would have increased the [number of] those who shed blood among Israel."

BT Makkot 7a

"Rabbi Tarfon and Rabbi Akiva say, 'Had we been, etc.' How would they proceed? Rabbi Yohanan and Rabbi Elazar both say [that they would have asked the witnesses:] "Did you see whether the victim was a *terefah*[18]

---

18. Someone suffering from any of certain physiological afflictions that are deemed to be fatal within twelve months. One who kills a *terefah* is exempt from capital punishment.

or whether he was intact? Rav Ashi [added]: And even if you should say he appeared intact, perhaps there had [already] been a puncture [at the point] where the blade [struck the body]?"

And [what would Rabbis Tarfon and Akiva have done in a case of] forbidden intercourse [to avoid imposing the death penalty]? Abaye and Rava both answered: [They would have asked the witnesses:] Did you witness the actual penetration?[19]

And how would the Rabbis [disagreeing with Tarfon and Akiva] proceed [given that such eyewitness evidence is virtually impossible to obtain]? They would follow Shmu'el, for Shmu'el said: "In a case of [alleged] adulterers, when they appear as adulterers [lying together, the testimony is sufficient]."

Upholding the Law

11. Maimonides, *Commentary to the Mishnah* Makkot 1:10

Maimonides views capital punishment as an important means for ensuring social stability (see also ¢3, §11). While acknowledging that the court should strive for acquittal, his interpretation of the mishnah (§10 above) reaffirms the legal mandate for execution.

With regard to the [effort] to minimize executions (§10 above): the Sanhedrin ought to strive for that by pondering their judgment and avoiding haste. But if they were unable [to find grounds for acquittal] and the testimony stands condemning a person to death, they [should] proceed with the execution. Even a thousand individuals, day after day [should be executed], in the event that the law demands it.

---

19. Lit. a euphemism: "the insertion of a brush in the tube."

Requiring Formal Warning and Response
12. Tosefta Sanhedrin 11:1–4[20]

The rules of prior warning are a Rabbinic innovation and, as described here, are clearly designed to make it virtually impossible to execute anyone. (Or, better, they make it impossible to execute anyone according to the law, leaving only the extralegal possibilities.) Note especially the requirement that the criminal must not only violate the law but also consciously and explicitly defy it in order to be liable to capital punishment.

[1] Regarding all others liable to the death penalty,[21] they can only be executed on the basis of [the testimony of] witnesses and a warning. [The warning] must include informing him that he is [about to become] liable to the death penalty. Rabbi Yose b. Rabbi Yehudah says: [The warning] must include informing him of the particular [form of] execution with which he will be put to death.

[Having received a warning,] he is liable, regardless of whether he was warned by all the witnesses or only by some of them. Rabbi Yose declares him exempt, unless he was warned by all the witnesses, as written, "[A person shall be put to death only] on the [word of] mouth of two [or more] witnesses" (Deut. 17:6)—only if the mouths of two witnesses warn him as one. The sages agree with Rabbi Yose that if the first [witness] warned him and left, and the second [warned him] and left—he is exempt.[22]

[2] If they warn him and he keeps silent, or if they warn him and he nods his head, or even if he says, "I know," he is exempt [from the death penalty] unless he says: "I know, and it is with that in mind that I act."

[3] How so? [If] they saw him desecrating the Shabbat [and] said to him, "You should know that today is Shabbat, and it is written, 'He who desecrates [the Shabbat] shall be put to death' (Exod. 31:14)"; even though he says, "I know," he is exempt unless he says, "I know, and it is it is with that in mind that I act."

---

20. The text here follows Vienna: Cod. Hebr. 20 at the Austrian National Library.
21. I.e., except for the enticer; see §23 below.
22. Other manuscripts read: "Rabbi Yose agrees that if the first [witness] warned him, and left, and the second [warned him] and left, he is liable."

[4] How so? [If] they saw him killing a person [and] said to him, "You should know that he is a member of the covenant, and it is written, 'Whoever sheds the blood of man, By man shall his blood be shed' (Gen. 9:6)," even though he says, "I know," he is exempt unless he says, "I know, and it is it is with that in mind that I act."

Alternative Measures

13. Mishnah Sanhedrin 9:5; BT Sanhedrin 81b

The virtual disarming of the criminal procedure leads to compensatory solutions such as the one below. The price, however. seems to be that of creating an extralegal penal system without clear rules to determine what proof is sufficient for conviction and death.

Mishnah Sanhedrin 9:5

One who kills a person not in [the presence of] witnesses is put in the cell and put on a diet of "meager bread and scant water" (Isa. 30:20).

BT Sanhedrin 81b

[If there are no witnesses], how do we know?

Rav said: By separated witnesses. [*Rashi:* There are two witnesses delivering a true testimony, but the court has no warrant to execute him—e.g., if two witnesses saw him, one from one window and the other from another window. In tractate Makkot (7a) it is stated that he cannot be executed on the basis of such testimony.]

Shmu'el said: [If] there was no warning.

Rav Hisda in the name of Avdimi said: If the witnesses, for example, contradicted each other in the examinations but not in the investigations.[23]

23. See Mishnah Sanhedrin 5:1–2 (§9 above).

Commentary. Diminishing the Divine Image

The final mishnah of Makkot, Chapter 1 (§10), which completes the corpus of laws dealing with capital jurisdiction (*dinei nefashot*), records an explicit repudiation of capital punishment.

At first blush, this mishnah is perplexing. Having presented the entire criminal procedure regulating the modes of judicial execution and the twenty-eight offenses punishable by death, the mishnah concludes with views holding that convictions and executions are rare and undesirable events. There is no dispute among the anonymous first opinion and Elazar b. Azariah, Akiva, and Tarfon. The ascending order of their views ("once in seven years," "once in seventy years," "never") is a rhetorical device that expresses an essential opposition to capital punishment. But a reader familiar with the procedural laws used, according to the *tanna'im,* to adjudicate capital crimes will not be surprised by this opposition. The formidable array of procedural obstacles in capital cases makes conviction by law highly unlikely, if not impossible. To mention but a few of these laws:

1. The tannaitic sages instituted punctilious methods of examining witnesses: "Once [Rabban Yohanan] ben Zakai examined [the witnesses] regarding the stems of figs" (§9), which Rashi explains, "They testified against him that he had killed a person under a fig tree and Ben Zakai asked whether the stems were thin or thick." Yohanan b. Zakai examined the two necessary witnesses with regard to the minutest details and would have disqualified their testimony had he found discrepancies between the two. This meticulous examination is part of the broader rules prescribed by the *tanna'im* for disqualifying testimony: "Any [judge] who engages in extensive examinations is to be praised. . . . Whether in the investigations [questions relating to the time and place of the crime, which are relevant for the possible refutation of the witness] or in the examinations [other circumstances pertaining to the actual offense], if the witnesses contradict each other [in any detail], their testimony is nullified" (§9; cf. also §10). In contrast to modern criminal law, the judge here has no discretion to choose those elements of the testi-

mony that he believes to be reliable and substantiated as the basis of a judicial conviction.

2. According to tannaitic *halakhah,* circumstantial evidence, confessions, and self-incriminations are inadmissible.

3. Tannaitic *halakhah* also establishes blanket rules concerning the disqualification of witnesses: "Just as with two witnesses, if one of them is a relative or [otherwise] disqualified, their entire testimony is invalid, so too is it with three witnesses, if one of them is a relative or [otherwise] disqualified, their entire testimony is invalidated" (Mishnah Makkot 1:8). Most important, the accused must be warned by the witnesses prior to the commission of the offense. Moreover, according to the Tosefta (§12) he is liable only if he responded, "I know, and it is with that in mind that I act." Clearly, the requirement of warning almost completely eliminates any possibility of conviction.

These laws don't only protect the wrongfully accused; they also prevent the conviction of the guilty. I am not claiming that this was the original purpose of these requirements. Some of them may have originally been aimed to protect innocent suspects, and some may have been based on other plausible considerations. Reviewing the procedure in its entirety, however, highlights its "failure" to distinguish between the innocent and the guilty. The system as a whole is intentionally structured to lead to the acquittal of all persons accused.

Elazar b. Azariah, Akiva, and Tarfon did not make their statements in a vacuum. The ultimate purpose of the minutiae governing criminal procedure is expressed explicitly in their own words, placed by the editors of the Mishnah at the conclusion of this corpus of rules. Indeed, the *amora'im* (§10) explained that this purpose would be achieved by means of that very procedure.

The approach of Tarfon and Akiva (and Akiva's students, whose views constitute the Mishnah's main text) to judicial executions was not shared by all the other tannaitic sages. Already in this very mishnah, Shimon b. Gamaliel rebukes them, saying: "They, too, would have increased the [number of] those who shed blood among Israel." A similar argument also appears in a midrashic comment: "'Do not take pity on him' (Deut. 19:13) — this is a warning not to have mercy on a murderer; let them not say, 'That one has already been killed and what use is there in killing the other?' Rather, he must be executed" (*Midrash Tanna'im* 19:13, p. 115). In the same midrashic passage, a similar view is attributed to Rabbi Eli'ezer.

These comments concern a murderer whose guilt is beyond doubt, and in the background we are aware of the approach taken by Akiva and his colleagues. Eli'ezer and Shimon b. Gamaliel refuse to forego the social benefit of deterrence that results from the implementation of the death sentence.

Talmudic literature doesn't tell us what Shimon and Eli'ezer thought of the criminal procedures described above, which cohere closely with the approach taken by Elazar b. Azariah, Tarfon, and Akiva. Did Shimon and Eli'ezer subscribe to alternative procedures? In the absence of sources, we cannot answer this question.

The position adopted by Eli'ezer and Shimon b. Gamaliel serves to highlight the radicalism of Akiva and his colleagues. Shimon's criticism of Akiva demonstrates that Akiva's opposition to judicial executions extended even to cases of murder. Note that in antiquity capital punishment was everywhere perceived as an effective means of deterrence. No one argued, as many do today, that it was commonly ineffective. To the best of my knowledge, Mishnah Makkot 1:10 is the first principled opposition to capital punishment. This is even more astonishing given that the Bible perceives it as the primary mode of punishment.

What is the reason for this bold position? The Mishnah does not suggest any reason, but the answer may be found in a passage in Tosefta Yevamot (8:7, ¢18, §9): "Rabbi Akiva says: Anyone who sheds blood thereby annuls the [divine] image [*demut*], as written, 'Whoever sheds the blood of man, by man shall his blood be shed; for in His image did God make man' (Gen. 9:6)." In this *derashah*, Akiva interprets Genesis 9:6, which brings together the idea that humanity is created in God's image and the claim that murder is a transgression that requires capital punishment. The conception of the image as presence forms the basis of this *derashah*. The "image," *demut,* is the figurative likeness of God, which is the configuration of man's form. The iconic connection between the prototype (God) and its images (humanity) enables Akiva to argue that harm to man is in effect harm to God, who inheres in his likeness. Relying on Genesis 9:6, he maintains that the act of murder is not just the "annulment" of the man; it also "annuls the image [of God]."

The verse upon which Akiva's *derashah* is based stands at the heart of the covenant concluded between God and Noah after the flood, a covenant that structures the postdiluvian world. This verse is the basis of biblical criminal law, as Moshe Greenberg writes in his classical essay "Some Postulates of Biblical Criminal Law":

> That man was made in the image of God is expressive of the peculiar and supreme worth of man. This view of the uniqueness and supremacy of human life has yet another consequence. It places life beyond the reach of other values. The idea that life may be measured in terms of money or other property and a fortiori the idea that persons may be evaluated as equivalences of other persons, is excluded. Compensation of any kind is ruled out. The guilt of the murderer is infinite because the murdered life is invaluable. An absolute wrong has been committed, a sin against God which is not subject to human discussion. (*Studies in the Bible and Jewish Thought* [Philadelphia: JPS, 1995], pp. 25–41)

In contrast with conceptions prevalent in the ancient Near East, the Bible holds that human life is infinitely valuable. The legal consequence of this conception is that a murderer must be put to death. This rule is not grounded in considerations of deterrence, which could be overridden by other (utilitarian) considerations, as indeed was common in most ancient law codes. In cases of murder, for example, these codes at times grant discretion to the victim's family to replace capital punishment with pecuniary compensation. By contrast, Genesis 9:6 insists on the immeasurable value of human life. Given that human life cannot be quantified, only the ultimate punishment—death—is commensurate with murder.

Scholars (Greenberg among them) argue that the effect of this view is paradoxical: because human life is invaluable, to take it entails the death penalty; in order to express the sanctity of human life, the Bible orders that a life be taken.

Akiva's opposition to capital punishment and his homily that portrays spilling blood as a diminution of the divine image implicitly address the paradox imbedded in Genesis 9:6. The implication for capital punishment of Akiva's reading of that text is evident. If bloodshed affects the Divine, then there is no difference between "permitted" killing (by the court) and "prohibited" killing (by a murderer). The killing of any person created in the divine image "diminishes" God and must be avoided. Given his bold homily in Tosefta Yevamot, it is easy to see why Akiva says here that were he "in a Sanhedrin, no person would ever have been executed by it."

The roots of Akiva's move against capital punishment already exist in the Bible. The paradox implicit in the biblical justification for capital punishment in the case of murder, the *imago dei* theosophy, provides the grounds for overturning the justification. The recognition that one who commits murder "diminishes the image" leads to the conclusion that the court, when it punishes with death, is doing the same thing. Indeed, anchoring capital punishment in the idea of creation in God's image produces an inherent tension, even without assuming a strong sense of iconic presence. Akiva's interpretation of the verse sharpens the paradox to the extent that considerations of deterrence and the need for blood expiation cannot stand in the way of the argument for abolishing capital punishment.

Eli'ezer, by contrast, as some midrashic passages suggest, rejects Akiva's *imago dei* theosophy and consequently sees no reason to abolish capital punishment. In his view, judicial execution does not diminish the Divine image—when it comes to murder, what it diminishes is bloodshed.

Akiva's approach to capital punishment could be described as theosophy in a legal-halakhic disguise. This "theological" structure of thought, with its legal-social implications, was invented in a period when the Jews in Palestine lacked authority in legal and especially in criminal matters. No wonder that medieval interpreters and halakhists such as Nissim Gerondi (Ran) argued that the laws of the Torah—mainly the talmudic laws regarding capital punishment—are aimed not to enhance political order (*tikkun seder medini*) but "to induce the appearance of divine affluence (*shefa' elohi*) within our nation and [to make it] cleave unto us." Gerondi argued that for the purpose of law and order, the Torah instituted the law of the king (see ¢3, §16).

The modern reader will probably approach Akiva's *dinei nefashot* and the theosophy underlying it with some ambivalence. On the one hand, the renunciation of deterrence and presumably other devices of social control—as far as one can tell, Akiva and his colleagues do not replace execution with other forms of punishment—suggest a kind of religious anarchism (as Shimon b. Gamaliel argues). On the other hand, modern readers cannot but admire this very early abolition of capital punishment, especially when it is portrayed as a continuation of the biblical tradition. Though we do not share the theological premises of Akiva (the bold anthropomorphism, the notion of image as presence, and so on), his words about the creation of humanity in God's image can be viewed as a mythic-symbolic source for the modern belief in the "sanctity of life," which is the basis of contemporary criticism of capital punishment. It is worth noting that in the early 1950s, immediately after the establishment of the state of Israel, the Knesset—explicitly inspired by Mishnah Makkot 1:10 and Akiva's teachings—abolished capital punishment (inherited from British Mandate law) in virtually all criminal cases, including murder (§22). The legislation was supported by almost all parties, including the secular majority, and since then has never been changed.

Akiva's theological structure of thought elevated humanity to the level of a divine image, which ultimately made possible the idea of "sanctity of life." After all, sanctity is first of all a religious idea, attributed to divinity. The *imago dei* theosophy allows attributing sanctity to human beings as well. Roman *dignitas,* interpreted by Cicero as the intrinsic value of human beings, did not have this status and power. It seems that once the notion of the "sanctity of life" was made available (in the Western tradition), it became a constitutive idea, even when the theological scaffold on which it was first erected was long removed—and even forgotten.

Yair Lorberbaum

Necessity and Special Powers

Extralegal Punishments: Talmudic Beginnings

14. BT Sanhedrin 27a, 46a

Under halakhic criminal procedure, few criminals can be convicted. In the previous selection, the Mishnah described alternative measures by which the authorities might deal with murderers. But could such measures be employed in the Diaspora, where Jewish courts were altogether deemed as lacking true judicial authority (cf. ¢24, §§5–6)? And what of offenders other than murderers? This pair of talmudic texts shows that ways were found to escape the restrictions on punishment.

BT Sanhedrin 27a

Bar Hama committed murder. The exilarch said to Rav Aba b. Ya'akov:

"Go forth and examine the case.

"If it is certain that he committed murder, let him be blinded."[24]

[*Rashi:* "Let him be blinded." For capital punishment by the court has been abrogated,[25] and this is an [extralegal] penalty imposed upon him, for a court may impose flagellation and [other] punishments not [warranted] by the Torah.]

BT Sanhedrin 46a

It has been taught: Rabbi Eli'ezer b. Ya'akov said: I have received by tradition that a court may impose flagellation and [other] punishments not [warranted] by the Torah; not to transgress against the words of the Torah, but rather to erect a fence[26] [s'yag] around the Torah.

---

24. Lit., "let them dim his eyes." Some alternative and even metaphorical interpretations have been offered for this irregular phrase, but Rashi—and the other commentators quoted below—took it to mean blinding.

25. With the loss of Jewish sovereignty (cf. §9 headnote, above).

26. "Erecting a fence" is a Rabbinic term of art for measures designed to protect against

Thus there was a case in which a man rode a horse on Shabbat[27] in the days of the Greeks, and was brought before the court and stoned [executed], not because he deserved it, but because it was required by the times. Similarly there was a case of a man who had intercourse with his wife under a fig tree; he was brought before the court and flogged, not because he deserved it, but because the times required it.

Special Measures by King and Court

15. Maimonides, MT Laws Concerning Murder and Preservation of Life 2:1–5

The Code of Maimonides, Book Eleven: The Book of Torts, translated by Hyman Klein, YJS (New Haven: Yale University Press, 1954), pp. 198–200.

Maimonides here provides his summary of the basic attitude toward the punishment of murderous criminals. Taking his cue from the commitment to social order in the spirit of Shimon b. Gamaliel (§10 above) and from the alternative measures delineated by the Mishnah (§13 above), he effectively marginalizes the abolitionist voice.

(1) If one person kills [his fellow] himself, such as by striking him with a sword or a deadly stone, or by strangling him, or by thrusting him into a fire, he must be put to death by the court, seeing that he himself killed another in some manner.

(2) If, however, one hires an assassin to kill [his fellow], or sends his slaves to kill him, or ties [his fellow] up and leaves him in front of a lion or another animal, and the animal kills him and, similarly, if one commits suicide, [the initiator] in each of these cases . . . is a shedder of blood, has committed the crime of murder, and is liable for death at the hand of Heaven; but there is no capital punishment at the hands of the court.

(3) How do we know that this is the [law]? Because Scripture says,

---

breach of the Torah. See Mishnah Avot 1:1, where this is depicted as one of the classical injunctions of Rabbinic Judaism.

27. A minor offense; cf. MT Shabbat 21:1, 9.

"Whoso sheddeth man's blood by man shall his blood be shed" (Gen. 9:6), referring to one who commits the murder himself and not through an agent. [It also says] "And surely your blood of your lives will I require" (Gen. 9:5), referring to suicide. [And also] "At the hand of every beast will I require it" (ibid.), referring to one who places [his fellow] before a wild animal for it to devour. [And finally] "At the hand of man, even at the hand of every man's brother, will I require the life of man" (ibid.), referring to one who hires others to kill [his fellow]. In these last three cases, the verb "require" is explicitly used to show that the judgment is reserved for Heaven.

(4) Regarding any of these or similar murderers who are not subject to being condemned to die by verdict of the court, if a king of Israel wishes to put them to death by royal [law] for the benefit of society, he has a right to do so. Similarly, if the court deems it proper to put them to death as an emergency measure [hora'at sha'ah], it has the authority to do so as it deems fit, if the times require it.

(5) If the king does not kill them, and the times do not require their death as a preventive measure, it is nevertheless the duty of the court to flog them almost to the point of death, to imprison them in a fortress or a prison for many years, and to inflict severe punishment on them in order to frighten and terrify other wicked persons, lest such a case become a pitfall and a snare, enticing one to say, "I will arrange to kill my enemy in a round-about way, as did so-and-so; then I will be acquitted."

Herem: *Theory and Operation*
16. Nahmanides, *Mishpat ha-Herem*

Punishment by herem, *"ostracism" (and the less severe ban,* niddui*), was the most important sanction employed by the medieval Jewish community: in the exilic world, where there was no religiously neutral civic space, an ostracized individual had nowhere to turn. But* herem *is not just the punishment; the term denotes first of all a communal decree, conceptualized as a conditional punishment. Enactment by* herem *served as the cen-*

*tral means of public legislation in medieval Jewish communities (see ¢8). Its mechanism
is akin to a stringent oath undertaken collectively by the* kahal *and binding on its individual members. This text, written in thirteenth-century Aragon, is the definitive treatise
on the* herem. *In light of the sacral character of enactment through* herem, *Nahmanides
labors to explain how communal enactments can ever be modified or revoked. Strikingly,
he grounds the* herem *in one of several meanings of the term in biblical law. He then asserts that regarding a* herem *of national scope—imposed by a king or by the Sanhedrin—
transgression is punishable by death.*

The *herem* mentioned in *aggadot* and in the Talmud means that a *bet din* imposes a ban, using the following words: "Whoever does such-and-such . . . ,"
or "Whoever breaches the fence with regard to this matter, shall be under
herem." This is the general meaning of the term *herem*. But when a person
applies this term to property, stating, for example, "My property is under
herem," the name of Heaven is laid upon it, and it is thereby dedicated to [the
fund for] temple maintenance or to the priests. This is stated explicitly in the
Torah, as written: "Nothing that he has proscribed [*herem*] for the Lord may
be sold or redeemed . . ." (Lev. 27:28).

    Similarly, a person can forbid his fellow [to derive any benefit] from
his property, or forbid himself [to derive any benefit] from property that does
not belong to him—for example, by saying to the owner, "Your property is
herem unto me," thus forswearing the use and benefit of that property and
rendering it forbidden to him. This is the law [of vows] known as "*konamot*."

    This type of *herem*, i.e., one involving property, must be [explic-
itly] accepted by the oral articulation of an oath [by the one to be bound].
Release [from this type of *herem*] can be obtained either through referral to
a sage [for annulment] or through complete recantation. It is like all other
vows [*nedarim*]. . . .

    However, the law regarding a *bet din* that employs the term [*herem*]
to a specific person by saying, for example, that whoever does such-and-
such will be under *herem* is not taught [explicitly] in Moses' Torah; rather, it
is taught to us by tradition, as we shall see below.

... There is a dimension of severity to [the *herem*] not found in other oaths. [Ordinarily,] an oath has no effect [on a person] unless he [hears it and] replies "amen" [which is tantamount to articulating it himself]. In case of a *herem*, however, [a person is bound] even if he did not accept it upon himself and even if he was not present at the time of the decree. This is because a *bet din* has the authority to impose a *herem*, as written, "And I cursed them ... and adjured them by God" (Neh. 13:25). The *herem* therefore applies to the individual, who is thus prohibited from violating that decree as if he had [explicitly] taken an oath himself.

The law is the same if the townspeople agree unanimously, or by a majority, in the presence of the good men of the town, to impose a *herem*, since they have "the authority to enforce their enactments" (¢8, §2) and to issue a *herem*. [Hence,] their *herem* applies to all who are obligated to follow their ordinances. Should any of the townspeople violate their enactment, he is like one who violates an oath: the *herem* enters into his 248 organs,[28] "consuming him, his timber and stones,"[29] and he is like one ostracized vis-à-vis his townspeople.

The *herem* is more severe than the *niddui*, as the Talmud expressly states. All are obligated to act toward him as being *herem* and to separate themselves from him accordingly. They are forsworn from allowing him to benefit from their property, except as necessary to sustain his life. Whoever does not treat him in accordance with his legal status is like one who commits trespass against sacred objects.

So, too, an individual under *herem* is forbidden from certain activities in accordance with his status. [He is prohibited,] for example, from wearing leather shoes, or doing anything forbidden to someone in mourning. He is also prohibited from benefiting from the property of those who put him in *herem*. His status is spelled out in the Talmud and submitted to the authority of the sages, and if he takes his prohibitions lightly, he brings evil upon himself and transgresses the Torah's provisions.

... A *herem* cannot be constituted by less than a quorum of ten, be-

---

28. The number 248 is the Talmud's standard number of internal human organs.
29. I.e., all his possessions; following Zech. 5:4 regarding one who swears falsely.

cause they are not [considered] a public [*tzibbur*]; neither are they [considered] a *bet din* that stands in place of a public. [A group of fewer than ten] is not empowered to impose a *herem,* but can only have each individual swear explicitly, each one taking an oath upon himself.

If a certain *herem* was imposed by a king of Israel or a by a Sanhedrin in the presence of the majority of Israel, one who violates it is liable to [be put to] death, and the king or the Sanhedrin may subject him to whatever manner of execution they wish. This was the law followed by Joshua, who judged Akhan as a capital offender for appropriating to himself [sacred] goods dedicated [*herem*] to heaven (Josh. 7:10–26). And so, too, in the verbal oath of *herem* we have [the precedent of King] Saul saying, "You shall be put to death, Jonathan!" (1 Sam. 14:44). And Israel, in the days of the concubine of Givah, killed the men of Jabesh-gilead, as written: "For a solemn oath had been taken concerning anyone who did not go up to the Lord at Mitzpah: 'He shall be put to death'" (Judg. 21:5). In the [Midrash] Yelamdenu, Rabbi Akiva asks, "And was there an oath there? [No!] Rather, it comes to teach you that the *herem* is the oath, and the oath is the *herem.* The men of Jabesh-gilead did not go up and were culpable of death."

Indeed I propose—while apologizing [for my audacity]—that perhaps this is the plain meaning of the text in the Torah, "No human being who has been put in *herem* can be ransomed; he shall be put to death" (Lev. 27:29); that is to say, whenever a matter is agreed upon by all, and they knowingly proscribed it as *herem,* whosoever violates it cannot redeem himself with money but is liable to [be put to] death. . . .

Moreover, in case a *bet din* imposes a *herem* on the men of a city and on their offspring, the *herem* applies to future generations. Such is the decree of Joshua bin Nun cited in declarations of *herem,* as written, "At that time Joshua pronounced this oath: 'Cursed of the Lord be the man who shall undertake to fortify this city of Jericho'" (Josh. 6:26), and this [curse] remained in force for several generations. . . .

We have found, then, four characteristics applicable to the *herem* that do not apply to oaths and vows: (1) that it need not be specifically uttered by the individual [on whom it will be binding]; (2) that it is effective [in binding the individual even] against his will and [even] if he is not present; (3) that one who violates it separates himself from the public, [and he is thereby to be treated] according to the rules applicable to the *niddui;* and (4) even more [than the *niddui,* that the violator of a *herem*] might be liable [to be put] to death in some cases. But with respect to its imposition upon future generations, it seems that such is also the case with respect to all vows accepted by the public [*rabim*], as we find [in the cases of] the acceptance of the Torah, the reading of Megillat [Esther], and [the establishment of] fast days.[30]

There is, however, one leniency with regard to the *herem* not found in oaths and vows: if the violator of the *herem* repents and comes to the *bet din* or to the good men of the town in the presence of the townspeople, they themselves may release him. . . . Similarly, if some of the townspeople have died, or have left the city,[31] those [who remain] may release him with no misgivings, as it is written in Avel Rabbati (5:15),[32] "If one of the excommunicators dies, so long as he gave the authority to his fellows, they can release [the person who was excommunicated]." We may assume the authority to be [invested] in the hands of the townspeople and the good [men of the town] and not in the hands of those who have left it. Similarly, if the generation [that imposed the *herem*] dies, their successors [have the authority to] release, so long as they are as great as them in wisdom and in numbers.[33] . . .

Nevertheless, a portion of the public cannot effect a release; nor can a majority, unless this is done in the presence of all those who imposed the *herem* or their representatives, who must be of equal stature. . . . And this particular release is like the release of a vow by three [people] or by one expert, like the *herem* or *niddui* of an individual. . . .

And we have found a responsum of Rav Hai Gaon on this matter, which states as follows: "With regard to your question about a public [*rabim*] that has taken upon itself a fast or undertaken enactments, and it later becomes apparent to them that it is good and fitting for them to change course—[may they do so? The answer is that] they may do so; how much

30. Cf. ¢1 §§12, 8.
31. Lit., "gone across the seas."
32. Avel Rabbati is another name for tractate Semahot, one of the Minor Tractates, which deals with the laws of mourning.
33. Cf. ¢7, §2.

more so if what they seek to do is [merely] to add to or subtract [from their original enactment]. And if they imposed a *herem* regarding that matter, they are permitted to release it. There is no [problem] with this, as long as the release or the change appears to them to be good and equitable." His wording in this responsum seems to indicate that they need not seek a release from a sage.

Similarly, in the case of a *herem* imposed by a king of Israel or a Sanhedrin, even though one who violates [the *herem*] is liable [to be put] to death, if they should all wish to pardon him, they may do so. . . .

When a *bet din,* the public, or [a group of] individuals says, "We swear that none of us will do such-and-such," this expression represents an oath uttered by others, and whoever replies "amen" is bound as if he had uttered the oath himself. If he violates it deliberately, he is punishable by lashes; if [he does so] unknowingly, he must bring an [appropriate] sacrifice. When he seeks release, he must come to a sage and make a request and a renunciation, like the [regular procedure for the] dissolution of vows and oaths. And anyone who did not reply "amen" is not bound at all, because one cannot be sworn to something by others. . . .

Contemporary Extralegal Punishment Only by Royal Authorization
17. Nissim Gerondi (Ran), *Novellae on Sanhedrin* 27a, 46a

These two passages discuss the two talmudic readings reproduced above (§14). His position, emphasizing (gentile) royal authorization, has some affinity with—but is distinct from—the detailed doctrine of monarchic function preached by the more famous Ran (to whom these novellae were once wrongly attributed), Nissim b. Reuben Gerondi (cf. ¢3, §16). Arguing that powers of extralegal punishment require a court with the highest authority, the author rejects Rashi's explanation that the exilarch in Babylonia could claim such powers. After citing Rashi's commentary to BT Sanhedrin 27a (see §14), he retorts:

Ran, BT Sanhedrin 27a

This is implausible, since the authorization for the court to impose flagellation and [other] punishments not [warranted] by the Torah is of greater gravity than [imposing punishments] prescribed by Torah law—therefore requiring greater and fully authorized [mumhin] judges. How then can this be done [by judges] in Babylonia[34] who have no authority with regard to capital cases even where [capital punishment is] mandated by Torah law?

Therefore Rabbi David of blessed memory explained that the exilarch was not acting with the authority of a bet din, as he was not a judge; rather, he acted with the authority of the [non-Jewish] sovereign [malkhut]. For it is the law of the kingdom to sweep out evildoers, and [the ruler] authorized the exilarch to do so as he saw fit.

Ran, BT Sanhedrin 46a

"A court may impose flagellation and [other] punishments not [warranted] by the Torah; not to transgress against the words of the Torah, but rather to erect a fence [s'yag] around the Torah" (§14 above). Rashi explains: "Not that they can intentionally violate the Torah and simply invent capital punishment for one not liable, but [rather] that for the needs of the hour they may erect a fence."

An interpretation of his interpretation: The sages may not prescribe capital punishment for the violation of a Rabbinic prohibition as a permanent ordinance, because to do so would be to add to the Torah.[35] But they may punish specifically, whether by lashes or execution, as the needs of the hour require, if the generation is unrestrained. Maimonides (MT Laws Concerning Rebels 2) wrote in a similar vein.

And from this it seems [to follow] that the courts which execute someone who is not culpable [by Torah law]—to erect a fence—ought to

---

34. "Babylonia" for these purposes encompasses every place outside the Land of Israel; see note 36, below.
35. See Deut. 4:2.

be ordained and fully authorized, as were Shimon b. Shatah and his fellows, since this is of greater gravity than the punishments of Torah law. [Ran refers the reader to his previous comments to BT Sanhedrin 27a.]

But in those [Jewish communities] that administer the death penalty outside the land [of Israel,] this grounding that ["that a court may impose flagellation and other punishments not warranted by the Torah"] cannot suffice, since they are not [truly a court].[36] If, however, they have royal authorization to try capital cases according the laws of Israel, it seems fair to say that in all capital cases where the death penalty is warranted both by the law of the kingdom[37] and by our laws, they may proceed as mandated by the royal authorization (as with Rabbi Elazar b. Shimon, BT Bava Metzia 83b). But in a case where [the defendant] is not liable under their laws but only under ours, it is certainly forbidden, because the requirement of a fully authorized *bet din* is not met.

However, in the case of betrayers and informers, the commonly established practice is to kill them once they are confirmed as betrayers, even outside the land [of Israel,] under the rule of *rodef* [the pursuer; §§30–32 below]. This is what seems right to me in these matters.

The Judge, the Public, and Criminal Law: Deterrence

18. Yom Tov Ishbili (Ritba), *Responsa* 131

This responsum from early fourteenth-century Spain gives us a full account of the normal protections provided for defendants in Jewish law — and then demonstrates how those protections could be overridden in what were deemed to be exceptional cases. It isn't clear, though, how exceptional this sort of case actually was. Shaul, the defendant here, seems to be an ordinary criminal; he is also called an "informer," but his punishment is dictated by his violent behavior, while "informing" seems to provide only an argument a fortiori.

36. "Elohim" — a word denoting God but also a fully authorized court; see ¢24, §§4–5.
37. *Din ha-malkhut;* Gerondi's careful formulation might be alluding to Jacob Tam's concerns, cf. ¢9, §5.

Note that the judge acts in consultation with a sage, for the sake of the common good. The gentile king of Aragon asked Rabbi Yom Tov to confirm the verdict and punishment rendered against the said Shaul, who apparently petitioned to have the case reconsidered. The text is the rabbi's reply to the king.

I have heard the complaints of the defendant Shaul regarding the judgment. They number eight:

(1) [The judge] judged him without bringing the complainants before him to complain [to his face] and put forth their case. For no person should be judged until the complaints of the parties be heard.

(2) The testimonies against him were not read to him so he could respond and, possibly, disprove them.

(3) The receipt of testimony was invalid since [the witnesses] included people who were related to one another, and some of them were complainants and interested parties, which according to the law of our Torah invalidate the testimony.

(4) Testimony was received from people who did not complain against him when the *herem,* [which called for] each person to come forward and present their complaint, was imposed.

(5) Some of the testimonies proffered against him [were invalid because they] concerned wrongdoings toward people who had already forgiven him the particular assaults [he inflicted on them].

(6) Even if the testimonies were truthful, they could not justify the imposition of corporal punishment or the cutting off of his arm. How much more so, given that the enactment of [the town of] Balaguer specifies the punishments for assault, pulling of hair, and the other acts in question—and he was only liable accordingly.

(7) Our law does not permit us to punish a person twice [and the judge in this case cut his hand off, disqualified him from testimony, and imposed banishment upon him].

(8) He requested leave from the judge to appeal the verdict to Your Majesty or to the master Rabbi Don Astruc, and he refused.

[The judge's replies to these complaints are listed, following which Ishbili states his own position:]

And now my lord, Your Majesty the King, I say that even if there has been an error in this judgment, the judge who sentenced him to have his arm and tongue[38] cut off, and disqualified him as witness, bears no guilt and should not be punished on the basis of [Shaul's] complaint. This is due to his oral argument and the written [record], which shows that he acted by the counsel of a person who is regarded in the land as a wise and truthful man, someone upon whom the judges of his land rely.

With respect to the substance of the judgment [and points 2–6 of Shaul's complaint], they all pertain to judgment according to the law so as to pacify the parties or to adjudicate [in private litigation] between them. However, with respect to the actions undertaken by the judge to deal with public [rabim] complaints, by way of chastisement for the public welfare [le-takken harabim], to rid the land of evil, and as a fence around the Torah, none of [the items recounted in the defendant's complaint] serve as impediments under our law. For the judgment is not for the sake of the injured parties, which would demand meticulous [procedure], but for the sake of the people, so evildoers should not become accustomed to behaving in this way, and the others will hear and fear. [Thus] if one wrongs [others] and they forgive him and he nevertheless persists in such behavior, he is all the more culpable and should be chastised. The judge can convict such a one without a complainant, for he is the father of the public [tzibbur] and is responsible to repair [le-takken] this just as he is obligated to repair obstructions in the roads and other such matters, so that people should not be injured. Indeed, one judge among our sages cut off the arm of a man who regularly hit people (BT Sanhedrin 58b).

[Shaul's] argument that the enactments of the kahal do not provide for corporal punishment plays no role here, for the reason stated previously — that it was done by way of chastisement of a habitual offender who repeated his evil acts three or four times. With regard to [the defendant's] claim that a person cannot be penalized twice, this is wrong; for we do so for two [dif-

---

38. It appears that his tongue was not in fact cut off, because this is not mentioned among the complaints.

ferent] transgressions. Moreover, in judgment by way of chastisement as we said, we most certainly [can] apply a combination of punishments in order to discipline the people. Furthermore, according to the testimony in the communal records, he has the publicly announced status of an informer and betrayer, and the execution of such a person or of one who causes suffering to the community, is the common norm among us. How much more so this [particular defendant] regarding whom there is testimony in the communal records that he is involved in other transgressions, from accepting bribes to [giving] false testimony, assaulting people, etc. In a case like this we are permitted to put a person to death, all the more so are we permitted to impose judgment by severing one of his limbs in accordance with his transgressions, seeing as death is the most severe of all.

With respect to Shaul's complaint that the receipt of testimony and the written [indictment] of the *kahal* are invalid because they are signed by relatives and interested parties, here [we see that] the judge produced a communal enactment that the entire *kahal* had accepted upon itself, which directed the communal officers that relatives can sign in any public business. Also were we to invalidate the testimony of interested parties in a matter such as this regarding public [*rabim*] complaints . . . as we do in other cases, where we disqualify all interested parties and any person affected by the testimony, the *kahal* would not be able to punish informers or anyone who causes suffering to the public for they are all interested parties. Thus the practice is to prosecute these matters with witnesses from the *kahal* and, at times, even with relatives.

It is also for this reason that sometimes we impose a sentence as a matter of chastisement without [the required] warning, as when we see someone who habitually commits transgressions and who is prepared to [continue transgressing] and who will clearly not acknowledge the warning. . . .

Thus, from all these perspectives, [it is clear that] there is no guilt in, and should be no punishment for, the judge so long as he imposed this chastisement by way of discipline [and out of] fear of God, for the sake of social order [*tikkun olam*] and to erect a fence around the law.[39] For if he has acted

39. *Dat;* the primary meaning of which is law.

cruelly, and not for the sake of heaven, God, who sees inside his heart, will exact retribution from him. . . .

However, my Lord, Your Majesty the King, I see that the judge exceeded the [penalties] advised by the wise man, his adviser, and expelled [the defendant] from the land of his residence and of his family—and decreed that [shedding] his blood be permitted to all who find him.[40] This is excessive cruelty. Once [the judge] had decided to spare his life rather than putting him to death according to the law of the informer, should we then expel him from the land of his residence, and from those who know him, and from his relatives? What kind of work will he do once his arm is cut off? We are severing his livelihood. . . . It therefore seems appropriate to nullify this decree, and in addition to command the *kahal* to provide for his livelihood to [enable him to] support his children once he has been subjected to these penalties. In addition, he should [continue to] live in the place [where he committed his] evil acts so that the others will always see [him] and be afraid.

Thus, after they have given him a warning that he should keep away from all evil things, not do business with any person who might be suspected of informing or betraying, and be humble in all his dealings—should he [nevertheless] transgress, [the community] will continue to chastise him. Perhaps following all this he will repent, and his Maker will have mercy on him as he is merciful and gracious.

Capital Punishment—Reservations
19. Asher b. Yehi'el (Rosh), *Responsa* 17:8

Coming to Spain from Germany in the late thirteenth century, Asher was surprised to find how powerful Jewish courts were in Spain and how ready they were to set aside the restrictions on capital punishment. This case was from Córdoba: after buying his way out of imprisonment by the gentiles, a Jew was heard cursing the divinity, employing the

40. Alluding to Cain's fear, Gen. 4:14.

Arabic divine name. Responding to a request to back the community's decision to execute the blasphemer, Asher defends the powers of the court while also expressing his personal reservations about the death penalty. The letter was to be presented to the king's local representative, Don Juan Manuel, as part of the communal effort to persuade him to support the action.

Your question regarding capital crimes is astonishing, because capital crimes are not judged [by Jewish communities] in any land I have ever heard of, except here in the land of Spain. I was very puzzled when I came here [initially], wondering how capital crimes were being judged in the absence of a Sanhedrin. I was told that this is by royal authorization and, moreover, that the community judges [with an intent] to save lives inasmuch as a great deal more blood would be shed if [such cases] were judged by the Arabs. I allowed them to continue as was their custom, although I have never agreed with them on the destruction of life. Nevertheless, I see that all of you share the opinion that this evildoer should be eliminated from your midst. [The defendant in this case] has certainly desecrated the name [of God] in public, and the matter is already known among the Ishmaelites, who are very strict with one who speaks against their law and faith. The desecration would be [even] greater if justice were not done for the sake of erecting a fence [*lemigdar milta*]. It is also appropriate to sanctify [God's] name by punishing this evil person.

[Rosh cites classic talmudic precedents of extralegal punishment, and concludes:]

Do as you see fit. Had I been party to the decision, my opinion would have leaned toward pulling his tongue from his mouth and cutting off most of it in order to mute his lips, thereby imposing a measure that befits his conduct. Indeed, this would be a striking [form of] vengeance, observed continually by all. But you should act in this matter as you see fit, for I know that your intent is to sanctify the name of Heaven. I hope that the will of God will succeed by your hands.

Restrictive Interpretation of "Needs of the Hour"
20. Joseph ibn Migash, *Responsa* 161

The extent of the judge's emergency power is the subject of the next two texts, the first from Spain in the early Middle Ages, the second from seventeenth-century Poland. Here ibn Migash attempts to set limits on the "needs of the hour" argument. What makes an emergency, he argues, is something like what we would call a "crime wave." Nothing less than that can justify the suspension of Torah law. He is also wary of extending judicial powers to the community and its officers.

Regarding the [talmudic] dictum, "One who hires false witnesses for another is exempt[41] in human judgment yet liable in divine judgment": . . . Nevertheless, if in that town there is a formally appointed judge, and he sees fit to punish him for it, he may do so. As stated by the Rabbis, "I have received by tradition that a court may impose flagellation and [other] punishments not [warranted] by the Torah; not to transgress against the words of the Torah, but rather to erect a fence [*s'yag*] around the Torah" (§14 above). This [holds], however, only provided that the hour requires it, namely, that this hirer had previously done this deed several times, or that in that [particular] province [*medinah*],[42] there are [repeated] instances of this deed; so that there are grounds for concern that if they fail to punish [the guilty ones], similar deeds would multiply. But if neither of these conditions obtains, the court may not impose anything upon one who does this; a fortiori, one who doesn't have the status of a court [cannot impose penalties] — and the community is not, in this matter, like a formally appointed judge.[43]

41. I.e., from paying compensation to whoever suffered a loss through giving testimony.
42. This can also be taken to mean "town" or "polity."
43. Cf. ¢8, §8.

Wide Interpretation of "Needs of the Hour"
21. Meir b. Gedaliah of Lublin, *Responsa* 138

Meir was asked about a murderer who had been apprehended and tried and was now awaiting punishment. The (non-Jewish) "official" inquired of the head of the bet din *whether to execute the prisoner—he was prepared to abide by the ruling of the Jewish court. The court decided against capital punishment, and its head asked Meir for his opinion. Meir forcefully continues the line of argument we have seen in the selections above permitting capital punishment of criminals even in the present times and outside of the Land of Israel. Citing a number of other authorities, Meir makes the needs of the hour into the needs of virtually all the hours. He begins by citing a case of Rav Nahman imposing a fine on a habitual robber in Babylonia, which Isaac Alfasi had linked to the famous statement of Rabbi Eli'ezer b. Ya'akov (§14 above).*

Alfasi must have interpreted Rabbi Eli'ezer b. Ya'akov's [statement to apply] even in case of a diaspora court, since otherwise he would not have cited it as a proof text. Indeed this was the very reasoning behind Rav Nahman's [own decision] to impose a penalty—he was in the Diaspora and relied on Rabbi Eli'ezer b. Ya'akov's tannaitic statement.

Tur HM 2, too, relies on this, stating simply that diaspora judges impose penalties, whether monetary or capital, according to the needs of the hour. Likewise in section HM 425, commenting on the statement of Natronai Gaon that "in our days we do not have the authority to flog or to banish those deserving of capital punishment," he states: "It may be that he wrote thus only with regard to the law, but not with regard to whatever it may be necessary to do to [the offender] in order to erect a fence [*lemigdar milta*], for who would dispute the statement of Rabbi Eli'ezer b. Ya'akov?"

[Meir goes on to cite Solomon b. Abraham Adret, Isaac b. Sheshet Perfet, and Asher b. Yehi'el as precedents. He then turns to the case of the exilarch (§14 above) and argues:]

From the fact that the exilarch imposed blinding as an extralegal penalty rather than imposing the death penalty, it might perhaps be inferred that a diaspora court may not impose capital punishment, even to erect a fence. Perfet [however] has already addressed this (*Responsa* 291), writing: . . . "As the exilarch assessed that according to the needs of that hour blinding him was sufficient, he did not decree his execution. And even so blinding him put him in danger of death since 'the eye is [directly linked] to the heart' (BT Avodah Zarah 28b)." . . .

It thus seems clear to me, as a halakhic principle that should be followed in practice, that even in these times a court has the authority to impose the death penalty for the needs of the hour even for other transgressions, and certainly for murder, which especially calls for imposing penalties for the needs of the hour. Proof of this was provided by Perfet, namely: That even in the times when capital crimes were judged, murder was treated more grievously and adjudicated beyond what is warranted by Torah law. Thus [a criminal tried for murder] with insufficient testimony was put in the cell (BT Sanhedrin 81b [§13 above])—a penalty not imposed in other capital crimes. The reason for this severity regarding the crime of murder is because, as Maimonides wrote (MT Laws Concerning Murder and Preservation of Life 4:9), murder is tantamount to the destruction of the world; and he expounded on this at some length. This is the proper ruling in my view, contrary to what you seem to hold.

It is however true that each court must consider the matter carefully, weighing it with the scales of their intellects—whether the needs of that [particular] hour really are so great as to merit imposing capital punishment. . . . But it seems obvious to me that the "needs of the hour" does not refer only to [a situation] where many of the people are in violation of the law in question. Seeing as your eminence has cited [to such an effect the precedent of] "the days of the Greeks" (§14 above), thus holding that the case at hand cannot be considered in terms of "the needs of the hour." But this is wrong: rather, even if at the time he transgressed violation of the law in question was not [common among] the people, if—in the court's assessment—failure in this case to impose capital punishment, or some other grievous measure, would bring about a breakdown and would lead the people from now on to treat this law lightly and to common violations—this is termed "the needs of the hour."

[Meir cites the above precedent by Rosh (§19 above) and goes on to cite an additional ruling of his (*Responsa* 18:13):]

And so too in the case of the widow who was made pregnant by a gentile, [Asher] permitted her nose to be cut off to destroy her beauty. This not because violation of that law was common among the people but lest news of this harlot should spread among the gentiles and be degrading to our religion, and as a warning to all other women, as he expounded in that responsum.

And even in a case where neither of these purposes are relevant, but the court sees that a certain individual is habituated to a specific transgression, and will certainly perpetrate such [criminal] acts upon many others, the Talmud makes clear that penalties are imposed, not in accordance with the law [*she-lo min ha-din*] but in order to erect a fence. For example, the case of the habitual robber whom Rav Nahman punished, though it is nowhere attested that the rest of the people were, like him, especially prone to robbery. Rather Rav Nahman [merely] stated that he was a habitual robber and he had decided to punish him. And that undoubtedly was so that he should not go on to perpetrate such [criminal] acts upon many others. . . .

Now, you wrote: "Can [capital punishment be justified] because he has acted brazenly, killing two people in cold blood, and [also] desecrating the Shabbat?—We find no indication in the Talmud or the decisors that such [factors] determine [a mandate for extralegal punishment]; rather, it is determined solely by the needs of the hour, insofar as it is required for repairing the public condition,[44] in which case it does not matter whether the transgression was great or small, or [whether it was] willful."

Yet Perfet (*Responsa* 291) explicitly states that [the issue] is to be determined also by taking account of the willfulness and guilt of the individual and the gravity of his sin in the particular transgression. He says: "If you choose to put them to death to erect a fence [*lemigdar milta*] since they killed cold bloodedly, brazenly, and willfully . . . you have the authority to do so." Thus clearly for [Perfet], much is determined by the gravity of the individual's guilt in the particular transgression. The reason is simple and

---

44. *Tikkun ha-dor*—lit., "repairing the generation"; i.e., the people in their present condition.

self-evident, since the more the offender was willful and criminal, commit-ting the evil deed in public and [thus] causing great desecration of God's name—the greater is the need of the hour to erect a fence, and thus the hour requires that he be punished, even extralegally [she-lo min ha-din]. Should they be lenient with his punishment for such great crimes, God's name would be desecrated. As a result, from that time onward such crimes would become common among the people, causing a breach for the many [rabim]; it is there-fore the need of the many to erect a fence against the breach by punishing him severely, as is self-evident—this seems clear to me.

And so, turning to the ugly case at hand, of course I am an outsider, whereas you—being within—must weigh in the scales of your clear intel-lects the urgency of the needs of the hour along the lines I have charted. But it seems that nearly all those breaches that I mentioned pertaining to the future regarding needs of the hour are applicable in the present case of wickedness—especially since it emerges from your report that in the pre-vious year a similar crime took place in the same area, and [the perpetrator] went unpunished and [as a result] the lawbreakers may, God forbid, multi-ply. Additionally, seeing that this evil business has become public knowledge among the gentiles, and the said criminal is imprisoned in [the hands of] the gentiles, keeping him alive is a desecration of God's name, as in the respon-sum of Rosh mentioned above. Furthermore, and this is readily understood, the gentiles might, heaven forfend, come to make light of spilling the blood of Israel. . . .

Now since God has already brought it about that he is in the hands of the gentiles, the best approach would be that the hand of the Jewish court not be upon him.[45] Rather, the victim's relatives should demand that the blood he spilled be avenged by the [gentile] official, who will eradicate him from the world, and thereby the breaches will be fenced, God's name will be sanctified, and all Israel shall be immaculate.

45. See 1 Sam. 24:14.

Commentary. Rabbinic Law and the Preventive State

Every society that aspires to govern within the rule of law finds it necessary to create (or discover) exceptions to the formal rules for what its leaders deem to be emergencies, extraordinary situations, or the "needs of the hour." This is because codified rules of law cannot anticipate all contingencies and threats and because formal rules often make it difficult to incapacitate all dangerous people. We see this phenomenon operating in post-9/11 America, where Guantanamo has filled gaps left by the criminal law, and in Israel, where administrative detention serves to confine dangerous terrorists who cannot be convicted of past crimes.

Rabbinic authorities anticipated this issue and provided what they believed were proper responses within the Jewish tradition. Their questions have endured the test of time. Their answers, for the most part, have not.

Classical Jewish law, which is one of the most ambitious attempts to function within the constraint of formal rules set out in the Torah and its authoritative interpretations, is also among the most innovative in creating (or discovering) ways around these constraints.

During different periods of Jewish history, rabbinical authorities have authorized practices—some of which appear to be in direct contradiction to the clear words of the biblical and talmudic texts—empowering the authorities to do what needs to be done to prevent grave harm to the community.

These practices invariably do several things: they weaken the protections afforded those suspected of criminal or deviant behavior; they strengthen the power of the authorities; they pander to the ever-present popular fear of disorder; and they do so in the benign name of "prevention."

Preventive action—ad hoc practices devised to go beyond what is authorized by the formal code of laws in order to prevent grave harms—has a long and troubling history within the Jewish tradition (as it does generally in Western traditions). Western parlance distinguished between what it considers "punishment" (which is backward looking) and "coercion" (which is forward looking). But this distinction is at best imprecise because punishment coerces (and looks forward as well, to deter) and coercion punishes (and looks backward, for evidence of danger). A more apt distinction is between formal laws that err on the side of protecting the accused and informal practices that err on the side of empowering the authorities—in the name of protecting the community.

For example, the Torah explicitly requires the testimony of two witnesses before a defendant can be convicted of a capital crime and executed. This daunting procedural protection makes it difficult to convict the guilty and so to assure a high level of protection for the innocent. What then should be done with an obviously guilty and dangerous murderer whose crime was witnessed by, let's say, only one highly credible witness? Should he simply be acquitted and allowed to return to the community, perhaps to kill again—taking care again not to be seen by a second witness? The literal words of the Torah would suggest that "dangerous" result. So the Rabbis devised a series of informal, preventive measures designed to satisfy the needs of the hour without purporting to violate the letter of biblical law. (The Talmud additionally requires a prior warning, thus making it even more difficult to convict a guilty murderer. But what the Talmud "gives" to the accused defendant with one hand it often takes back with the other, as demonstrated in the texts.)

These measures, which include the accordionlike concept of "the *rodef*" (pursuer, §30), are so broad and open-ended that they threaten to swallow up the very concept of the rule of law and to substitute vigilante justice (an oxymoron if there ever was one) for thoughtfully calibrated codes that strike the balance between community safety and due process in favor of that safety.

The expansive use of emergency measures also demonstrates the danger of making it too difficult to convict the guilty, thereby necessitating informal "safety nets." It suggests the need for the kind of balance reflected in Abraham's argument with God over the sinners of Sodom. The "world's first Jewish lawyer" (as I've called him in a book by that name) persuaded God to spare the city of Sodom if he found ten righteous people therein. By stopping at ten and not insisting that all the guilty be spared if there were as few as one or two innocent townfolk, Abraham (and God) recognized the need for proportionality in any just legal system. At the same time, they expressed a preference that some guilty go free rather than some innocents be wrongly condemned. But proportionality and nuance are often the first casualties of perceived emergencies. Jewish law may have been among the first to acknowledge the conflict between formal rules that offer extraordinary protection to the accused and the needs of the community threatened by such heightened protection. But other rule-oriented systems have also addressed this problem, and experience provides some generalizations.

History suggests that, all other factors being equal, the necessity for and emergence of informal preventative mechanisms will increase as it becomes more difficult to secure convictions against dangerous persons thought to be guilty of serious crimes. Mechanisms of social control, more specifically of coercion and prevention, frequently operate on a balloon principle: if you squeeze the air out of one end, the other will become more inflated. Thus it is a fairly constant phenomenon in most societies that dangerous people will be incapacitated by one means or another. If the formal law makes it easy to convict such people, there will be less need for informal preventive or coercive measures; if the formal law makes conviction difficult—as it does under Jewish law—then there will be greater need for informal measures. This principle is useful, at least, as a caveat: when a particular mechanism of confinement is rendered useless (or less useful), one should search to see if the slack has been picked up, in whole or in part, by other mechanisms.

The most disturbing lesson of history is that although preventive confinement has always been and will always be practiced, no systematic and widely accepted jurisprudence of prevention has ever been developed. There are some rules and precedents, to be sure, but they seem to reflect the ad hoc practices of the rabbis rather than a fully articulated legal or moral philosophy. It may sound surprising, even arrogant to say this, but it appears to be true. No philosopher, legal writer, or political theorist has ever, to this writer's knowledge, attempted to construct a systematic theory of when it is appropriate for the state to confine or otherwise incapacitate preventively. This is so for a number of reasons. The mechanisms of prevention have been, for the most part, informal; accordingly, they have not required articulate defense or justification. Moreover, there are many scholars who simply deny that preventive intervention, especially preventive confinement, really exists—or, if they acknowledge the existence of these mechanisms, they deny their legitimacy, thus obviating the need for a theory. Finally, it is extremely difficult to construct a theory of preventive confinement that neatly fits into existing theories of criminal law and democracy or into the jurisprudence of the Torah.

The upshot, however, is that there has always existed a widespread series of practices, involving significant restraints on human liberty, without an articulated jurisprudence circumscribing and limiting its application. People are confined or otherwise incapacitated to prevent predicted harms without any systematic effort to decide what kinds of harms warrant preventive confinement, or what degree of likelihood should be required, or what relationship should exist among the harm, the likelihood, and the confinement's duration. This is not to say that there currently exists a completely satisfactory jurisprudence justifying the imposition of punishment for *past* acts. But at least many of the right questions have been asked, and some interesting answers have been attempted. Even the primitive statement "It is better that ten guilty persons escape than that one innocent suffer" (which may have been derived loosely from the Sodom story) tells us something important about how to devise rules of evidence and procedure. There is no comparable aphorism for preventive confinement: Is it better for x number of false positives to be erroneously confined (and for how long?) than for y number of preventable harms (and of what kind?) to occur? What relationship between x and y does justice require? The Rabbis failed to ask these kinds of questions in a nuanced and systematic way or to develop modes of analysis for answering them, beyond clichés extolling the virtues of building fences, satisfying needs, and protecting the community. We must come to understand and acknowledge the harms that could be caused by ounces of preventive coercion or by stitches of preventive confinement.

The relationship between the formal criminal procedures set out in the Bible and the Talmud and the less formal mechanisms for dealing with the needs of the hour presents a fascinating area for future study, since it is an ongoing area of conflict in all contemporary nations governed by the rule of law.

The formal rules that make it difficult to convict not only the innocent but also the guilty are often used as an example of the "liberal" values reflected in the Torah. But there is a dark side of this moon, often hidden from view by apologists for Jewish law or preventive law in general. This dark side is the broad, discretionary power arrogated by the Rabbis to themselves in the name of protecting the community from danger. Invoking such talismanic phrases as "the needs of the hour," a "fence around the Torah," and "emergency measures," the Rabbis essentially created a supplement to the Torah that has virtually erased the safeguards contained in the law itself. The fence has become a *black hole;* the needs of the hour have become the convenience of *every* hour; and the emergency is always *now.* Necessity has replaced rules; discretion has substituted for procedure; and the need for prevention has trumped the presumption of innocence. This is not a system of which liberals should be proud.

Consider the case of Rav Kahana (§32), who "tore out [the] windpipe" of a man who threatened to inform against a fellow Jew's property. How can such an act of disproportionate vigilante injustice be justified by the principles of the Torah? In words reminiscent of Jesus', Rabbi Eli'ezer b. Ya'akov said: "I have received by tradition that a court may impose flagellation and [other] punishments not [warranted] by the Torah; not to transgress against the words of the Torah, but rather to erect a fence around the Torah." But what about fences around those parts of the Torah that demand protection of the accused? Why not three witnesses? Why do all the fences make it easier, not more difficult, to punish or coerce? Why do the needs of the hour never seem to require greater protection of the accused from the likes of Rabbi Kahana or the biblical vigilante Phinehas? The concept of fences is largely a ploy to give the Rabbis more power. (Some current Haredi rabbis have ruled that "the fence" prohibits smart phones, because such technology may give its owner "outside" information with which to challenge the authority of the Rabbis.) In this regard, the fence is reminiscent of the oven of Akhnai story that elevates the power of the Rabbis over God's voice (¢6, §10). The fence elevates the power of the Rabbis over the clear words of the Torah.

The power grabs reflected by fences and needs have been repeated throughout history. The U.S. Supreme Court demanded the authority to interpret the words of the Constitution in the famous case of *Marbury v. Madison.* It too has built fences and created exceptions for emergencies. The British courts authorized extralegal measures during the world wars. The Israeli courts—without a written constitution or Torah to constrain them— have allowed exceptions during periods of emergency.

What is needed is a thoughtful jurisprudence of prevention and emergencies. (The Israeli Supreme Court, more than any other, has at least begun to develop such a jurisprudence.) We live in an age of continuing, perhaps permanent, emergencies. The needs of the hour are daunting. We are experiencing the emergence of what I call "the preventive state." We need a jurisprudence to cabin the enormous power of such a Leviathan.

This jurisprudence should contain both substantive and procedural rules governing all actions—formal and informal, punitive and preventive— taken by officials to prevent harmful conduct, such as terrorism. Black holes in the law—whether they are created by rabbis, judges, or other functionaries—are anathema to democracy, accountability, human rights, and the rule of law.

The Rabbis, as usual, posed the right questions, but their answers were less than satisfactory. Experience—mostly bad experience—has given us the wisdom to do better. We must do better, if the values explicit and implicit in the Torah are to be served, along with those of democracy and the rule of law.

Alan M. Dershowitz

The Modern Israeli Debate

22. Zerah Warhaftig, "Revoking Capital Punishment"

Hukkah le-Yisrael Dat u-Medinah (Jerusalem: Mesilot, 1988), pp. 110–14.

Warhaftig was for many years a member of Knesset for the National Religious Party (NRP) and served also in various ministerial posts. In this essay, he recounts the main lines of the debate concerning capital punishment that he helped initiate early in 1948, shortly before the founding of the state of Israel. Capital punishment had been carried over from the British Mandate to the newly created state as the existing law of the land. The ruling Mapai Party, which dominated the first three decades of Israeli politics, favored capital punishment for reasons of deterrence and a "realistic" assessment of human moti-

vation. The United Religious Front, an alliance of orthodox parties, was its most out-spoken opponent. The effort to abolish capital punishment is no doubt the great moral moment of the orthodox parties in Israel.

I. Jewish *halakhah* takes a negative view of capital punishment. Human life is sacred: "And God created man in His image, in the image of God He created him" (Gen. 1:27). "Therefore Adam was created alone, to teach you that whoever destroys a single life is deemed by Scripture as if he had destroyed a whole world" (Mishnah Sanhedrin 4:5, §9 above).

[Warhaftig now cites Mishnah Makkot 1:10 (§10 above), which radically curtails capital punishment.]

For considerations of *tikkun olam,* however, "punishing criminals in this way alone would completely undermine political order: murderers would multiply, having no fear of punishment. [That is why God ordered the appointment of a king for the sake of civilization]" (Nissim Gerondi, *De-rashot* 11, ¢3, §16). . . . It has been taught: Rabbi Eli'ezer b. Ya'akov said: I have received by tradition that a court may impose flagellation and [other] punishments not [warranted] by the Torah; not to transgress against the words of the Torah, but rather to erect a fence around the Torah" (BT Sanhedrin 46a, §14 above). This [is done] as a temporary ruling, when the hour calls for it, as an enactment for emergencies, but not as a permanent statute in the law books and not when the government has in its hands, as it does today, alternative and serious measures of deterrence such as long-term imprisonment.

The chief rabbis of Israel, when asked by us for their opinions concerning the constitutional principles of [the state of] Israel, expressed their absolute rejection of capital punishment. Rabbi Ben Zion Meir Hai Uziel, the chief Sephardi rabbi of the Land of Israel, . . . wrote in the addenda of his reply to my constitutional memoranda: . . . "The state of the Land of Israel does not recognize the authority of a court to impose and to execute capital punishments in any manner whatsoever. . . . So too it rejects any judicial acts of bodily torture, or of lashing, etc. But the state will punish by the severe penalty of imprisonment and expropriation of the murderer's property for the good of the victim's heirs." Rabbi Isaac Herzog, chief [Ashkenazi] rabbi

of Israel, also denies a place to capital or corporal punishment in the constitution. . . .

III. On March 7, 1950, Minister of Justice Phinehas Rosen presented
the first Knesset with the proposed Capital Punishment Annulment Law–
1950, according to which there will be no capital punishment in the state save
for the crime of treason committed during a state of emergency. All existing
statutes demanding capital punishment will be viewed as imposing life imprisonment. A person awaiting execution will, as of the enactment of this
law, be treated as having a life sentence. The minister of justice concluded his
detailed presentation stating that by the acceptance of this law, we will have
proven that we do not seek the death of the wicked; [we seek] rather that he
repents of his ways and lives.[46]

. . . The MKs in the discussion divided into two camps:

1. Those absolutely rejecting capital punishment, or at least
rejecting it with regard to murder while retaining it with regard to
treason.

2. Those generally favoring capital punishment, or at least
favoring it temporarily.

The opposition to capital punishment was led by speakers from the
United Religious Front while those favoring were led by . . . the speakers
from the Mapai faction.

. . . Following are some excerpts from my speech as the lead speaker
in the discussion for the United Religious Front:[47]

This is an extraordinary discussion. In it we are not only legislators
but judges too. . . . There are seven prisoners today who, sentenced to death,
are sitting and waiting while their execution depends on the outcome of this
discussion. The government has given its word not to execute the sentences
so as to allow the Knesset the time to decide. . . . Imprisoned human beings
depend upon the outcome of our discussion today. . . .

I welcome the cabinet's proposal to abolish capital punishment. I am

46. Paraphrasing Ezek. 18:23.
47. Warhaftig cites the speech from the Knesset protocol, and the ellipses in it are his own.

sad to say that it is only a partial abolition, and I intend to propose that it be broadened by dropping . . . the exclusion of treason committed in a state of emergency. . . . Religious Judaism rejects capital punishment. . . . The number of offenses in the Torah for which a person might be liable to capital punishment is very limited. Up to a hundred years ago there were states where 150–200 crimes were considered capital offenses (as was the case in England and France)—in Torah law, however, there are only a few such offenses. . . . The Torah places very stringent demands on the evidence that is required for a capital sentence. . . . Add to this the warning [that must be] given to the criminal before committing the crime. . . . Special mention must be made of the Torah's injunction "Let the hands of the witnesses be the first against him [to put him to death]" (Deut. 17:7); the witnesses who brought about the sentence by their testimony—if they be confident of their testimony—are obliged to be the first to cast the stones at the accused. . . . In the [traditional] laws of [the people of] Israel we have reached a de facto abolition of capital punishment. . . .

Humans are created in the image of God, and only by the Lord's command may their life be denied them. . . . Would anyone in our society justify the execution of prisoners of war? Is it not the case that the criminals that society combats are themselves waging war against society, and as soon as they are apprehended by society, they are its prisoners, and they should be treated as such.

The main reason for capital punishment was—and to a large degree remains—that of instilling fear: "all the people will hear and be afraid and will not act presumptuously again" (Deut. 17:13). . . . Are there no more drastic ways of creating fear? Indeed there are, but no person would recommend their use. There were times when severing limbs was considered a less severe punishment than death. [Warhaftig cites as an example Isaac b. Sheshet Perfet (Rivash); cf. §21 above.] Today, the attitude toward such punishment has changed. . . . And if someone were to argue that [severing a limb] is more frightening—would we enact severing limbs? No one would dare suggest this, for its severity and barbarism is recognized. But with regard to capital punishment specifically there is a desensitization. . . .

It is proposed to retain capital punishment for traitors. But these are the very [criminals] who will not fear this punishment. A felon might be deterred by this sort of punishment, but not a traitor who sees himself acting for an ideal—for in many cases it is not money that is the motive. . . .

The goal of punishment . . . is the isolation of the criminal, to make further criminal activity impossible, . . . and imprisonment, whether for a term or for life, is absolutely sufficient for this.

The important goal of . . . abolishing capital punishment . . . is the revaluation of human life. In our age, human life is treated very cheaply . . . and it is beginning to be treated cheaply here in the state of Israel too. Among the people of Israel for many generations human life was treated as very dear. . . . For centuries the cases of murder . . . were few . . . chiefly due to the wondrous phenomenon of the love of Israel. Every Israelite, even a criminal, felt that the other person had some sublime love toward him and for that reason could not easily take his life from him. It is the task of the state of Israel to revalue human life in Israel and to bring about the feeling that the life of the other is holy, so that the [potential] murderer will feel this too. If society would treat human life with a trembling sanctity, this could be the case. . . . We are the nation who received the Ten Commandments from the mouth of the Lord and gave them to the world at large, including "You shall not murder" (Exod. 20:13). With our [national] revival, the renewed establishment of our state, we must bring again to the world the commandment "You shall not murder."

Coercion

The Use of Entrapment
23. Mishnah Sanhedrin 7:10

Entrapment is a practice in which the agents of the law, in this case, the "witness," causes or at least encourages the crime in order to catch the criminal. It is generally prohibited in halakhah, as in other legal systems. But in the case of incitement to idolatry, which will often involve only private speech, the law permits the use of subterfuge to lead the inciter to commit the crime in such a way that punishment is authorized.

An inciter is a layperson who has incites another layperson [to idolatry. For example,] if he said, "There is a deity in a certain place that eats in such a way, and drinks in such a way, that does good in such a way, and that does harm in such a way." In no capital cases in Torah [law] are [the suspects] entrapped, except in the case of the inciter. If he spoke [such things] to two [people], they become the witnesses against him: they bring him to court and stone him. [However,] if he spoke to [only] one [person], the latter [should] say, "I have friends who [also] want [to hear] this." If [the inciter] was prudent and avoids speaking before [others], he hides witnesses behind a fence and says to [the inciter], "Clarify what you said." Once he does so, he responds, "How can we abandon our God in heaven and go and worship wood and stones?" If [the inciter] turns back, all is well; however, if he responds, "This is right and good for us!," those standing behind the fence bring him to court and stone him.

Morality Patrols

24. Maimonides, MT Laws Concerning Repose on a Festival 6:21

The Code of Maimonides, Book Three: The Book of Seasons, translated by Solomon Gandz and Hyman Klein (New Haven: Yale University Press, 1961), p.304.

The officers described here are supposed to prevent sexual immorality, not to punish it. They seem to operate only in public places. An admonishment to "the people" — that is, to the heads of households — reflects an expectation that they will enforce sexual morality in private spaces.

It is the duty of the court to appoint officers for festival days to patrol and inspect parks, orchards, and river banks, to make sure that men and women do not congregate there to eat and drink together and thus be led to immorality. The court should also admonish all the people not to allow men and women to mix together freely inside their houses while engaged in rejoicing, nor to overindulge in wine, lest they should be led to immorality.

Coerced Consent

25. BT Bava Batra 47b–48a

Can a person's consent be valid even if it is not given freely? The talmudic discussion starts with a statement validating a sale made under duress and proceeds to examine whether this is similar to the mandate for legal coercion of deeds whose validity requires that the agent act willingly. This apparently paradoxical teaching is explored in the following selections, with regard to both its theoretical underpinnings and its practical ramifications.

Rav Huna said: If one consents to a sale under physical duress,[48] the sale is a [valid] sale. — What is the reason?

— In every case where a person sells, were he not under duress [by the need for money], he would not sell; nevertheless, the sale is a [valid] sale.

— But perhaps self-imposed duress is different from duress by others! Rather, [the reason the sale is valid is derived] from the following *baraita:*

> "He shall bring it forth" (Lev. 1:3) — this implies that they coerce him [to bring the offering he has vowed].
>
> Can it be [that it is valid] even against his will? We learn from what is written, "willingly" [*lirtzono*].[49] How so? They coerce him until he says, "I consent."

— But perhaps it is different there [in the case of a sacrifice], for he is content that [the sacrifice] will be an atonement for him. Rather, [the reason the coerced sale is valid is derived] from the end of that *baraita,* [which states:]

> The same is the case with regard to writs of divorce [*gittin*]: They coerce him until he says, "I consent."[50]

---

48. Lit., if they strung him up and he sold.
49. The plain reference of the word *lirtzono* is God's will, i.e., that the sacrifice be accepted. The midrashic rendition here relates it to the will of the person bringing the sacrifice.
50. See ¢18, §8.

—But perhaps it is different there [in the case of divorce], for it is a *mitzvah* to adhere to the words of the sages. Rather, [the rule] is derived by *sevara:* following the duress he consents to sell.

Value in Discharging One's Obligation

26. Tosafot Bava Batra 48a, s.v. *eleima*

The Tosafot postulate that the validation of a coerced transaction does not extend to a forced gift: even when given under duress, consent requires that something be received in exchange for what is relinquished. But then, what is received by the person coerced to bring a sacrifice or to deliver a get?

You may ask: if [we deduce] from [a coerced sacrifice that a forced sale is valid], then even if he gives a gift under physical duress, is it too [valid]? . . .

Rabbi Isaac thought to answer [this question] by saying that [bringing a sacrifice] is [not analogous to a gift but is rather] like a sale; since the sacrifice yields atonement, he thus obtains the atonement. And the case of divorce, from which [the Talmud also] sought to deduce [the validity of a coerced transaction], is like a sale, too. For by means of [the divorce], he is released from [his obligation to provide his wife with] food and clothing, and from his conjugal duties.

This however cannot be maintained, for if it were so, a *get* forced not in accordance with the law would also be valid, whereas in BT Gittin 88b (¢18, §8) Shmu'el stated that it is invalid.

Rabbi Isaac retorts that whatever one is obligated to do is like a sale: Here he is obligated to bring a sacrifice, and further on [in the next case] he is obligated to divorce his wife—for the case at hand concerns one of those who are "compelled to divorce" (¢18, §25). However, if [the coercion] is not in accordance with the law [*she-lo ka-din*], it is [rather] like [a case where] they torture him and he gives, which is not [considered] a [valid] gift.

Coercion Liberates from the Evil Inclination

27. Maimonides, MT Laws Concerning Divorce 2:20

The Code of Maimonides, Book Four: The Book of Women, edited by Leon Nemoy and translated by Isaac Klein, YJS (New Haven: Yale University Press, 1972), pp. 177–78 (with slight changes).

Here is the Maimonidean version of what Jean-Jacques Rousseau called "being forced to be free." The case is of a woman who is legally entitled to a divorce. Her husband refuses to write the get, and for it to be valid, he must give it willingly (cf. ¢18, §§7–8). The Talmud taught that he is coerced "until he says: 'I consent.'" Maimonides explains that the coerced husband is only doing what, as a good Jew committed to the commandments, he really wants to do.

If a person who may be legally compelled to divorce his wife refuses to do so, an Israelite court in any place and at any time may scourge him until he says, "I consent." He may then write a *get,* and it is a valid *get.* . . .

And why is this get not null and void, seeing that it is the product of duress . . . ? Because duress applies only to him who is compelled and pressed to do something that the Torah does not obligate him to do, for example, one who is lashed until he consents to sell something or give it away as a gift. On the other hand, he whose evil inclination induces him to violate a commandment or commit a transgression, and who is lashed until he does what he is obligated to do, or refrains from what he is forbidden to do, is not under duress by us; rather, his wicked character has brought duress upon his own self. Therefore this man who refuses to divorce his wife, inasmuch as he desires to be of the Israelites, to abide by all the commandments, and to keep away from transgressions (it is only his inclination that has overwhelmed him), and seeing that he was lashed until his inclination is weakened, and he says, "I consent"—he has indeed, divorced voluntarily.

Empirical Limits: Excluding an Apostate

28. Yom Tov b. Moses Tzahalon, *Responsa* 83

The received justification for coerced consent, as formulated by Maimonides (§27 above), has a troubling implication, since it apparently precludes coercive measures against an apostate who abandons his wife without issuing a get.

I have responded to the query posed by my reflections, whether an apostate can be coerced to divorce. . . . Specifically, my misgivings pertain to [the following issue:] If an apostate [proves to] be among those who are compelled to divorce—as in the case of one who states, "I will provide no food or sustenance" (cf. ¢18, §§24–25), where the law provides that we coerce an Israelite—[and] if we possess the power to coerce him to divorce [his wife even though] he has become an apostate [and left the community], can we do so or not?

Prima facie, it would seem that we [ought to] coerce him. For why should [our response] be less [severe] because he has become an apostate? Should his apostasy justify a sinner receiving gain? . . . If the law provides that we coerce an Israelite, how much more so should an apostate be coerced!

However, a close examination of Maimonides' position (§27 above) indicates that we cannot coerce. [Tzahalon cites Maimonides and continues:] . . . The only reason Maimonides found [to argue that coercion is permissible] is "inasmuch as he desires to be of the Israelites, etc." We see that [Maimonides] could not find a reason apart from the fact that "he desires to be of the Israelites," but "his inclination . . . overwhelmed him." It follows that with regard to one who becomes an apostate and thus does not desire to be of the Israelites, for he has already removed himself from the whole, this reason [for authorizing coercion] does not apply. Therefore, a forced *get* that is extracted from an apostate . . . is void. For the reason explicated by Maimonides . . . is irrelevant. It does not apply to an apostate, seeing that he has thrown off the yoke of Torah and *mitzvot* and does not desire to be of the Israelites. . . . The [apostate's] *get* is void because he is under duress. This appears, in my humble opinion, to derive from Maimonides' statements.

Normative Versus Punitive Coercion

29. Meir Simhah Cohen, *Or Same'ah* Laws Concerning Divorce 2:20

Disallowing coercion against an apostate who leaves his Jewish wife behind posed a difficult challenge for rabbinic authorities, particularly following emancipation and widespread assimilation. Rabbi Meir Simhah sets out to defend the traditional mandate for such coercion. Going back to the talmudic sugya, *he argues that coerced consent can be valid in two very different ways. When a court seeks to apply sanctions to members of the community, its power is restricted by the law, and hence in coercing a* get *it must rely on Maimonides' postulate of an inner desire to comply. No such restriction applies to the court's treatment of an apostate. Like the victim of a ruffian, the apostate thus faces unfettered violence, inducing complete capitulation*

It is the widespread [practice of] *halakhah* in Israel [i.e., among Jews] that apostates too are coerced [to divorce]. And yet, in his *Responsa,* Yom Tov b. Moses Tzahalon (§28 above), basing himself on the words of our master [Maimonides (§27 above)] . . . challenged this, [arguing] that an apostate cannot be coerced. . . . For after he has been beaten and has divorced [his wife] in accordance with the law, his mind will have no rest and he will be enraged with those who brought him to this, even though he has [in fact] fulfilled a *mitzvah.* Verily, the soul of the wicked craves wickedness and the wicked praises the lust of his soul;[51] he is thus under complete duress [and the necessary consent is absent]. . . .

      As a point of departure let us note [an inherent difficulty in the talmudic discussion in BT Bava Batra (§25):] "Rav Huna said: If one consents to a sale under physical duress, the sale is a [valid] sale." [The reason provided, namely that] "following the duress he consents to sell," [renders redundant the reasoning with regard to divorce in that very talmudic discussion: that] "it is a *mitzvah* to adhere to the words of the sages." . . .

      I would therefore submit that Rav Huna is stating a *sevara:* Every sale

51. Merging Prov. 21:10 with Ps. 10:3.

involves compulsion, since the person [selling] needs the funds derived from the sale. If he had the money, he would not sell. It is only because he needs the money that he sells his land. So too here [in the case of the person who consents to a sale under physical duress], he is not interested in the sale per se; [he sells] only because he fears for his life because of [the threat] of being beaten and pursued by the ruffian. In order to avoid this, he sells his land so as to be relieved of the [fear of] a beating. . . . [Rav Huna thus compares] the duress from a threat to one's life to universal [economic] duress. [He argues] that it makes no difference in [terms of the] acquiescence to the sale whether the [seller] has to solicit the [buyer] holding the money and entreat him so as to receive it or if someone else comes along and compels him and subjugates him with harsh chastisements because he does not sell.

All this holds however only in a case where the seller knows that if he does not sell the extortionist will chastise him harshly for not selling. [Even if] it is absolutely clear to the ruffian that the [owner] does not wish to sell and that he would rather sacrifice his life, he [the ruffian] will nevertheless beat him without limit due to his wrath at his refusal—therefore to avoid all this, he sells his land. [Having understood this argument, we may] now look into coercion by a court. [The law is that if, for example,] a person committed a transgression [punishable by] lashing, he cannot [simply] be beaten [without limit] until his soul departs, [but only in accordance with the prescribed punishment].[52] And if he transgressed a positive commandment, he is not liable at all [to punishment by a court], and so on. Only [in a case] where [the court] tells someone to carry out a specific [directive,] which is within his power, can he be beaten until his soul departs.[53] For it is not the court that is making him liable [to death]; he himself is [doing that]. At any moment, it is in his hands to rid himself of this bitterness—if he would agree to carry out [the directive]. Now would the court possess divine-like certainty that he will not concede and . . . that there [will be] no pragmatic result to their compulsion, since he [is prepared to] sacrifice his life for this, they are forbidden to raise a hand against him.

52. See §8 above.
53. See BT Ketubot 86a.

... This is why the Talmud must argue that "it is a *mitzvah* to adhere to the words of the sages." This Maimonides interpreted to mean that an Israelite who wishes to follow God's Torah and commandments has a fundamental volition to fulfill the laws of the Torah; only his desires momentarily harden his heart, and his mind cannot prevail over the power of his material nature. We bear witness to the fact that when he ultimately brings forth his sacrifice or gives the divorce, he will be happy that the court coerced him concerning this [matter] and that he fulfilled God's command. Therefore when he says, "I am willing," most especially now that he prevailed over the power of his material nature, he is performing this *mitzvah* wholeheartedly, his decision being made in free will. . . . [But it is] only in the case of a person who upholds God's Torah and wishes to walk in the straight path that [the Talmud and Maimonides need to] argue that "it is a *mitzvah* to adhere to the words of the sages." This is not so, however, in case of a defiant *mumar*.

[Hakohen here cites Maimonides' codification mandating uncurtailed force against apostates who act defiantly (see ¢15, §6). This mandate suffices to turn the argument around.]

Therefore even would the court have known [regarding] an apostate that coercion will not induce him to divorce willingly . . . although coercing him would [in this sense] be ineffective—still it would be permitted to kill him and divest him of his life. Therefore an Israelite court in relation to an apostate is like a ruffian in relation to an Israelite, and the apostate's decision to divorce is just like the Israelite's decision to sell in a coercive sale. . . . The same applies even in these times when our only authority is that granted by state law. If the Israelite *bet din* has been granted authority by the kingdom to coerce him, the court would not desist even if they knew that he would not acquiesce [inwardly] while granting the divorce. This being so, we can well say [as argued above] that the apostate, [realizing this,] will acquiesce and divorce [his wife] to rid himself [of the court's coercion], just as in a sale under physical duress, and the *get* is valid.

Commentary. Positive Freedom

These texts raise the central philosophical issue of positive and negative freedom. Do we enjoy freedom only when we are unhindered on our way to do whatever it is we want to do (the negative view)? Or are we really free (the positive view) only when we do what we ought to do? On the second view, freedom simply means acting in the right way, whether we act "freely" or not. But this is a hard definition to accept, even to understand, for those of us raised within a liberal political tradition.

Isaiah Berlin did not refer to the Jewish tradition when he wrote his classic critique of positive freedom, but he could easily have done so. True freedom, the Rabbis believed, lies in service to God. Israel was liberated from Egyptian bondage for the sake of this service—which did not, however, make the liberation any less liberating. The exodus was still a journey, as the Haggadah says, from slavery to freedom, even if it was also a journey from pharaonic to divine servitude. Thus Judah Halevi:

> The slaves of time
>   are the slaves of slaves;
> The slave of God
>   he alone is free.

Reduce this claim to the paradoxical equation "freedom = slavery," and we seem to have entered the nightmare world of George Orwell, where words have lost their meaning. How can it be that the content of my freedom is determined by someone else? It hardly matters whether the determination is the work of God or pharaoh, history or fate, or even the general will of the democratic state; it is plainly not the work of the individual who is said to be "free." The paradox is invincible. So it seems to us—and so it seemed to many of the Rabbis as well. That freedom doesn't sit easily with servitude is not a peculiarly modern insight. Paradoxes are paradoxes across time and space.

The Rabbis (or some of them) attempted to deal with the paradox by claiming that the servitude is voluntary, that the Jews agreed to it at Sinai. I won't consider the problems of this claim; I only want to stress its seriousness (see the extended discussion of the Sinai covenant in ¢1). But Sinai lies in the distant past: What about now? If the servitude is renewed in each generation, doesn't the consent also have to be renewed? This question is addressed again and again in Rabbinic literature, but one of the most illuminating discussions has to do with the laws of divorce. In traditional Jewish law, marriage is a patriarchal institution, and divorce is possible only with the agreement of the husband—formally recorded in a *get* (cf. ¢18). But there were cases where the rabbis and judges recognized that the wife was entitled to a divorce whether or not the husband agreed. He ought to agree, and they decided that he could be coerced to do so.

Maimonides sums up the argument in the following way: "If a person who may be legally compelled to divorce his wife refuses to do so, an Israelite court . . . may scourge him until he says I consent. He may then write a *get,* and it is a valid *get.*" But how can consent be valid if it is coerced, if the husband is literally beaten into agreement? Doesn't the beating, like God's threat to drop the mountain on the Jews at Sinai (see ¢1, §8), "furnish a powerful disclaimer" to the agreement?

There are two standard answers to these questions, and Maimonides offers both of them. First, he makes what I want to call the idealist defense. Why is the *get* not null and void seeing that it is (apparently) the product of duress? "Because duress applies only to him who is compelled . . . to do something which the Torah does not obligate him to do." Someone who is compelled to do what he ought to do can't be said to be under duress when he does it. Strictly speaking, only his "evil inclination" is compelled, for he himself, we assume, wants to do what is right and to live in accordance with divine command. "It is only his inclination that has overwhelmed him." He has an ideal will that we respect even when we deny his actual inclination. And so he is "free," he acts "voluntarily," despite the denial. But where does this assumption come from? How do we know that this particular recalcitrant husband really wants (behind the recalcitrance, so to speak) to write the *get* he ought to write? If he insists that his inclination expresses his will, what can we say to him?

These questions must have worried Maimonides, for he supplies an alternative argument, suggesting something like a communitarian defense of positive liberty. "This man who refuses to divorce his wife," he argues, "*inasmuch as he desires to be of the Israelites,* to abide by all the commandments, and to keep away from transgressions—it is only his inclination that has over-whelmed him." Now we don't assume an ideal will; we search for the practical involvement of the individual in the community. Ongoing membership is a kind of tacit consent. Maimonides doesn't look—as John Locke would later do—for such material signs of tacit consent as residence in the country or ownership of land. Signs like these might be ambiguous in a community in exile. He looks instead for a moral sign, namely, the manifest desire to be a member of such a community. The will to be a member takes precedence over temporary inclinations, not because it is ideal, but because it is real. We remain free despite this or that act of coercion, not because we *should* agree to what we are coerced to do, but because, if only in a general way, we *do* agree. But what we agree to is not whatever the community wants us to do; the community can coerce us only when it is acting according to its own law—so Maimonides' first argument sets limits on his second argument.

Maimonides does not say what it might mean not to agree—that is, to refuse communal membership. But the question arose in the responsa literature and in later commentaries with regard to converts to Islam or Christianity. Clearly a convert is someone who desires not to be "of the Israelites," who explicitly withdraws from the community. It would seem to follow from the communitarian defense that he cannot then be coerced (or, rather, that a *get* obtained by coercion would not be a valid *get*), and though there was disagreement, some of the rabbis apparently reached just this conclusion. We find it defended in the responsum of Yom Tov b. Moses Tzahalon in the early seventeenth century (and then cited, paraphrased, and rejected in the early twentieth-century *Or Same'ah*). Tzahalon, interpreting Maimonides roughly as I have done, argues that a convert who is compelled to write a *get* "consents only under duress"—which is to say, he doesn't really consent: "his soul will not rest and he will be full of anger toward those who brought him to do this." He is "just like someone forced to give a present"—that is, the present is not a genuine gift, and the *get* does not make for a morally or legally effective divorce.

This assumes, of course, the right or at least the possibility of conversion—distinctly a minority view. In the greater part by far of the responsa literature, over many centuries, conversion away from Judaism, called apostasy, was said to have no legal effects at all. Menachem Meiri is the only major figure to argue against this view, and even he makes an exception in the case of marriage and divorce (see ¢15, §12). But Meiri's claim, "Whoever has completely removed himself from the community and become a member of another religion is regarded by us as a member of the religion that he has joined," provides a background against which Tzahalon can be understood. I would suggest that the argument about consent and conversion has the following form: The Jewish community is a community of religious faith and lawful conduct. Members of this community take on certain obligations and can be coerced to act in line with those obligations. Converts have opted out of the community and the obligations, and so they can no longer be coerced.

Members can only be coerced in accordance with the established laws of the community and by its authorized agents. A *get* forcibly obtained by an unauthorized and non-Jewish court is an invalid *get,* whether or not the husband ought to agree. What justifies coercion is membership; therefore the members can only be coerced by one another. As long as they are coerced only by their fellows and only in the name of communal norms, they remain personally free. We might want to say of a particular individual, "He is free as a Jew but not as a husband." But Maimonides seems to take a different view. Being a Jew entails a certain way of being a husband, and insofar as one has freely chosen to be a Jew, one has also freely chosen to be a husband in that way. Hence Jews and husbands are alike free, even though they can't decide for themselves how to behave as either Jews or husbands. The community decides, through its courts.

The value of the communitarian defense of positive freedom is that it enables us to locate, rather than merely assume, the agreement by virtue of which the individual is said to be free. The actual agreement displaces the assumed agreement—and sets limits on the extremism of the idealist defense. It is not the case that individuals are free only if they do the right thing, for converts who refuse the morally or legally required divorce act freely; while if they are forced to grant the divorce, even though that is the right thing to do, they are denied their freedom. The communitarian defense, carried to its necessary conclusion by Tzahalon, is both consistent and powerful. It rests on what we might think of as a political and moral fact—that we are indeed members of communities, and commonly want to be, whether we have ideal wills or not.

But the argument faces severe problems too, for it seems to require a unitary community and all-or-nothing commitment from the individual. One is either in the community or not, a member or a stranger, and if one is in, one is wholly bound: no act of communal coercion, so long as the community acts within its laws, can possibly be called duress. But what if there is disagreement among the members about the meaning of their laws or about the proper extent of coercive enforcement? What if the community is pluralist in character—so that individuals who share a "desire to be of the Israelites" have in fact different desires? Pluralism multiplies the choices that individuals have to make, and the more choices there are, the more likely it is that coercion will challenge rather than confirm individual freedom. That's why the negative view of freedom, which acknowledges the challenge, gains strength as communal ties loosen. But so long as membership has any agreed-upon meaning at all, it makes sense to require members to live up to that meaning and to deny, at the same time, that the requirement renders them unfree.

Michael Walzer

Preemption and Zealotry

Rodef—*the Pursuer*

30. Mishnah Sanhedrin 8:5–7; BT Sanhedrin 73a

The Rabbis clearly advocate lethal intervention by a private citizen to prevent particular crimes: specifically, murder and capital rape. Note the ambiguity as to who is being saved: according to the mishnah's syntax, it is the perpetrator, yet victimless crimes—however severe—are explicitly excluded. The clause authorizing lethal intervention follows the mishnaic interpretation of the biblical permission for a homeowner to kill a tunneling burglar (Exod. 22:1-2).

Mishnah Sanhedrin 8:5–7

5. The rebellious son is judged in accordance with the [projected] outcome: let him die while [yet] innocent rather than when [already] guilty, for the death of the wicked [and the wicked-to-be] is beneficial for them and beneficial for the world, whereas the death of the righteous is bad for them and bad for the world.[54] . . .

6. The tunneling [burglar] is judged in accordance with the [projected] outcome [as he is deemed prepared to slay the homeowner].[55] . . .

7. These are saved by their lives: one who pursues [*rodef*] his fellow to kill him, and [one who pursues] a male, and [one who pursues] a betrothed maiden. But one who pursues an animal [to copulate with it], or a desecrator of Shabbat, or an idolater are not saved by their lives.

BT Sanhedrin 73a

Our Rabbis taught, "Whence is it that one who pursues his fellow to kill him may be saved by his life? We learn from what is written, 'Do not stand by the blood of your neighbor'"[56] (Lev. 19:16).

Is [the verse teaching] that? [Rather,] it is required for that which has been taught: "Whence is it that one who sees his fellow drowning in the river, or being dragged by a [wild] animal, or attacked by robbers, is obligated to save him? We learn from what is written, 'Do not stand by the blood of your neighbor'" (Lev. 19:16) [i.e., to establish the duty of rescue itself].

Indeed this is so; and [thus] whence that he is [to be] saved by his life? That is derived a fortiori from the [law mandating rescue of] the betrothed maiden (Deut. 22:25–27): If [in the case of] a betrothed maiden, whom [the pursuer] chases only to debase, the Torah stated that she should

54. See ¢19, §§1–3.
55. The Rabbis seem agreed that an attempt to steal property is not in itself sufficient to warrant lethal action by the homeowner, but their views diverge regarding the requisite degree of probability in ascribing lethal intent to the burglar.
56. The plain meaning of the verse is uncertain; thus NJPS: "Do not profit by the blood of your fellow."

be saved by his life, how much more so [does this apply to] one who pursues his fellow to kill him!

But can penal [liability] be established [in the absence of explicit statute, merely] by [a fortiori] reasoning?

[Instead,] the School of Rabbi [Judah the Prince] taught, "It is [derived by the explicit] analogy: "[But if the man comes upon the betrothed maiden in the open country, and the man lies with her by force, only the man who lay with her shall die, but you shall do nothing to the maiden. The maiden did not incur the death penalty,] for the case is like that of a man attacking another and murdering him" (Deut. 22:25–26). What is it that we derive from the murderer? Indeed, this [case of the murderer seems] intended to inform, but is itself informed. The case of a murderer is analogized to the case of a betrothed maiden; just as in the case of a betrothed maiden she should be saved by his life, so in the case of a murderer [the victim] should be saved by his life.

And whence do we derive [such a mandate regarding] the [case of] betrothed maiden itself?

As was taught by the School of Rabbi Yishmael . . . , [Scripture states, "though the betrothed maiden cried] there was no one to save her" (Deut. 22:27)—thus if there is someone to save her, [he should do so] with any means available to save her, [including the killing of the pursuer].

An Informer Is a Pursuer

31. Yeruham b. Meshulam, *Mesharim* 31:5

This section of Yeruham's influential legal compendium is mostly composed of Maimonides' earlier formulation. But leading up to that, it incorporates a crucial argument based on talmudic sources, identifying an informer as a "pursuer" and thus mandating killing him preemptively. This applies even if the informer directly endangers only property: his actions are construed as posing a latent threat to his victim's person. Notably, the same root (m.s.r., to convey or hand over) is used both for the terms denoting an informer and his actions and for the community's act of dealing with him by denouncing him to the gentile authorities.

If two people had a dispute over a thing [of value], and one caused it to be seized [*masar*] by the gentiles, he is to be placed under a ban until he removes the illicit force so that the property is subject to Jewish jurisdiction. . . .

One who says: "I will inform"; and they tell him: "Do not inform!"—and yet he says: "I will [indeed] inform!"—should be put to death immediately. Anyone who is able to do so first may kill him before he [goes on to] inform, even outside the Land [of Israel, where *halakhah* generally precludes capital punishment], since he is a pursuer [*rodef*]: In the short run [the gentiles] will seize [the victim's] property, bit by bit, and eventually they will seize his person ([as stated in BT Bava] Kama [117a]). Maimonides [MT Laws of Battery and Assault 8:11] wrote: "Once the informer [*moser*] has carried out his design and informed, it seems to me he may not be killed, unless he is known to be a [habitual] informer—who should be killed, lest he inform on others. The standard practice in the towns of the Magreb is to kill those who are known as [repeated] informers with regard to Jewish property, to turn them over [*limsor*] to the hands of the gentiles so that they be killed or beaten or incarcerated in accordance with their guilt. Likewise anyone who informs against the community and causes them suffering may be handed over to the gentiles to be beaten, incarcerated, and fined. On account of an individual's suffering, however, it is not permitted to hand over [a troublemaker]."

Threats of Informing: Defending the Community
32. Simeon b. Zemah Duran, *Tashbetz* 3:158

Duran reaffirms the policy of treating a confirmed informer as a pursuer, basing it both on extensive talmudic precedents and on the customary law of the kahal, *whose source he posits as an ancient* herem. *Yet in the case at hand, he insists that threats uttered in anger do not render their author an informer—even though the threatened party ("Reuven") was evidently a rabbi with some authority and the threats included denouncing his teachings about the trustworthiness of the gentile court.*

[Responding to a query from] Tunis. You asked as follows: Reuven quarreled with his fellow Shimon. In the course of the quarrel Shimon said to him: "You fornicate with gentile women! I will submit an affidavit about that to their court so that they shall stone you. I will moreover go to the judge and tell him that you declare that all documents signed by Ishmaelite witnesses are fraudulent, and that he applies his seal to them fraudulently!"—[Shimon] wanted to go tell [the judge] so. The Jews got him to turn back, yet he still threatens to inform. . . .

Answer: It is common knowledge that one who is known to be a [repeated] informer is liable to death under the law of the pursuer [*rodef*]. Moreover, anyone who says, "I will go and inform," forfeits his life, as recorded in [BT] tractate Berakhot [58a], and likewise in tractate Gittin [56a, ¢27], in the story about Kamsta and Bar-Kamsta, wherein they proposed to kill him. Similarly in [BT] tractate Bava Kama [117a], ". . . Once an Israelite's property falls into the hands of gentiles, they will show him no pity." Apart from all this, you well know that Israel's customary law is to ban and excommunicate informers, as [authorized] by an ancient *herem,* promulgated by the [rabbis] of old.

There are, however, two categories within this [law]. First, regarding a person who is known to be a [repeated] informer, causing the loss of Israelites' property two or three times. Such a person may be killed or handed over to the gentiles; he is among those who should be pushed down and not pulled up, as stated in [BT] Avodah Zarah 26a (¢15, §6). Second, regarding a person who says, "I will go and inform"—such a one may not be killed except after a warning. If they have warned him and he does not relent, they kill him, as in the case of the person who said: "I will go and point out [another Jew's] wheat to the government]!"; Rav Kahana told him: "Do not point it out!," but he replied: "I will certainly point it out!"—So Rav Kahana tore out his windpipe, killing him, as stated in [BT] Bava Kama (117a). Therefore the proper course for the community [*tzibbur*] in the case at hand is to warn this person, who has uttered these [threats of] informing; perhaps he spoke them out of anger and without criminal intent—though [admittedly] it is difficult to extend [such] understanding in these matters. Then if after he has been thus warned he repeats his folly, the community must spread the word that he is under a ban and all must separate from him; and that anyone who does not treat him as being under a ban [thereby] transgresses the teachings of the sages.

All Israel have a stake in this, for if you fail to repair this breach, what he has done to this one he will do to every one of you, and you will cause informers to gain power over the decent, powerless [people]. If, however, these statements [only] arose out of a quarrel between the parties about some other matters, let them go to court, and [the judges] shall find in favor of the righteous and find against the culprit. The elders should say to him: "Defend your rights against your fellow, but do not give away the secrets of another" (Prov. 25:9).

Phinehas: God's Knight
33. Numbers 25:1–15

Phinehas is the original zealot, and his story is the basis for all further discussions of zealotry. He acts without any kind of official authorization, alone, and in anger, defending what he takes to be God's law.

While Israel was staying at Shittim, the people profaned themselves by whoring with the Moabite women, who invited the people to the sacrifices for their god. The people partook of them and worshiped that god. Thus Israel attached itself to Baal-peor, and the Lord was incensed with Israel. The Lord said to Moses, "Take all the ringleaders and have them publicly impaled before the Lord, so that the Lord's wrath may turn away from Israel." So Moses said to Israel's officials, "Each of you slay those of his men who attached themselves to Baal-peor."

Just then one of the Israelites [Zimri] came and brought a Midianite woman over to his companions, in the sight of Moses and of the whole

Israelite community who were weeping at the entrance of the Tent of Meeting. When Phinehas, son of Eleazar son of Aaron the priest, saw this, he left the assembly, and taking a spear in his hand, he followed the Israelite into the chamber and stabbed both of them, the Israelite and the woman, through the belly. Then the plague against the Israelites was checked. Those who died of the plague numbered twenty-four thousand.

The Lord spoke to Moses, saying, "Phinehas, son of Eleazar son of Aaron the priest, has turned back My wrath from the Israelites by displaying among them his passion for Me, so that I did not wipe out the Israelite people in My passion.[57] Say, therefore, 'I grant him My pact of friendship [shalom]. It shall be for him and his descendants after him a pact of priesthood for all time, because he took impassioned action for his God, thus making expiation for the Israelites.'"

The Zealous Moment
34. BT Sanhedrin 82a

The Talmud here defines the contours of the moment when a zealot takes the law into his own hands by invoking the rule of the rodef, *"pursuer," discussed above (§30). It is a spontaneous reaction to a perceived transgression, and the zealot is also thereby exposed to legitimate self-defense by the person he attacks.*

Rav Hisda said: If someone [enraged by witnessing a transgression perpetrated] comes to consult [the court as to how to react], they do not instruct him. . . .

Moreover, had Zimri separated [from the Midianite woman] and Phinehas had slain him [thereafter], Phinehas would have been executed on account of [murdering] him. Had Zimri turned over and slain Phinehas, he would not have been executed, seeing as [Phinehas] was a *rodef.*

57. The word translated as "passion" is often translated as "jealousy" and also sometimes "zeal."

Zealotry

35. Maimonides, MT Laws of Mixed Kinds 10:29

The Code of Maimonides, Book Seven: The Book of Agriculture, translated by Isaac Klein, YJS (New Haven: Yale University Press, 1979), p. 43.

Zealotry and respect for people's dignity come into conflict in the cases discussed here regarding garments forbidden because they are woven from mixed kinds (see Deut. 22:12).

If one sees his companion wearing a garment of diverse kinds forbidden by the Torah, even when the latter is walking in the market, he should immediately accost him and rip it off him. He should do so even if it is his master who had taught him wisdom, because respect for people's dignity does not set aside a negative commandment explicitly stated in the Torah. . . .

Anything forbidden by scribal law, however, may be set aside . . . when the dignity of people is involved. Even though Scripture says, "You must not deviate from the verdict" (Deut. 17:11, ¢6, §1), this negative commandment is set aside when the dignity of people is involved. Therefore, if one's companion is wearing a garment of diverse kinds forbidden only by scribal law, he may not rip it and take it off him in the market. Nor need one remove [such a garment] until he reaches his home. If, however, the diverse kinds are forbidden by the Torah, he must remove the garment immediately.

Commentary. The Power and Failure of Zealotry

What happens when law fails to deter? What can be done? We can assume a prospective injured party to have legitimate recourse to self-defense, but what of a third party? May such an individual stand in for a prospective injured party? Can he stand in for the law? May a concerned citizen reinstate the claim of law?

The statute of the *rodef,* the pursuer, states that a third party not only may take preemptory action on the part of a prospective injured party but is obligated to do so if he judges the danger imminent. Here is the Mishnah's classic presentation:

These are saved by their lives: one who pursues [*rodef*] his fellow to kill him, and [one who pursues] a male, and [one who pursues] a betrothed maiden. (Mishnah Sanhedrin 8:7, §30)

The Mishnah's formulation is opaque. Who is being saved and at the price of which life?

On Maimonides' reading, the Mishnah calls for the saving of the lives of the pursued. In his code Maimonides contextualizes preemption in the larger setting of his discussion of murder and provides a reconstruction of the text:

If a murderer kills willfully, he may not be put to death by the witnesses or the spectators before he is brought to court and condemned. . . . The above rule applies when the offender has already transgressed and committed the crime. . . . But if one pursues his fellow to kill him, even if the pursuer is a minor, all of Israel are thus commanded to save the pursued, even by [the cost of] the pursuer's life. (MT Laws Concerning Murder and Preservation of Life 1:5–6)

According to Maimonides' reading of the Mishnah, "These" endangered individuals "are saved by" virtue of the imminent danger to their lives even at the cost of the "lives" of the pursuers.

Elaborating the moral rationale of the Mishnah, the Talmud argues that the obligation is to one's fellow in danger:

Whence is it that one who sees his fellow drowning in the river, or being dragged by a [wild] animal, or attacked by robbers, is obligated to save him? We learn from what is written, "Do not stand by the blood of your neighbor" (Lev. 19:16). (BT Sanhedrin 73a, §30)

One cannot stand indifferent to the shedding of innocent blood even if it means shedding the blood of the pursuer. (Note the consistent depiction of the prospective victim as "fellow." A murderer overlooks the fellowship of the "other"; it is when one becomes aware of fellowship that saving becomes vital.)

According to Rashi, however, the rhetorical staging of the case by the Mishnah is as follows: "These are saved by their lives." "These"—the following criminals—"are saved" from grievous sin "by their"—own—"lives." In the law of *rodef* the Mishnah pushes the dilemma of saving a life at the cost of a life to its ultimate, but exits the dilemma through a paternalistic conception of saving the potential criminal from sinning. That is to say, the third party here may not be able to avoid the shedding of blood, but he does succeed in maintaining the loyalty of fellowship to both parties: to the one by saving his life, to the other by saving him from sinning.

Has the Mishnah succeeded in completely cleansing the third party of the blood on his hands? Notice that in preceding cases of the death of a prospective criminal, that of the rebellious son by the court and that of the threatening burglar by the homeowner, the argument for their preemptory death is that each of them "is judged according to the [projected] outcome." If extended to the case of *rodef* this consequentialist argument would empower the second party acting in self-defense. But Rashi seems to imply that the argument cannot be extended to a third party. A third party acts on *behalf* of his fellow and therefore is not engaged in (self) defense. The case of *rodef* could arguably be construed as an action of defense, as an extension of this basic right in the interest of the other. Yet the Mishnah—holding, perhaps, that the right of self-defense, precisely because it is a right, is personal and not transitive—does not argue so. Rather, it casts the justification in terms of the obligation to rescue.

In contradistinction, the zealot wants more; he acts for God, on behalf of his passion and wrath. The paradigmatic case is that of Phinehas.

> The Lord spoke to Moses, saying, "Phinehas, son of Eleazar son of Aaron the priest, has turned back My wrath from the Israelites by displaying among them his passion for Me, so that I did not wipe out the Israelite people in My passion. (Num. 25:10–11, §33)

It is God's honor that has been affronted; the divine countenance, as it were, has been tarnished by the sinners' outrageous insult. In a theocratic setting, where the divine is the pinnacle and thereby the ultimate principle of the regime, this is an affront to the very notion of a legal order—and therefore the affront threatens a suspension of the Law. The zealot thus acts on behalf of the order preventing the wiping out of the Israelite people. In the case of *rodef,* it is the life and limb of the prospective injured party that are at stake. In that of the zealot, it is the entirety of the order. The killing of the pursuer saves an endangered individual; the act of zealotry reconstitutes the order and thereby saves the people.

The pursuer has taken the law into his hands. The law hence has remained intact. The zealot operates in the realm preceding law. The zealot is therefore construed by the Talmud as one acting on the spur of the moment:

> Rav Hisda said: If someone [enraged by witnessing a transgression perpetrated] comes to consult [the court as to how to react], they do not instruct him. (BT Sanhedrin 82a, §34)

Zealotry is a spontaneous upsurge of the moment before reason begins; it precedes law. The very fact that one has come for instruction proves that he is not a zealot; by reflection, he has forfeited the zealous passion of the moment.

The zealot seeks to save and thereby reconstitute the legal order's legitimacy. Viewed as it were from within, he is not a criminal because his prima facie "breaking" of law is construed as acting outside the law for the law. But this comes at a price: placing himself outside the law, he cannot enjoy the defense of law.

> Moreover, had Zimri [the Israelite man] separated [from Cozbi the Midianite woman] and Phinehas had slain him [thereafter], Phinehas would have been executed on account of [murdering] him. Had Zimri turned over and slain Phinehas, he would not have been executed seeing as [Phinehas] was a *rodef.*

Timing is of the essence. The zealot responds to the moment of sin. He counters villainous outrage with zealous rage. If time passes, he has lost his moment. Had Zimri separated from Cozbi and Phinehas had slain him, Phinehas would have been culpable of murder. (Put otherwise: Zimri enjoys a presumption of innocence as soon as the moment of sin has passed. This presumption assumes the stability of the legal order and attests to its power.)

Moreover, had Zimri succeeded in turning the table on Phinehas, he would be recognized as exercising his right of self-defense! Paradoxically, Zimri as criminal assumes the law he is breaking. That is what makes him a criminal. Phinehas is acting outside the law, and as long as that is clear, he is not declared a criminal himself. The zealot puts his life on the line; his work will be judged ultimately by its eventual success, but in real time, it cannot be said to be just; the zealot forfeits the claims of right.

Thus far we have considered the Talmud's reading of the story in its presentation of the delicate workings of the asymmetry of zealot and criminal. The semiotic construction by the Torah of this disturbing foundational myth of priestly custodianship of the sacred also conveys unease about, perhaps even a critique of, Phinehas and his deed.

> When Phinehas, son of Eleazar son of Aaron the priest, saw this, he left the assembly and, taking a spear in his hand, he followed the Israelite into the chamber and stabbed both of them, the Israelite and the woman, through the belly. Then the plague against the Israelites was checked. (Num. 25:7–8, §33)

Zimri is engaged in a negative ritual, perhaps an antiritual. He publicly copulates with Cozbi at the entrance to the Tent of Meeting, thereby defying the deity at the threshold of the sacred, of God's abode. The intended consequence seems to be the emasculation as it were of the Deity. (Cf. the Rabbinic story of Titus's desecration of the innermost sanctum sanctorium of the Second Temple in its hour of destruction in BT Gittin 56b.) It is an act of desacralization and thereby also a draining of the sacred of its power. Indeed, God's representative Moses weeps helplessly as though emptied of all strength and subjugated to Zimri and his antiritual. At this point, Phinehas enters the stage with his spear in hand and thrusts it through the entangled bodies of the couple. He seeks to reinstate the balance undermined by the negative ritual by a counter-ritual that seeks to retrieve the symbolic capital lost to the sinner. His phallic instrument unites with the phallic consummation of Zimri and Cozbi in the immolating of the sinners. Phinehas attempts to restore symbolic order by reinstating it in an act of retribution. It is meant to restore the divine countenance and reempower the presence of God in the world.

But what is so disturbing is not only the extreme violence of the story. The seeming hero of the myth, Phinehas, undermines Zimri's ritual regicide. The retribution, however, is guided by a principle of parity, and here Phinehas is constantly and consistently operating within the semiotic horizon constructed by Zimri! Phinehas counters phallic ritual with phallic violence. He fails to redeem himself or the viewers from the horizon of the sinner; he is enmeshed in the circularity of the new symbolic order created by the sinner. This priestly zealot does not sublimate the wellspring of sin; he is completely overtaken by it in his own rage. (We may recall here with bitter irony the Rabbinic equation of rage and idolatry in BT Shabbat 105b.) Phinehas therefore does not succeed in breaking loose from the pagan moment of idolatry. God must hand him a covenant of peace not only for the defense of his life but for his redemption and purification. God's word of peace goes beyond retribution. It is a gesture aimed at dismantling the impossible circle of sinful sexuality and violence. It is the human zealot who enacts the moment of exception but fails thereby to reinstate order. This is left to God in the benevolence of his covenant of peace. I suggest we interpret this gesture as a reaffirmation of the giving of Torah, the law, as an act of redeeming love.

This theological/political presaging of terroristic rage in modernity is uncanny. But it's not only the typology of the affliction that we see here but also the indication of an antidote: the idea of the political creates the conditions of peace by freeing politics from violence by the invocation of law. The zealous priest (along with his modern progeny) is caught in the web of a rage that undermines the political. Returning to the biblical text as its epic unfolds, we learn later on that the son of Eli the priest of Shilo (1 Sam. 2), whose name is Phinehas, is guilty of sexual abuse in the Temple. Might this be a typological suggestion that this lineage does not succeed in freeing itself from the atavistic phallic entanglement? The story of Eli and the demise of this priestly dynasty is part of the biblical stage-setting for the founding of the monarchy in ancient Israel. Could it be then that in these stories we hear the echo of a profound critique of the priestly by the monarchic tradition? If so, the monarchists seem to argue that politics cannot be reduced to semiotic capital. "A king by law shall constitute a land" (Prov. 29:4).

Menachem Lorberbaum

Introduction

Foundations: Building a System for Justice

The Judge's Responsibility

Orthodox Rejection of Secular Law
20. Ovadyah Yosef, *Responsa Yehave Da'at* 4:65
    Commentary. Noam J. Zohar, "Who Are the 'Others'? The Courts
    and the Political Community"

Introduction

In its early days, when it was an association in search of a legitimating idea, the *kahal* was often described as a *bet din,* a court. And then the authority of the "good men" was justified as if they were judges (see ¢8). Judgment is the political act most readily understood within the Jewish tradition.
If God is the lawgiver (and sometimes also the king), then all that is left to
his people is the interpretation and application of the law. In fact, however,
the Bible describes political actors of many different sorts, some of whom
were certainly involved in lawmaking and policy decisions: scribes, counselors, elders, generals, priests, prophets, and kings as well as judges. Though
the *kahal* could hardly provide room for all these—for it was a community
in exile, without land, temple, or sovereignty—it nonetheless required more
than one kind of official. Hence if it was in some sense conceived as a court,
it also *included* courts among its institutions. The law court in this specific
sense, with its own officers and procedures, is our subject in this chapter. At
the same time, because of the centrality of judgment, the literature dealing
with the court system also addresses, as we have seen, general issues about
the nature of political life: the use of punishment to deal with the "needs of
the hour" was a central theme of Chapter 23; those same "needs" figure here
in discussions of judicial authority.

We begin with some basic texts dealing with the importance of
courts, the appointment and qualifications of the judge, and the moral character of the act of judgment. It is worth noting that the distinction suggested in the selection from Chronicles between "all matters of the Lord"
and "the king's matters," and so presumably between religious and secular
law, may have been reflected in the maxim *dina de-malkhuta dina* (¢9), but it

had no direct application to the Jewish courts. There talmudic law reigned supreme and judges were scholars and rabbis, whenever such people could be found. But the authority of the rabbis was sometimes challenged by laymen, especially with regard to economic matters (*mamona,* issues of property and wealth). We saw this most clearly in the Ordinances of the Livorno Community (¢8, §17), which held that the "customs of the merchants" took precedence over talmudic law and should be adjudicated by lay leaders (*parnasim*).

The religious/secular distinction was indirectly reflected in two other distinctions having to do with judgment itself: between justice and necessity and between justice and compromise ("settlement" in some of our texts). Both emergency decision-making and compromise, since they were meant to provide an escape from the strictness and specificity of God's law, were plausibly the work of laymen. But they are most often assigned, in the literature, at least, to the rabbinic authorities, who are presumed best able to judge their value and their limits. Outside the *kahal,* of course, there were royal and secular courts, but resort to these was commonly condemned—as by Maimonides in the text that introduces the next to last section of this chapter. Indeed, one of the main concerns in the elaboration of the legal system was to preclude appeals to gentile rulers and secular law. How this concern plays out in the state of Israel today is the subject of our final selections.

The existence and power of gentile courts was not the only difficulty associated with the experience of exile. The legitimacy of Jewish courts was also in question, for the Talmud seemed to allow the full range of halakhic adjudication only in the Land of Israel. And yet judgment across the range was necessary if the exilic communities were to govern themselves. This necessity was recognized and partly addressed in the Talmud itself; medieval rabbis developed a wide array of methods for dealing with this problem. Their arguments are most clearly summarized by Menachem Meiri in the selection below. Notice in his text and in later ones, too, that though diaspora Jewish courts operated, as it were, under a cloud, Jewish judges displayed remarkable confidence in their own authority.

It was crucial to find judges who commanded respect within the community and to develop procedures that really worked—and not only for the most powerful members of the *kahal.* Though Issac b. Sheshet Perfet's account of how judges are chosen is obviously at odds with the biblical versions, it suggests the kind of adaptation to medieval social conditions that was necessary to secure the legitimacy of the judge. Legitimacy did not depend on appointment only, however, but on conduct as well. Hence the argument in the texts from Maimonides, Jacob Weil, and Yoel Sirkes about the courage required of a judge also addresses the problem of legitimation. At issue here is the judge's independence and the integrity of his judgments. How could he fulfill the negative command (best translated in the King James Version): "Thou shalt not respect persons" (Deut. 16:19), when he was himself without police powers, dependent on the "good men," who were also, as we have seen, the richest and most powerful men in the community? But if he were merely the tool of such men, what would prevent weaker members of the *kahal* from (legitimately) seeking justice at the hands of the gentile authorities?

Under conditions of sovereignty, judicial independence is a constitutional issue. It has to do with the standing of judges vis-à-vis executive officers (kings, presidents, prime ministers) and members of legislative bodies (assemblies, parliaments, congresses). How can they be protected against the imperious demands of state power? But where sovereignty is absent, as in the *kahal,* judicial independence is a social and moral issue. It has to do with the judge's standing vis-à-vis the litigants who come before him. Suppose that one of these litigants is what Maimonides calls a "hard man" with the power and will to seek revenge on anyone who rules against him. How many judges are brave enough to refuse in such a case to "respect persons," that is, to defer to wealth and power—social rather than political imperiousness?

The realism of the Rabbis is nicely displayed in their response to this problem, which cannot have been uncommon. They resist the preemptory character of the biblical rule while still recognizing and struggling to accommodate its moral point. Their argument draws on a distinction between inaction and wicked action—in this case, between backing off from judgment and judging unjustly. Neither, to be sure, meets the ideal of righteous (impartial) judgment, but the first failure is less bad than the second and may be acceptable if the physical safety of the judge himself is at risk. It would seem, however, that a poor man or woman denied justice by the intimidated judges of the *bet din* would have a right to seek it elsewhere.

Jewish law was strict not only with regard to the judge's duty but also with regard to the court's procedures. Here it was criminal defendants rather than poor or weak litigants to whom protection was extended—especially in capital cases, where the Rabbis seem genuinely uncertain whether conviction, given what must follow, could ever be justified (see the discussion in ¢23). At the same time, they also believed that capital punishment, and other corporal punishments too, were necessary for the maintenance of social order. The logic of deterrence seems never to have been questioned within the tradition. And thus necessity and justice were at odds; and sometimes justice was also at odds with itself, procedure against substance, as in cases where the talmudic rules of evidence—Torah law—made it impossible to do anything at all to a defendant about whose guilt the judges felt certain. Confronting these oppositions (as we saw in ¢23), the Rabbis invoked the doctrines of equity and emergency.

But how could they maintain communities for whose daily needs the Torah made no satisfactory provision? The obvious answer was to separate divine and secular law. This is what happened in Christendom and what would probably have happened in the Jewish world too, had there been Jewish kings and Jewish states (rather than only kings-in-books, theoretical kings of nonexistent states) to seize upon the "needs of the hour." The Rabbis were forced instead to find justifications in the Torah for deviations from it. But they knew that this was a dangerous thing to do: How to prevent the deviations from overwhelming the Torah? There was no church-state boundary to argue about, so other limits had to be sought. Two of these are especially important. First, some of the Rabbis insisted that judges required special authorization (from the people of the *kahal* or even from the gentile king) before they could act beyond or against divine law. And second, some of them argued, as we have seen, for highly restrictive definitions of "needs" and "hours"—but this only provoked counterarguments and looser definitions. Ultimately, in the absence of institutional constraints, there was no recourse except, as Solomon Luria argues, to the standard of *sevara,* reasonableness or common sense. Popular consent and expert knowledge, which Luria also insists on, help to ensure that judicial sense and common sense coincide more often than not. So the question of "needs" and "hours," which is properly a political question, was dealt with in the Jewish exile by stressing the authority and qualifications of the judges.

The alternative to all this was the gentile court, which could do whatever needed to be done without putting Jewish law at risk. But the *kahal* authorities, who quite reasonably were wary of gentile "help," did everything they could to prevent Jews from using the non-Jewish courts, at least as a means of adjudication. The authorities themselves, however, often turned to the gentiles in search of a means of enforcement. There was an odd symbiosis here: if gentile overlords were reluctant to allow their Jewish subjects to inflict corporal punishment (capital punishment was hardly ever allowed), the Jews were similarly reluctant to punish outside their own law. They could recognize the needs of the hour but were happy enough to turn offenders over to non-Jews for the necessary but, strictly speaking, illegal discipline. In a sovereign Jewish state, this would presumably have been the work of the king, not the *bet din*.

In somewhat similar fashion, Jewish laymen might also stand in for the rabbis—first of all where rabbis and scholars were unavailable and also (in civil cases) where compromises were called for that fell short of strict justice. Most of the rabbis preferred to negotiate such compromises themselves, but they were prepared to accept lay negotiators: the choice commonly was made by the parties themselves. The *Hazon Ish,* defending secular "judges" of this sort as one of the lesser evils of Jewish life, insists only that they must not subscribe to any alternative (secular) laws. As in cases of emergency, the judges must do the best they can—but without claiming to interpret the Torah. Here indeed we can see a line being drawn between "the matters of the Lord" and the everyday requirements of the political community. Writing in 1948, a few months before the establishment of the state of Israel, Shlomo Goren finds different ways to recognize and accommodate the everyday requirements. By contrast, Ovadyah Yosef refuses to do that; he denies the legitimacy of state courts that are not rabbinic courts. But he doesn't address the tension between Torah law and modern conceptions of justice that leads Goren to argue for accommodation. These two views, both of which have religious justification, suggest the cultural struggle brought on by the realization of Jewish sovereignty.

Foundations: Building a System for Justice

Divine Law, Human Judges
1. Exodus 18:13–26; Deuteronomy 1:9–17, 16:18–20

Moses alone conveys God's laws, and at first it is also he alone who sits in judgment;
but necessity leads to the establishment of a many-tiered hierarchy of judges. These men
(Deborah is the exceptional woman; cf. ¢13, §20) are not prophets yet are authorized to
apply God's law on their own, at least in "minor matters" — hence the emphasis here on
their qualifications. The last two passages are from Deuteronomy, framed as Moses' de-
parting address; in the first of these, he recapitulates the creation of the judicial system,
adding his exhortations toward judicial integrity. (But note the difference from Exodus:
the meritocratic description of the selection process, "Moses chose capable men from out of
all Israel," is replaced by "I took your tribal leaders.") In the third passage, similar injunc-
tions are coupled with a commandment to set up judicial institutions in the promised land
(this is followed by other constitutional provisions: cf. ¢3, §5; ¢4, §§5–6; ¢5, §9; ¢6, §1).

Exodus 18:13–26

Next day, Moses sat as magistrate among the people, while the people stood about Moses from morning until evening. But when Moses' father-in-law [Jethro] saw how much he had to do for the people, he said, "What is this thing that you are doing to the people? Why do you act alone, while all the people stand about you from morning until evening?" Moses replied to his father-in-law, "It is because the people come to me to inquire of God. When they have a dispute, it comes before me, and I decide between one person and another, and I make known the laws and teachings of God."

But Moses' father-in-law said to him, "The thing you are doing is not right. You will surely wear yourself out, and these people as well. For the task is too heavy for you; you cannot do it alone. Now listen to me. I will give you counsel, and God be with you! You represent the people before God; you bring the disputes before God, and enjoin upon them the laws and teachings, and make known to them the way they are to go and the practices they are to follow. You shall also seek out from among all the people capable men who fear God, trustworthy men who spurn ill-gotten gain. Set these over them as chiefs of thousands, hundreds, fifties, and tens, and let them judge the people at all times. Have them bring every major dispute to you, but let them decide every minor dispute themselves. Make it easier for yourself by letting them share the burden with you. If you do this—and God so commands you—you will be able to bear up; and all these people too will go home unwearied."

Moses heeded his father-in-law and did just as he had said. Moses chose capable men out of all Israel and appointed them heads over the people—chiefs of thousands, hundreds, fifties, and tens; and they judged the people at all times: the difficult matters they would bring to Moses, and all the minor matters they would decide themselves.

Deuteronomy 1:9–17

Thereupon I said to you, "I cannot bear the burden of you by myself. The Lord your God has multiplied you until you are today as numerous as the stars in the sky. May the Lord, the God of your fathers, increase your numbers a thousandfold, and bless you as He promised you. How can I bear unaided the trouble of you, and the burden, and the bickering! Pick from each of your tribes men who are wise, discerning, and experienced, and I will appoint them as your heads." You answered me and said, "What you propose to do is good." So I took your tribal leaders, wise and experienced men, and appointed them heads over you: chiefs of thousands, chiefs of hundreds, chiefs of fifties, and chiefs of tens, and officials for your tribes. I charged your magistrates at that time as follows, "Hear out your fellow men, and decide justly between any man and a fellow Israelite or a stranger. You shall not be partial in judgment: hear out low and high alike. Fear no man, for judgment is God's. And any matter that is too difficult for you, you shall bring to me and I will hear it.

Deuteronomy 16:18–20

You shall appoint magistrates and officials for your tribes, in all the settlements that the Lord your God is giving you, and they shall govern the people with due justice. You shall not judge unfairly: you shall show no partiality; you shall not take bribes, for bribes blind the eyes of the discerning and upset the plea of the just. Justice, justice shall you pursue, that you may thrive and occupy the land that the Lord your God is giving you.

Judges for God and King
2. 2 Chronicles 19:4–11

The author of Chronicles makes a crucial distinction between two kinds of "cases" — those dealing with God's affairs and those dealing with the affairs of the king. The same judges, drawn from priestly and lay (clan) leaders, deal with both kinds, but under different presiding officers.

[King] Jehoshaphat remained in Jerusalem a while and then went out among the people from Beer-sheba to the hill country of Ephraim; he brought them back to the Lord God of their fathers. He appointed judges in the land in all the fortified towns of Judah, in each and every town. He charged the judges: "Consider what you are doing, for you judge not on behalf of man, but on behalf of the Lord, and He is with you when you pass judgment. Now let the dread of the Lord be upon you; act with care, for there is no injustice or favoritism or bribe-taking with the Lord our God." Jehoshaphat also appointed in Jerusalem some Levites and priests and heads of the clans of Israelites for rendering judgment in matters of the Lord, and for disputes. Then they returned to Jerusalem. He charged them, "This is how you shall act: in fear of the Lord, with fidelity, and with whole heart. When a dispute comes before you from your brothers living in their towns, whether about homicide, or about ritual, or laws or rules, you must instruct them so that they do not incur guilt before the Lord and wrath be upon your brothers. See, Ama-

riah the chief priest is over you in all cases concerning the Lord, and Zeba-
diah son of Ishmael is the commander of the house of Judah in all cases concerning the king; the Levitical officials are at your disposal; act with resolve
and the Lord be with the good."

Integrity in Appointments and in Judgment

3. Sifre Deuteronomy 15–17

Sifre: A Tannaitic Commentary on the Book of Deuteronomy, translated by Reuven Hammer, YJS
(New Haven: Yale University Press, 1986), pp. 38–41.

*This midrash on Deuteronomy's account of judicial office addresses key questions about
the necessary character of the judge and the moral requirements of judgment. Evidently,
the Rabbis had considerable experience with both nepotism and favoritism, but the remedies they suggest are moral and prudential rather than institutional in character.*

15. *So I took the heads of your tribes, wise men, etc., and I charged your judges* (1:15–16):
I attracted them with words, saying, "How fortunate you are! Over whom are
you about to be appointed! Over the children of Abraham, Isaac, and Jacob,
men who have been called brothers and friends, a pleasant vineyard and portion, sheep of His pasture, and all kinds of such endearing terms."

    Wise men, and full of knowledge (1:15): This is one of the seven quali-
ties which Jethro had mentioned to Moses, of which Moses found only three,
wise men and full of knowledge.

    And made them heads over you (1:15): Meaning that they should be held
in honor by you, leaders in buying and selling, in mutual negotiation, in
coming in and in going out, such as come in first and go out last. . . .

    16. *And I charged your judges at that time saying, "Hear the causes between
your brethren, and judge righteously"* (1:16): I said to them, "Be deliberate in judgment. If a case comes before you two or three times, do not say, 'Such a case
has already come before me repeatedly,' but be deliberate in judgment." The
men of the Great Assembly likewise said, "Be deliberate in judgment, raise
up many disciples, and make a fence for the Torah" (Mishnah Avot 1:1)." . . .

    17. *Ye shall not respect persons in judgment* (1:17): This refers to him who

appoints judges. You might say, "So-and-so is a fine man—I will appoint him judge"; "So-and-so is a mighty man—I will appoint him judge"; "So-and-so is a kinsman of mine—I will appoint him judge"; "So-and-so had lent me money—I will appoint him judge"; "So-and-so is a polyglot—I will appoint him judge." The result might be that such a judge would free the guilty and convict the innocent, not because he is wicked but because he is simply not knowledgeable: yet he will be regarded as having respected persons in judgment.

Ye shall hear the small and the great alike (1:17): You might say, "Since A is poor and B is rich, and it is our duty to sustain the poor, I will therefore rule in A's favor, so that he may be sustained honorably." Hence, *Ye shall hear the small and the great alike.*

Another interpretation: *Ye shall hear the small and the great alike:* You might say, "How can I dishonor this rich man A for a mere *denar?* I shall therefore rule in his favor, and then, when he goes outside, I will tell him, 'Give B (the *denar*), for you really owe it to him.'" Hence, *Ye shall hear the small and the great alike. . . .*

Ye shall not be afraid of the face of any man (1:17): You might say, "I am afraid of So-and-so, lest he slay my children, or set fire to my stacks of grain, or uproot my planting." Hence *Ye shall not be afraid of the face of any man, for the judgment is God's.* So also Jehoshaphat said to the judges, "Consider what ye do; for ye judge not for man, but for the Lord" (2 Chr. 19:6).

Settlement: Justice Versus Peace
4. BT Sanhedrin 6b–7a

The Rabbis were primarily religious leaders and teachers, but they were also occasional judges. When approached by parties to a dispute, they could respond either by encouraging an out-of-court settlement or by proceeding to render judgment. The former course might better promote peace, or it might only be less burdensome for the judge. But is it not the judge's duty to enforce justice?

Our Rabbis taught: Just as judgment requires [a court of] three, so too does [overseeing a] settlement require three. [But] after a judgment has been rendered, you may not [oversee a] settlement.

Rabbi Eli'ezer the son of Rabbi Yose the Galilean says: It is forbidden to [oversee a] settlement and anyone who [does so] is a sinner . . . rather let judgment bore through the mountain, as written: "For judgment is God's" (Deut. 1:17). So ran Moses' maxim: "Let judgment bore through the mountain." Aaron, however, loved peace and pursued peace and brought about peace among people, as written, "True instruction was in his mouth, and nothing perverse was on his lips, he walked with Me in peace and equity and turned many away from iniquity" (Mal. 2:6). . . .

[But] Rabbi Yehoshua b. Korha says: [Overseeing a] settlement is a meritorious act [*mitzvah*], as written, "Faithfully render judgment with peace in your gates" (Zech. 8:16). Surely where there is [legal] judgment there is no peace, and where there is peace, there is no judgment. What then is the kind of judgment that incorporates peace? It is [overseeing] a settlement. . . .

Rabbi Shimon b. Menasya says: Should two come before you for judgment, before you have heard their arguments, or [even] afterwards, if you do not [yet] know which way the judgment inclines, you may say to them: "Go out and settle." But once you have heard their arguments and know which way the judgment inclines, you may not say to them: "Go out and settle." . . .

Rabbi Yehudah b. Lakish says: Should two come before you for judgment, one gentle and the other hard, before you have heard their arguments, or [even] afterwards, if you do not [yet] know which way the judgment inclines, you may say to them: "I will not deal with you"—lest the hard one be found liable, and go after [the judge]. But once you have heard their arguments and know which way the judgment inclines, you may not say to them: "I will not deal with you"—as written: "You shall not be afraid of the face of any man" (Deut. 1:17). . . .

The witnesses should realize against whom they are giving evidence, before whom they are giving evidence, and who will call them to account. As written: "The two men between whom the controversy is, shall stand before the Lord" (Deut. 19:17).[1] The judges should [realize] whom it is they are judging, before whom they are judging, and who will call them to account, as written: "God stands in the divine assembly, among divine beings He pronounces judgment" (Ps. 82:1). Similarly it is written, regarding Jehoshaphat: "He charged the judges: 'Consider what you are doing, for you judge not on behalf of man [*la-adam*], but on behalf of the Lord" (2 Chron. 19:6). And lest the judge should say: "Why should I undertake this burden?" [the text goes on to say:] "and He is with you when you pass judgment." A judge need be [concerned] only with what he sees with his eyes.

"Elohim" — Divine Judges?

5. Mekhilta Derabbi Yishmael, *Kaspa* 19

A key passage regarding disputes over property held in safekeeping (Exod. 22:6–8) prescribes adjudication before and by elohim — *a word that regularly denotes God (sometimes also: gods) but which in that passage is rendered by many translations as "judges."[2]* *This* Mekhilta *selection addresses a subsequent verse from the same chapter, one that seems to prohibit first blasphemy and then cursing a political leader. Rabbi Yishmael, however, interprets* elohim *here too as specifically denoting the judges. Thus — uniquely among officeholders — judges are designated by this divine epithet.*

"You shall not revile *elohim*, [nor curse a ruler of your people]" (Exod. 22:27). Why was this written? — Whereas it is written, "[Anyone who blasphemes his God . . .] shall be put to death" (Lev. 24:16), we have been told of the punishment; [but] whence the prohibition? We learn from what is written [here], "You shall not revile God [*elohim*]" in any way; these are the words of Rabbi

---

1. This verse was midrashically construed as referring to the witnesses; cf. BT Shevuot 30a (¢13, §19).
2. Thus in KJV (and partly already in the Vulgate). NJPS prefers "God" throughout but adds footnotes referring to the alternative "judges" that it noted at Exod. 21:6.

Akiva. Rabbi Yishmael says: This verse refers to the judges, as written, "the case of both parties shall come before the judges [*elohim*]" (Exod. 22:8). . . . Rabbi Yehuda b. Betera says: . . . I might have thought that one is not liable unless [the object of his curse] is both a judge and a ruler; [against this, the full verse] teaches that there is [separate] liability for [cursing] a judge and for [cursing] a ruler.

Exile: Extending Partial Authorization
6. BT Gittin 88b; Bava Kama 84a–b

Given the centrality of law as the carrier of the divine word in the Jewish tradition, it was a fundamental expectation of the Rabbis that Jews turn only to authorized Jewish courts to resolve their disputes. But are the courts of Jews in exile authorized? Are they any better than gentile courts? The Rabbis recognized that exile had severed the chain of ordination and so produced a crisis of legitimacy. Formally, all contemporary scholars are "laymen" without judicial authority: they cannot be deemed "elohim" (cf. §5 above). Yet necessity called for finding a way to assert judicial authority.

BT Gittin 88b

Abaye encountered Rav Yosef, who was sitting [in judgment] and employing coercion regarding writs of divorce [*gittin*]. [Abaye] said to him: Behold, we are laymen [since the chain of formal ordination has been severed], and it was taught "Rabbi Tarfon used to say: Anywhere you encounter gentile courts, even though their laws are the same as Israel's laws,[3] you are not permitted to have recourse to them, as written, 'These are the laws that you shall set before them' (Exod. 21:1) — 'before them,' and not before gentiles; another interpretation: 'before them,' and not before laymen"! He re-

3. This could also be translated: "their judgments are the same as Israel's judgments."

plied: We act as agents for [the authorized judges[4]], just as is the case regarding [monetary] obligations and loans.

—If so, [let us do so] regarding robbery and assault as well! We act as their agents in matters that are common [that arise frequently]; in matters that are not common, we do not act as their agents.

BT Bava Kama 84a–b

Rava said: "Damage caused to an ox by [another] ox, or damage caused to an ox by a person—can be [adjudicated] in Babylonia; whereas damage caused to a person by [another] person or damage caused to a person by an ox—cannot be [adjudicated] in Babylonia." [But] what is the difference? [Damage caused to] a person by a person or by an ox cannot [be adjudicated in exile], since *"elohim"* are required yet lacking; likewise, [regarding damage caused to] an ox by an ox or by a person—*"elohim"* are required yet lacking! Conversely, if the reason [we can adjudicate damage caused to] an ox by an ox or by a person is that we act as agents for [the authorized judges], just as is the case regarding [monetary] obligations and loans—[then regarding damage caused to] a person by a person or by an ox as well, we [can] act as agents for [the authorized judges], just as is the case regarding [monetary] obligations and loans! . . .

We act as their agents in matters that are both common and involve [compensation for] monetary loss; in a matter that is common yet does not involve monetary loss, or a matter that is not common though it involves monetary loss—we do not act as their agents. Therefore [regarding damage caused to] a person by a person, even though it involves monetary loss, since it is not common—we do not act as their agents. Regarding [acts of interpersonal] dishonoring, although they are common, since they do not involve monetary loss—we do not act as their agents.

---

4. According to Rashi, these Babylonian sages are the agents of the authorized rabbis in the Land of Israel; the Tosafot note that in their own time, there were no longer such rabbis in the Land of Israel and explain that "we act as agents of the earlier [authorized] rabbis."

Range of Legitimate Halakhic Adjudication
7. Menachem Meiri, *Bet ha-Behirah* Bava Kama 84b

The distinction drawn by the Talmud at the end of the previous selection is also articulated as a distinction between pecuniary penalties (kenas) and monetary compensation (mamona). The basic rule is that kenas can be imposed only by judges who have been formally ordained and reside in the Land of Israel, excluding all judges abroad ("Babylonia"). Medieval commentators sought to explain why the actual practice of Jewish courts, from talmudic times onward, seems hardly affected by these formal restrictions. Meiri summarizes their accounts here. Relying on the "agency" argument, but drawing also on the authority invested in courts by the consent of the litigants or by the members of the kahal (or by the gentile authorities), and finally on "the needs of the hour," Meiri manages to allow a full range of judicial activity (see also the discussions in ¢8 alluded to by Meiri).

Remunerations required [by law] in cases of injury are not imposed [by a *bet din*] in Babylonia. Not that these are pecuniary penalties: they are monetary [compensation] for injuries, but even so they require three authorized judges [*mumhin*], as I explained at the beginning of tractate Sanhedrin; and only judges ordained in the Land of Israel are considered *mumhin*.

And yet you ought to be aware that this is not the case with regard to all injuries. The rule in such matters is as follows: Uncommon matters such as injuries caused to a person by an ox or by another person . . . even though they involve loss—compensation is not imposed in Babylonia; so too all common matters that do not involve [monetary] loss such as shame and dishonor. It follows then that only [payments in] common matters that involve loss are imposed. Therefore [with regard to] all common injuries involving loss, compensation is imposed in Babylonia. Such are: [an injury caused by] an ox to another ox—for [oxen] goring one another are quite common—and so too an ox [injured] by a person. So too [one person] ripping his fellow's garment, breaking his utensils, or uprooting his saplings. Similarly, all indirect damages are not subject to pecuniary penalties and are [therefore] tried outside of the Land [of Israel] . . . as are [infractions of] the laws of safekeeping and rental objects. . . .

Even in such cases, it is not that we ourselves are formally competent [to judge] but we [act] as agents of the judges of the Land of Israel. For we may assume that they indeed grant us authority for all matters of loss regarding common injuries so that wrongdoers not abound in Israel. Even nowadays when there are no [longer] authorized judges extant, [such cases] are nevertheless tried outside the Land [of Israel] in virtue of the original agency. So too in cases of [monetary] obligations and loans . . . we are authorized [to act] so that the door not be shut in the face of loan seekers.[5] Robbery and theft however are uncommon matters, and so even though they involve loss, they are not tried in Babylonia . . . and [so too] all cases involving pecuniary penalties.

With regard to this, the French sages [the tosafists] have raised the question: Is it not the case that the [Talmud records] several instances of trying such cases in Babylonia?

Some reply that all those reports . . . relate to cases where the litigants came before us to judge them. Seeing that they accepted our adjudication upon themselves, we may judge whatever it is that [leads them to] come before us. But in any case that they do not [together] bring before us, we cannot rule regarding one party even if the other party brings suit. Such cases can only be addressed on the basis of a novel ordinance [takkanah], namely, the gaonic enactment that nowadays we judge cases of robbery, theft, and injury for the sake of social order [tikkun olam]. . . . The great Geonim have written [authorizing] pecuniary punishments and floggings as well, according to the needs of the hour. They argue that in localities where [the courts] are authorized by the [local] kingdom to judge by Jewish law [dine yisrael], and all the [Jewish] people consent to this, [every case] is assumed to enjoy the tacit acceptance of the litigants to be adjudicated according to Jewish law. Even capital cases are tried in virtue of their consent, according to the needs of the hour. . . . Some authorities[6] have explained this issue [by assert-

5. Cf. ¢6, §15.
6. Nahmanides, *Novellae to Sanhedrin* 23a.

ing] that the demand for authorized judges . . . pertains only to such a time that such judges are extant, but if they are not extant, [our] judges adjudicate these matters acting as their agents, as it were, for otherwise there would be no law and the world will be desolate.

Four Paths to Judicial Office
8. Isaac b. Sheshet Perfet (Rivash), *Responsa 271*

This responsum is the result of a struggle between two scholars for the position of chief rabbi of France after the death of Rabbi Matitya, who had enjoyed the support of the Jewish communities and of the French government. With the approval of the government, Matitya's son Yohanan succeeded him. Isaiah, a disciple of the late Matitya, opposed Yohanan's appointment on the basis of an old takkanah *prohibiting anyone from accepting a communal appointment from the gentile government. Meir Levi of Vienna supported Isaiah and issued a decree that no one in France has the authority to establish* yeshivot *or to grant divorces without first obtaining permission from him. Yohanan turned to Perfet, a Spanish scholar, for support. Perfet's response describes four paths to judicial office: inheritance, communal appointment, royal appointment, and scholarly achievement and recognition. The responsum begins with a detailed account of the controversy and an extensive discussion of rabbinic legal authority. We excerpt its summation.*

The upshot of all that was said is that the decree issued by our teacher Rabbi Meir Levi is unlawful [*she-lo ka-din*] and against halakhic [practice]. [While] respect is due to him, his [decree] need not be heeded. It is only his own students and those of Rabbi Isaiah, who owe the greater part of their wisdom to them, who are not to rule or establish a hall of study or head a yeshiva unless they obtain his permission . . . [But] by declaring [Yohanan's] divorces and *halitzah* invalid, he [Meir] exceeded the measure. We have striven to find some grounds or a sound reason for [his position]; we sought to justify him, but to no avail.

We will now approach [the matter] from a different angle, thus: Even if it were in Rabbi Levi's power to appoint a rabbi and judge to administer justice and instruct the communities of France, . . . in choosing Rabbi Isaiah and removing Rabbi Yohanan from his office, he would have acted in violation of *halakhah* for several reasons.

First, even if Rabbi Yohanan had not [yet established his] hold[7] on [his office], but was only beginning his appointment, he would be worthy of this authority since his father, Rabbi Matitya, previously functioned in the same capacity—pursuant to the will of the *kehillot* and the authorization of the king. [Rabbi Matitya] exceeded [all others] in that entire kingdom "in wisdom and in numbers" [that is, in the support of the majority: see ¢7, §2]. And in accordance with the law, his son took his place. As is written in Sifre [Deuteronomy] (Shoftim 162), "'He and his sons [in the midst of Israel]' (Deut. 17:20)—if he dies, his son will reign in his place. This applies only to kings; whence do we learn that it applies also to all leaders in Israel, in that their sons will fill their places? From the verse, 'He and his sons, in the midst of Israel'—anyone who is in the midst of Israel, his son will fill his place." . . . And as Maimonides wrote (MT Laws of Kings 1:7), "But not only the office of king but every position or appointive office held by the father descends to his son and son's son in perpetuity, provided that the son is entitled to fill the vacancy by reason of wisdom and piety." . . .

Second, even if Rabbi Yohanan did not rely on the claim of [inheritance from] his father, and [even] if Rabbi Isaiah was worthy of precedence in appointment, nevertheless, since he [Yohanan] was already exercising this authority, which he assumed on his own and held, he was entitled to it. As we learn from [JT Horayot 3:5] . . . one who holds a [position of] authority or [enjoys some] priority, even of his own accord, it is not to be taken from him in order to give it to someone greater than he. He has already become entitled to it, unless he is an *am ha-aretz* and the other person is a scholar. However, if he is a scholar, he is not to be removed, even if the one who seeks to take [over the position] is greater than him. . . . The wise ought to shy

---

7. In its original talmudic context, this term means "took possession" and refers to establishing ownership of real estate.

away from [positions of] authority, but in fact when scholars were appointed thereto, they were strict about not withdrawing from them.

Third, because Rabbi Yohanan was already appointed to this position with the agreement of the *kehillot* of France, and they accepted him [as the authority] over them. At this point, he should not be demoted [because of the principle] that one increases sanctity but does not decrease it (BT Berakhot 28a). . . .

Fourth, because he was appointed by authorization of the king, and *dina de-malkhuta dina.* Even legal documents made in gentile courts are legitimate by reason of *dina de-malkhuta dina* (¢9, §§1 and 3). How much more so—when the king appoints an Israelite judge in his kingdom, to adjudicate between a person and his fellow, and when he is an expert in the laws—should his judgments be law. And litigants can be forced to adjudicate [their claims] before him. . . .

Truly, one ought not receive authorization from the king if it is against the will of the *kehillot,* and one who does so is causing suffering to the public and will certainly be brought to [divine] justice.

This is much more the case when he is not worthy of judging because he lacks adequate knowledge or because of unseemly conduct, since for such [a one] authorization is ineffectual, even if the *nasi* or the exilarch grants him authorization, as Maimonides says (MT Laws Concerning Sanhedrin 4:15): "If a man who is not qualified to discharge judicial duties, either because of lack of adequate knowledge or because of unseemly conduct, has been clothed by the exilarch with authority to act as judge, in disregard of the would-be incumbent's unfitness, or has obtained authorization from the court, the latter having been ignorant of his unfitness, the authority vested in him is of no avail. It is as though one would dedicate on the altar a blemished animal, in which case no sacredness attaches to it." Maimonides also wrote in the Laws Concerning Sanhedrin (6:4), "But if he is not well qualified and the litigants did not accept him, even though he received authorization, he is to be classified not as a judge but as a man of violence. Therefore, the decisions he has rendered, whether erroneous or correct, are void. The litigants may reject his verdicts and take the cases to court." . . .

But in any event, Rabbi Yohanan was appointed by the king in accordance with the will of the *kehillot,* and everyone was desirous of and happy with his greatness.

The Judge's Responsibility

The Necessary Courage of a Judge

9. Maimonides, MT Laws Concerning Sanhedrin 22:1

The Code of Maimonides, Book Fourteen: The Book of Judges, translated by Abraham M. Hershman, YJS (New Haven: Yale University Press, 1949), p. 66.

For the Rabbis (§§3–4 above), judicial courage was essentially an issue of integrity: a duty of conscience not to hold back from a risk-prone judgment once it had become clear in the judge's mind. Maimonides adds a crucial distinction: the option of sidestepping confrontation is not open to a judge holding public appointment.

1. When two litigants come before you, one of whom is gentle, the other hard, before you have heard their statements, or even after you have heard them, so long as you are uncertain in whose favor the verdict will be, you have a right to say to them, "I am not bound to decide your case," lest the hard man be found guilty and persecute you. Once, however, you have heard their statements and know in whose favor the verdict will be, you no longer have the right to say, "I am not bound to decide your case," for it is written: "Ye shall not be afraid of the face of any man" (Deut. 1:17). Say not, "So-and-so is wicked, he may slay my son, set fire to my shock of grain, or cut down my plants." But if he has been appointed to act as judge, he is bound to try all cases.

Opposing Dangerous Offenders
10. Jacob Weil, *Responsa 157*

Beyond sitting in courts to adjudicate disputes, a rabbi's role was taken to include a duty of proactive intervention against evildoers. Weil here is replying to a colleague—the rabbi of Neustadt—regarding the limits of the obligation to protest (see ¢17, §§16-17), an obligation pertaining especially to the communal religious leadership. As we will see in the next selection, his argument was taken to hold with regard to the obligation to judge as well.

Best wishes to the dear Rabbi Mesterlein, may God protect him. Your honor wrote, regarding our rabbis' statement "Whosoever has the power to protest [against a sinner] and does not—[is punished on his account]" (BT Avodah Zarah 18a, see ¢17, §17); [your honor is] seeking an explanation and wondering whether we fulfill our obligation, given that [today in fact] we do not protest?

Seeing that the offenders among our people, those who mock and insult the Torah and its scholars, have multiplied and they do not heed rebukes, if we were to protest, there are grounds to fear that they would act against our person and our property. The [talmudic] statement refers to situations in which there is no danger.

So too [with regard to investigating genealogical purity], the Talmud states: "They started investigating [local lineages to root out the supposed impurities] until they were faced with danger [*Rashi:* the danger of disqualifying powerful families that would kill them]; then they desisted" (BT Kiddushin 71a, ¢12, §3).

. . . For it is clear that with respect to physical attack, after even the slightest blow, one is no longer obligated to protest.[8]

---

8. Following BT Arakhin 16b.

The Limits of Judicial Responsibility

11. Yoel Sirkes (Bah), *Tur* HM 12:1

How is Jacob Weil's permission (§10 above) to retreat in the face of violence to be squared with Maimonides' crucial qualification regarding the obligation of a judge holding public office (§9 above)? Sirkes plausibly assumes that Weil himself held a public appointment and hence proceeds to offer two alternative distinctions: one regarding the type of offense, the other considering the source of the threatening force. Having said that, he reiterates Maimonides' ruling, elaborating its manifest rationale.

Jacob Weil wrote . . . that it is customary nowadays not to protest against sinners because of the danger that the sinner will deliver [the judge] into the hands of the [non-Jewish] government.[9] This is surprising! It is explicitly stated in Sifre Deuteronomy (1:17, §3 above) that even when there is danger of loss of life or of all one's property, [the judge] must deal with them. And Maimonides (§9 above) explicitly [applies this demand] even when [the litigant] is known to be wicked. . . .

Perhaps Weil draws the following distinction: The Sifre's position applies only to judgment pertaining to laws between a person and his fellow. This is where the judge is obligated to judge in righteousness even where there are [grounds for] concern involving risk to life. It is in such a case that [Sifre states], "Fear no man [for judgment is God's]." However, with respect to those who transgress a norm between a person and God, against whom we are obligated to protest in accordance with [the scriptural] commandment "You shall surely rebuke [your fellow]" (Lev. 19:17), there is room for leniency in cases of danger. For it is clear to us that [the wrongdoers] would not heed [our rebuke]; on the contrary, they would threaten our persons and our property. Thus, even if they are intentional [sinners], one ought to keep silent, as stated [by Moses of Coucy] (*Sefer Mitzvot Gadol*, positive commandment 11). Even in case of public appointment, like that of Weil [himself],

---

9. By informing against him, or otherwise employing political connections or influence; though not stated explicitly, Weil's rhetoric seems to suggest this kind of threat.

who was surely so appointed, it is implied that despite [the public obligation], one should not protest transgressions between a person and God.

Alternatively, a distinction may be drawn between earlier generations and the current exilic generation rather than between [different types of sins]. For the verse "Fear no man," pertains only to fear of danger threatened by a [fellow] Israelite, even if he is wicked. However, where there is fear of danger from the [non-Jewish] government through informing, where harm is certain [to come] "Like an antelope caught in a net" (Isa. 51:20)[10]—of this it has already been taught "'by the pursuit of which man shall live' (Lev. 18:5)—not that he shall die" (BT Sanhedrin 74a, ¢11, §17).

Maimonides has written, "But if he has been [publicly] appointed to act as judge, he is bound to try all cases" (§9 above). It appears that his rationale is [as follows:] Seeing that it is a positive commandment to appoint judges, both in the Land of Israel and outside it, if one who is publicly appointed a judge would be permitted to withdraw from a case whenever one or both [of the litigants] are hard men, there would be no one to deal with [such men]. Thus "the violent would have the upper hand" and "the world would become desolate" (¢h8, §11), since it would be lawless. Therefore, one who is appointed to public office is required to deal with them.

Commentary. Judicial Responsibility: A Perennial Challenge

Implicit in the foregoing passages is a recognition that a central component of a judge's responsibility—namely, impartiality—is not easy to achieve. It requires, among other preconditions, that the judge believe he has the power and protection necessary to be independent, free to decide the merits of a dispute without fear or favor, but at the same time fully cabined by the law and by the procedures and traditions of the institution of which he is a part. Even federal judges in the United States, the most powerful judiciary in the world, find this balance sometimes difficult to achieve. For Jewish judges in prior centuries, it must often have required delicacy and courage.

10. See BT Bava Kama 117a, ¢23, §§31–32.

The contrast is worth further exploration. The hallmark of the federal judiciary in the United States is independence. Buttressed by the constitutional guarantee of life tenure and by the early established power to review the constitutionality of legislation and executive actions, federal judges feel free to disregard the power and position of particular litigants, the demands of the government, and even the dictates of public opinion, in favor of deciding cases "on the merits," that is, in accordance with the facts as they (or a jury) determine the facts and the law as they (or prior or higher courts) construe the law. Rarely, if ever, do U.S. judges think about the fact that it is only because of the willingness of the government to enforce such decisions that judicial power and independence are sustained.

From the Diaspora to the mid-twentieth century, judges in many Jewish courts and communities enjoyed no such security. Quite aside from their submission to whatever secular power ruled over their communities, Jewish judges had to fear reprisals from powerful men within their own communities—the "hard men" to whom Maimonides refers—and had to be wary of offending the tight-knit community from which they were drawn. The readings in this and the subsequent section reflect some of the accommodations that were made to adjust to these realities; yet it is remarkable how much deference was still accorded to the ideals of independent judging. Being a Jewish judge in these circumstances was not for the faint of heart.

To be sure, as the readings reflect, judges could sometimes "duck" difficult cases. Maimonides, for example (following the talmudic teaching, §4), gives an unofficial judge the option of avoiding a case involving a party who may persecute the judge; but he adds that once the judge has accepted public appointment, that option disappears. Similarly, once any judge has heard the evidence and knows that the verdict will be adverse to the "hard man," he can no longer avoid deciding the case on the merits, regardless of his fear of retaliation.

As some of the post-Maimonides readings suggest, it was not always so easy to adhere to these aspirations, and refined (perhaps overly refined) distinctions were suggested to justify a judge's avoiding a case where the threat of retaliation was real. Moreover, as the readings in the subsequent section indicate, complex rules of evidence and procedure regarding who could testify, who was presumed credible, what level of proof was required, and so forth, gave a less-than-courageous Jewish judge many ways to avoid difficult decisions without appearing to avoid his duty to decide a case on the merits.

Intimidation of judges is not unheard of even in the United States: many judges receive occasional physical threats during their tenure, federal judges enforcing civil rights in the South in the 1960s regularly received death threats, and, more systemically, elected state judges must always weigh the possibility that an unpopular decision will invite retaliation at the polls. Overall, however, American judges are remarkably free of the pressures that Jewish judges in the *kehillot* and the ghetto must have commonly encountered.

Nevertheless, there are some rough parallels in U.S. law to some of the distinctions that Jewish judges made to avoid controversy and retaliation. For example, U.S. judges must recuse themselves from a case in which their impartiality might reasonably be questioned. Usually, however, this refers to their having a conflict of interest (as, for example, by owning shares of a corporate party's securities); and the decisions are legion that judges should not recuse themselves if they have been threatened by someone associated with a party, since this would only encourage such behavior.

More apt, perhaps, is the well-established precept that judges should avoid constitutional issues if they can fairly decide the case on some other ground. The rationale for this is the implicit corollary to judicial independence: judges, not being directly subservient to the people, should not abuse that independence to decide fundamental constitutional issues (many of which involve heated public controversies) that need not be decided in the particular case before them.

Still, while there were far greater pressures on the Jewish judge of yore to compromise his independence, the fundamental expectation was still that he would decide cases with impartiality, and this expectation runs through Maimonides and the Talmud and back to the Torah. But if a judge is to be independent in the sense of judging all parties equally and impartially, that is, in the sense of not being responsive to wrongful pressures, the question then is: To whom or what is a judge rightly responsible? For if he is responsible to no one and nothing, his rulings are no better than capricious fiats.

Put most broadly, judges are more than mediators or arbitrators, simply seeking to resolve disputes on the basis of what is "fair" and "just" between the parties. Judges also have a responsibility to the past and to the future: the "past" consists of the laws that they must apply (whether they appear in the U.S. Code or in the Torah), the interpretations of those laws that prior judges have made (whether recorded in U.S. Reports or the Talmud), and the overarching purposes that those laws are designed to serve (whether it be the preservation of individual liberty in a relatively secure nation like the United States or the preservation of communal cohesion and, ultimately, communal existence in the much less secure reality of the Jewish diaspora).

The "future" consists of assessing how a given decision in a case before a judge will affect future cases — that is, whether it will fulfill the policies that the aforesaid laws, interpretations, and intentions sought to bring about. This exercise of foresight is the hardest thing a judge is called upon to do, but it is no less inherent in the work of a Jewish judge in a rabbinical court than of a U.S. judge in a secular court.

Some of the extreme rulings described by Maimonides in the next section (§12) will strike most readers as irrational and cruel:

> Thus we are told that a man was flogged for cohabiting with his wife under a fig tree. There is also the incident of a man who, during the days of the Greeks, rode a horse on the Sabbath and was brought before the court and stoned. There is also the incident of Shimon b. Shatah (at whose instance) eighty women were hanged on the same day at Askhelon, without the legally prescribed inquiry and query, due warning, and conclusive evidence.

Maimonides says, in effect, that these decisions were the product of emergency situations that either required dispensing with due process or called for what we would now call general deterrence. In that regard, it is worth remembering that in many of these old Jewish communities, executive authority was weak, so that the judges sometimes had to act as, in effect, both judges and administrators. Without commenting on whether the individual decisions were right, Maimonides describes such decisions as, overall, the product of a broad discretion that, he says, is necessarily given to a Jewish judge to deal with dire circumstances and the threat of future transgressions. Unopposed violence and disruption of the community's way of life threaten its identity and very survival; it is the necessity of preventing this that justifies giving judges such broad discretion, even if it at times leads to questionable decisions. When, in national security cases, U.S. judges invoke Justice Robert H. Jackson's aphorism that "the Constitution is not a suicide pact," they are, rightly or wrongly, making the same kind of argument.

The discretion afforded U.S. judges is more typically akin to a check on executive authority than an exercise of such authority, but it is still substantial and often involves policy choices that are more commonly thought of as being reserved for the legislature. As a general matter, judges interpreting statutes cannot avoid the exercise of some discretion, since even the most careful legislators will fail to foresee all the situations that might, or might not, fall within the ambit of their enactments. In the United States, moreover, it is not uncommon in the case of controversial laws for Congress, by enacting vague (and therefore less controversial) provisions, to pass responsibility to the courts for determining how those laws will apply even in fully foreseeable but controversial situations.

No one has devised a satisfactory—that is, neutral and objective—method for exercising such discretion. Various "canons" of statutory interpretation come and go, complete with names like "textualist," "originalist," "purposiveist," and the like, but in practice most judges will apply differing modes of statutory interpretation on different occasions, in the way that a carpenter might choose differing tools from a toolbox depending on the job. This kind of exercise of discretion may, in some instances, be nothing more than a "cover" for a judge's policy preferences (or, worse, personal biases); but in most instances most judges are simply trying to "get it right"—as evidenced by the fact that nearly all judges will openly admit to having decided cases, not as they would have preferred in terms of outcome, but because "the law demanded it." In such instances, indeed, the judges often take pride in having "played by the rules," even though the choice of applicable rules will often involve some exercise of discretion. The exercise of discretion, then, is bounded, not so much by canons of construction, but by a professional fidelity to the abstract but powerful ideal of the rule of law.

The Jewish people are frequently called the "people of the book"— the book in question being the Torah, which, especially as interpreted in the Mishnah and Talmud, is not just a history but also a book of laws. It is sometimes inferred that this makes Jewish people especially respectful of the law. Whether or not this is true, the history of the Jewish people has given them a thirst for justice. Is it not then the responsibility of every Jewish judge to exercise independence, impartiality, and courage within the framework of the law?

Jed S. Rakoff

The Judge's Power

Judicial Discretion

12. Maimonides, MT Laws Concerning Sanhedrin 24

The Code of Maimonides, Book Fourteen: The Book of Judges, translated by Abraham M. Hershman, YJS (New Haven: Yale University Press 1949), pp. 71–75.

This is Maimonides' summary statement about the judge's authority, incorporating arguments that we included in ¢23 regarding necessity and the "needs of the hour." Judicial procedure is boldly set aside for the sake of judicial discretion. The discretion is extensive, indeed, extraordinarily so, and only at the end of our selection does Maimonides turn to the question of its limits. As in other arguments of this sort (see ¢3, §16), the limits rely heavily upon the personal piety of the judge.

1. In monetary matters [*mamon*], the judge should act in accordance with what he is inclined to believe is the truth when he [is convinced] that his belief is justified, though he has no actual proof of it. It is hardly necessary to say that if he is certain that the opinion he has formed is correct, he should act upon it. The following are cases in point.

If the court imposes an oath upon the defendant and a person whom the judge regards as trustworthy and by whose opinion he sets much store tells him that the defendant is suspected of perjury, it is the duty of the judge to transfer the oath to the claimant, and the latter swears and recovers his due. This ruling holds good even if the informant be a woman or a slave; since the suspicion has a firm hold on him, he may rely upon the informant and act accordingly. It goes without saying that he is to follow this course if he himself knows that the suspicion is warranted.

So too, if a note of indebtedness is produced in court and a person who enjoys the confidence of the judge, even if that person is a woman or a kinsman, says to him, "This note is paid up," since the judge trusts that person, he is to advise the defendant not to pay it, unless the claimant takes an oath. If in addition to the impaired note an unimpaired note is produced against the same defendant by another claimant, the judge is to order payment of the unimpaired one, and put away (undisposed) the one that according to his informant is impaired, or throw it out of court, as the judge sees fit.

Similarly, in case a person appears before the judge claiming that he had entrusted a (valuable) object to the safekeeping of one who has since died intestate, and identifies the object by unmistakable marks, and it is known that he was not a frequent visitor at the house of the deceased, if the judge knows that the departed was not wealthy enough to own such a costly object and is satisfied in his mind that it did not belong to him, he takes it away from the heirs and gives it to the claimant who is a man of means and has identified it by unmistakable marks. This applies to like cases. Matters of this kind are matters committed to [the judge's reason], who in pronouncing judgment is to be guided by what appears to him to be a true judgment.

If this be so, why does the Torah require two witnesses? The answer is: when two witnesses give testimony, the judge is bound to decide on their evidence, although he does not know whether the evidence submitted by them is true or false.

2. What has been said before constitutes a fundamental of (Jewish) law. But with the increase of courts whose members are lacking the requisite moral qualifications, and when even those whose conduct entitles them to the office do not possess adequate knowledge and understanding, most courts

have decided neither to transfer an oath (from the defendant to the plaintiff), unless there is clear evidence (to warrant such a procedure), nor to impair a note, causing it to lose its validity on the evidence of a woman or otherwise ineligible witness.

So too with reference to other legal matters (it was decided) that the judge should not be guided by his own opinion or that of one in whom he reposes confidence, lest any [layman] say, "I believe it is so" or "I put credence in this man."

Likewise, it was decided not to take away things from orphans—unless there is ample warrant for such seizure—on the strength of an opinion formed by the judge or on an estimate of the wealth of the deceased or of the claimant.

Nevertheless, if a trustworthy person testifies concerning any of these matters, and the judge feels that he speaks the truth, he will deliberate before giving his opinion, will not disregard the evidence, but will [pursue] the matter with the litigants until they acknowledge the truth of the statement made by the informant, or will have the suit arbitrated; else he will withdraw from the case.

3. Whence do we derive that a judge who has reason to suspect one of the litigants of misrepresentation should not say, "I will decide the case according to the evidence and let the witnesses bear the responsibility"? Because it is said: "Keep thee far from a false matter" (Exod. 23:7). How is he to proceed in such a case? Let him sedulously investigate the witnesses with the inquiries and queries to which witnesses in capital offenses are subjected (¢23, §9). If after this thoroughgoing examination, he concludes [that there is nothing fraudulent about the suit, he gives his decision on the basis of the evidence. But if he has any scruples about it,] suspecting dishonesty, or has no confidence in the witnesses, although he has no valid ground on which to disqualify them, or he is inclined to believe that the litigant is a subtle fraud, that the witnesses are honest men, giving their evidence in all innocence, but were led astray by the litigant, or if it appears to him from the whole tenor of the proceedings that some information is withheld, not brought into the open—in any of these or similar circumstances—the judge is forbidden to render a decision. He should withdraw from the case and let another judge,

who can without qualms of conscience pronounce judgment, handle it. For matters of this nature are committed to [one's conscience], and Scripture says: "For the judgment is God's" (Deut. 1:17).

4. The court is empowered to flog him who is not liable to flagellation and to mete out the death penalty to him who is not liable to death. This extensive power is granted to the court not with the intention of disregarding the Law but in order to build a fence around it. Whenever the court sees that a command has fallen into general disuse, the duty devolves upon it to safeguard and strengthen the command in any way which in its judgment will achieve the desired result. But whatever measure it adopts is only a temporary one [so long as they do not impart to it] the force of a law, binding for all time to come.

Thus we are told that a man was flogged for cohabiting with his wife under a fig tree. There is also the incident of a man who, during the days of the Greeks, rode a horse on the Sabbath and was brought before the court and stoned. There is also the incident of Shimon b. Shatah (at whose instance) eighty women were hanged on the same day at Askhelon, without the legally prescribed inquiry and query, due warning, and conclusive evidence. He (Rabbi Shimon b. Shatah) felt that the emergency of the hour [hora'at sha'ah] demanded drastic action.

5. So too the court may in all places and at all times flog a man whose reputation is unsavory, about whom the people are talking, accusing him of immoral conduct, provided that the rumor with respect to him is persistent, as has already been stated, and that he has no avowed enemies who spread an evil report about him. Similarly, a person of evil repute may be despised, and she that bore him reviled in his presence.

6. Likewise, the judge may at all times expropriate money from its owner, destroy it, or give it away, disposing of it in any way which in his judgment will halt the breakdown of religion, repair its breaches, or bring to terms the defier of the Law. Thus it is written in the book of Ezra (10:8): "Whosoever come not within three days, according to the counsel of the princes and the elders, all his substance should be forfeited." From this we infer that it is within the jurisdiction of the court to confiscate property.

7. So too the judge may lay the ban and invoke the *herem* upon him who is not liable to these penalties in order to check the breakdown of religion, if in his opinion these disciplinary measures will achieve the desired end or meet the exigency of the hour. He shall say that he bans or excommunicates him by his authority, and make public the details of the offense, as it is written: "Curse ye Meroz, said the angel of the Lord, curse ye bitterly the inhabitants thereof, because they came not to the help of the Lord" (Judg. 5:23).

8. So too the judge may quarrel with him who deserves to be quarreled with, curse him, smite him, pluck his hair, and compel him to take an oath that he will desist from committing the offense again or that he has not committed it, as it is written: "And I contended with them, and I cursed them, and smote certain of them and plucked off their hair, and made them swear by God" (Neh. 13:25).

9. Likewise the judge may fetter the hands and feet of the offender, imprison him, knock him down, and drag him on the ground, as it is written: "Let judgment be executed upon him with all diligence, whether it be unto death, or to be banished, or to confiscation of goods, or to imprisonment" (Ezra 7:26).

10. With regard to all these disciplinary measures, discretionary power is vested in the judge. He is to decide whether the offender deserves these punishments and whether the emergency of the hour demands their application. But whatever the expedient he sees fit to resort to, all his deeds should be done for the sake of Heaven. Let not human dignity be light in his eyes; for the respect due to man supersedes a negative Rabbinical command. This applies with even greater force to the dignity of the children of Abraham, Isaac, and Jacob, who adhere to the True Law. The judge must be careful not to do aught calculated to destroy their self-respect. His sole concern should be to enhance the glory of God, for whosoever dishonors the Torah is himself dishonored by men, and whosoever honors the Torah is himself honored by men. To honor the Torah means to follow its statutes and laws.

Unlearned Judges

13. Solomon b. Abraham Adret (Rashba), *Responsa* 2:290[11]

The Rabbis wanted Jews to resort always to Jewish courts to resolve their disputes; as we saw above (§§6–7), they found ways of authorizing such courts in exile despite the lack of formal authority. But in some small or remote Jewish communities, the problem was not just formal: they had no members who met the standards described in the classic texts for judges or were even minimally literate. And yet there too it was necessary to resolve disputes. Adret relies on communal consent on the one hand and royal authorization on the other to legitimate nonprofessional conflict resolution and even lay decisions in criminal cases. He thus underscores the difference between the rabbis' professional legal knowledge and lay views of equity that were frequently relied on in adjudication.

To Rabbi Jacob b. Kadjaf, Toledo: You have asked: It is stated that appointing an unworthy judge is tantamount to planting an *asherah* [a tree serving as an idol] (BT Avodah Zarah 52a). What then should be done in towns where not one [of them] knows even a single letter, but [some] must be appointed to adjudicate and arbitrate with coercive [authority] over litigants? If we do not appoint [them, the people] will go instead to the gentile courts, and violations [of justice] will abound. Perhaps we should require at any rate that local judges be appointed unanimously or by a majority [of community members]—certainly so in capital cases. It is the practice in this [central] city to send [our] elders to appoint elders in other [peripheral communities] who will judge both civil and capital cases. Should we endorse [this practice] or not?

Answer: Strictly by the law, one cannot appoint judges who are not authorized without the consent of the litigants; but the judges authorized by the town's court can compel litigants to submit to adjudication before them, as long as there are none more learned in that town—provided that they are knowledgeable in the law.

It is therefore necessary that you obtain the consent of the towns-

---

11. The text in the printed editions is partly corrupt; we have relied also on the version of this responsum cited by Joseph Karo in *Bet Yosef* HM 8.

people to appoint these [judges] despite the fact that they are not knowledgeable, [the rule being that we act] in accordance with the needs of the hour—"and all your actions should be done for the sake of heaven" (Mishnah Avot 2:12). If the townspeople accept the judges you appoint, they may [adjudicate], and then nobody can disqualify them. This is precisely an instance of "tribunals of Syria" [arkhaot she-besuriya], regarding whom the Talmud states, "If [the judges are] worthy, they are regarded as authorized by [a competent] court [bet din] and cannot be disqualified. For no one has power to disqualify a judge authorized by public acceptance."

At any rate, one must seek out upright [kesherim], God-fearing men "who spurn ill-gotten gain,"[12] men of keen perception. And in capital cases, they must be careful to proceed with the approval of the elders of your city, so that what they do will be done with deliberation, as a last resort [lit., "in response to great need"]. Given that, they may act [as they see fit], since to my mind you have [effective] authority from the king for this and whoever acts with the king's authority is permitted [to judge].

[Adret concludes by referring to his previous responsum (3:393, ¢8, §11) to the addressee a year earlier.]

Stature and Communal Acceptance
14. Jacob b. Asher, *Tur* HM 2

The codifiers of the tradition continued to uphold and support a range of extralegal activity with regard to both procedure and competence. Jacob begins by citing Isaac Alfasi's broadening of discretionary powers beyond the Land of Israel provided that they are exercised by judges of stature, renowned for their learning, or by those appointed by the good men of the town—thus following his father, Asher b. Yehi'el, cited in the next selection. But he goes on to endorse the recognition of extralegal authority, applying it effectively to all judges.

12. One of the biblical requirements for judges: Exod. 18:21 (§1 above).

Although [criminal] cases, whether capital, corporal, or fiscal, are not tried outside the Land [of Israel], if the court understands it to be a need of the hour—because the people are lax with regard to various prohibitions—it may try them and impose [penalties of] death, or money, or indeed any kind of penalty. If the transgressor is a violent man, they [may] have the gentiles beat him and say to him, "Do what the Israelites are telling you" (¢19, §8).

Rabbi [Isaac] Alfasi (*Alfasi* Bava Kama 34a) wrote . . . regarding the case in which Rav Nahman penalized a person on account of being a habitual robber (BT Bava Kama 96b, cf. §15 below): "Hence we deduce that in cases like this we [may] assign penalties even outside the Land" providing [the judge] is a great man of the generation, such as Rav Nahman, who was married into the exilarch's family and was appointed by the exilarch; or [the penalty is imposed by] the good men of the town whom the public have accepted [as judges] over them—but ordinary judges [cannot impose penalties].

It seems that even in a case lacking halakhically recognized testimonies whereby the defendant could have been convicted in a court of law at the time when capital punishment was imposed[13]—still, if [the accusation] has a basis and [is supported by] a persistent rumor, and if the judge considers it to be the need of the hour to impose such a penalty, he has the authority [to do so].

[Jacob goes on to excerpt Maimonides, MT Sanhedrin 24:4–10 (§12).]

The Judge and the Good Men

15. Solomon Luria, *Yam Shel Shelomo* Bava Kama 9:7

Solomon b. Abraham Adret's and Jacob b. Asher's expansion of judicial authority is animated by a concern for social order: conflicts have to be resolved and criminal activity must be curtailed. Luria underscores the theme we have already seen in Maimonides—that

13. See ¢3, §11; ¢23, §15.

judicial competence includes knowing not only when to apply the law but when not to. Luria continues the discussion of Isaac Alfasi's view of judicial authority (quoted in §14 above), arguing that beside professional expertise, the legal exercise of emergency powers requires both the political consent of the good men of the town and their active partici-pation in authorizing and imposing the necessary sanctions. But it seems that expertise matters most, in the end.

A judge may penalize [impose punitive damages] extra-legally, provided they are reasonable and if he has been duly appointed.

[We read in BT Bava Kama 96b:][14] "A man seized a pair of oxen, plowed and sowed his entire plot with them and then returned them [when he was done].[15] This was brought before Rav Nahman, who ordered an esti-mate of the gain and ordered him to forward that to the owner of the oxen.

Said Rava to Rav Nahman, 'Were the oxen alone the source of his profit? Did not the land [also] produce the profit?'

Rav Nahman replied, 'I too did not assess the full gain, only half of it.'

Said Rava: 'But the robber is in fact returning the oxen intact and the owner is therefore not entitled to profit!' . . .

Rav Nahman replied: 'Have I not told you not to say anything while I'm sitting in judgment? For my colleague [Rav] Huna has stated that Shmu'el and I are brethren in the court.[16] I know that this man is a habitual robber, and so I wish to punish him.'"

Seeing that Rav Nahman was in Babylonia, Isaac Alfasi (Alfasi Bava Kama 34a) concluded that one can impose punitive damages in such circum-stances even outside the Land of Israel. And moreover it was taught: "Rabbi Eli'ezer b. Ya'akov said: I have received by tradition that a court may impose flagellation and [other] punishments not [warranted] by the Torah; not to transgress against the words of the Torah, but rather to erect a fence around the Torah" (BT Sanhedrin 46a, ¢23, §14). . . .

14. The talmudic dialogue is reproduced here following Luria's light paraphrasing.
15. By Torah law, there is no punishment beyond returning the stolen property.
16. The significance of this seemingly obscure line is discussed at the end of this selection.

Now when Alfasi said that damages may be imposed "in such circumstances," he did not mean to exclude other cases, inasmuch as he quotes Rabbi Eli'ezer, who says that in all manner of cases authority has been given to the court to impose punishment and erect fences as needed. Rather the exclusionary import is [meant to emphasize] that a judge should only do as reason indicates, as in the case at hand of Rav Nahman, who imposed only a partial [fine, proportionate to the gain]. . . . This implies that though these were punitive impositions, he did not have authority to charge him the full sum. This is what Alfasi meant by "in such circumstances." Asher b. Yehi'el (*Piskei ha-Rosh* Bava Kama 9:5) added that "only the great man of the generation, like Rav Nahman, whom the exilarch had appointed or one appointed by the good men of the town—those accepted by the community—[can act in this way], but an ordinary judge cannot."

Now this is obviously correct because not just anyone can pronounce penalties, even if he is a singular person of his time, so long as he is not acceptable to the people and given authority by them. [He may do so only if] he has been appointed to judge, so that not just anyone can go ahead and erect his own platform.

Still, it does not seem to me that everything depends on having been appointed, because even one appointed by the good men cannot judge on his own if he is not an expert well versed in adjudication—unless he is joined by the good men of the town, who may enforce their decree (see ¢8, §2) and unless they concur in penalizing [culprits] and imposing decrees. . . . But there is no authority in the hands of the judge alone to penalize unless he is authorized [*mumhe*] and a renowned halakhic decisor. And note the wording of Rav Nahman's reply to Rava (BT Bava Kama 113a–b, cf. ¢9): [This is as if to say:] "Do not be surprised that I judge and rule against the Torah law enunciated in our Mishnah; I can judge on my own and penalize for I am [fully] authorized by the public to judge, just like Shmu'el in his time, who was thus authorized. . . . It follows clearly then that any [lesser] judge does not [have such powers], even if he is [publicly] appointed.

Alternative Mechanisms

Against Non-Jewish Courts

16. Maimonides, MT Laws Concerning Sanhedrin 26:7

The Code of Maimonides, Book Fourteen, The Book of Judges, translated by Abraham M. Hershman, YJS (New Haven: Yale University Press, 1949), p. 80.

For most of their history, Jews were subjects of non-Jewish political systems, and they commonly had the option of recourse to non-Jewish courts. As we have seen (§6 above), the Rabbis regarded such recourse as forbidden. Here Maimonides reiterates the classic Jewish position, condemning any move outside the halakhic system. In the end, however, he acknowledges the possible necessity of such a move and tries to regulate it.

7. Whoever submits a suit for adjudication to heathen judges in their courts, even if the judgment rendered by them is in consonance with Jewish law, is a wicked man. It is as though he reviled, blasphemed, and rebelled against the Law of Moses, our teacher, for it is said, "Now these are the ordinances which thou shalt set before them" (Exod. 21:1)—before them, not before heathens, and not before ordinary men. If the hand of the heathens is powerful and his opponent is a man of violence and the claimant is unable to recover what is due to him through the Jewish court, he must first summon him to appear before Jewish judges; if his opponent refuses to appear, the plaintiff obtains permission from the court to recover his claim through the heathen court.

Disadvantages of Professional Judges

17. Jacob b. Joseph Reischer, *Shevut Ya'akov* 143

The tradition of agreed-upon judges goes back to the Mishnah. In Metz in the seventeenth century, this was the traditional practice, preferred over "permanent"—that is, official and professional courts. Some of the good men of the town sought to initiate official courts. Reischer defends the established custom by arguing, first, that appointments by the leader-

ship of the kahal *were more often than not corrupt and, second, that mutually agreed upon adjudication is more conducive to finding the truth.*

Question: Here in the holy *kahal* of Metz it has forever and of old been the practice not to appoint permanent judges but to adjudicate thus: One [party] chooses one [judge] for himself, and the other [party] chooses one for himself, and a third [is chosen independently] to make up a court.[17] It has now occurred to some of the good men of the town to establish a permanent court. Is this [a] worthy [proposal]?

Answer: It appears, at first glance, that the heads of the *kahal* and the good men of the town do have the power [to do this]. Since the public has, whether unanimously or by majority, authorized them for all matters, what they do is done [and is] an enactment of the *kahal*. [And this is true] even where there was no custom previously and even where it is not a case of creating a fence . . . , and even with respect to matters that result in a benefit to one and a loss to another. . . . Such is the opinion of most great men of the world [sages], ancients and moderns. Even if they chose a single individual to [sit as judge], what they have done is done. . . .

I have written elsewhere that there are those who disagree regarding [the scope of the *kahal*'s powers, disallowing enactments that yield] a benefit to some at the expense of others.[18] Here, however, there is no [expense or] loss; it is simply [a matter of] complying with the Torah's commandment, as written: "You shall appoint magistrates and officials for your tribes, in all [your] settlements" (Deut. 16:18). Even though this verse refers to the Sanhedrin, nevertheless, the common practice of most Jewish communities is to appoint permanent judges on the basis of this verse.

However, upon closer examination it appears that [the established practice] cannot be changed in any way, for [the *kahal*] has forever and of old functioned this way. Not a single person recalls there ever having been a professional court. It is [in fact] a virtuous practice as indicated by the talmudic discussion at the beginning of the third chapter of BT Sanhedrin (23a),

---

17. Following Mishnah Sanhedrin 3:1. Three judges make up the quorum of a court. See also Mishnah Avot 4:8.

18. Compare ¢10, §3.

[which states] that since "this [party] chooses one for himself and this other [party] chooses one for himself . . . the judgment comes out according to the truth." . . .

Nowadays especially, [the appointment of professional judges should be rejected since] the leaders and the good men of the town mostly appoint their relatives and intimates as judges, despite the fact that they are neither suitable nor worthy to judge. This however is not the case when [the custom is that] each [litigant] chooses [a judge], for even if one of [the judges] is not suitable, in that he rules in favor of his litigant when this is not warranted by the law, nevertheless, since the second [litigant] also chooses whomever he wants, we treat the forum as accepted by the litigants so as to bring the truth to light. And for this reason, I have seen in many *kehillot*, even in those with permanent judges, that major disputes[19] are mostly arbitrated according to [the practice of] "this [party] chooses" so as to bring the truth to light.

Therefore, it seems clear to me that this practice should not be changed, as it is a virtuous practice established in accordance with the letter of the law and the *halakhah*.

Secular Courts in a Jewish State

The founding of the state of Israel awakened many primordial hopes and aspirations. For most Jewish communities, autonomous courts had been defunct since the advent of emancipation. Yet given the centrality of law in Judaism, reconstituting a legal system based at least in part on Jewish law was a dream shared by both secular (or cultural) Zionists following Ahad Ha'am and orthodox Jews committed to halakhah *as a way of life. Previous chapters have already dealt with the intricacies of Jewish law confronting modern civil law (¢9, §§11–13) and with the attempts to incorporate elements of* halakhah *into the laws of the modern state of Israel (¢10, §§1–3, 10–13). Here we follow an internal debate*

19. Echoing Exod. 18:22 (see §1 above).

among protagonists of halakhah *regarding the status and legitimacy of the new state's secular courts.*

Permitting Secular Adjudication of Cases, but No Legislation

18. Abraham Yeshayah Karelitz, *Hazon Ish* HM Sanhedrin 15:4

The basic mandate of Jewish courts is to apply Torah law, and thus judges must be learned. Still, Karelitz recognizes that lack of sufficient learning can be compensated, at least in part, by the authority endowed through public appointment. But can there be courts consisting of Jewish judges who judge independently of Torah law (the Israeli court system provides the subtext)? Are secular Jewish courts any different from gentile courts? Karelitz reconsiders Solomon b. Abraham Adret's endorsement of unlearned judges (§13 above) and boldly describes a court system operating without a set of laws.

A judge who was not appointed according to the *halakhah*—[such as one] not appointed by the seven good men of the town, or [regarding whom] the selectors' motivation was not for the sake of heaven but for a factional advantage, or [whose appointment was motivated by] one of the many other vices that human inclination devises—is not authorized to coerce [litigants to] appear before him when [sitting as a] single [judge]. [This is so] even if he is sufficiently learned to be eligible to join in a [court of] three [which is so authorized]—all the more so if he is not learned and depends upon public appointment [for his very eligibility]. No person is obligated to appear before him for judgment, even at a time when there is no one greater than him in the town. All the more so if he is unworthy—[e.g.,] he tends to judge in favor of his cronies and to ingratiate those whom he needs. This falls under the general rule regarding an "unworthy judge."[20]

    ... There is another [type of] authorization of people who have not

20. As cited in the question posed to Adret; cf. §13 above.

learned any Torah at all, who judge by their intellect according to human justice [*mishpat*]. This is in a location where there is no learned person at all; [the appointment is made] in the public interest [*takkanot ha-tzibbur*] so that [cases] shall not be brought before the gentile courts [*arkhaot*].

This is all expounded in Adret's responsum (§13 above) . . . which makes reference to the talmudic "Tribunals of Syria." His language seems to indicate that the judge in [these] Tribunals of Syria judges with no reference to the laws of the Torah. The talmudic context, however, suggests that this judge is [supposed to] adjudicate in accordance with the laws of the Torah; he is [therefore] disqualified because, due to the paucity of his knowledge of Torah, he is prone to error—and [can act as judge] only by virtue of public authorization. Perhaps Adret concluded from this that public authorization is effective [in any case] . . . even if he does not know Torah law at all, because it is in the public interest.

Yet even though they do not have among them a judge who can adjudicate according to the statutes of the Torah, and they are forced to appoint a person of intellect who will judge according to human morality, they are not permitted to accept upon themselves the laws of [other] peoples or to legislate [their own] laws. For one who judges each [individual] case coming before him according to what appears [right] to him is [in fact] enforcing a settlement. When a community resorts to such judgment, they do not broadcast that they have "forsaken . . . the fount of living waters, and hewed them out broken cisterns" (Jer. 2:13). Should [the public] however adopt laws, they are desecrating the Torah. It is regarding this that it has been stated, "'[These are the laws] that you shall set before them' (Exod. 21: 1)—'before them,' and not before laymen" (BT Gittin 88b, §6 above).

There is no difference between appearing before [judges who] are not Israelites [or before] an Israelite who judges according to fabricated laws. The latter is even more deplorable, since they have replaced the laws of the Torah with worthless laws. And if the townspeople agree upon this, their compact [*haskamah*] has no effect; if enforced, this constitutes misappropriation and robbery, and they [thereby] raise their hand against the Torah of Moses.

Civil and Criminal Law Courts in a Democracy

19. Shlomo Goren [Gorontchick], "A Torah Constitution—How So?"

Hatzofeh, 19 Shevat 5708 (January 30, 1948), p. 4.

Goren, who was (at the time of writing this column) about to be appointed chief rabbi of the Israel Defense Forces, presents a pro-Zionist and realist argument endorsing the very system castigated by the ultra-Orthodox leader Abraham Yeshayah Karelitz. Recognizing that the formal rules and procedures of halakhah *cannot be adopted in constituting the courts of the nascent state, he presents halakhic, consent-based grounds for endorsing a democratically constituted legal system.*

Upon proclamation of political independence for the Jewish people in the Land of Israel, religious Judaism is faced with an onerous challenge. It must determine how to conduct the struggle of instilling the spirit of Torah and its laws in the state. . . . It is necessary to work out detailed legislation, offering for each problem an appropriate solution, one that will be acceptable to all segments of the public and be practical. Those formulating the legislation will have also to take into account the charter of the United Nations, and ensure that the legislation not contravene international law, which requires equal rights for all segments of the population.[21]

One of the most important problems demanding a comprehensive solution is that of the courts in the Jewish state. It is usually the courts that determine the character of states or peoples. If we are able to ensure that this central aspect of the state's affairs shall be administered according to the Torah, we can hope for success in other aspects as well. . . .

The prevailing opinion in the religious community is that the Torah laws of old are to be instituted as the basis of legislation for the renewed courts [of the soon-to-be-founded state of Israel]. In fact, [however,] this cannot easily be realized. The laws of judges and witnesses would violate the rights of minorities, women, and others, and would arouse strong opposition from the secular part of the *yishuv* and from the United Nations. Torah

---

21. A similar line of reasoning, focusing on the status of non-Jewish citizens, was advanced at roughly the same time by Chief Rabbi Herzog; cf. ¢16, §36.

law disqualifies transgressors and, needless to say, non-Jews [literally: those who are not party to the covenant] from serving as witnesses or judges. It [generally] disqualifies women from giving testimony except in certain circumstances. These difficulties make it almost impossible [to adopt] legislation entirely following the Torah in setting up the renewed courts.

With certain Torah innovations, however, we can establish "courts of settlement" [i.e., binding arbitration]. In such courts, both transgressors and non-Jews can serve as judges and witnesses. It is stated in *Shulhan Arukh* HM 22:1: "[Even if] someone specifies for himself a relative disqualified [by Torah law], whether as judge or as witness, even someone disqualified due to transgression, [the single specified person counts] as two qualified witnesses to deliver testimony or as three authorized [judges] to judge him. . . ."

Moreover, [the option] of rendering disqualified judges and witnesses competent is not [restricted] to a single instance of specification by an individual, for a particular dispute. . . . There also exists the possibility of a general specification by an entire public, appointing disqualified judges for itself. HM 8:1 states: "Any public may accept upon [itself] a court that is not [considered] competent by Torah [law]." We see therefore that a public is empowered to specify for itself judges who are not competent [by Torah law], and given that they were accepted by the townspeople, no one can disqualify them.

This authority makes it likewise possible to qualify through pre-established communal *takkanot* persons who are disqualified [by Torah] as witnesses. . . .

Following such an appointment [procedure], we would be able to have judges deal . . . with civil cases—seeing that they were appointed by the public. It should be emphasized that such a court would not be deemed a *bet din* since it would not really have *Torah* authority but rather *public* authority.

Neither do criminal courts present great difficulty. . . . Is it not stated in *Shulhan Arukh* HM 2, "The good men of the town are considered, for their town, like the Great Court, and can administer corporal and all manner of punishment, even without complete [formal] evidence"?—"[Two qualified] witnesses and warning are needed only for judging according to Torah law, but if one transgresses the laws of the polity [*tikkunei ha-medinah*], [the public] may act in accordance with the needs of the hour."[22] In virtue of this authority, the public may make laws and fix penalties regarding criminal transgressions—punishing by imprisonment and similar [penalties] in accordance with what the judges or the legislators see [as necessary] for the sake of public order.

Orthodox Rejection of Secular Law

20. Ovadyah Yosef, *Responsa Yehave Da'at* 4:65

Ovadyah Yosef here delivers a militant critique of secular Israeli civil courts. Although he served in the dual state office of chief rabbi and head of the High Rabbinic Court, he denies the legitimacy of Israel's secular courts and decrees it a grievous sin to file any suit before them. The argument is made in the specific context of the laws of inheritance—a long-standing issue of contention regarding the legitimacy of non-halakhic jurisdictions[23]—but is formulated as a sweeping rejection applying to all civil litigation, if not to criminal justice as well.

Query: Since it is known that under Torah law daughters do not inherit from their father if there are sons—in contrast to [Israeli] state law followed in the secular courts, whereby daughters inherit with sons equally—are the daughters permitted by *halakhah* to sue in a secular court for their portion in the inheritance, relying on the Rabbis' statement, "The law of the kingdom is law" (BT Bava Kama 113a–b, cf. ¢9)?

Answer:

[Yosef begins with a detailed discussion regarding the scope of the rule recognizing "the law of the kingdom" (cf. ¢9, §10). He cites a thread of

---

22. Goren refers to the Responsa of Nahmanides, evidently having in mind the text found in *The Responsa of Adret Attributed to Nahmanides* 279. See also ¢8, §§11–12.

23. This is especially true regarding the issue of gender equity (the subject of the query here as well); see above ¢19, §§22–26, and particularly the discussion there by Herzog (§26).

Rabbinic teachings that excluded the laws of inheritance and emphasized the prohibition of going to gentile courts in such matters. He then applies the same approach to Israeli secular courts:]

Know that even though legal authority is given by the government to the secular courts to adjudicate civil cases and inheritance, and even though the judges sitting are Jews, it is clear that according to our holy Torah, the sin of someone who sues his fellow in their courts is "too great to bear" (Gen. 4:13). [As ruled by both Maimonides (MT, Sanhedrin 26:7, §16 above) and Joseph Karo (*Shulhan Arukh* HM 26:1)]: Anyone who seeks adjudication before the courts of the others [lit., "their courts"] is an evildoer, and it is as though he has blasphemed and raised his hand against the Torah of Moses.

For first of all, the judges are totally unversed in the laws of the Torah [and unable] to judge between persons in accordance with *Hoshen Mishpat* and the decisors. Our rabbis have stated: "'These are the laws that you shall set before them' (Exod. 21:1) — 'before them,' and not before gentiles; and not before laymen"! (BT Gittin 88a, §6 above). It is furthermore known that they rule according to gentile law and also allow [testimony by] a single witness, relatives, women, and [other individuals] disqualified according to *halakhah*. Many of the judges are themselves halakhically disqualified from serving as judges.

I will not deny that I have heard the false words of those who deviate from the path of intellect and facetiously claim that since the judges are Jews and the government has granted them the authority to try and judge civil cases and inheritance, [then] "the law of the kingdom is law" (BT Bava Kama 113a–b) . . . but their mouths emit hot air. "Were they wise, they would think upon this" (Deut. 32:29). Indeed, this is precisely what renders the matter severe: the judges are Jews sworn from Mount Sinai to judge according to Torah law (if they are at all competent to judge). But "they have forsaken the fount of living waters" — the Talmud and the codifiers — "and hewed them out cisterns, broken cisterns, which cannot even hold water" (Jer. 2:13), ruling according to the laws of the gentiles, [following] their judges and law books. [Going to their courts] is sevenfold [worse] than going to gentile judges who have never been commanded to rule according to our Torah. For even though Noahides are commanded to institute justice, they may judge in accordance with human intellect and their discretion; they are not obligated to judge according to the details of Torah law. . . .[24]

Now although [gentile courts are mandated by the Torah's Noahide code], it is absolutely prohibited for an Israelite to turn to them for adjudication. A fortiori, [it is prohibited to turn] to Jewish judges who . . . instead of judging according to the laws of the Torah — "that man should follow and live by them" (Lev. 18:5) — rule according to Ottoman and [British] Mandate law. It is like a maidservant who has inherited the place of the lady: "They have followed worthless things and become worthless themselves" (Jer. 2:5). They thereby lend respect and importance to the laws of the gentile idol worshippers, honoring and elevating their idols. . . . Therefore, according to *halakhah* a God-fearing lawyer asked to represent in their court a person suing another ought to refrain from doing so, for he is aiding transgressors. . . . But a lawyer may represent a party forced to appear in court because the [other] claimant refused to adjudicate by Torah law [in a rabbinic court]. [He acts] to save the victim from the victimizer.

Commentary. Who Are the "Others"? The Courts and the Political Community

The discussion in this section starts from a point of view that appears quite plausible from one perspective yet breathtakingly audacious from another. From the internal perspective of learned Torah discourse, it seems perfectly natural to ask whether the state courts have any authority — whether they can be construed as halakhically valid institutions. Yet from the perspective of a modern state, denying the legitimacy of its courts of law amounts to a seditious repudiation of its sovereign authority.

Would Hazon Ish (Abraham Yeshayah Karelitz) be alarmed at the accusation that his teachings constitute sedition? I suspect he might respond serenely that, of course, denying the legitimacy of the Zionist state was part of the message. But although this theological/political issue is the crux of the

24. See the discussion of this Noahide law in ¢16, §§4–7.

matter, I shall leave it aside for the moment and take up the arguments of Ka-relitz—and of the other two prominent rabbis presented here—on their own terms, as a halakhic analysis.

Karelitz rightly focuses at the outset on the question of coercive authority. For a court to wield that kind of power, two conditions must be met. One condition pertains to the court itself: it must be properly constituted, the judges both qualified and appointed by the appropriate procedure. The second condition is more fundamental: the court must be tasked with applying and enforcing a set of laws that are binding upon those under its jurisdiction, "the law of the land."

From the perspective of traditional *halakhah,* no judge "in present times" can claim authority to enforce divine law simply by virtue of his stature and learning. This point, stated in the Talmud regarding the talmudic sages themselves (§6), has been an accepted premise of subsequent halakhic jurisprudence. Necessarily, a variety of means were found in order to overcome the lack of authority, so as to avoid both social chaos and recourse to non-Jewish courts. As evident in the earlier sections of this chapter, central among these means was reliance on collective consent—that is, on authorization of the judges by virtue of their appointment by the community's accepted leadership.

Citing Solomon b. Abraham Adret's influential application of the talmudic precedent regarding the "tribunals of Syria" (§13), Karelitz readily acknowledges that appointment by the community can confer authority upon judges who are quite ignorant of Torah law. Like Adret, he is sure that this should be done only as a last resort, where no learned judges are available, since the normative practice is judgment by the laws of Torah. It seems that Karelitz would want even such judges to attempt to apply Torah law, however incompetently; but he reluctantly acknowledges that according to Adret, this is not a necessary condition. Communal acceptance in and of itself can mandate coercive judgments.

What keeps him, then, from endorsing the courts of the reborn Jewish state? After all, the Israeli democracy and its institutions, including its court system, reflect the consent of the governed at least as much as the *kahal* at its best. Even if the judges are "ignorant" (i.e., of *halakhah*)—if not quite as

ignorant as those endorsed by Adret, who did not know "even one letter"—
are they not fully authorized by virtue of being appointed by the public? Karelitz's response is emphatically negative, transferring his attention from the
first condition for judicial authority to the second. Israeli secular courts lack
authority, not because of the judges' qualifications or their mode of appointment, but because the law they enforce is not Torah law, and it is therefore
inherently illegitimate for any Jewish community.

What laws, then, served the "tribunals of Syria," or the lay, unlearned judges allowed by Adret? Here Karelitz comes up with an astonishing
solution: they were to follow no law at all. It is not that the Torah provides
an exclusive key to justice: rather, this can be attained by "human intellect."
Indeed, the Noahides are required to use their moral understanding in order
to devise laws and construct legal systems. But Jewish lay judges must refrain
from doing so, adhering instead strictly to a practice of ad hoc adjudication,
without adopting or employing any fixed laws.

If the courts neither subscribe to a given set of laws nor are permitted to develop their own rules, people will be unable to anticipate legal
outcomes, and the judicial system will thus fail to fulfill one of its chief functions. Yet Karelitz seems oblivious to the serious social and economic costs
of the volatility of judgments that he in effect requires. His major concern is
theological: Jewish loyalty to God is expressed in a commitment to his Torah;
conversely, replacing the Torah with any alternative set of laws is tantamount
to idolatry. His quest for ultimate denunciation is satisfied with nothing less
than the famous words of Jeremiah, who in God's name condemned the idol-
worshipping Israelites (Jer. 2:13):

> For my people have done a twofold wrong:
> They have forsaken Me, the Fount of living waters,
> And hewed them out cisterns, broken cisterns,
> Which cannot even hold water.

It is perhaps understandable that in a religious culture where fidelity
to God's authority as lawgiver has become the chief mode of commitment,
establishing a secular legal system is perceived as the ultimate betrayal. This

perception trumps the tradition's own endorsement of consent as a decisive legitimating force: "if the townspeople agree upon this, their compact has no effect."

Shlomo Goren, too, seeks to incorporate "the spirit of the Torah and its laws into the state" and believes that achieving this with regard to the courts is a key to broader success. But he differs from Karelitz in (at least) two crucial points. First—whether motivated by pragmatism, principle, or some combination thereof—his premise is fundamentally democratic: the Torah-backed legal system must "be acceptable to all segments of the public" and, moreover, cannot allow ethnic or gender discrimination, as it must comply with international law.

Second, starting from the above premise, Rabbi (later, Chief Rabbi of Israel) Goren is prepared to subject received halakhic norms to critical examination. His critique here focuses on norms constituting discrimination in the qualification of judges and witnesses, and on the unrealistic hurdles of criminal procedure; he could easily have added the lack of effective sanctions for offenses such as stealing (as proclaimed in the talmudic source regarding Rav Nahman, discussed in §§14–15). The Israeli legal system can be set up in accordance with Jewish law, but this requires "innovations of Torah"—that is, creative interpretations and applications. The clash between rival legal systems—which for Karelitz embodies the clash between the True God and false idols—is averted by extending the Torah so that it can encompass the secular courts of the state of Israel.

The problem of usurpation is resolved by what may seem a merely semantic ruse: Goren emphasizes that these courts are not true Torah courts; they cannot be called "*bet din*." But his insistence that they are in fact another entity entirely, "courts of settlement," serves also to underline that their authority derives exclusively from the consent of the people—not the ad hoc consent of individual parties agreeing to arbitration but sweeping public authorization.

Now, Kaerlitz too had recognized the legitimizing force of consent, granted through public authorization. For him the sticking point was loyalty to the Torah's laws, whereas for Goren it is precisely the inadequacy of

those laws (as received) that makes it essential to seek alternative legitimiza-
tion. And he does not find it difficult to provide ample support for his assertion that the community and its officers are authorized not only to judge and
punish but also to enact legislation, "in accordance with what the judges or
the legislators see [as necessary] for the sake of social order." Because all this
is mandated by halakhic sources, it is by no means a "forsaking" of God or his
Torah; on the contrary, this is how commitment to the Torah is to be realized
in the contemporary democratic Jewish state.

Strangest among these three texts is the responsum by Chief Rabbi
Ovadyah Yosef. Clearly endorsing the position of Karelitz, he cites against
Israeli courts the same verse from Jeremiah, reiterating the comparison to
idol worship (and, as if that were not enough, he cites the verse from Genesis proclaiming the unbearable guilt of Cain, the first murderer). Moreover,
he provides an explanation (which harks back to the medieval commentator
Rashi): by seeking adjudication according to non-Jewish laws, one is lending
"respect and importance to the laws of the gentile idol worshippers, honoring
and elevating their idols." What is strange here is that this statement follows
a discussion of non-Jewish law in terms of the Noahide code, which requires
each gentile society to maintain a legal system. Yosef affirms the legitimacy
(for the gentiles) of these diverse laws, which are based upon "human intellect and discretion." His specific complaint against Israeli law is that it is based
on the adoption of Ottoman and British law; yet it is far from clear that these
are idolatrous nations. Yosef, in any event, offers no arguments to that effect.

Interestingly, the exposition here does not include Karelitz's explicit rejection of "fabricated laws." The emphasis on the alien origins of the
Israeli legal code seems to imply that were the Knesset (Israel's parliament)
to enact its own, independent code, adjudicating by that code would not be
quite so sinful.

The general course of Yosef's argument suggests, however, that the
Knesset could have no justification to adopt any laws other than those of the
"Talmud and the codifiers." Indeed, in contrast to Goren—and even to Karelitz—he makes no mention of public authorization or consent, and hence
does not even engage the possibility that Israel's laws and courts might attain
legitimacy on that basis. Instead, he goes along with the tone set by whoever

sent in this question, formulated entirely in terms of *dina de-malkhuta,* as if the state of Israel is some alien kingdom.

To be fair, we should probably note that, although the reponsum deals with law as such, and its concluding ruling speaks of monetary matters generally, the issue directly at stake here is inheritance, a realm of law that halakhists—from the High Middle Ages onward—famously strove to protect against any encroachment by the "law of the kingdom." By the same token, however, notice that the specific question is about gender equality. Obviously, in this matter the Knesset could hardly be expected to adopt traditional halakhic norms, since they embody gender discrimination. It was precisely problems like this that led Goren to assert that it would not do to simply legislate a wholesale adoption of *halakhah* as the law of the nascent state. For Goren, a main reason precluding such an adoption is that, under the received tradition, women cannot serve as witnesses or judges. For Yosef, however, a major complaint against "their courts" is that they allow testimony "by women and [other individuals] disqualified according to *halakhah.*"

To my mind, the most problematic aspect of Yosef's discussion is connected to his biography in public life. He served ten years as chief rabbi (until forced by term limits to leave that office), a position established by Israeli law, whose occupant is entrusted with a wide range of legal powers and responsibilities. How could he in good faith seek election and exercise power under a system of law that he castigates as idolatrous? Subsequently, he initiated the founding of a powerful political party (Shas), whose representatives took active part in the Knesset's work of legislation, often consulting with Yosef—their undisputed spiritual leader—about how to cast their votes. How could that be undertaken in good faith, with as little regard for democracy as evident in the text before us?

We should not be surprised, then, if for many Israelis the real question is not whether *halakhah* can (or should) recognize Israel's secular courts of law but rather whether the Israeli polity should continue to allow the exercise of power by rabbis who do not share its democratic commitments. More fundamentally, the question is less about political ideology than about the sense of community. Courts are nested in a legal system, which in turn is nested in a political community—a constitutive element of its social fabric. For Yosef, and perhaps for Karelitz, the Israeli courts belong to "others" and should be opposed and shunned. For Goren, the selfsame courts and the laws they apply are fully legitimate, because they were endorsed by "the public"—that is, the citizens of the state through their elected representatives. For him, as for most Israelis—both secular and religious—that is the real community today.

Noam J. Zohar

Glossary of Names

Abraham b. David of Posquieres; Rabad—(Provence, c. 1125–98), talmudic scholar. Born in Narbonne, Rabad moved to Posquieres, where he established a yeshiva that became a center for the study of Talmud in Provence. His works include commentaries on talmudic literature, responsa, homiletic discourses, and critical glosses (*hassagot*) on famous works of Rabbinic literature, including Maimonides' *Mishneh Torah,* for which he became known as *ba'al ha-hassagot* (master of the glosses).

Adret, Solomon b. Abraham; Rashba—(Barcelona, c. 1235–c. 1310), Spanish rabbi, communal leader, halakhic authority, and kabbalist. Adret, a disciple of Nahmanides (see entry), was a central figure in the development of what may be called the "constitutional law" of the *kahal.* He wrote commentaries on the Talmud and other halakhic books, but he is probably best known for his thousands of responsa, many of which deal with communal matters—most importantly, the authority of *berurim* and rabbinic courts.

Alashkar, Joseph b. Moses—(Spain–Algeria, c. 1470–1540), scholar and Hebrew poet. Born in Seville, Alashkar moved with his family to Tlemcen, Algeria, owing to the expulsion from Spain in 1492. There he became the head of a yeshiva. Among his writings is *Mirkevet ha-Mishneh* (Chariot of the Mishneh), in which he presents his commentary on Mishnah Avot with constant reference to previous commentaries. Alashkar also wrote poems and several religious hymns.

Alshekh, Moshe—(Turkey–Palestine, d. after 1593), halakhic authority and biblical exegete. Born in Adrianople, Alshekh settled in Safed, Palestine; there he was a member of the rabbinical court of Joseph Karo and he ordained Ḥayyim Vital, who was his halakhic disciple. He is known mainly for his commentaries on the Bible.

Asher b. Yehi'el; Rosh (also known as Asheri)—(Germany–Spain, c. 1250–1327), rabbi and halakhist. Asher was born into an Ashkenazi pietist family. In Worms he studied under Meir b. Baruch of Rothenburg (see entry), who appointed him a member of the city's *bet din*. After the imprisonment of Meir, Asher was probably the leading figure of German Jewry. But, fearing Meir's fate, he left with his family for Spain, settling finally in Toledo, where he accepted the position of rabbi. He promoted the methodology of the tosafists in Spain and tried to establish Ashkenazic *minhag* (customs) there. Among his writings are *Piskei ha-Rosh,* in which he collected and codified previous halakhic decisions and commentaries, and about a thousand surviving responsa. His son Jacob was the author of the *Tur.*

Avoth Yeshurun (Yehiel Perlmutter) — (Niskhish, Ukraine — Israel, 1904–92). Yeshurun was a powerful expressionist Hebrew poet living in Tel Aviv. Born Yehiel Perlmutter, he was scion to an important Ukrainian hasidic family against whose traditions he rebelled. After experiencing the fate of a refugee as a child in the First World War, he immigrated as a young man to Palestine, leaving his family behind. As the years passed and the situation in Europe turned gloomier, and the possibility of facilitating his family's immigration became more and more remote, he experienced his own move as an abandonment. The experience of a redeeming immigration changing its hues is starkly encapsulated in his poem, which speaks for an entire generation of youth leaving home for the utopian home of Zion.

Bonfils (Tov Elem), Joseph b. Samuel — (French, 11th century), halakhic scholar and poet. Bonfils was born in Narbonne but lived in Limoges. He is best known for his decisions with regard to taxation which served as a basis for the later *takkanot* (regulations) of the Jewish communities in France and Germany. Some of his *piyyutim* (liturgical poems) appear in the *mahzor* (the liturgical arrangements), according to the French rite.

Capsali, Elijah — (Crete, c. 1483–1555), rabbi, communal leader and historian. Born in Candia, Crete, Capsali left his native city in 1508 to study at Padua and Venice. After two years, he returned to Crete, served as constable of the Jewish community, and became the rabbi in Candia (c. 1528). One of the few Jewish historians of the 16th century, Capsali wrote a short chronicle about the history of Venice in 1517. Five years later, he wrote his best-known work, *Seder Eliyahu Zuta,* whose main subject is the history of the Ottoman Empire up to his lifetime, with special reference to the Jews. Capsali also wrote various responsa and a book about honoring one's parents, *Me'ah Shearim.*

Cohen, Meir Simhah—(Latvia, 1843–1926), talmudic scholar and biblical commentator. Cohen served as the rabbi of Dvinsk for forty years and was recognized as one of the leading rabbinic scholars of eastern Europe. *Or Same'ah,* his commentary on Maimonides' *Mishneh Torah,* is a modern classic of this genre. He also wrote a commentary on the Pentateuch, *Meshekh Hokhmah.*

David b. Solomon Ben Zimra; Radbaz—(Spain–Egypt–Palestine, 1479–1573), halakhic authority, talmudic scholar, and kabbalist. Born into a wealthy family, David b. Zimra settled in Egypt and was appointed the Rabbinic leader of Egyptian Jewry. He eventually moved to Safed, Palestine, becoming an active member of this center of Kabbalah. He was a prolific author who composed works in many areas, including seven volumes of responsa.

Dubnow, Simon—(Belorussia–Saint Petersburg–Berlin–Riga, 1860–1941), Jewish historian and ideologist. Born in Mstislavl, Dubnow settled after extensive travels in Saint Petersburg, where he taught Jewish history. Dubnow was largely self-educated. He was one of the founders and directors of the Jewish Historico-Ethnographical Society, and when the Bolsheviks came to power, he was asked to prepare several publications, none of which was ever published. In 1922 he moved to Berlin. When Hitler rose to power Dubnow went to Riga, Latvia, where he remained at work until killed by the Gestapo. Among Dubnow's numerous works are *History of the Jews in Russia and Poland* and the multivolume *History of the Jews,* in which he maintained that Jewish survival had resulted from the communal and spiritual independence of Jews in the diaspora. Dubnow's ideology of autonomism proposed that Jews must develop an autonomous community, language, and schools in the separate areas of the diaspora and placed him in strong opposition to both Zionism and assimilation.

Duran, Simeon b. Zemah; Tashbetz — (Majorca–Algiers, 1361–1444), halakhic authority, religious philosopher, and physician. In his youth in Palma, Duran studied Talmud and *halakhah* as well as medicine. After the persecutions of 1391, he left for Algiers and became a member of Isaac b. Sheshet Perfet's (see entry) *bet din*. Duran served on a commission appointed by the Algiers community to deal with questions of matrimonial status, and he was the chief author of its ordinances, observed in North Africa for hundreds of years. He succeeded Perfet as chief rabbi of Algiers and was considered the supreme halakhic authority of his generation. He is known mostly for his responsa.

Eli'ezer b. Samuel of Metz — (France, c. 1115–98), tosafist and halakhic authority. Eli'ezer made his living by moneylending and was in charge of the distribution of charity. He is best known for his *Sefer Yere'im* (Book of the [God-]Fearing), which explores the 613 commandments.

Emden, Jacob — (Germany, 1697–1776), talmudic scholar, halakhic authority, and kabbalist. Emden studied under his father, Zevi Hirsch Ashkenazi (Hakham Zevi). Apart from a few years as rabbi of Emden, he never held any official position. Publishing numerous works in diverse fields, including *halakhah,* Kabbalah, and liturgy, he was regarded as one of the leading but also one of the most controversial scholars of his generation. Particularly contentious was his controversy with Jonathan Eybeschütz, another leading German scholar, whom Emden accused of crypto-Sabbatean beliefs.

Epstein, Yehiel Mikhel b. Aaron Isaac Ha-Levi — (Belorussia, 1829–1908), rabbi and halakhic authority. Born in Bobruisk, Epstein was appointed rabbi of Novogrudok in 1862; he remained there for the rest of his life. Abraham Isaac Kook (see entry in Vol. I) and Shelomo Yosef Zevin were among his disciples. He is best known for his *Arukh ha-Shulhan,* consisting of novellae and halakhic rulings on Joseph Karo's *Shulhan Arukh.*

Falk, Joshua b. Alexander Ha-Kohen; Sma — (Poland, c. 1555–1614), halakhic authority and *rosh yeshiva.* Born in Lublin, Falk studied under Moses

Isserles and Solomon Luria (see entries). He headed a yeshiva in Lemberg and took an active part in the Council of the Four Lands. He is usually referred to by the initials of the title of his book *Sefer Me'irat Einayim,* a commentary on Joseph Karo's *Shulhan Arukh* (see entries), *Hoshen Mishpat,* which includes extensive exposition and elaboration on Moses Isserles's glosses.

Feldblum, Meir Simcha Hakohen — (Lithuania–United States–Israel, 1927–2002), rabbi and professor of Talmud. Born in Lithuania, Feldblum immigrated to the United States in 1948. He received both rabbinical ordination and a Ph.D. from Yeshiva University, where he continued teaching for more than 20 years. Feldblum immigrated to Israel in 1985 and taught Talmud at Bar-Ilan University.

Gerondi, Nissim b. Reuben; Ran — (Spain, 1310–1375?), talmudist, halakhic authority, and physician in the royal court. Born in Gerona, he later moved to Barcelona, where he played a leading role in communal affairs and headed a yeshiva. Among his disciples were Isaac b. Sheshet Perfet (see entry) and Hasdai Crescas. Gerondi's main works are his commentaries on the Talmud (in which he followed the tradition of Nahmanides and Solomon b. Abraham Adret: see entries), a commentary on Isaac Alfasi's *halakhot,* and *Derashot HaRan,* twelve sermons or public lectures, one of them devoted to kingship.

Gershom b. Judah; Me'or Ha-Golah — (Germany, c. 960–1028), one of the first talmudic scholars in Ashkenaz. Probably born in Metz, he later headed a yeshiva in Mainz; among his pupils were the teachers of Rashi (see entry), who summed up Gershom's reputation: "Rabbenu Gershom . . . who enlightened the eyes of the exile (*me'or ha-golah*), and upon whom we all depend." Gershom is known in later literature as the author of many *takkanot;* both the ban on bigamy and the prohibition of the divorce of a wife against her will are attributed to him.

Goren [Gorontchick], Shlomo — (Poland–Israel, 1917–1994), rabbinic scholar, first chief rabbi of the Israel Defense Forces, and Ashkenazi chief rabbi of Israel. Born in Zambrów, he moved in 1925 to Palestine, where he studied in Hebron Yeshiva in Jerusalem. He joined the

Haganah paramilitary organization in 1936 and fought in the 1948 Israeli War of Independence. During the war Goren was appointed as chief chaplain of the newly formed army, a position he held until 1968. He was responsible for the organization of the military chaplaincy and the way in which halakhic rulings and religious themes permeate various levels of IDF practice. In the 1967 Six-Day War, Goren sounded a shofar at the Western Wall to celebrate its liberation. In 1968 he was elected Ashkenazi chief rabbi of Tel Aviv–Jaffa and in 1972 was elected Ashkenazi chief rabbi of Israel. He was a prolific author who composed works in many areas, including numerous responsa concerning problems of observance due to conditions of active warfare and technological progress.

Hanover, Nathan Nata — (Galicia–Moravia, d. 1683), preacher, kabbalist, lexicographer, and chronicler. The Chmielnicki uprising and the attendant persecutions of 1648–49 forced Hanover to flee his birthplace in Volhynia and wander through Poland, Germany, and Holland for several years. In 1653 in Italy he published *Yeven Metzulah* (Abyss of Despair), which documented the Chmielnicki persecutions. In 1662 he was appointed head of the *bet din* in Jassy, Walachia. After about ten years, he was appointed preacher and *dayan* in Ungarisch Brod, Moravia, where he was killed by Turkish soldiers who raided the town. Among his writings are *Safah Berurah* (Pure Language), a Hebrew-German-Latin-Italian lexicon for travelers, and the kabbalistic prayer book *Sha'are Ziyyon.*

Herzog, Isaac Halevi — (Poland–Ireland–Israel, 1888–1959), rabbinic scholar and chief Ashkenazi rabbi of Israel. Born in Poland, Herzog moved to Ireland and served as rabbi in Belfast and Dublin. In 1936 he went to Palestine, succeeding Abraham Isaac Kook (see entry in Vol. I) as chief rabbi. A fervent Zionist, Herzog founded the Mizrahi Federation of Great Britain and Ireland. In Israel he sought to meet the challenges posed to the halakhic tradition by the prospect of political sovereignty. Herzog was responsible for the enactment of important *takkanot* on matters of personal status.

Ibn Aknin, Joseph b. Judah—(Spain–North-Africa, c. 1150–1220), philosopher and poet. Born in Barcelona, he later moved to North Africa, probably due to the Almohad persecutions. There he lived as a crypto-Jew. He wrote several halakhic and philosophical works. In *Sefer ha-Musar* (The Book of Morality), which is a commentary on Mishnah Avot, he follows the views of his master, Maimonides, on many issues.

Ibn Migash, Joseph b. Meir Ha-Levi—(North Africa–Spain, 1077–1141), talmudic scholar. Ibn Migash studied under Isaac Alfasi and succeeded him as head of the yeshiva in Lucena, Spain, occupying this position until his death. Maimon, Maimonides' father, may have been one of his pupils, and Maimonides, who held him in high esteem, relies upon his views. Ibn Migash had a significant impact on the study of Talmud in Spain and Provence, but very little of his work has survived.

Isaac b. Moses of Vienna; Isaac Or Zaru'a—(Bohemia–Germany, c. 1180–c. 1250), halakhic authority. Isaac is usually referred to by the title of his halakhic compendium, *Or Zaru'a*. Because of its great length, the book had a limited circulation, but it was frequently quoted in secondary sources and in this way had an impact on later scholars. *Or Zaru'a* is a valuable collection of halakhic rulings and customary practices from the High Middle Ages including a section dedicated to *tzedakah*.

Isaac b. Yeda'ayah—(southern France, 13th century), scholar. At age fifteen (c. 1230), Yeda'ayah entered the yeshiva of Meshullam b. Moses in Beziers. Later he had a debate with an unnamed Christian polemicist who tried to use the talmudic *aggadot* to prove that the Messiah had already come. Among his writings are his commentaries on the *aggadot* of the Talmud and Midrash Rabbah.

Ishbili, Yom Tov b. Abraham—(Asbili; i.e., of Seville; known as Ritba)—(Spain, c. 1250–1330), rabbi, communal leader, and halakhic authority. A disciple of Solomon b. Abraham Adret (see entry), Ishbili served as rabbi in Saragossa and Seville, and rendered halakhic decisions on many matters. His best-known work is his novellae to the Talmud, *Hiddushei ha-Ritba*. Ishbili also wrote *Sefer ha-Zikkaron* to defend *The Guide of the Perplexed* against Nahmanides' criticism.

Isserles, Moses; Rema—(Poland, c. 1530–72), codifier and rabbi. Isserles was a member of the Kraków *bet din* and head of a yeshiva there. His glosses on Joseph Karo's *Shulhan Arukh* (see entries), the *Mappah* (Tablecloth), became authoritative for Ashkenazi Jewry. He also composed responsa, talmudic commentaries, and works that attempted to build a synthesis between Kabbalah and philosophy.

Jacob b. Asher—(Germany–Spain, 1270?–1340), halakhic authority. The son of Asher b. Yehi'el (Rosh; see entry), under whom he studied, Jacob moved with his father to Toledo (1303), where he lived in poverty, shunning rabbinical office and devoting his time to study. He wrote commentaries on the Pentateuch and various halakhic books, but he is best known for the *Arba'ah Turim* (see entry *Tur*), as a result of which he is commonly referred to as "the Ba'al ha-Turim" (the author of the *Turim*).

Josephus Flavius—(Palestine–Rome, c. 38–after 100 C.E.), general, historian, apologist; writer in the Jewish-Hellenistic tradition. Josephus was born in Jerusalem into a priestly family related to the Hasmonean dynasty. At the beginning of the rebellion in 66 C.E., he was appointed commander of the Galilee, but when the war in the north was almost lost—in what seems to have been an act of treachery toward his comrades—he went over to the Roman side, becoming an adviser to Titus and Vespasian. After the war, Josephus moved to Rome, where he wrote (in Greek) a history of the rebellion and an account of the history, culture, and religion of the Jewish people (*Antiquities*). In this work, and also in his response to critics of Judaism, *Against Apion,* he appears as a defender of his people, arguing for the spiritual value and practical utility of their religion and its ethical superiority to Hellenism.

Judah b. Samuel Halevi—(Spain–Palestine (?), before 1075–1141), Hebrew poet and philosopher. Born in Toledo, he settled in southern Spain after years of studying and traveling, working as a physician. Around

1140 Halevi decided to emigrate to Eretz Israel, a decision that reflected a lifetime's yearning, expressed in both his religious/philosophical and poetic writings. Halevi's philosophy is contained in his famous book *The Kuzari* (finished c. 1140), which is subtitled *The Book of Argument and Proof in Defense of the Despised Faith*. *The Kuzari* is both an argument against the Karaites (see entry in Vol. I) and a critique of efforts to provide a fully rationalist account of Judaism. His philosophy emphasized the bond between God and Israel, to be fully realized in the Land of Israel.

Karelitz, Abraham Yeshayah; Hazon Ish—(Lithuania–Palestine, 1878–1953), talmudic scholar and halakhic authority. Karelitz resided in a number of east European communities, including Vilna, where he devoted himself almost exclusively to the study of rabbinic texts and the composition of halakhic works. He immigrated to Palestine, where he continued to shun all official communal positions. He was, nevertheless, recognized as the leading Torah scholar in Palestine and is considered one of the principal architects of the Israel ultra-orthodox community. He is best known for his wide-ranging and erudite commentary on various rabbinic texts, entitled *Hazon Ish*.

Karo, Joseph b. Ephraim—(Castile?–Turkey–Palestine, 1488–1575), talmudic scholar, codifier, and kabbalist. After establishing himself as a distinguished talmudist, he left Turkey for Safed, Palestine (1536). There he headed a large yeshiva, wrote hundreds of responsa and was regarded as the leader of the scholars. Karo's main works are his magnum opus, the halakhic code *Bet Yosef* (see entry), its more abridged version, *Shulhan Arukh* (see entry), *Kesef Mishneh* (see entry), and his mystical diary, *Maggid Mesharim* (One Who Announces What Is True). Karo's pupils included Moshe Alshekh and Moses Cordovero.

Kisch, Abraham—(Prague–Breslau–Berlin–Prague, 1725–1803), physician. Kisch was the first Prague Jew to receive a doctorate in medicine (at Halle University in 1749). He founded the Jewish hospital in Breslau and was the head of the Prague community's hospital.

Krochmal, Menahem Mendel b. Abraham—(Poland–Moravia, c. 1600–1661), rabbi and halakhic authority. Born in Kraków, he was a student of

Yoel Sirkes (see entry), and from 1630 he attended the Council of Four Lands. In 1650 he was elected chief rabbi (*Landesrabbiner*) of Moravia, an appointment he held until his death. He formulated the Shai Takkanot, which regulated the organization of the Moravian communities until the Revolution of 1848, and his responsa *Tzemah Tzedek* reflect Jewish suffering during the Thirty Years' War (1618–48).

Lamm, Norman—(New York, 1927–), scholar and communal leader. Lamm received his ordination from the Rabbi Isaac Elchanan Theological Seminary (RIETS, the Yeshiva University rabbinical school) in 1951 and has held leading positions at Yeshiva University, serving as its third president (1976–2003). Lamm was the founding editor of *Tradition,* the major journal of orthodox thought. He writes extensively on Jewish philosophy and law, especially in relation to problems involving science, technology, and philosophy in the modern world.

Landau, Ezekiel b. Judah; Noda Bihudah—(Poland–Bohemia, 1713–93), halakhic authority and rabbinic figure. Landau was born in Opatow to a wealthy and distinguished family that traced its descent back to Rashi. He received his talmudic education at Vladimir and Brody. After serving as *dayan* in Brody (1734) and as a rabbi in Yampol (1746), he was appointed rabbi of Prague and the whole of Bohemia, occupying this position from 1754 until his death. Though an advocate of Kabbalah and secular studies, he actively opposed Hasidism and the *haskalah.* Landau is known as the Noda Bihudah, after his responsa bearing that title.

Lazarus, Emma—(New York, 1849–87), poet, essayist, translator, and activist whose 1883 poem "The New Colossus" is inscribed on the pedestal of the *Statue of Liberty.* Lazarus's interest in the Jewish tradition began in the late 1870s. She studied Hebrew and published translations of the medieval Spanish Jewish poets. In the 1880s Lazarus was moved by the news of the Russian persecution of Jews to become an active advocate for Jewish immigrants. A decade before Theodore

Herzl, she argued in her writing for making Palestine a safe shelter for oppressed Jews everywhere.

Loeb, Morris—(United States, 1863–1912), physical chemist and philanthropist. Born in Cincinnati into a wealthy family, Loeb became a professor of chemistry at New York University in 1891. In 1910 he resigned his chair to devote himself to scientific research and public activities. He had been active not only as a donor but also as a leader in many of the Jewish communal undertakings that marked the period of intensive immigration of Jews into the United States. Among other things, he was president of the Hebrew Technical Institute, trustee of the Jewish Theological Seminary of America, and founder of the American Jewish Committee and of the Educational Alliance.

Loew, Judah b. Bezalel; Maharal—(Prague, c. 1525–1609), rabbi, talmudist, kabbalist, and moralist. A scholar of both Jewish and secular studies (particularly mathematics), Loew is a transitional figure between medieval and early modern Jewish thought. In his voluminous works in the fields of ethics and theology, he interprets Rabbinic *aggadah* in light of his mystical philosophy. He wrote extensively on the relationship between God and Israel, on the mediating role of the Torah, and on the moral and political meaning of the Jewish exile.

Lublin, Meir b. Gedaliah; Maharam of Lublin—(Poland, 1558–1616), rabbi, talmudic scholar, and halakhic authority. Born into a rabbinical family, Meir served as a rabbi and *rosh yeshiva* in Lublin, Kraków, and Lemberg. He is mostly known for his commentary on most of the tractates of the Talmud, *Me'ir Einei Ḥakhamim.* His responsa, *Manhir Einei Hakhamim,* is one of the earliest sources for knowledge of the Council of the Four Lands.

Luria, Solomon b. Yehiel (also known as Rashal or Maharshal)—(Poland, 1510?–74), rabbi, halakhic authority, and talmudic scholar. Luria served as a rabbi for various Polish communities. In 1567 he established his own yeshiva in Lublin. He is best known for his *Yam Shel*

Shelomo (Solomon's Sea), a halakhic compendium that follows the order of the Talmud, and his *Hokhmat Shelomo* (Solomon's Wisdom), glosses, short comments, and textual emendations that appear in most editions of the Talmud.

Luz [Lozinsky], Kaddish — (Belorussia–Israel, 1895–1972), politician and pioneer. Luz was one of the leaders of the *kibbutz* movement. He studied agriculture, economics, and social sciences at the Economics Institute in Saint Petersburg and in other institutions, served in the Russian army during World War I, and was a founder of the Hebrew Soldier Association and the HeHalutz [lit., The Pioneer] movement. After immigrating to Palestine in 1920, he joined *kibbutz* Degania Bet. He was one of the leaders of the Histadrut [lit., Federation (of labor)], as well as the secretariat of Tel Aviv's workers' council. Luz was elected to the Knesset in 1951 on Mapai's [Workers' Party of Eretz Yisrael] list and later was appointed minister of agriculture and Speaker of the Knesset.

Maimonides, Moses; Moses b. Maimon; Rambam — (Spain–Egypt, 1135–1204), rabbi, codifier, philosopher, and physician; the most prominent Jewish thinker in the post-talmudic era. Born in Córdoba, Maimonides wandered with his family through North Africa; they settled in Cairo, where he later headed the Jewish community. Maimonides' first important work was his *Commentary to the Mishnah,* completed at age thirty-three. His greatest achievements were the halakhic code *Mishneh Torah* (1180) and the philosophical treatise *The Guide of the Perplexed* (1190). The *Mishneh Torah,* written in Hebrew, systematically organizes the whole of Jewish law. The *Guide,* written in Arabic, was designed for readers whose faith had been undermined by philosophical criticism. The book aimed to harmonize philosophy and Judaism, thus enabling a renewed, but also a refined, religious faith. Although his philosophical views were the subject of fierce opposition, his influence on the development of Judaism was enormous.

Meir b. Baruch of Rothenburg; Maharam — (Germany, c. 1215–93), tosafist, halakhic authority, and communal leader. Meir was born in Worms

and died in prison after an eight-year incarceration ordered by the
Emperor Rudolf. He played a critical role in establishing the public law of the German communities. More than a thousand of his
responsa survive, most of them dealing with matters of *mamona,* including business transactions, real estate, inheritance, partnerships,
community property, and taxation. He greatly influenced later
codifiers, particularly Jacob b. Asher, author of the *Tur* (see entries),
whose father was Meir's student (see also ¢9, §8 headnote).

Meiri, Menachem b. Shlomo—(Provence, 1249–1316), rabbi and commentator on the Talmud. Meiri is best known for his interpretive summary of the Talmud, *Bet ha-Behirah,* which untypically includes
halakhic conclusions. He was a follower of Maimonides, both in
philosophical bent and in *halakhah;* like him, he engaged in secular
and scientific studies. He was apparently in touch with Christian
scholars and was one of the earliest advocates of tolerance toward
gentile society.

Mizrahi, Elijah (Re'em)—(Constantinople, c. 1450–1526), in his time, the
most prominent rabbi in the Ottoman Empire. Mizrahi played a
leading role in the Jewish community of Constantinople, headed a
yeshiva where both Talmud and secular subjects were taught, and
rendered halakhic decisions on many matters. He was actively involved in the absorption of exiles from Spain and Portugal following the expulsion. As a writer, he is chiefly known for his supercom-
mentary to Rashi's commentary on the Torah.

Modena, Samuel b. Moses de; Maharshdam—(Ottoman Empire, 1506–89),
rabbi, halakhic authority, and talmudic scholar. De Modena established a yeshiva in Salonika, where he was also the communal and
spiritual leader. He wrote more than a thousand responsa, many of
which adjudicated the disputes that emerged between the different groups of Jewish immigrants that inhabited Salonika in his day.

Nahmanides, Moses b. Nahman; Ramban—(Spain–Palestine, 1194–1270),
rabbi, prominent talmudist, kabbalist, and biblical commentator;
also a poet and physician. Born in Gerona, Nahmanides was the
chief rabbi of Catalonia and the most influential Jewish figure of

his generation. In 1263 he was forced by the king to participate in a public disputation in Barcelona with the apostate Pablo Christiani, in which Nahmanides gained the upper hand. Late in life he emigrated to Palestine. Many leading halakhists of the next generation, including Solomon b. Abraham Adret (see entry), were his students. His works include interpretations of the Talmud, halakhic monographs, e.g., *Mishpat ha-Herem* (Laws Concerning Bans), responsa, sermons, and letters. He also wrote a classic commentary on the Torah that incorporates kabbalistic readings of the text.

Oshry, Ephraim — (Lithuania–New York, 1914–2003), rabbi and halakhic authority. During the Holocaust, Oshry carefully recorded questions from the Kovno ghetto as well as his responses, burying them in tin cans for retrieval and publication. They were eventually published in his *She'elot u-Teshuvot mi-Ma'amakim* (Responsa out of the Depths). After the war he moved to Rome where he founded a yeshiva for orphaned refugee children. Later he transferred the yeshiva to Montreal, and eventually moved it to New York City, where he became rabbi of the Beit Midrash Hagodol on the Lower East Side.

Perfet, Isaac b. Sheshet; Rivash — (Spain–North Africa, 1326–1408), rabbi and halakhic authority. Perfet was born and studied in Barcelona — under, among others, Nissim Gerondi (see entry) — where he acted unofficially as rabbi. Later he moved to Saragossa; driven from there by the anti-Jewish riots of 1391, he came eventually to Algiers. Perfet is best known for his responsa, which influenced subsequent *halakhah* — including Joseph Karo's (see entry) *Shulhan Arukh*.

Rashi; Shlomo b. Isaac — (France, 1040–1105), the most prominent Jewish exegete of both the Bible and the Talmud. He was born and lived in Troyes, but his reputation extended throughout the Jewish world. Through his line-by-line interpretation of the Talmud, Rashi opened the text to a much wider audience than ever before. His work gained such authority and popularity that almost all printed editions of the Talmud include it. No less influential is Rashi's biblical commentary, which follows Scripture line by line and interprets it both according to the *peshat* (literal meaning) and the midrashic understanding. Besides being the ultimate exegete, Rashi was also a halakhic authority; some of his rulings are scattered in his talmudic commentaries, and some appear in his responsa.

Reischer, Jacob b. Joseph (aka Jacob Backofen) — (Prague–France, c. 1670–1733), *rosh yeshiva* and halakhic authority. After serving as a member of the great *bet din* of Prague, Reischer served as head of the rabbinic court and *rosh yeshiva* in various cities, including Worms and Metz. He is mostly known for his responsa *Shevut Ya'akov* (The Return of Ya'akov).

Rubinow, Issac Max — (Russia–New York, 1875–1936), social reformer, economic statistician, physician, and Zionist activist. Born in Grodno, Rubinow arrived in New York City in 1893. He qualified at New York Medical College (1898) but abandoned medical practice in favor of statistics and social work. As America's first major theorist of social insurance, he argued that social insurance, national in scope, covering health, unemployment, accidents, and old age, should replace charity and other forms of voluntary relief. In 1935 he was appointed by President Franklin D. Roosevelt as a consultant for the committee that drafted social security legislation. As a Jewish welfare work activist Rubinow argued that poverty among Jews must not be isolated from conditions in America generally, calling for Jewish participation in national progressive social movements. In addition as an active Zionist, he helped establish the first modern health services in Palestine as director of the Hadassah Medical Unit (1918–22) and served as executive director of the Zionist Organization of America (1928). His works include *Social Insurance: With Special Reference to American Conditions* (1913) and *The Quest for Security* (1934).

Shabbetai b. Meir Ha-Kohen; Shakh — (Lithuania–Bohemia, 1621–62), rabbi and halakhic authority. Served as *dayan* in the *bet din* of Vilna. Shabbetai lived during the Chmielnicki persecutions of 1648–49. Because of these massacres, in 1655 he fled from Vilna to Lublin, to Prague, and then to Dresnitz, Moravia. Shortly before he died he was appointed rabbi of Holesov, Bohemia. Shabbetai is usually referred by the initials of the title of his book *Siftei Kohen,* a commentary on Joseph Karo's *Shulhan Arukh* (see entries), *Yoreh De'ah.* Among his other writings is *Megillat Efah,* in which he documented the Chmielnicki persecutions.

Shapira, Yeshayahu—(Poland–Palestine, 1891–1945), rabbi and religious Zionist who was known as the "Pioneering Rebbe." Born into a hasidic family, Shapira emigrated to Palestine (1914), but on the outbreak of the First World War, he hastened back to Poland, where in 1917 he participated in the foundation of Mizrachi, a religious Zionist organization. He settled in Palestine in 1920 and became the head of the Immigration and Labor Department of the Mizrachi center in Jerusalem. He was one of the founders and leaders of Ha-Po'el ha-Mizrachi [lit., Mizrachi Workers] and wrote extensively on economic problems of settlement and cooperation.

Sirkes, Yoel; Bah—(Poland, 1561–1640), rabbi and halakhist. Born in Lublin, Sirkes was a rabbi in a number of communities and was appointed *av bet din* [head of court] and head of the yeshiva at Kraków in 1619. Though opposed to philosophy and an adherent of Kabbalah, he rejected kabbalistic practices that were contrary to *halakhah.* He is best known for the *Bayit Ḥadash* (Bah).

Sofer [Schreiber], Moses; Hatam Sofer—(Germany–Hungary, 1762–1839), rabbi, halakhic authority, and a founding leader of orthodox Jewry. Born in Frankfurt, in 1806 Sofer was appointed rabbi of Pressberg, where he remained for the rest of his life, founding a yeshiva that became a center of orthodoxy. Sofer was uncompromising in his struggle against *haskalah* and the early Reform movement. He wrote commentaries on several tractates of the Talmud and many responsa.

Solomon b. Abraham Hakohen; Maharshakh—(Ottoman Empire, c. 1520–1601), rabbi and halakhic authority. Born in Sérres (near Salonika), Hakohen served as rabbi in Bitola, Macedonia, and later as the rabbi of the Castilian Jewish community in Salonika. He is best known for his responsa *Shut Maharshakh.*

Soloveitchik, Joseph Baer—(Pruzhana, Poland–Boston, 1903–93), rabbi, talmudist, philosopher, and a leading figure of modern orthodoxy in the second half of the 20th century. Trained in the Lithuanian analytic method of Talmud study, Soloveitchik graduated from the University of Berlin with a doctorate in philosophy. In 1932 he emigrated to the United States, where he became a leading authority at the Rabbi Isaac Elchanan Theological Seminary (RIETS), which later became known as Yeshiva University. Soloveitchik's philosophical position can be characterized as religious existentialism; he often strives to endow halakhic concepts and traditional terms with spiritual significance. His essays and public lectures enabled a wider audience to be inspired by his instruction.

Tam, Jacob b. Meir; Rabbenu Tam—(France, c. 1100–1171), talmudic scholar and halakhic authority. The grandson of Rashi, Tam was the most prominent scholar of his generation. He settled in Ramepert, a small town, but exercised halakhic authority all over France and Ashkenaz. Tam lived through the persecutions and murders of the Second Crusade, which devastated the Ramepert community. Many of the Tosafot are based on his interpretations and rulings. Among his other works is *Sefer ha-Yashar,* which includes responsa and talmudic commentaries.

Trani, Moses b. Joseph di; Mabit—(Salonika–Safed, Palestine, 1500–1580), rabbi and halakhic authority. Born in Salonika into a family of Spanish origin, di Trani studied in Adrianople and later settled in Safed, Palestine, where he studied under Jacob Berab, who ordained him. After the death of Joseph Karo (1575, see entry), with whom he had many disputes, he was appointed spiritual head of the community of Safed. He penned fifty works, including more than eight hundred surviving responsa.

Tzahalon, Yom Tov b. Moses—(Safed, Palestine, 1559–1619/20), halakhic authority and emissary. One of the distinguished rabbis of Safed, Tzahalon served as the town's emissary, visiting Italy and Holland (1590–1600). After returning to Safed, he was sent to Egypt and Constantinople, where he wrote hundreds of responsa. Writing books in diverse fields, Tzahalon was a vocal opponent of Joseph Karo's *Shulhan Arukh* (see entries), despite being one of his students.

Waldenberg, Eli'ezer Judah—(Jerusalem, 1912–2006), halakhic authority. Born in Jerusalem, Waldenberg studied at Hebron Yeshiva, and beginning in 1957 served as a chief judge of the regional *bet din* in Jerusalem. From 1981 to 1985 he was a member of the High Rabbinical Court in Jerusalem. A premier authority on medical *halakhah,* Waldenberg is best known for his multivolume series of responsa, *Tsits Eli'ezer.* Waldenberg was awarded the Israel Prize for rabbinical scholarship in 1976.

Weil, Jacob b. Judah—(Germany, d. before 1456), rabbi and halakhic authority. After serving as a rabbi in Nuremberg, Weil moved to Augsburg, then to Bamberg for a short period, and from 1444 he was rabbi of Erfurt. He is best known for his responsa, which are a valuable source for the social and religious history of German Jewry, and for his *Hilkhot Shehitah u-Vedikah* (Laws of Slaughtering and Examination), which set the halakhic practice for Ashkenaz.

Weiss, Benjamin Aryeh Hakohen—(Ukraine, 1842–1913), talmudic scholar and halakhic authority. Born into a rabbinic family near Lvov, Weiss served as rabbi in Chernivtsi. He is best known for his responsa *Even Yekarah.*

Wolf [Wolfowicz], Shimon b.—(Lithuania, 1755–1830), businessman and social critic. Though born into the wealthy elite of Vilna, Wolf criticized the ways in which organizational leaders operated, and he demanded changes in the administrative system. During a dispute with the members of the city's kahal, he was placed under a *herem* and arrested by the *wojewoda* (provincial governor) of Vilna. While in prison (1788–90), he published an influential pamphlet arguing for the dissolution of Jewish self-rule. After his release he was appointed to the Vilna *kahal* (1796) and was actively engaged in opposing the hasidic movement.

Yosef, Ovadyah—(Iraq–Israel, 1920–2013), rabbi, halakhic authority, and leading figure of Israeli Sephardic ultraorthodoxy. Born in Baghdad, Yosef was brought to Jerusalem at age four. After serving as *dayan* in several courts—among them Cairo, Petah Tikvah, and Jerusalem—he was appointed Sephardi chief rabbi of Tel Aviv-

Jaffa (1968) and Sephardi chief rabbi of Israel (1972–83). In 1984 he founded Shas, an ultraorthodox Sephardi political party that deeply affected Israeli political and cultural life with its own school system, El ha-Ma'ayan. As its spiritual leader, Yosef became one of the most vocal opponents of Israel's Supreme Court.

Zevin, Shelomo Yosef—(Belorussia–Israel, 1885–1978), prominent rabbi and scholar among the adherents of religious Zionism. Zevin took an active role in the struggle to preserve Jewish identity in Soviet Russia after the Communist Revolution. In 1935 he immigrated to Palestine. He was one of the founders and editors of the *Talmudic Encyclopedia,* which reflected his unique style: a clear presentation of complex material in a form meaningful to knowledgeable lay-persons as well as to accomplished scholars. Zevin served as a member of the Israeli Chief Rabbinate Council and had a strong interest in applying *halakhah* to the modern world.

Glossary of Terms

aggadah (pl. *aggadot*)—lit., "legend, story (fiction)"; the non-halakhic part of
 Rabbinic literature.

aliyah—lit., "ascension" or "rising"; the immigration of Jews to the Land of
 Israel.

am ha-aretz (pl. *amme ha-aretz*)—lit., "people of the land." In Rabbinic Hebrew,
 a person without knowledge of Torah; applied pejoratively to those
 who did not belong to the class of the *hakhamim* (see entry *hakham*).

amora (pl. *amora'im*)—sages of the Talmud (Babylonian and Palestinian,
 roughly 200–600 C.E.); distinguished from the earlier *tanna'im* (see
 entry *tanna*).

Ashkenaz—Germany; Ashkenazi, a Jew from Ashkenaz (later, from central
 and eastern Europe); opp. Sephardi, lit., "a Jew from Spain" (by extension, a Jew from the Orient). Ashkenaz and Sepharad designate
 two distinct halakhic traditions within Judaism from the Middle
 Ages onward.

baraita (pl. *baraitot*)—lit., "external, not belonging to"; traditions and teachings of the *tanna'im* not embodied in the Mishnah but often quoted
 in the Gemara (see entries).

Bayit Ḥadash—lit., "new house"; 14th-century critical commentary to the
 Arba'ah Turim (see entry *Tur*) of Jacob b. Asher (see entry), written
 by Yoel Sirkes (Bah, see entry) in Poland.

berurim—selectmen, local officials elected (or appointed) to govern or represent the *kahal*.

bet din—court, sometimes high court or Sanhedrin (see entry in Vol. I).

bet midrash—house of learning.

Bet Yosef—a commentary to the *Tur* (see entry), written by Joseph Karo (see
 entry).

da'at torah—lit., the "opinion of Torah," and its companion phrase, *emunat
 hakhamim,* "faith in the sages" (see entry) designate, in modern ultraorthodoxy, the authority of leading scholars to decide in (all) areas

of policy that were not traditionally subject to halakhic jurisdiction (see also ¢6, §24 headnote).

din hamelekh—see *dina de-malkhuta.*

dina de-malkhuta—lit., "the law of the kingdom"; refers to the law of a foreign kingdom or a secular state. See Vol. I, ¢9.

dinar—denarius, basic monetary unit.

emunat hakhamim—faith in the sages; commitment to follow the opinion of a *hakham.* See also *da'at torah;* ¢6, §24 headnote.

eretz yisrael—Land of Israel.

gabbai (pl. *gabba'im*)—collector of taxes or charity, or treasurer; also *parnas* (see entry).

Gaon (pl. Geonim)—the title of the chiefs of the Babylonian academies in the post-talmudic period (roughly 750–1150).

Gemara—from the Aramaic, lit., "to learn or infer"; the main part of the Talmud.

gemilut hesed (pl. *gemilut hasadim*)—lit., "the giving of loving-kindness"; a voluntary assistance to one's fellow that an individual completes without the anticipation of receiving something in return, e.g., clothing the naked, visiting the sick, burying the dead.

gerah—a unit of weight and currency equivalent to one-twentieth of a *shekel* (see entry).

get (pl. *gittin*)—legal document, usually a writ of divorce.

hakham (pl. *hakhamim*)—sage, learned, scholar of the Torah; *talmid hakham* (pl. *talmide hakhamim*), lit., "student (disciple) of a learned," usually designates a scholar.

halakhah—lit., "practice, accepted opinion"; Jewish law in general or a specific instance of it.

halitzah—lit., "untying, removing"; the ceremony of removing the *yabam*'s (levir's) shoe, which exempts him and his brother's childless widow from marrying each other (see *yibbum*).

hallah—the portion of the dough that is set aside and given to the priest (see Num. 15:19).

hasid (pl. *hasidim*)—lit., "pious." The term designates members of pietistic groups, notably during the Second Commonwealth and in 13th-century Germany. More recently, and most of the time in this volume, it designates members of the movement known as Hasidism, inspired by Israel Ba'al Shem Tov (Besht) at the end of the 18th century in eastern Europe.

haver (pl. *haverim*)—friend, fellow; in Rabbinic literature, one who is strict in adherence to the law or initiated to special norms of piety, in contrast with *am ha-aretz;* hence also: scholar.

hazan (pl. *hazanim*)—official of the synagogue or the community of the talmudic period; also cantor.

hekdesh—consecrated donation or fund set aside for charitable purposes or for the fulfillment of any other *mitzvah.*

herem—ban, excommunication, boycott.

hevra (havurah) kadisha—lit., "holy brotherhood"; nonprofit society engaged in charitable activities. In a more restricted sense, an association for the reverential disposal of the dead in accordance with Jewish tradition.

issura—prohibition, primarily of a ritual nature; also, ritual matters in Jewish law. The term encompasses all realms of *halakhah* not defined as *mamona.*

kahal (pl. *kehillot*)—lit., "gathering, community"; in biblical literature, congregation of worship; in medieval Hebrew and thereafter, the local Jewish community, specifically as a political entity; sometimes, the assembly of its members.

kal vahomer (a fortiori)—an inference from minor to major, one of the thirteen means defined by the *tanna'im* for the interpretation of the Torah (the written law).

kasher (pl. *kasherim*)—lit., "proper, lawful"; kosher (e.g., food prepared according to the halakhic requirements); of an individual, upright in moral and religious behavior; sometimes used to denote proper lineage and personal status.

kashrut—noun derived from *kasher;* ritual lawfulness or good standing, especially of food.

karet—lit., "cutting off"; in talmudic law, divine punishment through premature or sudden death; distinguished from capital punishment.

Kenneset Yisrael—lit., "gathering of Israel"; the entire nation or community of Israel.

Kesef Mishneh—a commentary to Maimonides' *Mishneh Torah* (see entry in Vol. I), written by Joseph Karo (see entry).

ketubah (pl. *ketubot*)—marriage contract, fixing, among other things, the amount of money or other goods due to the wife on her husband's death or on being divorced; Ketubot, a tractate in the Mishnah and Talmud.

kibbutz—(pl. *kibbutzim*), a communal farm or settlement in Israel.

kibbutz medini—political society/community; a possible Hebrew translation of body politic.

log—a unit of liquid volume equal to 0.3 liter or 0.08 gallon.

lulav—twig, palm branch; one of the four species of plants used on Sukkot (see entry *sukkah*).

Mahzor Vitry—halakhic-liturgical composition by Simhah b. Samuel of Vitry (France, c. 1100).

ma'ah—silver coin equivalent in worth to a one-sixth dinar (see entry).

malkhut—kingdom, kingship, monarchy, empire, also government; the name of the tenth *sefirah* in Kabbalah; *malkhuti,* monarchical, kingly, majestic.

mamona (pl. *mamonot*)—lit., "accumulation, wealth, value"; civil matters in Jewish law, opp. *issura*.

mamzer (pl. *mamzerim*)—bastard, illegitimate child, also rejected, outcast; in biblical and Rabbinic law, a descendent of close relatives (brother-sister, son-mother, etc.) or of a married woman with a foreign man. A *mamzer* cannot marry an Israelite, but only another *mamzer* (or a convert to Judaism).

manè—a unit of weight or of currency equivalent in worth to one-hundredth of a *dinar*.

meshumadim—see *shmad*.

met mitzvah—lit., a deceased person of a commandment; a dead person who has no one to deal with his or her burial.

midrash (pl. *midrashim*)—commentary, sermon, study, textual interpretation;

homiletical interpretation of the scriptures (see M. Fishbane's Introduction to Vol. I).

min (pl. *minim*)—heretic.

minyan—religious quorum, consisting of at least ten Israelite adults.

Mishnah—lit., "repetition"; verbal teaching by repeated recitation; also, study, opinion; hence, codification of oral laws, compiled in six orders by Judah the Prince in the early 3rd century C.E. A section of the Mishnah is a mishnah.

Mishneh Torah—lit., "repetition of the Torah"; Hebrew name of the fifth book of the Pentateuch, Deuteronomy. Also, in most references here, the name of Maimonides' halakhic code.

miztvah (pl. *mitzvot*)—commandment, precept, law, religious duty, obligation.

mumar (pl. *mumarim*)—lit., "one who changes"; apostate or habitual violator of religious law.

nasi (pl. *nesi'im*)—in modern Hebrew, president; in biblical Hebrew, chieftain, ruler, officer; in talmudic Hebrew, head of the Sanhedrin, e.g., Judah the Prince.

Neturei Karta—lit., Guards of the City; the most radical anti-Zionist branch of ultraorthodox Jewry.

niddah—woman who is menstruating or who has not yet ritually immersed herself since her menstrual period. Sexual intercourse with a *niddah* is prohibited by *halakhah*.

niddui—isolation (to a lesser degree than that imposed by a *herem*), banishment.

nishtamed—see *shmad*.

Otzar ha-Poskim—lit., "treasure of decisors"; 20th-century halakhic responsa compendium, composed in Israel.

parnas—manager, administrator, chief, leader of the community.

peah—lit., "edge"; the edges of a farmer's field that must be reserved for the poor.

peshat—plain meaning (of text).

posek (pl. *poskim*)—lit., "arbiter, decider"; rabbinical scholar who pronounces in disputes about halakhic questions.

prosbul—(from the Greek: *pros boule*), a declaration made in court before the execution of a loan to the effect that the law of the sabbatical year shall not apply to the loan to be transacted; an innovation of Hillel the Elder (see ¢6, §15 headnote).

pundiyon—copper coin equivalent in worth to one-eighteenth *dinar* (see entry).

savora (pl. *savoraim*)—Babylonian scholars between the *amora'im* (see entry) and the Geonim (see entry).

schnorrer—lit., "beggar" (Yiddish); one who wheedles others into supplying his wants.

se'ah—a unit of dry volume equal to 7.3 liters or 1.9 gallons.

sela—silver coin equivalent in worth to a one-fourth *dinar* (see entry).

sevara—reason, something derived from logical or deductive argument; often with the connotation of innovative or speculative reasoning.

Shabbat—lit., "to rest, cease from labor"; Sabbath, seventh day of the week, day or period of rest (also a week).

shammash (pl. *shammashim*)—lit., "beadle"—a person who assists in the running of a synagogue, court, etc.

shehitah—slaughtering an animal, particularly in conformance with halakhic rules; *shohet* one who performs *shehitah*.

shekel—a unit of weight or of currency equal to 0.4 ounce.

shekhinah—divine presence, Godhead; royalty, royal residence; one of the names of the tenth *sefirah* in Kabbalah.

shohet—See *shehitah*.

shofar—instrument formed from the horn of an animal and blown ritually, particularly in the service of the New Year.

shmad—lit., "destruction"; religious persecution, forced apostasy, baptism.

Shulhan Arukh—lit., "prepared or set table"; authoritative code of Jewish religious and civil law written by Joseph Karo in the 16th century.

siddur (pl. *siddurim*)—lit., "order, arrangement"; Jewish prayer book.

sotah—lit., "wayward wife"; woman suspected of adultery.

sugya—talmudic pericope, a unit of talmudic discussion.

sukkah—lit., "booth"; the plural, Sukkot, is also the name of the Feast of

Tabernacles, for which booths are erected, where Jews dwell or eat for seven days.

takkanah (pl. *takkanot*)—regulation, remedy, rule, reform, improvement; an ordinance of the rabbis or the *kahal*; opposite of the law of the Torah. *Takkanot ha-medinah*—a regulation by the rabbis or the *kahal* for the sake of law and order or for the improvement of the state, society, or community. See also *tikkun*.

talmid hakham (pl. *talmide hakhamim*)—lit., "student (disciple) of a learned"; usually designates a scholar.

tanna (pl. *tanna'im*)—first generations of talmudic sages, whose sayings are recorded in the Mishnah, Tosefta, and the *baraitot*.

tartemar—a unit of weight or of currency equal to 6.4 oz.

terumah (pl. *terumot*)—lit., "offering, gift, donation"; heave offering, one of the sacrifices; priestly tithe on produce.

tikkun—repair; correction, reform; amendment, improvement; regulation; *tikkun olam*, lit., "repairing the world," reforming society; *tikkun hamedinah*, establishing law and order in the state or improving its well-being; *takanah la-olam*, general improvement to the order of society; *tikkun seder medini*, reform of the political order.

Tosafot—lit., "additions"; supplements to and commentaries on the Talmud written by rabbinic scholars (the tosafists) in Germany and France in the 11th to 13th centuries. They are printed along with Rashi's commentaries on either side of the traditional talmudic texts.

Tur (abbr. *Arba'ah Turim* [Four Columns])—early 14th-century codification of Rabbinic *halakhah*, written by Jacob b. Asher (Rosh, see entry) in Spain.

tzedakah—lit., "justness, fairness, righteousness"; charity; also good deed, piety, mercy.

tzibbur—public, community, congregation.

yibbum—levirate marriage: the obligatory marriage between a man and the widow of his childless, deceased brother (see Deut. 25:5).

yishuv—lit., "population, settlement"; *Ha-yishuv*, the Jewish population in the Land of Israel, particularly before 1948.

zuz—silver coin equivalent in worth to a *dinar* (see entry).

Commentators

Alan M. Dershowitz, Harvard Law School, Cambridge

Harry Frankfurt, Philosophy, Princeton University

Daniel Greenwood, Hofstra Law School, Long Island, New York

Amy Gutmann, President, University of Pennsylvania, Philadelphia

Ruth Halperin-Kaddari, Law, Bar Ilan University, Ramat Gan

Tova Hartman, Education, Ono Academic College, Kiryat Ono

David Heyd, Philosophy, Hebrew University, Jerusalem

Bonnie Honig, Political Science, Brown University, Providence

Ronit Irshay, Gender Studies, Bar Ilan University, Ramat Gan

Yuval Jobani, Education and Jewish Philosophy, Tel Aviv University

Menachem Lorberbaum, Jewish Philosophy, Tel Aviv University

Yair Lorberbaum, Law, Bar Ilan University, Ramat Gan

Fania Oz-Salzberger, Law, University of Haifa

Ruth Anna Putnam, Philosophy, Wellesley College

Jed S. Rakoff, United States District Judge, New York

Nancy L. Rosenblum, Government, Harvard University, Cambridge

Michael Sandel, Government, Harvard University, Cambridge

Pinhas Shifman, Law, Hebrew University, Jerusalem

Michael Walzer, Social Science, Institute for Advanced Study, Princeton

Noam J. Zohar, Philosophy, Bar Ilan University, Ramat Gan

Index of Biblical and Rabbinic Sources

Page numbers of selections in this volume are marked with §. Only the first page number is listed.

Index of Names

Page numbers of selections in this volume, listed under their authors' names, are marked with §; commentaries and introductary material are labeled "com" and "intro," respectively. Only the first page number is listed.

Concerning First Fruits, 195; Laws Concerning Gifts to the Poor, 46§, 264§, 272, 297–98, 610; Laws Concerning Marriage, 82§, 121§, 123–24, 200§; Laws Concerning Megillah and Hanukkah, 297; Laws Concerning Mourning, 50§; Laws Concerning Murder and Preservation of Life, 495§, 511, 544; Laws Concerning Original Acquisition and Gifts, 221, 243§, 380; Laws Concerning Rebels, 171, 193, 502; Laws Concerning Repose on a Festival, 524§; Laws Concerning Sanhedrin, 360, 570–71, 577, 579§, 589§, 586, 597; Laws Concerning the Foundations of the Torah, 60–61; Laws of Battery and Assault, 539; Laws of Fast Days, 25§; Laws of Inheritance, 217; Laws of Kings, 569, 365, 368, 374; Laws of Mixed Kinds, 543§; Laws of Shabbat, 364; Laws of the Study of Torah, 358§, 377§

Malachi, 78§, 96–97, 114

Manuel, Don Juan, 508

Mar Rav Hunay, 120

Mar Rav Raba, 120

Mar Ukva, 39, 277

Mar Zutra, 113

Marcus, Ivan, xv, xxi

Marcus, Jacob R., 304

Margolis, Moshe. Works: *Mareh ha-Panim,* 60–61

Marx, Karl, 350

Matitya, Rabbi, 568–69

Meir, Rabbi, 115, 119, 165, 199, 277

Meir b. Baruch of Rothenburg, 12, 34, 74, 103, 125, 135, 179, 184–85, 325, 350. Works: *Responsa,* 28§, 30§, 48§, 124§, 174§, 293§, 343§, 345§, 397§

Meir b. Gedaliah of Lublin (Maharam of Lublin), 138, 139, 430, 455. Works: *Responsa,* 510§

Meir b. Yekutiel ha-Cohen of Rothenburg. Works: *Hagahot Maymoniyot,* 416

Meir Levi of Vienna, 568–69

Meir of Padua (Maharim), 104

Meiri, Menachem b. Solomon, 27, 35, 329, 535, 553. Works: *Bet ha-Behirah,* 31§, 351§, 566§

Mesharshia, Rav, 18, 115

Mesterlein, Rabbi, 572

Mill, John Stuart, 413

Mirsky, Yehudah, xxiii

Mizrahi, Elijah (Re'em), 389, 424. Works: *Responsa,* 400§

Mordecai, 11, 15, 16, 27

Mordechai b. Hillel, 415. Works: *Mordechai,* 416

Moses, 20, 25, 88, 203, 233–35, 241, 332, 335, 354, 366, 395, 462, 497, 541–42, 545, 547, 557–58, 560, 589; Laws of, 75, 129–30, 340; maxim of, 562; rule of, 118; Torah of, 593, 597

Moses of Coucy. Works: *Sefer Mitzvot Gadol,* 573

Nadab, 393

Naeh, Shlomo, xxiii

Nahman, Rav, 85, 88, 91, 285, 295, 510, 512, 586–87, 601

Nahman b. Hisda, 113

Nahman b. Rav Hisda, 335

Nahman b. Yitzhak, 90, 91, 335

Nahmanides, 107, 310, 329, 455, 497. Works: *Commentary to the Torah,* 310; *Mishpat ha-Herem,* xxiii, 496§; *Novellae,* 567; *Pseudo-Nahmanides,* 110; *Torat ha-Adam,* 55

Nakdimon ben-Gurion, 347

Natan, Rabbi, 89

Natan b. Ami, 191, 200, 285–87

Natan b. Oshaia, 188

Nathan, Rabbi, 327, 337§

Natronai Gaon, 510

Nehemiah, 16, 605

Nehemiah, Rabbi, 276–77, 283–84

General Index

An alphabetical list of legal principles and sayings frequently invoked in traditional discourse appears under the entry "Maxims."